ASCENT
CENTER FOR TECHNICAL KNOWLEDGE

Autodesk® Civil 3D® 2023
Fundamentals for Land Developers
(Grading)

Learning Guide
Imperial Units - 2nd Edition

ASCENT - Center for Technical Knowledge®
Autodesk® Civil 3D® 2023
Fundamentals for Land Developers (Grading)
Imperial Units - 2nd Edition

Prepared and produced by:

ASCENT Center for Technical Knowledge
630 Peter Jefferson Parkway, Suite 175
Charlottesville, VA 22911

866-527-2368
www.ASCENTed.com

Lead Contributor: Jeff Morris

Contents

Preface

The Autodesk® Civil 3D® 2023 software supports a wide range of civil engineering tasks and creates intelligent relationships between objects. The *Autodesk Civil 3D 2023: Fundamentals for Land Developers (Grading)* guide is recommended for users that are required to create site grading plans using the Autodesk Civil 3D software. This guide is also suited for managers who require an overview and understanding of this aspect of the Autodesk Civil 3D software.

Users use feature lines, grading tools, and corridors to create a commercial site containing a parking lot, building pads, pond, and simple sewage lagoon. An existing road has been included in the survey and a survey team collected the existing conditions. Users also work on a residential site to grade a small subdivision for proper grading of each lot.

The learning content in this guide assumes the existing conditions are already processed. To learn how to create the existing conditions, refer to *Autodesk Civil 3D 2023: Fundamentals for Surveyors*.

Topics Covered

- Introduction to grading

- Parcel grading

- Grading using feature lines

- Grading using grading objects and grading groups

- Grading using corridors

- Combining surfaces

- Visualization in Autodesk® InfraWorks®

Prerequisites

- Access to the 2023.0 version of the software, to ensure compatibility with this guide. Future software updates that are released by Autodesk may include changes that are not reflected in this guide. The practices and files included with this guide might not be compatible with prior versions (e.g., 2022).

- Experience with AutoCAD® or AutoCAD-based products and a sound understanding and knowledge of civil engineering terminology is recommended.

Note on Software Setup

This guide assumes a standard installation of the software using the default preferences during installation. Lectures and practices use the standard software templates and default options for the Content Libraries.

Lead Contributor: Jeff Morris

Specializing in the civil engineering industry, Jeff authors training guides and provides instruction, support, and implementation on all Autodesk infrastructure solutions.

Jeff brings to bear over 20 years of diverse work experience in the civil engineering industry. He has played multiple roles, including Sales, Trainer, Application Specialist, Implementation and Customization Consultant, CAD Coordinator, and CAD/BIM Manager, in civil engineering and architecture firms, and Autodesk reseller organizations. He has worked for government organizations and private firms, small companies and large multinational corporations and in multiple geographies across the globe. Through his extensive experience in Building and Infrastructure design, Jeff has acquired a thorough understanding of CAD Standards and Procedures and an in-depth knowledge of CAD and BIM. Jeff studied Architecture and has a diploma in Systems Analysis and Programming. He is an Autodesk Certified Instructor (ACI) and holds the Autodesk Certified Professional certification for Civil 3D and Revit.

Jeff Morris has been the Lead Contributor for *Autodesk Civil 3D: Fundamentals for Land Developers (Grading)* since 2019.

In This Guide

The following highlights the key features of this guide.

Feature	Description
Practice Files	The Practice Files page includes a link to the practice files and instructions on how to download and install them. The practice files are required to complete the practices in this guide.
Chapters	A chapter consists of the following: Learning Objectives, Instructional Content, Practices, Chapter Review Questions, and Command Summary.
	• **Learning Objectives** define the skills you can acquire by learning the content provided in the chapter.
	• **Instructional Content**, which begins right after Learning Objectives, refers to the descriptive and procedural information related to various topics. Each main topic introduces a product feature, discusses various aspects of that feature, and provides step-by-step procedures on how to use that feature. Where relevant, examples, figures, helpful hints, and notes are provided.
	• **Practice** for a topic follows the instructional content. Practices enable you to use the software to perform a hands-on review of a topic. It is required that you download the practice files (using the link found on the Practice Files page) prior to starting the first practice.
	• **Chapter Review Questions**, located close to the end of a chapter, enable you to test your knowledge of the key concepts discussed in the chapter.
	• **Command Summary** concludes a chapter. It contains a list of the software commands that are used throughout the chapter and provides information on where the command can be found in the software.
Appendices	Appendices provide additional information to the main course content. It could be in the form of instructional content, practices, tables, projects, or skills assessment.

Practice Files

To download the practice files for this guide, use the following steps:

1. Type the URL **exactly as shown below** into the address bar of your Internet browser, to access the Course File Download page.

   Note: If you are using the ebook, you do not have to type the URL. Instead, you can access the page simply by clicking the URL below.

   ## https://www.ascented.com/getfile/id/devarioPF

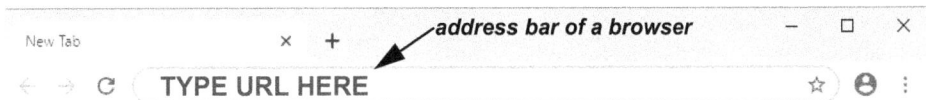

2. On the Course File Download page, click the **DOWNLOAD NOW** button, as shown below, to download the .ZIP file that contains the practice files.

   DOWNLOAD NOW ▶

3. Once the download is complete, unzip the file and extract its contents.

   The recommended practice files folder location is:
   C:\Civil 3D for Land Dev

   Note: It is recommended that you do not change the location of the practice files folder. Doing so may cause errors when completing the practices.

Stay Informed!

To receive information about upcoming events, promotional offers, and complimentary webcasts, visit:

www.ASCENTed.com/updates

Introduction to Grading for Land Developers

During the grading process, it is important for a designer to be able to visualize how the ground is affected when it gets reshaped. Designers need to understand where the water runs so that they can make any necessary changes. In this chapter, you will learn how to create styles that make it easier to visualize a ground surface and understand its impact on flowing water.

Learning Objectives in This Chapter

- State the purpose of grading and reshaping the earth's surface.
- List the tools in the Autodesk® Civil 3D® software that can be used for grading and the items that are affected by their changes.
- Identify the required settings to set up a new grading project.
- Set up feature line styles.
- Set up a grading group style for easy viewing of grading objects.
- Create grading criteria sets for multiple types of grading tasks.
- Create surface styles that make the effects of your grading easier to see and adjust.
- Create sites for managing common topology, such as parcels, alignments, grading groups, and feature lines.
- Create a drawing template specifically for grading.

1.1 Overview

Grading is used in construction to create the proper slope conditions for drainage, transportation, landscaping, and more. Its purpose is to provide stability for the site by minimizing soil erosion and sedimentation. When reshaping the ground surface, engineers and designers strive to prevent drainage problems, such as standing water on roads, flooding of homes and businesses, and having the ground wash away with storms, as shown in Figure 1–1. A properly graded project establishes drainage areas, directs drainage patterns, and affects runoff velocities.

Figure 1–1

Before creating a grading plan, the existing conditions of a site must be gathered. Land surveys, soil investigations, and storm data should all be studied before starting to consider where to create cut or fill areas. Another consideration is the newly created hard surfaces that create additional runoff.

Parts of the Grading Object

Grading objects contain several components. A basic grading object contains a footprint or base line, projection lines, daylight or target lines, and faces. Each of the parts are shown in Figure 1–2.

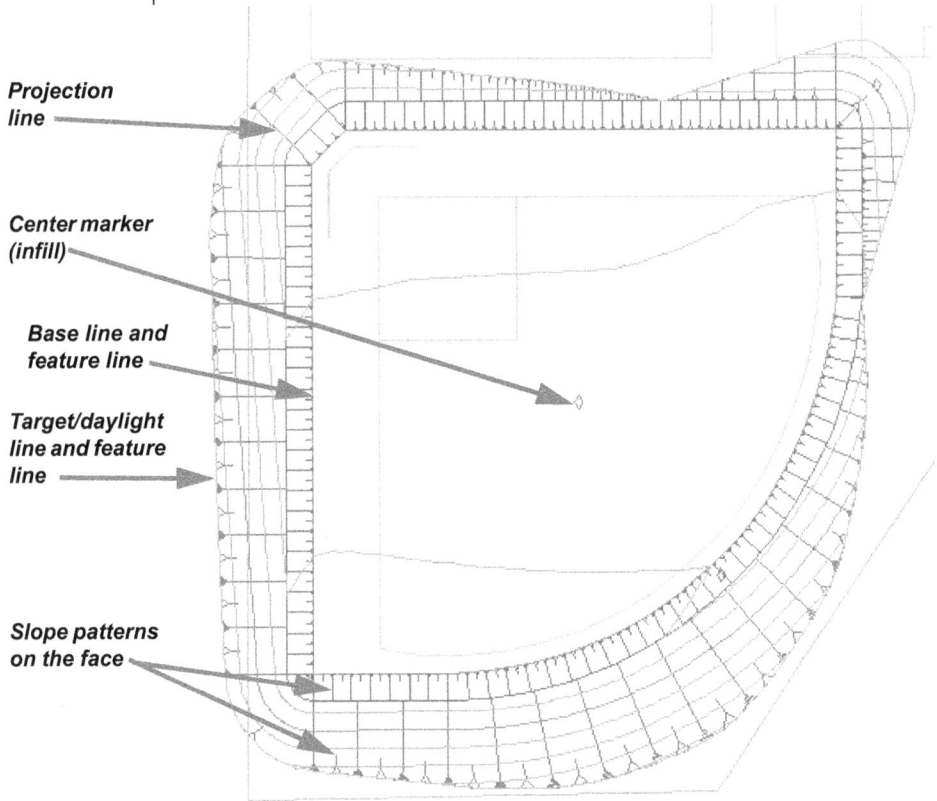

Projection line

Center marker (infill)

Base line and feature line

Target/daylight line and feature line

Slope patterns on the face

Figure 1–2

- **Base lines** act as the footprint for the grading object. They can be a parcel line or any open or closed feature line. Feature lines can represent ridge or swale lines, building footprints, parking lots, and a number of other design features.

- A **target line** is the end result of a grading object. It can be defined by a distance, elevation (relative or absolute), or surface. If a surface is used as the target, the result is a daylight line. In all cases, the target line will be a feature line that can then be used as the base line for another grading object.

- A **face** is the slope area created by the application of a grading criteria. Depending on the grading object's specified style, slope patterns might be displayed on each face according to the type of grading solution. The slope pattern for a distance grading object might look different than the slope pattern on a cut or fill slope, as shown in Figure 1–2.

- **Projection lines** define the face edges within a region of a grading object and are used for the facets along curves and break points on the base line and target line.

- The **center marker** is a diamond that marks a graded face's center and is used for display and selection purposes. When you edit each grading object, select the center marker that displays the *Grading* contextual tab in the ribbon. In most cases, this center marker designates a grading infill.

A **grading group** is a collection of grading objects that is used to organize gradings and make surface creation and volume calculations easier. By setting a volume base surface in the grading group properties (as shown in Figure 1–3), grading volume tools can be used to calculate a quick volume between the new grading surface and the existing ground surface.

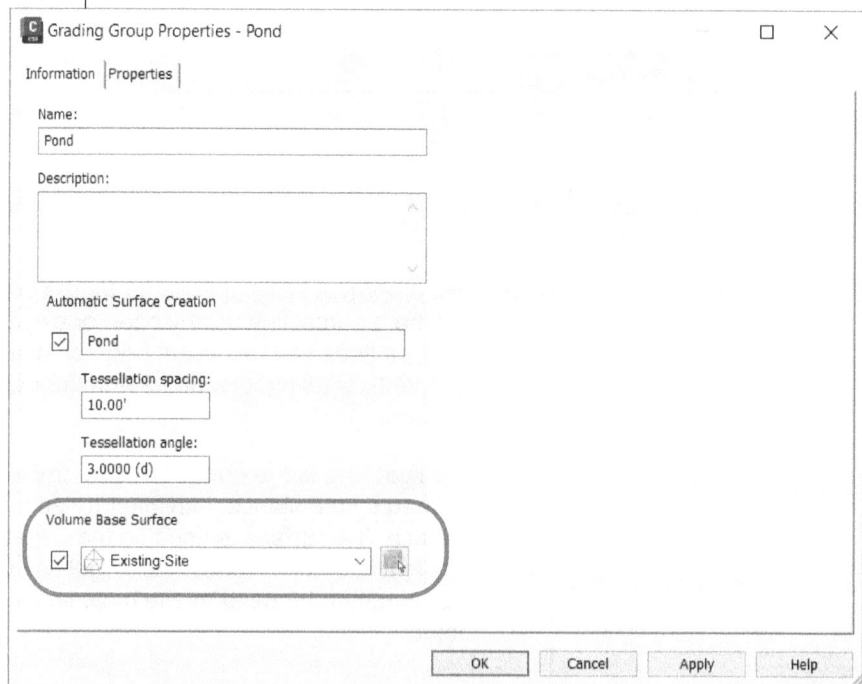

Figure 1–3

Grading Workflow

Setting Up Gradings

In the preliminary phase of a project, you can save a lot of time and effort if your drawing is set up beforehand with the settings and styles needed to convey design intent effectively. Then save it as a template.

1. **Establish Grading Settings:** This is where you will define units of measurement to be used throughout the project for gradings.
2. **Create Grading Styles:** Styles determine how feature lines, surfaces, and grading groups display in the drawing and on the printed sheet.
3. **Define Grading Criteria:** Predefining the methods and projections for grading saves time and ensures that the proper standards are followed.

Designing and Creating Gradings

The process used to create gradings might vary from one project to another. The list of tasks below is intended to be a high-level overview.

1. **Create a Site:** A site is where the grading information created resides in Civil 3D. This is where the interaction between Feature Lines and Grading Groups occur.
2. **Create Feature Lines:** Parcel lines can be used to create feature lines or convert existing linework into feature lines. Nearly every grading project contains at least one feature line.
3. **Create Grading Groups:** The interaction between feature lines can be controlled along with grading projections using grading groups.
4. **Create the Grading:** By creating multiple grading objects, you can determine the slope of the ground from the base line to the target line.
5. **Modify the Grading as Required:** Editing commands can be used to make easy adjustments to grading objects and feature lines as the design changes.

Outputting Grading Information

It is important to be able to convey the grading design to others. During the design phase, community leaders and the public might need to be able to visualize the finished project. Creating renderings for the public makes visualizing the project easier for them. However, contractors are more familiar with reading contour data with cut and fill slopes labeled or shaded to indicate how much ground needs to be moved from one area to another. They might also need cut and fill reports to help them order the correct volume of material for the site.

1. **Select the Grading Group Surface Creation:** Once the grading group satisfies your grading specifications, you need to create contours for it. This is only accomplished by creating a surface.
2. **Edit Grading Styles:** Viewing the surface in various ways assists in finding problems and communicating design intent.
3. **Plot and Publish the Drawings:** Drawings can be plotted onto paper or published electronically to send to interested parties more efficiently.
4. **Produce Reports:** Reports complement drawings to communicate design intent and volumes to interested parties.

1.2 Tools in Autodesk Civil 3D

The Autodesk Civil 3D software is a powerful application for civil engineering design. Although it runs in the familiar AutoCAD® environment, the software is based on a dynamic engineering model that contains all of the core geometry and integrates all of the data. When you make a change to the design, the Autodesk Civil 3D software automatically updates the related objects, views, annotations, tables, etc.

The objects used for grading in the Autodesk Civil 3D software establish intelligent relationships. The following table lists items that can be used for grading and shows these relationships and how a change made to one object is reflected in others.

When you edit these objects...	These objects are updated...
Points	Surfaces
Surfaces	Grading Groups, Profiles, Pipe Networks, and Corridors
Parcels	Grading Groups and Corridors
Alignments	Grading Groups, Corridors, Profiles, Parcels, Sections, and Pipe Networks
Profiles	Grading Groups, Corridors, Parcels, Sections, and Pipe Networks
Grading Groups	Surfaces and Corridors
Subassembly	Assembly, Corridors, and Surfaces
Assembly	Corridors and Surfaces
Feature Lines	Grading Groups, Alignments, Profiles, Corridors, and Surfaces
Sample Lines	Sections and Corridors

1.3 Settings and Defaults

In the Drawing Settings dialog box, the *Units and Zone* tab (as shown in Figure 1–4) sets the Model Space plotting scale and coordinate zone for the drawing. The scale can be a custom value or selected from a drop-down list. A zone is selected from a drop-down list of worldwide categories and coordinate systems.

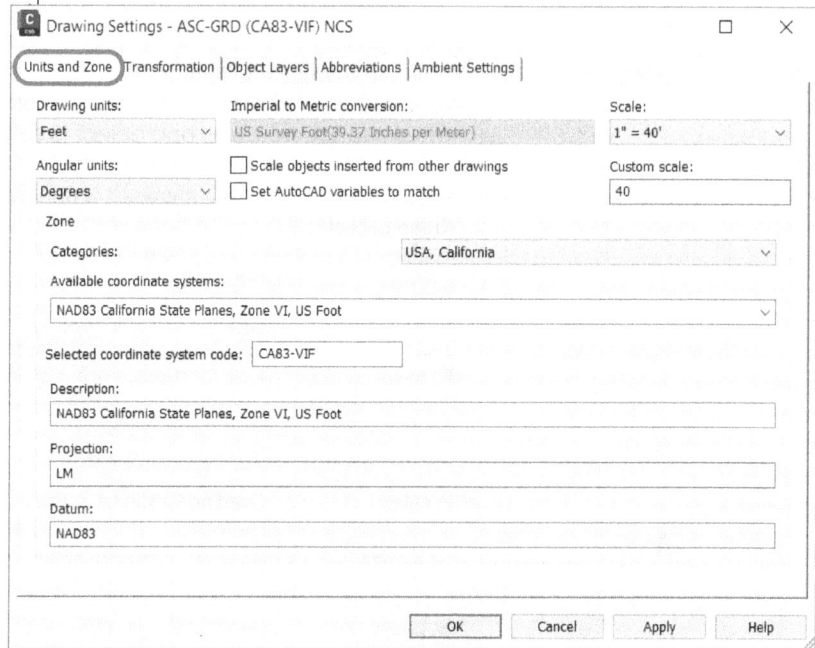

Figure 1–4

If you work predominantly in one Coordinate Zone, you can set your template to that zone.

A drawing that has been assigned a coordinate system enables points to report their grid coordinates and/or their longitude and latitude. Conversely, when assigning a coordinate system, grid coordinates and longitude and latitude data can create points in a drawing.

The Autodesk Civil 3D software has default drawing settings that control all of the basic commands for the drawing, unless there is a specific override at the feature or command level. In the Drawing Settings dialog box, **Ambient Settings** can be set to control the units for area and volume. For example, by changing the unit value, the software knows that you want the volume measurements to be in cubic yards rather than cubic meters, as shown in Figure 1–5.

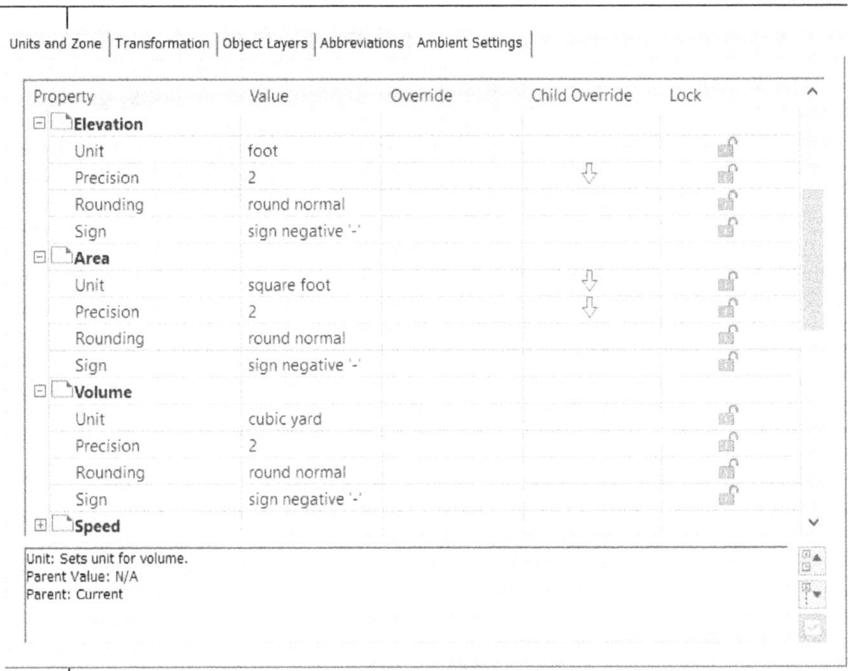

Units and Zone | Transformation | Object Layers | Abbreviations | Ambient Settings |

Property	Value	Override	Child Override	Lock	^
⊟ Elevation					
Unit	foot			🔓	
Precision	2		⇩	🔓	
Rounding	round normal			🔓	
Sign	sign negative '-'			🔓	
⊟ Area					
Unit	square foot		⇩	🔓	
Precision	2		⇩	🔓	
Rounding	round normal			🔓	
Sign	sign negative '-'			🔓	
⊟ Volume					
Unit	cubic yard			🔓	
Precision	2			🔓	
Rounding	round normal			🔓	
Sign	sign negative '-'			🔓	
⊞ Speed					⌄

Unit: Sets unit for volume.
Parent Value: N/A
Parent: Current

Figure 1–5

The *Object Layers* tab in the Drawing Settings dialog box enables you to specify layers for objects. By default, layers are named in accordance with the national CAD Standards if one of the Autodesk supplied templates is used. The object's name can be added at the beginning or end of the layer by selecting the prefix or suffix modifier and placing an asterisk (*) in the *Value* column, as shown in Figure 1–6.

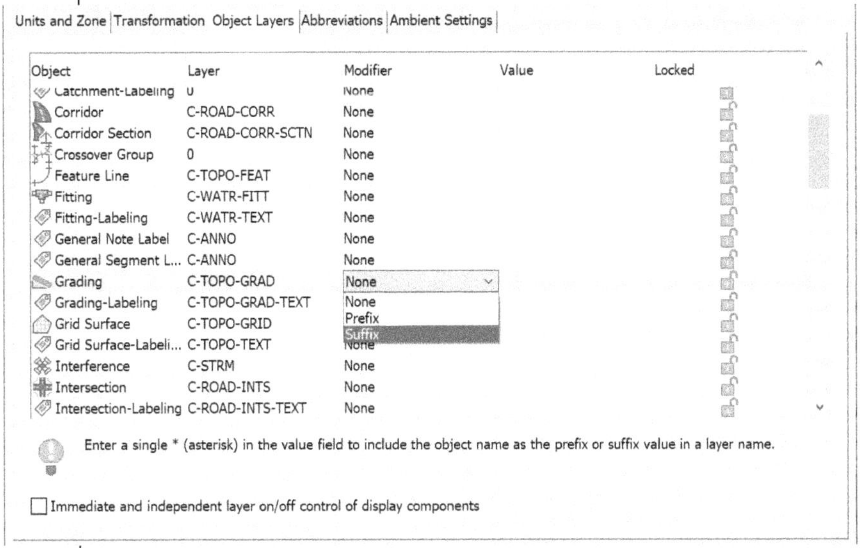

Units and Zone | Transformation | Object Layers | Abbreviations | Ambient Settings |

Object	Layer	Modifier	Value	Locked	^
Catchment-Labeling	0	None			
Corridor	C-ROAD-CORR	None		🔓	
Corridor Section	C-ROAD-CORR-SCTN	None		🔓	
Crossover Group	0	None		🔓	
Feature Line	C-TOPO-FEAT	None		🔓	
Fitting	C-WATR-FITT	None		🔓	
Fitting-Labeling	C-WATR-TEXT	None		🔓	
General Note Label	C-ANNO	None		🔓	
General Segment L...	C-ANNO	None		🔓	
Grading	C-TOPO-GRAD	None ⌄		🔓	
Grading-Labeling	C-TOPO-GRAD-TEXT	None		🔓	
Grid Surface	C-TOPO-GRID	Prefix		🔓	
Grid Surface-Labeli...	C-TOPO-TEXT	Suffix		🔓	
Interference	C-STRM	None		🔓	
Intersection	C-ROAD-INTS	None		🔓	
Intersection-Labeling	C-ROAD-INTS-TEXT	None		🔓	⌄

💡 Enter a single * (asterisk) in the value field to include the object name as the prefix or suffix value in a layer name.

☐ Immediate and independent layer on/off control of display components

Figure 1–6

Command settings enable you to set default styles for specific commands. This helps you save time by automatically setting the correct style for feature lines, grading styles, and cut and fill slopes, as shown in Figure 1–7.

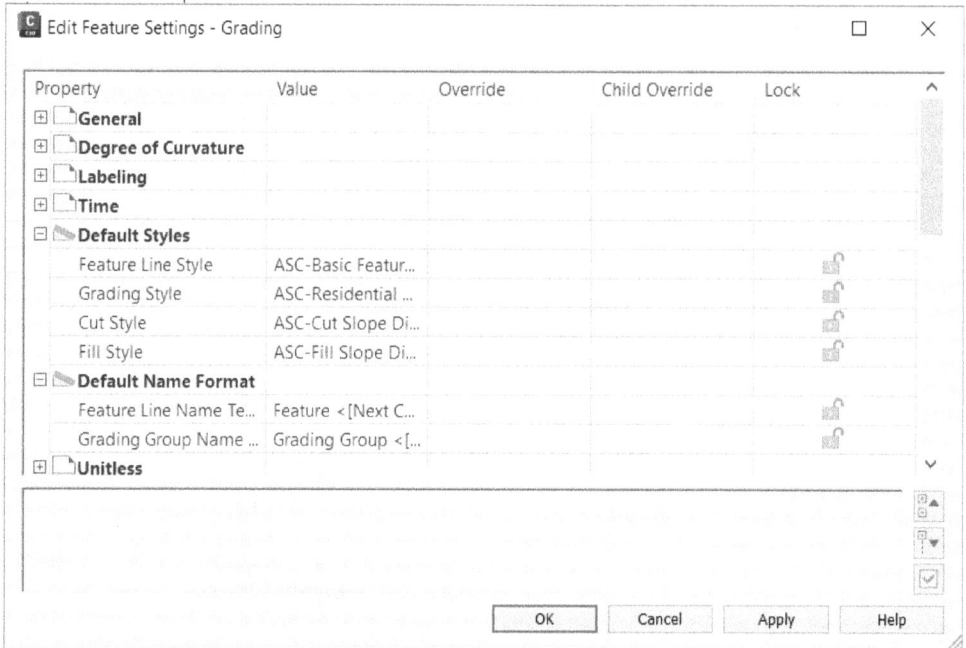

Figure 1–7

Practice 1a

Settings and Defaults

Practice Objectives

- Create a customized drawing template for grading.
- Identify the required settings to set up a new grading project.

In this practice, you will create a template based on National CAD Standards to include the correct settings and defaults for the types of grading done in the project.

Task 1 - Create preliminary drawing template.

Note: Having project files stored in a common folder structure emulates proper CAD Procedures. For training purposes, these folders reside on the local C drive, but in practice, these folders should be on a shared network drive so that the entire project team has access to them.

1. Open the Autodesk Civil 3D software. In the *Start* tab, click the **New** drop-down arrow and select **Autodesk Civil 3D (Imperial) NCS.dwt**, as shown in Figure 1–8, to start a new drawing using this template. This is one of the standard templates that come with the software.

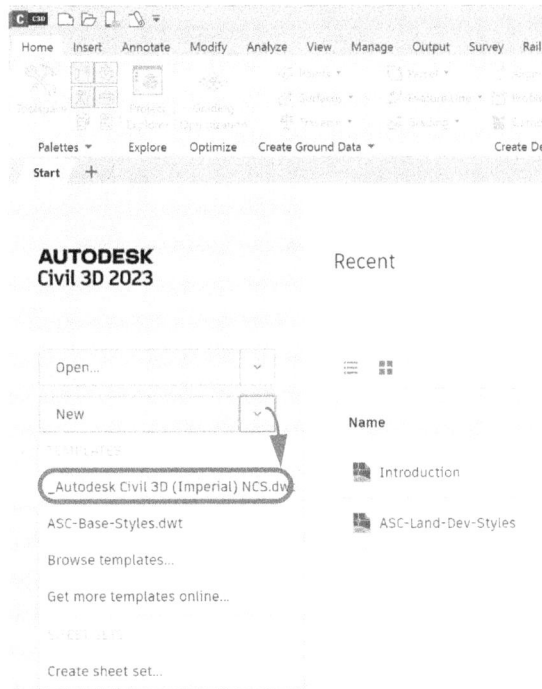

Figure 1–8

2. Click **C C3D** (Application Menu) and select **Save As> Drawing Template**, as shown in Figure 1–9.

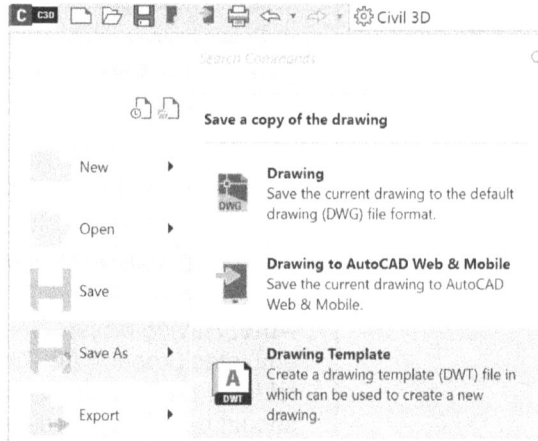

Figure 1–9

GRD is for Grading; CA83-VIF designates the coordinate zone we will set this template up for.

3. Browse to the *C:\Civil 3D for Land Dev\Ascent-Config* folder and type **XXX-GRD (CA83-VIF) NCS.dwt** as the template file name (replacing XXX with your initials). Click on the **Save** icon.

4. In the *Template Options* dialog box, add an appropriate description for this newly created template, for example: **Civil 3D Training template for Land Development**.

5. Select the Toolspace, *Settings* tab, as shown in Figure 1–10.

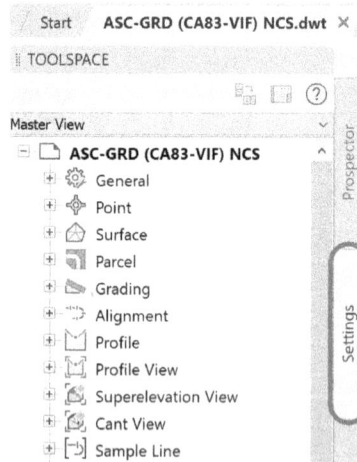

Figure 1–10

6. In the Toolspace, *Settings* tab, right-click on the drawing's name (**XXX-GRD (CA83-VIF) NCS**, at the top) and select **Edit Drawing Settings**. (Substitute your initials for XXX.)

7. In the Drawing Settings dialog box, select the *Units and Zone* tab, as shown in Figure 1–11.

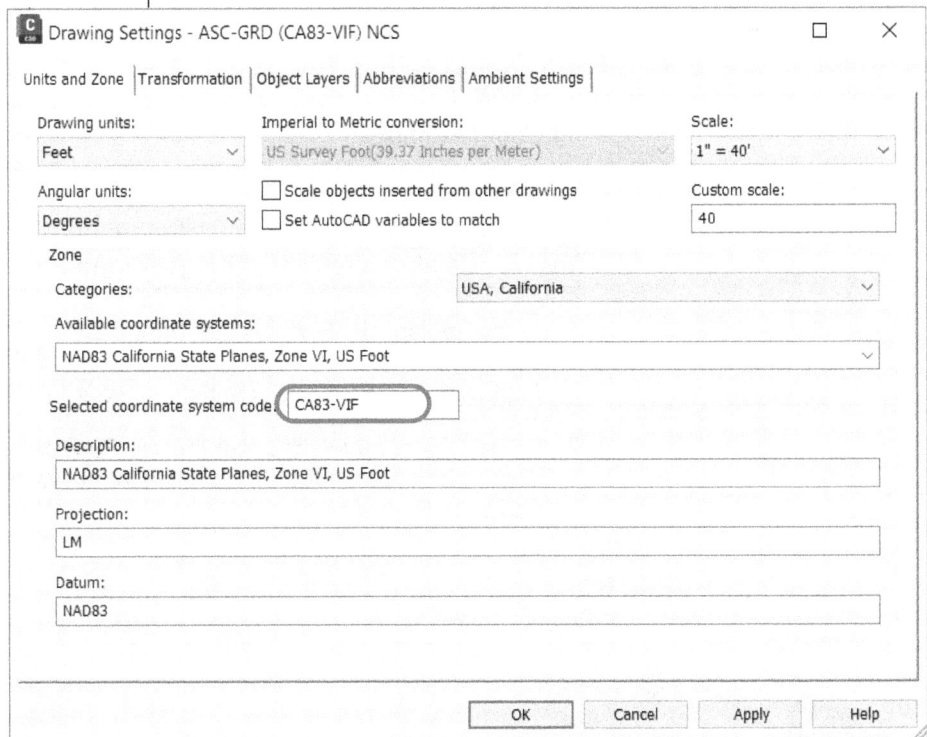

Figure 1–11

8. Type in **CA83-VIF** for the Selected coordinate system code. This is the code for *NAD83 California State Planes, Zone VI, US Foot*.

9. Click **OK** to close the Drawing Settings dialog box.

These coordinates are in the vicinity of the CA83-VIF coordinate zone.

10. Note the coordinates of the drawing are near 0,0. At the command line, type **Zoom** and press <Enter>, then type **C** (for Center) and press <Enter>. For the coordinates, type **6256700, 2036200**. At the ensuing *magnification or height* prompt, type **5300** and press <Enter>.

11. Start the **Single Line text** command (type in **DTEXT** at the command line or select in the ribbon>*Annotate* tab, *Multiline Text* drop down), then select the center of the display as the insertion point.

12. Set the *text height* to **150** and the *rotation angle* to **33**.

13. Type the following, pressing <Enter> after each line (when done typing the last line, press <Enter> twice to finish):

"GRADING TEMPLATE...

DRAWING SET TO CA83-VIF COORDINATE SYSTEM.

GO TO DRAWING SETTINGS TO MODIFY IF NEED BE.

DELETE THIS MESSAGE."

14. Zoom extents.

15. Save the drawing template.

Task 2 - Establish typical settings for grading.

1. In the Toolspace, *Settings* tab, right-click on the drawing's name (**XXX-GRD (CA83-VIF) NCS**, at the top) and select **Edit Drawing Settings**. (Substitute your initials for XXX.)

2. In the *Object Layers* tab, set the *Tin Surface Modifier* to a **Suffix**, and type **-*** (dash, asterisk) in the *Value* field, as shown in Figure 1–12.

Units and Zone | Transformation | Object Layers | Abbreviations | Ambient Settings |

Object	Layer	Modifier	Value	Locked	
Section View-Lab...	C-ROAD-SCTN-TEXT	None			
Section View Qu...	C-ROAD-SCTN-TABL	None			
Sheet	C-ANNO	None			
Structure	C-STRM-STRC	None			
Structure-Labeling	C-STRM-TEXT	None			
Subassembly	C-ROAD-ASSM	None			
Superelevation V...	C-ROAD-SE-VIEW	None			
Surface Legend ...	C-TOPO-TABL	None			
Survey Figure	V-SURV-FIGR	None			
Survey Figure-La...	0	None			
Survey Figure Se...	0	None			
Survey Network	V-SURV-NTWK	None			
Tin Surface	C-TOPO	Suffix	-*		
Tin Surface-Labe...	C-TOPO-TEXT	None			
View Frame	C-ANNO-VFRM	None			
View Frame-Lab...	C-ANNO-VFRM-TEXT	None			

Enter a single * (asterisk) in the value field to include the object name as the prefix or suffix value in a layer name.

☐ Immediate and independent layer on/off control of display components

Figure 1–12

3. In the *Ambient Settings* tab, verify that the *Volume Unit* is set to **Cubic yard**, the *Grade Format* is set to **percent**, and the *Slope Format* is set to **run:rise**, as shown in Figure 1–13.

Units and Zone | Transformation | Object Layers | Abbreviations Ambient Settings |

Property	Value	Override	Child Override	Lock	^
⊟ Volume					
Unit	cubic yard			🔓	
Precision	2			🔓	
Rounding	round normal			🔓	
Sign	sign negative '-'			🔓	
⊞ Speed					
⊞ Angle					
⊞ Direction					
⊞ Lat Long					
⊟ Grade					
Precision	2			🔓	
Rounding	round normal			🔓	
Format	percent			🔓	
Sign	sign negative '-'			🔓	
⊟ Slope					
Precision	2			🔓	
Rounding	round normal			🔓	
Format	run:rise			🔓	
Sign	sign negative '-'			🔓	⌄

Figure 1–13

4. Click **OK** to close the dialog box.

5. In the *Settings* tab, do the following:
   - Expand **Grading>Commands**.
   - Right-click on *CreateFeatureLines*.
   - Select **Edit Command Settings**.

You can also double-click on CreateFeatureLines.

6. In the Edit Command Settings dialog box, do the following, as shown in Figure 1–14:

    *   Select the Plus symbol next to *Feature Line Creation* to expand it.
    *   Select **True** for the values of the *Feature Line Name* and *Use Feature Line Style*.
    *   Expand *Default Styles* and set the *Feature Line Style* to **Basic**.
    *   Click **OK**.

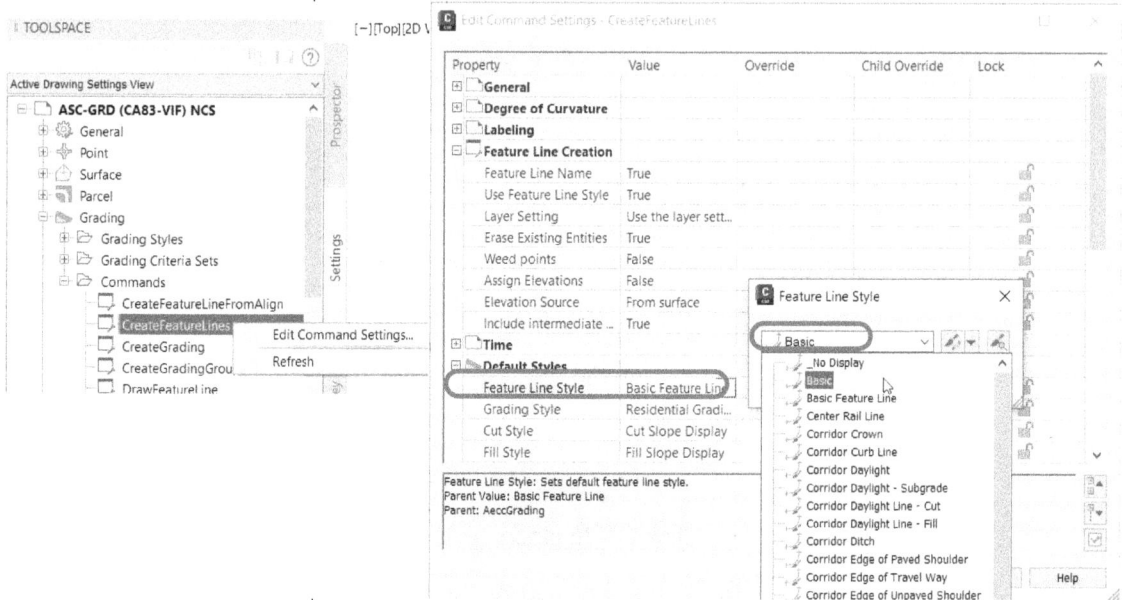

Figure 1–14

7. Save the drawing template.

1.4 Feature Line Styles

Styles assist you in creating the design documentation required for construction documents so that you can focus on the design rather than drafting standards.

Feature lines are complex, linear 3D objects that define a string of known or proposed elevations. Feature lines can be used as breaklines (or folds) in surfaces or as grading object baselines and are created during the corridor creation process. Corridor feature lines can be extracted for use in grading groups. When a drawing is created using one of the standard Autodesk Civil 3D templates, it contains a large number of feature line styles, as shown in Figure 1–15.

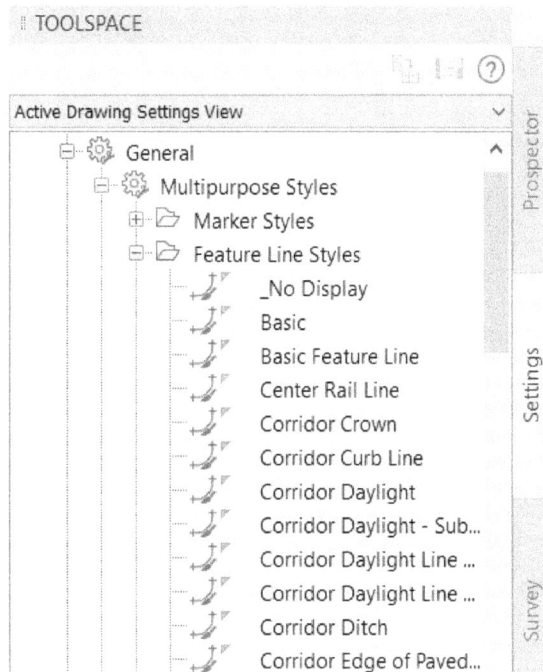

Figure 1–15

Additional feature line styles can easily be created. In the Settings tab, expand **General>Multipurpose Styles**, right-click on Feature Line Styles and select **New**. The Feature Line Styles dialog box opens, as shown in Figure 1–16.

The *Information* tab assigns a name and description. It also indicates who created the style and when it was last modified.

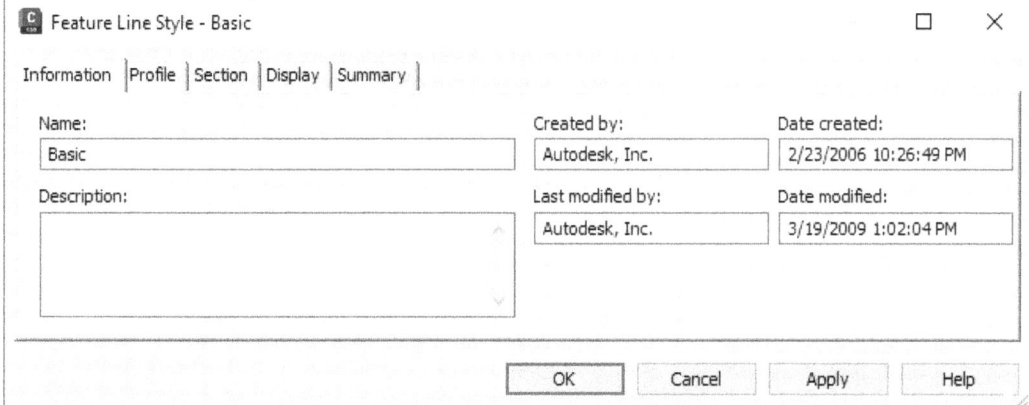

Figure 1–16

The *Profile* tab sets the marker symbol that displays at the end points and internal vertices of the feature line in the profile view, as shown in Figure 1–17. The markers are set to not display when the **_No Markers** style is selected.

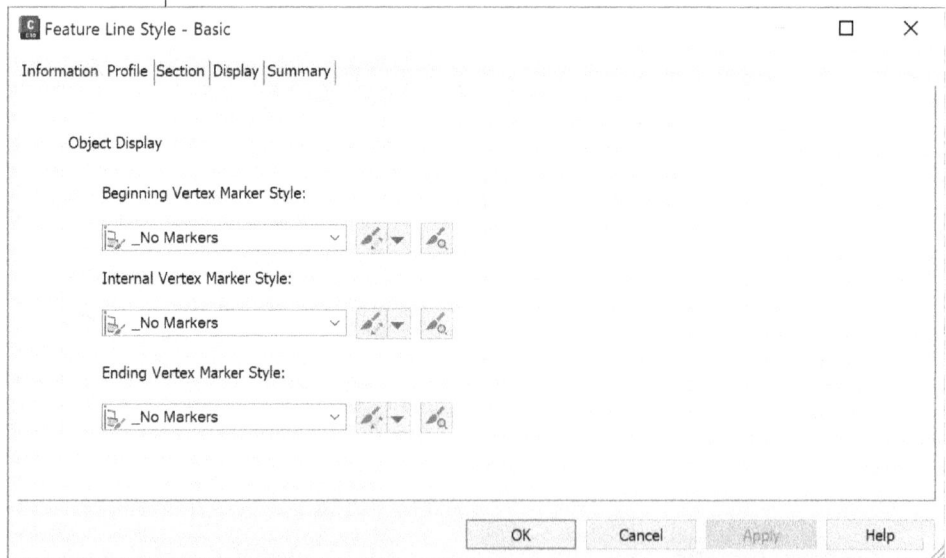

Figure 1–17

The *Sections* tab sets the marker symbol that displays in the section view, as shown in Figure 1–18. The markers are set to not display when the **_No Markers** style is selected.

Feature Line Style - Basic

Information | Profile | Section | Display | Summary

Object Display

Crossing Marker Style:

_No Markers

OK   Cancel   Apply   Help

Figure 1–18

The *Display* tab is where you set the layer, color, linetype, visibility, etc., of the feature line in the various views, as shown in Figure 1–19. If the layer is set to layer 0 (zero), the drawing settings determine the layer on which the feature line is located. If it is set to any other layer in the Feature Line Style dialog box, it overrides the drawing settings.

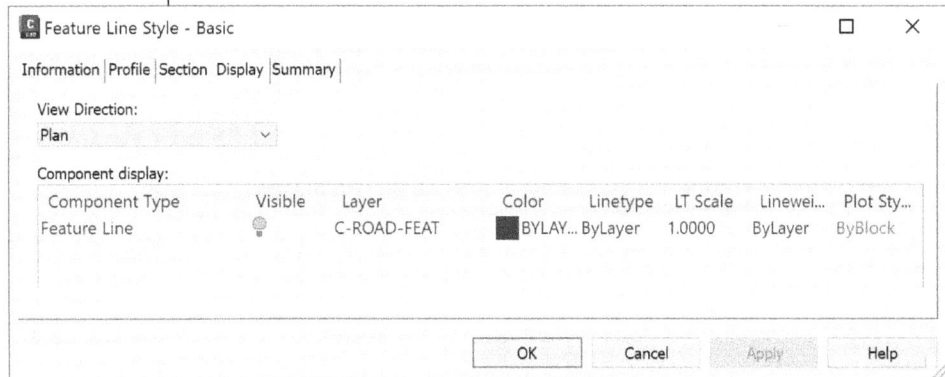

Feature Line Style - Basic

Information | Profile | Section | Display | Summary

View Direction:
Plan

Component display:

Component Type	Visible	Layer	Color	Linetype	LT Scale	Linewei...	Plot Sty...
Feature Line	💡	C-ROAD-FEAT	BYLAY...	ByLayer	1.0000	ByLayer	ByBlock

OK   Cancel   Apply   Help

Figure 1–19

The *Summary* tab displays the settings that are set on all of the other tabs and is useful for quickly referencing what is happening in a specific style.

1.5 Grading Group Styles

The grading group style determines what is displayed in the drawing. You can set the layers for the various grading components to a no plot layer in the *Display* tab of the Grading Style dialog box (as shown in Figure 1–20). This enables you to create grading groups, which enable the grading objects to be displayed while you are working and not when the drawing is printed or plotted. Therefore, only the contours and labels are displayed on the printed sheet.

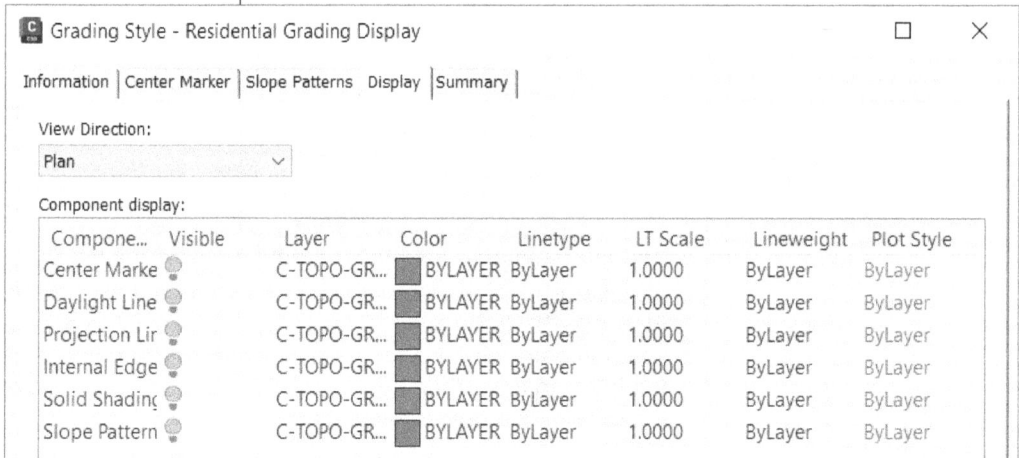

| C Grading Style - Residential Grading Display | | | | | | | □ ✕ |

| Information | Center Marker | Slope Patterns | Display | Summary |

View Direction:
Plan

Component display:

Compone...	Visible	Layer	Color	Linetype	LT Scale	Lineweight	Plot Style
Center Marke		C-TOPO-GR...	BYLAYER	ByLayer	1.0000	ByLayer	ByLayer
Daylight Line		C-TOPO-GR...	BYLAYER	ByLayer	1.0000	ByLayer	ByLayer
Projection Lir		C-TOPO-GR...	BYLAYER	ByLayer	1.0000	ByLayer	ByLayer
Internal Edge		C-TOPO-GR...	BYLAYER	ByLayer	1.0000	ByLayer	ByLayer
Solid Shadinç		C-TOPO-GR...	BYLAYER	ByLayer	1.0000	ByLayer	ByLayer
Slope Pattern		C-TOPO-GR...	BYLAYER	ByLayer	1.0000	ByLayer	ByLayer

Figure 1–20

The *Center Marker* tab determines the size of the center mark (diamond at the center of the grading face). The center mark size can be:

- A percentage of the screen, as shown in Figure 1–21.

- A fixed size (using feet or meters) according to the drawing units.

- Based on the drawing scale so that it plots a specific size.

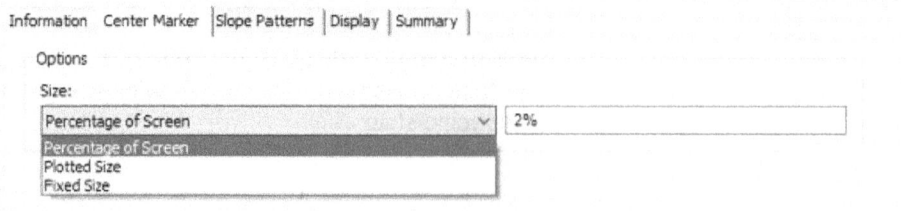

| Information | Center Marker | Slope Patterns | Display | Summary |

Options

Size:

Percentage of Screen	∨	2%
Percentage of Screen		
Plotted Size		
Fixed Size		

Figure 1–21

The *Slope Pattern* tab determines the patterns used to mark the grading slopes. If you select the option to display a slope pattern, an additional style needs to be created to define the number of components to use and the length of each of those components. To access this style, select the **Edit Current Selection** option as shown in Figure 1–22.

Alternatively, you can go to the *Settings* tab and expand **General>Multipurpose Styles>Slope Pattern Styles**. This enables a symbol to be placed at the beginning of the slope. The symbol can be a block, triangle (opened or closed), or tapered lines (with or without a gap). You can also have multiple components for the slope pattern with different symbols and line lengths for each.

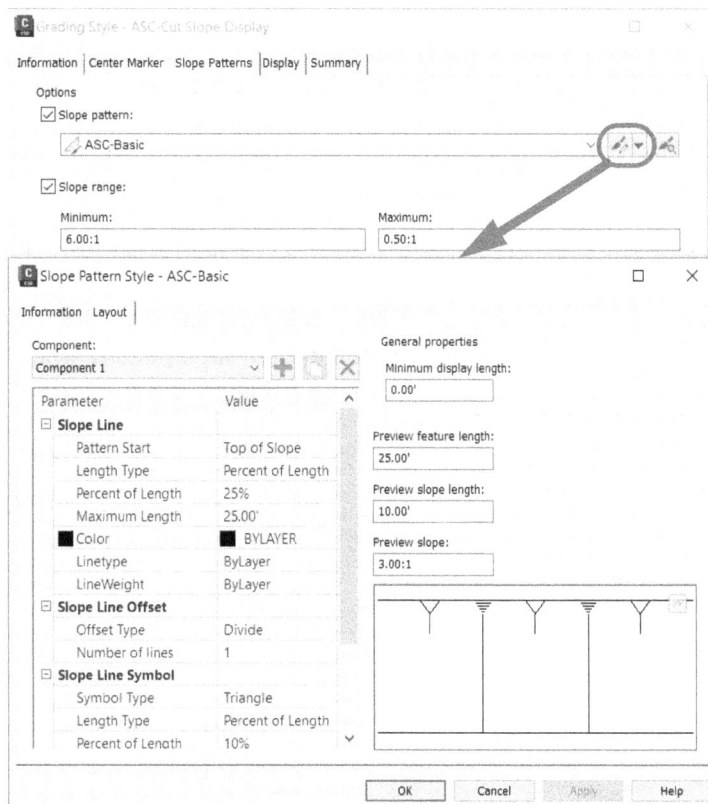

Figure 1–22

In the **Grading Style editor**, *Slope Pattern* tab, the slope ranges can also be turned on. This enables you to apply the slope patterns to a limited range of slope values that you specify.

In the *Display* tab, you can set the layer, color, linetype, visibility, etc., of the various components in the plan or model views, as shown in Figure 1–23. If the layer is set to layer **0** (zero), the drawing settings determine the layer on which the grading group components are placed. If it is set to any other layer in the Grading Style dialog box, it overrides the drawing settings.

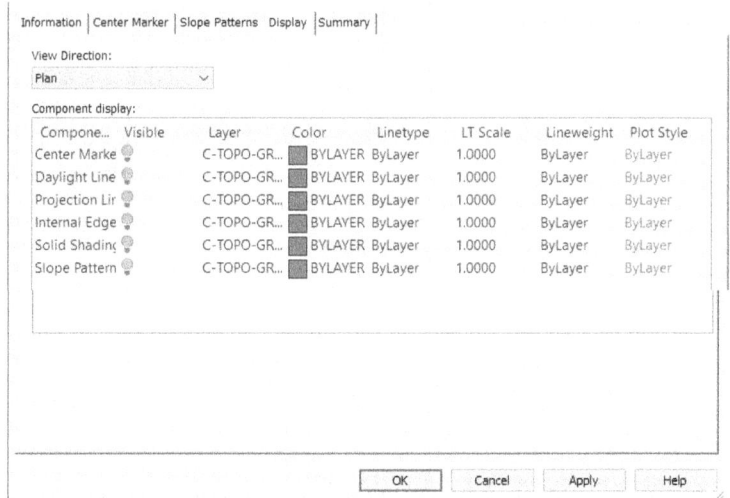

Figure 1–23

The *Summary* tab is a quick way of determining which center marker and slope pattern styles were set on previous pages, as shown in Figure 1–24.

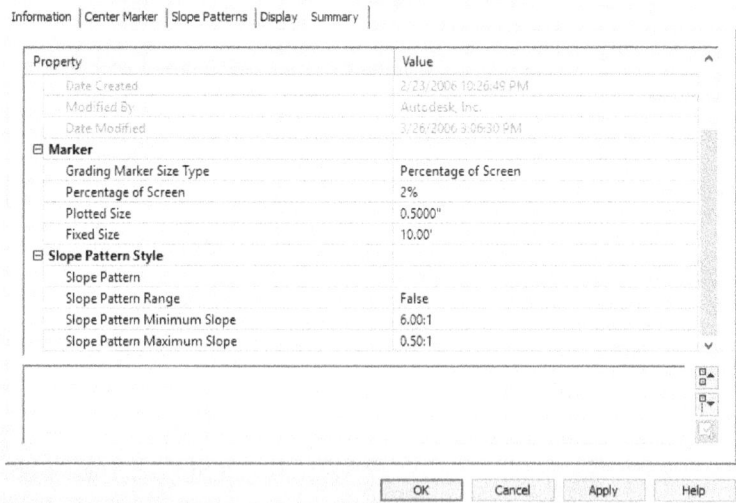

Figure 1–24

1.6 Grading Criteria Sets

Grading criteria is applied to a base line or footprint to create grading projections. Different types of projects require different grading criteria. A pond grading might require a 2:1 slope up to a specific elevation on the interior while the exterior of the pond might require a maximum of a 3:1 slope that daylights to a surface. Each of these criteria can be set in an Autodesk Civil 3D template to speed up and control the grading process during design.

Design criteria can be locked in the criteria to ensure that predefined design specifications are used every time. This also permits faster completion of grading projects by reducing the redundant typing of grading parameters. Once each type of grading criteria has been created, they can be included in a Grading Criteria Set so that they are in one location, making them easier to use (as shown in Figure 1–25).

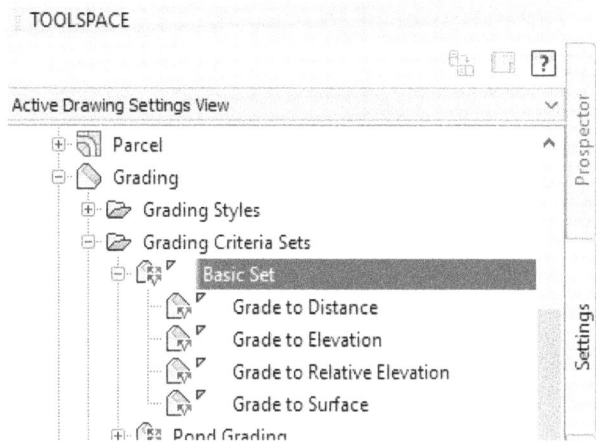

Figure 1–25

There are four different types of grading criteria:

1. Grade to a distance.
2. Grade to an elevation.
3. Grade to a relative elevation.
4. Grade to a surface.

Grade to Distance

When you need to keep a specific grade or slope for a specified horizontal distance, you use the Grade to Distance criteria (as shown in Figure 1–26). For example, a building pad for a house might require that the ground slope away from the house at a 2% grade for a specified distance to ensure that standing water is directed away from the foundation. Use this criteria to set the target at a specific distance and then lock that distance so that it cannot be changed.

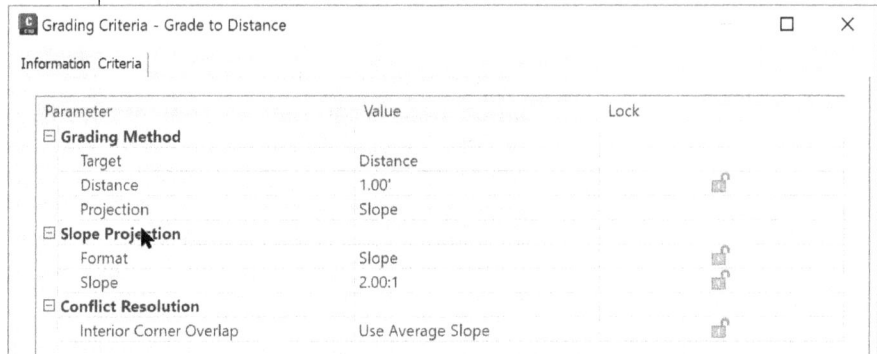

Figure 1–26

Grade to Elevation

When you need to keep a specific grade or slope to an absolute elevation, you need to use the Grade to Elevation criteria (as shown in Figure 1–27) to set the target to be a specific elevation. You can then decide which slope or grade to use for the fill slopes separate from the cut slopes. This is useful in pond grading since the top of the pond needs to be level.

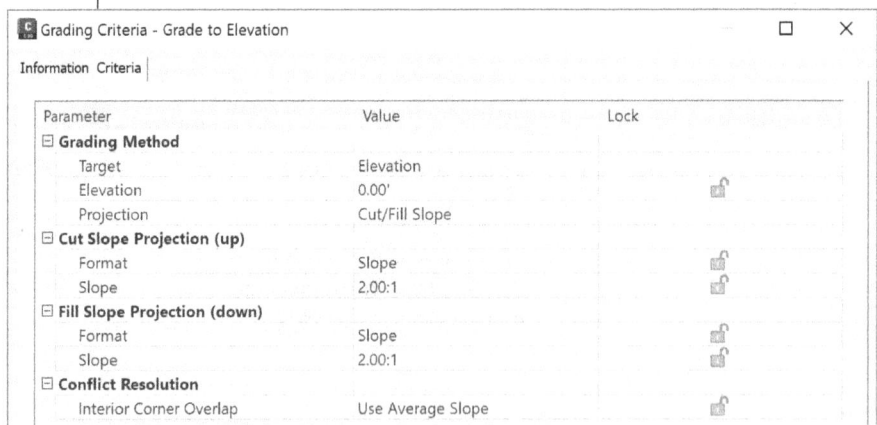

Figure 1–27

Grade to Relative Elevation

Sometimes it is necessary to project a grade up or down a specific vertical distance. This strategy requires using the Grade to Relative Elevation criteria (as shown in Figure 1–28), which enables you to set the target to a specific vertical distance and the slope or grade for that relative elevation. You can then lock the relative elevation so that it cannot be changed.

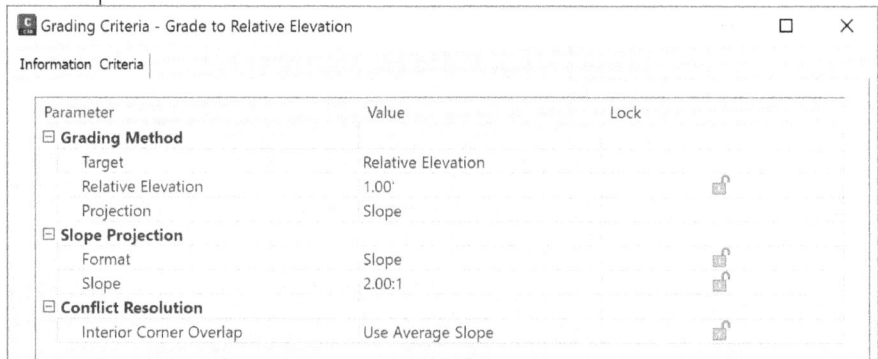

Figure 1–28

Grade to Surface

When you need to keep a specific slope until the projection finds daylight, you need to use the Grade to Surface criteria (as shown in Figure 1–29). It enables you to set the target to be a specific surface name. You can then decide which slope or grade to use for the separate fill and cut slope solutions. This criteria is typically used last to finish the grading solution.

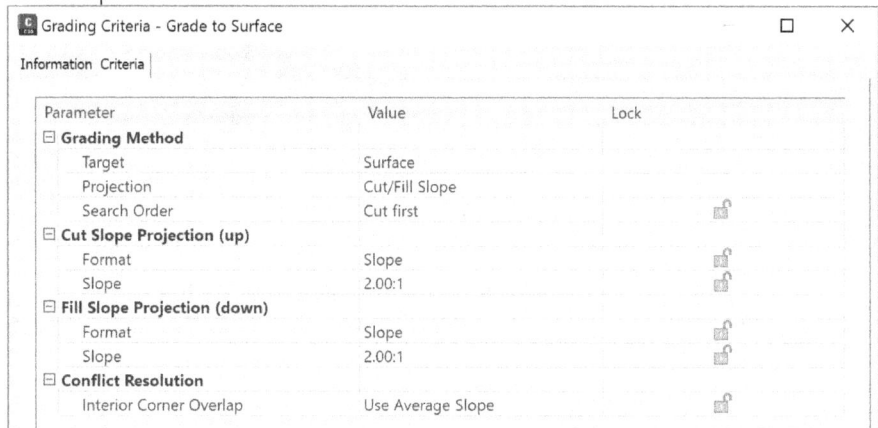

Figure 1–29

- When locking grading criteria parameters, note that once they are locked, they cannot be changed (not even during the editing process). If you change the design parameters, you might need to redefine the grading group rather than just edit it as you would if the grading criteria was not locked.

Practice 1b | Grading Styles

Practice Objective

- Create feature line styles, grading group styles, and a grading criteria set to be used in the project.

In this practice, you will add to the template to include the correct styles and grading criteria.

Task 1 - Create feature line styles.

1. Continue working in the drawing template from the previous practice.

2. In the *Settings* tab, expand the General tree, expand Multipurpose Styles, right-click on Feature Line Styles and select **New**, as shown in Figure 1–30.

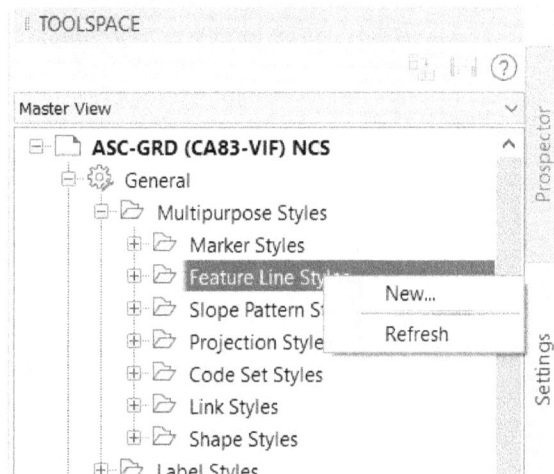

Figure 1–30

3. In the *Information* tab, for the *Name*, type **ASC-Parking Lot**. For the *Description*, type **Parking lot foot print**.

4. In the *Profile* tab, set each of the *Vertex Marker Styles* to **_No Markers**, as shown in Figure 1–31.

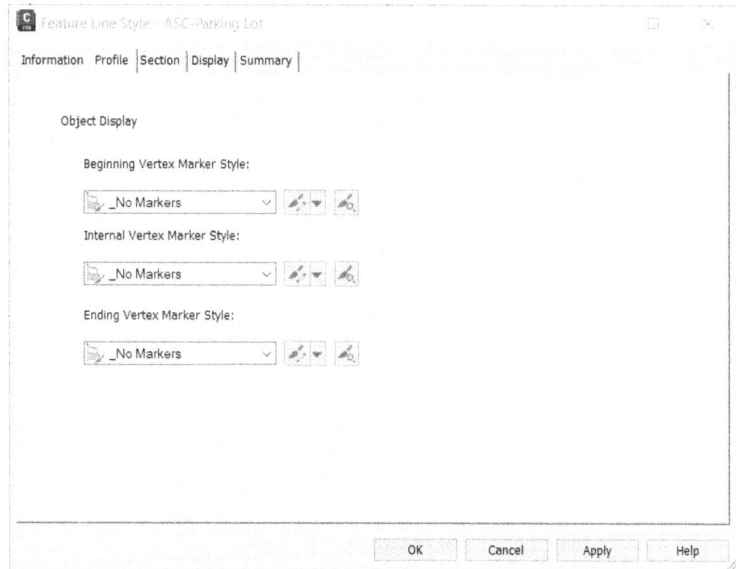

Figure 1–31

5. In the *Section* tab, set the *Crossing Marker Style* to **_No Markers**, as shown in Figure 1–32.

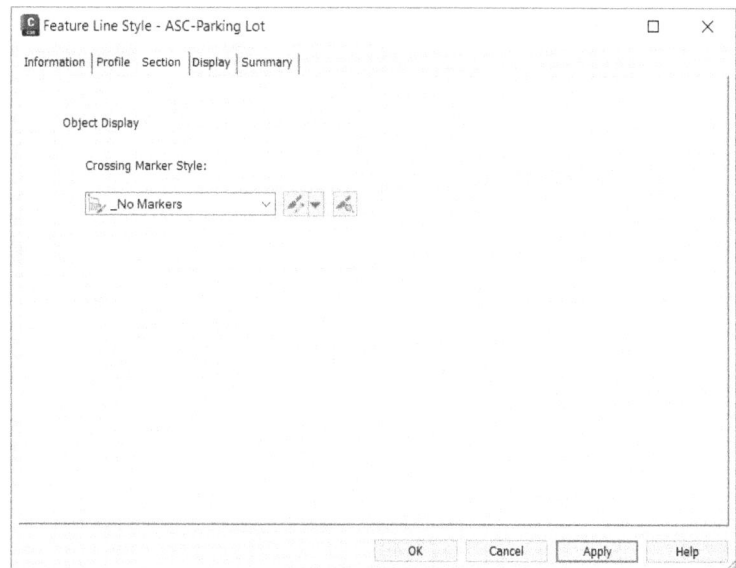

Figure 1–32

6. In the *Display* tab, select the Layer 0 to the right of the Feature Line component. In the Layer Selection dialog box, click the **New** button as shown in Figure 1–33.

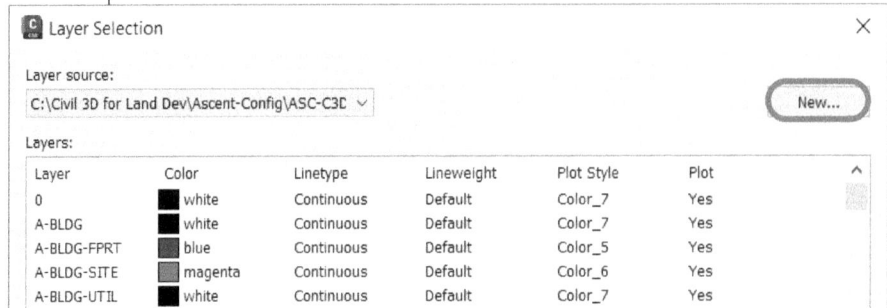

Figure 1–33

7. For the *Layer name*, type **C-GRAD-PARK** and set the *Color* to **40**, as shown in Figure 1–34. Click **OK** three times to close all of the dialog boxes.

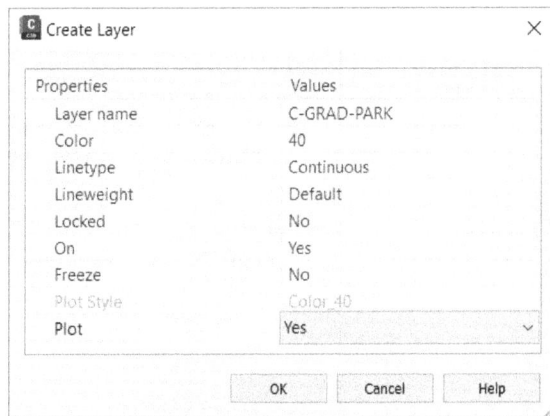

Figure 1–34

8. Repeat Steps 2 to 7 to create additional feature lines for the design objects listed in the following table. Keep the same settings unless otherwise noted.

Feature Line Style Name	Layer Name	Color
ASC-Building Pad	C-GRAD-BLDG	Blue (5)
ASC-Pond	C-GRAD-POND	Yellow (2)
ASC-Lagoon	C-GRAD-LGON	Green (3)

9. Save the drawing template.

Task 2 - Create grading group styles.

1. Continue working in the drawing template from the previous task.

2. In the Toolspace, in the *Settings* tab, expand **General> Multipurpose Styles**, right-click on Slope Pattern Styles and select **New**, as shown in Figure 1–35.

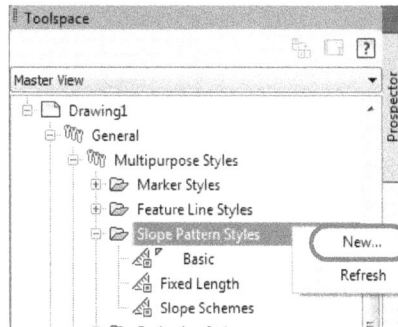

Figure 1–35

3. In the *Information* tab, type **ASC-Easy Viewing** for the name.

4. In the *Layout* tab, for Component 1, in the *Slope Line Symbol* area, set the following:
   - *Symbol Type*: **Triangle**
   - *Percent of Length*: **10%**

5. Set the *Component* to **Component 2**, as shown in Figure 1–36.

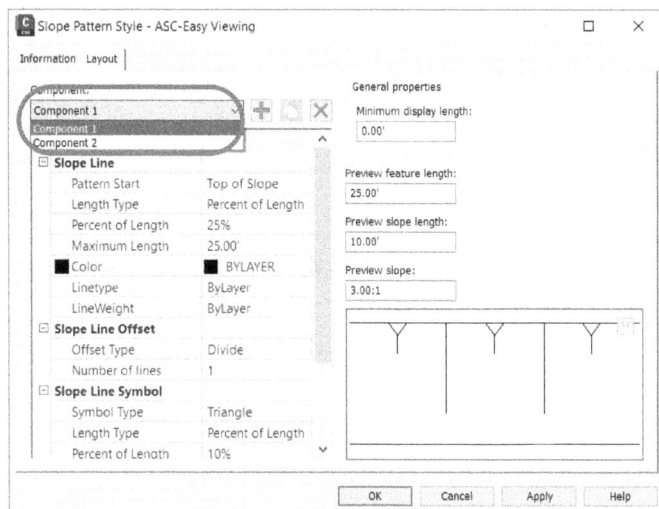

Figure 1–36

---

6. For Component 2, in the *Slope Line* area, set the *Percent of Length* to **75%**, as shown in Figure 1–37.

This will ensure that the slope lines are not mistaken for projection lines.

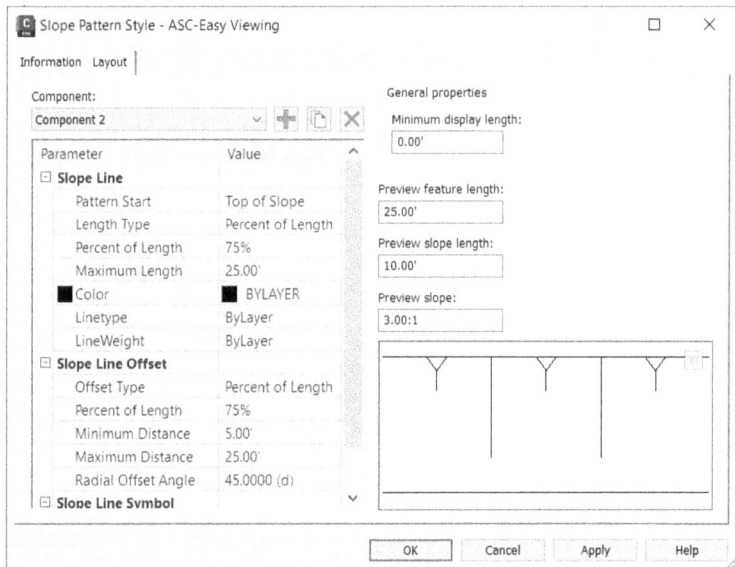

Figure 1–37

7. Click **OK**.

8. In the *Settings* tab, expand Grading, right-click on Grading Styles and select **New**, as shown in Figure 1–38.

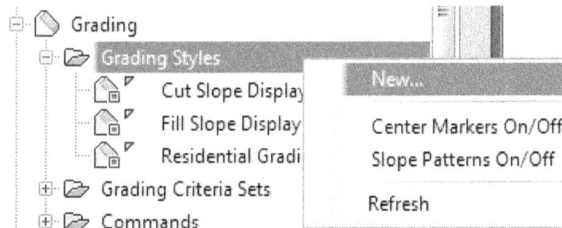

Figure 1–38

9. In the *Information* tab, type **ASC-Pond Grading Display**.

10. On the *Center Marker* tab, type **5** for the *Percentage of Screen* size.

11. In the *Slope Patterns* tab, select the **Slope pattern** option and set the *Style* to **ASC-Easy Viewing**, as shown in Figure 1–39.

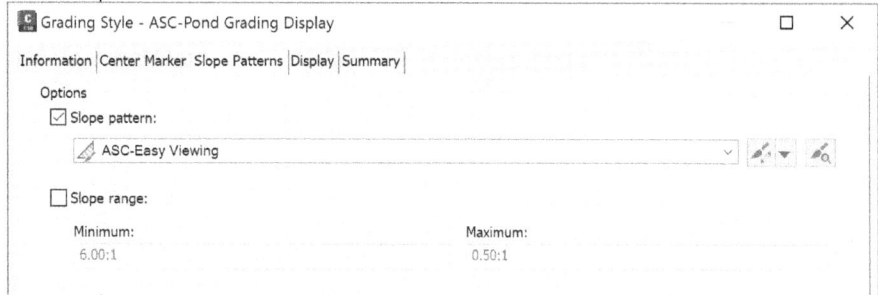

Figure 1–39

12. In the *Display* tab, select all of the components using <Shift>, and then select a **0** (zero) in the *Layer* column. In the Layer Selection dialog box, click the **New** button. For the *Layer name*, type **C-GRAD-NPLT** and set *Plot* to **No**, as shown in Figure 1–40.

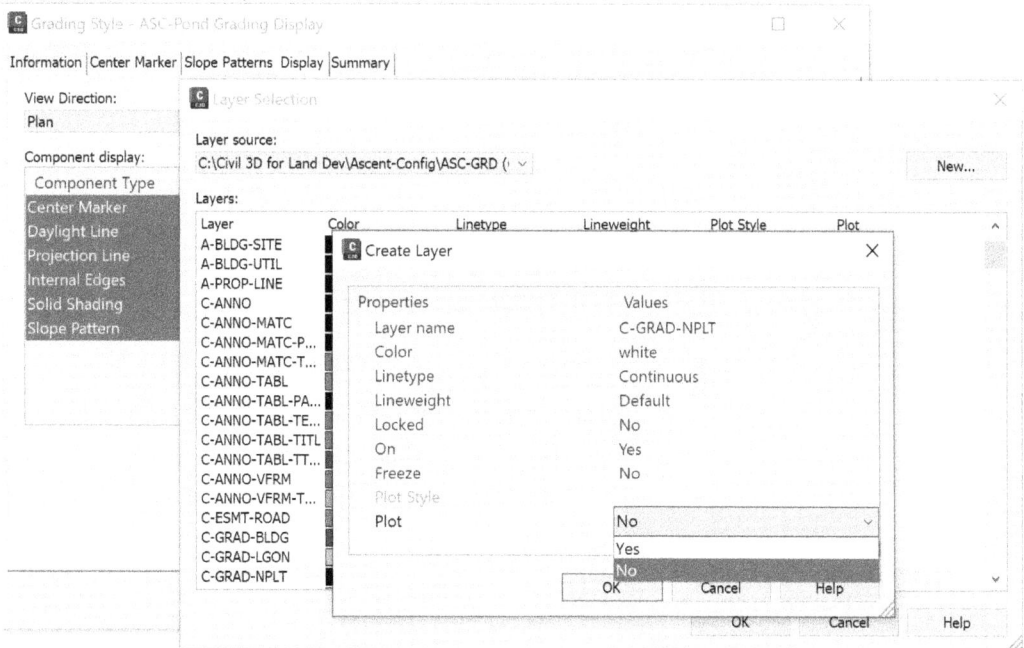

Figure 1–40

13. Click **OK** three times to close all of the dialog boxes.

14. Save the drawing template.

Task 3 - Create grading criteria sets.

1. Continue working in the drawing template from the previous task.

2. In the *Settings* tab, expand **Grading>Grading Criteria Set> Basic Set**.

   - Note that it includes the criteria for each type of projection that can be created in the Autodesk Civil 3D software. When this set is used, the designer can select which slope/grades to use and the distance to which to grade. For Pond grading, you will want more control of the slopes to ensure that the correct specifications are used.

3. Right-click on Grading Criteria Sets and select **New**, as shown in Figure 1–41.

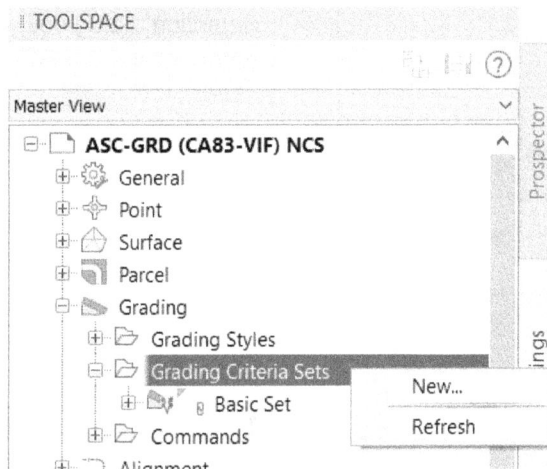

Figure 1–41

4. For the *Name*, type **Pond Grading**. Click **OK**.

5. In the *Settings* tab, right-click on the Pond Grading criteria that you just created and select **New**, as shown in Figure 1–42.

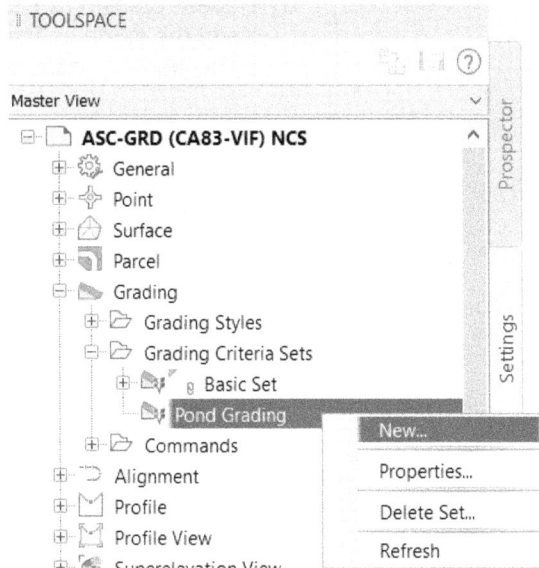

Figure 1–42

6. In the *Information* tab, for the *Name*, type **Interior**.

Note: You might have to save the drawing for the new criteria to be displayed.

7. In the *Criteria* tab, do the following, as shown in Figure 1–43:

- Set *Target* to **Elevation**.
- For *Elevation*, type **160**.
- Set the *Format* of both the Cut Slope and Fill Slope projections to **Slope**.
- For both the Cut Slope and Fill Slope, set *Slope* to **3**.
- Select each **Lock** icon to lock each parameter and ensure that it cannot be changed when used in a grading.
- Click **OK**.

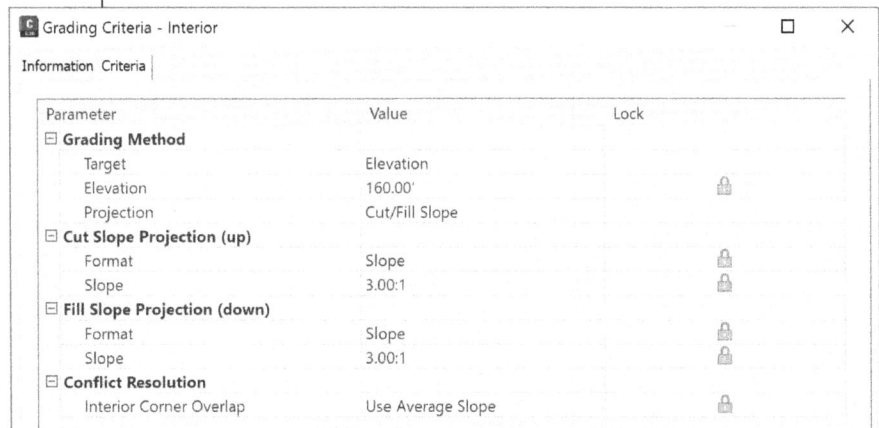

Figure 1–43

8. Repeat Steps 5 to 7 to create the following grading criteria. Keep the same settings unless otherwise noted in the following table and shown in Figure 1–44.

Grading Criteria Name	Grading Method	Slop Projection	Lock
Rim	Distance, 6', Slope	Grade, 2%	Yes
Outer Slope to Surface	Surface, Cut/Fill Slope, Cut first	Slope, 3:1 cut, 3:1 fill	Yes

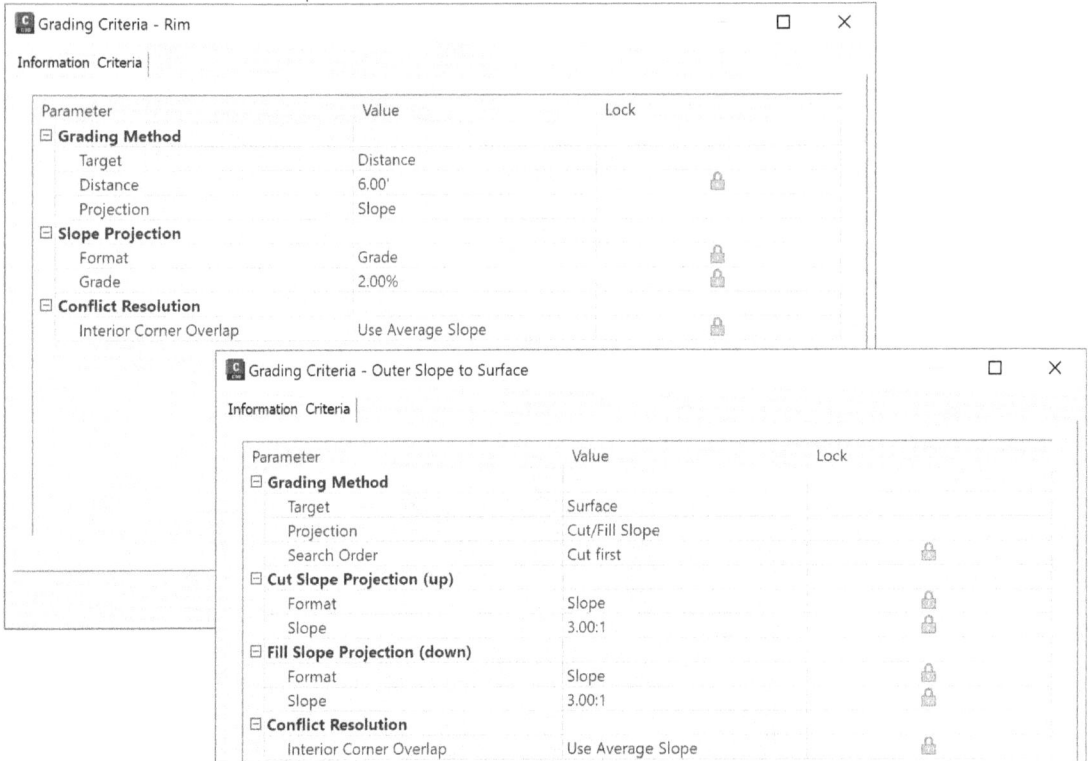

Figure 1–44

9. Save the drawing template.

1.7 Surface Styles

Visualizing the grading results is best done using a predefined surface style. Components, such as watershed boundaries, slope arrows, and slope directions, can be turned on in a surface style to visually indicate which way the ground is sloping and draining, as shown in Figure 1–45.

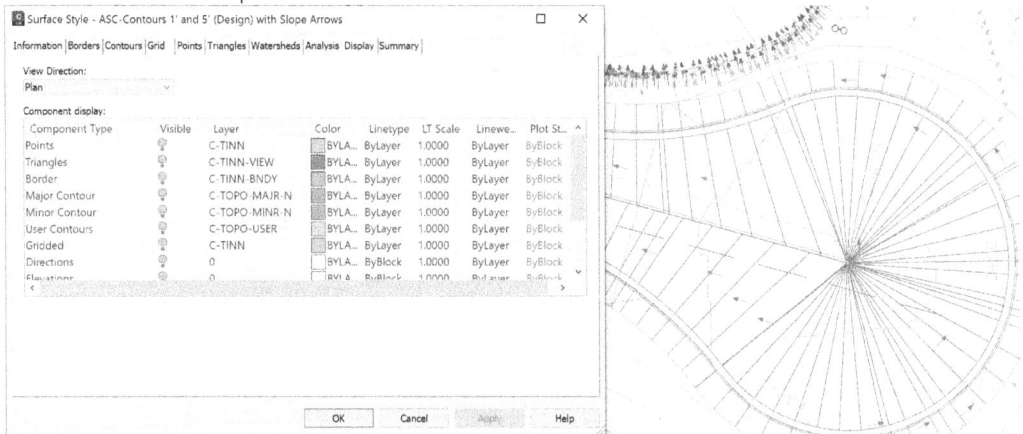

Figure 1–45

As with any styles, the *Display* tab determines which components are visible and how they display by setting their layer, color, linetype, etc., as shown above in Figure 1–45.

The Surface Styles dialog box has additional tabs that also control the display of various surface components. For example, in the *Watersheds* tab, the color, linetype, hatch pattern, etc. can be set for each watershed area type, as shown in Figure 1–46.

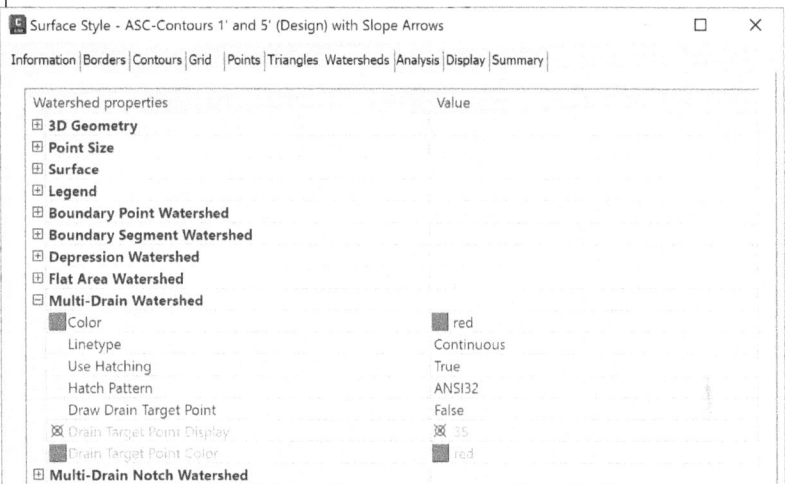

Figure 1–46

In the *Analysis* tab, the color scheme and method of division for the surface analysis ranges can be set, as shown in Figure 1–47. If the same number of ranges in for the slope analysis are constantly used, it can be set here. However, only equal interval, quantile, or standard deviation for the groups can be used. To set specific ranges, use the *Analysis* tab in the Surface Properties dialog box.

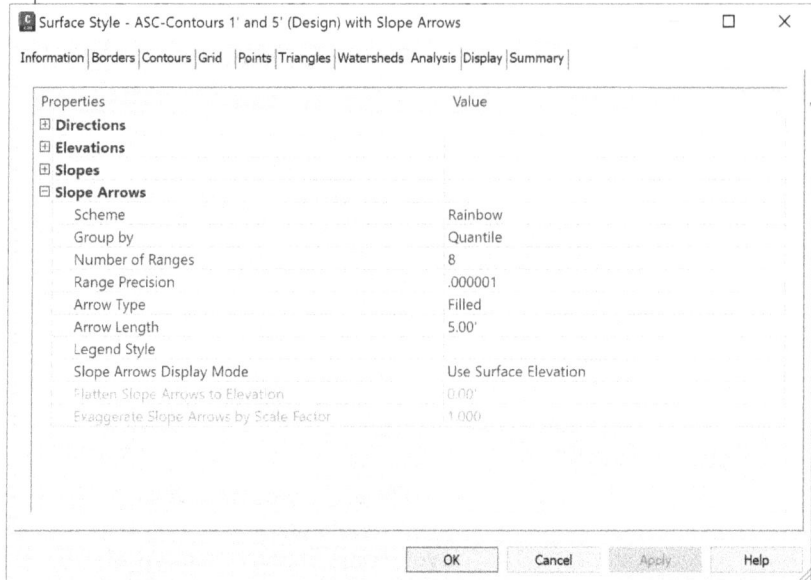

Figure 1–47

In the *Contours* tab, the contour interval, smoothing factor, and color scheme for ranges can be set. By default, only one range is defined, but more ranges can also be defined. With more contour ranges, the contours can be divided into groups similar to the *Analysis* tab, as shown in Figure 1–48.

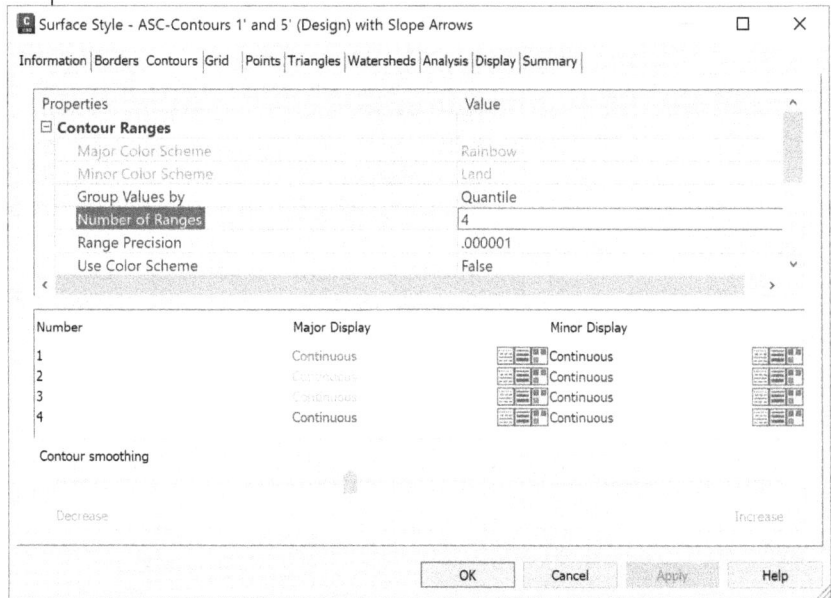

Figure 1–48

1.8 Sites Overview

In the Autodesk Civil 3D software, sites are used as a collection point for common topologies that share relationships with each other. When an alignment and a parcel reside in the same site, they interact with each other. An alignment that resides in the same site as a parcel subdivides the parcel. Grading groups and feature lines also reside in sites and interact with each other when they share the same site. Each drawing can have multiple sites for various purposes, as shown in Figure 1–49.

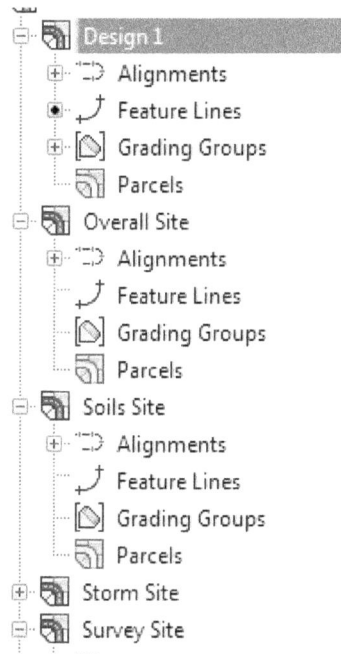

Figure 1–49

Sites for Design Options

It is recommended that you always start your project with an overall site in which you place all of the existing parcel linework. Then before adding alignments, feature lines, and grading groups to your design, you can create another site, label it **Design option 1**, and copy the parcels with which you are going to be working into that site, as shown in Figure 1–50.

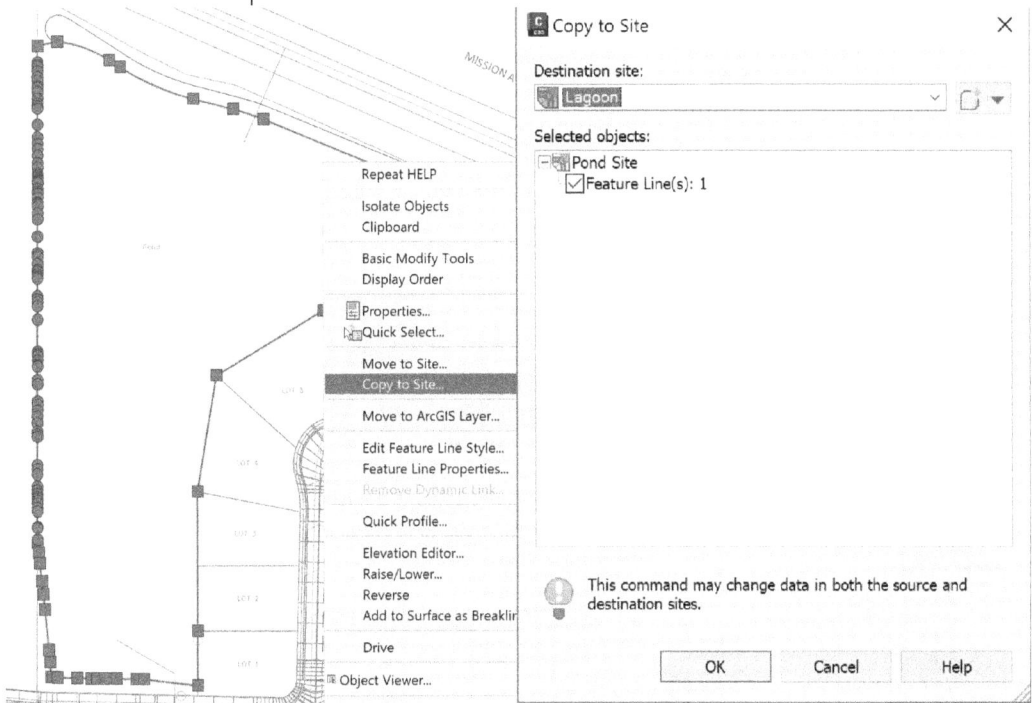

Figure 1–50

This enables you to provide more options to your clients without having many file versions in multiple drawings on a server. Once a client decides which design option to pursue, the other sites can easily be deleted, removing all of the design components within it at the same time, as shown in Figure 1–51.

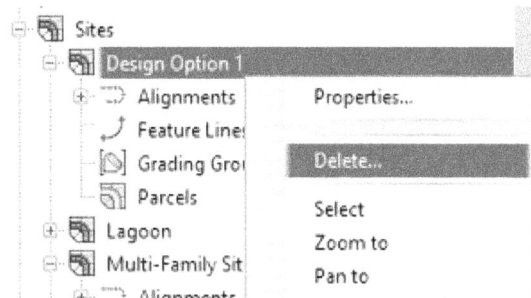

Figure 1–51

Creating Sites

To create a new site, select the *Prospector* tab in the Toolspace, right-click on Sites and select **New**. In the *Information* tab, type a name that is relevant to the entire team. In the *3D Geometry* tab, set the *Site Display Mode*, as shown in Figure 1–52.

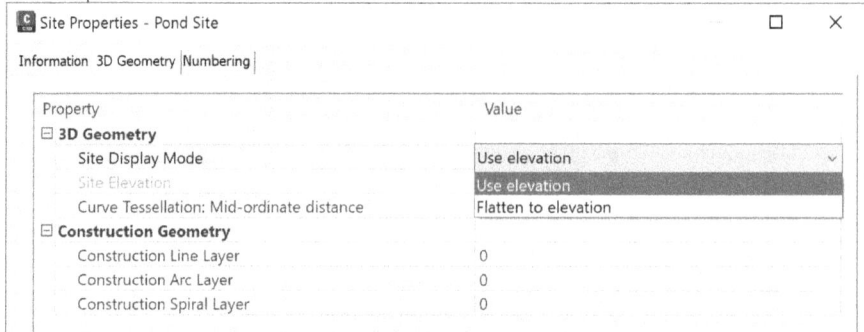

Figure 1–52

- It is recommended that you leave the default option as **Use elevation** so that the site's linework displays at its actual elevations, making it easier to view design intent from any direction in the Object Viewer.

- The optional **Flatten to elevation** option causes all of the site's linework to become 2D and to be located at the elevation that you set.

- In the *3D Geometry* tab, you can also set the layers on which the construction geometry is to be located.

The *Numbering* tab enables you to set the Automatic number for parcels and the counting interval to use for the next number, as shown in Figure 1–53.

*Note: If you do not take the time to create the project site(s) before starting to create feature lines, parcels, or grading groups, a default site is created automatically, called **Site 1**. By default, alignments are placed in the alignments tree rather than in a specific site.*

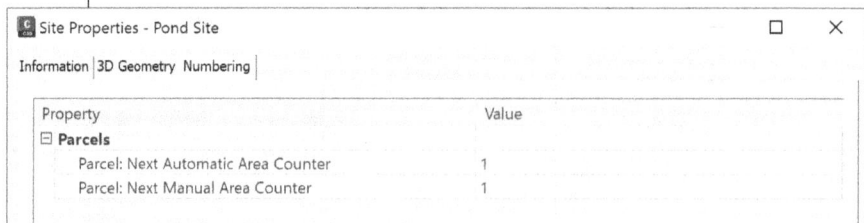

Figure 1–53

Practice 1c | Prepare for the Project

Practice Objective

- Create a surface style and sites in preparation for the grading project.

In this practice, you will add a surface style to the template to make it easier to display the site grading. You will also create some sites to give multiple design options to the client.

Task 1 - Create a surface style.

1. Continue working in the drawing template from the previous practice.

2. In the *Settings* tab, expand **Surfaces>Surface Styles**. Right-click on **Contours 2' and 10' (Design)** and select **Copy**, as shown in Figure 1–54.

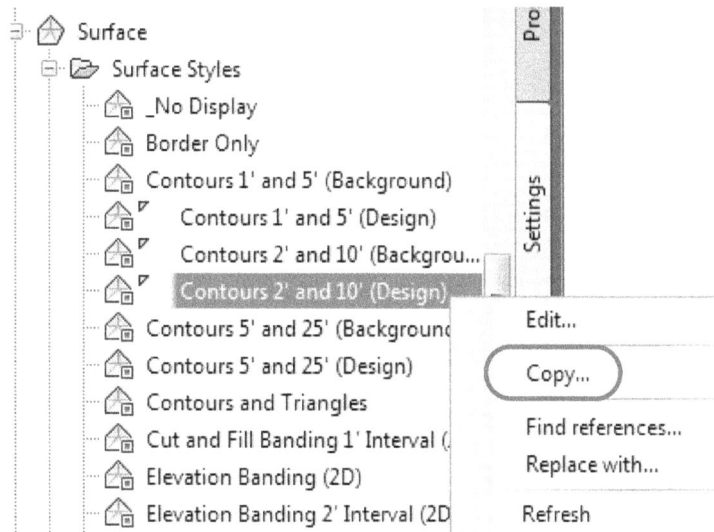

Figure 1–54

3. In the *Information* tab, type **ASC-Temporary Grading View**.

4. In the *Display* tab, turn on the layers **Slope Arrows** and **Watersheds**, as shown in Figure 1–55.

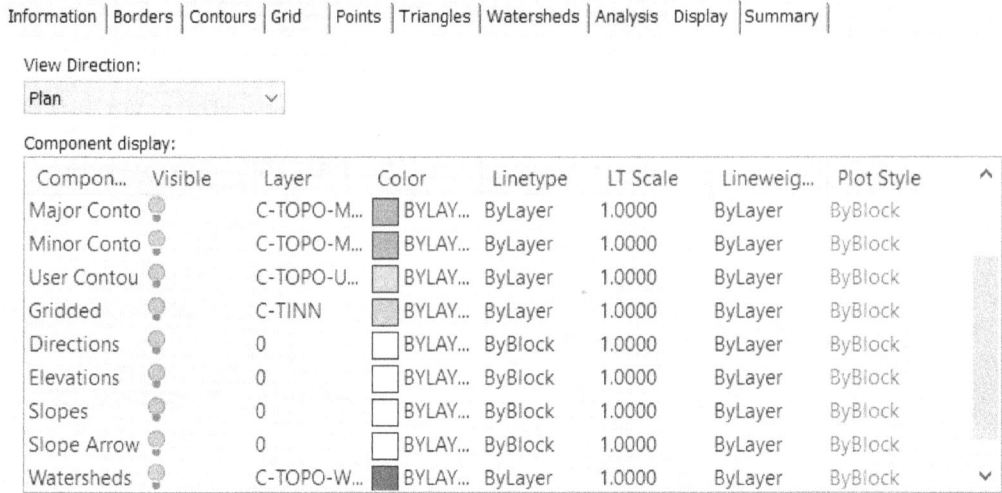

| Information | Borders | Contours | Grid | Points | Triangles | Watersheds | Analysis | Display | Summary |

View Direction:

Plan ⌄

Component display:

Compon...	Visible	Layer	Color	Linetype	LT Scale	Lineweig...	Plot Style	
Major Conto	💡	C-TOPO-M...	BYLAY...	ByLayer	1.0000	ByLayer	ByBlock	^
Minor Conto	💡	C-TOPO-M...	BYLAY...	ByLayer	1.0000	ByLayer	ByBlock	
User Contou	💡	C-TOPO-U...	BYLAY...	ByLayer	1.0000	ByLayer	ByBlock	
Gridded	💡	C-TINN	BYLAY...	ByLayer	1.0000	ByLayer	ByBlock	
Directions	💡	0	BYLAY...	ByBlock	1.0000	ByLayer	ByBlock	
Elevations	💡	0	BYLAY...	ByBlock	1.0000	ByLayer	ByBlock	
Slopes	💡	0	BYLAY...	ByBlock	1.0000	ByLayer	ByBlock	
Slope Arrow	💡	0	BYLAY...	ByBlock	1.0000	ByLayer	ByBlock	
Watersheds	💡	C-TOPO-W...	BYLAY...	ByLayer	1.0000	ByLayer	ByBlock	⌄

Figure 1–55

5. In the *Watersheds* tab, expand 3D Geometry. Verify that *Watershed Display Mode* is set to **Use Surface Elevation**, as shown in Figure 1–56.

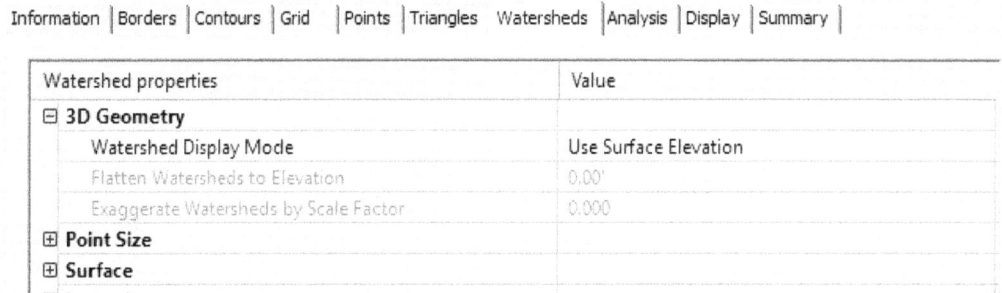

| Information | Borders | Contours | Grid | Points | Triangles | Watersheds | Analysis | Display | Summary |

Watershed properties	Value
⊟ **3D Geometry**	
Watershed Display Mode	Use Surface Elevation
Flatten Watersheds to Elevation	0.00'
Exaggerate Watersheds by Scale Factor	0.000
⊞ **Point Size**	
⊞ **Surface**	

Figure 1–56

6. Click **OK** to close the dialog box.

7. Save the drawing template.

Task 2 - Create sites.

1. In the *Prospector* tab, right-click on **Sites** and select **New**.

2. In the *Information* tab, for the *Name*, type **Multi-Family**. For the description, type **Parcels, building pads, and parking lots for multi-family property**.

3. Click **OK** to close the dialog box and accept the defaults on the other tabs.

4. Repeat Steps 1 to 3 to create the following sites. Keep the same settings unless otherwise noted in the following table.

Site Name	Description
Pond Site	Storm water retention pond
Lagoon	Lagoon and wetland grading
Residential Grading	Single family lot grading

5. Save the drawing template.

1.9 Autodesk Civil 3D Projects

There are multiple ways of organizing Autodesk Civil 3D project drawings. The ones used in this guide are through externally referenced (XREF) drawings and Data Shortcuts.

Single-Design Drawing Projects

Since Autodesk Civil 3D surfaces, alignments, and other AEC objects can be entirely drawing-based, you can have a single drawing file act as the repository for all design data. The only external data might be survey databases and XREF drawings.

Multiple Drawings Sharing Data Using Shortcuts

This approach permits multiple existing conditions and design drawings to share data. For example, a surface could exist in one drawing and an alignment in another. Both could be kept in sync with each other using Data Shortcuts.

This approach does not create any external project data other than XML data files that are used to share data between drawings.

Once an object has been referenced into the drawing and the drawing has been saved, the object is saved in the drawing.

1.10 Using Data Shortcuts for Project Management

Data Shortcuts can be used to share design data between drawing files through the use of XML files.

Data Shortcuts are managed using the Toolspace, *Prospector* tab, under the *Data Shortcuts* collection or in the *Manage* tab> Data Shortcuts panel, as shown in Figure 1–57. The shortcuts are stored in XML files in one or more working folders that you create.

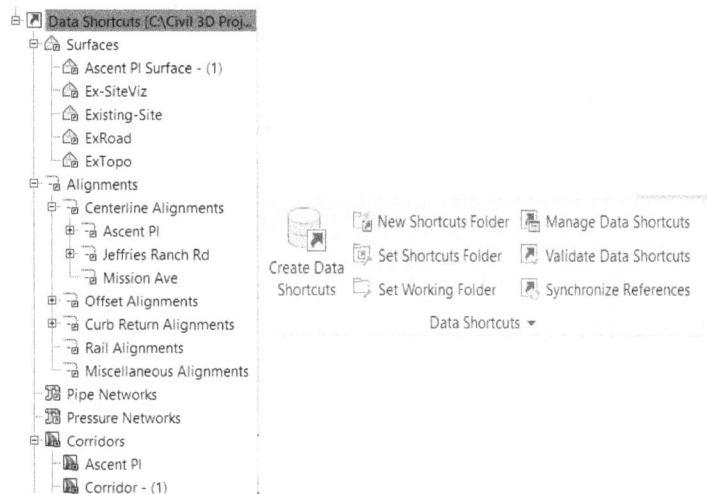

Figure 1–57

Using Data Shortcuts, the intelligent Autodesk Civil 3D object design data can be consumed and used on different levels. However, this referenced data can only be edited in the drawing that contains the original object.

Autodesk Docs Design Collaboration

The Autodesk Docs Design product includes a new entitlement called Autodesk Collaboration for Civil 3D. This enables Civil 3D to share External Reference Files (XREFs) and Data Shortcuts (DREFs) to be stored and shared within a project in a Autodesk Docs Hub. This allows you to collaborate your Civil 3D design through these references in the Autodesk Docs cloud with anyone anywhere.

Autodesk Docs Design Collaboration makes extensive use of the Autodesk Desktop Connector, which serves as a traffic director between the Autodesk Docs Project files in the cloud and the local caches on your hard drive.

When opening a Autodesk Docs based drawing for the first time (or after a long interlude), the Desktop Connector checks the local cache of the drawings and reference files to see if they are up to date. If not, the Desktop Connector downloads a fresh copy of the files. This can take some time, depending on the file sizes, your download speeds, and the traffic in the Autodesk Docs cloud.

Data Shortcut Workflow

1. In the Toolspace, *Prospector* tab, right-click on Data Shortcuts and select **Set the Working Folder...**.
2. In the Toolspace, *Prospector* tab, right-click on Data Shortcuts and select **Set Data Shortcuts Folder...** to select an existing project folder.
3. You might also want to add an XREF to the source drawing if there are additional AutoCAD® objects that you want to display in the downstream drawing.
4. The Autodesk Civil 3D tools for Data Shortcuts are located in the *Manage* tab (as shown in Figure 1–58) and in the Toolspace, *Prospector* tab.

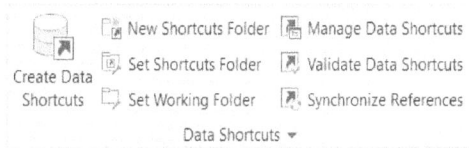

Figure 1–58

Workflow Details

- **Set Working Folder:** Sets a new working folder as the location in which to store the Data Shortcut project. The default working folder for Data Shortcut projects is *C:\Users\Public\Documents\Autodesk\Civil 3D Projects*.

- The default working folder is also used for Autodesk Vault projects and local (non-Vault) Survey projects. If you work with the Autodesk Vault software, local Survey, and Data Shortcut projects, you should have separate working folders for each project type for ease of management.

- **New Shortcuts Folder:** Creates a new folder for storing a set of related project drawings and Data Shortcuts.

- **Create Data Shortcuts:** Creates Data Shortcuts from the active drawing.

Data Shortcuts are stored in the _Shortcuts folder for the active project and used to create data references to source objects in other drawings. Each Data Shortcut is stored in a separate XML file.

When the data shortcuts reside in a Autodesk Docs project in the cloud, it is designated as such in the Toolspace, *Prospector* tab with a small cloud symbol and a path pointing to the Autodesk Docs Project, as shown in Figure 1–59.

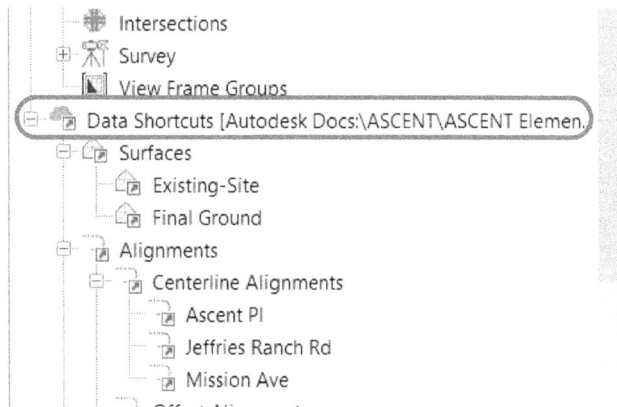

Figure 1–59

Similarly, when you are working in a drawing that resides in a Autodesk Docs project, in the Toolspace, *Prospector* tab, the drawing has a cloud symbol as a prefix, as shown in Figure 1–60.

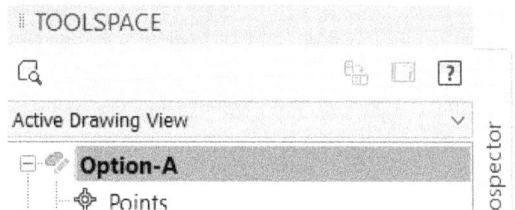

Figure 1–60

Practice 1d | Setting a Project

Practice Objective

- Create a new data shortcut project with the correct working folder for the project being worked on.

In this practice, you will walk through the steps of creating project-based Data Shortcuts folders.

Task 1 - Set the *Working* folder.

In this task, you will select a working folder as the location in which the project's Data Shortcut are stored. The default working folder for Data Shortcut projects is *C:\Users\Public\Documents\Autodesk\Civil 3D Projects*.

1. Start a new drawing from **XXX-GRD (CA83-VIF) NCS.dwt** (replacing XXX with your initials), from the *C:\Civil 3D for Land Dev\Ascent-Config* folder.

   - If you did not successfully complete the previous tasks creating that template, you can use **ASC-GRD (CA83-VIF) NCS.dwt**.

2. In the *Manage* tab>Data Shortcuts panel, click

   ⬜ (Set Working Folder), as shown in Figure 1–61.

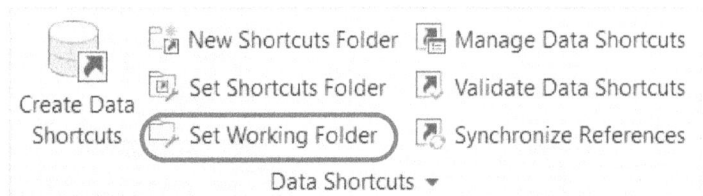

Figure 1–61

3. In the Browse For Folder dialog box, select the *Civil 3D for Land Dev\DataShortcuts\Fundamentals* folder. Click **Select Folder**.

Task 2 - Set the *Shortcuts* folder.

In this task, you will select a folder for referencing a set of related project drawings and Data Shortcuts.

1. In the *Manage* tab>Data Shortcuts panel, click ⬚ (Set Shortcuts Folder), as shown in Figure 1–62.

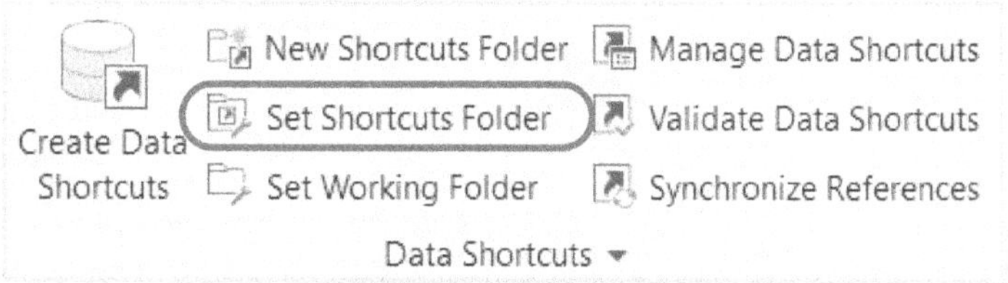

New Shortcuts Folder | Manage Data Shortcuts

Set Shortcuts Folder | Validate Data Shortcuts

Create Data Shortcuts | Set Working Folder | Synchronize References

Data Shortcuts ▾

Figure 1–62

2. In the Set Data Shortcut Folder dialog box, select the **Ascent-Development** project, as shown in Figure 1–63.

3. Click **OK**.

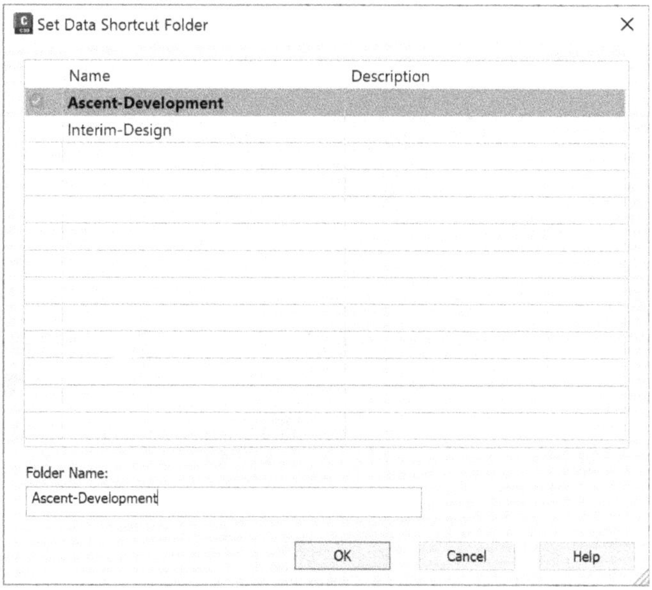

Set Data Shortcut Folder ✕

Name	Description
Ascent-Development	
Interim-Design	

Folder Name:

Ascent-Development

OK   Cancel   Help

Figure 1–63

4. In the Toolspace, *Prospector* tab, verify that the Data Shortcuts points to the correct folder, as shown in Figure 1–64. By hovering over the Data Shortcuts heading, the full path gets revealed in the tooltip. If it is not set to *Ascent-Development,* repeat the steps from the previous exercise.

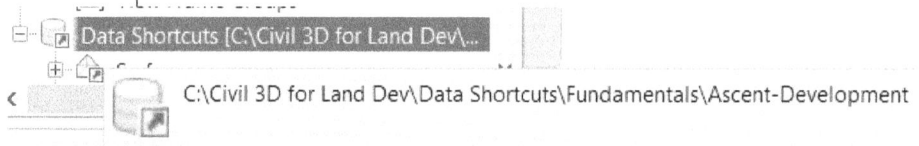

Data Shortcuts [C:\Civil 3D for Land Dev\...

C:\Civil 3D for Land Dev\Data Shortcuts\Fundamentals\Ascent-Development

Figure 1–64

Note that in the Toolspace, *Prospector* tab, under the *Data Shortcuts* and *Surfaces* collections, you can now access all of the surfaces. In the list view, the source file name and source path display, as shown in Figure 1–65.

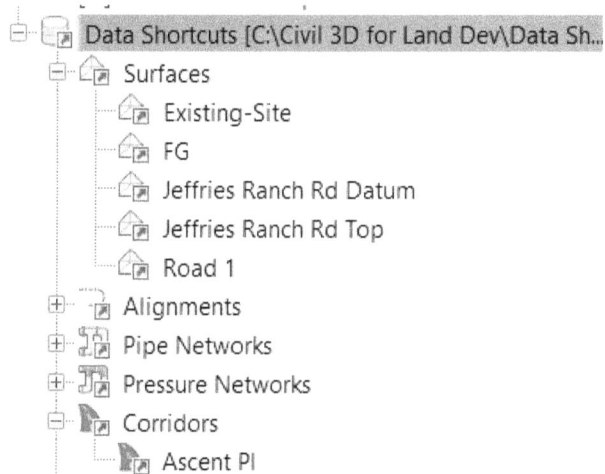

Data Shortcuts [C:\Civil 3D for Land Dev\Data Sh...
- Surfaces
  - Existing-Site
  - FG
  - Jeffries Ranch Rd Datum
  - Jeffries Ranch Rd Top
  - Road 1
- Alignments
- Pipe Networks
- Pressure Networks
- Corridors
  - Ascent Pl

Figure 1–65

5. Close the drawing, but do not save it.

Chapter Review Questions

1. What geometric shape is the Center Mark of a grading object?

   a. Diamond

   b. Circle

   c. Triangle

   d. Rectangle

2. Figure 1–66 shows each of the parts of a grading object. Match the numbers with their corresponding names.

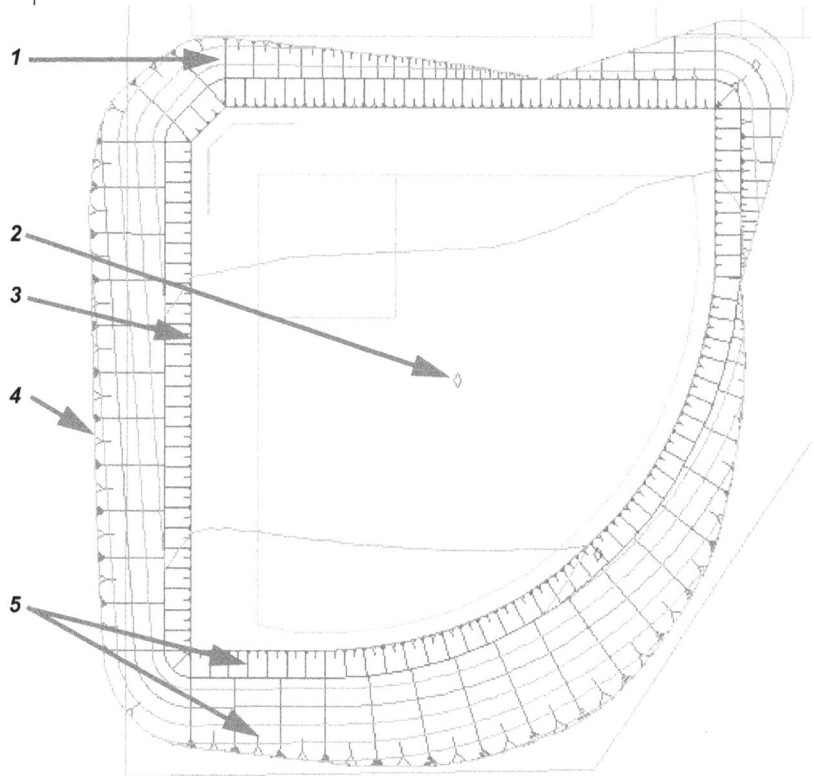

Figure 1–66

   a. Slope Pattern

   b. Center Mark (Infill)

   c. Target Line

   d. Projection Line

   e. Base Line

3. When you edit a grading group, which of the following objects are updated?

   a. Feature Lines, Alignments, and Surfaces.

   b. Points, Surfaces, and Corridors.

   c. Surfaces and Corridors.

   d. Assemblies, Profiles, and Feature Lines.

4. How can you have the software automatically use one style when creating a feature line from objects and a different style when creating a feature line from scratch?

   a. Set it in Drawing Settings, in the *Ambient Settings* tab.

   b. Set it in Command Settings.

   c. Set it in Drawing Settings, in the *Object Layers* tab.

   d. Set it in the grading group style.

5. If you create a grading criteria with locked parameters, you can still change the parameters during the editing process.

   a. True

   b. False

6. What are sites used for? (Select all that apply.)

   a. To group the collection of common topology that share relationships with each other.

   b. To provide different design options within the same project.

   c. To house the sample sections for a grading design.

   d. To set the settings and styles to use for grading projects.

Parcel Grading

Site properties enable you to assign elevations to lot lines or treat them as 2D representations of parcels. The advantage of assigning elevations to parcel lines is that it helps to speed up the building of a grading model and to finish the ground surface. In this chapter, you will create a residential grading plan in which the front of the lots take on elevations in reference to the corridor model. The back of the lots take on the existing ground surface elevations and designed elevations to accommodate walk out basements. Finally, retaining walls and other feature lines will be added to indicate where the building footprint causes a drastic change in grade.

Learning Objectives in This Chapter

- Set parcel line elevations using the feature line Edit Elevation tools.
- Create wall breaklines representing large grade breaks to add definition to the site.
- Edit surfaces to make them more accurate.
- Create split points where parcel lines cross feature lines or share elevation points.

2.1 Setting Parcel Line Elevations

You can create and edit parcel lines in the Autodesk® Civil 3D® software. If site properties are set correctly, parcels can be assigned elevations. Once parcel lines have been assigned elevations, they can be added to a surface as breaklines to grade a site. The tools that are used to edit feature lines can also be used to assign elevations to parcel lines.

There are two places that enable you to edit parcel, feature line, or survey figure elevations. The first is in the *Parcel Segment* contextual tab>Edit Elevations panel and the second is in the *Parcel Segment* contextual tab>Edit Elevations panel in the Edit Elevations vista. You can also use the Quick Elevation Tool.

Site Properties

Before you can edit parcel line elevations, you need to ensure that the site they are in is set up to use the elevations you assign. In the *Prospector* tab, expand the Sites tree, right-click on the site in which the parcels reside, and select **Properties**, as shown in Figure 2–1.

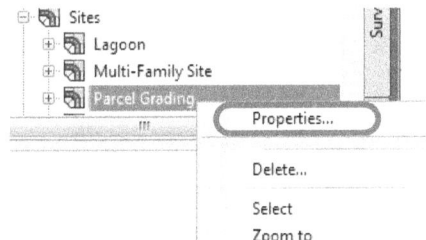

Figure 2–1

In the Site Properties dialog box, go to the *3D Geometry* tab. Change the *Site Display Mode* to **Use elevation**, as shown in Figure 2–2.

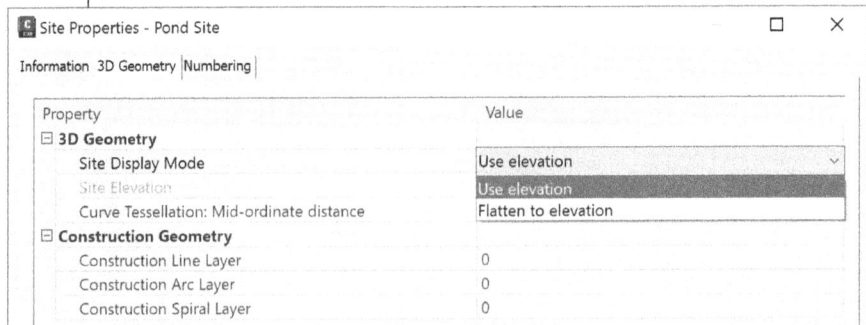

Figure 2–2

Move/Copy Parcels to Another Site

Next you need to ensure that all of the parcels are in the site in which you plan to work. To put them in the correct site you can move them or make a copy of them.

Move Parcels to Another Site

To move parcels to another site, select the parcel segment(s). In the *Parcel Segments* contextual tab>Modify panel, click

(Move to Site), as shown in Figure 2–3.

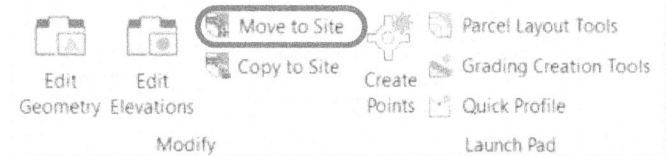

Figure 2–3

When parcels move to a new site, their style changes to the default parcel style for the drawing. A new parcel is also created in the original site that takes on the overall outline of all of the parcels moved, as shown in Figure 2–4.

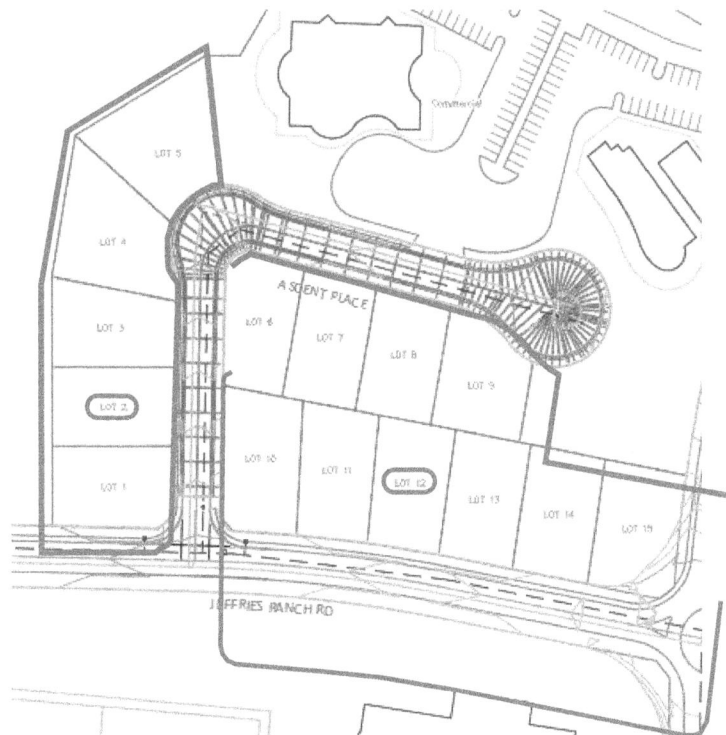

Figure 2–4

If your intention is not to create an overall parcel in place of the parcels you move to a new site, you can select the area label when selecting parcels. This moves the selected parcels along with any surrounding parcels without changing their styles.

Copy Parcels to Another Site

To copy parcels to another site, select the parcel segment(s) or their area labels. In the *Parcel Segments* contextual tab>Modify panel, click (Copy to Site), as shown in Figure 2–5.

Figure 2–5

Note that copying the parcels and placing them in a new site causes them to lose any interaction they have with other objects, such as feature lines, alignments, or grading groups. It is recommended that you create a style that turns off the display of parcel segments. You can then set the parcels in the site that you are not working with to that style to ensure that you are working with the correct site's parcels as you add elevations and make other edits.

Edit Elevations Panel

Select a parcel segment. In the *Parcel Segment* contextual tab> Modify panel, click (Edit Elevations) to display the Edit Elevations panel. The tools in the Edit Elevations panel are as follows:

Icon	Command	Description
	Elevation Editor	Opens the Elevation Editor vista in which you can edit each vertex elevation of feature lines, survey figures, and parcel lines.
	Insert Elevation Point	Adds an elevation control to the feature line. Elevation points provide an elevation control without creating a whole new vertex. These points are Z-controls without X- or Y-components.
	Delete Elevation Point	Permits vertical grade breaks to be removed anywhere other than horizontal vertices.

	Quick Elevation Edit	Displays elevation values at vertices and elevation points along a feature line or parcel line. Selecting one of these points enables you to edit it in the Command Line.
	Edit Elevations	Edits elevations at vertices along a feature line, parcel line, or 3D polyline as you step through each vertex in the Command Line.
	Set Grade/Slope Between Points	Sets the grade or slope between two points on a feature line, parcel line, or 3D polyline. The elevations of the points between the two selected points are interpolated to maintain the grade/slope/elevation/elevation difference entered.
	Insert High/Low Elevation Point	Inserts a high or low break point where two grades intersect on a feature line, survey figure, parcel line, or 3D polyline.
	Raise/Lower by Reference	Raises or lowers a feature line, survey figure, parcel line, or 3D polyline a specified grade or slope from a selected COGO point or surface elevation.
	Set Elevation by Reference	Sets a single vertex elevation on a feature line, survey figure, parcel line, or 3D polyline a specified grade or slope from a selected COGO point or surface elevation.
	Adjacent Elevations by Reference	Sets elevations of one feature line, survey figure, parcel line, or 3D polyline based on a grade/slope/elevation/elevation difference from points on another feature running alongside the first feature.
	Grade Extension by Reference	Extends the grade of one feature line, survey figure, parcel line, or 3D polyline across a gap to set the elevations of another feature and maintain the same slope.
	Elevations from Surface	Takes the elevations of all of the vertices from the surface if no vertices are selected. If a vertex is selected, it takes the surface elevation for just that vertex.
	Raise/Lower	Raises or lowers all of the feature line vertices by the elevation entered.

The second location where parcel line elevations can be assigned is in the Elevation Editor vista. To access these tools, select a parcel segment. This displays the *Parcel Segment* tab in the ribbon, as shown in Figure 2–6.

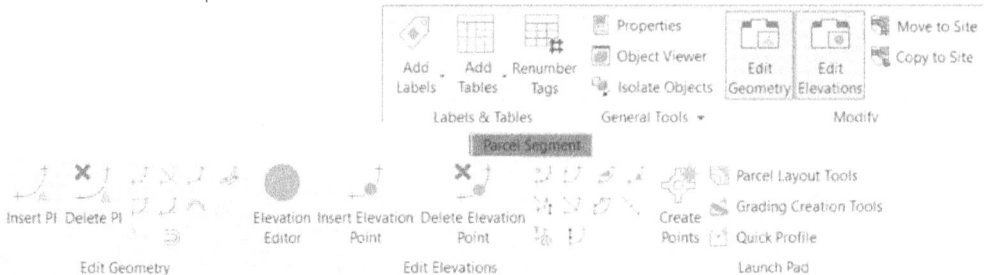

Figure 2–6

In the Modify panel, select **Edit Elevations** to display the Edit Elevations panel.

In the Edit Elevations panel, select the **Elevation Editor** to open the Elevation Editor panorama, as shown in Figure 2–7.

Station	Elevation(Actual)	Length	Grade Back	Grade Ahead
0+00.00	201.10'	80.86'		-16.20%
0+80.86	188.00'	171.73'	16.20%	-3.49%
2+52.60	182.00'	145.09'	3.49%	-1.03%
3+97.69	180.50'	157.55'	1.03%	0.00%
5+55.24	180.50'	35.79'	0.00%	0.00%
5+91.03	180.50'	179.76'	0.00%	-7.85%

Figure 2–7

The Elevation Editor contains the properties of the vertices of the selected feature lines or lot lines. The properties for each vertex include a station, elevation, length, grade ahead, and grade back. To make changes to a station's elevation, select the row in which it is located. Selecting one or more rows in the panorama causes a green triangle to display in the drawing indicating which vertex (or vertices) you are working with, as shown in Figure 2–8.

- Stations displaying a ▲ triangular symbol to the left of their station can be edited horizontally and vertically.

- Stations displaying a ◉ circular symbol to the left of their station are elevation points and can only be edited vertically.

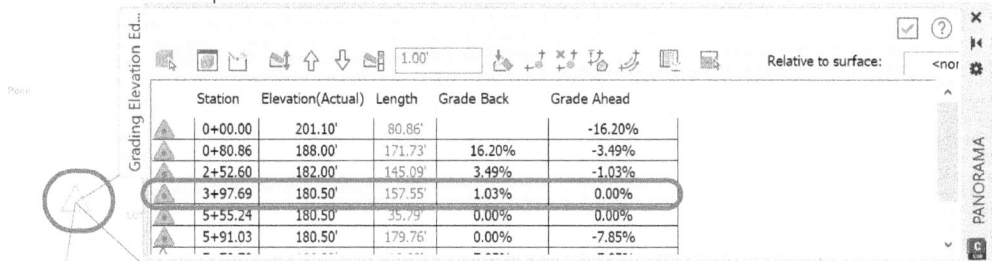

Figure 2–8

Once the required vertices have been selected, you can use the tools at the top of the panorama to change the elevation of each vertex or the slope between vertices. The function of each tool is as follows:

Icon	Command	Description
	Select Feature Line	Selects the feature line, parcel line, or survey figure.
	Zoom To	Zooms to the selected vertex or vertices.
	Quick Profile	Creates a profile view of the selected feature line.
	Raise/Lower	Enables you to type an elevation value in the input field to raise or lower selected vertices to the specified elevation.
	Raise Incrementally	Raises the vertex or vertices selected by the increment set in the input field.
	Lower Incrementally	Lowers the vertex or vertices selected by the increment set in the input field.
	Set Increment	Enables you to type a distance value in the input field to raise or lower selected vertices by a specified increment.
	Input Field	Type a distance or elevation to raise or lower selected vertices.
	Flatten Grade or Elevations	Flattens selected vertices to a constant elevation or sets a constant grade.
	Insert Elevation Point	Enables you to add additional vertical grade breaks without having to add additional horizontal vertices.
	Delete Elevation Point	Permits vertical grade breaks to be removed anywhere other than horizontal vertices.

	Elevations from Surface	Takes the vertex or vertices elevations from the specified surface.
	Reverse the Direction	Changes the direction from which the feature line is stationed.
	Show Grade Breaks Only	Reduces the number of vertices displayed in the table by only displaying feature line stations where the grade changes.
	Unselect All Rows	Removes all rows from the current selection.

How To: Use Elevations from Surface

1. In the *Modify* tab>Design panel, click 🖾 (Parcel) to open the *Parcel* contextual tab.

2. In the *Parcel* contextual tab>Modify panel, click 🖾 (Edit Elevations) to open the Edit Elevations panel.

3. In the *Parcel* contextual tab>Edit Elevations panel, click

   🖾 (Elevations from Surface) to assign surface elevations to the vertices of the parcels.

4. In the Set Elevations from Surface dialog box, select the surface from which to set the pull elevations.

5. Determine whether intermediate grade break points are required. If not, do not select the **Insert intermediate grade break points** option, as shown in Figure 2–9. Click **OK** to close the dialog box.

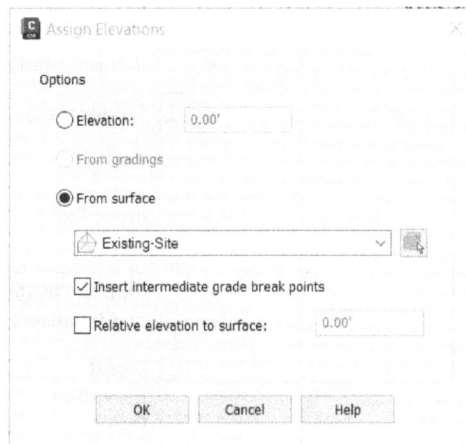

Figure 2–9

6. In the drawing, select the parcel segments that need to be changed.

How To: Use Edit Elevations

1. In the *Modify* tab>Design panel, click ⬒ (Parcel) to display the *Parcel* contextual tab.
2. In the *Parcel* contextual tab>Modify panel, click ⬓ (Edit Elevations) to open the Edit Elevations panel.
3. In the *Parcel* tab>Edit Elevations panel, click ↧ (Edit Elevations).
4. In the drawing, the current vertex is highlighted with a green triangle, as shown in Figure 2–10. In the Command Line, you have the following options: **Elevation**, **Previous**, **Grade**, **SLope**, **SUrface**, **Insert**, or **eXit**.

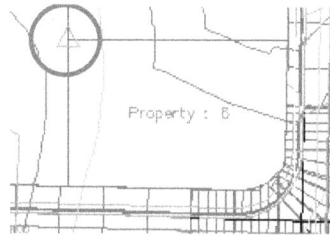

Figure 2–10

5. If the option is set to **Elevation** (the default until a different option is selected), the current elevation displays in brackets <188.000>. In the Command Line, you can press <Enter> to accept the elevation and go to the next vertex, type an elevation to override the current elevation, or type the capital letter(s) for the required option. The expected results for the selected options are as follows:

Type	Option	Description
E	Elevation	Sets the elevation to a typed in value.
P	Previous	Changes the selected vertex to the vertex just before the current one.
G	Grade	Sets the slope out to the percent typed in the Command Line.
SL	Slope	Sets the slope out to the rise/run ratio typed in the Command Line. (Note that you type the rise and the run is a default value of 1.)
SU	Surface	Sets the elevation at the selected surface value for that location.
I	Insert	Inserts a new vertex between the current and next vertex along the feature line, survey figure, or parcel.
X	Exit	Ends the command

How To: Use Set Elevation by Reference

1. In the *Modify* tab>Design panel, click ▨ (Parcel) to open the *Parcel* contextual tab.

2. In the *Parcel* contextual tab>Modify panel, click ▣ (Edit Elevations) to open the Edit Elevations panel.

3. In the *Parcel* tab>Edit Elevations panel, click ↗ (Set Elevations by Reference).

4. In the drawing, pick a point to reference (from a surface, feature line, another parcel, survey figure, or corridor model).

5. In the drawing, select the parcel segment, feature line, or survey figure to edit.

6. In the drawing, specify the vertex or elevation point to adjust by clicking near it.

7. In the Command Line, enter a grade or select one of the other two options for setting the elevation. You can type **S** to set the slope or **D** to set a difference in elevation.

8. Press <Esc> to end the command.

Setting elevations by reference does not create a link to the referenced point. If the referenced point changes, the parcel lines, feature line, or survey figures need to be updated manually.

Practice 2a

Set Parcel Line Elevations

Practice Objective

- Assign elevations to parcel lines using the Edit Elevation tools.

For the land development drawings in this guide, much of the preliminary work has already been done for the site development.

The completed corridors for Jeffries Ranch Road and Ascent Place, the Ascent Place knuckle and cul-de-sac target alignments, the Mission Avenue alignment, and the Existing-Site surface have been referenced through Data Shortcuts.

Another surface that has been referenced is Road-Tops, which is a combination of all the corridor top surfaces, including Jeffries Ranch Road, Ascent Place, Rand Boulevard and the roundabout at the juncture of Jeffries Ranch Road and Rand Boulevard.

In this practice, you will review the site and prepare the drawing. You will then set the parcel elevations to a surface, set parcel elevations by design, and set parcel elevations by reference.

Task 1 - Review the site and prepare the drawing.

1. In the *Start* screen, click **Open...**, or expand **C c3D** (Application Menu) and select **Open**.

2. In the Select File dialog box, browse to the *C:\Civil 3D for Land Dev\Working* folder, as shown in Figure 2–11.

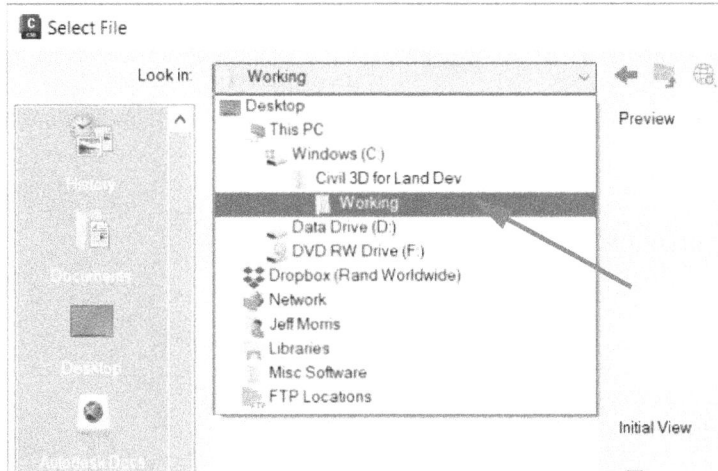

Figure 2–11

3. Expand the Tools drop-down list and select **Add Current Folder to Places**, as shown in Figure 2–12.

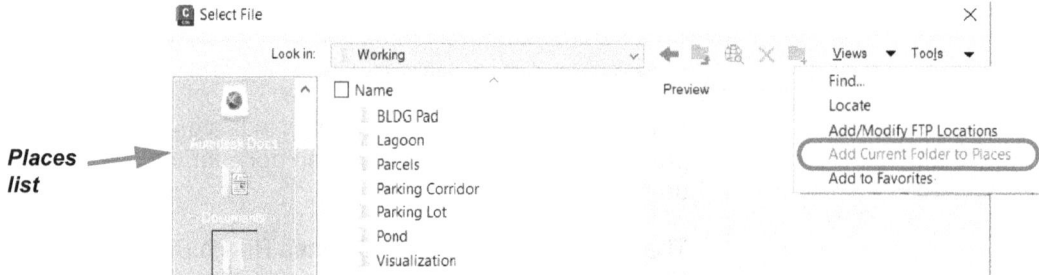

Figure 2–12

4. After you create the new entry into your *Places,* select the Parcels folder.

5. Open **PARCELS-A.dwg.**

6. Hover over the Data Shortcuts and look at the tooltip that appears, as shown in Figure 2–13. Ensure that your **Data Shortcuts Working Folder** is set to *C:\Civil 3D for Land Dev\Data Shortcuts\Fundamentals* and the **Data Shortcuts Project Folder** to *Ascent-Development*.

   If required, review the Setting a Project practice for how to set the working folder and the project folder.

   - If not, right-click on Data Shortcuts to set the **Working Folder** to *C:\Civil 3D for Land Dev\Data Shortcuts\ Fundamentals* and the **Data Shortcuts Project Folder** to *Ascent-Development*.

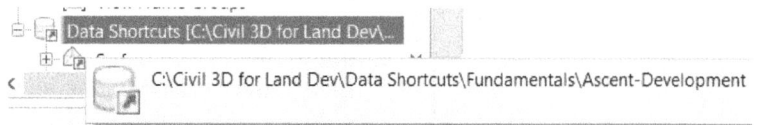

Figure 2–13

7. In the *Prospector* tab, expand **Sites>Residential Grading> Parcels**. Note which parcels reside in this site, as shown in Figure 2–14.

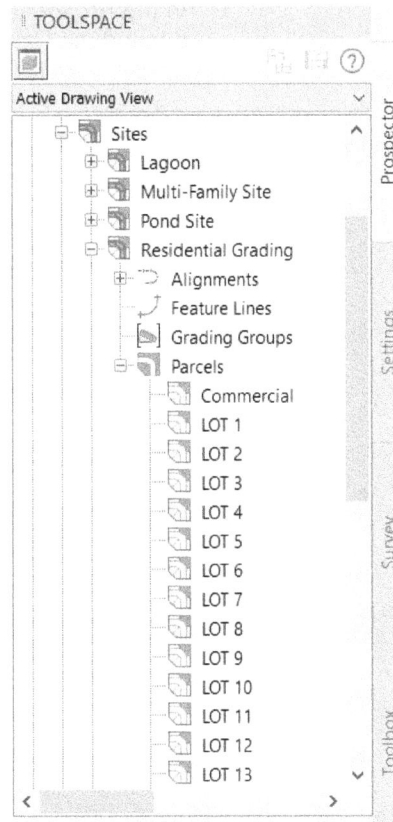

Figure 2–14

You can also select the view in the View tab> Views panel.

8. In the top-left corner of the drawing window, select **Top**, expand Custom Model Views and select **Site**, as shown in Figure 2–15. This will zoom into a preset view of the entire site.

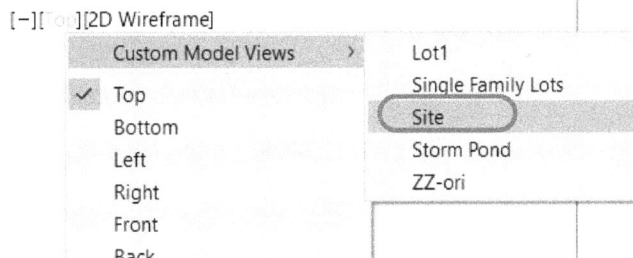

Figure 2–15

9. In the *Prospector* tab, select the **Residential Grading** site, expand the Parcels branch and select the **Commercial** parcel, then hold <Ctrl> as you select the **Pond** and **ROW** parcels. Right-click and select **Select**, as shown in Figure 2–16.

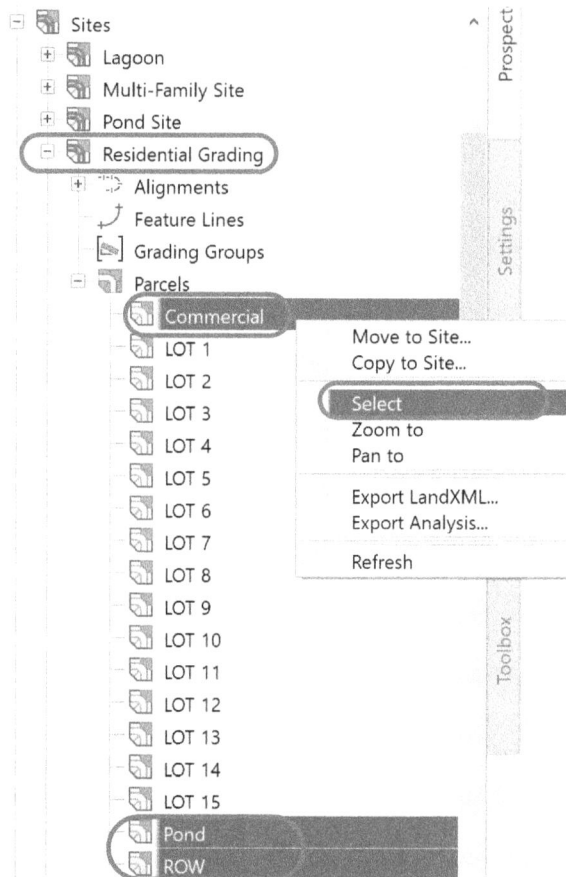

Figure 2–16

10. In the *Parcels* contextual tab>expanded General Tools panel, click ⬚ (Send to Back), as shown in Figure 2–17.

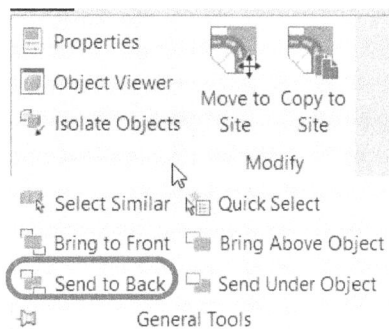

Figure 2–17

11. Press <Esc> to release the selection.

Task 2 - Set parcel elevations to a surface.

1. Continue working in the drawing from the previous task.

2. In the *View* tab>Views panel, select **Single Family Lots** to zoom in on the residential area to be graded.

3. In the drawing, select **Lot 10** by selecting its area label.

4. In the *Parcel* contextual tab>Modify panel, click 🗂 (Edit Elevations) to open the Edit Elevations panel.

5. In the *Parcel* contextual tab>Edit Elevations panel, click ⬚ (Elevations from Surface) to assign surface elevations to the vertices of the parcels.

6. In the Set Elevations from Surface dialog box, select **Road-Tops** for the surface. Do not select the **Insert intermediate grade break points** or **Relative elevation to surface** options, as shown in Figure 2–18. Click **OK** to close the dialog box.

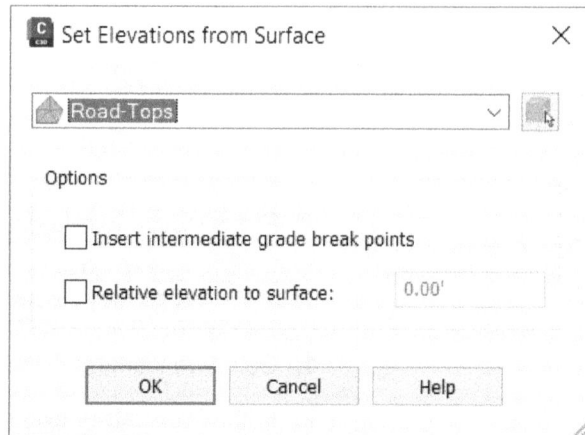

Figure 2–18

7. Select a parcel segment of **Lot 10**.

8. In the Command Line, you are prompted to select objects. Type **M** and press <Enter> to permit crossing window selections. Select all 15 single family lot segments, the Commercial parcel segments, and the Pond parcel segments (17 Total), as shown in Figure 2–19.

Figure 2–19

9. Press <Enter> to end the selection and exit the command.

10. In the drawing, select **Lot 10** by selecting its area label again.

11. In the *Parcel* contextual tab>Edit Elevations panel, click

    (Elevation Editor) to open the Elevation Editor vista to see what elevations were assigned to the parcel segments.

12. When prompted to select objects, select the parcel segments of **Lot 10.** Note that elevations are assigned to each vertex along the roads but not on the interior, as shown in Figure 2–20. This is because the road surfaces do not extend into the interior.

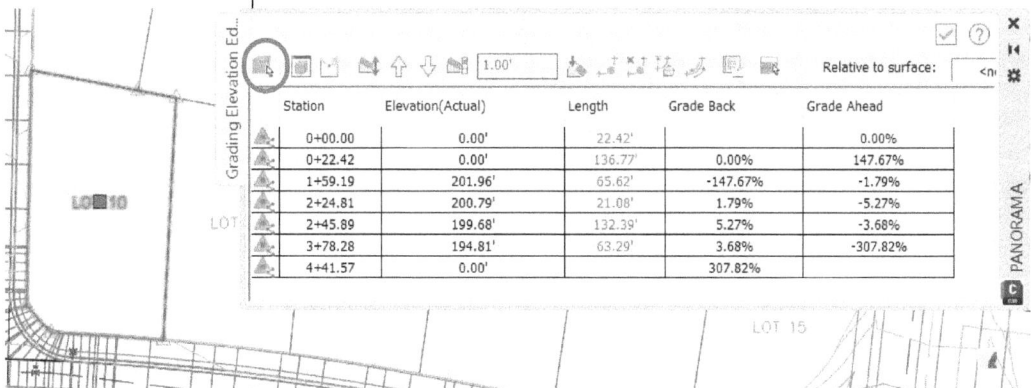

Station	Elevation(Actual)	Length	Grade Back	Grade Ahead
0+00.00	0.00'	22.42'		0.00%
0+22.42	0.00'	136.77'	0.00%	147.67%
1+59.19	201.96'	65.62'	-147.67%	-1.79%
2+24.81	200.79'	21.08'	1.79%	-5.27%
2+45.89	199.68'	132.39'	5.27%	-3.68%
3+78.28	194.81'	63.29'	3.68%	-307.82%
4+41.57	0.00'		307.82%	

Figure 2–20

13. Check other parcels by clicking (Select Feature), as shown above in Figure 2–20, to select them without closing the Elevation Editor vista.

14. In the Edit Elevations vista, click ☑ to close the vista.

15. The *Parcel* contextual tab should still be available since the parcel is still selected. In the Edit Elevations panel, click

    (Quick Elevation Edit).

16. Hover over a lot line and notice the grade which appears in a tooltip, as shown in Figure 2–21. Notice that if you are beyond the midpoint of the lot line, the grade changes from positive to negative, and the small green arrow changes direction.

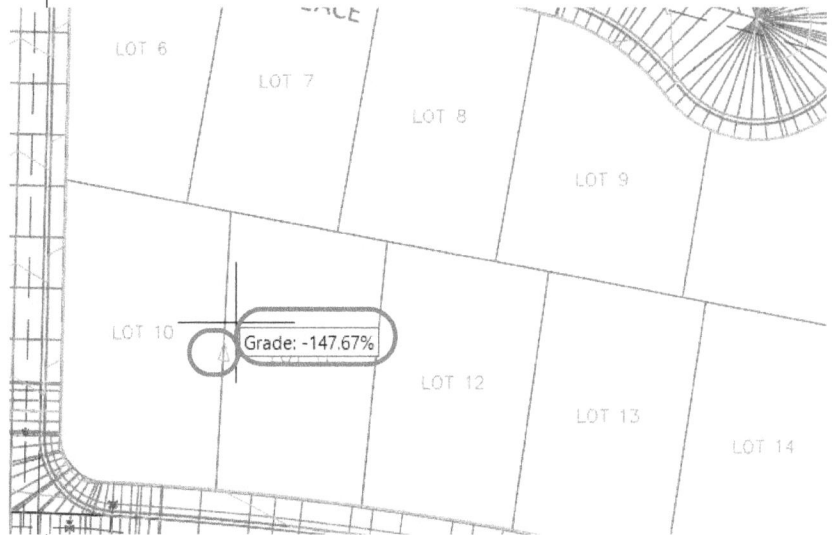

Grade: -147.67%

Figure 2–21

17. Ensure that the green arrow is pointing to the rear of the lot and click it, then type **-2 (minus 2)** to have the lot line lower with a 2% grade.

18. Hover over the endpoint of the rear of the lot line. Note that the elevation is no longer zero, but approximately **199**, as shown in Figure 2–22.

Elevation: 199.23'

Figure 2–22

19. Select the lot line between **Lot 6** and **Lot 7** near the rear of the lot and set that grade to **8**. Hover over the rear endpoint and note that the elevation is about **198.8**.

20. Change all lot lines running north-south of lots (near the rear of the lots) **10** through **15** to grade **-2 (minus 2)**.

21. Change all lot lines running north-south of lots (near the rear of the lots) **6** through **9** to grade **up 8%**.

22. Hover over the rear lot lines (running east-west) and note that the grades are acceptable.

23. Press <Enter> to finish.

24. **Lot 10** should still be selected. If not, select it by clicking its area label again.

25. In the *Parcel* contextual tab>Edit Elevations panel, click

    (Elevation Editor) to open the Elevation Editor vista to see what elevations are now assigned to the parcel segments.

26. When prompted to select objects, select the parcel segments of **Lot 10.** Note that the elevations and grades are acceptable, as shown in Figure 2–23.

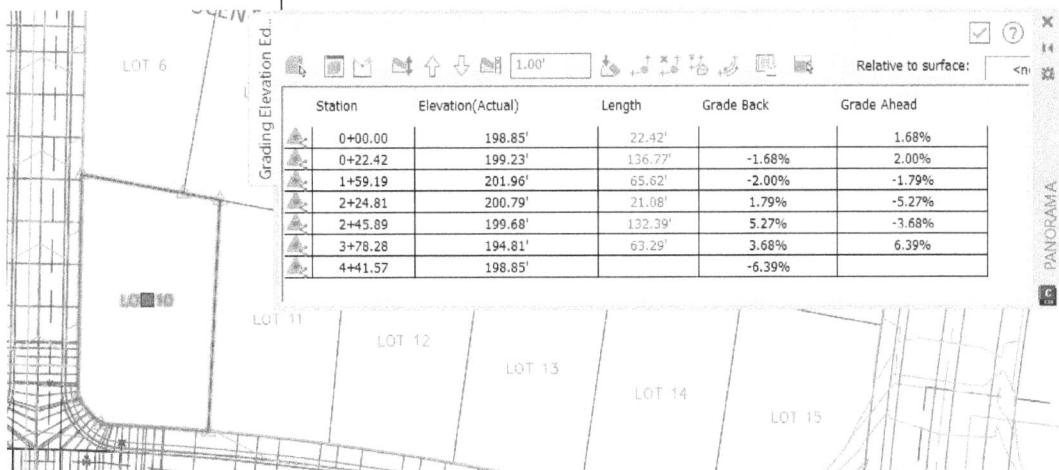

Station	Elevation(Actual)	Length	Grade Back	Grade Ahead
0+00.00	198.85'	22.42'		1.68%
0+22.42	199.23'	136.77'	-1.68%	2.00%
1+59.19	201.96'	65.62'	-2.00%	-1.79%
2+24.81	200.79'	21.08'	1.79%	-5.27%
2+45.89	199.68'	132.39'	5.27%	-3.68%
3+78.28	194.81'	63.29'	3.68%	6.39%
4+41.57	198.85'		-6.39%	

Figure 2–23

27. If time permits, check the other lots 6 though 15. Ensure that **Lot 9** (or **Lot 13**) has no vertices at elevation 0. If it has, set the elevation to **198**.

28. Save the drawing.

Task 3 - Set parcel elevations by design.

The lots on the west side of Ascent Pl have been assigned elevations to ensure that the pond grading elevations to their west coordinate with each other.

1. Continue working in the drawing from the previous practice or open **PARCELS-B.dwg** from the *C:\Civil 3D for Land Dev\ Working\Parcels* folder.

2. In the *View* tab>Views panel, select **Storm Pond** to zoom in on the pond area.

3. In the drawing, select the parcel segments representing the pond boundary. In the right-click menu, expand the **Display Order** drop-down list and select **Bring to Front**, as shown in Figure 2–24.

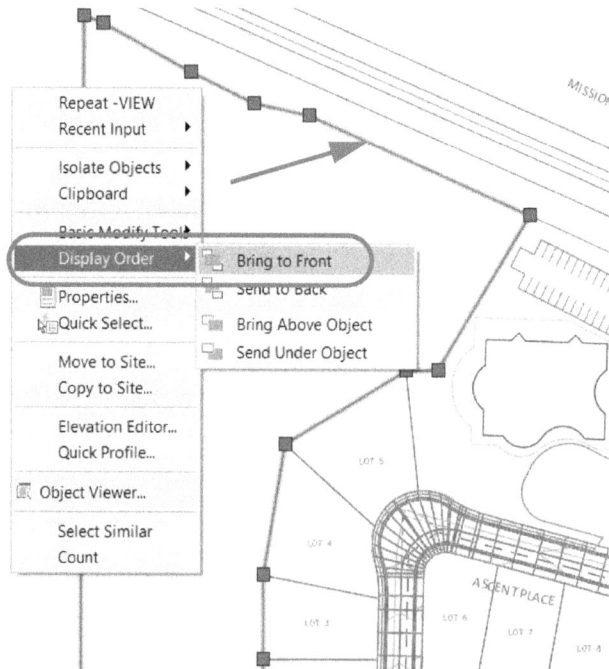

Figure 2–24

4. In the drawing, select the pond's parcel segments again if you released the selection.

5. In the *Parcel* tab>Edit Elevations panel, click ⏎ (Edit Elevations). Press <Enter> until the green triangle displays at the northernmost vertex of Lot 5, as shown in Figure 2–25.

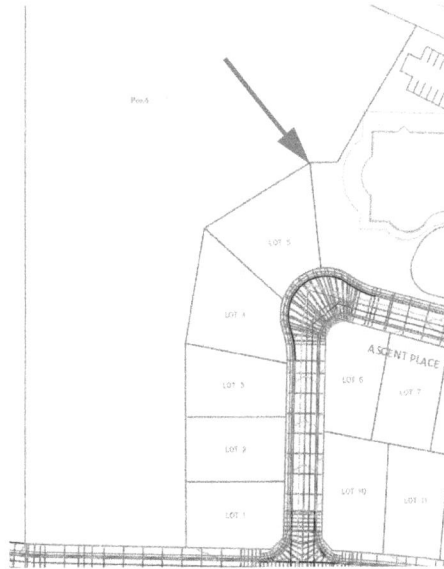

Figure 2–25

6. Type **180.5** and press <Enter> for the elevation. The green triangle should move to the next vertex when you press <Enter> to assign the remaining elevations, as shown in Figure 2–26. Press <Esc> twice when done to release the pond segments.

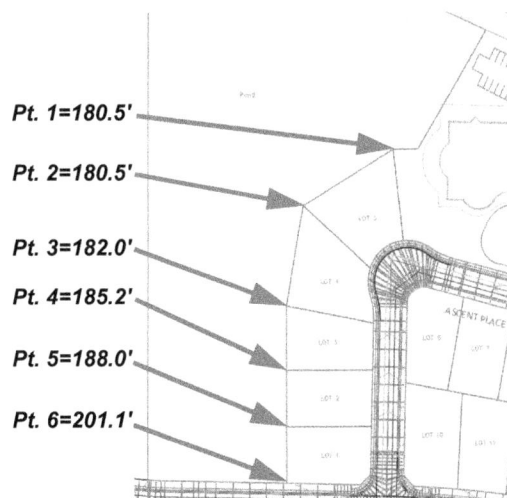

Pt. 1=180.5'
Pt. 2=180.5'
Pt. 3=182.0'
Pt. 4=185.2'
Pt. 5=188.0'
Pt. 6=201.1'

Figure 2–26

7. **Lots 1-5**, in the Residential Grading site, share these vertices. Therefore, their elevations also update. Verify this by opening the Elevation Editor vista and selecting the parcel segments of one of the parcels. In the *Parcel* contextual tab>

   Edit Elevations panel, click ⚪ (Elevation Editor) to open the Elevation Editor vista.

8. Save the drawing.

Task 4 - Set parcel elevations by reference.

In this task, you will assign elevations to the front of the lots according to the corridor elevations. At vertices that do not fall directly on the corridor model, use a -2% grade if it falls outside the corridor and a 2% grade if it falls inside the corridor model.

1. Continue working in the drawing from the previous task.

2. In the *View* tab>Views panel, select **Lot 1** to zoom in on the area to be graded.

3. In the drawing, select the Corridor models (**Ascent Pl** and **Jeffries Ranch Rd**). In the *Corridors* contextual tab> expanded General Tools panel, click

   🖥 (Bring to Front). Press <Esc> to end the selection.

4. In the drawing, select the **Lot 1** parcel segments. In the

   Parcel tab>Edit Elevations panel, click ⤴ (Set Elevations by Reference).

Setting elevations by reference does not create a link. If the corridor design changes, the parcel lines need to be updated manually.

*If you have difficulty selecting the **Lot 1** parcel segments, turn on Selection Cycling with the **<CTRL> W** keystrokes.*

5. In the drawing, select the endpoint of the corridor section line directly north of the first parcel corner for the reference point, marked **A** in Figure 2–27.

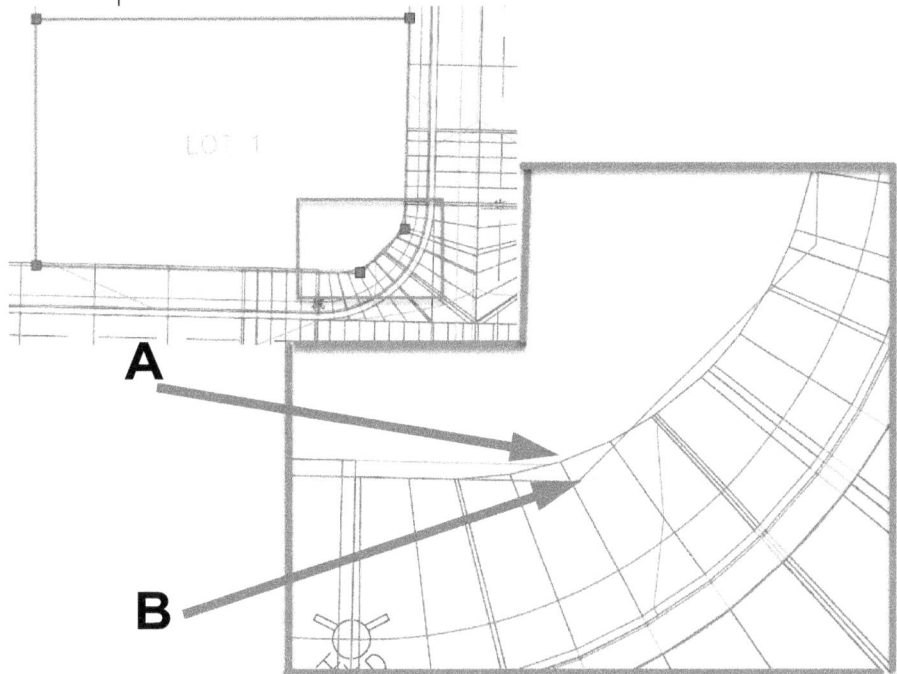

Figure 2–27

6. In the drawing, select the parcel vertex near the corridor section line that you selected for the reference point, marked **B** in Figure 2–27.

7. At the Command Line, verify that it is prompting you for the grade. If not, type **G** and press <Enter>. Since the parcel line is down slope from the end of the corridor, type **2** (for upslope) to maintain the corridor grade of 2%. Press <Esc> to end the command.

8. Repeat Steps 5 to 7 to set the elevation for the next vertex running counter-clockwise along the Lot 1 perimeter, as shown in Figure 2–28.

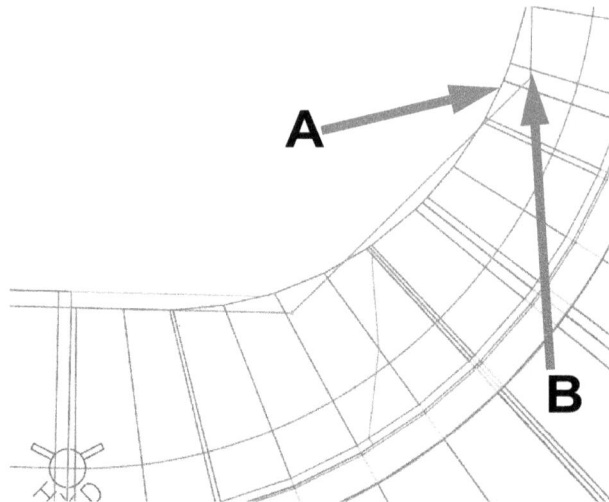

Figure 2–28

9. In the drawing, select the **Lot 1** parcel segments again. In the

   Parcel tab>Edit Elevations panel, click (Set Elevations by Reference).

10. In the drawing, select the nearest point on the corridor feature line at the north-east parcel corner for the reference point, using the **NEAR** Osnap setting, as shown in Figure 2–29.

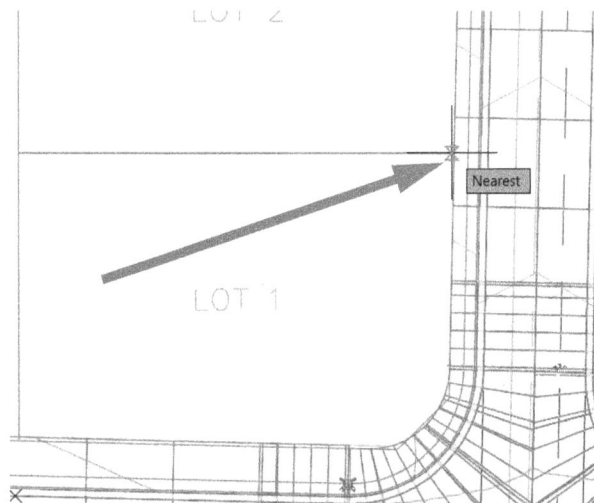

Figure 2–29

11. In the drawing, select the parcel corner near the reference point for the vertex to change,

12. Since the parcel line falls directly on the corridor being referenced, type **0** for the grade to indicate that there is no change in elevation. Press <Esc> to end the command.

13. Repeat this process for all of the lot corners adjacent to or touching the corridor model, including the Commercial parcel.

    - At vertices that do not fall directly on the corridor model, ensure you pick points that are perpendicular to the corridor model and then use a -2% grade if it falls outside of the corridor and a 2% grade if it falls inside the corridor model.

14. Lot 4 has some additional vertices. Select the **Lot 4** Parcel lines.

15. In the *Parcel* contextual tab>Edit Elevations panel, click

    (Elevation Editor) to open the Elevation Editor vista to see what elevations are now assigned to the parcel segments.

16. Note that the elevations and grades are acceptable, as shown in Figure 2–30.

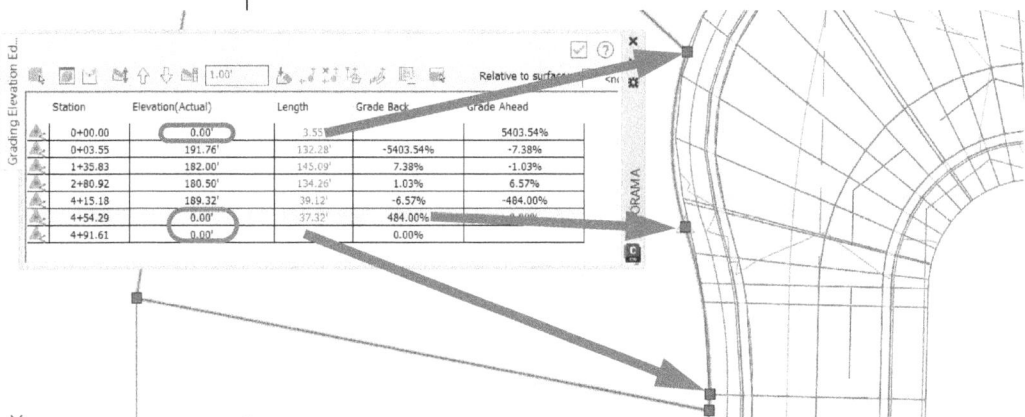

Station	Elevation(Actual)	Length	Grade Back	Grade Ahead
0+00.00	0.00'	3.55'		5403.54%
0+03.55	191.76'	132.28'	-5403.54%	-7.38%
1+35.83	182.00'	145.09'	7.38%	-1.03%
2+80.92	180.50'	134.26'	1.03%	6.57%
4+15.18	189.32'	39.12'	-6.57%	-484.00%
4+54.29	0.00'	37.32'	484.00%	0.00%
4+91.61	0.00'		0.00%	

Figure 2–30

17. Repeat the (Set Elevations by Reference) process for these three vertices, while keeping the Elevation Editor open.

18. When done, the results are shown in Figure 2–31.

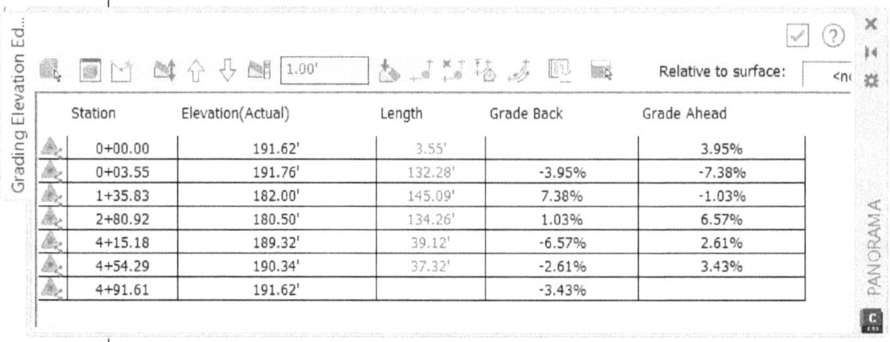

Station	Elevation(Actual)	Length	Grade Back	Grade Ahead
0+00.00	191.62'	3.55'		3.95%
0+03.55	191.76'	132.28'	-3.95%	-7.38%
1+35.83	182.00'	145.09'	7.38%	-1.03%
2+80.92	180.50'	134.26'	1.03%	6.57%
4+15.18	189.32'	39.12'	-6.57%	2.61%
4+54.29	190.34'	37.32'	-2.61%	3.43%
4+91.61	191.62'		-3.43%	

Figure 2–31

19. Time permitting, check the other lots 1 though 5.

20. Save the drawing.

2.2 Retaining Walls

Adding elevations to parcel segments helps define the finished grade. However, it does not do anything until you add them to a surface. This section covers adding breaklines to a surface since you add parcel segments to surfaces as breaklines.

Breaklines created by Proximity leave the original polylines in the drawing even though they are defined as a Standard breakline. This Standard definition can be inserted into the drawing and manipulated. The original line can be deleted.

A breakline created as a Standard breakline is linked to the original line in the drawing. If this line is deleted, the breakline definition is also deleted. The different breakline definitions are as follows:

Breakline Type	Description
Standard	Creates a breakline that is defined by selecting 3D lines, feature lines, parcel segments, survey figures, and 3D polylines.
Proximity	Creates a breakline that is defined by drawing or selecting a feature line, parcel segment, survey figure, or polyline within the extents of the surface boundary. The location and elevation of each vertex is determined by the nearest surface point.
Wall	A wall breakline is stored as a standard breakline but is defined differently. You provide an offset side, elevation difference at each vertex or along the entire breakline.
Non-destructive	Creates a breakline that is defined using grading feature lines and open or closed AutoCAD® objects. A non-destructive breakline does not affect the original surface.

How To: Add Parcel Segments to a Surface

1. To create a surface, in the *Home* tab>Create Ground Data panel, expand the Surfaces drop-down list and click

   (Create Surface).
2. In the Create Surface dialog box, type a name and description, and select a style. Click **OK** to close the dialog box.

3. In the *Prospector* tab, expand Surfaces>[Surface you are working with]>Definition. Right-click on **Breaklines** and select **Add**, as shown in Figure 2–32.

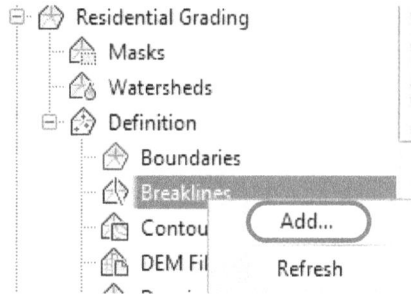

Figure 2–32

4. In the Add Breaklines dialog box, type a description and set the type to **Standard** if elevations are already assigned to the parcels. Add weeding and supplementing factors as required. Click **OK** to close the dialog box.
5. Select the parcel segments in the drawing. Press <Enter> when done.

How To: Add Wall Breaklines to a Surface

1. Draw a feature line, parcel line, survey figure, or 3D Polyline.
2. In the *Prospector* tab>expand Surfaces>[Surface you are working with]>Definition. Right-click on **Breaklines** and select **Add**, as shown in Figure 2–33.

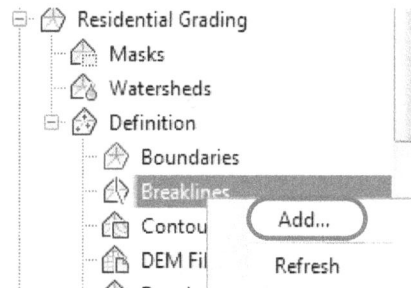

Figure 2–33

3. In the Add Breaklines dialog box, type a description and set the *Type* to **Wall**, as shown in Figure 2–34.

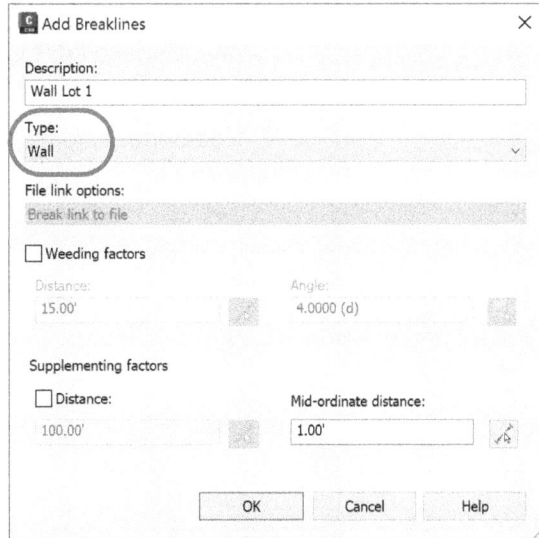

Figure 2–34

4. Add weeding and supplementing factors as required. Click **OK** to close the dialog box.
5. In the drawing, select the object you drew in Step 1. Press <Enter> when done.
6. Pick a point on the side to offset the original feature line.
7. Type **I** to set the height of the wall at each individual vertex or press <Enter> to accept the default **All** to set the height of all of the vertices at the same time.
8. In the Command Line, type a value for the difference in elevation or type **E** to set the actual elevation.

2.3 Editing Surfaces

Once the basic information has been added to a surface definition, you might need to edit the surface to make it more accurate. Surface edits can be done by selecting the surface. Then, in the *Tin Surface* contextual tab>Modify panel, expand

 (Edit Surface) to display the available tools, as shown in Figure 2–35.

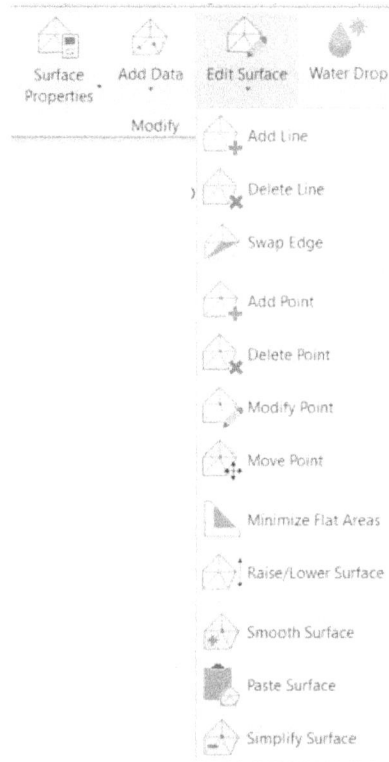

Figure 2–35

The tools in the Edit Surface drop-down list are as follows:

Icon	Command	Description
	Add Line	Adds additional triangle line to a surface to modify how the surface triangulates. Note that the surface triangles must be visible in the style to use this command.
	Delete Line	Removes triangle or grid lines from a surface to modify how the surface triangulates. Note that the surface triangles or grid lines must be visible in the style to use this command.

	Swap Edge	Changes the direction of two triangle faces within a surface to modify how the surface triangulates. Note that the surface triangles must be visible in the style to use this command.
	Add Point	Adds a point to a surface to modify how the surface triangulates. Note that the surface points must be visible in the style to use this command.
	Delete Point	Removes unnecessary or inaccurate points from a surface to modify how the surface triangulates. Note that the surface points must be visible in the style to use this command.
	Modify Point	Modifies the elevation of a surface point to modify how the surface triangulates. Note that the surface points must be visible in the style to use this command.
	Move Point	Moves a surface point to a new location without changing its elevation to modify how the surface triangulates. Note that the surface points must be visible in the style to use this command.
	Minimize Flat Areas	Reduces the number of adjacent triangles containing the same elevation and modifies how the surface triangulates to make it more accurately represent a real-world surface.
	Raise/Lower Surface	Adds/Subtracts a specified distance to a surface and changes the elevations of every triangle by the same amount.
	Smooth Surface	Adds points at system-determined elevations using Natural Neighbor Interpolation (NNI) or Kriging methods to smooth contour lines without making them overlap.
	Paste Surface	Combines two surfaces by overriding triangles in the destination surface with triangles from the pasted surface. Note that the paste order is key because elevations are taken from the last surface pasted.
	Simplify Surface	Removes unnecessary points from a surface to reduce its size while preserving its accuracy.

How To: Paste Surfaces Together

1. In the drawing, select the destination surface (it is going to be overridden by another surface.
2. In the *Tin Surface* contextual tab>Modify panel, expand the Edit Surface drop-down list and click (Paste Surface).
3. In the Select Surface dialog box, select the surface(s) to paste into the destination surface, as shown in Figure 2–36.

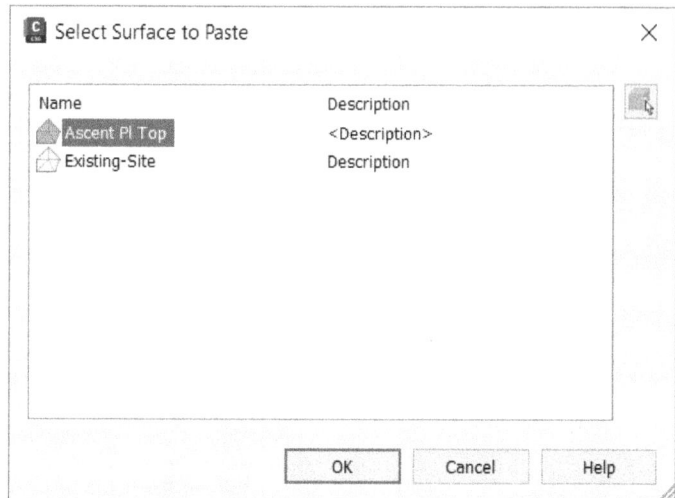

Figure 2–36

4. Click **OK** to close the dialog box.

Practice 2b

Create and Edit the Surface to Add Retaining Walls

Practice Objective

- Create wall breaklines to display drastic grade breaks and create a 7' minimum wall.

In this practice, you will create a finish ground surface to grade the single-family area. You will then paste the surfaces together and add wall breaklines to the surface.

Task 1 - Create a finish ground surface to grade the single-family area.

---

1. Open **PARCELS-C.dwg** from the *C:\Civil 3D for Land Dev\ Working\Parcels* folder. Do not continue working in the drawing from the previous practice, the parcel elevations have been fine-tuned in this drawing. Some more feature lines have been added as well.

2. In the *View* tab>Views panel, select **Single Family Lots** as the view to zoom into the residential area.

3. In the *Home* tab>Create Ground Data panel, click ⌂ (Create Surface).

4. In the Create Surface dialog box, for the *Name*, type **Residential Grading**, for the *Description*, type **Grading from parcel segment elevations and additional breaklines**, and for the *Style*, select **ASC-Temporary Grading View**, as shown in Figure 2–37.

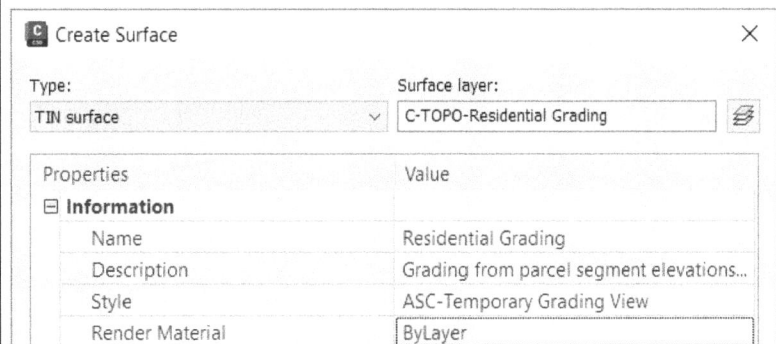

Type:		Surface layer:	
TIN surface	∨	C-TOPO-Residential Grading	🗐

Properties	Value
⊟ **Information**	
Name	Residential Grading
Description	Grading from parcel segment elevations...
Style	ASC-Temporary Grading View
Render Material	ByLayer

Figure 2–37

5. Click **OK** to close the dialog box.

---

6. In the *Prospector* tab, expand **Surfaces>Residential Grading>Definition**. Right-click on Breaklines and select **Add**. In the Add Breaklines dialog box, for the *Description*, type **Residential Parcels**, as shown in Figure 2–38. Click **OK** to accept the other defaults and close the dialog box.

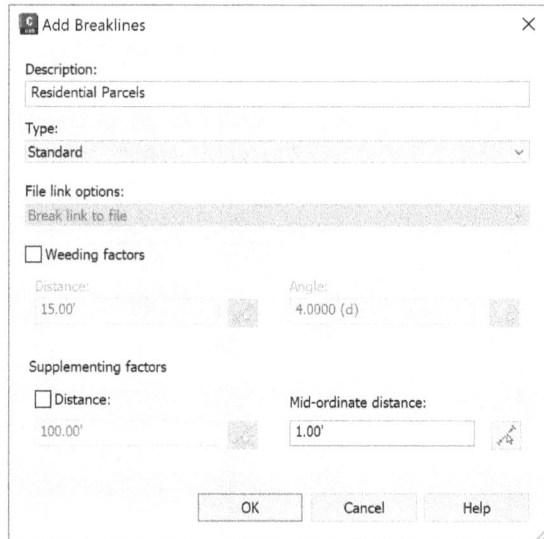

Figure 2–38

7. Select the 15 single-family parcel segments and the one Commercial parcel segment to the north (16 total), as shown in Figure 2–39. Press <Enter> to end the selection.

Figure 2–39

8. Save the drawing.

Task 2 - Paste the surfaces together.

1. Continue working in the drawing from the previous task.

2. In the drawing, select the **Residential Grading** surface.

3. In the *Tin Surface* contextual tab>Modify panel, expand the

   Edit Surface drop-down list and click ![icon] (Paste Surface).

4. In the Select Surface dialog box, select the **Road-Tops** surface, as shown in Figure 2–40.

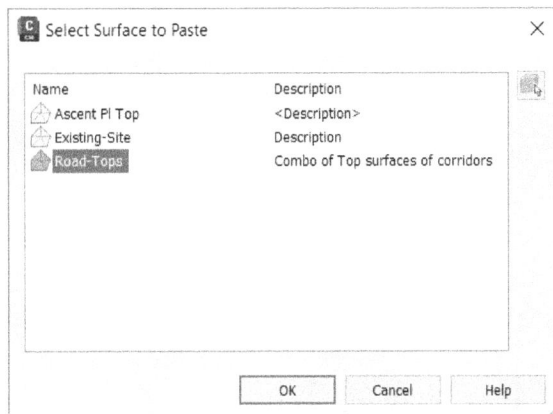

Figure 2–40

5. Click **OK** to close the dialog box.

6. Save the drawing. The drawing displays as shown in Figure 2–41.

Figure 2–41

Task 3 - Add wall breaklines to the surface.

1. Continue working in the drawing from the previous task.

The feature lines for the top of walls have already been created for you to speed up the process. This was done by creating stepped offsets of the parcels lines 55' from the back of lot at a positive 2% slope to ensure that the water drains away from the house toward the back property line and 30' from the street at a positive 4% grade to ensure that the water drains toward the street in front. At the front of the property, the wall is a minimum of 7' and tapers down from there. Figure 2–42 shows a cross section of a typical wall breakline.

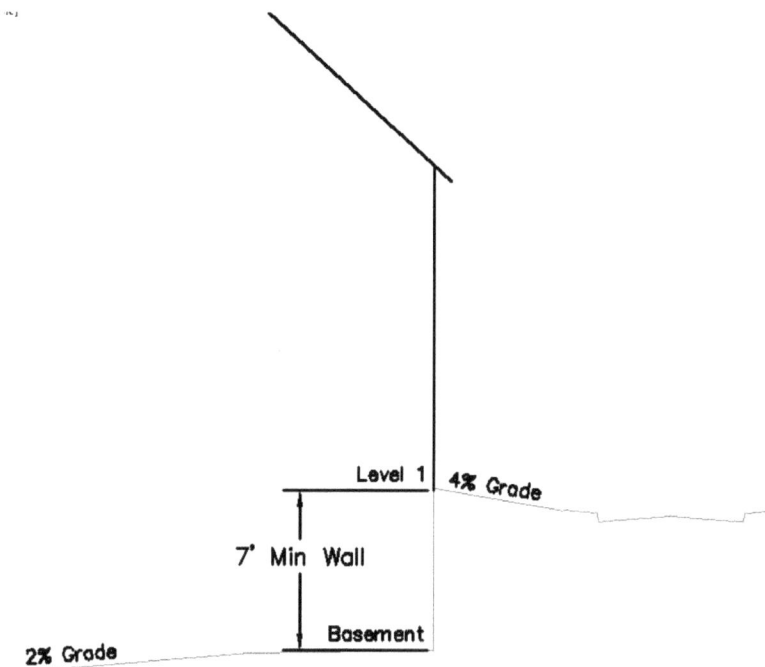

Figure 2–42

2. Thaw the **C-GRAD-BREK** layer which contains feature lines which you will convert to breaklines.

3. In the *View* tab>Views panel, select **Lot1** as the view to zoom into the first lot to grade.

4. Select the Residential Grading surface in the drawing. In the *Tin Surface* contextual tab>Modify panel, expand the Add Data drop-down list and click (Breaklines), as shown in Figure 2–43.

Figure 2–43

5. In the Add Breaklines dialog box, for the *Description* type **Wall Lot 1**. For the type select **Wall**, as shown in Figure 2–44. Click **OK** to accept all of the other defaults and close the dialog box.

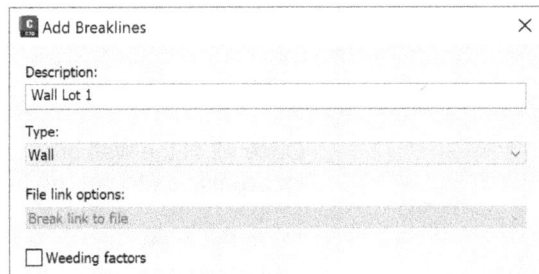

Figure 2–44

6. In the drawing, select the green C-shaped feature line inside Lot 1 and press <Enter>.

7. Pick a point to the inside of the C-shaped feature line for the offset side. Press <Enter> to accept the **All** option to set the height for all of the vertices at the same time.

8. In the Command Line, select the **Elevation** option.

9. For the elevation value type **196**. Note that the arrows on the surface indicate the direction in which the water will flow, as shown in Figure 2–45.

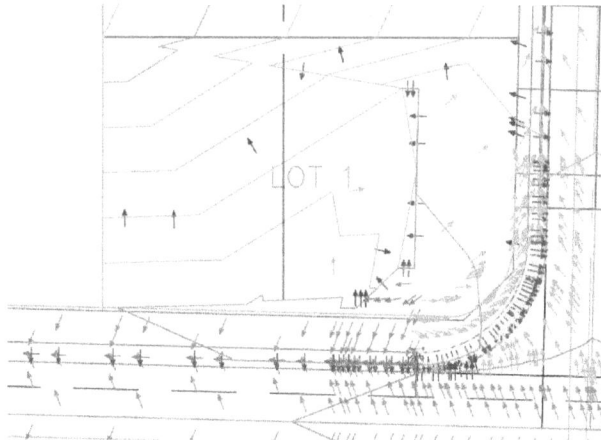

Figure 2–45

10. Repeat Steps 5 to 9 to add a retaining wall to Lots 2 to 5 using the following value for the target elevation in each lot.

Area	Target Elevation
Lot 2	188
Lot 3	186
Lot 4	183
Lot 5	182

Once all of the wall breaklines are in the surface, add the back of lot breaklines to set the back yard grades at 2%.

11. In the *View* tab>Views panel, select **Single Family Lots** as the view to zoom into.

12. Select the Residential Grading surface in the drawing. In the *Tin Surface* contextual tab>Modify panel, expand the Add

    Data drop-down list and click ⬙ (Breaklines).

13. In the Add Breaklines dialog box, for the *Description* type **Backyard Grade** and for the *Type* select **Standard**. Click **OK** to accept all of the other defaults and close the dialog box.

14. In the drawing, select the black feature lines in each lot, as shown in Figure 2–46. Press <Enter> to end the selection.

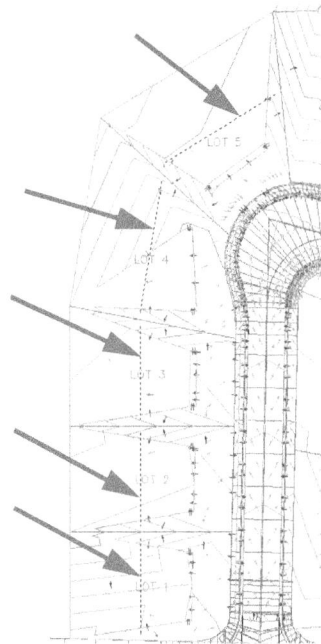

Figure 2–46

15. Press <Esc> to release the surface and then save the drawing.

2.4 Feature Line Interactions with Parcel Lines

When parcel lines and feature lines reside in the same site and intersect each other or share vertices, one line overrides the elevations of the other and creates a split point at the shared point of intersection. The *last* object edited automatically edits the elevations of the first. This is called the *last one wins* rule. Therefore, it is recommended that you create multiple sites for a grading plan. Keeping parcels in one site and feature lines in another site ensures that they do not unintentionally override each other as you are working.

When parcels share line segment(s), any edits to the elevations of one parcel affect the elevations of the second parcel along the shared segment(s). This includes any elevation points that might be added. Figure 2–47 shows the elevations of two lots that share a common segment. Elevation points have been inserted along the shared segment in Lot 1 (marked with circular symbols). Note that Lot 2 automatically picked up the same elevation points (marked with empty triangles) along the shared segment. These are known as split points.

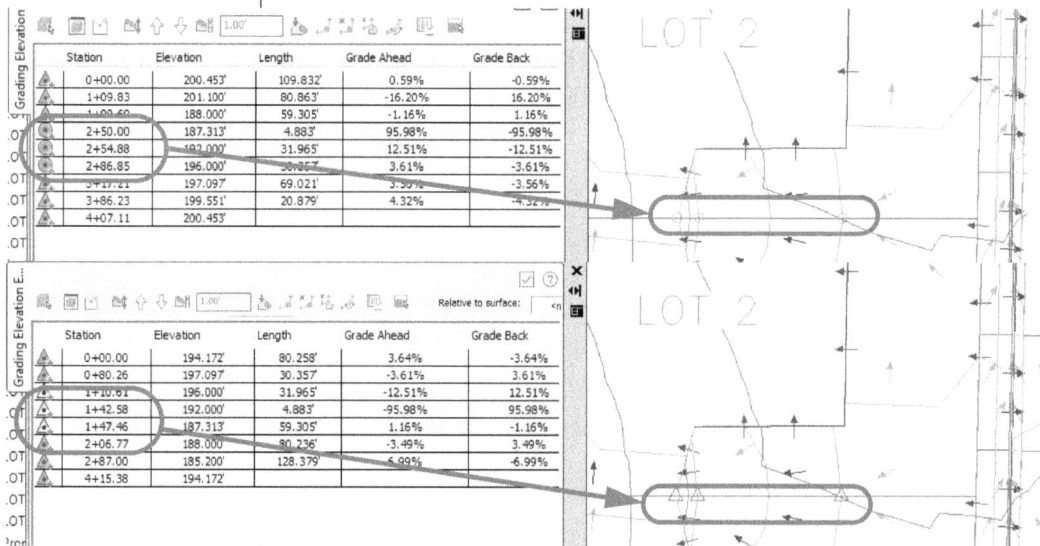

Figure 2–47

Practice 2c

Add Elevation Points to Parcels

Practice Objective

- Create split points along parcel lines by adding elevations to adjacent parcel segments.

In this practice, you will insert elevation points along the parcel segments.

1. Continue working in the drawing from the previous practice or open **PARCELS-D.dwg** from the *C:\Civil 3D for Land Dev\ Working\Parcels* folder.

2. In the *View* tab>Views panel, select **Lot1** as the view to zoom into the first lot to grade.

3. In the *Prospector* tab, expand Surfaces, right-click on **Residential Surface**, and select **Rebuild - Automatic**, as shown in Figure 2–48.

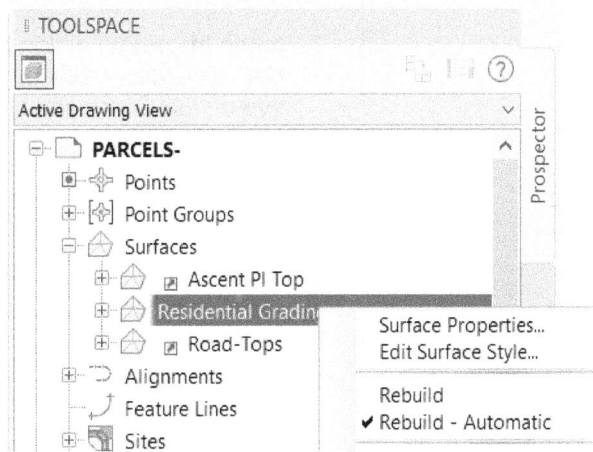

Figure 2–48

4. In the drawing, select the Lot 1 parcel segments. In the *Parcel Segments* contextual tab>Modify panel, click ⬜ (Edit Elevations). In the Edit Elevations panel, click ⬤ (Elevation Editor).

5. In the Elevation Editor vista, click ⊞ (Insert Elevation Point).

---

6. In the drawing, pick the endpoint of the walls at the front corner of the house in Lot 1, as shown in Figure 2–49.

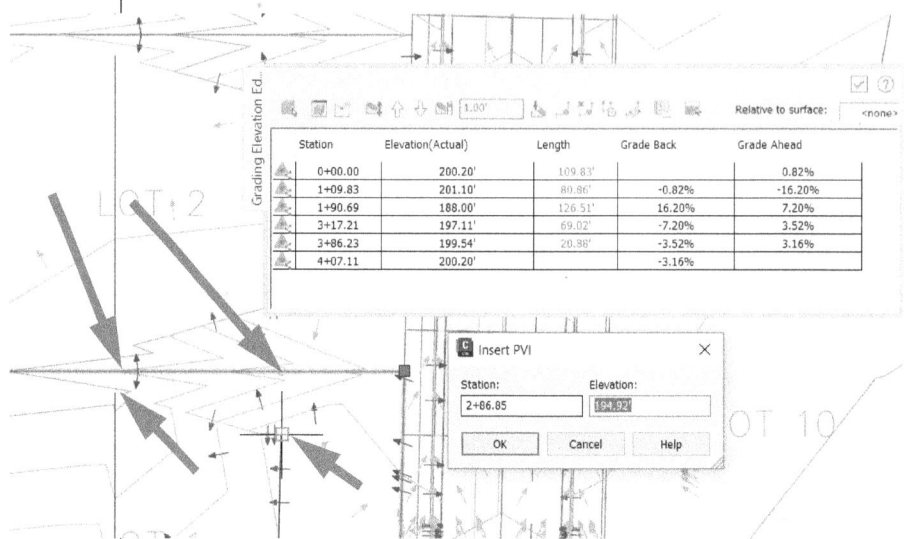

Station	Elevation(Actual)	Length	Grade Back	Grade Ahead
0+00.00	200.20'	109.83'		0.82%
1+09.83	201.10'	80.86'	-0.82%	-16.20%
1+90.69	188.00'	126.51'	16.20%	7.20%
3+17.21	197.11'	69.02'	-7.20%	3.52%
3+86.23	199.54'	20.86'	-3.52%	3.16%
4+07.11	200.20'		-3.16%	

Insert PVI

Station: 2+86.85   Elevation: 194.92'

OK   Cancel   Help

Figure 2–49

7. In the Insert PVI dialog box, for the *Elevation* type **198**. Click **OK**. (This dialog box might not open. If it does not, keep an eye on the Command Line because it will prompt you for the elevation instead.)

8. Repeat Steps 4 to 7 to add an elevation at the endpoint of the backyard feature lines for Lot 1 with an elevation of **190**.

   When finished, the Lot 1 elevations in the Elevation Editor vista should be as shown in Figure 2–50.

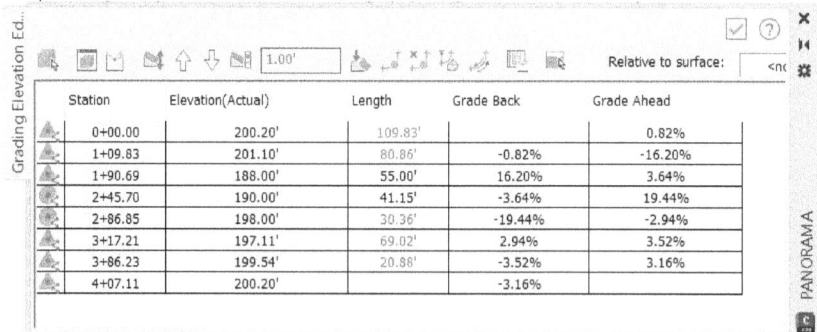

Station	Elevation(Actual)	Length	Grade Back	Grade Ahead
0+00.00	200.20'	109.83'		0.82%
1+09.83	201.10'	80.86'	-0.82%	-16.20%
1+90.69	188.00'	55.00'	16.20%	3.64%
2+45.70	190.00'	41.15'	-3.64%	19.44%
2+86.85	198.00'	30.36'	-19.44%	-2.94%
3+17.21	197.11'	69.02'	2.94%	3.52%
3+86.23	199.54'	20.88'	-3.52%	3.16%
4+07.11	200.20'		-3.16%	

Figure 2–50

9. In the Elevation Editor vista, click ⬛ (Select Feature).

10. In the drawing, select the Lot 2 parcel segments. Note the three split points marked with triangles along the south boundary line, as shown in Figure 2–51.

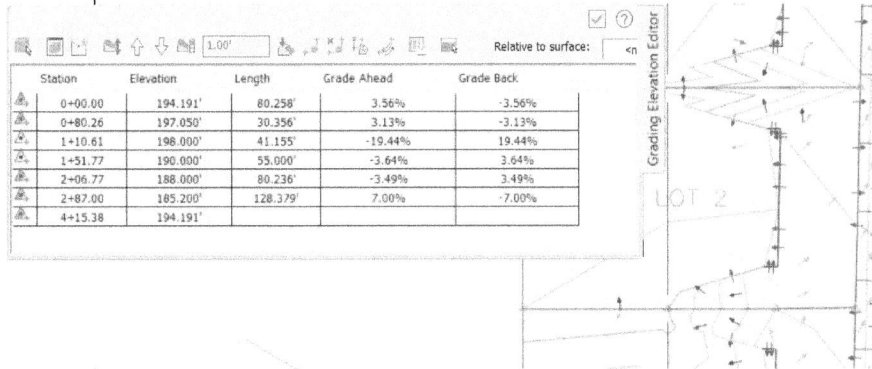

	Station	Elevation	Length	Grade Ahead	Grade Back
	0+00.00	194.191'	80.258'	3.56%	-3.56%
	0+80.26	197.050'	30.356'	3.13%	-3.13%
	1+10.61	198.000'	41.155'	-19.44%	19.44%
	1+51.77	190.000'	55.000'	-3.64%	3.64%
	2+06.77	188.000'	80.236'	-3.49%	3.49%
	2+87.00	185.200'	128.379'	7.00%	-7.00%
	4+15.38	194.191'			

Figure 2–51

11. Repeat Steps 4 to 8 to add elevation points to the north line of Lot 2, as shown in Figure 2–52.

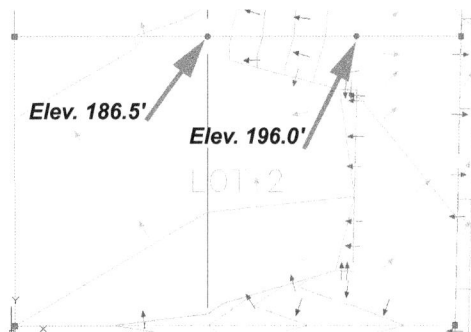

Elev. 186.5'
Elev. 196.0'

Figure 2–52

12. Repeat Steps 4 to 8 to add elevation points to the north line of Lot 3, as shown in Figure 2–53.

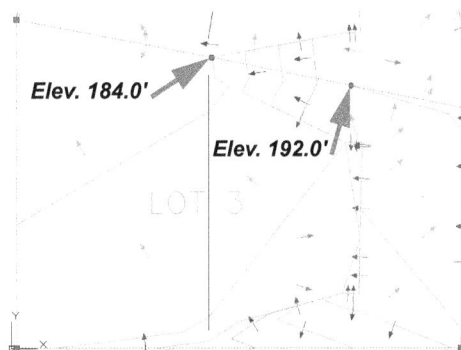

Elev. 184.0'
Elev. 192.0'

Figure 2–53

13. Repeat Steps 4 to 8 to add elevation points to the north line of Lot 4, as shown in Figure 2–54.

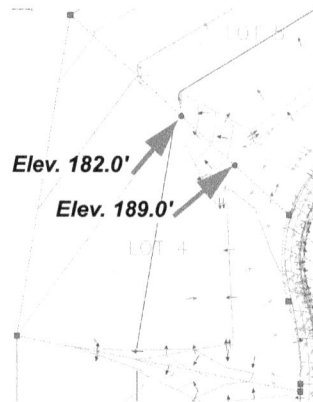

Elev. 182.0'

Elev. 189.0'

Figure 2–54

14. Repeat Steps 4 to 8 to add elevation points to the north line of Lot 5, as shown in Figure 2–55.

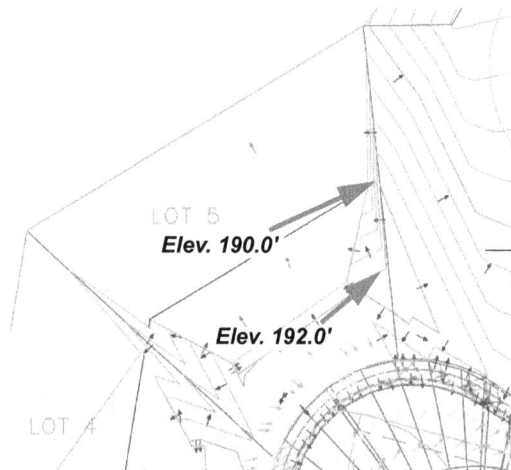

LOT 5

Elev. 190.0'

Elev. 192.0'

LOT 4

Figure 2–55

15. Save the drawing. (Before opening the Object Viewer in the next step, it is always prudent to save the drawing.)

16. Select the Residential Grading surface (select one of its contour lines).

17. In the *Surface* contextual tab, click ▣ (Object Viewer). Set the view direction to **SW Isometric** and the style to **Conceptual**. Note the hole in the surface, as shown in Figure 2–56.

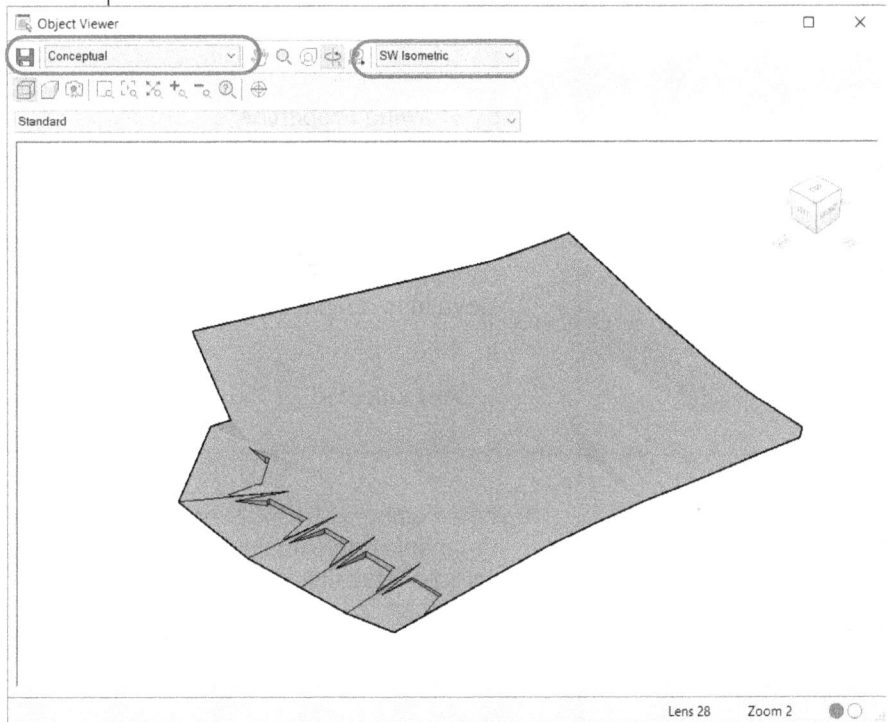

Figure 2–56

18. Press <Esc> twice to close the Object Viewer and release the selection.

Chapter Review Questions

1. Where do you set the option to use parcel elevations in the drawing?

   a. Parcel Properties

   b. Site Properties

   c. Drawing Properties

   d. Feature Line Properties

2. When using (Edit Elevations) in the *Parcel Segments* contextual tab>Edit Elevations panel, how many vertices' elevations do you set at a time?

   a. One

   b. Any selected

   c. All

3. When using (Set Elevations by Reference) in the *Parcel Segments* contextual tab>Edit Elevations panel, how many vertices' elevations do you set at a time?

   a. One

   b. Any selected

   c. All

4. When creating a wall breakline, you can use the following to set the elevations of the offset points at each vertex? (Select all that apply.)

   a. Elevation

   b. Difference in Elevation

   c. By Reference

   d. Surface

5. When feature lines, parcel segments, or survey figures cross each other, what is the elevation point assigned called?

   a. Point of Intersection

   b. Crossing Point

   c. Elevation Point

   d. Split Point

Command Summary

Button	Command	Location
	Breakline	• **Ribbon**: *Tin Surface* contextual tab> Modify panel, expanded Add Data drop-down list • **Command Prompt:** AddSurfaceBreaklines
	Bring to Front	• **Ribbon**: *Parcel Segments* contextual tab>expanded General Tools panel • **Command Prompt:** DrawOrder
	Edit Elevations	• **Ribbon**: *Parcel Segments* contextual tab>Edit Elevations panel • **Command Prompt:** EditFeatureElevs
	Elevations from Surface	• **Ribbon**: *Parcel Segments* contextual tab>Edit Elevations panel • **Command Prompt:** FeatureElevsFromSurf
	Move to Site	• **Ribbon**: *Parcel* contextual tab>Modify panel • **Command Prompt:** MoveToSite
	Paste Surface	• **Ribbon**: *Tin Surface* contextual tab> Modify panel, expanded Edit Surface drop-down list • **Command Prompt:** EditSurfacePaste
	Send to Back	• **Ribbon**: *Parcel Segments* contextual tab>expanded General Tools panel • **Command Prompt:** DrawOrder
	Set Elevations by Reference	• **Ribbon**: *Parcel Segments* contextual tab>Edit Elevations panel • **Command Prompt:** SetFeatureRefElev

Building Pad Design

Setting the elevation of a building pad and grading out a specified slope from that pad is important to fully understand how much cut and fill a site is going to have. In this chapter, you will learn how to assign elevations to a building footprint, and then create a simple grading object to calculate how much cut/fill is going to be required for the building at that elevation.

Learning Objectives in This Chapter

- List the five ways in which feature lines can be created.
- Create a feature line from objects in a drawing or external reference file.
- Project a specific slope from a baseline to a specific target in a drawing.
- Change the grading criteria of an existing grading solution.
- Calculate the earthwork volumes for a grading group or a single grading object using the Grading Volume Tools.

3.1 Feature Lines Overview

The Autodesk® Civil 3D® software uses 3D polylines known as *Feature Lines* for grading footprints, corridor modeling, and surface breaklines. A feature line can represent a building footprint, parking lot perimeter, swale, or ridgeline. The benefit of using a feature line over an AutoCAD 3D polyline is its ease of editing and its ability to support arcs without tessellation. Tessellated curves are undesirable in grading because of their many small grading faces around radial corners.

To access commands for creating feature lines, select the *Home* tab>Create Design panel and select **Feature Line**, as shown in Figure 3–1.

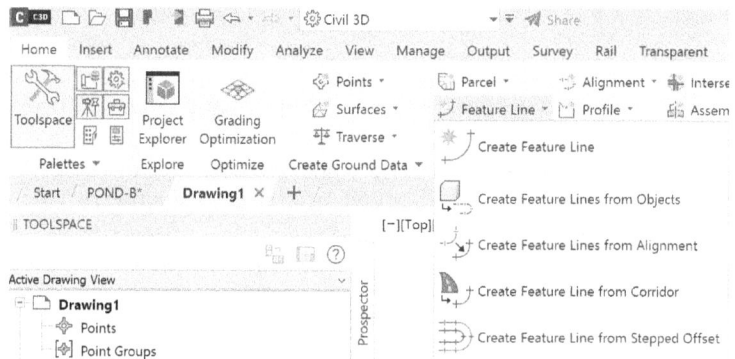

Figure 3–1

Feature lines can be created in five different ways:

1. Create Feature Line manually
2. Create Feature Lines from Objects
3. Create Feature Lines from Alignment
4. Create Feature Line from Corridor
5. Create Feature Line from Stepped Offset

3.2 Create Feature Lines from Objects

Designs often start out as 2D conceptual drawings to help determine where to locate design components. In these cases, you can easily convert existing 2D or 3D polylines, lines, or arcs into feature lines. During the conversion process, a name and style are assigned to the feature line along with elevations for each of the vertices. To edit the elevations of a feature line, you use the same tools used for editing parcel segment elevations.

How To: Create a Feature Line from Existing Objects

1. In the *Home* tab>Create Design panel, in the Feature Line drop-down list, select ⌐꜀ (Create Feature Lines from Objects).
2. Select the arcs, lines, or polylines in the drawing to convert or type **X** and press <Enter> to select objects in an external reference file.
3. In the Create Feature Lines dialog box, set the **Site** to ensure that other feature lines, parcels, and grading groups interact with the new feature line. Type a name for the feature line. Set the style, layer, and conversion options, as shown in Figure 3–2.

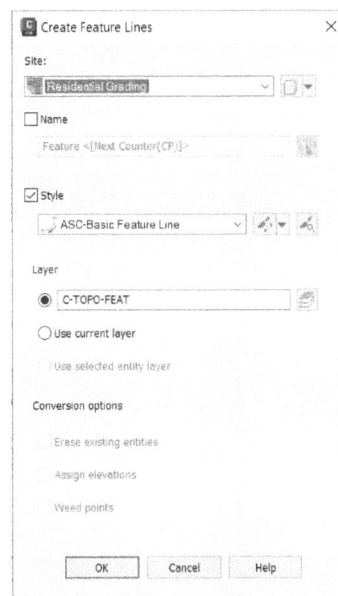

Figure 3–2

4. If the option to assign elevations is selected in the Conversion options, a dialog box opens that enables you to assign elevations to the vertices, as shown in Figure 3–3.

- Select the **Elevation** option and type the required elevation value or set the vertex elevations to be assigned from other gradings or surfaces that exist in the drawing.
- By selecting the option to insert intermediate grade break points, additional elevation points are added to the feature line anywhere the line crosses a surface triangle.

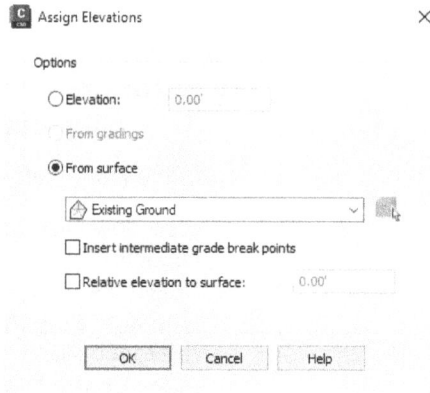

Figure 3–3

5. If the **Weed Points** option is selected under Conversion options, a third dialog box opens, as shown in Figure 3–4.

- Set the minimum angle, grade, or length that is required between the elevation points. This causes any points closer than the set minimums to be removed.
- You can also set the minimum 3D distance between elevation points.
- At the bottom of the dialog box, an information line indicates how many vertices are going to be weeded out.

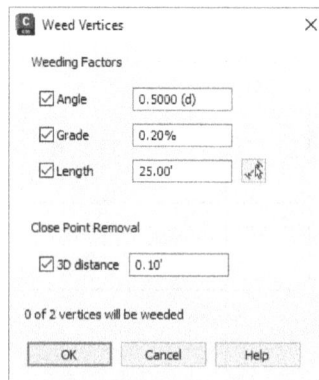

Figure 3–4

Practice 3a

Create a Feature Line from Objects in an XREF

Practice Objective

- Create a feature line from objects in an external reference file.

In this practice, you will create a feature line from objects and then edit the feature line elevations.

For the land development drawings in this guide, much of the preliminary work has already been done for the site development.

The completed corridors for Jeffries Ranch Road and Ascent Place, the Ascent Place knuckle and cul-de-sac target alignments, the Mission Avenue alignment, and the Existing-Site surface have been referenced through Data Shortcuts.

The Residential Grading surface created in the *Parcel Grading* chapter has been referenced as well; its surface style is set to *_No Display*.

In the sequence of construction projects, the parking lots usually are graded first to form a reference for building pads grading. For this reason, the parking lot has already been graded and a surface created for you. You will learn how to grade the parking lot in subsequent chapters.

Task 1 - Create a feature line from objects.

In this task, you will convert a drawing's polyline into a grading feature line. The feature line is the basis for the future grading object baseline. There are two building platforms to be converted, one for the office building, the other for the hotel.

1. Open **BLDG-A**.dwg from the *C:\Civil 3D for Land Dev\ Working\BLDG Pad* folder.

2. Hover over the Data Shortcuts and look at the tooltip that appears, as shown in Figure 3–5. Ensure that your **Data Shortcuts Working Folder** is set to *C:\Civil 3D for Land Dev\ Data Shortcuts\Fundamentals* and the **Data Shortcuts Project Folder** to *Ascent-Development*.

If required, review the Setting a Project practice for how to set the working folder and the project folder.

- If not, right-click on Data Shortcuts to set the **Working Folder** to *C:\Civil 3D for Land Dev\Data Shortcuts\ Fundamentals* and the **Data Shortcuts Project Folder** to *Ascent-Development*.

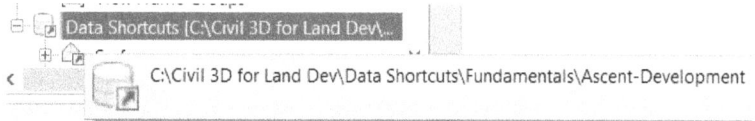

Figure 3–5

3. In the *View* tab>Views panel, select **Office** as the view to zoom into the outline that represents the office building platform surrounding the office building, as shown in Figure 3–6.

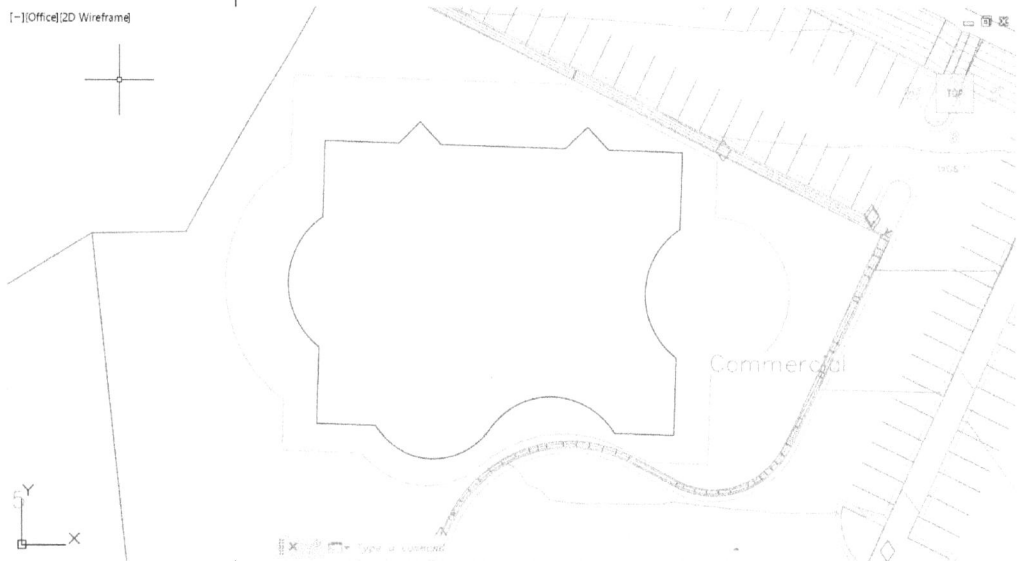

Figure 3–6

4. In the *Home* tab>Create Design panel, expand the Feature Line drop-down list and select ⬚ (Create Feature Lines from Objects), as shown in Figure 3–7.

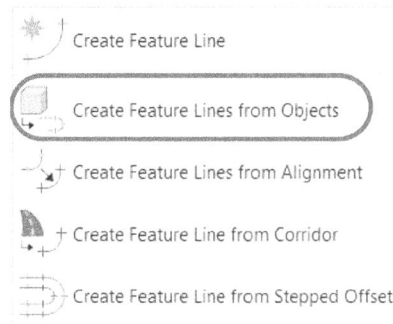

Figure 3–7

5. In the Command Line, select **Xref** to select linework from the XREF.

6. Select the cyan polyline, as shown in Figure 3–8. Press <Enter> to end the object selection process.

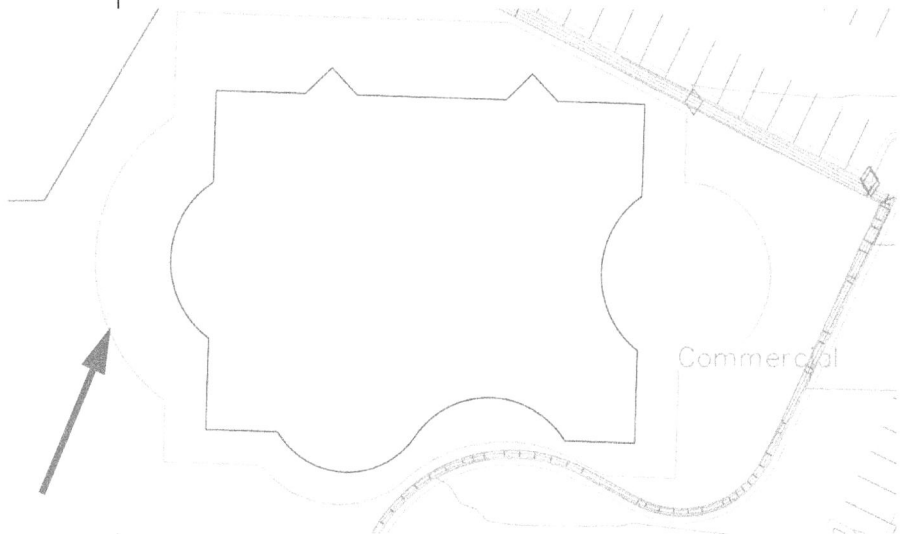

Figure 3–8

7. In the Create Feature Lines dialog box, complete the following, as shown in Figure 3–9:

   - Set the *Site* to **Multi-Family Site**.
   - For the *Name*, type **Office**.
   - Set the *Style* to **ASC_Building Pad**.
   - Set the *Conversion options* to **Assign elevations**.
   - Click **OK** to close the dialog box.

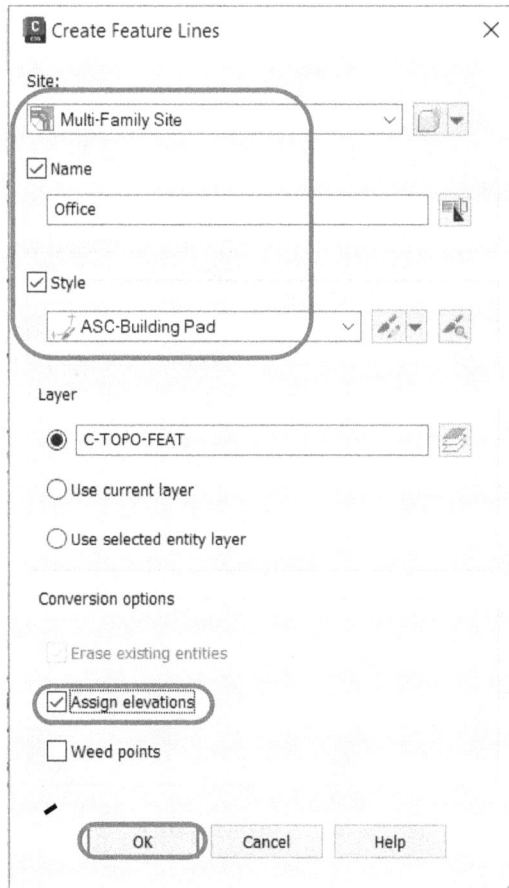

Figure 3–9

8. In the Assign Elevations dialog box, complete the following, as shown in Figure 3–10:

- Select **From Surface** for the surface.
- Select **Residential Grading**.
- Clear the **Insert intermediate grade break points** and **Relative elevation to surface** options.
- Click **OK** to close the dialog box.

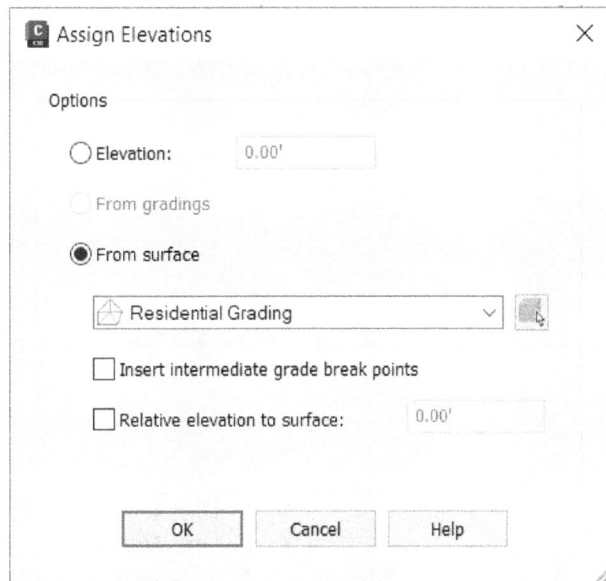

Figure 3–10

Repeat steps for the hotel, as follows:

9. In the *View* tab>Views panel, select **Hotel**.

10. In the *Home* tab>Create Design panel, expand the Feature Line drop-down list and select 📐 (Create Feature Lines from Objects).

11. In the Command Line, select **Xref** to select linework from the XREF.

12. Select the cyan polyline representing the pad for the hotel and pool, as shown in Figure 3–11. Press <Enter> to end the object selection process.

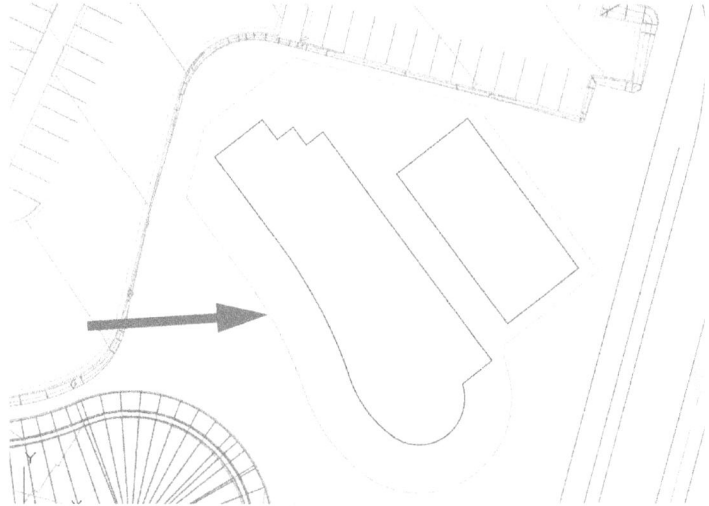

Figure 3–11

13. In the Create Feature Lines dialog box, complete the following:

   - Set the *Site* to **Multi-Family Site**.
   - For the *Name*, type **Hotel**.
   - Set the *Style* to **ASC_Building Pad**.
   - Set the *Conversion options* to **Assign elevations**.
   - Click **OK** to close the dialog box.

14. In the Assign Elevations dialog box, complete the following:

   - Select **From Surface** for the surface.
   - Select **Residential Grading.**
   - Clear the **Insert intermediate grade break points** and **Relative elevation to surface** options.
   - Click **OK** to close the dialog box.

15. Save the drawing.

Task 2 - Edit the feature line elevations.

1. Continue working in the drawing.

2. Select the Office feature line created in the previous task. (In the *Feature Line* contextual tab>Modify panel, select **Edit Elevations**, as shown in Figure 3–12.

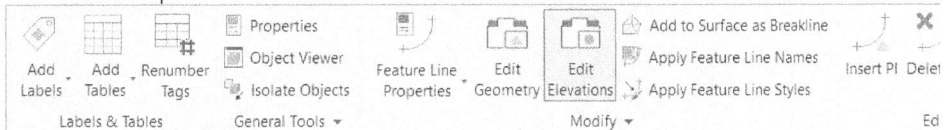

Figure 3–12

3. In the Edit Elevations panel, select **Elevation Edito**r, as shown in Figure 3–13.

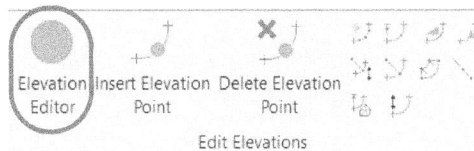

Figure 3–13

4. In the Elevation Editor panorama, select any row and hold down <Ctrl> as you type **A** to select every row, as shown in Figure 3–14.

Alternatively, you don't have to select any rows and can go straight to the next step. When none of the rows are selected, the Elevation Editor acts on all rows.

Station	Elevation(Actual)	Length	Grade Back	Grade Ahead
0+00.00	180.60'	59.03'		-0.79%
0+59.03	180.13'	24.00'	0.79%	-0.93%
0+83.03	179.91'	30.08'	0.93%	-7.65%
1+13.11	177.61'	58.96'	7.65%	-6.48%
1+72.07	173.79'	30.00'	6.48%	-7.65%
2+02.07	171.50'	29.79'	7.65%	0.93%
2+31.86	171.77'	12.21'	-0.93%	-5.77%
2+44.07	171.07'	12.12'	5.77%	4.72%
2+56.19	171.64'	49.71'	-4.72%	-2.32%
3+05.90	170.49'	12.21'	2.32%	-7.97%
3+18.11	169.52'	12.13'	7.97%	4.72%
3+30.23	170.09'	29.91'	-4.72%	-1.38%
3+60.14	169.68'	29.82'	1.38%	8.06%
3+89.96	172.08'	59.58'	-8.06%	7.62%
4+49.54	176.62'	29.71'	-7.62%	9.00%
4+79.25	179.30'	24.00'	-9.00%	2.32%
5+03.25	179.85'	54.31'	-2.32%	1.38%
5+57.56	180.60'		-1.38%	

Figure 3–14

5. In the Elevation Editor, click (Flatten Grade or Elevation). Select **Constant Elevation**, as shown in Figure 3–15. Click **OK** to close the dialog box.

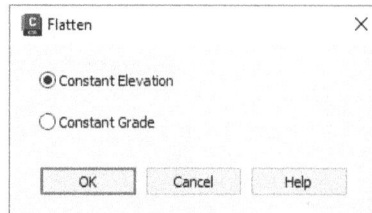

Figure 3–15

6. In the Elevation Editor, click (Raise/Lower). In the *Input* field, type **180** and press <Enter>, as shown in Figure 3–16.

Figure 3–16

7. Click to close the Elevation Editor panorama.

8. Repeat the same steps for the Hotel pad, with the elevation of **179.0.**

9. Save the drawing.

3.3 Grading Creation Tools

This section focuses on grading to a surface. To start the
Grading command, go to the *Home* tab>Create Design panel,
expand the Grading drop-down list, and select a command in the
Grading Creation Tools toolbar, as shown at the top of
Figure 3–17.

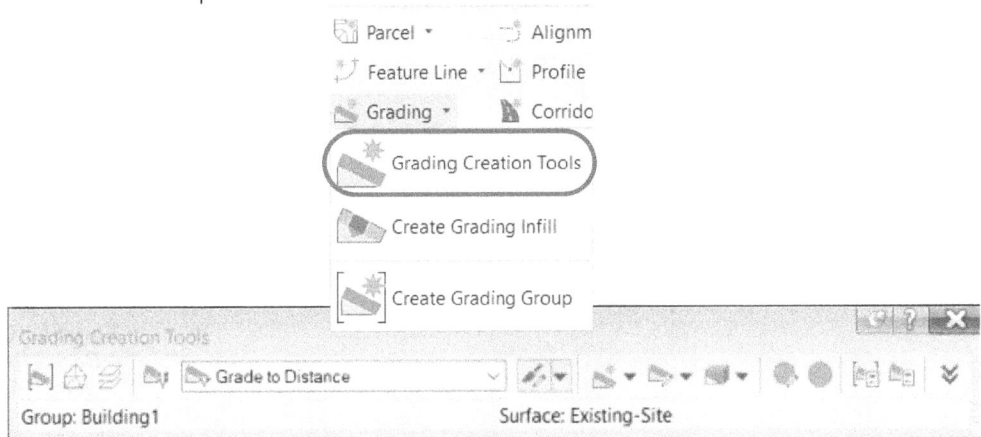

Figure 3–17

It is recommended that you start on the left and work to the right
in command specific toolbars. The Grading Creation Tools
toolbar is no exception to this recommended process. Therefore,
the first thing you need to do is define or set the Grading Group.

Grading Groups

A grading object consists of a base line, projection lines, target lines, and faces. Combining multiple grading objects into a group enables you to create complex grading schemes. A grading group calculates a volume for an entire grading area, rather than one object at a time. Figure 3–18 shows each part of a grading group.

Each time a grading object is created, a new feature line is created as a projected target line. The resulting target line can then be used as a baseline for a new grading object within the same group.

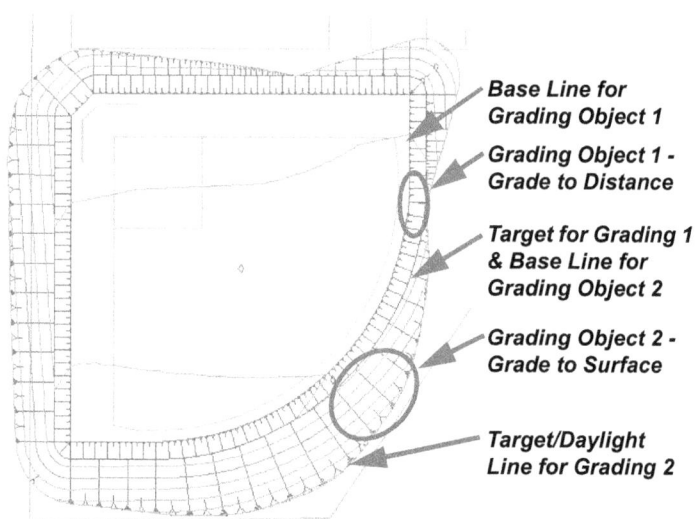

Base Line for Grading Object 1

Grading Object 1 - Grade to Distance

Target for Grading 1 & Base Line for Grading Object 2

Grading Object 2 - Grade to Surface

Target/Daylight Line for Grading 2

Figure 3–18

To create a new grading group, click ⬠ (Set Grading Group) in the Grading Creation Tools toolbar. The first entry is the site in which you want to work, as shown in Figure 3–19. Sites can be created in the template to keep constancy across all of the projects. If a site does not already exist, one called Site 1 is created automatically.

Figure 3–19

Once the site has been set, another dialog box opens enabling you to create a grading group, as shown in Figure 3–20. The first task is to type a name and a description. Next you decide whether you want to predefine a surface for the grading group. If simple grading groups are being created with one or two projections, creating a surface immediately should not be a problem. However, if a grading group is complex with three or more grading objects, it is recommended that you wait until the grading group is complete before creating the group's surface.

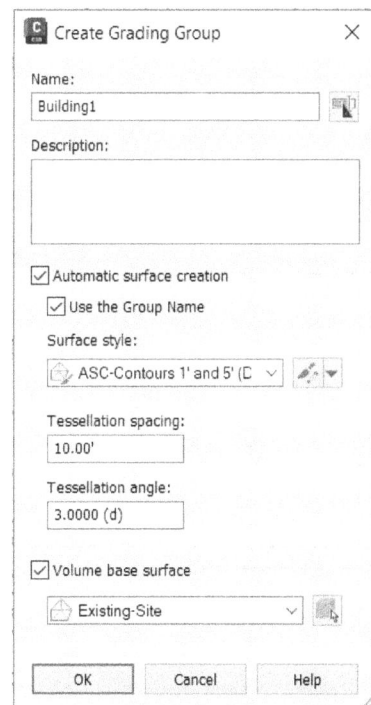

Figure 3–20

The last option to consider in the Create Grading Group dialog box is whether or not to set a Volume base surface. By selecting this option, a volume for the entire grading group can be calculated between this base surface and the grading group's surface. The base surface is usually set to the existing ground surface.

If the **Automatic surface creation** option is selected, a Create Surface dialog box opens, as shown in Figure 3–21. If you also selected the **Use the Group Name** option, the surface name field is already filled in with the grading group's name. Using the grading group's name as the surface ensures consistency and makes communication between other team members easy because they recognize that the grading group and surface are the same. As with any Autodesk Civil 3D surface, you can assign a style to the grading group surface.

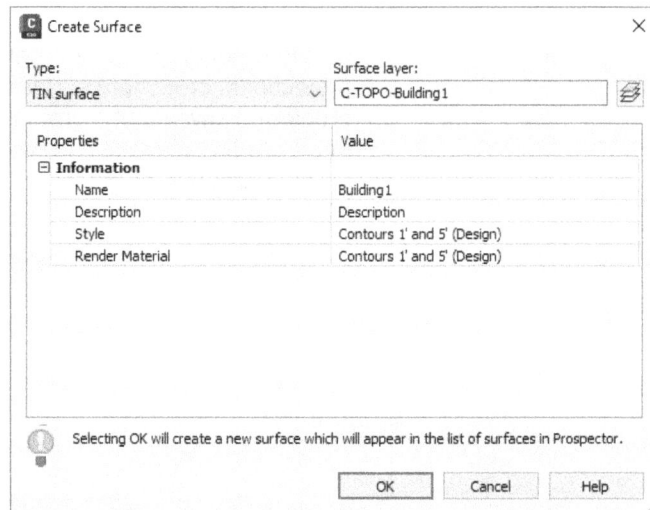

Figure 3–21

Grading Setup

The next task in the Grading Creation Tools toolbar is to set the target surface ⬦ . This is especially important if you want to grade to a surface because this surface is the Grade to Surface criteria's target. If a volume base surface was set in the Create Grading Group dialog box, the surface is set in the Grading Creation Tools toolbar, as shown in Figure 3–22.

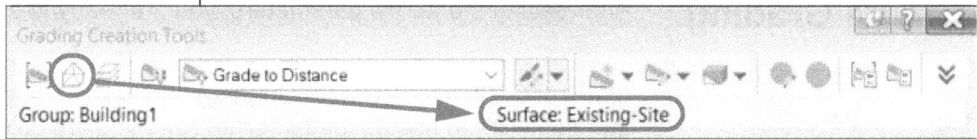

Figure 3–22

The next tool in the Grading Creation Tools toolbar is ⬙ (Set Grading Layer). Although you can use this tool to set the Layer for the grading objects, it is recommended that you use the drawing settings and grading styles to set the layer.

The next tool is ◥ (Select a Criteria Set). The standard Autodesk Civil 3D template includes a Basic criteria set that incorporates all four grading criteria without any locks toggled on. If you or someone in your company has added additional grading criteria sets to prevent unnecessary parameter entries, you can select the grading criteria set that you want to use, as shown in Figure 3–23.

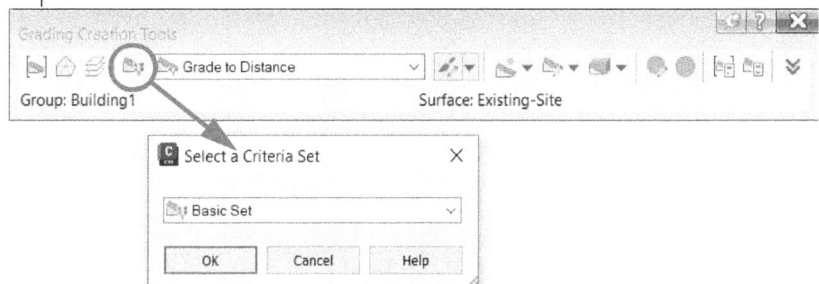

Figure 3–23

Depending on the selected Criteria Set, different grading criteria might be available. Figure 3–24 shows the available criteria from the Basic Set. Select the required criteria for the type of project you are doing. If the required criteria is not available, you can create new criteria on the fly by clicking ◢▼ (Create New Criteria).

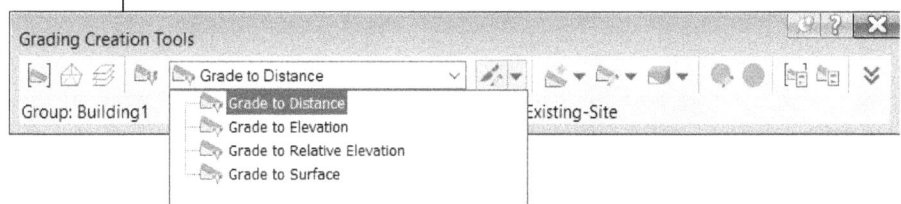

Figure 3–24

Create Grading

After setting the above parameters, you are ready to start grading. Click (Create Grading) and select the feature line that you want to use as the baseline. Next you are prompted for the side to which to grade if you want the grading to apply to the entire length of the feature line. After you have set the length to apply the grading criteria, the next prompt is for the grading parameters. This only occurs if the criteria you are using is not locked. Grading can be done on either side even if you have an open feature line or a closed feature line. If grading to the inside of a closed feature line, projections continue until the target is reached or the grading grades to itself, as shown in Figure 3–25.

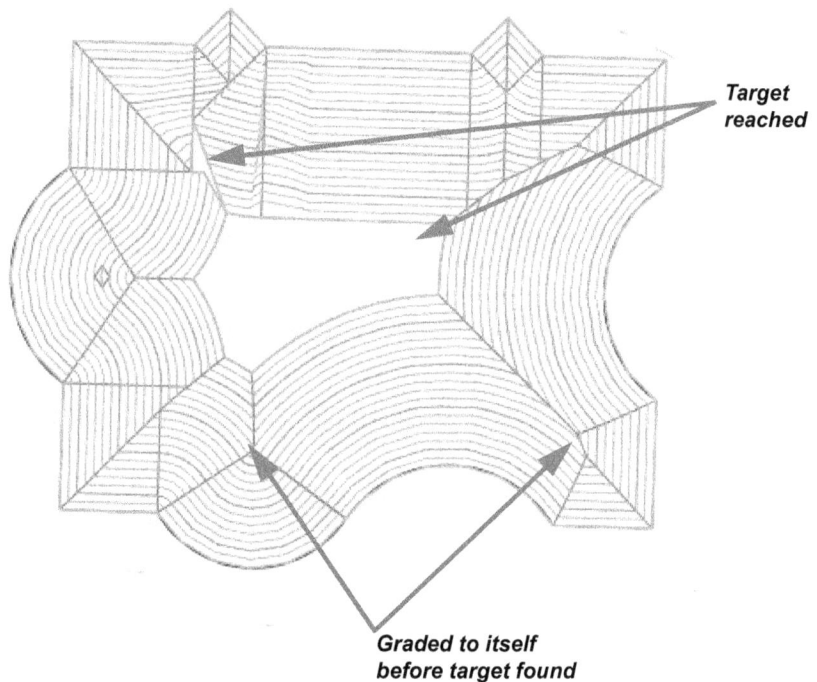

Target reached

Graded to itself before target found

Figure 3–25

Grading Infill

Sometimes there is a need to fill in an area between two grading objects or feature lines. A grading infill is a grading face that eliminates holes in grading groups and ensures that the finished ground surface covers the entire grading area. To create an infill, click ![icon] (Create Infill) in the Create Grading drop-down list in the Grading Creation toolbar. The routine prompts you to pick a point in the open area to infill with a grading face (similar to picking a point to hatch an area), as shown in Figure 3–26.

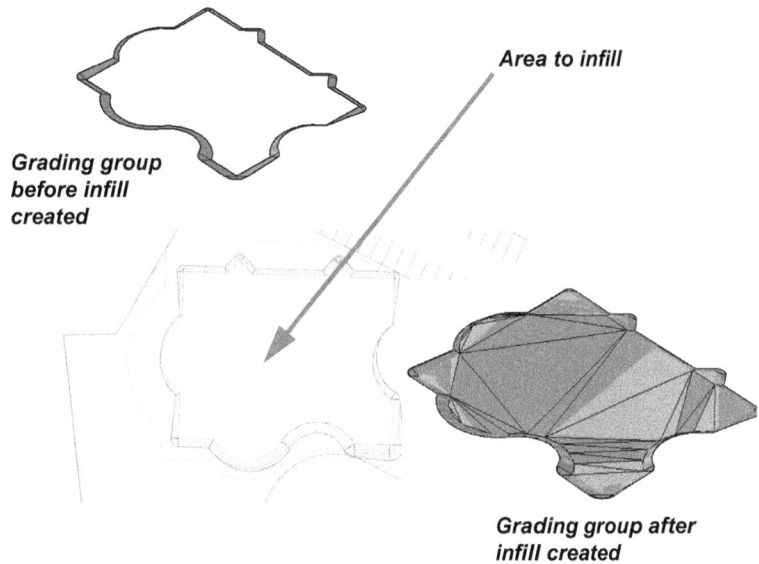

Area to infill

Grading group before infill created

Grading group after infill created

Figure 3–26

3.4 Editing the Grading

After creating a grading group, you might need to change one or more of the grading parameters. Some changes are required due to a mistake when creating the original grading place or due to a design change. In either case, the grading criteria used during the creation of the grading object determines what can change. If you used a Grade to Distance criteria but meant to use a Grade to Surface criteria, then you must delete the original grading object and replace it with a new grading object.

Delete Grading Objects

To delete a grading object and not corrupt your drawing, you should first select the grading object and, in the *Grading* contextual tab>Modify panel, click ✎ (Delete Grading), as shown in Figure 3–27. It is important that you delete the outer most grading object before deleting the interior grading objects. This is because if an interior grading object is used by other grading objects as a baseline, the exterior grading object becomes corrupt and unusable.

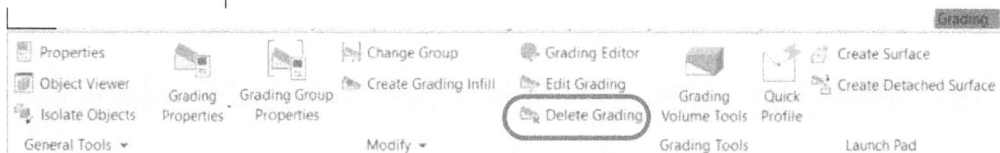

Figure 3–27

Modify Grading Object Criteria

To modify the input parameters of a grading object, you must first ensure that the criteria used was not locked; locks prevent editing. To check this and make the required changes at the same time, you use the Grading Editor. In the *Grading* contextual tab>Modify panel, click 🖱 (Grading Editor), as shown in Figure 3–28.

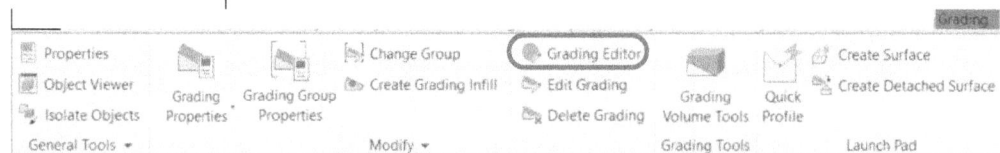

Figure 3–28

The Panorama's Grading Editor vista enables you to modify a grading's parameters. Any parameters that were locked when creating the grading object have a lock symbol to the left indicating that they cannot be changed. Anything without a lock can be changed by selecting the value field to the right of the parameter, as shown in Figure 3–29.

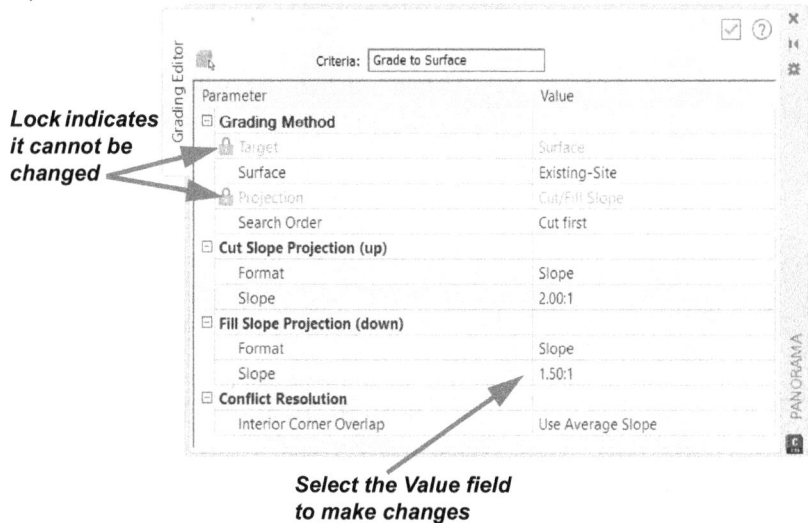

Lock indicates it cannot be changed

Select the Value field to make changes

Figure 3–29

Alternatively, you can click 🖾 (Edit Grading) on the *Grading* contextual tab>Modify panel to use the Grading Editor to change the grading parameters, as shown in Figure 3–30. This routine prompts you for the parameters in the Command Line. Note that you are only prompted for parameters that are not locked.

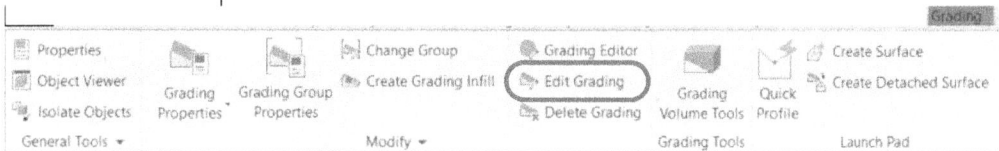

Figure 3–30

Practice 3b | Grading Creation Tools

Practice Objectives

- Project a feature line at a specific slope to a surface.
- Project another feature line to a surface on a temporary site.
- Adjust the grading.
- Create infills.

In this practice, you will grade to a surface, create infills, and modify the grading criteria.

Task 1 - Grade to a surface.

In this task, you will use the feature line as a baseline for your Grading Object and use the Grading Creation Tools toolbar to create a grading that slopes into the existing ground surface.

1. Continue working in the drawing from the last practice or open **BLDG-B.dwg** from the *C:\Civil 3D for Land Dev\ Working\BLDG Pad* folder.

2. In the *Home* tab>Create Design panel, expand the Grading drop-down list and click ![icon] (Grading Creation Tools). The Grading Creation Tools toolbar displays.

3. In the Grading Creation Tools toolbar, click ![icon] (Set Group). Select **Multi-Family Site**, and click ![icon] (Create a Grading Group) as shown in Figure 3–31.

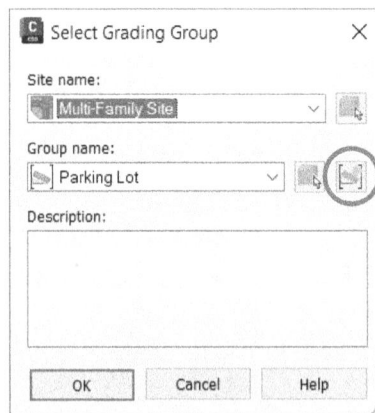

Figure 3–31

4. In the Create Grading Group dialog box, do the following, as shown in Figure 3–32:

- For the *Name*, type **Building Pads**.
- For the *Description*, type **Commercial building platforms**.
- Select the option to automatically create a surface.
- Set the *Volume base surface* to **Residential Grading**.
- Click **OK** to close the dialog box.

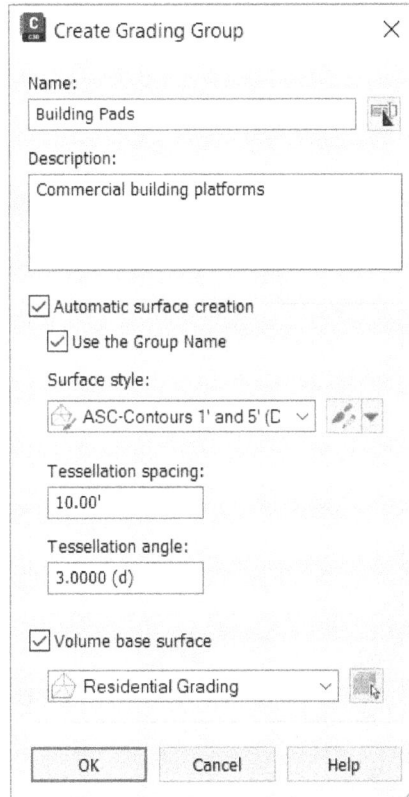

Figure 3–32

5. In the Create Surface dialog box, leave all of the default values and click **OK**.

6. Click **OK** to close the Select Grading Group dialog box.

7. In the Grading Creation Tools toolbar, verify that the *Criteria Set* is set to **Basic Set** by hovering over (Select a Criteria Set). Set the grading criteria to **Grade to Surface**, as shown in Figure 3–33.

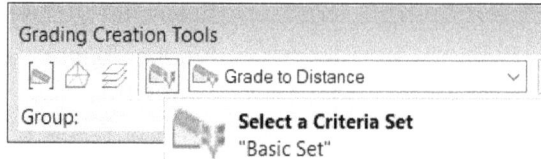

Figure 3–33

8. In the Grading Creation Tools toolbar, click (Create Grading).

9. In the model, select the blue hotel pad feature line marked as **A** in Figure 3–34.

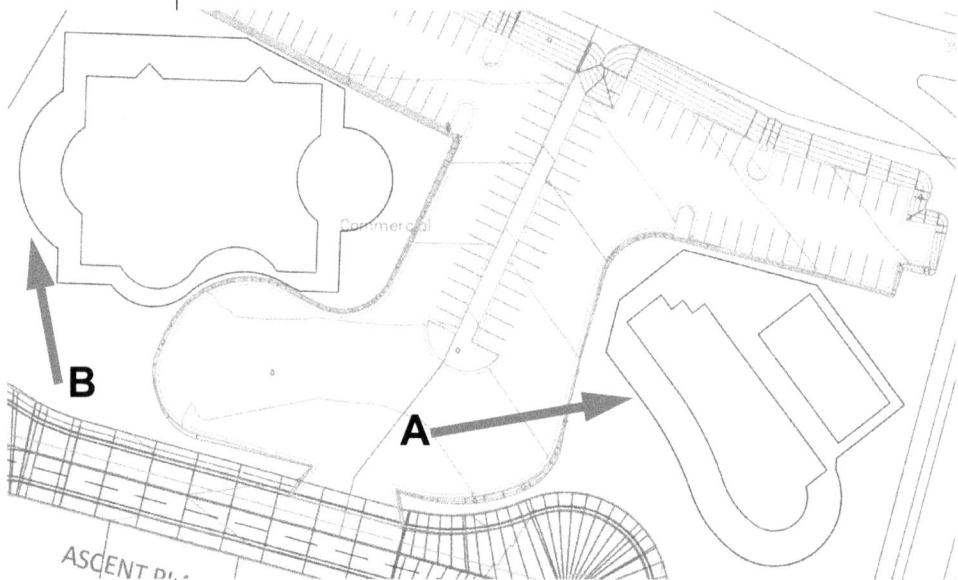

Figure 3–34

10. When prompted for a grading side, pick a point outside the building footprint.

11. When prompted to apply it to the entire length, press <Enter> to accept the default of **Yes**.

12. Press <Enter> to accept the default format of slope for both cut and fill.

13. Press <Enter> to accept the default 2:1 slopes for both cut and fill.

14. Click ✔ to close the Events Vista if it displays. Press <Esc> to end the command. The drawing should display as shown in Figure 3–35.

15. Press <Esc> to finish the grading command.

16. Note that the grading between the parking curb and the hotel pad neatly coincides, as shown in Figure 3–35. This is because both grading groups reside in the same site.

17. There are issues with this solution, as shown in Figure 3–35 where it gets too close to the property line. This will get fixed later in this exercise.

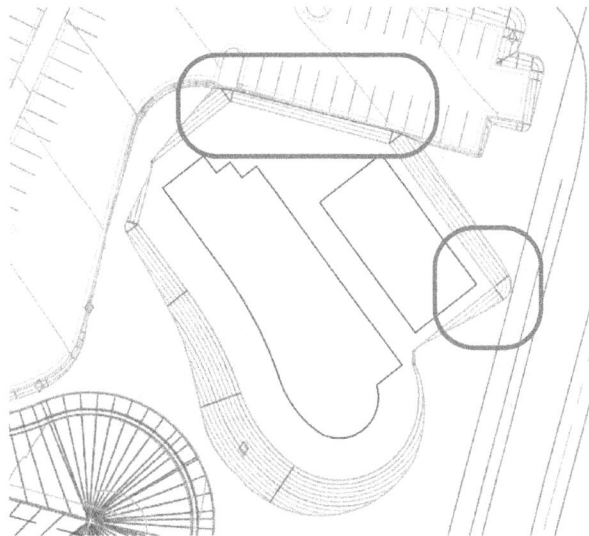

Figure 3–35

18. Save the drawing.

Task 2 - (Optional) Attempt to grade the office pad.

Civil 3D's grading tools and procedures as well as creating surfaces from grading groups can be somewhat unpredictable at times. When grading scenarios get complex and other grading groups within the same site are present, Civil 3D may not be able to solve the grading and either give unexpected results or even crash the program.

Such is the case when trying to grade the office pad as you have done with the hotel pad. You can attempt to preform this task in the following steps, but if there are time constraints or your system becomes too unstable, you can review the result by opening **BLDG-B1.dwg** from the *C:\Civil 3D for Land Dev\ Working\BLDG-Pad* folder.

The next task (3) will start with the completed drawing from the previous task (1).

Repeat the same steps you did in the previous task for the office pad feature line, as follows:

1. If need be, in the *Home* tab>Create Design panel, expand the Grading drop-down list and click (Grading Creation Tools).

2. In the *View* tab>Views panel, select **Office**.

3. In the Grading Creation Tools toolbar, verify that the grading criteria to **Grade to Surface**.

4. In the Grading Creation Tools toolbar, click (Create Grading).

5. In the model, select the blue office pad feature line., marked as **B** in Figure 3–34.When prompted for a grading side, pick a point outside the building footprint.

6. When prompted to apply it to the entire length, press <Enter> to accept the default of **Yes**.

7. Press <Enter> to accept the default format of slope for both cut and fill.

8. Type **1 (One)** to set the slope to 1:1 for both cut and fill.

9. Click to close the Events Vista if it displays. Press <Esc> to end the command. The drawing should display, as shown in Figure 3–36.

10. Press <Esc> to finish the grading command.

11. There are major issues with this solution, as shown in Figure 3–36. Initially they may not be apparent, except where the grading is incomplete in the North-west corner of the pad, as marked **A**. However, notice what has happened to the surface over at the hotel pad and in the parking area north of the hotel, as marked **B**. This is unacceptable.

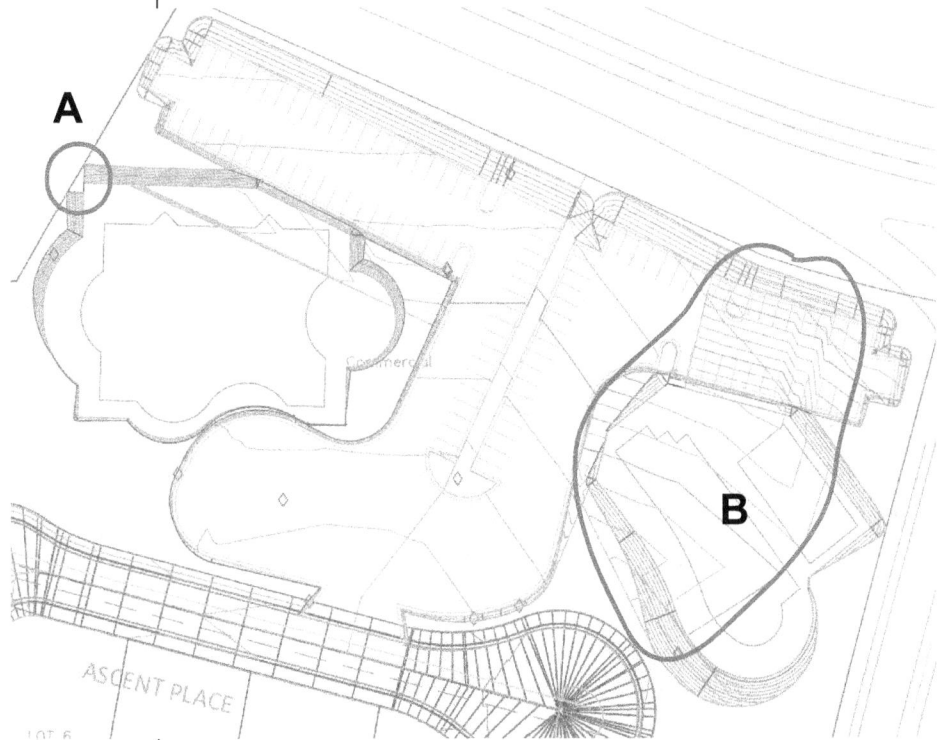

Figure 3–36

12. We will find another solution in the next task. For now, quit the drawing without saving.

Task 3 - Alternative way to grade the office pad.

While it is convenient to have grading groups interact when they belong to the same site, at times it can become impossible for Civil 3D to grade properly with such interdependent grading groups. When this occurs, it is advisable to create the grading groups on different sites (usually a temporary site) and later paste the resulting surfaces together to form a combined surface.

1. Open **BLDG-C**.dwg from the *C:\Civil 3D for Land Dev\ Working\BLDG Pad* folder.

2. In the *Prospector* tab, right-click on **Sites** and select **New**, as shown in Figure 3–37.

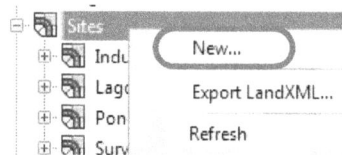

Figure 3–37

3. In the *Information* tab, for the *Name*, type **Temp** and click **OK**.

4. In the *View* tab>Views panel, select **Office**.

5. Select the **Office** feature line and in the right-click menu, select **Move to Site...**, as shown in Figure 3–38.

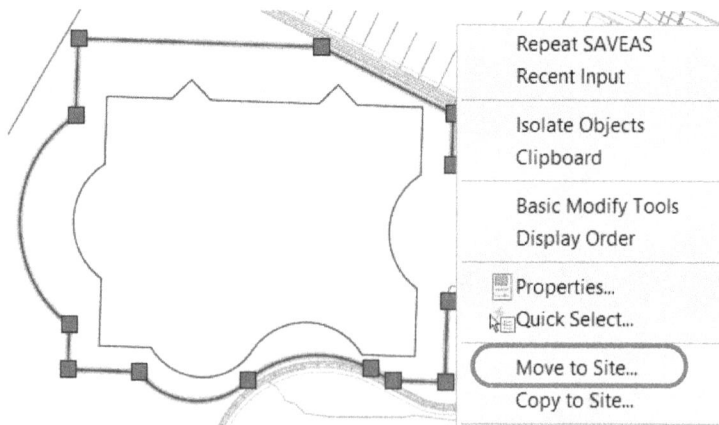

Figure 3–38

6. In the *Move to Site* dialog box, use the drop-down arrow to select the **Temp** site, as shown in Figure 3–39.

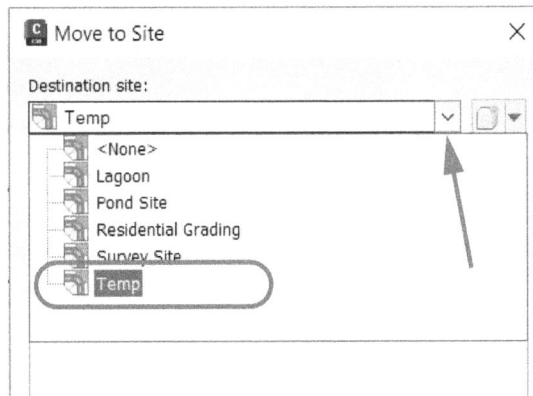

Figure 3–39

7. Click **OK** to dismiss the *Move to Site* dialog box.

8. Note that after the move, the name of the feature line has changed to **Office (1)**.

Repeat the same steps you did in Task 1, as follows:

9. If need be, in the *Home* tab>Create Design panel, expand the Grading drop-down list and click (Grading Creation Tools).

10. In the Grading Creation Tools toolbar, click (Set Group).

11. The *Select Grading Group* dialog box opens. Select the **Temp** site, then click (Create a Grading Group), as shown in Figure 3–40.

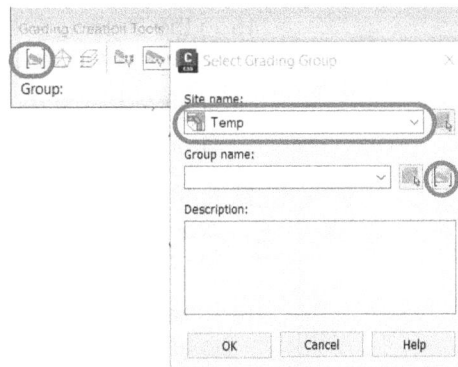

Figure 3–40

12. In the *Create Grading Group* dialog box, do the following, as shown in Figure 3–41:

   • For the *Name*, type **Office Pad**.
   • Select the **Automatic surface creation** option.
   • Set the *Volume base surface* to **Residential Grading**.
   • Click **OK** to close the dialog box.

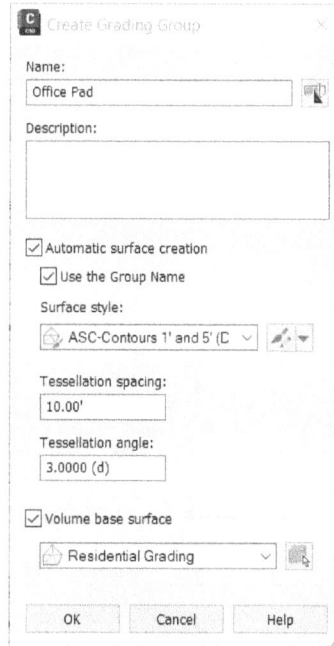

Figure 3–41

13. In the Create Surface dialog box, leave all of the default values and click **OK**.

14. Click **OK** to dismiss the *Select Grading Group* dialog box.

15. In the Grading Creation Tools toolbar, verify that the grading criteria to **Grade to Surface**.

16. In the Grading Creation Tools toolbar, click (Create Grading).

17. In the model, select the **Office (1)** feature line. When prompted for a grading side, pick a point outside the building footprint.

18. When prompted to apply it to the entire length, press <Enter> to accept the default of **Yes**.

19. Press <Enter> to accept the default format of slope for both cut and fill.

20. Type **1 (One)** to set the slope to 1:1 for both cut and fill.

21. Click ✔ to close the Events Vista if it displays. Press <Esc> to end the command. The drawing should display, as shown in Figure 3–42.

22. Press <Esc> to finish the grading command.

23. There are some issues with this solution, as shown in Figure 3–42. The grading is incomplete in the North-west corner of the pad, as marked **A**. This can be solved with transitional grading tools, which will be covered later in this guide.

24. The grading between the parking lot and the office pad overlaps since they are on different sites, as marked **B**. This will get resolved later when pasting the separate surfaces into a combination surface.

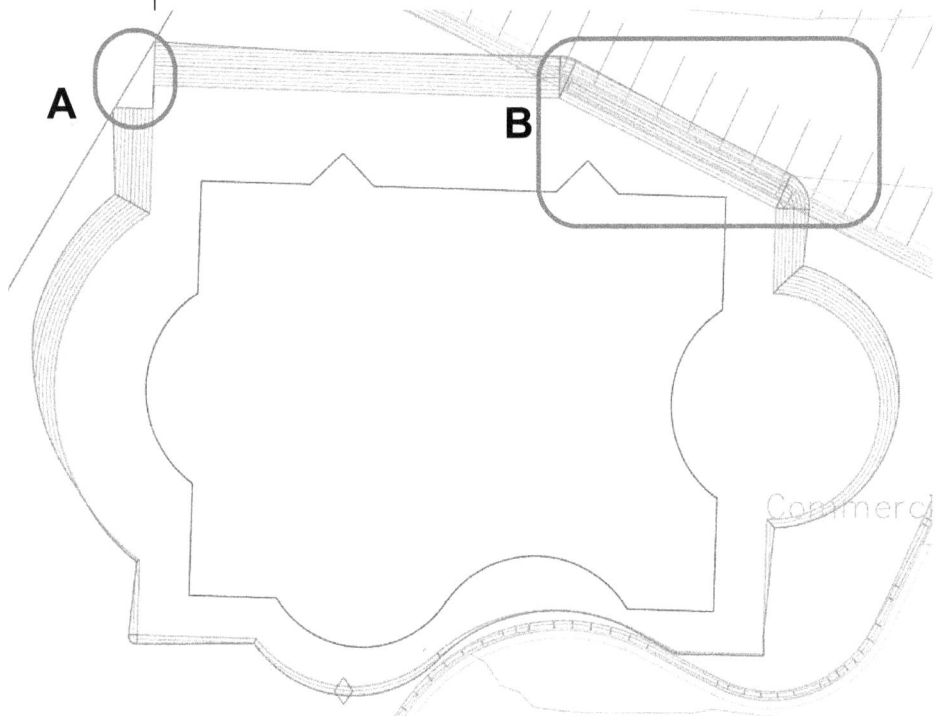

Figure 3–42

25. Save the drawing.

Task 4 - Create infill.

1. Open **BLDG-D.dwg** from the *C:\Civil 3D for Land Dev\ Working\BLDG-Pad* folder. Do not continue working in the drawing from the previous practice, the office building pad grading has been fine-tuned in this drawing. The transitional grading tools used will be covered later in this guide.

2. In the Grading Creation Tools toolbar, verify that the *Grading Group* is set to **Office Pad**, as shown in Figure 3–43.

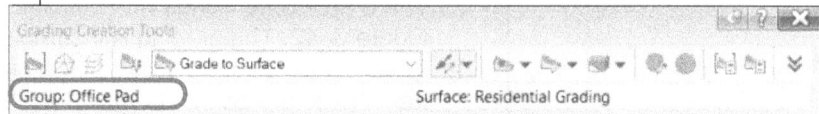

Figure 3–43

3. In the Grading Creation Tools toolbar, expand the Create Grading drop-down list and click (Create Infill). Pick a point in the center of the office pad, as marked **A** in Figure 3–44.

A green diamond indicating that the area now has a grading face should display.

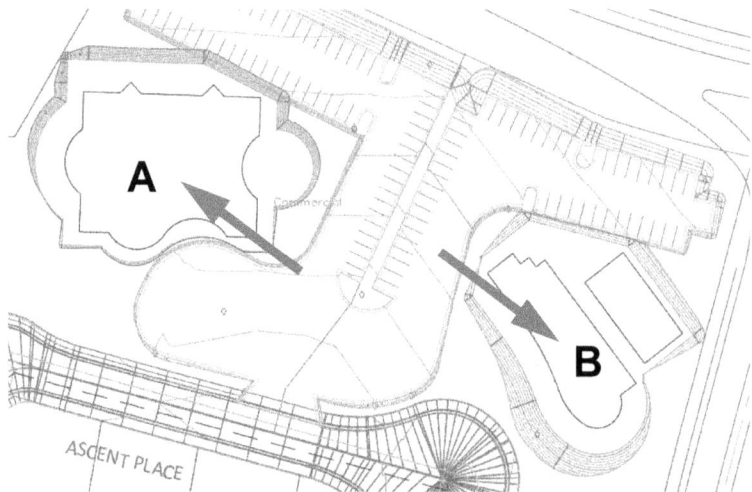

Figure 3–44

4. Press <Enter> to end the command. If the Events Vista displays, click to close it.

5. In the Grading Creation Tools toolbar, change the *Grading Group* to **Building Pads**, as shown in Figure 3–45.

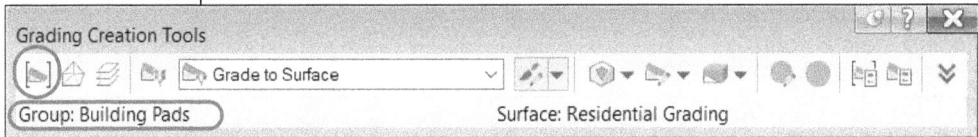

Figure 3–45

6. In the Grading Creation Tools toolbar, expand the Create Grading drop-down list and click [Create Infill icon] (Create Infill). Pick a point in the center of the office pad, as marked **B** in Figure 3–44.

7. Press <Enter> to end the command. If the Events Vista displays, click [checkmark icon] to close it.

8. Save the drawing.

Task 5 - Modify the grading criteria.

After completing the grading, for the office pad, note that the fill slope on the northwest side of the building pad is encroaching the property line, and the other fill slopes are a bit too steep. Rather than moving the building or the pad, you will decrease the corner grading to **0.3** and increase the other fill slope to **1.50:1**.

1. Continue to work in the drawing from the previous task.

2. Select the grading object center mark (diamond symbol) created by grading marked **A** in Figure 3–46.

*If you have problems finding the diamond grip, zoom out and **REGEN** the drawing. This will resize the diamond grips.*

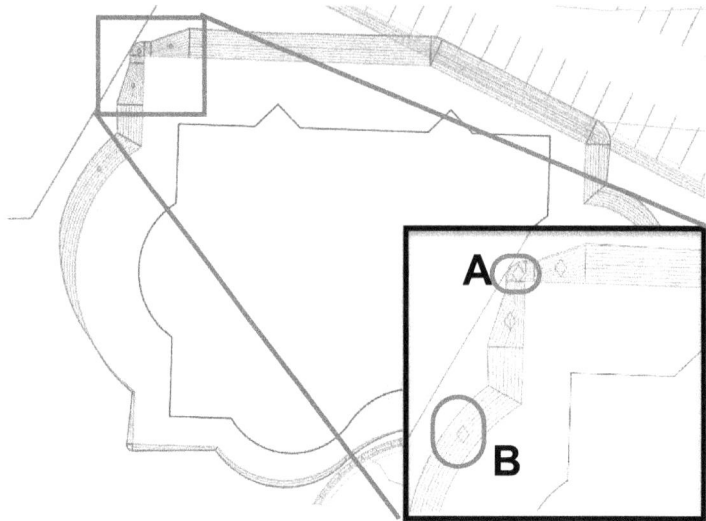

Figure 3–46

3. In the *Grading* contextual tab>Modify panel, click (Grading Editor).

4. In the Grading Editor panorama, change the *Fill Slope* to **0.3:1**, as shown in Figure 3–47, and press <Enter>. Note that the results are immediate; the grading recalculates after you press <Enter>.

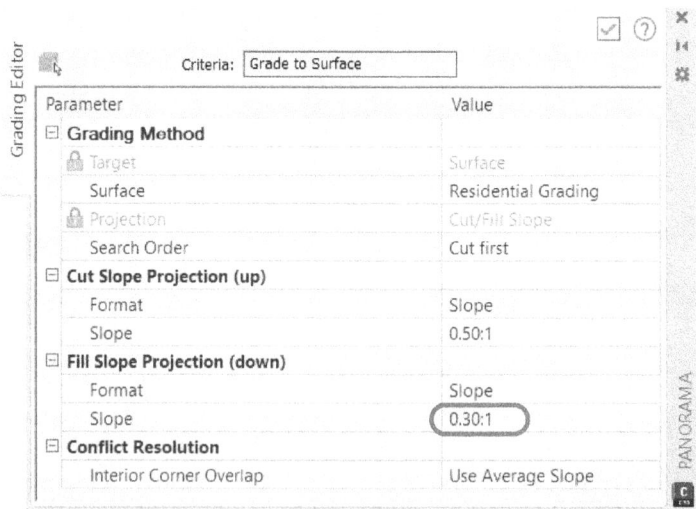

Parameter	Value
Grading Method	
Target	Surface
Surface	Residential Grading
Projection	Cut/Fill Slope
Search Order	Cut first
Cut Slope Projection (up)	
Format	Slope
Slope	0.50:1
Fill Slope Projection (down)	
Format	Slope
Slope	0.30:1
Conflict Resolution	
Interior Corner Overlap	Use Average Slope

Criteria: Grade to Surface

Figure 3–47

5. Click ✔ to close the Grading Editor panorama. Press <Esc> to release the grading object.

6. Repeat steps with the grading object center mark marked **A** in Figure 3–46. Give this a fill slope of **1.50:1**.

7. The final result is displayed in Figure 3–48.

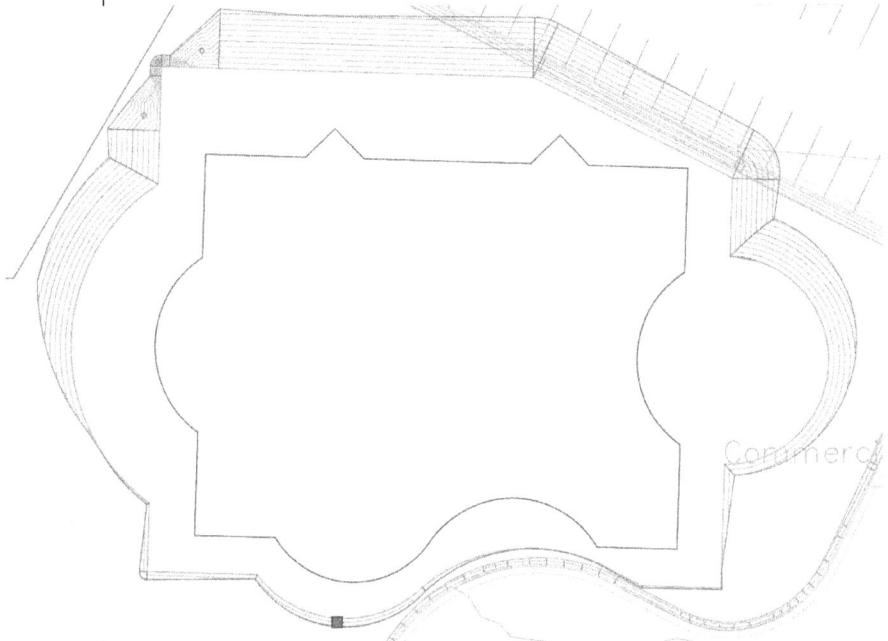

Figure 3–48

8. Save the drawing. (Before opening the Object Viewer in the next step, it is always prudent to save the drawing.)

9. Zoom out to see both building pads.

10. Select the Building Pads surface (select one of its contour lines) and the Office Pad surface.

11. In the *Surface* contextual tab, click ▦ (Object Viewer). Set the view direction to **SW Isometric** and the style to **Conceptual**. Note the hole in the surface, as shown in Figure 3–49.

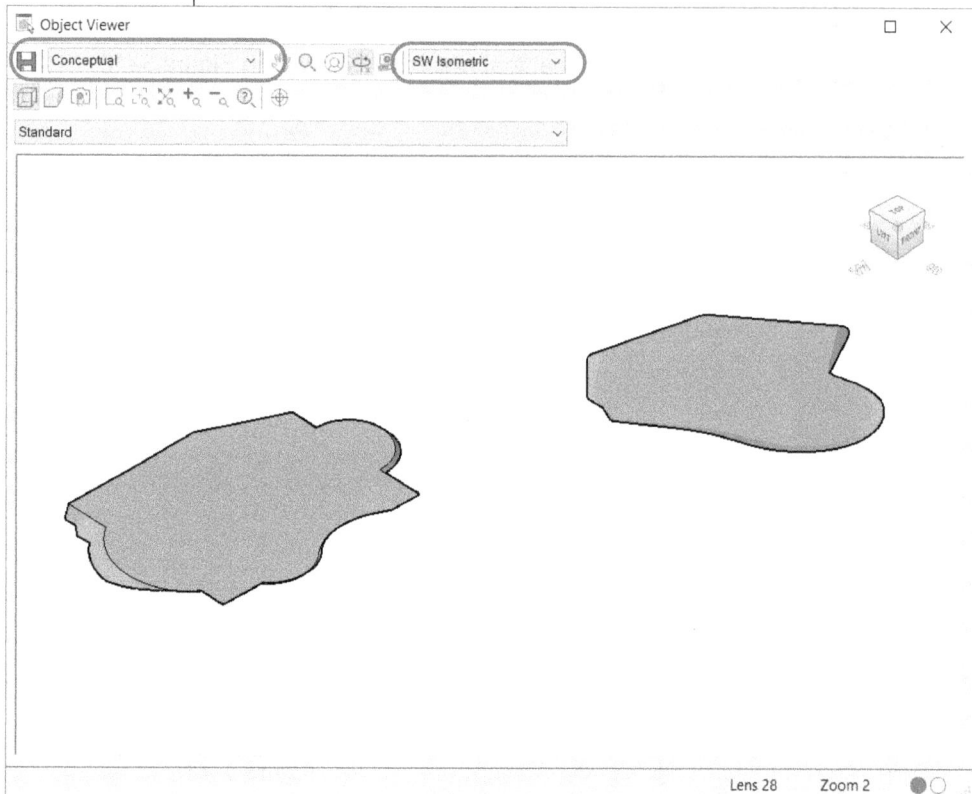

Figure 3–49

12. Press <Esc> twice to close the Object Viewer and release the selection.

13. Save the drawing.

3.5 Grading Volume Tools

The biggest benefit to using grading groups to create future grading plans is the ease in which they can be modified and their volumes calculated. The Grading Volume Tools assist in calculating the earthwork volumes for the grading group and assist in balancing the cut and fill volumes.

Calculate Volumes

Selecting a grading object displays the *Grading* contextual tab. You also access this tab by going to the *Modify* tab>Design panel and clicking 🔲 (Grading). In the *Grading* tab>Grading Tools panel, click 🔲 (Grading Volume Tools) to access the Grading Volume Tools toolbar, as shown in Figure 3–50.

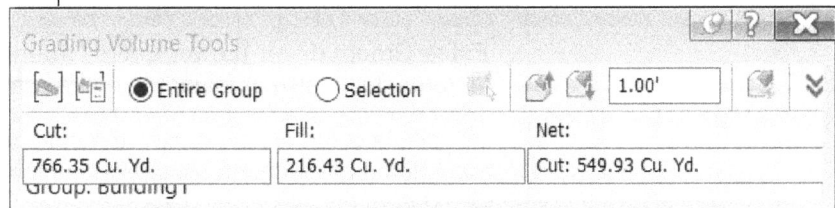

Figure 3–50

The group whose calculation displays in the toolbar is listed in the bottom left corner. To change which group is being calculated, click 🔲 (Set Group) at the top left. By default, the **Entire Group** option is set so that the volume for all of the grading objects within the group is calculated as one item. To find the volume of a single grading object, change the option to **Selection** and pick a grading object in the drawing by clicking 🔲, as shown in Figure 3–51.

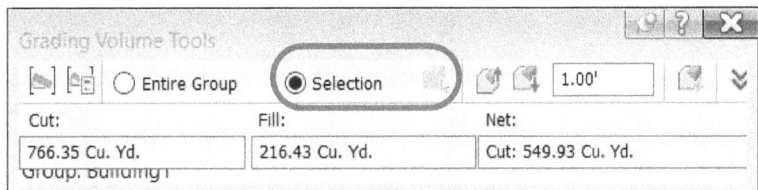

Figure 3–51

Balance Volumes

Grading groups can be adjusted vertically using the Grading Volume Tools to balance the cut and fill volumes and reduce the cost of hauling material in or out of the site. To do so, the **Entire Group** option must be selected. The option to raise or lower the group becomes available, as shown in Figure 3–52.

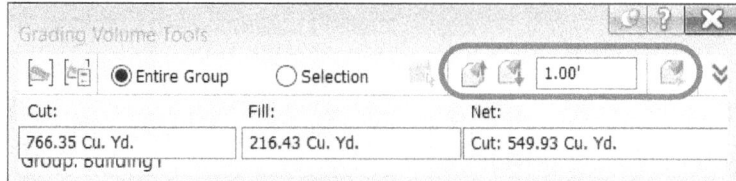

Figure 3–52

Incremental Changes

Typing an increment in the input field and clicking ⬆ (Raise Entire Group) or ⬇ (Lower Entire Group) enables you to incrementally raise or lower the entire grading group. Clicking

⋁ displays the history of how the incremental changes affect the volume calculations, as shown in Figure 3–53.

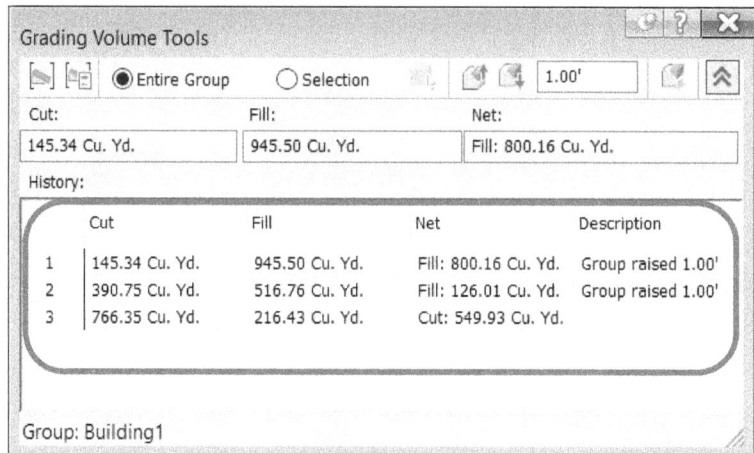

Figure 3–53

Automatically Balance Cut and Fill

Many projects require that the cut and fill for the project be minimized as much as possible to reduce costs. If that is the case on your project, you can use ⬚ (Auto Balance) to automatically raise or lower the entire grading group to balance the volumes. If this option is selected, a dialog box opens prompting you to set the required volume, as shown in Figure 3–54.

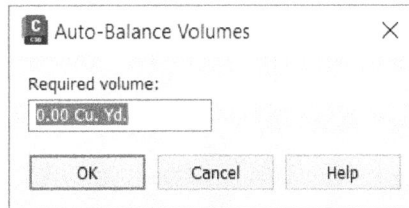

Figure 3–54

If you enter a specific volume in the *Required volume* field and click **OK** but the resulting volume does not match your entered target volume, you can click ⬚ (Auto Balance) again to get it closer. There might be times when you need to click this option more than once to get the required result.

Practice 3c

Grading Volume Tools

Practice Objective

- Calculate and balance the cut and fill volumes of a grading group.

In this practice, you will calculate the grading group volume.

1. Continue working in the drawing from the previous practice or open **BLDG-E**.dwg from the *C:\Civil 3D for Land Dev\ Working\BLDG Pad* folder.

2. In the *Home* tab>Create Design panel, expand the Grading drop-down list and click ⚒ (Grading Creation Tools).

3. In the Grading Creation Tools toolbar, click ✉ (Grading Volume Tools), as shown in Figure 3–55.

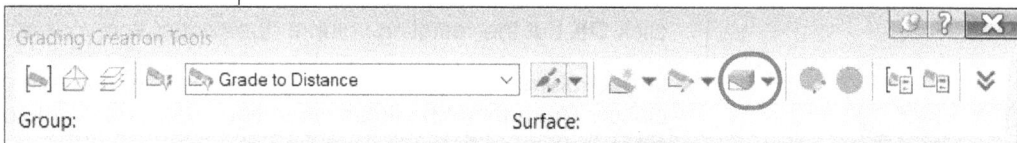

Figure 3–55

4. In the *Select Grading Group* dialog box, ensure that the **Office Pad** group in the **Temp** site is selected, as shown in Figure 3–56.

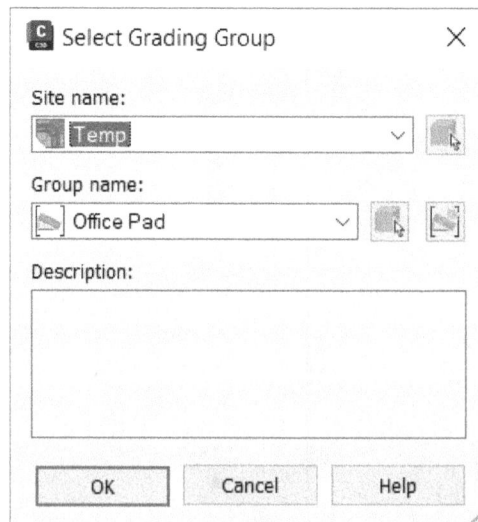

Figure 3–56

5. Click **OK** to dismiss the *Select Grading Group* dialog box.

6. Click [icon] (Raise Group) to raise the entire group by **1'**, as shown in Figure 3–57.

7. Click [icon] (Expand Toolbar) to display the grading calculation history, as shown in Figure 3–57.

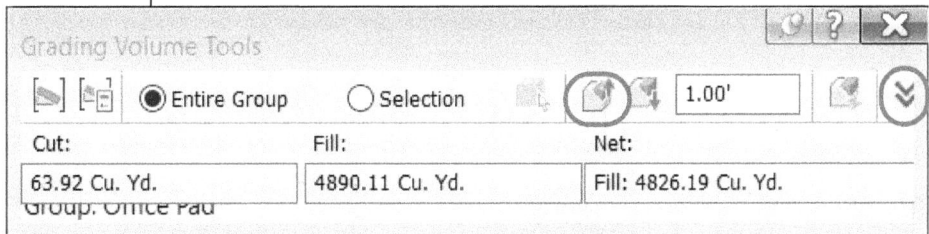

Figure 3–57

8. Click [icon] (Auto-Balance) to automatically balance the cut and fill volumes for the entire group. Take the default of **0.00 Cu. Yd.** (zero), as shown in Figure 3–58. Click **OK** to close the dialog box.

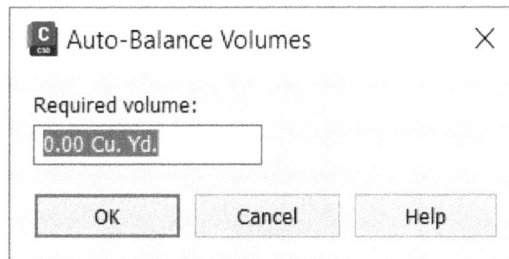

Figure 3–58

9. Click [icon] to close the Events Vista if it displays.

10. Review the final volume calculation, as shown in Figure 3–59 and Figure 3–60.

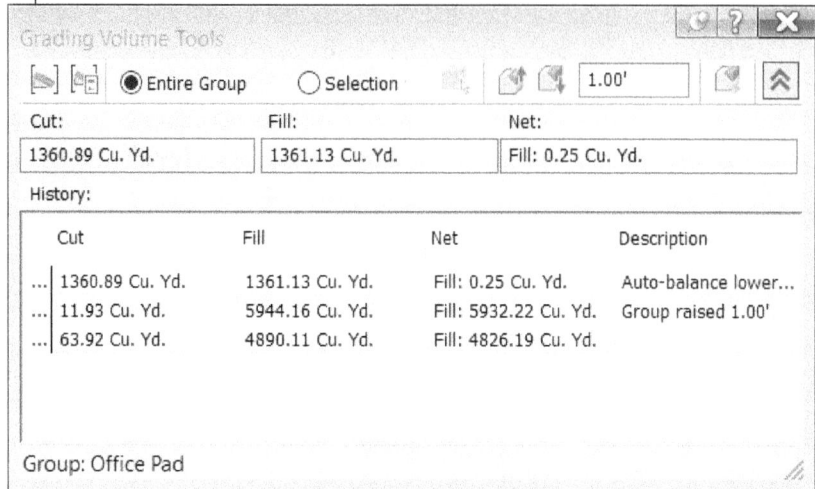

Figure 3–59

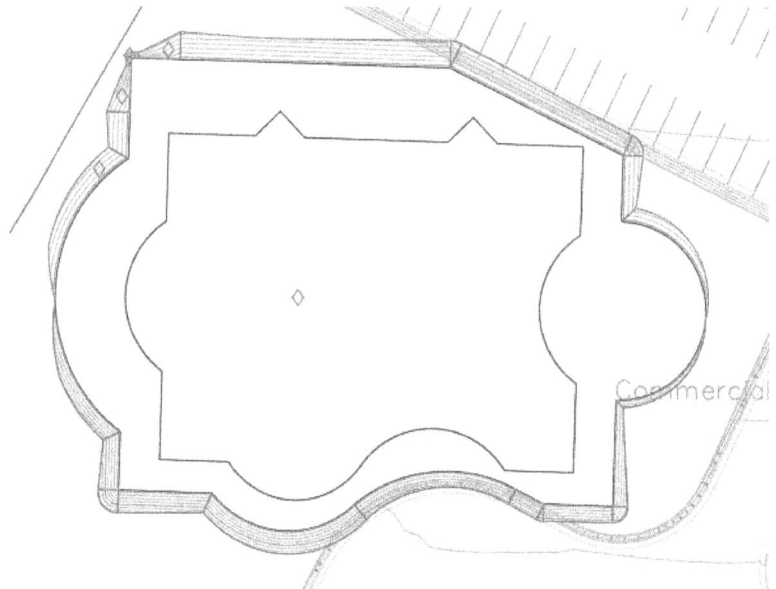

Figure 3–60

11. Save the drawing.

Chapter Review Questions

1. Which is not an option for creating a feature line?

    a. **Create Feature Lines from Objects**

    b. **Create Feature Lines from Alignment**

    c. **Create Feature Line from Corridor**

    d. **Create Feature Lines from Profile**

2. When creating a feature line from objects, which object cannot be used?

    a. Lines

    b. Circles

    c. Arcs

    d. Polylines or 3D Polylines

3. Which icon in the Elevation Editor represents an elevation point?

    a. (Circle)

    b. (Triangle)

4. Which icon fills in an area that has not been graded with a grading face?

    a.

    b.

    c.

    d.

5. Which icon in the Grading Volume Tools toolbar enables you to display a history of the grading volume calculations?

a.

b.

c.

d.

Command Summary

Button	Command	Location
	Auto-Balance	• **Toolbar**: Grading Volume Tools (*contextual*)
	Create Feature Lines from Objects	• **Ribbon**: *Home* tab>Create Design panel, expand Feature Line drop-down list and click Create Feature Lines From Objects • **Command Prompt**: CreateFeatureLines
	Create Grading	• **Toolbar**: Grading Creation Tools (*contextual*)
	Create Grading Infill	• **Toolbar**: Grading Creation Tools (*contextual*) • **Ribbon**: *Home* tab>Create Design panel, expand Grading drop-down list and click Create Grading Infill • **Command Prompt**: CreateGradingInfill
	Elevation Editor	• **Ribbon**: *Feature Line* contextual tab>Edit Elevations panel>Elevation Editor • **Command Prompt**: GradingElevEditor
	Grading Creation Tools	• **Ribbon**: *Home* tab>Create Design panel, expand Grading drop-down list and click Grading Creation Tools • **Command Prompt**: GradingTools
	Grading Volume Tools	• **Ribbon**: *Grading* contextual tab>Grading Tools panel>Grading Volume Tools • **Command Prompt**: GradingVolumeTools
	Lower Grading Features	• **Toolbar**: Grading Volume Tools (*contextual*)
	Raise Grading Features	• **Toolbar**: Grading Volume Tools (*contextual*)
	Set Group	• **Toolbar**: Grading Volume Tools (*contextual*)
	Set Surface	• **Toolbar**: Grading Volume Tools (*contextual*)

Parking Lot Design

Parking lots can be more challenging to grade than a building since you need to ensure that they drain properly across the parking surface. In this chapter, you will learn how to easily set slopes along a parking lot perimeter using a temporary surface. Then, you will explore the first of the two options on how to grade the parking lot. You will also create a series of feature lines representing the curb returns to grade to the existing ground at various slopes.

The second option is explored in a separate chapter. Using the same base feature line created for the back of curb, you will create a corridor for the curb in that chapter.

Learning Objectives in This Chapter

- Draw a feature line from scratch.
- Create a temporary surface to assist in setting feature line elevations and slopes.
- Edit feature lines using the geometry editing tools.
- Copy or move feature lines from one site to another.
- Create a grading group that transitions from one grade to another along a feature line.
- Create a surface from a grading group.
- Create feature lines that affect the grading group surface.

4.1 Draw Feature Lines

When creating feature lines, ⤵ (Create Feature Line) creates both straight and curved segments. Elevations are assigned at each vertex by typing an elevation value or by assigning an elevation from a surface that exists in the drawing.

How To: Draw a Feature Line

1. In the *Home* tab>Create Design panel, click ⤵ (Create Feature Line).
2. In the Create Feature Line dialog box, set the site, enter a name for the feature line, and select a style for the feature line, as shown in Figure 4–1. Click **OK**.

Note that the conversion options are unavailable since the feature line is being drawn rather than created from an existing object.

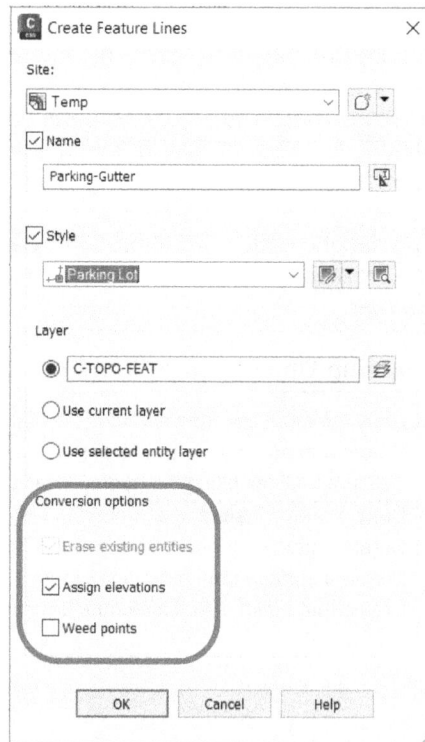

Figure 4–1

3. In the Command Line you are prompted to *Specify start point*. Pick a point in the drawing or type a coordinate value where the feature line starts.
4. In the Command Line you are prompted to *Specify elevation*. You can either type an elevation value or type **S** and press <Enter> to obtain a surface elevation at that point.

5. In the Command Line you are prompted to *Specify the next point*. Pick a point in the drawing or type a coordinate value to define the next end point.

6. Type the capital letter(s) from the following options to set the elevation:

Option	Description
Grade	A grade percentage is applied between the previous point and the next point.
SLope	A rise:run slope is applied between the previous point and the next point.
Elevation	The typed elevation is given to the next point.
Difference	An elevation is calculated for the next point by adding an amount to the previous point's elevation value.
SUrface	Obtain the elevation from a selected surface at the next point in the drawing.
Transition	Skips setting the elevation of the next point and subsequent points by pressing <Enter> until an elevation is assigned to the last point. The elevations for all intermediate vertices is calculated from a grade based on the distance between the first and last point and the change in elevation.

7. In the Command Line you are prompted to *Specify the next point*. Type **A** and press <Enter> to draw an arc.

8. Type the capitol letter from the following options to create the arc according to the required design parameters.

Option	Description
Arc end point	Pick an arc end point to complete the arc. The arc is automatically tangential to the previous segment.
Radius	Enter a radius and then pick the end point of the arc or type **L** to enter the arc length. The arc is automatically tangential to the previous segment.
Secondpnt	Pick a point to specify the second point through which the arc must pass. Then specify the arc endpoint by picking another point or typing **L** to set the arc length. This enables the arc to not be tangential to the previous segment.
Line	Returns to drawing straight line segments.
Undo	Undoes the last segment of the feature line.

Using feature line arcs avoids creating tessellated arcs. This is preferred when working with grading footprints because it creates many small grading faces joined by radial corners. If you use 3D polylines as surface breaklines for grading, tessellation occurs and slows down your drawing. You can use the **Fit Curve** command to convert tessellated arcs to true arcs.

4.2 Create a Temporary Surface

Creating a temporary surface can help set elevations of a complex feature line. For example, a feature line that has to follow a specific slope across a site can be created from the elevations of a temporary surface. Parking lots are examples of this strategy because they often slope to one side or to the center for drainage management.

To create a temporary surface, it is recommended that you create a temporary site for the temporary feature lines and grading groups. Once the design feature line has been created it is used for the final grading and the elevations are obtained from the temporary surface. You can then delete the temporary site without losing any design information. This helps to keep the drawing clean and efficient.

How To: Create a Temporary Surface

1. Create a temporary site for all of the feature lines and grading groups that are going to be deleted later. Define the site by going to the *Prospector* tab, right-clicking on Sites, and selecting **New**.
2. Decide whether you start from the center and grade out in both directions or start on one side and create multiple grading objects going in the same direction at different slopes. Figure 4–2 shows an example of grading from the center out in both directions.

Figure 4–2

3. Create the base feature line.

4. Create a grading group with the **Automatic surface creation** option selected, as shown in Figure 4–3.

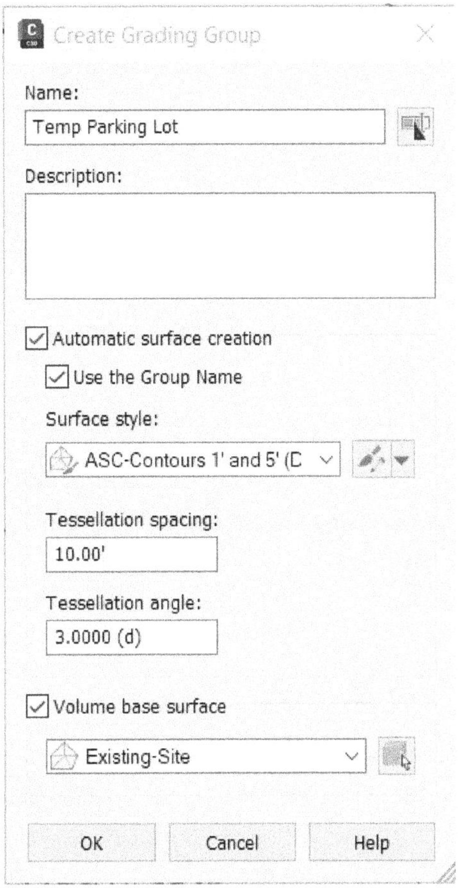

Figure 4–3

5. Create grading from the base feature line out each side at a required distance to cover the entire site. Set a grade in each direction to provides the required slopes.
6. Use the surface elevations from this temporary surface to assign elevations for the actual grading design feature line.

Practice 4a	# Draw a Feature Line and Create a Temporary Surface

Practice Objective

- Create a feature line and temporary surface which will be used to assign elevations to the vertices of another feature line.

For the land development drawings in this guide, much of the preliminary work has already been done for the site development.

The completed corridors for Jeffries Ranch Road and Ascent Place, the Ascent Place knuckle and cul-de-sac target alignments, the Mission Avenue alignment, and the Existing-Site surface have been referenced through Data Shortcuts.

The Residential Grading surface created in the *Parcel Grading* chapter has been referenced as well; its surface style is set to *_No Display*.

In this practice, you will create a temporary site, draw a feature line, create a temporary surface, and create a feature line and set elevations by grading.

Task 1 - Create a temporary site.

1. Open **PKLOT-A.dwg** from the *C:\Civil 3D for Land Dev\ Working\Parking Lot* folder.

2. Hover over the Data Shortcuts and look at the tooltip that appears, as shown in Figure 4–4. Ensure that your **Data Shortcuts Working Folder** is set to *C:\Civil 3D for Land Dev\Data Shortcuts\Fundamentals* and the **Data Shortcuts Project Folder** to *Ascent-Development*.

   - If not, right-click on Data Shortcuts to set the **Working Folder** to *C:\Civil 3D for Land Dev\Data Shortcuts\ Fundamentals* and the **Data Shortcuts Project Folder** to *Ascent-Development*.

If required, review the Setting a Project practice for how to set the working folder and the project folder.

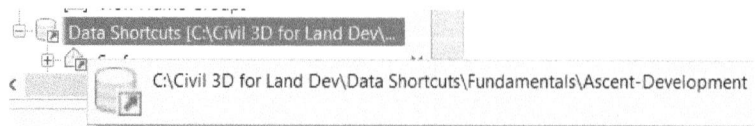

Figure 4–4

3. In the *View* tab>Views panel, select **Parking Lot** as the view to zoom into the parking lot area, as shown in Figure 4–5.

Figure 4–5

4. In the *Prospector* tab, right-click on **Sites** and select **New**, as shown in Figure 4–6.

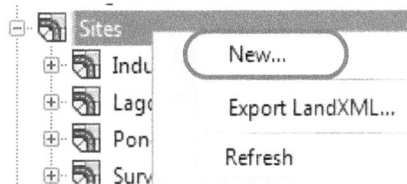

Figure 4–6

5. In the *Information* tab, for the *Name*, type **Temp**. Click **OK**.

Task 2 - Draw a feature line.

1. Continue working in the drawing from the previous task.

2. In the *Home* tab>Create Design panel, click ☀ (Create Feature Line).

3. In the Create Feature Lines dialog box, complete the following, as shown in Figure 4–7:

   - For the *Site*, select **Temp**.
   - For the feature line *Name,* type **CenterLine**.
   - For the *Style,* select **ASC-Basic Feature Line**.
   - Click **OK**.

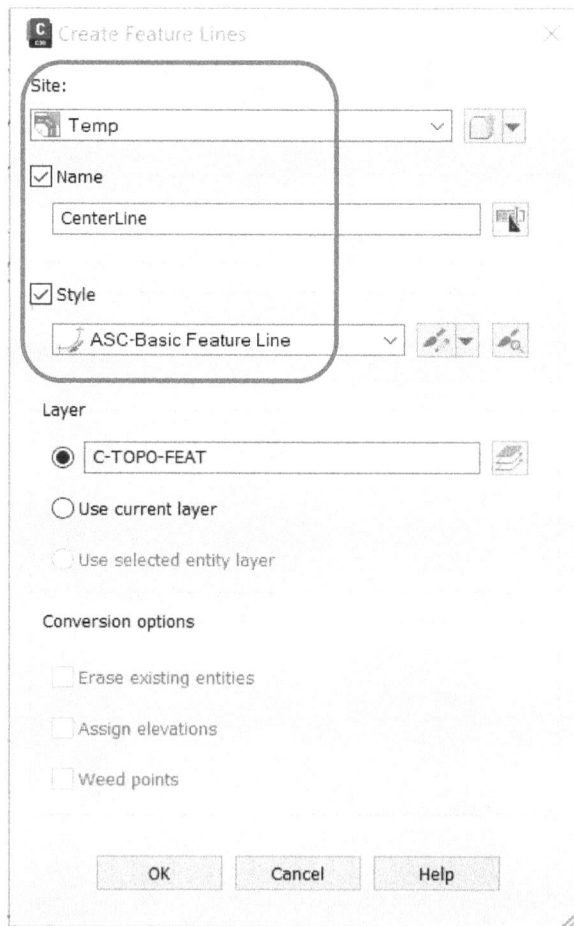

Figure 4–7

4. At the Command Prompt, you will be prompted to pick a point. Using the **Endpoint** Osnap, click point one on the parking lot center line, as shown in Figure 4–8.

Figure 4–8

5. Type **S** and press <Enter> to have it find the elevation of a surface at that point.

6. When prompted for the surface, select **Ascent Pl-Top**, as shown in Figure 4–9, and click **OK**.

*If this dialog box does not open, type **S** and press <Enter> to select the surface.*

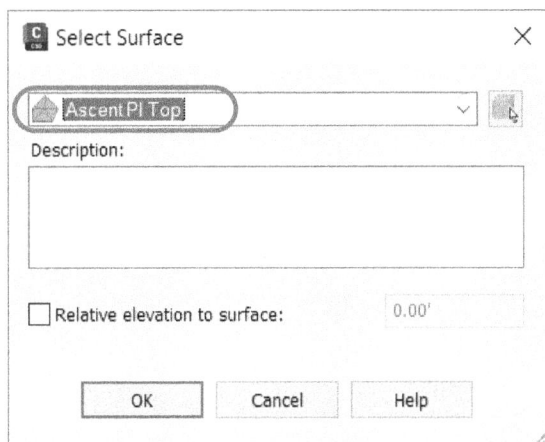

Figure 4–9

*If grade is not the default, type **G** and press <Enter> before setting the negative 2% grade.*

7. For the next point, use the **Endpoint** Osnap to pick point 2, as shown in Figure 4–8.

8. For the elevation, the default will be to set the grade. Type **-2 (minus 2)** and press <Enter> to set the grade at 2% going down.

9. For the next point, use the **Endpoint** Osnap to pick point 3, as shown in Figure 4–8.

10. For the elevation, the default will be to set the grade. Type **-2 (minus 2)** and press <Enter> to set the grade at 2% going down.

11. For the next point, use the **Endpoint** Osnap to pick point 4, as shown in Figure 4–8.

12. For the elevation, the default will be to set the grade. Type **-4 (minus 4)** and press <Enter> to set the grade at 4% going down.

13. Press <Enter> to end the command.

14. Save the drawing.

Task 3 - Create a temporary surface.

---

1. Continue working in the drawing from the previous task.

2. In the *Home* tab>Create Design panel, click ✎ (Grading Creation Tools).

3. In the Grading Creations Tools toolbar, click ▨ (Set Group).

4. In the Site dialog box, select **Temp**, as shown in Figure 4–10. Click **OK**.

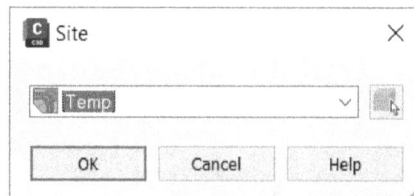

Figure 4–10

5. In the Create Grading Group dialog box, do the following, as shown in Figure 4–11:

- For the *Name*, type **Temp Parking Lot**.
- Select the **Automatic surface creation** option.
- Select the **Volume Base Surface** option and ensure *Existing Site* is listed.
- Click **OK**.

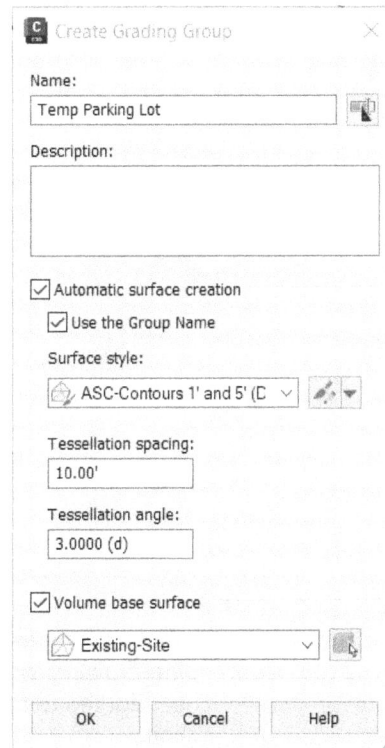

Figure 4–11

6. In the Create Surface dialog box, click **OK** to the defaults.

7. In the Grading Creation Tools toolbar, select **Grade to Distance** for the criteria, as shown in Figure 4–12.

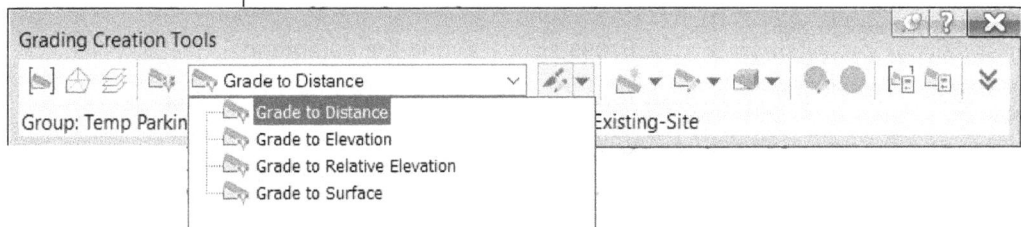

Figure 4–12

8. In the Grading Creation Tools toolbar, click ▨ (Create Grading.

9. In the drawing, select the CenterLine feature line that you created in the last task, as shown in Figure 4–13.

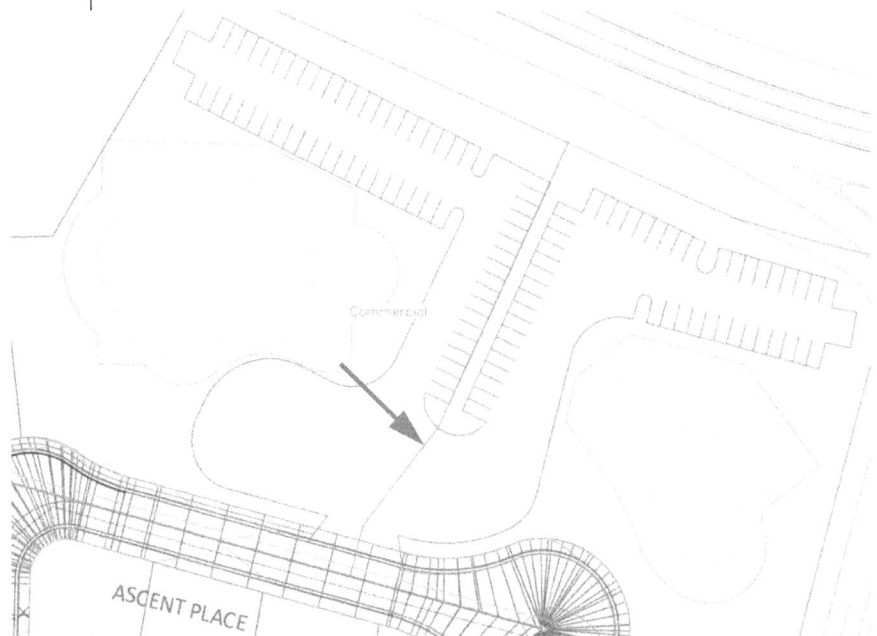

Figure 4–13

10. When prompted for a side to which to grade, pick a point in the drawing to the right of the feature line. Press <Enter> to accept the default to grade the entire length of the feature line.

- For the *Distance*, type **235** and press <Enter>.
- For the *Format*, type **G** and press <Enter> for grade.
- For the *Grade*, type -**2 (Minus 2)** for a negative 2% slope.

11. Repeat Steps 3 to 10 to grade to the left side **265'** at a **-2%(minus 2)** grade.

12. Press <Esc> to end the command.

13. Close the Grading Creation Tools toolbar.

14. Save the drawing.

Note: If selecting the feature line is difficult, you might need to set the drawing order of the grading surface to the back.

Task 4 - Create a feature line and set elevations by grading.

1. Continue working in the drawing from the previous task.

2. In the *Home* tab>Create Design panel, expand the Feature Line drop-down list and click ✳ (Create Feature Line from Objects).

3. Type **X** and press <Enter> to select linework from the external reference file. Select the magenta line that represents the parking lot perimeter, as highlighted in blue in Figure 4–14. Press <Enter> to continue.

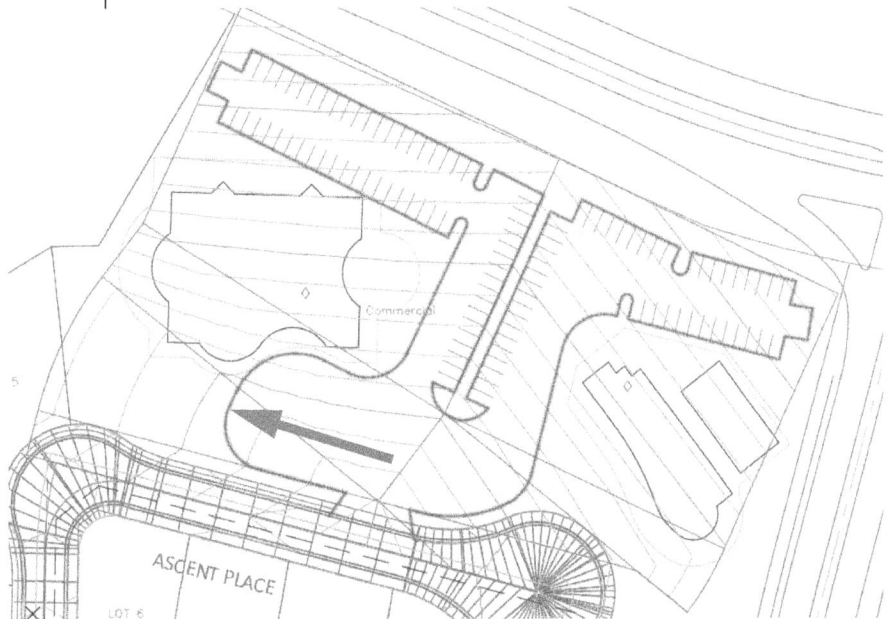

Figure 4–14

4. In the Create Feature Lines dialog box, complete the following, as shown in Figure 4–15:

- Leave the *Site* set to **Temp**.
- For the *Name*, type **Parking-Gutter**.
- Set the *Style* to **ASC-Parking Lot**.
- Verify that **Assign elevations** is selected.
- Click **OK**.

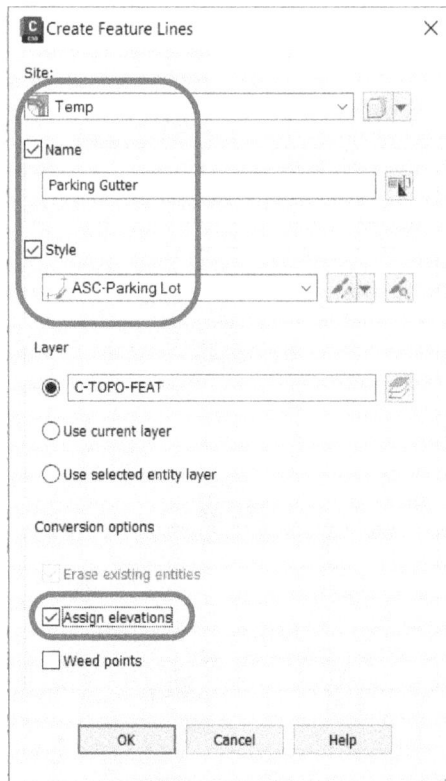

Figure 4–15

5. In the Assign Elevations dialog box, select **From gradings**, as shown in Figure 4–16. Click **OK**.

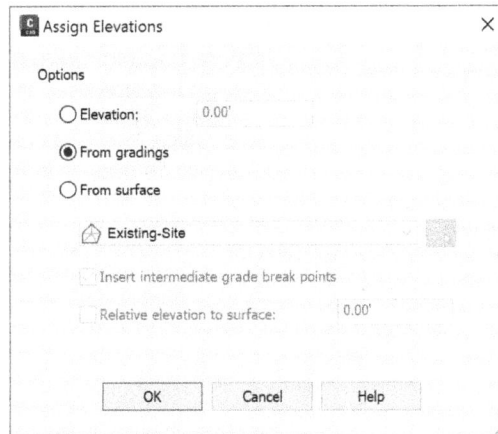

Figure 4–16

6. Save the drawing.

4.3 Edit Feature Line Geometry

Working with feature lines is similar to working with standard AutoCAD lines and polylines. The differences are with the tools that are used to make the required changes. To access the tools, select a feature line. In the *Feature Line* contextual tab>Modify panel, click ▣ (Edit Geometry). The Edit Geometry panel displays, as shown in Figure 4–17.

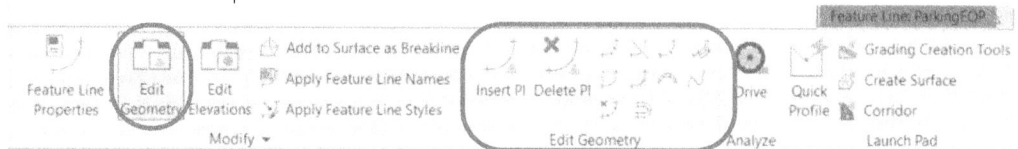

Figure 4–17

The tool functions are as follows:

Icon	Command	Description
	Insert PI	Adds a new vertex to a feature line, survey figure, parcel line, polyline, or 3D polyline, giving you additional horizontal and vertical control.
	Delete PI	Removes a selected vertex from a feature line, survey figure, parcel line, polyline, or 3D polyline.
	Break	Creates a gap or break in a feature line, survey figure, or parcel line. The location selected when picking the object is the first point of the break, unless otherwise specified.
	Trim	Removes part of a feature line, survey figure, or parcel line at the specified boundary edge.
	Join	Combines two feature lines, survey figures, parcel lines, polylines, or 3D polylines that fall within the tolerance distance set in the command settings.
	Reverse	Changes the direction of the stationing along a feature line, survey figure, parcel line, polyline, or 3D polyline.
	Edit Curve	Changes the radius of a feature line arc, parcel line arc, or survey figure arc.
	Fillet	Creates a curve between two segments of selected feature line(s), survey figures, parcel lines, or 3D polylines.

	Fit Curve	Places a curve between the selected vertices of a feature line, survey figure, parcel line, or 3D polyline while removing vertices between the selected vertices. Useful for converting tessellated lines to true arcs.
	Smooth	Adds multiple arcs to feature lines or survey figures to assist in smoothing tessellated lines.
	Weed	Removes unnecessary vertices along feature lines, polylines, or 3D polylines based on defined angle, grade, length, and 3D distance values.
	Stepped Offset	Creates copies of a selected feature line, survey figure, polyline, or 3D polyline at a specified horizontal and vertical distance away from the original object.

Delete PI

Reshaping a feature line is easily done by removing vertices where lines intersect or where lines connect to arcs. This is similar to removing vertices in regular polylines.

How To: Modify a Feature Line Using the Delete PI Command

1. In the Drawing, select a feature line.
2. In the *Feature Line* contextual tab>Modify panel, click

   (Edit Geometry). In the Edit Geometry panel that

   displays, click (Delete PI).
3. In the drawing, click near the vertex you wish to remove.

Stepped Offsets

When working in the standard AutoCAD® software, you can use the **Offset** command to make copies of lines, arcs, and polylines at a specific horizontal distance away from the original object. However, when working in 3D, a horizontal and vertical offset is often required. Therefore, the **Stepped Offset** command is available in Civil 3D for feature lines. You can use it to make copies of feature lines, survey figures, and parcel lines a specified distance away from the original object both horizontally and vertically.

How To: Create Stepped Offsets

1. In the *Home* tab>Create Design panel, expand the Feature Line drop-down list and click ⬚ (Stepped Offset), as shown in Figure 4–18.

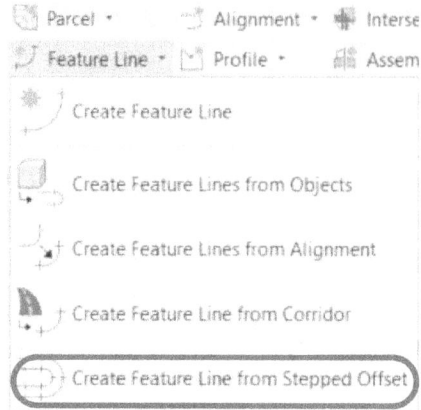

Figure 4–18

2. Specify the distance to offset the new object by typing a numeric value or type **T** (for Through) to specify the point the new object should pass through.
3. Select the feature line, survey figure, or parcel line to offset from the drawing.
4. Specify which side to offset to by picking a point in the drawing.
5. Type the capitol letter from the following options to set the elevation of the new object.

Option	Description
Grade	A grade percentage is applied between the original object and the newly offset object.
Slope	A rise:run slope is applied between the original object and the newly offset object.
Elevation	The typed elevation is assigned to the new object.
Difference	An elevation is calculated for the new object's vertices by adding the amount entered to the original feature line, parcel line, or survey figure's vertex elevations.
Variable	Enables you to enter a new elevation or a difference in elevation for each vertex along the new feature line, survey figure, or parcel line.

• The default option is set to **Difference** or the last option used.

4.4 Copy or Move Feature Lines from One Site to Another

Feature lines must reside in a site to be created and used. If you use feature lines for grading, it is important that they reside in the same site as their grading group. Sometimes feature lines are created in the wrong site or need to be reused in other sites. In these cases you can move or copy a feature line from one site to another. You are able to copy or move the contents of an entire site (alignments, grading groups, parcels, and feature lines) to another site.

How To: Move or Copy Feature Lines

1. Select the object(s) to move or copy.
2. Right-click and select **Move to Site** or **Copy to Site**, as shown in Figure 4–19.

Figure 4–19

- Another option is to select **Move to Site** or **Copy to Site** by expanding the *Feature Line* contextual tab>Modify panel, as shown in Figure 4–20.

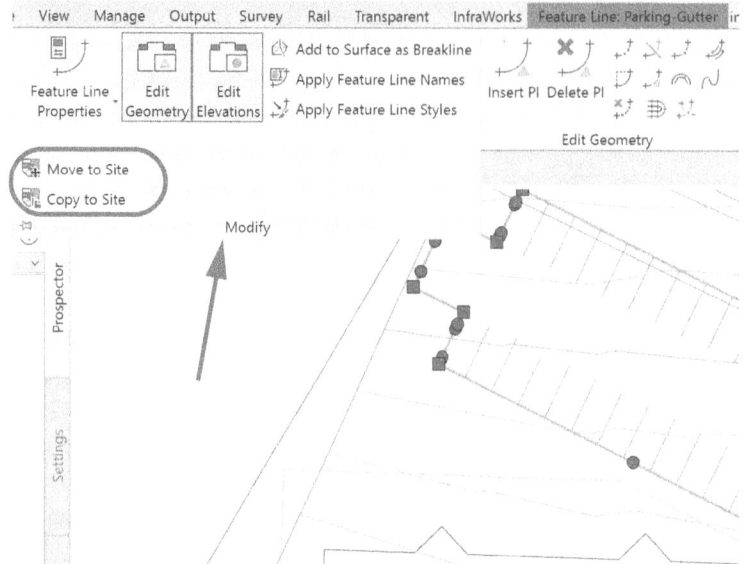

Figure 4–20

3. In the dialog box, select an option for the *Destination site*, as shown in Figure 4–21.

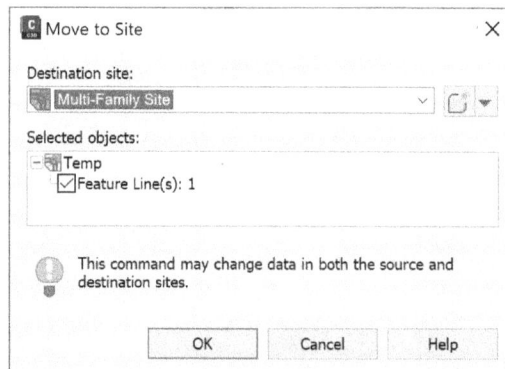

Figure 4–21

4. Civil 3D appends the name with a (1) (or the next available number) so as to ensure the feature line name remains unique. This is true of moving or copying the features line to another site.

4.5 Create a Transitional Grading Group

So far you have only created grading groups that follow the same slope the entire length of the feature line. Some designs require a transition from one slope to another to accommodate differences in elevation without an ample amount of grading area. For example, you have a target slope for a site of 5:1, but can grade as steep as 2:1 if needed. You might need to use a 2:1 slope to ensure that you do not encroach on an easement, another building, or a property line.

To fit a building on the property, you can grade the front to the preferred slope of 5:1, and then grade the back at 2:1 to ensure that you stay within the property line. In between the two slopes, you use a transitional grading object and have the computer calculate the transitional slopes between the building's front and back, as shown in Figure 4–22. In this example, you had to change grading slopes to ensure that the building to the north is not encroached on by the cut or fill slopes from the building to the south.

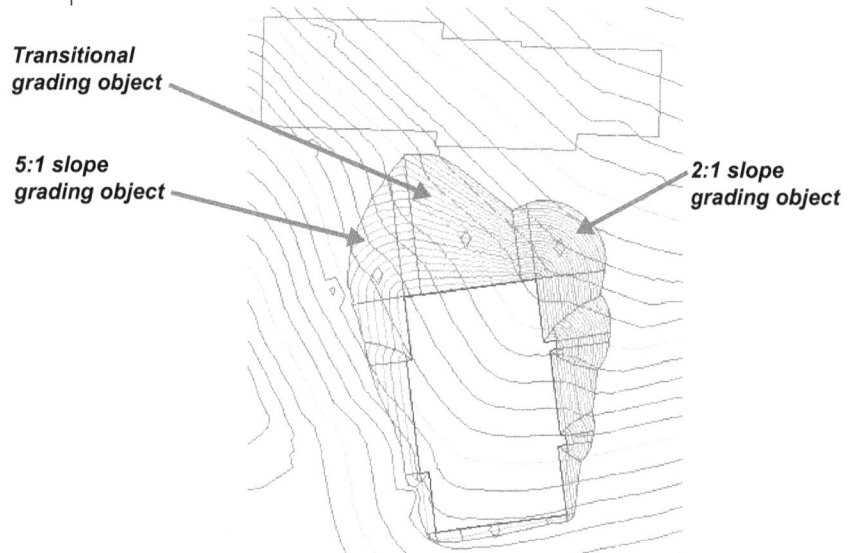

Transitional grading object

5:1 slope grading object

2:1 slope grading object

Figure 4–22

How To: Create Transitional Grading Groups

1. In the *Home* tab>Create Design panel, expand the Grading

   drop-down list and click (Grading Creation Tools).

2. In the Grading Creation Tools toolbar, click (Set Group)
   on the far left. Select the *Site name* in which you want to
   work, as shown in Figure 4–23.

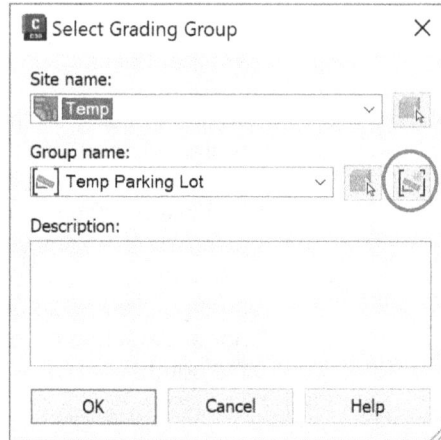

Figure 4–23

3. To create a new grading group, click (Create a Grading
   Group), as shown above in Figure 4–23.
4. In the Create Grading Group dialog box, type a name in the
   Name field. Do not select the **Automatic surface creation**
   option, as shown in Figure 4–24. Click **OK**.

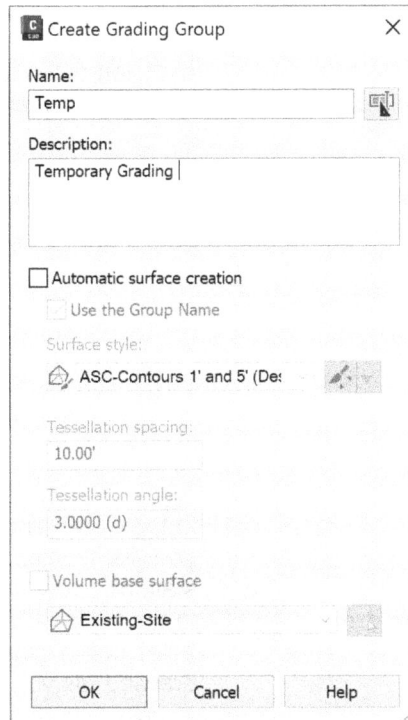

Figure 4–24

5. In the Grading Creation Tools toolbar, click (Select a Criteria Set) to select the grading criteria set that is required for the project.
6. Set the required grading criteria, as shown in Figure 4–25.

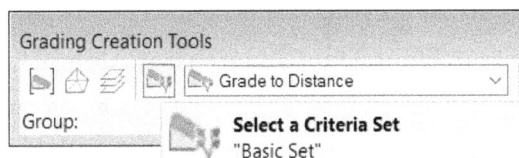

Figure 4–25

7. In the Grading Creation Tools toolbar, click (Create Grading). Select the feature line to use as the baseline.
8. When prompted for a grading side, pick a point in the drawing.
9. When prompted to apply it to the entire length, type **N** (for No) and press <Enter>.

You can use any Osnap commands or type the feature line station value.

10. In the Command Line, the routine prompts you to *Select the start point*. In the drawing, an arrow displays pointing in the direction of the feature line stations to help you pick the point to start your first slope, as shown in Figure 4–26.

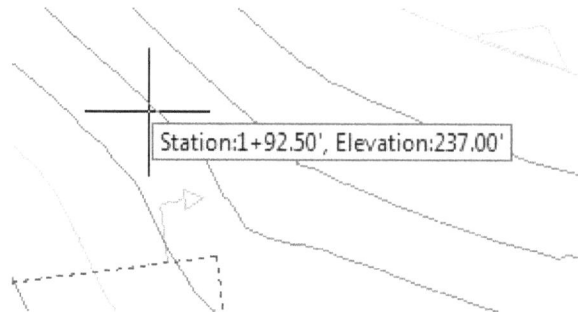

Station:1+92.50', Elevation:237.00'

Figure 4–26

11. In the Command Line, the station you selected displays for your verification (this occurs even if you are typing the station). Press <Enter> to accept.

12. In the Command Line, you are prompted to specify the end point for the grading. You can either pick a point in the drawing (as you did in Step 10), or proceed as follows:

- Type a feature line station.

    OR

- Type **L** and press <Enter> to set the length of the grading.

In the drawing, an arrow displays pointing in the opposite direction as the starting point for the grading, as shown in Figure 4–27.

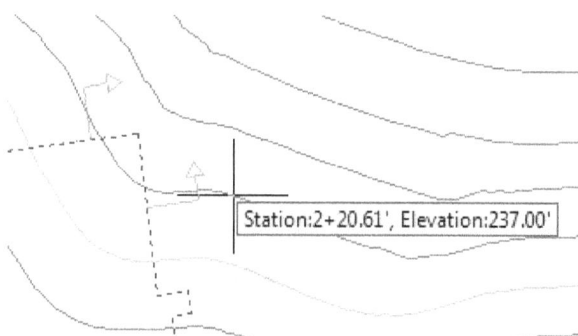

Station:2+20.61', Elevation:237.00'

Figure 4–27

13. In the Command Line, the station displays for verification even if you are typing the station value. Press <Enter> to accept it.

14. Repeat Steps 1 to 12 to set another grading criteria on the same feature line. Your results should be similar to those shown in Figure 4–28.

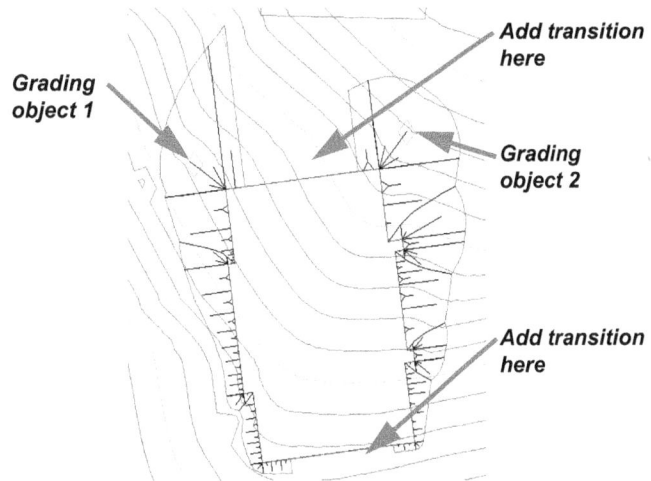

Figure 4–28

15. In the Grading Creation Tools toolbar, expand the Create Grading drop-down list and click 🔷 (Create Transition).
16. In the Command Line, you are prompted to *Select the feature*. Select the feature line that has been partially graded.
17. In the Command Line, you are prompted to pick a point between the gradings. Select between any previously created grading objects, as shown in Figure 4–28.
18. Repeat Steps 15 and 16 as needed to complete all of the transitions.
19. Press <Esc> to end the command.

Practice 4b

Create Stepped Offsets and Transitional Gradings

Practice Objective

- Create curb returns using stepped offsets and incorporate them into a parking lot grading group.

In this practice, you will create stepped offsets. You will also move feature lines to a different site, grade to a surface with varying slopes along one feature line, and create transitions between predefined grading objects along the same feature line.

Task 1 - Create stepped offsets.

1. Continue working in the drawing from the last practice or open **PKLOT-B.dwg** from the *C:\Civil 3D for Land Dev\ Working\Parking Lot* folder.

2. In the *Prospector* tab, expand **Sites>Temp** and select the feature lines. In the preview window in the lower part of the Prospector, select **Parking-Gutter**, then right-click and select **Select**, as shown in Figure 4–29.

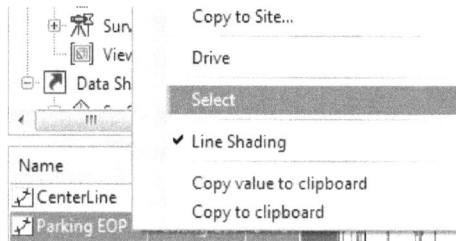

Figure 4–29

If the Edit Geometry panel is not displayed,

click ⊓ᵣ (Edit Geometry) in the Feature Line contextual tab>Modify panel.

3. In the *Feature Line* contextual tab>Edit Geometry panel, click ⊐ (Stepped Offset).

4. For the *Offset Distance*, type **2** and press <Enter>.

5. In the drawing, pick a point inside the parking area for the side to which to offset.

6. To set the elevation, type **G** and press <Enter> for grade.

7. For the grade, type **2** to set the grade at 2%. (This will act as the lip of curb.)

8. Press <Esc> to end the command.

9. In the preview window in the lower part of the Prospector, select the lowest feature line, then right-click and select **Properties**, as shown in Figure 4–30.

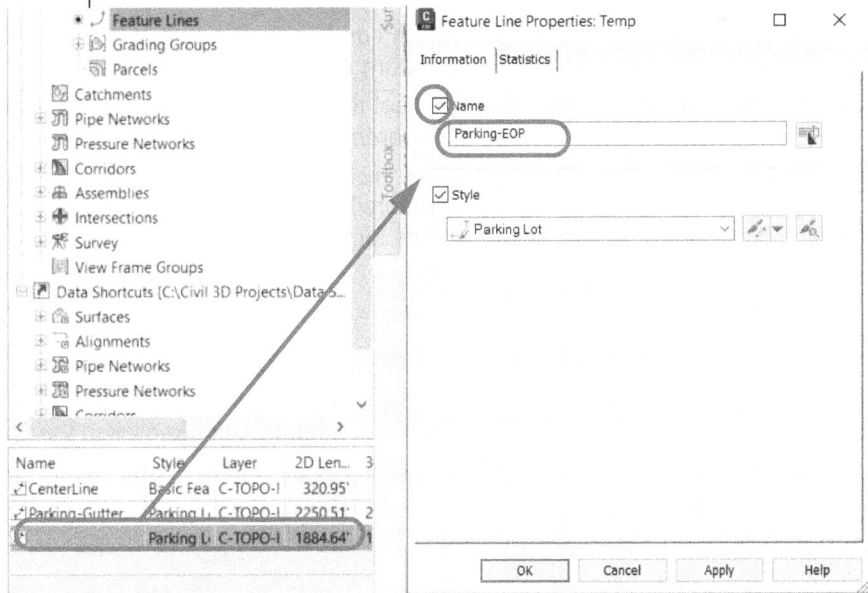

Figure 4–30

It is recommended that you rename the newly created feature line to a meaningful name so you can easily identify it later.

10. In the Feature Line Properties dialog box, click on the *Name* checkmark (which enables the *Name* box) and name the newly created feature line **Parking-EOP**, as shown in Figure 4–30.

You are going to start the Stepped Offset command again in the next step, but first you have to exit and then restart the command to set a different offset value for the next feature line.

11. In the *Prospector* tab, expand **Sites>Temp**, and select the feature lines. In the preview window, select **Parking-Gutter**, then right-click and select **Select**, as shown in Figure 4–31.

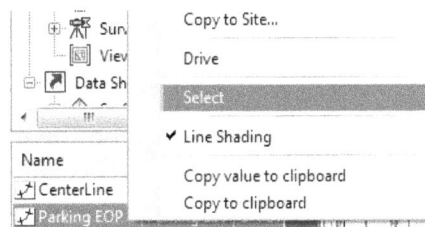

Figure 4–31

12. In the *Feature Line* contextual tab>Edit Geometry panel, click
    ⬝ (Stepped Offset).
    - For the *Offset Distance*, type **0.1**.
    - In the drawing, pick a point outside the Parking-Gutter feature line for the side to which to offset.
    - To set the elevation, type **D** and press <Enter> for *Difference*.
    - For the difference in elevation, type **0.5** to set the new feature line 6" above the other one. (This creates the curb face for the parking lot.)
    - Press <Esc> to end the command.
    - Press <Esc> again to release the selection.

13. In the *Prospector* tab, expand **Sites>Temp**, and select the feature lines. In the preview window, select the last feature line without a name, double-click in the *Name* field (as shown in Figure 4–32), and type **Top of Curb** and press <Enter>.

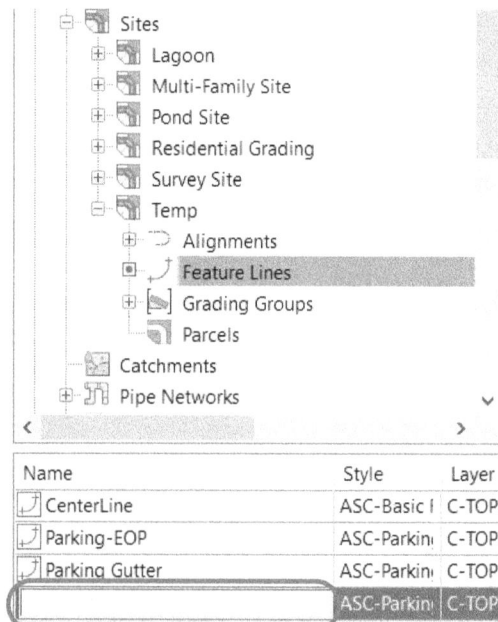

Name	Style	Layer
CenterLine	ASC-Basic F	C-TOP
Parking-EOP	ASC-Parkin	C-TOP
Parking Gutter	ASC-Parkin	C-TOP
	ASC-Parkin	C-TOP

Figure 4–32

14. Select the **Top of Curb** feature line.

*You could also select **G** for Grade and **0** for the grade, the result will be the same.*

15. In the *Feature Line* contextual tab>Edit Geometry panel, click

    (Stepped Offset).
    - For the *Offset Distance*, type **0.5**.
    - In the drawing, pick a point outside the Parking-Gutter feature line for the side to which to offset.
    - To set the elevation, type **D** and press <Enter> for *Difference*.
    - For the difference in elevation, type **0** to set the new feature line at the same elevation as the other one. (This creates the top back of curb for the parking lot.)
    - Press <Esc> to end the command.

16. Name the feature line **Back of Curb**, using either method as done previously.

17. If you zoom in, the four lines representing the curb are displayed, as shown in Figure 4–33.

Figure 4–33

18. Save the drawing.

Task 2 - Move feature lines to a different site.

You now have all of the necessary feature lines in the Temp site. However, you need to move them to the Multi-Family site so they interact when grading the building pads (done in earlier practices).

1. Continue working in the drawing from the previous task.

2. Select the last feature line created from the stepped offset (**Back of Curb**), as shown in Figure 4–34.

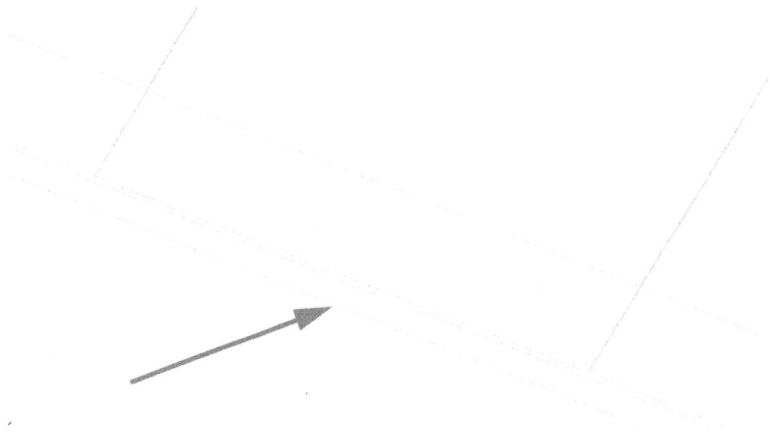

Figure 4–34

3. Right-click and select **Move to Site**, as shown in Figure 4–35.

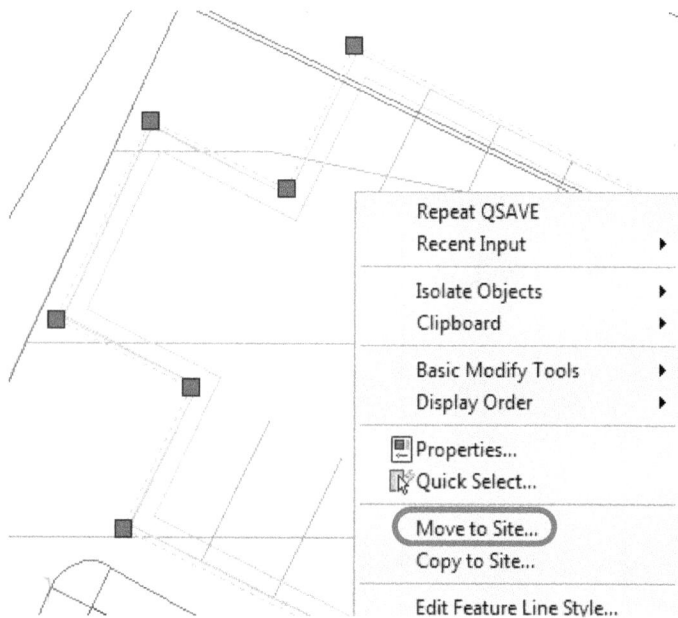

Figure 4–35

4. Set the *Destination site* to **Multi-Family Site**, as shown in Figure 4–36. Click **OK**.

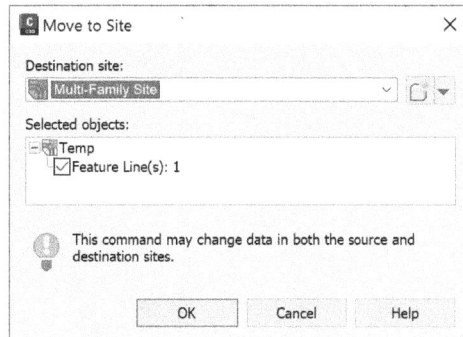

Figure 4–36

5. Note that the name of the feature line is now **Back of curb (1)**. Rename the feature line to **Back of Curb.**

6. In the drawing, select the **Back of Curb** feature line.

7. In the Edit Geometry panel that displays, click (Delete PI).

If the Edit Geometry panel is not displayed, in the Feature Line contextual tab>Modify panel, click (Edit Geometry).

8. In the drawing, remove the ten vertices circled in Figure 4–37.

Figure 4–37

9. Delete the vertex marked **A** in Figure 4–38. (The vertex marked **B** will be moved in the next step.)

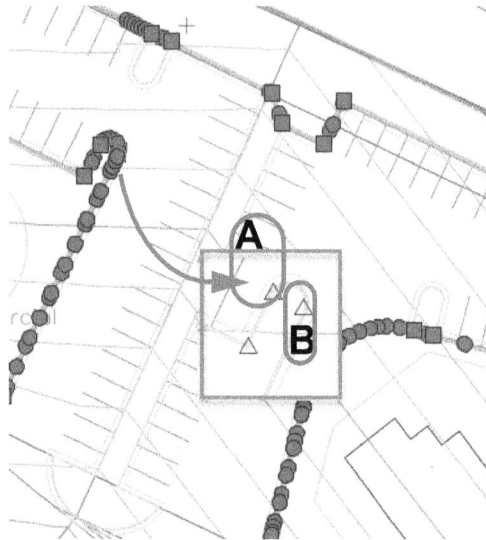

Figure 4–38

10. Press <Esc> to clear the selection and finish the command.

11. Move the vertex marked **A** in Figure 4–39. You can use the Extension Osnap to make it perpendicular to be precise.

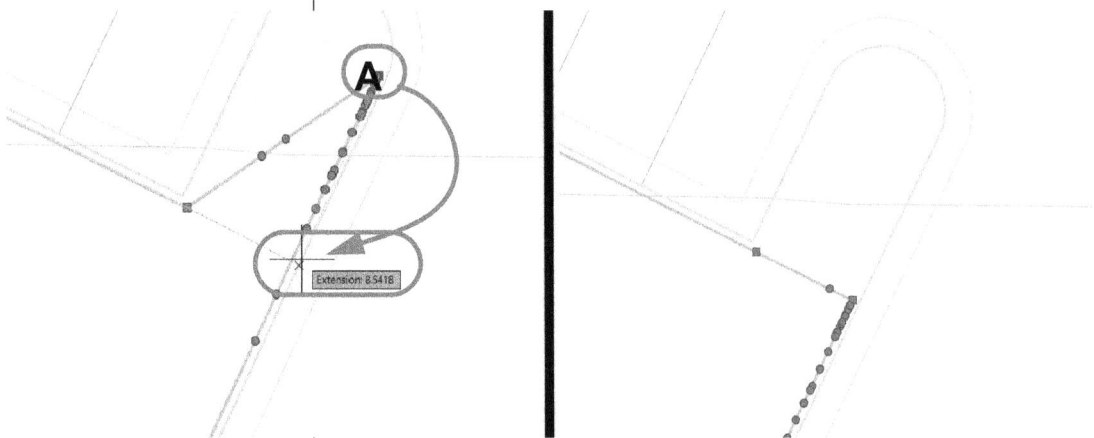

Figure 4–39

12. Press <Esc> to clear the selection.

13. The final result is shown in Figure 4–40.

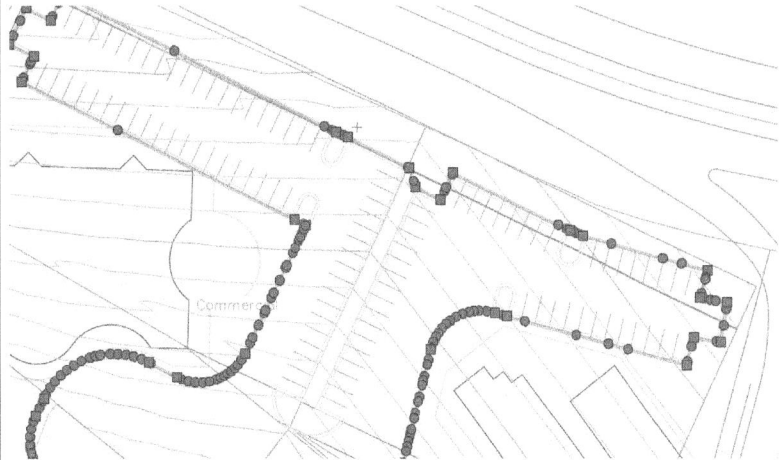

Figure 4–40

14. Select the **Temp Parking Lot** surface and set the surface style to **_No Display**, as shown in Figure 4–41.

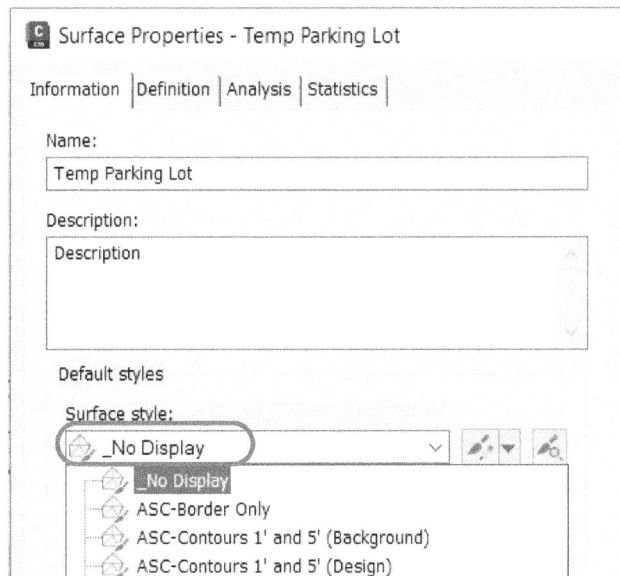

Figure 4–41

15. Save the drawing.

Task 3 - Grade to a surface with varying slopes along one feature line.

This task is quite intensive for computer processing. It is recommended that you save often, as well as audit your drawing on a regular basis. You will grade only the beginning of the parking lot, with the rest being optional, depending on your time and your computer's performance.

If you are unable to complete this task, you can skip to the next task, where the grading has been completed for you.

1. Continue working in the drawing from the last practice or open **PKLOT-C.dwg** from the *C:\Civil 3D for Land Dev\ Working\Parking Lot* folder.

2. In the *Home* tab>Create Design panel, expand the Grading drop-down list and click (Grading Creation Tools).

3. In the Grading Creation Tools toolbar, click (Set Group) on the far left to open the Select Grading Group dialog box.

4. In the Select Grading Group dialog box, select the **Multi-Family Site** and click (Create Grading Group), as shown in Figure 4–42.

Figure 4–42

5. In the Create Grading Group dialog box, complete the following, as shown in Figure 4–43:

- In the *Name* field, type **Parking Lot**.
- Do not select the **Automatic surface creation** option.
- Click **OK** twice to return to the Grading Creation Tools toolbar.

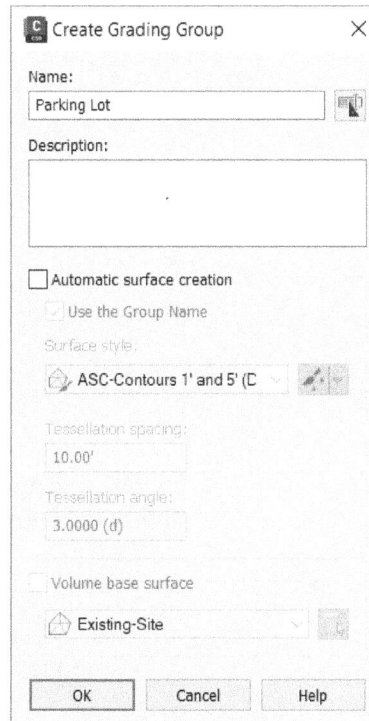

Figure 4–43

6. In the Grading Creation Tools toolbar, click ⬠ (Set Surface) In the Select surface dialog box, select **Residential Grading**. Click **OK**.

7. In the Grading Creation Tools toolbar, verify that the grading criteria set is set to **Basic Set**. Then set the grading criteria to **Grade to Surface**, as shown in Figure 4–44.

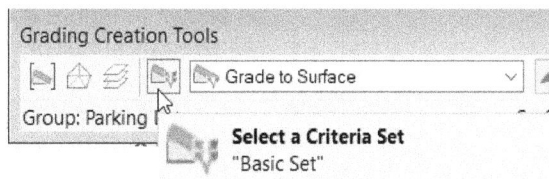

Figure 4–44

8. In the Grading Creation Tools toolbar, click (Create Grading). Select the **Back of Curb** feature line to use as the baseline, as shown in Figure 4–45.

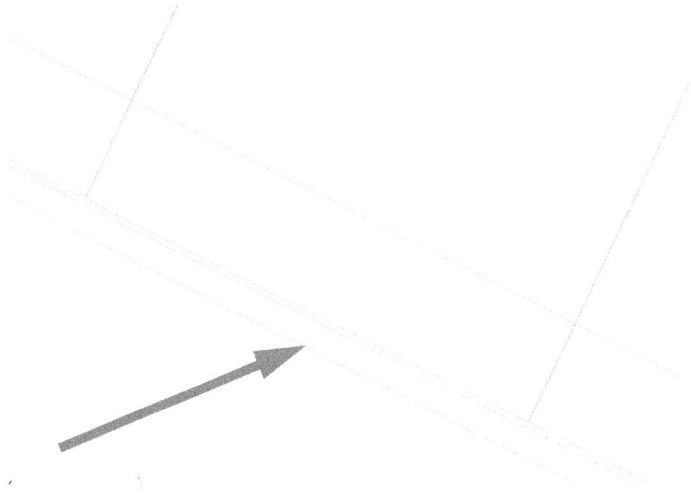

Figure 4–45

9. In the Grading - Weed Feature Line dialog box, select **Weed the feature line**, as shown in Figure 4–46.

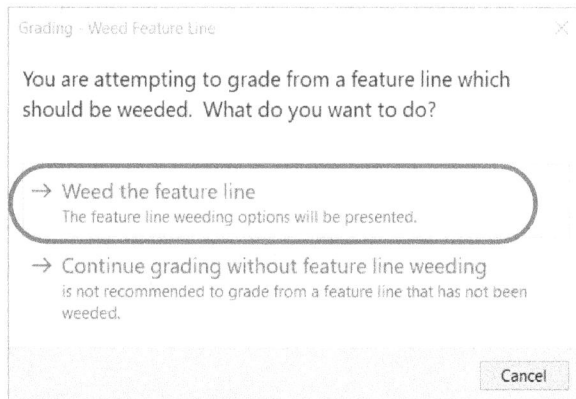

Figure 4–46

10. In the Weed Vertices dialog box, set the *3D distance* to **1.00'**, as shown in Figure 4–47. Note that 95 vertices will be removed (number of vertices may vary).

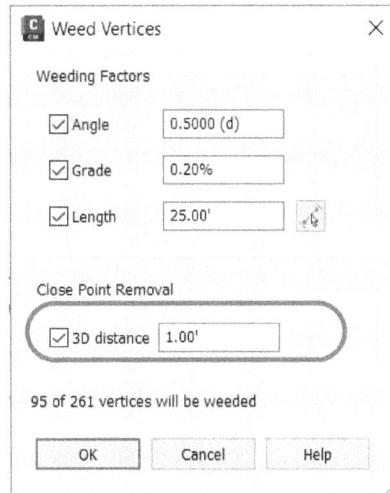

Figure 4–47

11. Click **OK** to continue.

12. When prompted for a grading side, pick a point on the outside of the parking lot.

13. When prompted to apply it to the entire length, type **N** (for No) and press <Enter>.

14. Using the **Endpoint** Osnap, select the endpoint at the beginning of the feature line. Press <Enter> to accept <0+00.00> as the beginning value.

15. Using the **Midpoint** Osnap, select the midpoint of the first curve, as shown in Figure 4–48. Press <Enter> to accept <0+70.54'> as the ending value.

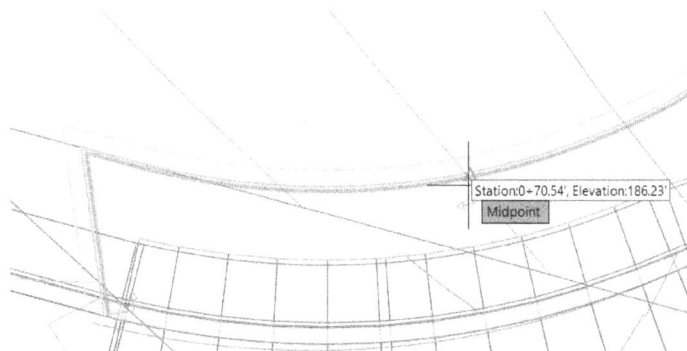

Figure 4–48

16. Press <Enter> to accept **Slope** as the cut format. Type **1** for a 1:1 slope.

The command continues until you press <Esc>. Rather than end the command, select the same feature line again to continue grading until prompted to press <Esc>.

17. Press <Enter> to accept **Slope** as the fill format. Type **1** for a 1:1 slope.

18. Select the **Back of Curb** feature line again.

19. Select a point on the outside of the parking lot to which to grade.

20. In the Command Line, type **135** for the start point. Press <Enter> to accept the beginning value. This is near the beginning of the building 2 footprint.

21. Using the **Endpoint** Osnap, select the south corner of the parking lot north of building 2 for the endpoint, as shown in Figure 4–49. Press <Enter> to accept <4+01.70'> as the end value.

Figure 4–49

22. Press <Enter> to accept **Slope** as the cut format. Type **0.5** for a 0.5:1 slope.

23. Press <Enter> to accept **Slope** as the fill format. Type **0.5** for a 0.5:1 slope.

Optional steps:

The following steps are optional, depending on your computer's capabilities and the time you have. In the next task, you can open a drawing where these optional steps have been completed.

24. Select the **Back of Curb** feature line again.

25. Select a point on the outside of the parking lot to which to grade.

26. For the beginning point, select the endpoint at the top right corner of the parking lot north of the last endpoint selected, as shown in Figure 4–50.

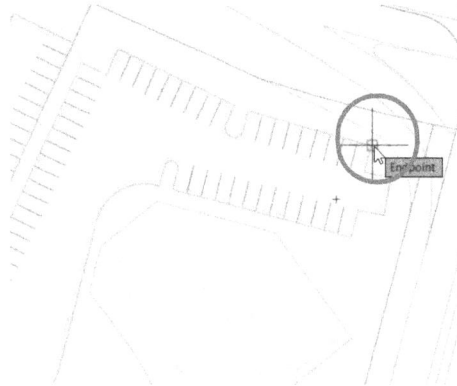

Figure 4–50

27. Press <Enter> to accept <4+96.39'> as the station.

28. For the ending point, select the endpoint at the top left corner on the far north west side of the parking lot, as shown in Figure 4–51.

Figure 4–51

29. Press <Enter> to accept <9+66.94'> as the station.

30. Press <Enter> to accept **Slope** as the cut format. Type **2** for a 2:1 slope.

31. Press <Enter> to accept **Slope** as the fill format. Type **1.5** for a 1.5:1 slope.

32. Select the curb feature line again and select a point on the outside of the parking lot to which to grade.

33. Using the **Endpoint** Osnap, select the south corner of the parking lot north of building 1 as the start point, as shown in Figure 4–52. Press <Enter> to accept <10+61.87'> as the start point.

Figure 4–52

34. In the Command Line, type **1500** for the end point. Press <Enter> to accept it.

35. Press <Enter> to accept **Slope** as the cut format. Type **0.5** for a 0.5:1 slope.

36. Press <Enter> to accept **Slope** as the fill format. Type **0.5** for a 0.5:1 slope.

37. Select the curb feature line again and pick a point on the outside to which to grade.

38. Using Osnaps, select the endpoint of the last curve near the parking lot entrance, as shown in Figure 4–53.

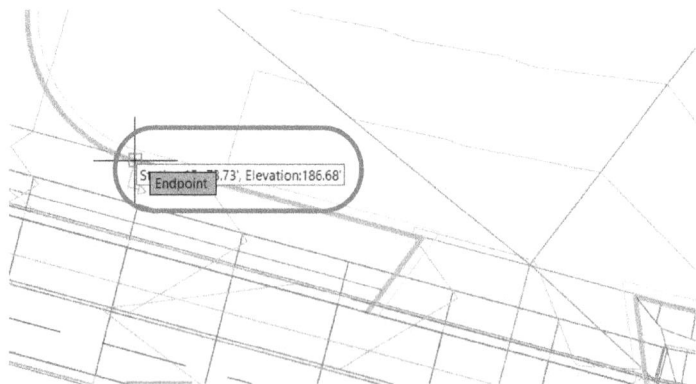

Figure 4–53

39. Press <Enter> to accept <15+73.77'> as the station.

40. Using Osnaps, select the endpoint of the feature line at the parking lot entrance, as shown in Figure 4–54.

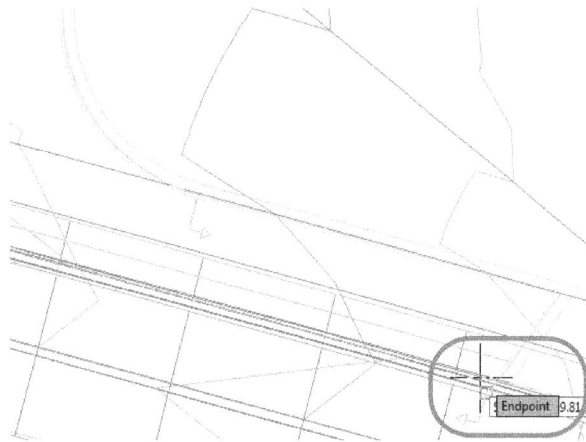

Figure 4–54

41. Press <Enter> to accept the value given.

42. Press <Enter> to accept **Slope** as the cut format. Type **2** for a 2:1 slope.

43. Press <Enter> to accept **Slope** as the fill format. Type **2** for a 2:1 slope.

44. Press <Esc> to end the command.

45. Save the drawing.

Task 4 - Create transitions between predefined grading objects along the same feature line.

---

1. Continue working in the drawing from the previous task, or open **PKLOT-D.dwg** from the *C:\Civil 3D for Land Dev\ Working\Parking Lot* folder.

2. In the *Home* tab>Create Design panel, expand the Grading drop-down list and click (Grading Creation Tools).

3. In the Grading Creation Tools toolbar, set the grading group to **Parking Lot** within the **Multi-Family** site, and the surface to **Residential Grading**, if necessary.

4. Expand the Create Grading drop-down list and click
   ⬡ (Create Transition).

5. Select the curb feature line that contains the previously created grading objects.

6. In the Command Line, you are prompted to pick a point between the gradings. Select between two previously created grading objects, as shown in Figure 4–55.

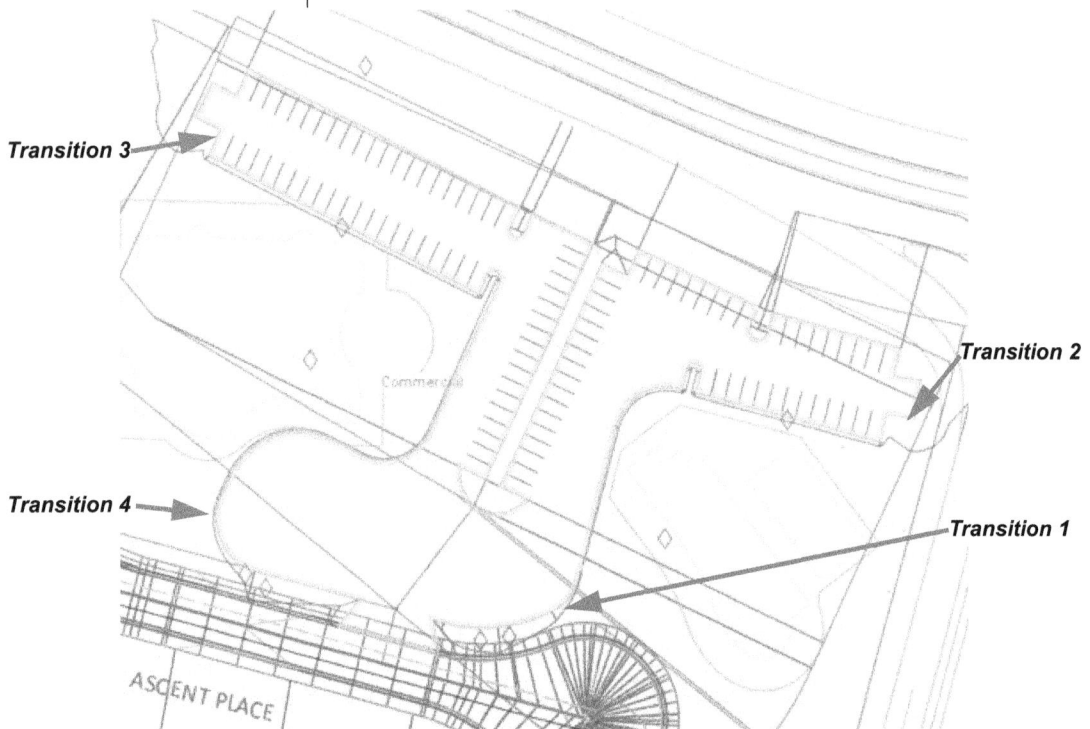

Figure 4–55

7. Repeat Steps 5 and 6 as needed to complete all four transitions.

8. Press <Esc> to end the command.

9. Save the drawing.

4.6 Create a Grading Surface

When working with complex grading objects, it is better to completely design the grading group before creating its surface. In most design workflows, as you first create the grading group, you clear the option to create a surface automatically and then build a surface from the grading group at a later time.

When you are ready to build the surface, you can select any part of the grading group. In the *Grading* contextual tab, click

(Grading Group Properties). In the Grading Group Properties dialog box, select the **Automatic Surface Creation** option to create a surface and click **OK**, as shown in Figure 4–56. You can also select the **Volume Base Surface** option if needed.

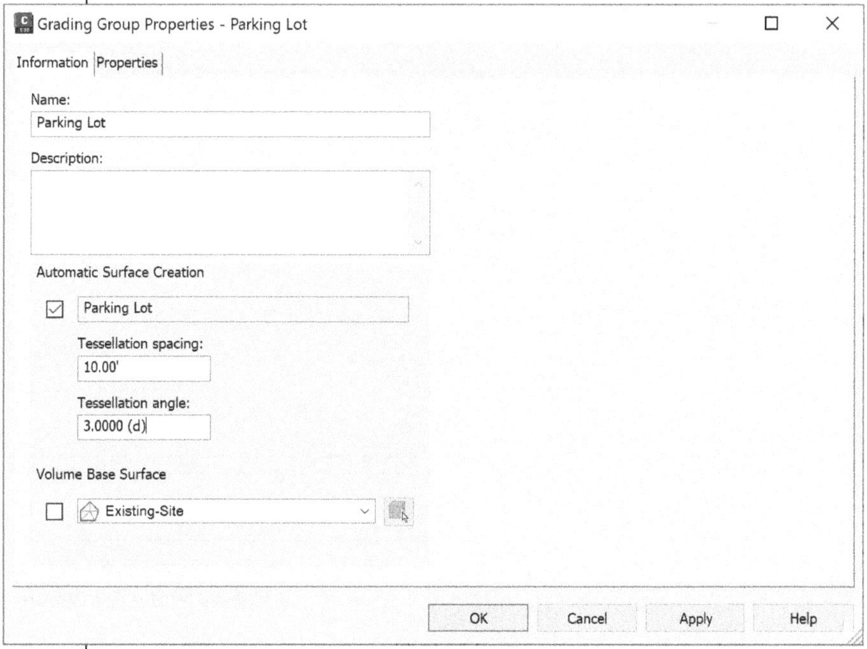

Figure 4–56

The Create Surface dialog box opens and you enter a surface name (the grading group name is the default surface name), type a description, set a style, and set a render material. Clicking **OK** creates the surface and displays the contours.

4.7 Add Feature Lines to a Grading Surface

After creating a grading group, any feature lines in the same area affects the surface that was created by the grading group. The key to making this work is to ensure that the grading group and feature lines are in the same site. Figure 4–57 shows what happens when feature lines are drawn on top of a grading object in the same site.

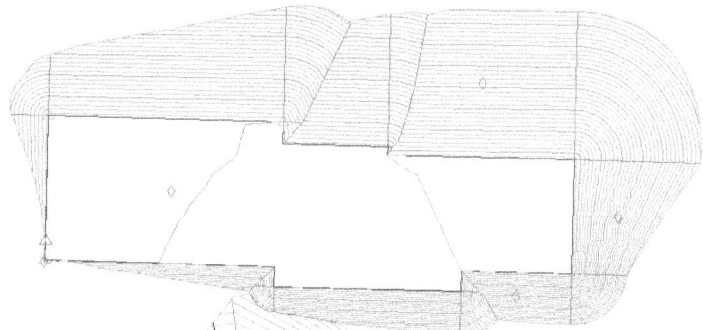

Before adding a feature line

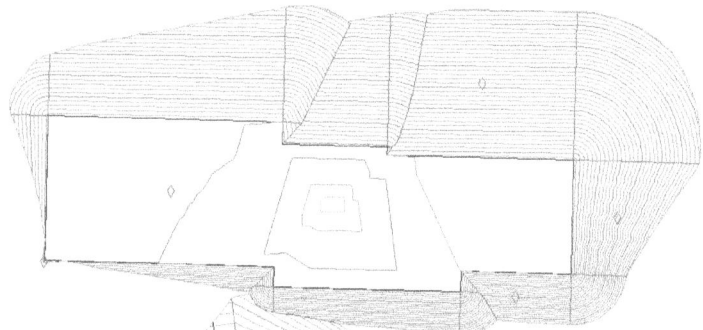

After adding a feature line

Figure 4–57

Practice 4c

Create a Surface with Proper Drainage

Practice Objective

- Create a grading group surface and add feature lines for proper drainage.

In this practice, you will prepare to create a grading surface, create the grading surface, and add feature lines to a grading surface.

Task 1 - Prepare to create a grading surface.

Before creating a finished ground surface, you need to clean up and finish the grading group. So far you have created multiple feature lines to represent the curb and gutter of the parking area.But during the offset procedure you never "capped" off the feature lines. You have also created grading objects all the way around the parking lot. Next you need to draw a feature line at to close the parking lot off, then infill the center of the parking lot to add the pavement's grading.

For convenience, the Parking-EOP feature line has been trimmed back to the Ascent Place EOP. Therefore, you need to open the next drawing. More elevation points were weeded as well.

1. Open **PKLOT-E.dwg** from the *C:\Civil 3D for Land Dev\ Working\Parking Lot* folder. Do not continue working in the drawing from the previous practice.

2. In the *View* tab>Views panel, select **Parking-Entrance** to zoom to the entrance of the parking lot.

3. In the *Home* tab>Create Design panel, click ⌇ (Create Feature Line).

4. In the Create Feature Lines dialog box, complete the following:

   - For the *Site*, select **Multi-Family Site**.
   - For the feature line *Name,* type **Parking-Endcap**.
   - For the *Style,* select **ASC-Parking Lot**.

5. Click **OK**.

6. Use the endpoint Osnap to snap to the following eight points at the end of the feature lines, as shown in Figure 4–58. Accept the elevations and grades that are calculated.

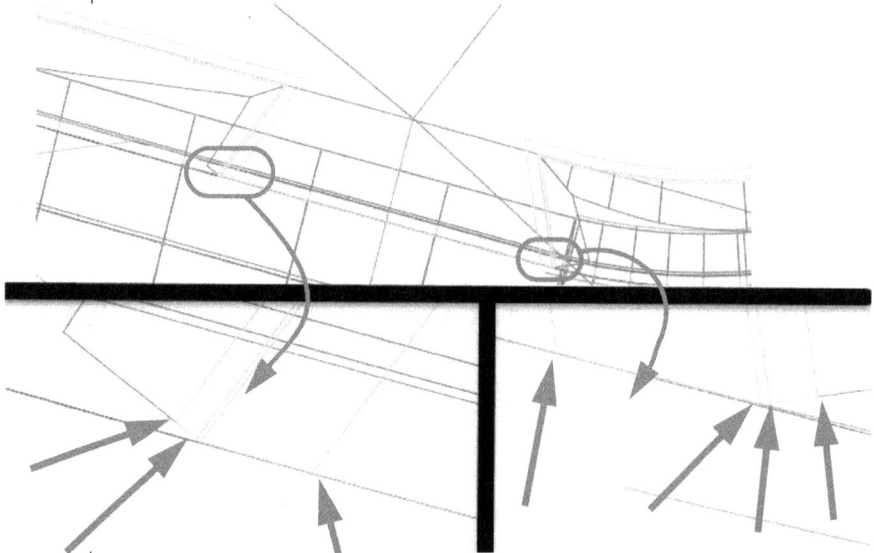

Figure 4–58

7. In the *View* tab>Views panel, select **Parking-Lot**.

8. In the *Home* tab>Create Design panel, expand the Grading drop-down list and click (Create Infill).

9. In the *Select Grading Group* dialog box, ensure that the **Parking Lot** grading group (in the Multi-Family Site) is set, as shown in Figure 4–59.

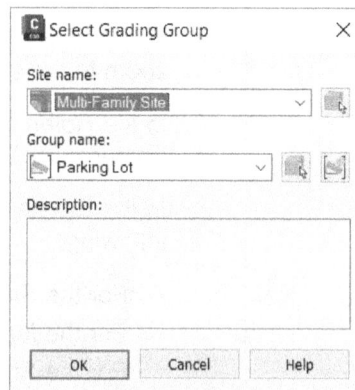

Figure 4–59

10. Click **OK** to close the Select Grading Group dialog box.

11. In the Grading Style dialog box, accept the default and click **OK**.

12. Pick a point in the center of the parking lot area, as shown in Figure 4–60.

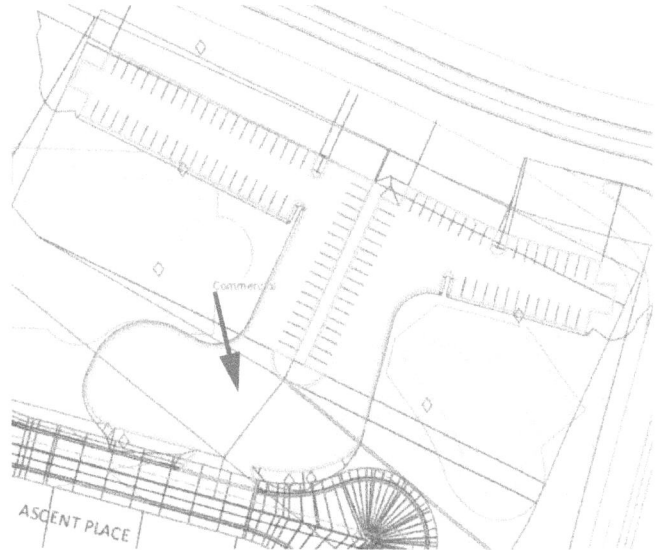

Figure 4–60

13. Press <Esc> to end the command.

14. Save the drawing.

Task 2 - Create the grading surface.

1. Continue working in the drawing from the previous task.

2. Select the diamond shape representing the infill center mark of the parking lot (or any part of the grading group). In the

   Grading contextual tab>Modify panel, click (Grading Group Properties).

3. In the Grading Group Properties dialog box, in the *Information* tab, select the **Automatic Surface Creation** option, as shown in Figure 4–61.

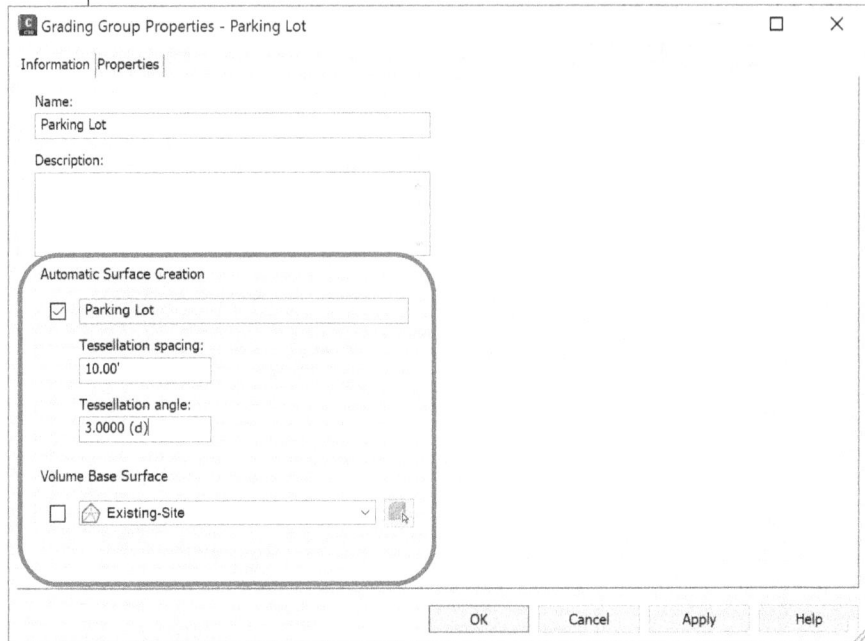

Figure 4–61

4. When the Create Surface dialog box opens, click **OK** to accept the defaults.

5. Select the **Volume Base Surface** option and select **Existing-Site** for the base surface.

6. Click **OK** and save the drawing.

Task 3 - Add feature lines to a grading surface.

1. Continue working in the drawing from the previous task.

2. In the *Prospector* tab, expand **Sites>Temp**. Select the Feature Lines collection to view them in the preview. Select all of the feature lines except **CenterLine**, right-click, and select **Move to Site**, as shown in Figure 4–62.

Figure 4–62

3. In the Move to Site dialog box, select **Multi-Family Site** as the *Destination site*, as shown in Figure 4–63, and click **OK**.

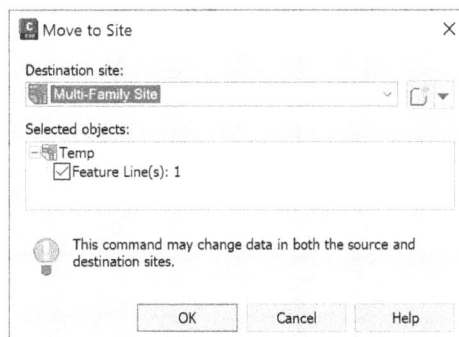

Figure 4–63

The original infill grading object automatically fills in the center island of the parking lot. You need to add additional infill grading objects to fill in the surface of the asphalt and the curbs.

4. In the *Home* tab>Create Design panel, expand the Grading drop-down list and click (Create Infill).

5. Pick a point in the center of the parking lot area, as shown in Figure 4–64.

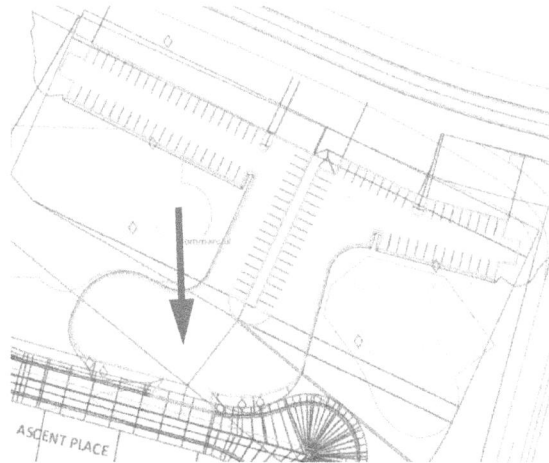

Figure 4–64

6. Repeat Steps 4 and 5 to add infill between each of the curb lines. When you are done, you should see that the grading is slightly affected along the edge of the parking lot where the feature lines have caused more definition, as shown in Figure 4–65.

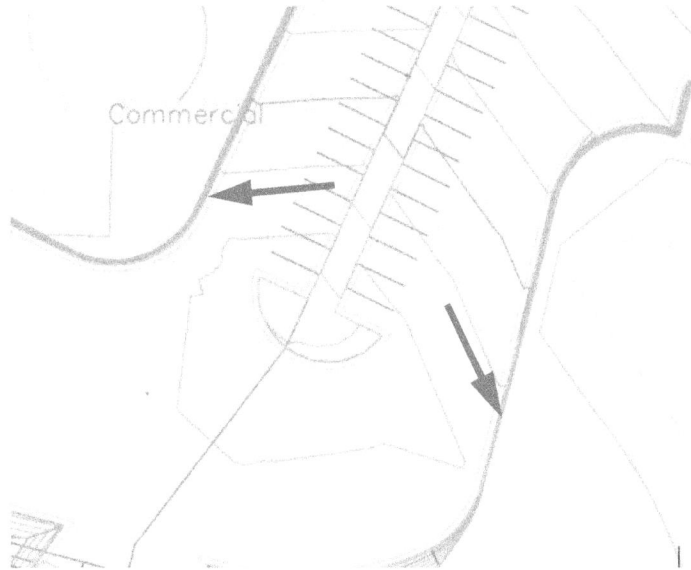

Figure 4–65

7. You can now delete the Temp site. In the *Prospector* tab, expand **Sites**. Right-click on **Temp** and select **Delete**, as shown in Figure 4–66. Confirm **Yes** in the alert box.

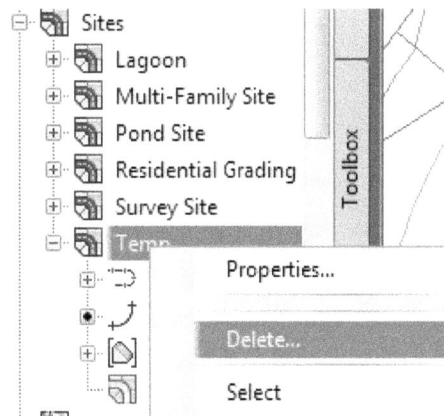

Figure 4–66

Note: If you wish to keep the Temp site for later use, you can freeze the following layers instead:

*   C-TOPO-GRAD
*   C-TOPO-GRAD-CUTS
*   C-TOPO-GRAD-FILL
*   C-TOPO-GRAD-TEXT

8. Save the drawing. (Before opening the Object Viewer in the next step, it is always prudent to save the drawing.)

9. Select the **Parking Lot** surface (select one of its contour lines).

10. In the *Surface* contextual tab, click ▦ (Object Viewer). Set the view direction to **SW Isometric** and the style to **Conceptual**. Note the hole in the surface, as shown in Figure 4–67.

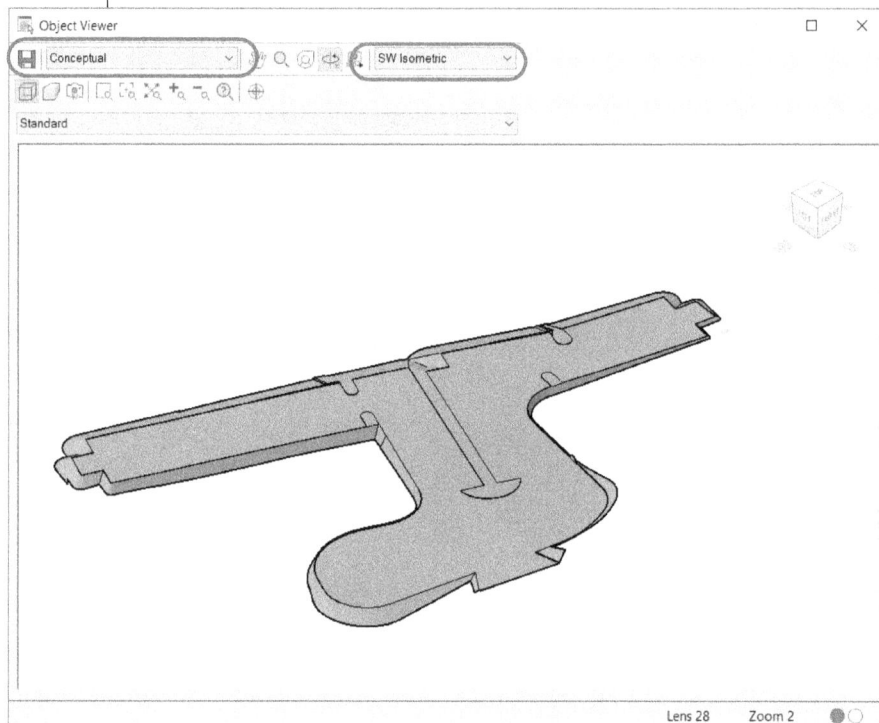

Figure 4–67

11. Press <Esc> twice to close the Object Viewer and release the selection.

Chapter Review Questions

1. Which of the following is NOT an option for setting the elevation a feature line vertex as you draw it?

   a. Slope

   b. Transition

   c. Surface

   d. Grading Object

2. Which of the following is NOT an option for creating curves within feature lines as you draw them?

   a. Secondpnt

   b. Diameter

   c. Radius

   d. Arc end point

3. The **Stepped Offset** command is the same as the AutoCAD **Offset** command. These commands can be used interchangeably.

   a. True

   b. False

4. Which of the following is not an option for setting elevations when using the **Stepped Offset** command?

   a. Grade

   b. Slope

   c. Difference

   d. Surface

5. Which icon in the Grading Creation Tools toolbar enables you to create transitions between two grading objects of varying slopes?

a.

b.

c.

d.

Command Summary

Button	Command	Location
	Create Feature Line	• **Ribbon**: *Home* tab>Create Design panel, expand Feature Line drop-down list • **Command Prompt:** DrawFeatureLine
	Create Infill	• **Ribbon**: *Home* tab>Create Design panel, expand Grading drop-down list • **Toolbar**: Grading Creation Tools (*contextual*), expand Create Grading drop-down list
	Delete PI	• **Ribbon**: *Grading* contextual tab>Edit Geometry panel • **Command Prompt:** DeleteFeaturePI
	Grading Group Properties	• **Ribbon**: *Grading* contextual tab>Modify panel
	Stepped Offset	• **Ribbon**: *Feature Line* contextual tab> Edit Geometry panel • **Command Prompt:** GradingElevEditor

Parking Lot Option

Parking lots can be designed either with grading tools and feature lines or by using corridors. In a previous chapter, the parking lot was graded using feature lines and a temporary surface. Various feature lines were created representing the back of curb, top of curb, gutter line, and edge of pavement. From these, the parking lot surface was generated.

The second option is explored in this chapter. Using the linework on the XREF for the back of the curb, you will create feature lines and a corridor for the curb and build a surface from the corridor.

Corridors are 3D representations of a road design. In this chapter, you will create a typical cross-section of the curb (called an assembly). Next, you will apply the assembly to the back of curb feature line created earlier, then you will create the parking surfaces.

Learning Objectives in This Chapter

- Create assemblies.
- Create feature lines from an XREF file.
- Create a corridor representing the parking lot.
- Clear bowties from the corridor.
- Edit the feature line.
- Create a surface from the corridor.
- Create a boundary for the corridor surface.

5.1 Assembly Overview

Assemblies

An *assembly* defines the attachment point of a roadway cross-section to the horizontal and vertical alignments. This attachment point occurs at the midpoint of the assembly marker (or assembly baseline), as shown in Figure 5–1. The 3D progression of the attachment point along the corridor is also sometimes referred to as the *profile grade line*.

Figure 5–1

Assemblies can be placed anywhere in a drawing (centerline of roads, curb returns, sidewalks, off ramps, railways, etc.). Assembly styles only affect the display of the marker itself (e.g., color, layer, etc.).

Subassemblies

Assemblies are assigned *subassemblies*, which represent individual components of the proposed cross-section (such as lane or curb subassemblies). Subassemblies attach to the left or right side of an assembly's attachment point. When building an assembly, you build from the middle out to the left or right edges.

The library of stock subassemblies supplied with the Autodesk Civil 3D® software uses a wide array of dynamic parameters (e.g., dimensions of lane width and slope). When these values change, the road model gets updated. Custom dynamic subassemblies can be created using the .net programming language, using the Subassembly Composer, which is an additional program that is included with Autodesk Civil 3D.

The example in Figure 5–2 shows an assembly containing lane, curb, and daylight subassemblies. This assembly has been assigned to display an offset and elevation marker (point) label at the edge of the lane, a pavement slope (link) label, and shape labels displaying the area of the sub-base.

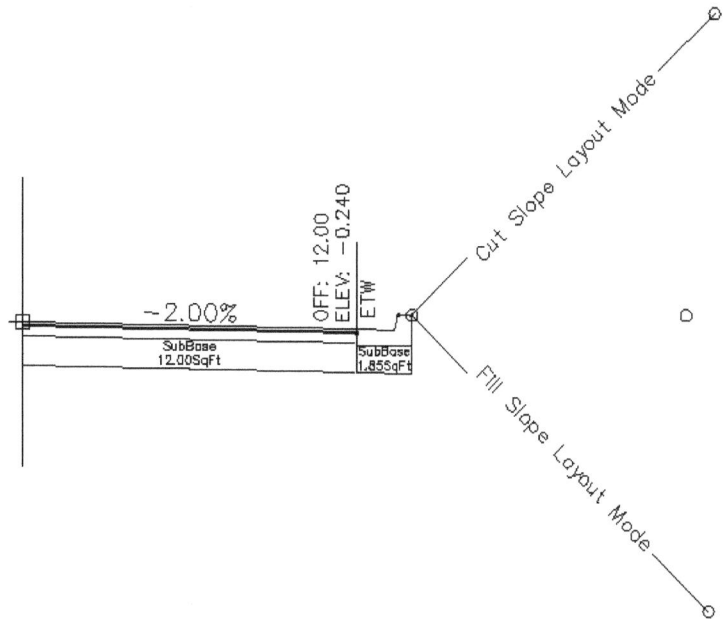

Figure 5–2

- Each subassembly attaches to the assembly connection point or to a point on an adjacent subassembly. You should assign each assembly a logical, unique name during creation. This is helpful later in the corridor creation process when you are working with very complex corridors that include intersections, transitions, and other components.

The Toolspace, *Prospector* tab lists each assembly with a further breakdown of each subassembly associated with it in a tree structure, as shown in Figure 5–3.

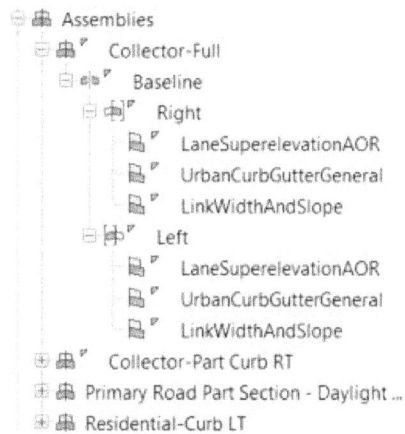

Figure 5–3

To review their interconnections and parameters, select the assembly, then right-click and select **Assembly Properties**. The Assembly Properties dialog box opens, as shown in Figure 5–4.

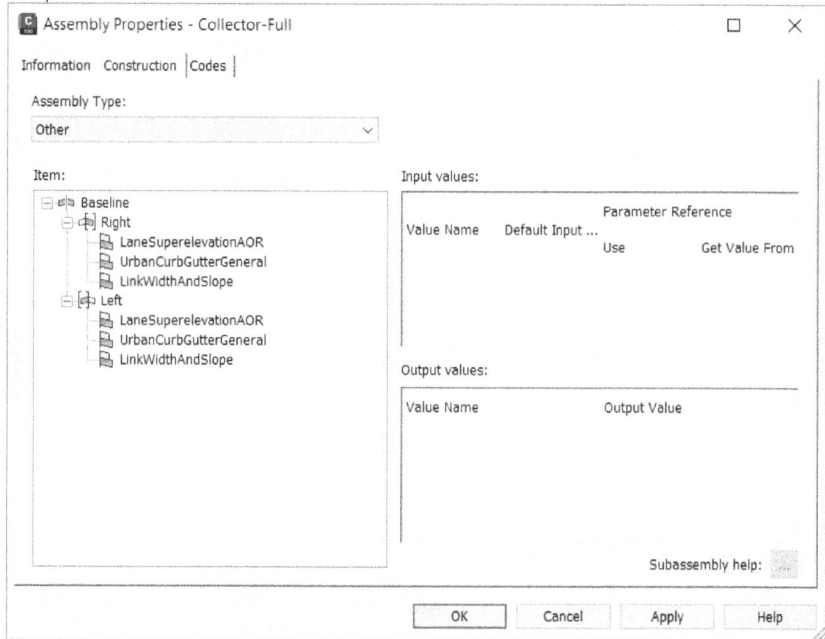

Figure 5–4

5.2 Modifying Assemblies

Attaching Subassemblies

The easiest way to add an Autodesk Civil 3D subassembly to an assembly is using the Tool Palettes. You can open the Tool Palettes by clicking ⬚ (Tool Palettes) in the *Home* tab>Palettes panel (as shown in Figure 5–5) or in the *View* tab>Palettes panel. You can also use <Ctrl>+<3>.

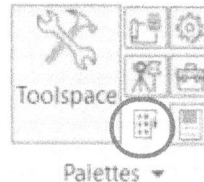

Figure 5–5

The Autodesk Civil 3D software provides a number of stock subassembly tool palettes, as shown in Figure 5–6. In addition, it is continually updating and adding new subassemblies with every release.

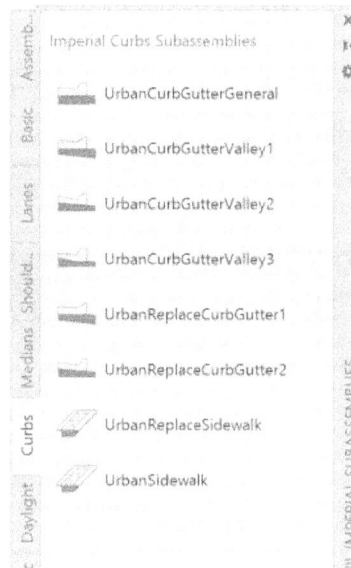

Figure 5–6

There are separate tool palettes for Metric and Imperial. Care must be taken that you are using the proper one. Right-click on the Tool Palettes band to select the proper tool palette, as shown in Figure 5–7.

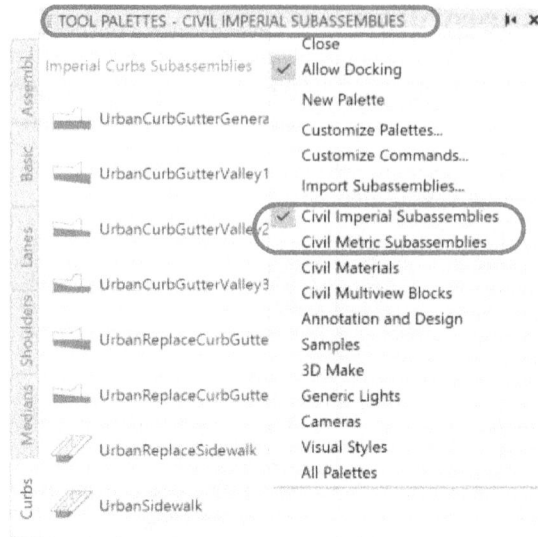

Figure 5–7

Copying Assemblies

Assemblies can be copied with the AutoCAD **Copy** command. Copying an assembly creates an independent assembly without a relationship to the original. Select the assembly by selecting the **Assembly Baseline**.

Mirroring Subassemblies

In the Autodesk Civil 3D software, subassemblies can be mirrored, copied, and moved across the assembly to which they are attached by selecting the subassemblies, right-clicking, and selecting **Mirror**, **Copy to**, or **Move to**. You can also click

(Mirror), (Copy), or (Move) in the *Assembly* tab> Modify Subassembly panel. This enables you to create one side of the roadway and to create a mirrored image for the other side in one step.

> **Hint: AutoCAD Mirror, Move, or Copy Commands**
>
> The basic AutoCAD **Mirror**, **Move**, or **Copy** commands do not work for subassemblies. You need to use the special commands from the shortcut menu or the Modify Subassembly panel.

Practice 5a

Creating Assemblies and Feature Lines

Practice Objectives

- Create and modify curb assemblies for use in a corridor model.
- Replace base engineering XREF with a drawing depicting an alternative parking lot layout.
- Create feature lines for a corridor.

For the land development drawings in this guide, much of the preliminary work has already been done for the site development.

The completed corridors for Jeffries Ranch Road and Ascent Place, the Ascent Place knuckle and cul-de-sac target alignments, the Mission Avenue alignment, and the Existing-Site surface have been referenced through Data Shortcuts.

In this practice, you will create an assembly for the curb of the parking lot. A typical cross-section of the desired curb is shown in Figure 5–8.

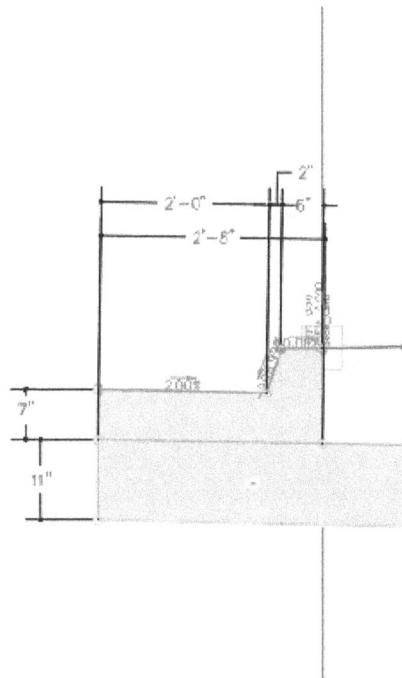

Figure 5–8

Task 1 - Create an assembly.

1. Open **PKCOR-A.dwg** from the *C:\Civil 3D for Land Dev\ Grading\Parking Corridor* folder.

2. Hover over the Data Shortcuts and look at the tooltip that appears, as shown in Figure 5–9. Ensure that the **Working Folder** is set to *C:\Civil 3D for Land Dev\Data Shortcuts\ Fundamentals* and the **Data Shortcuts Project Folder** is set to *Ascent-Development*.

   If required, review the Setting a Project practice for how to set the working folder and the project folder.

   - If not, right-click on Data Shortcuts to set the **Working Folder** to *C:\Civil 3D for Land Dev\Data Shortcuts\ Fundamentals* and the **Data Shortcuts Project Folder** to *Ascent-Development*.

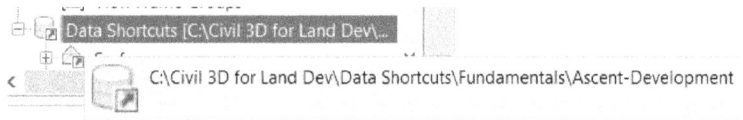

Figure 5–9

3. In the *Home* tab>Create Design panel, click ![icon] (Create Assembly).

4. In the Create Assembly dialog box, name the new assembly **Parking-Curb-Back**. Set the *Assembly Type* to **Other** and leave the other settings at their defaults, as shown in Figure 5–10. Click **OK** to close the dialog box.

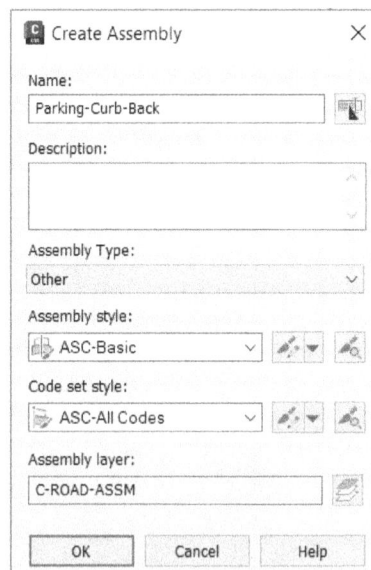

Figure 5–10

Once you specify the assembly baseline location, the Autodesk Civil 3D software will change the view to zoom into the assembly baseline location.

5. When prompted, place the assembly baseline to the right of the profile view of Jeffries Ranch Rd in the current drawing, as shown in Figure 5–11.

Figure 5–11

6. Open the Tool Palettes by clicking (Tool Palettes) in the *Home* tab>Palettes panel.

7. In the Subassemblies Tool Palette, select the *Curbs* tab and select the **UrbanCurbGutterGeneral** subassembly.

8. Prior to selecting the marker point to attach the subassembly, in the AutoCAD Properties palette, in the *Advanced* section, set the following (as shown in Figure 5–12):

- *Side*: **Left**
- *Dimension B*: **24"**
- *Insertion Point:* **Curb Back** (use the drop-down list to pick)

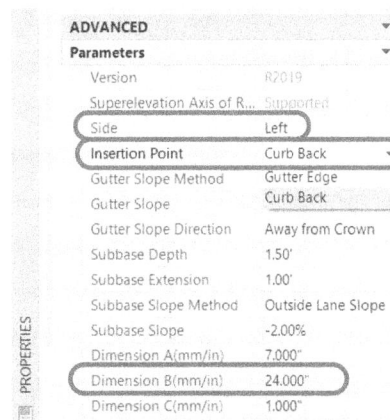

Figure 5–12

9. You will now create a subassembly that links the back of curb to the property line. In the Subassemblies Tool Palette, select the *Generic* tab, then select the **LinkWidthAndSlope** subassembly.

10. In the *Advanced* section of the Properties palette, set the following:

  - *Side parameter:* **Right**
  - *Width:* **1.0'**
  - *Slope:* **2%**

11. Insert the subassembly by selecting the circle at the end of the **UrbanCurbGutterGeneral** subassembly, as shown in Figure 5–13.

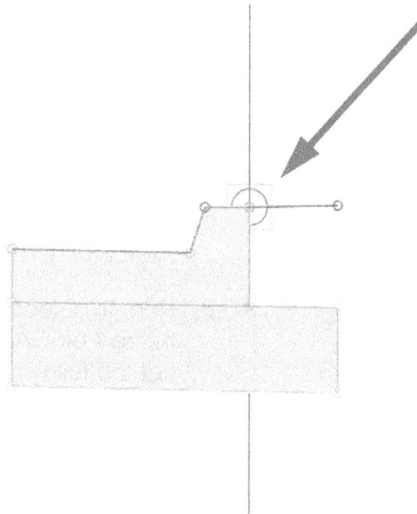

Figure 5–13

12. Press <Esc> to exit the subassembly command.

13. Save the drawing.

Task 2 - Replace base engineering XREF.

The original Base-Proposed Engineering XREF needs to be swapped with an XREF showing an alternative parking lot layout.

1. Zoom and pan over to the Ascent Place development area.

2. Select the temporary surface (Temp Parking Lot), as shown in Figure 5–14.

*This temporary surface
and grading object were
generated in an earlier
chapter.*

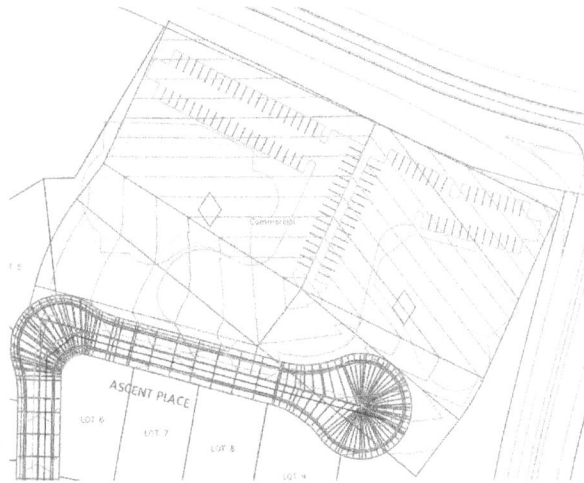

Figure 5–14

3. Go to Surface Properties in the contextual ribbon and set the
   Surface style to **_No Display**.

4. Click **OK** to exit the Surface Properties dialog box.

5. Invoke the External References panel by typing **XREF** at the
   command prompt.

6. Select the Base-Proposed Engineering link in the upper part
   of the panel, as shown in Figure 5–15.

7. In the lower part of the panel, select the ellipses (...) in the
   Saved Path, as shown in Figure 5–15.

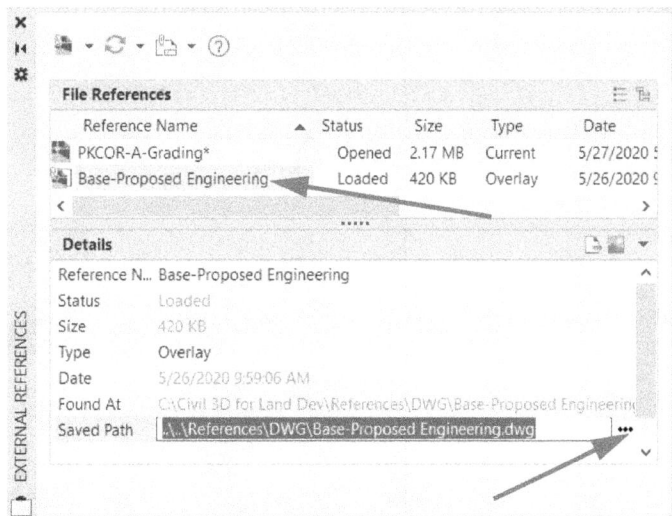

Figure 5–15

8. Select **Base-Proposed Alternate.dwg** from the same folder as the original XREF (*C:\Civil 3D for Land Dev\References\ DWG*).

9. Close the External References panel.

10. Save the drawing.

Task 3 - Create a feature line and set elevations by grading.

In this task, you will create feature lines representing the back of curbs of the alternate parking lot and set elevations by grading. While the previous parking lot layout was designed to slope downward toward Mission Ave, this layout explores another drainage option of the parking lot sloping towards Ascent Place.

1. Continue working in the drawing from the previous task.

2. In the *Home* tab>Create Design panel, expand the Feature Line drop-down list and click ⬚ (Create Feature Line from Objects).

3. Type **X** and press <Enter> to select linework from the external reference file. Select the line that represents the parking lot perimeter back of curb, designated as **A** in Figure 5–16. Press <Enter> to continue.

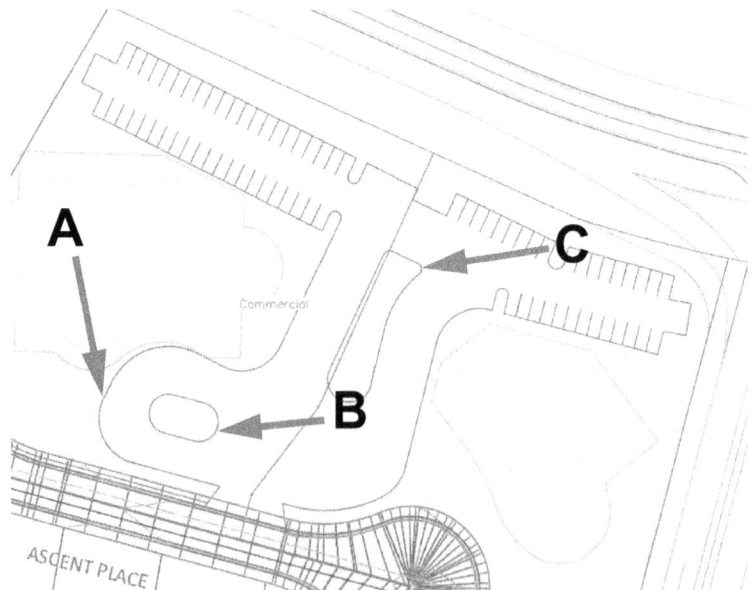

Figure 5–16

Be sure you check the
Name *option to enable*
you to type in a name
for the feature line.

4. In the Create Feature Lines dialog box, complete the following, as shown in Figure 5–17:

   - Set the *Site* to **Multi-Family Site**.
   - For the *Name*, type **Perimeter-BOC**.
   - Set the *Style* to **ASC-Parking Lot**.
   - Verify that **Assign elevations** is selected.
   - Click **OK**.

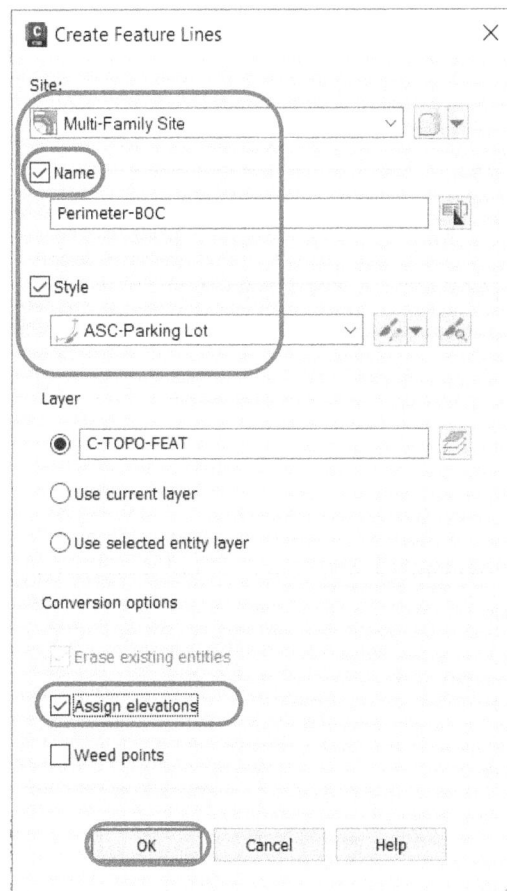

Figure 5–17

5. In the Assign Elevations dialog box, select **From surface**, then select **Temp Parking Lot** from the list, as shown in Figure 5–18.

6. Click **Insert intermediate grade break points**, then click on **OK**.

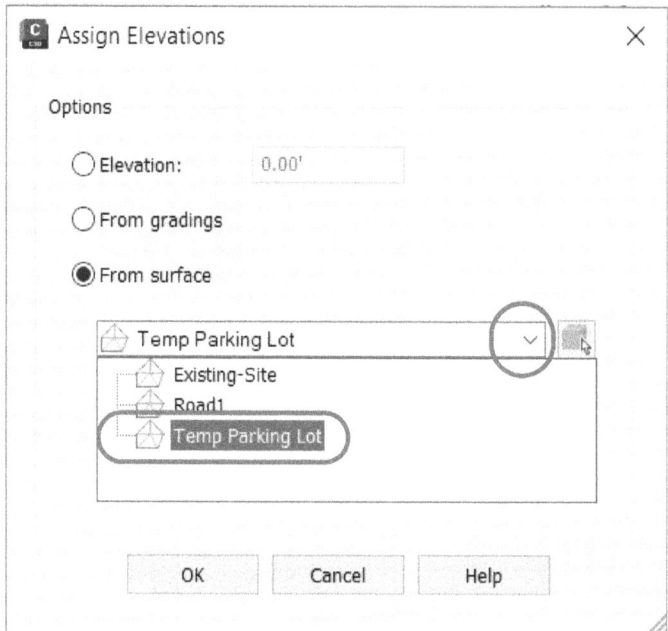

Figure 5–18

7. Repeat Steps 2 to 6 to create:

- **B** (as shown in Figure 5–16): Name it **Island-1-BOC** and click **Insert intermediate grade break points**.
- **C** (as shown in Figure 5–16): Name it **Island-2-BOC** and click **Insert intermediate grade break points**.

8. Freeze the **C-TOPO-GRAD** layer, on which the grading objects reside.

9. Save the drawing.

5.3 Creating a Corridor

A corridor is a 3D model of a proposed design based on alignments and profiles (or feature lines) and assemblies. Corridors can be used to create terrain models (such as a finished ground terrain model) and generate section data. Corridors display as complex drawing objects consisting of individual cross-sections, feature lines that connect marker points (locations where point codes are assigned), and other related data, as shown in Figure 5–19.

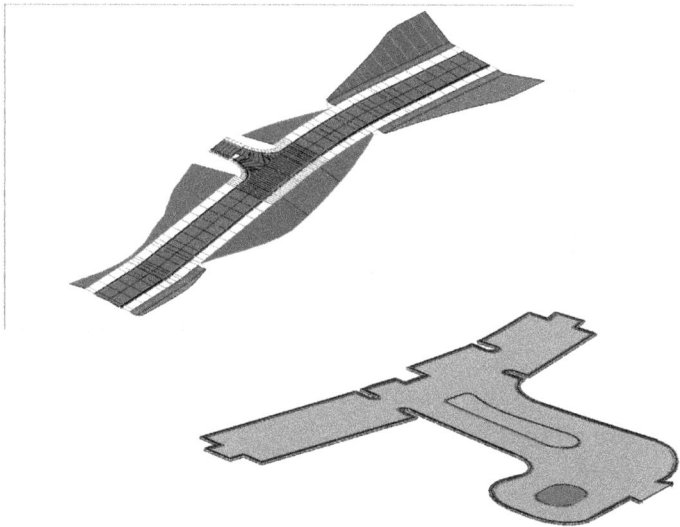

Figure 5–19

Corridors can consist of an individual alignment and profile (or a feature line) and assemblies (such as for a single road) or can contain multiples of each. You can have any number of corridors present in the same drawing file.

To create a corridor, click in the *Home* tab> Create Design panel. A dialog box opens in which you can enter a description, corridor style, layer, alignment or feature line, profile, assembly, and target surface, as shown on the left in Figure 5–20. It also has an option that enables you to set the baseline and region parameters. If you select this, a second dialog box will open when you click **OK**, as shown on the right in Figure 5–20.

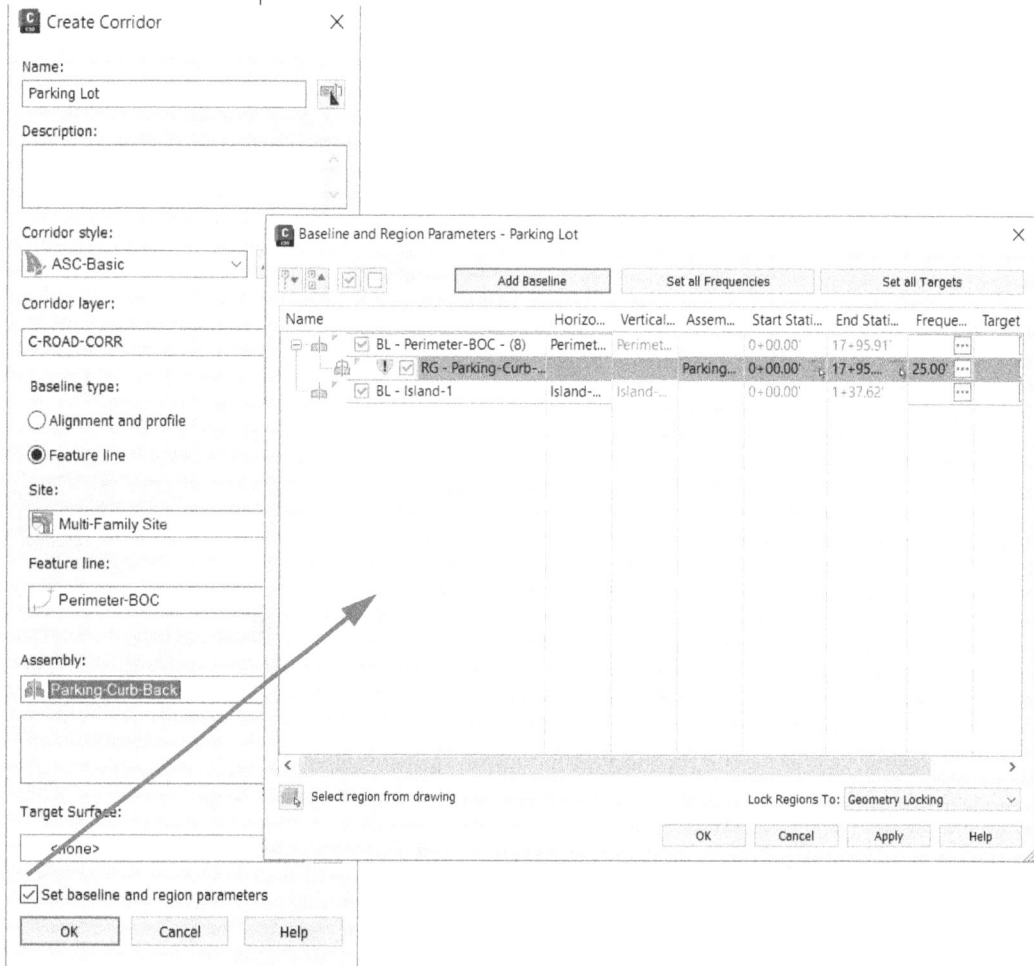

Figure 5–20

Corridor Frequency

The corridor frequency determines how often assemblies are applied to the corridor model, as shown in Figure 5–21. The frequency can be set for tangents separate from curves to provide more control over the model's size and accuracy. The more frequently the assembly is applied to the corridor model, the more accurate the model. However, a higher frequency also causes the model to require more computer resources, as it increases the size of the model. It is important to set the frequency at a level that balances the level of required accuracy with a reasonably sized corridor model.

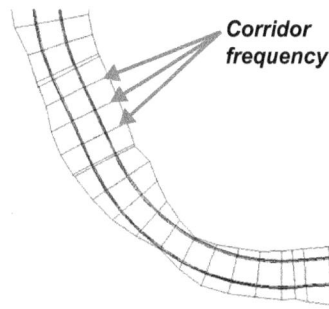

Figure 5–21

*These can be preset through the Edit Command Settings dialog box for the various **CreateCorridor** commands.*

Frequency locations for curved baselines can be set **By curvature**, **At an increment**, or **Both**, as shown in Figure 5–22. If the **At an increment** option is selected, assemblies are applied at a specified number of units along the curve. If the **By curvature** option is selected, the radius of the curve determines how frequently the assemblies are applied to the corridor model.

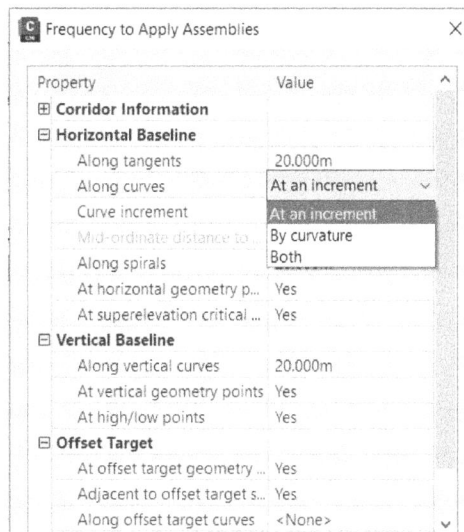

Figure 5–22

5.4 Corridor Properties

Once created, corridors are adjusted in the Corridor Properties dialog box.

Information Tab

The *Information* tab enables you to name the corridor (recommended) and add a description. The corridor style is not very pertinent since the **Code Set Styles** will control the appearance of the corridor.

Parameters Tab

The *Parameters* tab enables you to review and adjust corridor parameters, including which alignments, profiles, and assemblies are being used. Each unique road center line is listed as a *baseline*. In each baseline, there is at least one *region*. Each region is an area over which a specific assembly is applied. You can have multiple baselines and multiple regions in the same baseline as required. The *Parameters* tab is shown in Figure 5–23.

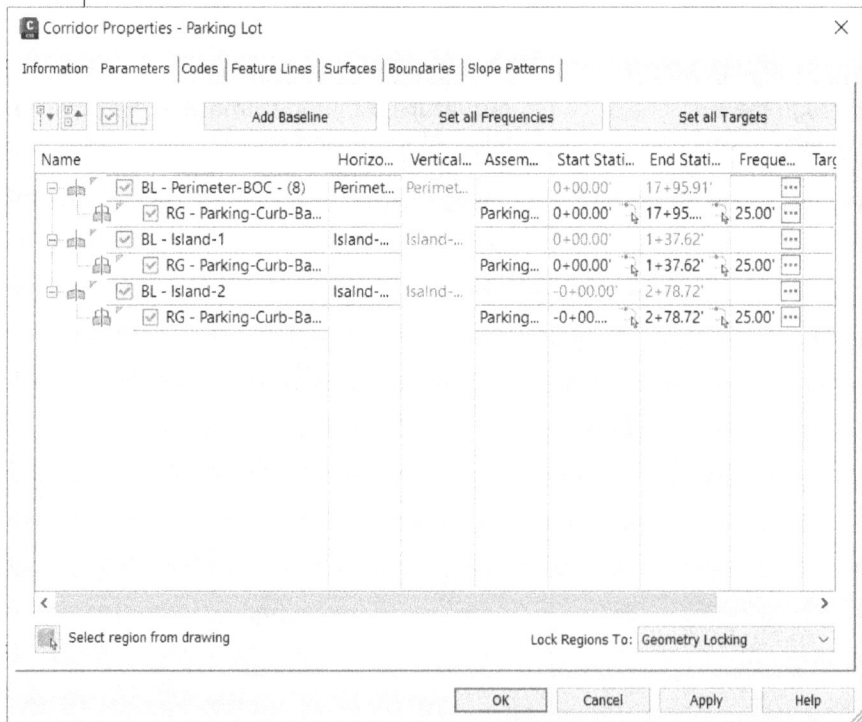

Figure 5–23

Each region has controls that enable you to review the Target Mapping, and the *Frequency* at which corridor sections should be created. If the corridor has had overrides applied using the Corridor Section Editor (select the corridor, *Corridor* tab> Modify panel), those can be reviewed here as well.

At the top of the dialog box are two important buttons: **Set all Frequencies** and **Set all Targets**. These can be used to assign frequencies and targets to all corridor regions. Otherwise, these properties can be adjusted for individual regions using ⊡ (Ellipsis), which is available in the *Frequency* and *Targets* columns.

Codes

*These can be preset through the Edit Command Settings dialog box for the various **CreateCorridor** commands.*

The *Codes* tab lists all of the codes that are available in the corridor based on the subassemblies in the assembly, as shown in Figure 5–24. These codes are combined into Code set styles.

They control the appearance of the corridor (and cross sections and assemblies) by applying styles to each of the subassemblies. Codes are also used to set section labels and for quantity take-off.

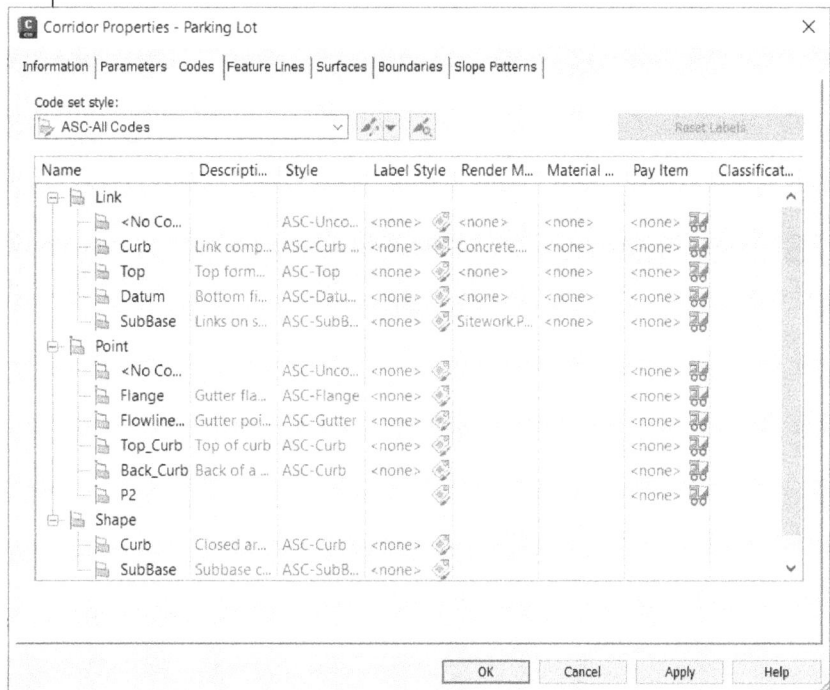

Figure 5–24

Feature Lines

Feature lines are named 3D linework that connect marker points (locations assigned point codes) in your assemblies, as shown in Figure 5–25. From any feature line listed in the *Feature Lines* tab, you can export a polyline or extract a linked or unlinked feature line (such as for grading purposes).

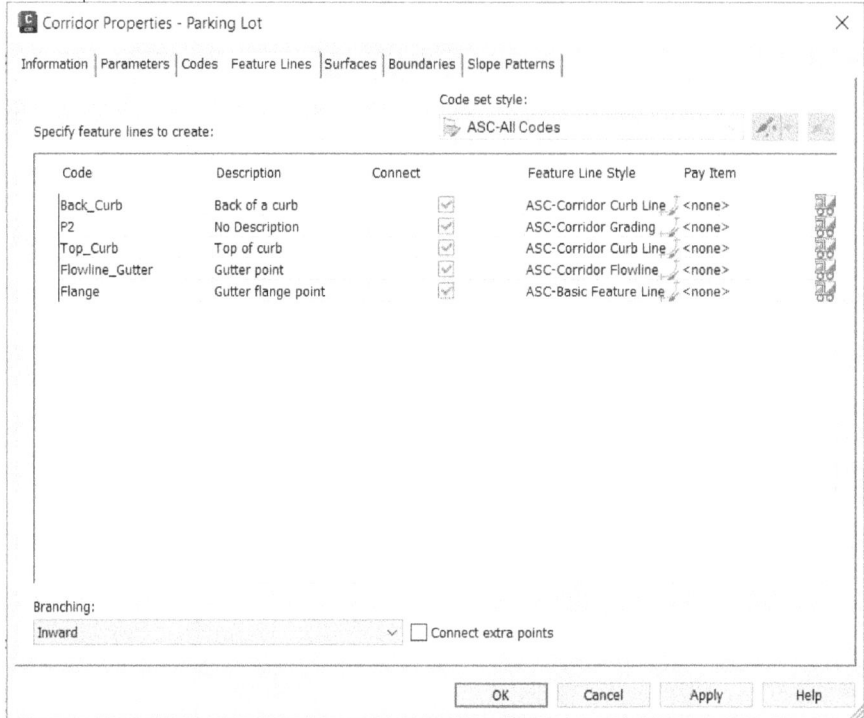

Figure 5–25

Slope Patterns

Slope patterns can be used to indicate whether an area of side slope is a cut or fill. The *Slope Patterns* tab is shown in Figure 5–26.

Figure 5–26

Corridor Contextual Ribbon

Most of the functions performed in the *Corridors Parameters* tab are also available in the ribbon in the *Corridor* contextual tab> Modify Region panel, as shown in Figure 5–27. For many users, this is the preferred option; they find it more intuitive because they can pick the regions of the corridor in the drawing and view the results.

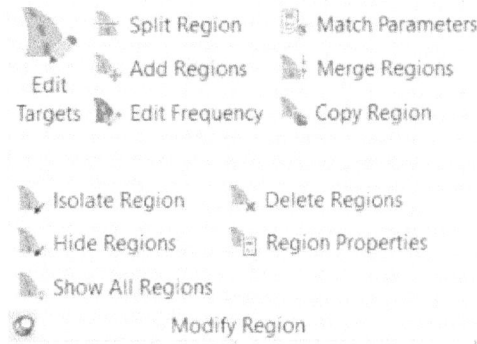

Edit Targets

- Split Region
- Add Regions
- Edit Frequency
- Match Parameters
- Merge Regions
- Copy Region

- Isolate Region
- Hide Regions
- Show All Regions
- Delete Regions
- Region Properties

Modify Region

Figure 5–27

The *Corridor* contextual tab>Modify Corridor panel also has **Corridor Surfaces**, **Code Sets**, **Feature Lines**, and **Slope Patterns**, as shown in Figure 5–28.

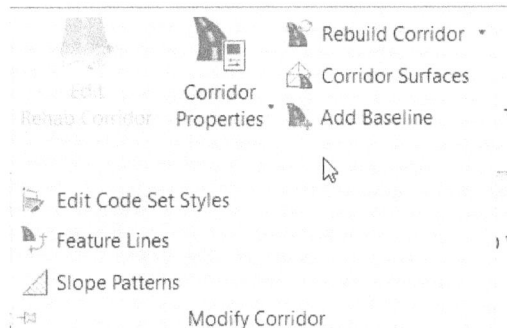

Rebuild Corridor

Corridor Properties

- Rebuild Corridor
- Corridor Surfaces
- Add Baseline

- Edit Code Set Styles
- Feature Lines
- Slope Patterns

Modify Corridor

Figure 5–28

Practice 5b

Create the Corridor

Practice Objectives

* Create a corridor model using previously created feature lines and assemblies.
* Add baselines and regions for the islands using Corridor Parameters.

In this practice, you will use the perimeter feature line to create a corridor for the overall parking lot.

Task 1 - Create a corridor representing the overall parking lot.

1. Continue working with the drawing from the previous practice or open **PKCOR-B.dwg** from the *C:\Civil 3D for Land Dev\Grading\Parking Corridor* folder.

2. In the *Home* tab>Create Design panel, click   (Corridor). Do the following (as shown in Figure 5–29):

    * For the *Name*, type **Parking Lot**.
    * For the *Baseline type*, select **Feature line**.
    * For the *Site*, select **Multi-Family Site**.
    * For the *Feature line*, select **Perimeter-BOC**.
    * For the *Assembly*, select **Parking-Curb-Back**.
    * Verify that the **Set baseline and region parameters** option is *not* selected.

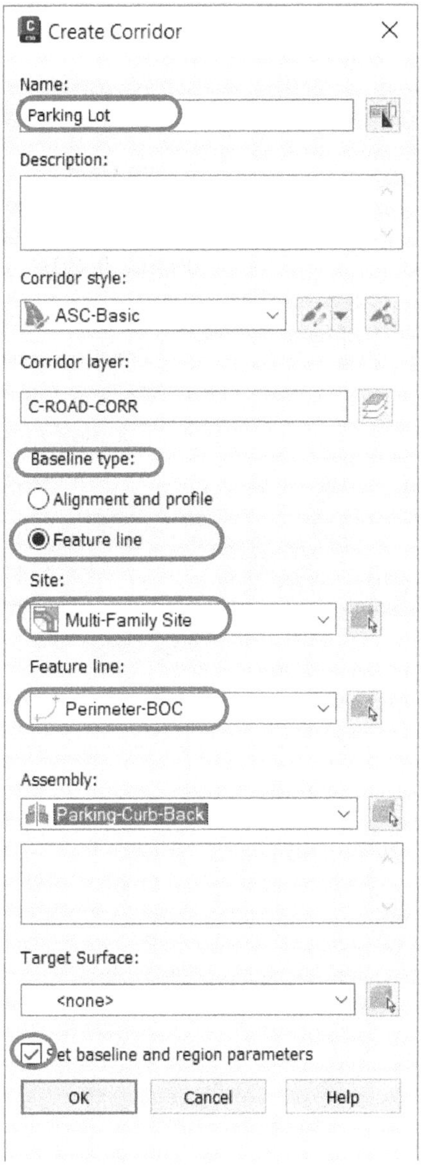

Figure 5–29

For now, ignore the inconsistencies within the corridor. They will be fixed later.

3. Click **OK**. The corridor is built.

4. Save the drawing.

Task 2 - Add islands to the corridor.

1. Select the corridor. In either the right-click menu or the contextual ribbon, select **Corridor Properties**.

2. In the Corridor Properties dialog box, in the *Parameters* tab, click the **Add Baseline** button. Then, in the Create Corridor Baseline dialog box, do the following (as shown in Figure 5–30):

   - For the *Baseline name*, enter **BL - Island-1**.
   - For the *Baseline type*, select **Feature line**.
   - For the *Site*, select **Multi-Family Site**.
   - For the *Feature line*, select **Island-1-BOC**.

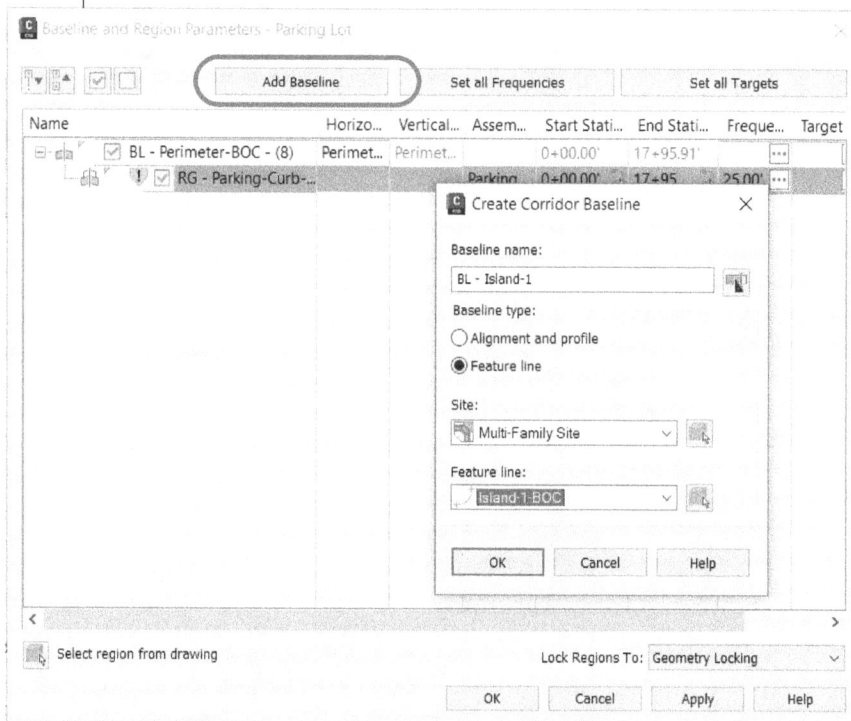

Figure 5–30

3. Click **OK** to close the Create Corridor Baseline dialog box.

4. In the Corridor Properties dialog box, right-click on the newly created baseline to add a region. In the Create Corridor Region dialog box, accept all the defaults as they are (as shown in Figure 5–31) and click **OK**.

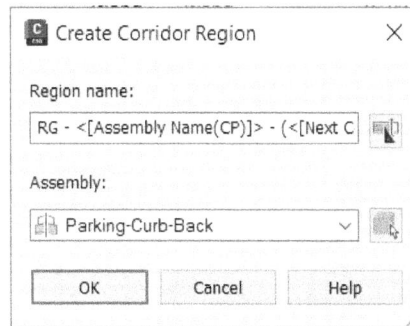

Figure 5–31

5. Click **OK** to close the Corridor Properties dialog box. When the warning box displays, select the **Rebuild the corridor** option, as shown in Figure 5–32.

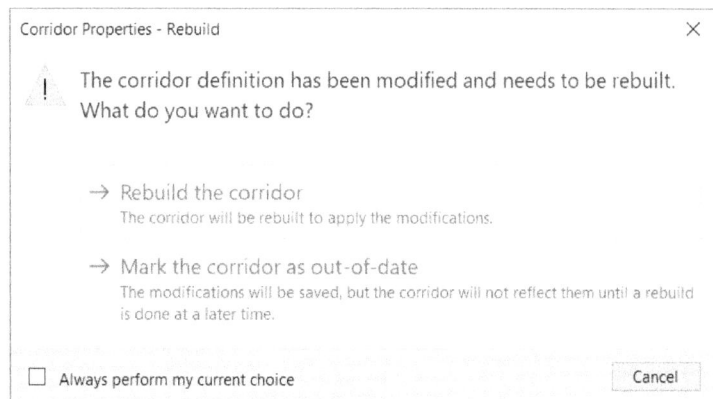

Figure 5–32

For now, ignore the inconsistencies within the corridor. They will be fixed later.

6. Save the drawing.

7. Repeat the same steps as before for the second island by selecting the corridor again. In either the right-click menu or the contextual ribbon, select **Corridor Properties**.

8. In the Corridor Properties dialog box, click the **Add Baseline** button. Then, in the Create Corridor Baseline dialog box, do the following (as shown in Figure 5–33):

- For the *Baseline name*, type **BL - Island-2**.
- For the *Baseline type*, select **Feature line**.
- For the *Site*, leave this blank.
- For the *Feature line*, click the green cube to select the feature line from the drawing.
- Once the elongated feature line is picked in the drawing, the Site and Feature line names will be populated in the Create Corridor Baseline dialog box.

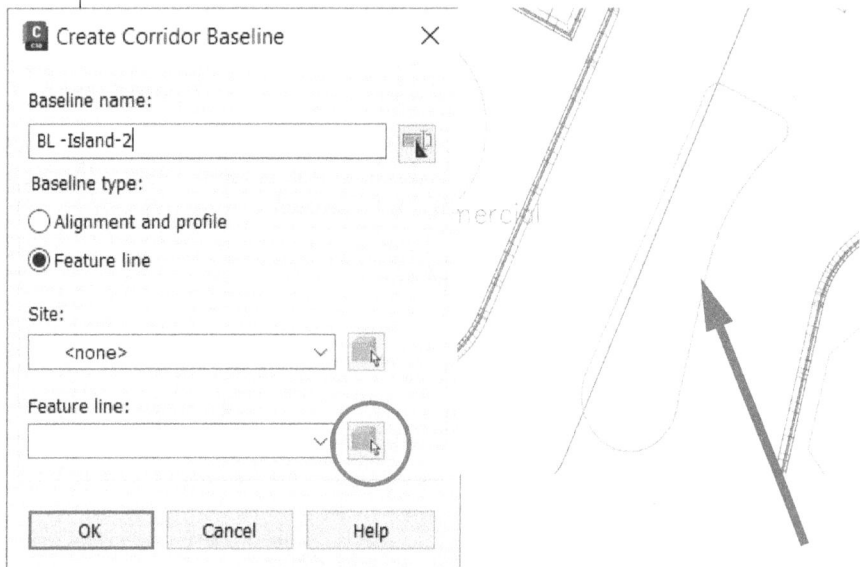

Figure 5–33

9. Click **OK** to close the Create Corridor Baseline dialog box.

10. In the Corridor Properties dialog box, right-click on the newly created Baseline to add a region. In the Create Corridor Baseline dialog box, accept all the defaults as they are and click **OK**.

For now, ignore the inconsistencies within the corridor. They will be fixed later.

11. Click **OK** to close the Corridor Properties dialog box. When the warning box displays, select the **Rebuild the corridor** option.

12. Save the drawing.

5.5 Corridor Editing

In the typical Civil 3D workflow, you create the initial corridor, then edit and refine it. Corridors are perhaps the most complicated of all the Civil 3D (AEC) objects, with a multitude of settings and defaults. These settings are available in the different tabs of the Corridor Properties dialog box.

Corridor Bowties

In situations where there are tight curves or abrupt direction changes (such as corners) in the control line of the corridor, the corridor links can cross each other, resulting in links resembling bowties.

You can edit the feature settings of corridors to automatically clean bowties in corridors, as shown in Figure 5–34.

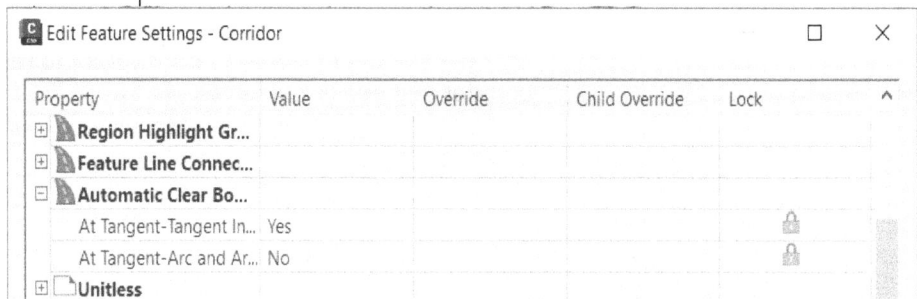

Figure 5–34

But bowties may still persist. In the *Corridor* contextual ribbon, there is a tool to fix such bowties, as shown in Figure 5–35.

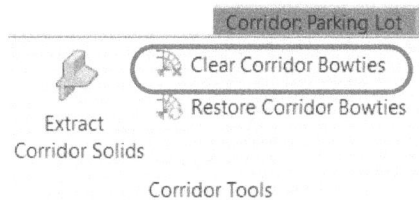

Figure 5–35

How To: Fix Bowties

1. In the *Corridor* contextual tab>Corridor Tools panel, click
   (Clear Corridor Bowties), as shown previously in
   Figure 5–35.
2. You are prompted to select the corridor baseline (either an
   alignment or a feature line). See **A** in Figure 5–36.
3. You are prompted for the starting subentity. Select the same
   baseline as you did previously, just *before* the bowtie. Take
   care that you understand the direction of the corridor and that
   the stationing of the starting subentity is lower than the
   ending subentity (next step). See **B** in Figure 5–36. The
   selected line segment highlights in red.
4. Specify the ending subentity, then select the baseline just
   after the bowtie. See **C** in Figure 5–36.
5. Next you determine where you want the resulting corridor
   feature lines to intersect. See **D** in Figure 5–36.
6. If there are more bowties to be cleared, you can move on to
   the next starting entity, or press <Enter> to rebuild the
   corridor and see the results.

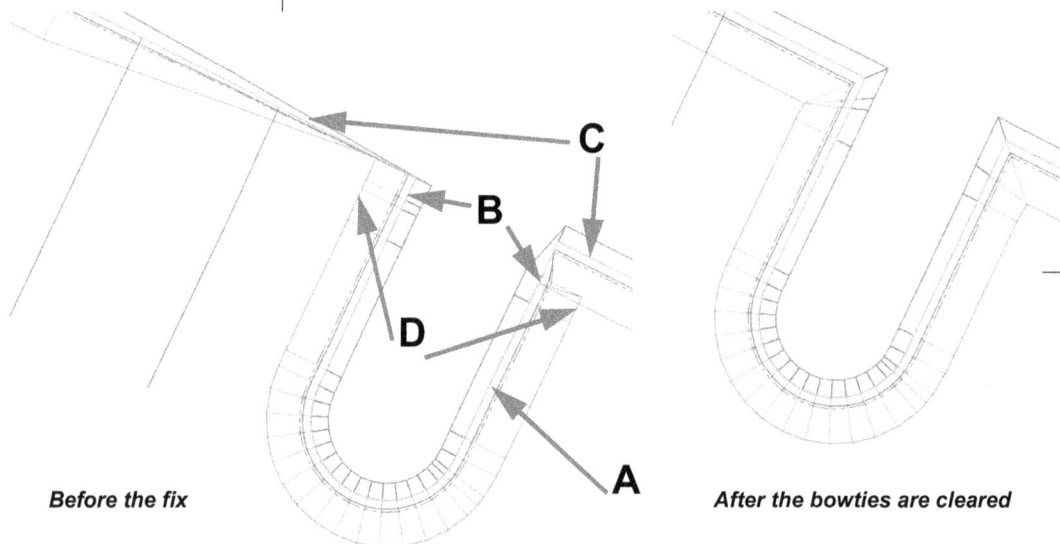

Before the fix   *After the bowties are cleared*

Figure 5–36

Sometimes when the baselines change directions, the cleared
bowties will remain and result in unsatisfactory conditions. For
this reason, you can restore the original bowtie conditions.

It is the adding of an elevation point at the POTENTIAL
intersection point of the flange point of the incoming and
outgoing flange. It is not always perfect, but by adding elevation
points almost all bowties are removed.

How To: Restore Bowties

1. In the *Corridor* contextual tab>Corridor Tools panel, click ▣ (Restore Corridor Bowties), as shown in Figure 5–37.

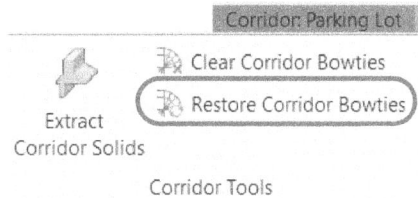

Figure 5–37

2. Since you invoked this command from the contextual corridor ribbon, Civil 3D already knows how many bowties have been cleared and highlights the first one. On the command line, it informs you how many bowties are cleared and the number of the current one.
3. You can choose to restore the current bowtie by simply pressing <Enter>, and it will move on to the next bowtie.
4. You can choose to ignore the bowtie by clicking **Skip** and it will move on to the next bowtie.
5. Once you are done selecting the bowties to be restored, select **Rebuild and restore** at the command line. The command terminates and the selected bowties are restored.
6. You can choose all bowties by clicking **All**. The command terminates and the bowties are restored.

5.6 Reversing Feature Lines

Working with feature lines is similar to working with standard AutoCAD polylines and, like polylines, the direction of feature lines can be reversed. However, it is not the standard AutoCAD **Reverse** command, but a specialized command specific to feature lines, which is accessible through a contextual ribbon.

The direction of the feature line that is the baseline of a corridor will determine the stationing of the corridor as well as the "left" and "right" sides of attached assemblies. When picking objects to create feature lines, it is difficult to know the direction of the picked objects and the resulting feature lines.

How To: Reverse a Feature Line

1. Select the feature line.
2. In the *Feature Line* contextual tab>Modify panel, click

   (Edit Geometry). The Edit Geometry panel displays, as shown in Figure 5–38.

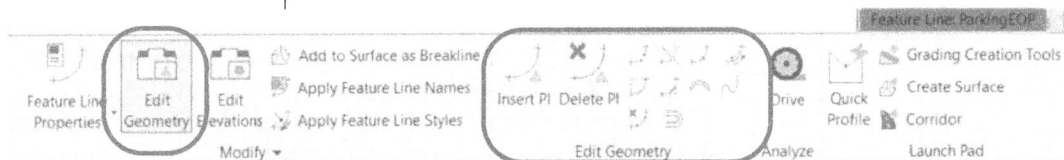

Figure 5–38

3. Click the (Reverse) command.
4. Each time you click the command, the feature line changes direction. When assemblies are attached to the feature line (baseline of the corridor), they will change sides.

Practice 5c | Corridor Editing

Practice Objectives

- Change the frequency of the corridor.
- Clean up the various bowties along the perimeter.
- Reverse the direction of the Island feature lines.

In the previous practice, you created the preliminary corridor. In this practice, you will fine tune the corridor by cleaning up the bowties and modifying some feature lines so the curbs are created correctly.

Task 1 - Changing corridor frequencies.

For the drawings in these exercises, the frequencies were preset through the Edit Command Settings dialog box for the various **CreateCorridor** commands for a satisfactory corridor. You will change them to see the results.

1. Continue working with the drawing from the previous practice or open **PKCOR-C.dwg** from the *C:\Civil 3D for Land Dev\ Grading\Parking Corridor* folder.

2. Select the corridor. In either the right-click menu or the contextual ribbon, select **Corridor Properties**. In the Corridor Properties dialog box, select the **Set all Frequencies** button. In the Frequency to Apply Assemblies dialog box, change the *Horizontal Baseline>Along curves* to **Both** (using the drop-down list), as shown in Figure 5–39.

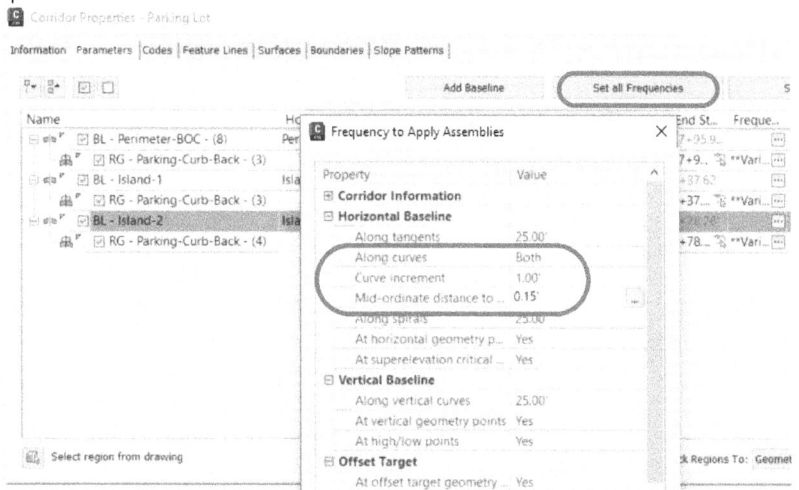

Figure 5–39

3. Change the *Curve increment* to **1.00'** and the *Mid-ordinate distance* to **0.15'**.

4. Click **OK** to close the Frequency to Apply Assemblies dialog box.

Note the increased placement along the curves, causing a smoother curve.

5. Click **OK** to close the Corridor Properties dialog box. When the warning box displays, select the **Rebuild the corridor** option.

6. Save the drawing.

Task 2 - Clearing bowties.

---

1. Select the corridor and using either the right-click menu or the *Corridor* contextual tab>General Tools expanded panel, send the corridor to the back. This will simplify picking the corridor baseline when clearing bowties.

2. In the *View* tab>Views panel, select **Problem Area** to view where some bowties might have occurred.

3. In the *Corridor* contextual tab>Corridor Tools panel, click

    ⚠ (Clear Corridor Bowties), as shown in Figure 5–40.

Your corridor and bowties may differ from the figure, depending on how the corridor is built.

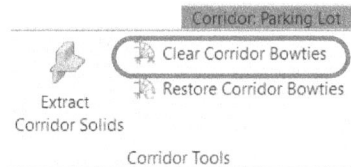

Figure 5–40

4. Select the corridor baseline **A**, as shown in Figure 5–41.

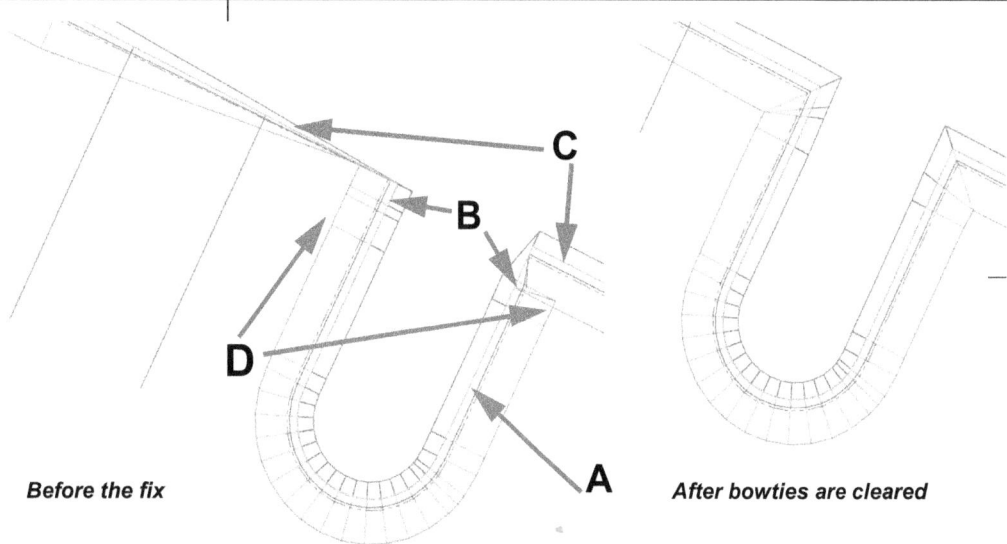

Before the fix

After bowties are cleared

Figure 5–41

5. When prompted to specify the starting subentity, select the same baseline as you did previously, just *before* the bowtie. See **B** in Figure 5–41. The selected line segment highlights in red.

6. When prompted to specify the ending subentity, select the baseline just *after* the bowtie. See **C** in Figure 5–41.

7. Next select the point where the resulting corridor feature lines are to intersect. See **D** in Figure 5–41.

8. At the command line, click **Specify another bowtie** to move on to the next corner. Repeat the same steps.

9. Press <Enter> to rebuild the corridor and study the results.

10. In the *View* tab>Views panel, select **Problem Area 2** to view where other bowties might have occurred.

11. Try to fix these as you did above. Chances are the left one will not clear properly. In the *Corridor* contextual tab>Corridor Tools panel, click (Restore Corridor Bowties), as shown in Figure 5–42.

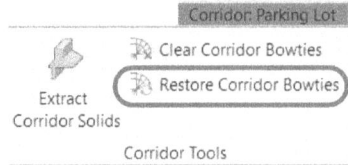

Figure 5–42

12. To move to the errant bowtie, keep selecting **Skip** (on the command line) until it is highlighted. You can pan and zoom to keep up with the bowties, then select **Rebuild and restore** at the command line, as shown in Figure 5–43.

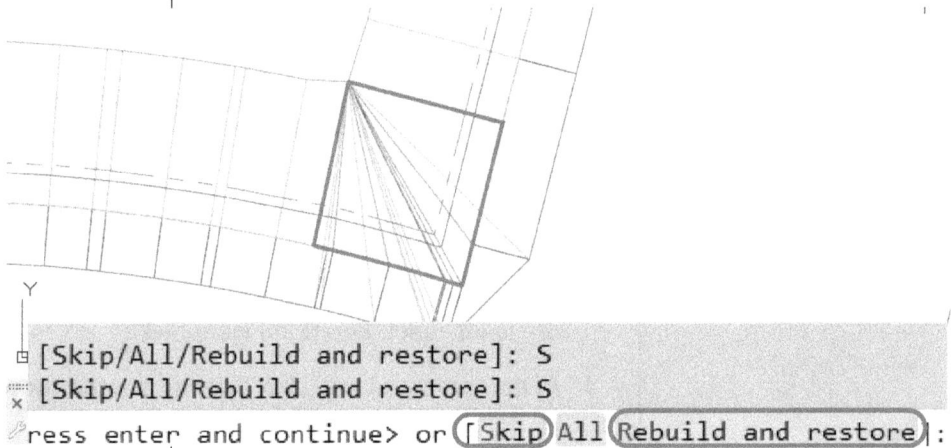

Figure 5–43

13. Select the feature line. The circular grips are *Elevation Points* of the feature line and reveal the problem of why the bowtie will not clear properly. As seen in Figure 5–44, the elevation point just after the intersection is too close to the intersection and needs to be eliminated.

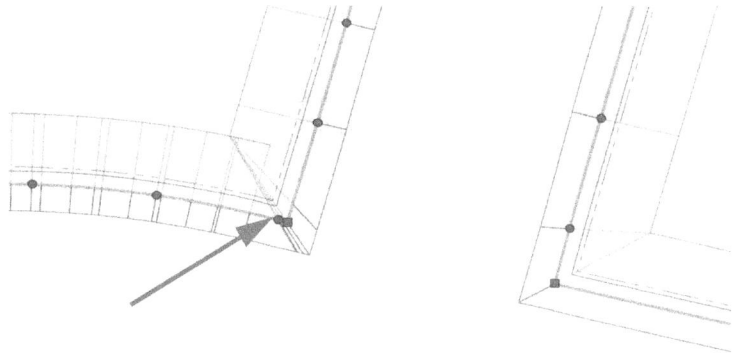

Figure 5–44

14. In the *Feature Line* contextual tab>Modify panel, click
    (Edit Elevations) to display the Edit Elevations panel.

15. In the Edit Elevations panel, click (Delete Elevation
    Point), as shown in Figure 5–45.

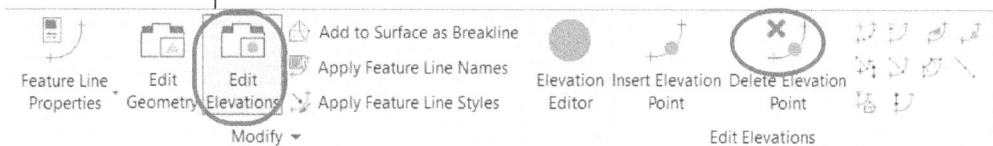

Figure 5–45

16. Select the errant elevation point and press <Enter> twice.
    You will notice that the circular grip has now been eliminated.

17. In the *Prospector* tab, note that the **Parking Lot** corridor is
    marked Out of Date (the yellow warning sign). Right-click on
    the name and select **Rebuild**, as shown in Figure 5–46.

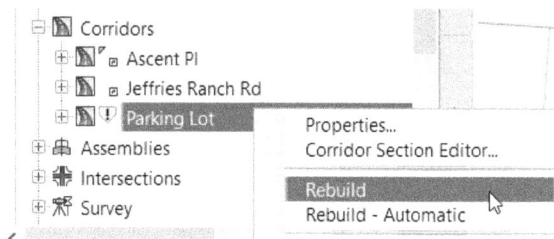

Figure 5–46

18. Click to close the Events Vista if it displays. Press <Esc>
    to end the command.

19. Clear the bowtie as done previously.

20. In the *View* tab>Views panel, select **Problem-Area2**.

21. Select the **Perimeter-BOC** feature line and note the elevation points (circular grips), as shown in Figure 5–47. They are quite sparse.

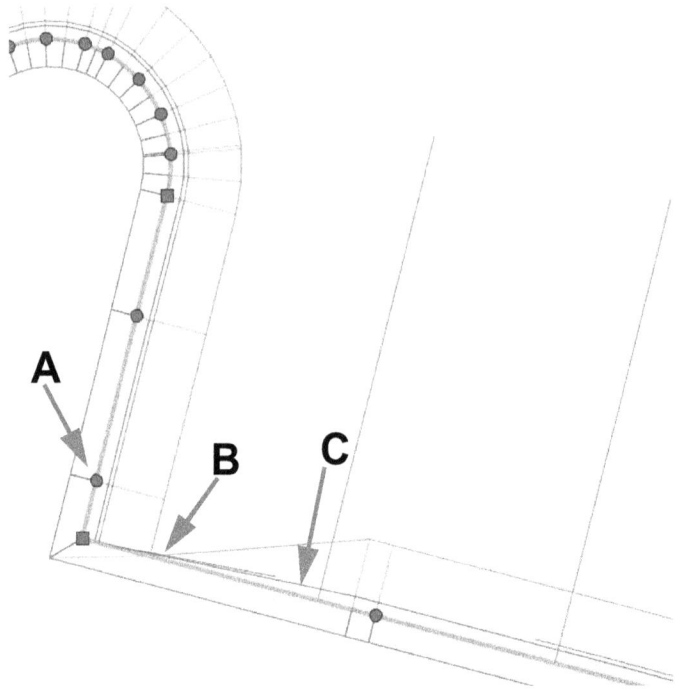

Figure 5–47

- It is the lack of such elevation points at corners that can create the bowties. Often, by adding an elevation point near the overlapping flange, bowties can be removed.

22. Select the elevation point marked **A** in Figure 5–47 above and move it above the intersection of the gutters, as shown in Figure 5–48.

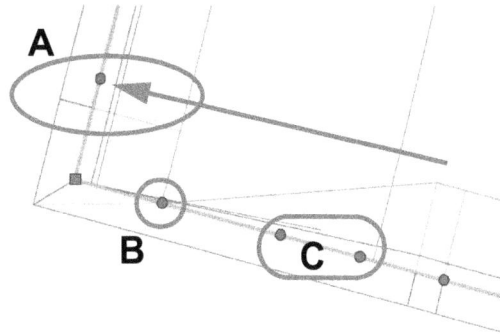

Figure 5–48

23. In the *Feature Line* contextual tab>Edit Elevations panel, click ⊞ (Insert Elevation Point).

24. For the point, select the endpoint of the green EOP (Edge of Pavement) line, marked as **B** in Figure 5–48 above. When prompted for the elevation, accept the default.

25. Add two more elevation points as marked **C** in Figure 5–48 above. When prompted for the elevation, accept the default.

26. Press <Enter> to finish adding elevation points.

27. In the *Prospector* tab, note that the **Parking Lot** corridor may be marked Out of Date (the yellow warning sign). If it is, right-click on the name and select **Rebuild**, as shown in Figure 5–49.

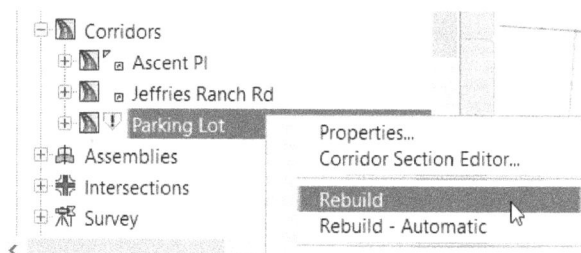

Figure 5–49

28. The bowtie gets resolved, as shown in Figure 5–50.

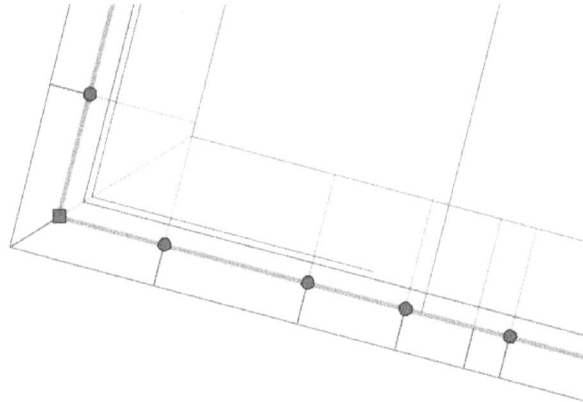

Figure 5–50

29. In the *View* tab>Views panel, select **Parking Entrance** to view another troubling bowtie.

30. Clear the bowtie in the regular manner, but select the point on the outside where the resulting corridor feature lines are to intersect, as shown in Figure 5–51.

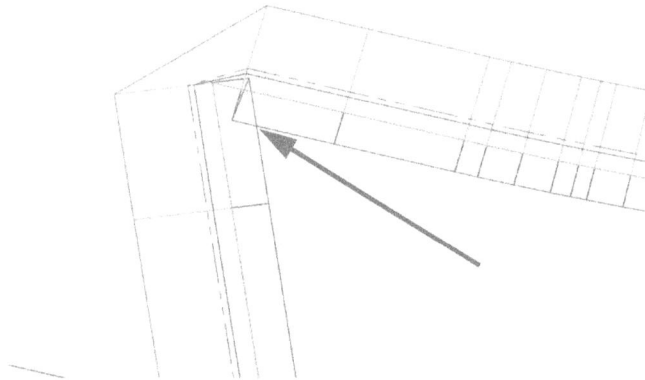

Figure 5–51

31. Continue clearing the rest of the bowties.

32. Save the drawing.

Task 3 - Reversing feature lines.

Careful inspection will reveal that the assemblies in the two island regions are attached to the wrong side (the curbs are facing inward). The feature lines need to be reversed and the corridor updated.

1. Note that the magenta links of the corridor representing the **LinkWidthAndSlope** subassembly, as shown in Figure 5–52, fall on the wrong side in the islands.

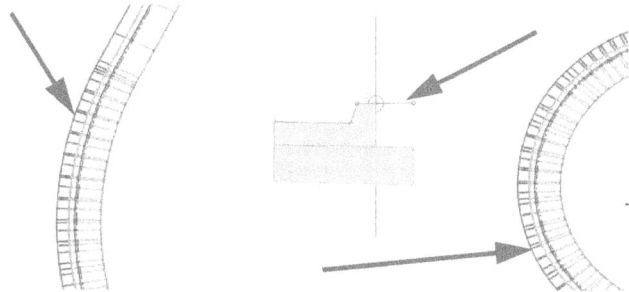

Figure 5–52

2. You need to reverse the island feature lines. Select the first feature line (you need to reverse them one at a time).

3. In the *Feature Line* contextual tab>Modify panel, click

   (Edit Geometry). The Edit Geometry panel displays, as shown in Figure 5–53.

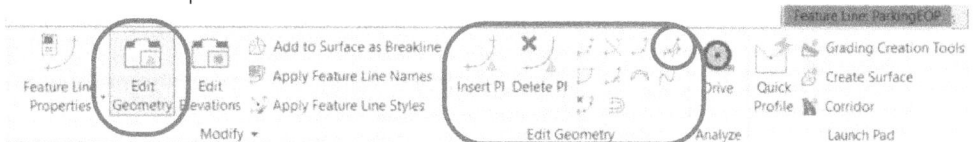

Figure 5–53

4. Click the (Reverse) command. The assemblies swap sides but are not yet connected (until the corridor is rebuilt).

5. Press <Esc> to clear the first feature line, then repeat the procedure for the other island feature line.

6. As before, rebuild the Parking Lot corridor.

7. Click to close the Events Vista if it displays. Press <Esc> to end the command.

8. Save the drawing.

5.7 Corridor Surfaces

The *Surfaces* tab in the Corridor Properties dialog box enables you to build the proposed surfaces based on corridor geometry. You can create these surfaces from corridor links or from feature lines based on marker points (point codes). As the corridor changes, its surfaces automatically update.

The two most common types of corridor surfaces are **top** and **datum** surfaces.

- **Top surfaces** follow the uppermost geometry of the corridor. These are useful for many purposes, such as in the display of finished ground contours or as a way of determining rim elevations of proposed utility structures.

- **Datum surfaces** generally follow the bottommost corridor geometry, where the corridor and the existing surface meet. These can be used in both Surface-to-Surface volume calculations and Section-based Earthworks calculations to determine site cut and fill totals (when compared to existing ground).

Other surfaces may be created and assigned materials for rendering purposes. Rendering can be done in Civil 3D; however, better results are achieved when using rendering-specific programs like Autodesk® 3DS Max®, Autodesk® Navisworks® , etc.

- **Corridor surfaces:** As with all Autodesk Civil 3D surfaces, these cannot contain vertical elements. Include slight offsets so that vertical curbing and similar geometry are not absolutely vertical.

Overhang Correction

In some configurations, Autodesk Civil 3D assemblies might have top or datum points or links in locations that might lead to incorrect surfaces, such as the datum surface represented by the heavy line in Figure 5–54.

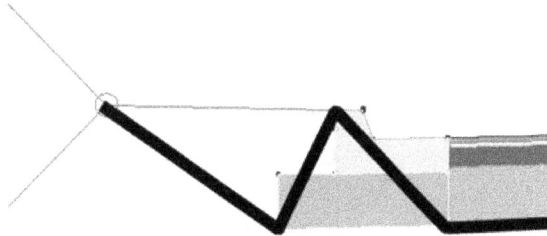

Figure 5–54

In these cases, the **Overhang Correction** option forces these surfaces to follow either the top or bottom of the corridor geometry, as shown in Figure 5–55. This setting is typically only required for top and datum surfaces.

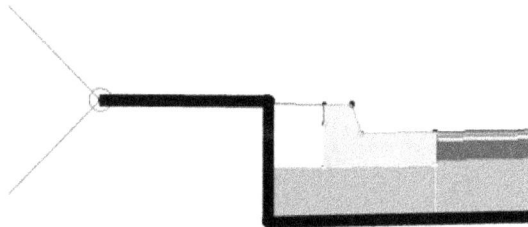

Figure 5–55

Surface Boundaries

Corridor surfaces, as with all Autodesk Civil 3D surfaces, often benefit from a boundary to remove unwanted interpolation between points. The *Boundaries* tab in the Corridor Surfaces dialog box enables you to add these boundaries in a couple of ways: by selecting a closed polyline or by interactively tracing the boundary using a jig.

The best option for top and datum surfaces is often to *automatically* add a boundary that follows the outermost edge on both sides. This can be done using the **Create Boundary from Corridor Extents** command.

For rendering specific surfaces (such as Asphalt, Concrete, etc.), you need to either trace the boundary or pick a polyline representing the boundary.

Practice 5d

Adding Surfaces and Boundaries

Practice Objectives

- Adding the top surface to the corridor.
- Extracting a feature line from the corridor.
- Add a boundary to the corridor surface.

In this practice, you will create the finished parking surface from the corridor and apply a boundary.

Task 1 - Creating the top surface of the corridor.

1. Continue working with the drawing from the previous practice or open **PKCOR-D.dwg** from the *C:\Civil 3D for Land Dev\Grading\Parking Corridor* folder.

2. Select the corridor. In either the right-click menu or the contextual ribbon, select **Corridor Properties**.

3. In the Corridor Properties dialog box, select the *Surfaces* tab.

4. Click (Create a Corridor Surface). In the Corridor Surfaces dialog box, do the following, as shown in Figure 5–56:

   - Name it **Parking Lot Surface - TOP**.
   - Set *Overhang Correction* to **Top Links**.
   - Change *Data type* to **Feature Lines**.
   - In the *Specify code* section, select **Back_Curb** and click
     (Add Surface Item).
   - Repeat for the **Flange, Flowline_Gutter**, and **Top_Curb**, one by one.
   - Click **OK**.

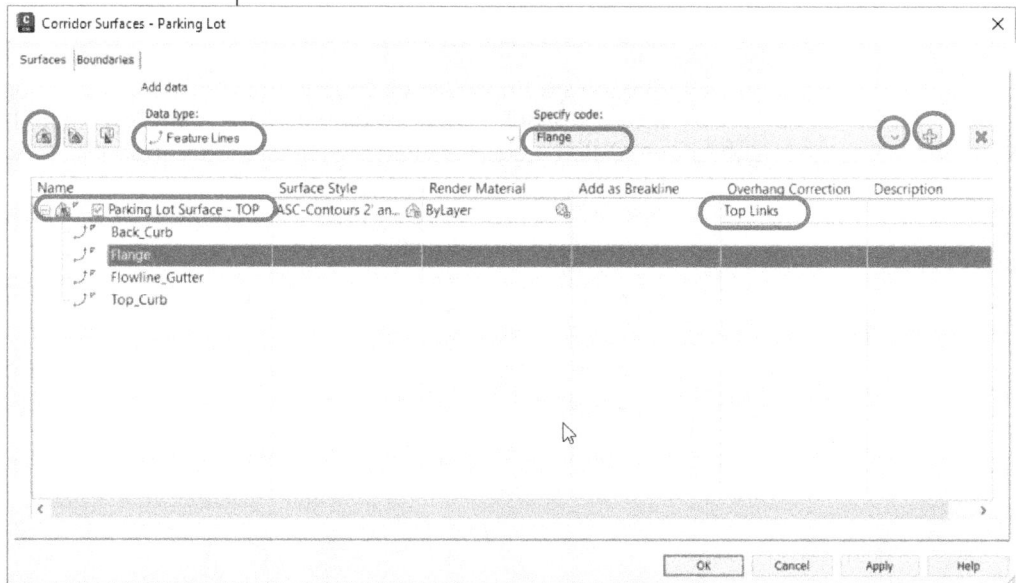

Figure 5–56

5. Click **OK** to close the Corridor Properties dialog box. When the warning box displays, select the **Rebuild the corridor** option.

6. The top surface is built, as shown in Figure 5–57.

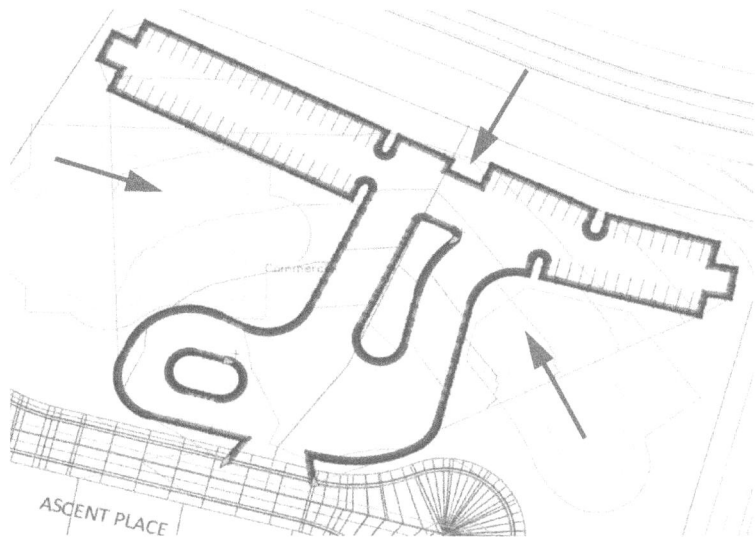

Figure 5–57

7. Save the drawing.

Task 2 - Extract corridor feature line.

The top surface expands beyond the parking lot and triangulates across the outer concave curves of the corridor. A boundary needs to be added to trim the surface back. In order to create the boundary, you will extract a feature line from the corridor and convert it to a closed polyline, which then can be chosen as the boundary of the surface.

1. Select the corridor. In the contextual ribbon>Launch Pad panel (far right), select ![icon] (Feature Lines from Corridor), as shown in Figure 5–58.

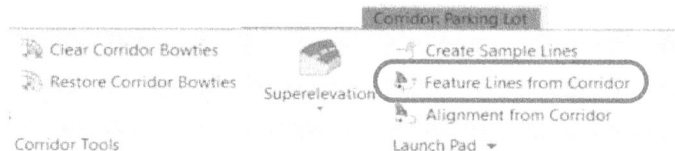

Figure 5–58

2. Hover over the outer edge of the corridor until you see the tooltip displaying **P2** and the outer edge highlights in red, as shown in Figure 5–59.

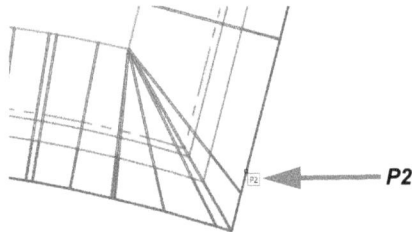

Figure 5–59

3. In the Extract Corridor Feature Lines dialog box, click the **Settings...** button in the upper-right corner.

4. In the Extract Corridor Feature Line Settings dialog box, do the following, as shown in Figure 5–60:

   • Clear the *Dynamic link to corridor* checkbox.
   • Clear the *Apply Smoothing* checkbox.
   • Check the *Name* checkbox and name it **FL-Outer Limits**.
   • Click **OK** to close the Extract Corridor Feature Line Settings dialog box.

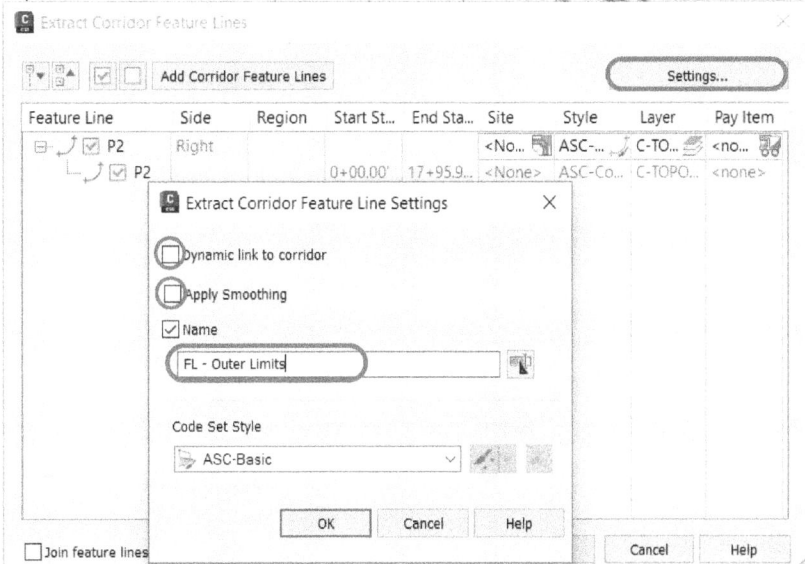

Figure 5–60

5. In the Extract Corridor Feature Lines dialog box, click **Extract**.

Since you are going to explode the feature line, there is no need to name it or change any of the settings.

6. Invoke the AutoCAD Explode command (type **X** at the command line and press <Enter>) and select the extracted feature line. It becomes an AutoCAD 3D polyline.

7. Select the 3D polyline and, in the AutoCAD Properties palette, close the polyline (as shown in Figure 5–61).

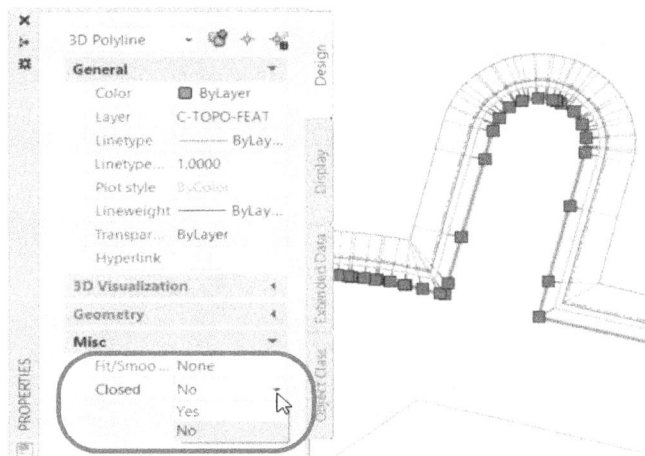

Figure 5–61

8. Save the drawing.

Task 3 - Create the corridor surface boundary.

1. Select the corridor. In either the right-click menu or the contextual ribbon, select **Corridor Properties**.

2. In the Corridor Properties dialog box, select the *Boundaries* tab.

3. Right-click on **Parking Lot Surface - TOP** and select **Add From Polygon...**, as shown in Figure 5–62.

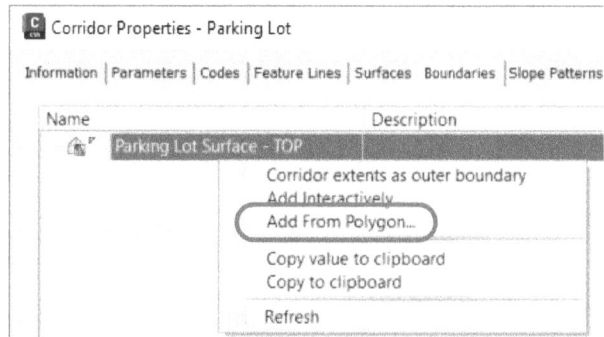

Figure 5–62

4. Select the 3D polyline from the previous task.

5. Click **OK** to close the Corridor Properties dialog box. When the warning box displays, select the **Rebuild the corridor** option.

6. Save the drawing. (Before opening the Object Viewer in the next step, it is always prudent to save the drawing.)

7. Select the **Parking Lot Surface - TOP** surface (select one of its contour lines).

8. In the *Surface* contextual tab, click ▣ (Object Viewer). Set the view direction to **SW Isometric** and the style to **Conceptual**. Note the hole in the surface, as shown in Figure 5–63.

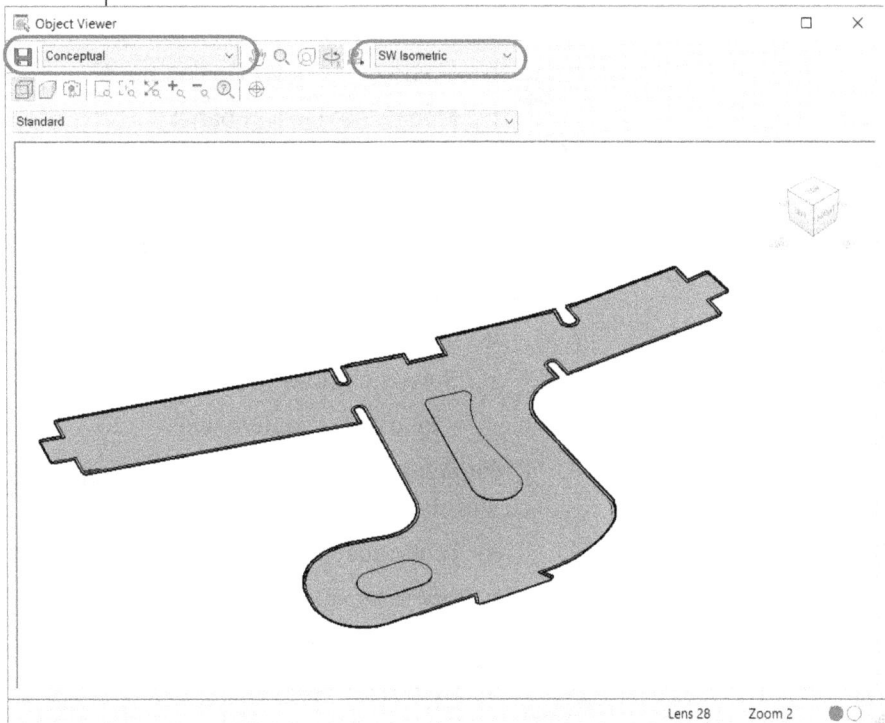

Figure 5–63

9. Press <Esc> twice to close the Object Viewer and release the selection.

Chapter Review Questions

1. Where would you find subassemblies to attach to an assembly?

   a. Tool Palettes

   b. *Home* tab>Create Design panel

   c. *Modify* tab>Design panel

   d. *Insert* tab>Block panel

2. Which of the following items must you have before you can create a corridor model? (Select all that apply.)

   a. Assembly

   b. Grading object

   c. Survey database

   d. Alignment or feature line

3. Where would you go to create a surface representing the finished ground of a corridor model?

   a. Toolspace, *Prospector* tab>*Surfaces* collection

   b. *Home* tab>Create Ground Data panel

   c. *Home* tab>Create Design panel

   d. Corridor Properties

4. How do you create a polyline from a corridor line efficiently?

   a. Manually draw it over the corridor.

   b. Use the **Pline Follower**.

   c. Extract a feature line from the corridor and explode it.

   d. Export the corridor to LandXML.

5. Can corridor bowties be restored once they are cleared?

   a. Only by undoing the **Clear Bowtie** command.

   b. No, it will corrupt the corridor.

   c. By using the **Restore Bowtie** command.

   d. By unchecking the cleared bowtie in Corridor Properties.

Command Summary

Button	Command	Location
	Assembly Properties	• **Contextual Ribbon:** *Assembly* tab> Modify Assembly panel • **Command Prompt:** editassemblyproperties
	Clear Bowties	• **Contextual Ribbon:** *Corridor* tab> Corridor Tools panel • **Command Prompt:** ClearCorridorBowTie
	Corridor Properties	• **Contextual Ribbon:** *Corridor* tab> Modify Corridor panel • **Command Prompt:** editcorridorproperties
	Create Corridor	• **Ribbon:** *Home* tab>Create Design panel • **Command Prompt:** createcorridor
	Create Feature Line	• **Ribbon:** *Home* tab>Create Design panel, expand Feature Line drop-down list • **Command Prompt:** DrawFeatureLine
	Create Infill	• **Ribbon:** *Home* tab>Create Design panel, expand Grading drop-down list • **Toolbar:** Grading Creation Tools (*contextual*), expand Create Grading drop-down list
	Delete Elevation Point	• **Ribbon:** *Feature Line* contextual tab> Edit Geometry panel • **Command Prompt:** DeleteElevPoint
	Restore Bowties	• **Contextual Ribbon:** *Corridor* tab> Corridor Tools panel • **Command Prompt:** RestoreCorridorBowTie
	Reverse Feature Line	• **Ribbon:** *Feature Line* contextual tab> Edit Geometry panel • **Command Prompt:** ReverseFeature
	Tool Palettes	• **Ribbon:** *Home* tab>Palettes panel • **Command Prompt:** <Ctrl>+<3>

Pond Design

Grading ponds can be some of the most difficult grading projects. Ponds often require grading one object from another and combining various feature lines to use as a baseline. In this chapter, you will learn more feature line editing tools and work with complex grading groups.

Learning Objectives in This Chapter

- Review what you have already learned about creating feature lines.
- Change the elevations of a feature line using the Elevation Editor panel tools.
- Create feature lines from corridors to take advantage of existing design data.
- Edit feature lines using geometry editing tools, such as break, trim, join, etc.
- Create a grading object from another previously created grading object.
- Calculate pond staging quantities.

6.1 Feature Line Review

There are times when you cannot create a simple grading object. For example, the design criteria required for the pond cross-section shown in Figure 6–1 is too complex for just a grading group.

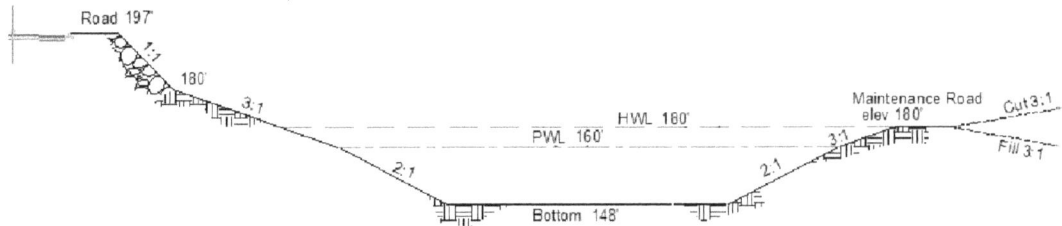

Figure 6–1

Each side of the pond requires different grading criteria:

- At the **South end** of the pond site is a road which has an elevation of 197'. The road is elevated at an average of 20' above the adjacent parcels. As a result, you use a 1:1 slope from the road so that you can create a pond base elevation of 180'.

- At the **North end** of the pond site, a maintenance access road is designed that is elevated 3' above the Permanent Water Level (PWL).

To grade the pond as shown in the cross-section, you must establish a base feature line that uses a common grading criteria. This involves the following:

- Creating a base feature line to the South (1:1 to elev 180').

- Creating a base feature line to the North (3:1 to elev 164').

- Joining the trimmed east and west feature lines to the north and south control feature lines.

- Grading the pond based on this new combined feature line.

Feature Line Contextual Tab

The *Feature Line* contextual tab (shown in Figure 6–2) contains commands that enable you to edit and modify feature lines. These include tools to edit feature line elevations and feature line geometry, such as **Break**, **Trim**, **Join**, and **Fillet** (which creates a true 3D curve).

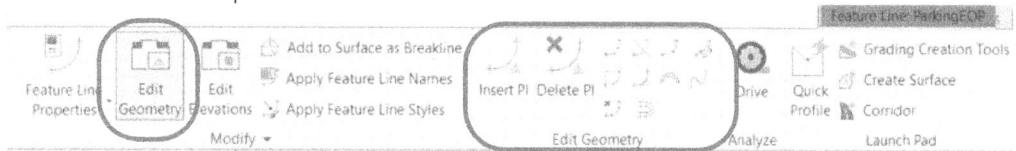

Figure 6–2

The **Create Feature Line** and **Create Feature Lines from Objects** commands are accessed in the *Home* tab>Create Design panel, expanded Feature Line drop-down list, as shown in Figure 6–3.

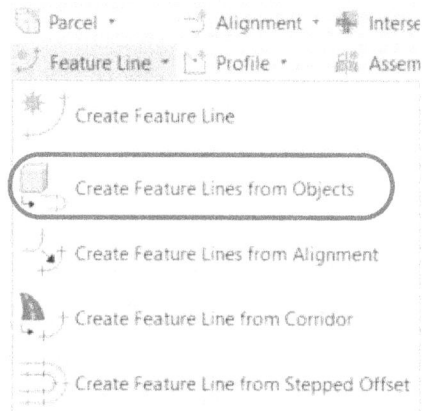

Figure 6–3

These commands can be used to draw feature lines from scratch and to establish an elevation at each vertex. You can also use existing objects to create feature lines and set the elevations of their vertices from surfaces and grading objects.

Practice 6a	# Feature Lines I

Practice Objective

- Create and edit feature lines using various tools.

For the land development drawings in this guide, much of the preliminary work has already been done for the site development.

The completed corridors for Jeffries Ranch Road and Ascent Place, the Ascent Place knuckle and cul-de-sac target alignments, the Mission Avenue alignment, and the Existing-Site surface have been referenced through Data Shortcuts.

In this practice, you will define the perimeter of the pond using two methods of defining a feature line: you will create a feature line from a surface and then create a feature based on design elevations.

Task 1 - Create a feature line from a surface.

Mission Avenue is the northern boundary of the site and an existing subdivision bounds the western side. To establish a design control line for the north and west perimeters of the site, you will create a feature line that extracts elevations from the existing surface.

1. Open **POND-A.dwg** from the *C:\Civil 3D for Land Dev\Working\Pond* folder.

2. Hover over the Data Shortcuts and look at the tooltip that appears, as shown in Figure 6–4. Ensure that your **Data Shortcuts Working Folder** is set to *C:\Civil 3D for Land Dev\Data Shortcuts\Fundamentals* and the **Data Shortcuts Project Folder** to *Ascent-Development*.

   - If not, right-click on Data Shortcuts to set the **Working Folder** to *C:\Civil 3D for Land Dev\Data Shortcuts\Fundamentals* and the **Data Shortcuts Project Folder** to *Ascent-Development*.

If required, review the Setting a Project practice for how to set the working folder and the project folder.

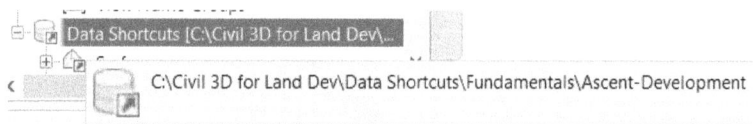

C:\Civil 3D for Land Dev\Data Shortcuts\Fundamentals\Ascent-Development

Figure 6–4

3. In the *View* tab>Views panel, select the preset view **Storm Pond**. A red polyline displays along the north and west property lines, as shown in Figure 6–5.

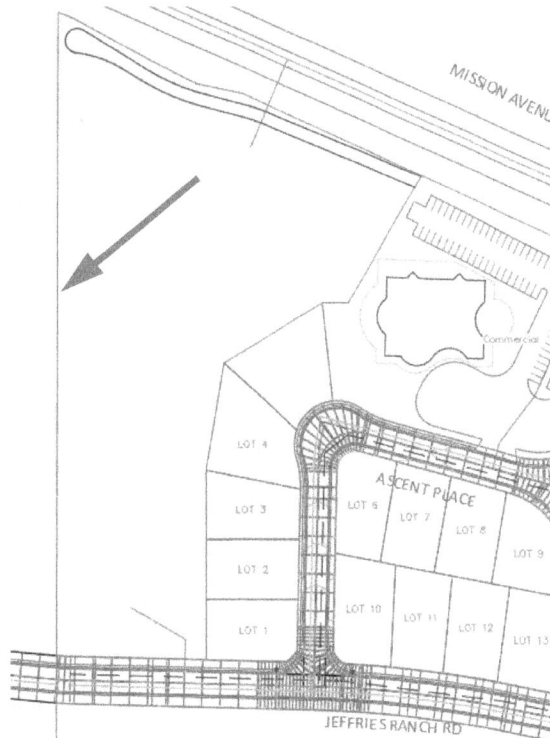

You might need to type **Regen** *in the Command Line to display this polyline.*

Figure 6–5

4. In the *Home* tab>Create Design panel, expand the Feature Line drop-down list and click (Create Feature Lines from Objects).

5. When prompted to *Select the object*, select the red polyline shown above in Figure 6–5. Press <Enter> when done.

6. In the Create Feature Lines dialog box, complete the following, as shown in Figure 6–6:

- For the *Site,* select **Pond Site**
- For the *Name,* type **North-West-Boundary**
- In the *Conversion options* area select the **Erase existing entities**, **Assign elevations**, and **Weed Points** options.
- Accept all of the other defaults and click **OK** when done.

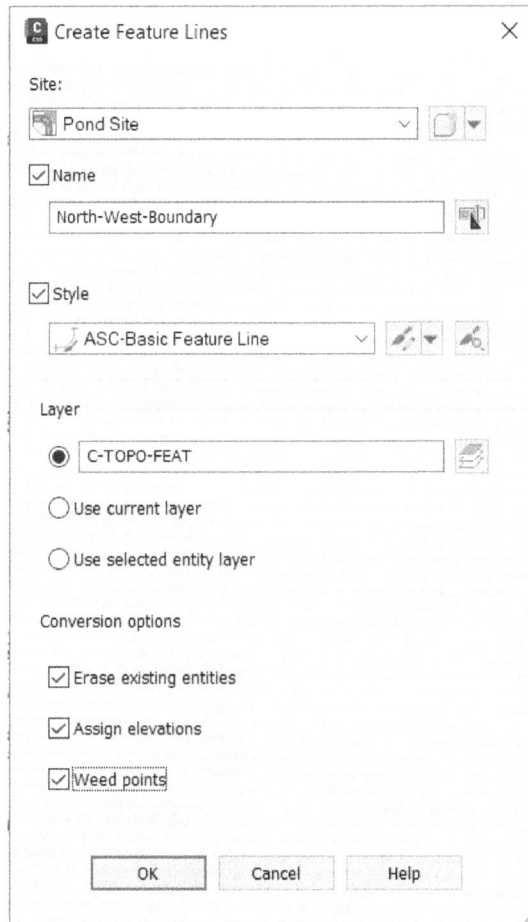

Figure 6–6

7. In the Assign Elevations dialog box, complete the following, as shown in Figure 6–7:

- Select the **From surface** option.
- In the drop-down list, select **Existing-Site**.
- Select the **Insert intermediate grade break points** option.
- Click **OK** to accept the changes and close the dialog box.

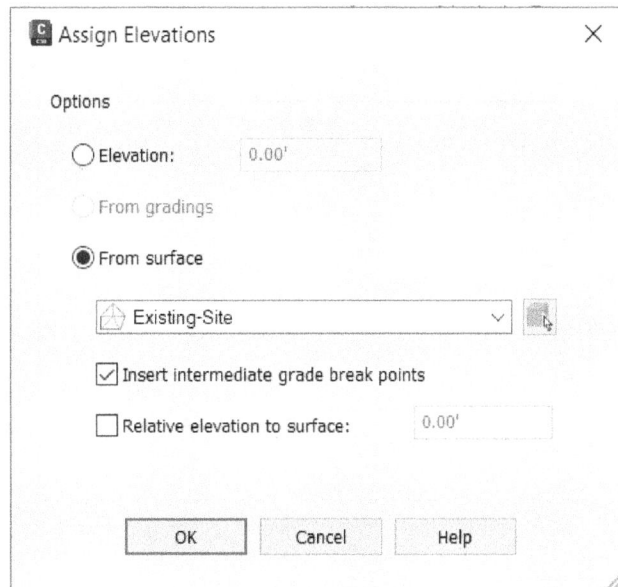

Figure 6–7

8. In the Weed Vertices dialog box, accept the defaults, as shown in Figure 6–8, and click **OK**.

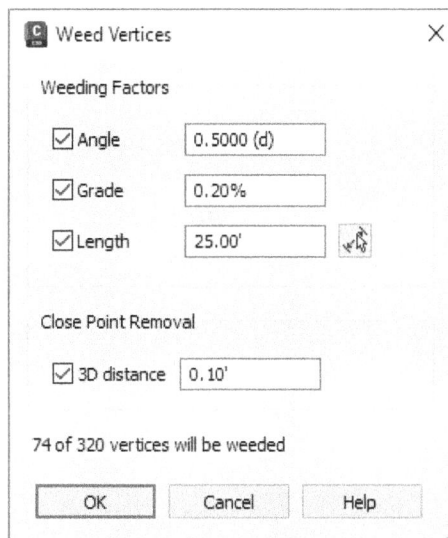

Figure 6–8

9. A feature line has been created for the north and west property lines of the site, with elevations matching the existing ground surface. Save the drawing.

Task 2 - Create a feature based on design elevations.

In this task, you will create a feature line of the east perimeter of the pond. The grades at the east perimeter of the pond are governed by the rear grades of the lots or parcels.

1. Continue working with the drawing from the previous task.

   Based on the street grades and types of lots that are required (Walkout Basements), elevations for the east property line have been roughly calculated. The last point (Pt. 7) ties into the existing ground elevation that is controlled by Mission Avenue, as shown in Figure 6–9.

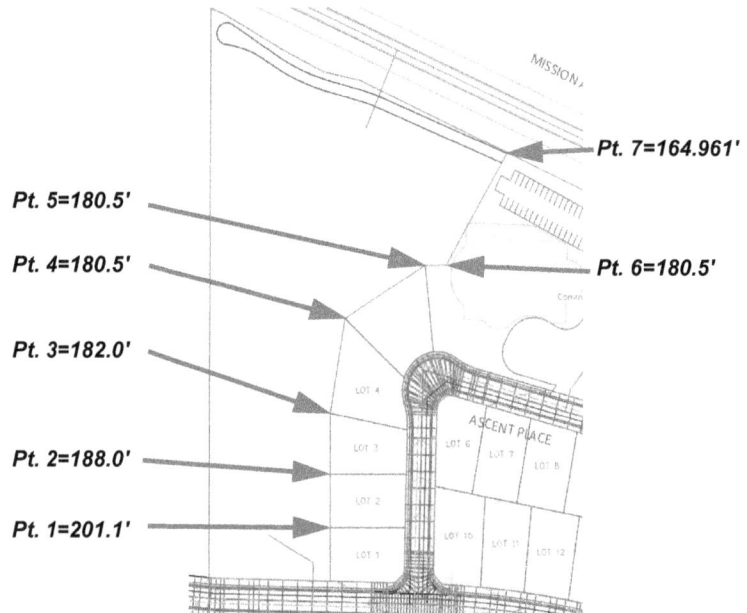

Figure 6–9

2. In the *Home* tab>Create Design panel, expand the Feature Line drop-down list and click ✏ (Create Feature Line).

3. In the Create Feature Lines dialog box, complete the following:

   - Select **Pond Site** for the site and select the option to name it.
   - For the *Name* type **East-Boundary**.
   - Accept all of the other defaults.
   - Click **OK**.

4. When prompted for the feature line points, using the **Endpoint** Osnap, select **Pt. 1**, as shown above in Figure 6–9.

5. When prompted to *Specify elevation or [surface] <0.000>*, type **201.1** and press <Enter>.

6. When prompted for the next point, using the **Endpoint** Osnap, select **Pt. 2**, as shown above in Figure 6–9.

7. You are prompted to *Specify grade or [SLope/Elevation/ Difference/SUrface/Transition] <0.00>*. If the option is not set to accept elevations, type **E** and press <Enter> to set the default as the elevation.

8. Once the option has been set to accept elevations, you are prompted to *Specify elevation or [Grade/SLope/Difference/ SUrface/ Transition] <61.300>*. Type **188.0** and press <Enter>.

9. Continue selecting endpoints and entering elevations for all of the points as shown in Figure 6–9. When finished entering the elevation for the last point, Pt. 7 (**164.961**), press <Enter> to exit the command.

10. Save the drawing.

6.2 Edit Elevations

The Grading Elevation Editor vista (as shown in Figure 6–10) enables you to add, modify, or vary the elevations of a feature line. The feature line data is organized into rows, where one row lists the data for an individual vertex.

Station	Elevation(Actual)	Length	Grade Back	Grade Ahead
0+00.00	201.10'	80.86'		-16.20%
0+80.86	188.00'	171.73'	16.20%	-3.49%
2+52.60	182.00'	145.09'	3.49%	-1.03%
3+97.69	180.50'	157.55'	1.03%	0.00%
5+55.24	180.50'	35.79'	0.00%	0.00%
5+91.03	180.50'	179.76'	0.00%	-7.85%

Figure 6–10

Other elevation editing tools are available on the *Feature Line* contextual tab>Edit Elevations panel. To access this panel, in the *Modify* tab>Design panel, click $\curvearrowleft$ (Feature Line). The *Feature Line* contextual tab displays, click $\boxed{\cdot}$ (Edit Elevations). The Edit Elevations panel displays, as shown in Figure 6–11.

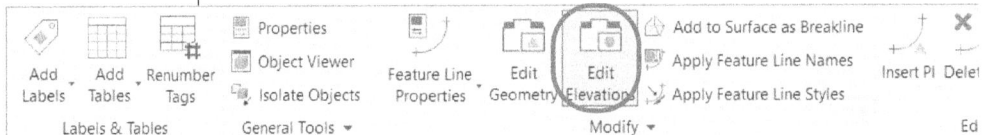

Figure 6–11

Each icon's function is as follows:

Icon	Command	Description
	Elevation Editor	Opens the Elevation Editor vista where you edit the vertex elevations of feature lines, survey figures, and parcel lines.
	Insert Elevation Point	Adds an elevation control to the feature line. Elevation points provide an elevation control without creating a new vertex. These points are Z-controls without X- or Y-components.
	Delete Elevation Point	Vertical grade breaks are anywhere other than horizontal vertices.

	Quick Elevation Edit	Displays elevation values at vertices and elevation points along a feature line or parcel line. Selecting one of these points enables you to edit it in the Command Line.
	Edit Elevations	Edits elevations at vertices along a feature line, parcel line, or 3D polyline as you step through each vertex in the Command Line.
	Set Grade/Slope Between Points	Sets the grade or slope between two points on a feature line, parcel line, or 3D polyline. The elevations between the two selected points are interpolated to maintain the grade/slope/ elevation/elevation difference entered.
	Insert High/Low Elevation Point	Inserts a high or low break point where two grades intersect on a feature line, survey figure, parcel line, or 3D polyline.
	Raise/Lower by Reference	Raises or lowers a feature line, survey figure, parcel line, or 3D polyline a specified grade or slope from a selected COGO point or surface elevation.
	Set Elevation by Reference	Sets a single vertex elevation on a feature line, survey figure, parcel line, or 3D polyline a specified grade or slope from a selected COGO point or surface elevation.
	Adjacent Elevations by Reference	Sets elevations of one feature line, survey figure, parcel line, or 3D polyline based on a grade/ slope/elevation/elevation difference from points on another feature running alongside the first feature.
	Grade Extension by Reference	Extends the grade of one feature line, survey figure, parcel line, or 3D Polyline across a gap to set the elevations of another feature and maintain the same slope.
	Elevations from Surface	Takes the elevations of all vertices from the surface if no vertices are selected. If a vertex is selected, it takes the surface elevation for just that vertex.
	Raise/Lower	Raises or lowers all of the feature line vertices by the elevation entered.

- You can edit the elevations of a feature line or parcel line before or after it becomes part of a grading group.

How To: Insert Elevation Points

1. In the *Feature Line* contextual tab>Modify panel, click
   ⬜ (Edit Elevations).
2. In the Elevation Editor or in the *Feature Line* contextual tab>
   Edit Elevations panel, click ⬜ (Insert Elevation Point).
3. Either pick a point along the feature line or enter a station
   where you want the new elevation point to be located.
4. At the Command Line, type the station and press <Enter>,
   then type the elevation and press <Enter>.
5. In the Grading Elevation Editor vista, the new station should
   be displayed, as shown in Figure 6–12.

Station	Elevation	Length	Grade Ahead	Grade Back
0+00.00	201.100'	13.000'	-100.77%	100.77%
0+13.00	188.000'	67.863'	0.00%	0.00%
0+80.86	188.000'	168.805'	-3.55%	3.55%
2+49.67	182.000'	147.637'	-1.02%	1.02%

Figure 6–12

6.3 Create Feature Lines from Corridors

When corridors are created, the sub-assemblies point codes create feature lines. These feature lines can be used in grading groups but they must be extracted from the corridor for the

Grading command to recognize them. ![icon] (Create Feature Line from Corridor) in the Feature Line drop-down list in the *Home* tab>Create Design panel extracts the feature lines from a corridor model. During the extraction process, you determine whether the new feature line automatically updates if the corridor changes. The **Create dynamic link to the corridor** option in the Create Feature Line from Corridor dialog box creates this dynamic link.

How To: Create a Feature Line from a Corridor

1. In the *Home* tab>Create Design panel, expand the Feature Line drop-down list and click ![icon] (Create Feature Line from Corridor), as shown in Figure 6–13.

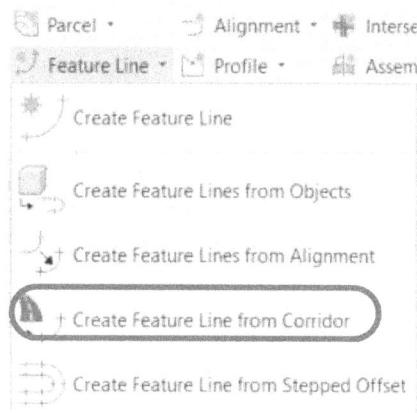

Parcel ▾   Alignment ▾ ✦ Interse
Feature Line ▾ Profile ▾   Assem

　✳ Create Feature Line

　 Create Feature Lines from Objects

　 Create Feature Lines from Alignment

　 Create Feature Line from Corridor

　 Create Feature Line from Stepped Offset

Figure 6–13

2. When prompted, select the corridor that you want to use.

3. When prompted, select the corridor feature line that you want to use, as shown in Figure 6–14.
4. In the Extract Corridor Feature Line dialog box, select a *Site*.
5. Click **Settings** and determine whether you want to have the feature line automatically update or not with the **Create dynamic link to the corridor** option, as shown in Figure 6–14.

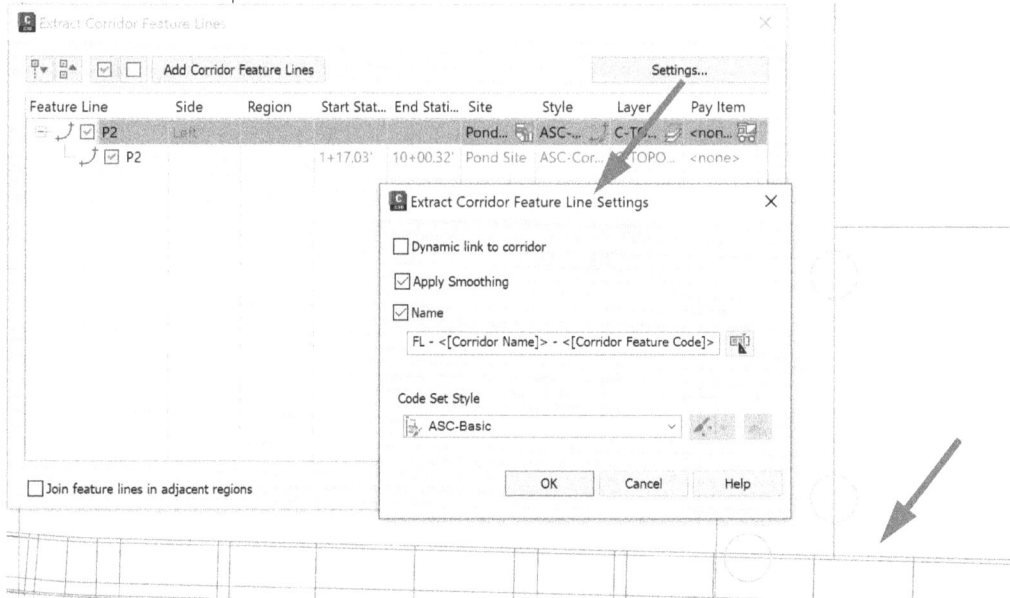

Figure 6–14

It is recommended to name feature lines in complex models for easy identification.

6. If you want to give the feature line a name, select the **Name** option and type a name in the *Name* field.
7. Click **OK** to accept and close the dialog box.
8. A message displays in the Command Line indicating that a feature line has been created. Press <Enter> to exit the **Selection** command.

6.4 Edit Geometry

The Edit Geometry panel (shown in Figure 6–15) enables you to modify feature lines, survey figures, parcel lines, polylines, and 3D polylines. When working with feature lines, you must use these commands to make edits to feature line geometry, rather than the **Polyline Edit** command. To open the Edit Geometry panel, in the *Feature Line* contextual tab>Modify panel, click

🔲 (Edit Geometry).

Figure 6–15

The tool functions are as follows:

Icon	Command	Description
	Insert PI	Adds a new vertex to a feature line, survey figure, parcel line, polyline, or 3D polyline giving you additional horizontal and vertical control.
	Delete PI	Removes a selected vertex from a feature line, survey figure, parcel line, polyline, or 3D polyline.
	Break	Creates a gap or break in a feature line, survey figure, or parcel line. The location selected when picking the object is the first point of the break unless otherwise specified.
	Trim	Removes part of a feature line, survey figure, or parcel line at the specified boundary edge.
	Join	Combines two feature lines, survey figures, parcel lines, polylines, or 3D polylines that fall within the tolerance distance set in the command settings.
	Reverse	Changes the direction of the stationing along a feature line, survey figure, parcel line, polyline, or 3D polyline.
	Edit Curve	Changes the radius of a feature line arc, parcel line arc, or survey figure arc.

	Fillet	Creates a curve between two segments of selected feature line(s), survey figures, parcel lines, or 3D polylines.
	Fit Curve	Places a curve between selected vertices of a feature line, survey figure, parcel line, or 3D polyline while removing vertices between the selected vertices. Useful for converting tessellated lines to true arcs.
	Smooth	Adds multiple arcs to feature lines or survey figures to assist in smoothing tessellated lines.
	Weed	Removes unnecessary vertices along feature lines, polylines, or 3D polylines based on defined angle, grade, length, and 3D distance values.
	Stepped Offset	Creates copies of a selected feature line, survey figure, polyline, or 3D polyline a specified horizontal and vertical distance away from the original object.

Break Feature Lines

Feature lines can be broken into two or more segments in order to have more control over surface elevations. It is common for existing ground surface contours or corridor feature lines to be used in a finish ground grading plan. However, the entire feature line might not be required. It is in these instances that it becomes

necessary to use the feature line ⌐ (Break) or ⌐ (Trim) commands. The **Break** command allows you to break the feature line at selected points, as shown in Figure 6–16.

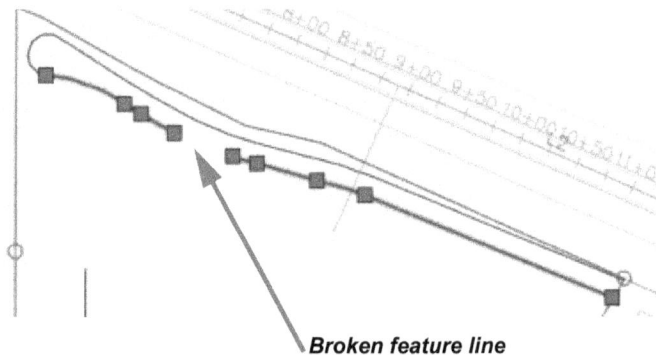

Broken feature line

Figure 6–16

How To: Break a Feature Line

1. In Model Space, select the feature line that needs to be split into two feature lines.
2. In the *Feature Line* contextual tab>Modify panel, click ▦ (Edit Geometry) to display the Edit Geometry panel.

3. In the Edit Geometry panel, click ⤚ (Break), as shown in Figure 6–17.

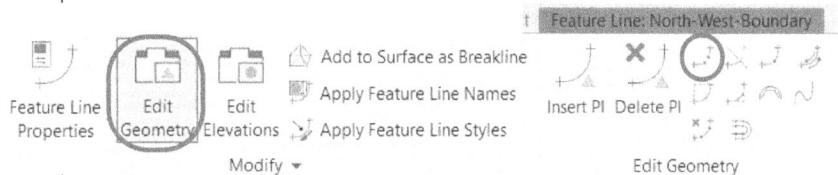

Figure 6–17

4. When prompted to select an object to break, select the feature line at the location where you want to place the first break point.
5. When prompted to select the second break point, click on the line at the second point.
   - If you need to provide a different first point, type **F** and press <Enter>. Click on the feature line to re-select the first break point, and then click on the feature line at the second break point location.

Trim Feature Lines

Feature lines can be trimmed at specified cutting edges. This allows you to ensure that feature lines do not go beyond a specific boundary. The specified boundary becomes the cutting edge, and then the feature line is removed up to the cutting edge, as shown in Figure 6–18.

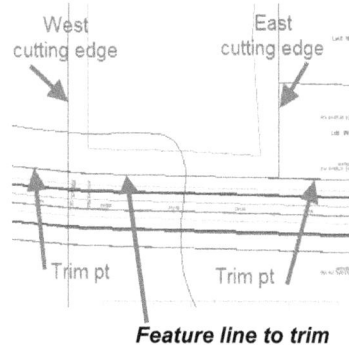

Feature line to trim

Figure 6–18

How To: Trim a Feature Line

1. In Model Space, select the feature line requiring trimming.
2. In the *Feature Line* contextual tab>Modify panel, click
   (Edit Geometry) to display the Edit Geometry panel.

3. In the Edit Geometry panel, click (Trim), as shown in
   Figure 6–19.

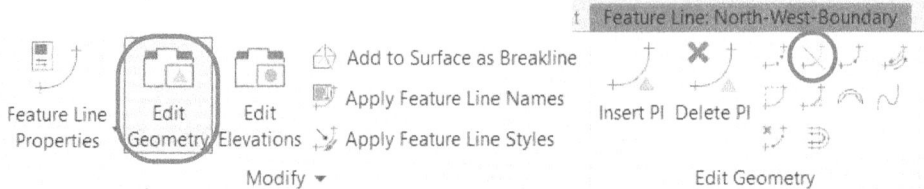

Figure 6–19

4. When prompted to select the cutting edge, select an object to
   trim to and press <Enter>.
5. When prompted to select the object to trim, select the feature
   line to trim on the side you wish to remove from the drawing.

Join Feature Lines

When two feature lines touch each other, end to end, at the
same elevation, you can join them into one feature line, as
shown in Figure 6–20. This is especially useful when you have
used various commands to create the base feature lines, such
as **Create Feature Line from Objects** or **Create Feature Line
from Corridor**.

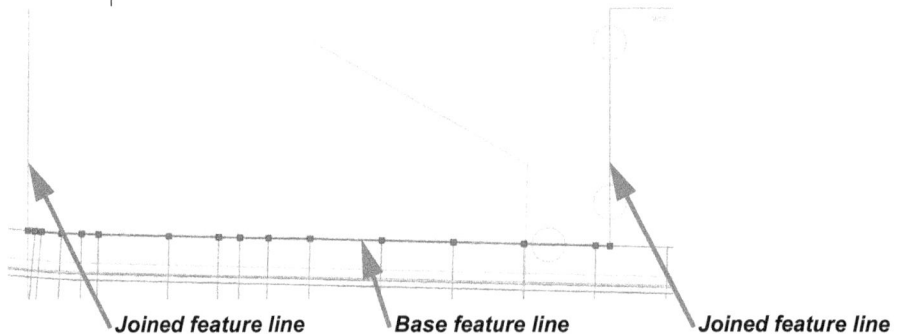

Joined feature line   *Base feature line*   *Joined feature line*

Figure 6–20

How To: Join Feature Lines Together

1. In the *Feature Line* contextual tab>Modify panel, click
   (Edit Geometry) to display the Edit Geometry panel.

2. In the Edit Geometry panel, click (Join), as shown in
   Figure 6–21.

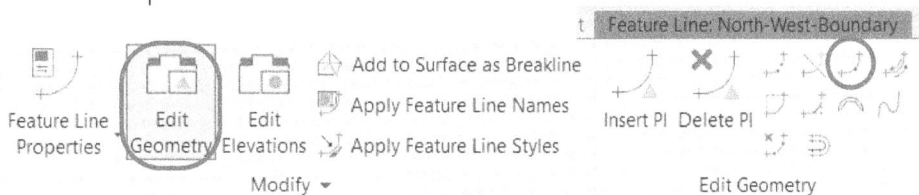

Figure 6–21

3. When prompted, select all the feature lines in the drawing
   that you want to join.
4. Press <Enter> to end the command
5. Press <Esc> to exit the feature line selection.

Hint: Fixing Feature Lines Which Fail to Join

If the (Join) command does not join the selected feature
lines, some grip editing might be required where lines do not
intersect perfectly.

Alternatively, you can change the command settings to set a
tolerance factor. Changing the tolerance factor allows feature
lines with a gap between them to join together as long as the
gap is within the selected tolerance.

Practice 6b

Feature Lines II

Practice Objectives

- Edit feature line elevations by adding additional elevation points at locations other than the vertices.
- Create feature lines from corridors to speed up the creation process and ensure design coordination.

In this practice, you will modify feature line elevations, create a feature line from a corridor, and edit feature line geometry.

Task 1 - Modify feature line elevations.

In the Grading Elevation Editor vista, you can make changes to the feature line design. Due to the grade difference between Jeffries Ranch Rd and the adjacent lot grade, the start of the feature line must be adjusted to display a 1:1 slope.

1. Continue working with the drawing from the previous practice or open **POND-B.dwg** from the *C:\Civil 3D for Land Dev\ Working\Pond* folder.

2. In Model Space, select the East-Boundary feature line you created in the last practice. In the *Feature Line* contextual tab>Modify panel, click 📷 (Edit Elevations) to display the Edit Elevations panel, and then click ⊹ (Insert Elevation Point).

3. When prompted for a point, type **13** and press <Enter> at the Command Line (this is the distance/station along the feature line).

4. When prompted for the *Elevation*, type **188.0'** and press <Enter>.

5. Press <Enter> to finish the command.

6. In the *Feature Line* contextual tab>Edit Elevations panel, click ⬤ (Elevation Editor) to open the vista. The new station should display with a circle icon indicating that it is an elevation point rather than a vertex, as shown in Figure 6–22.

Station	Elevation	Length	Grade Ahead	Grade Back
0+00.00	201.100'	13.000'	-100.77%	100.77%
0+13.00	188.000'	67.863'	0.00%	0.00%
0+80.86	188.000'	168.805'	-3.55%	3.55%
2+49.67	182.000'	147.637'	-1.02%	1.02%

Figure 6–22

7. Save the drawing.

Task 2 - Create a feature line from corridor.

The grades at the south end of the pond are controlled by Jeffries Ranch Rd. In this task, you will extract a feature from the corridor to establish the elevation of the south property line.

1. Continue working with the drawing from the previous task.

2. In the *View* tab>Views panel, select the preset view **Storm Pond**.

3. In the *Home* tab>Layers panel, ensure that the **C-ROAD-CORR** layer is toggled on. Regen the drawing by typing **RE** in the Command Line.

4. In Model Space, select the Jeffries Ranch Rd corridor object, right-click, and select **Display Order>Bring to Front**.

5. In the *Home* tab>Create Design panel, expand the Feature Line drop-down list and click ![icon] (Create Feature Line from Corridor), as shown in Figure 6–23.

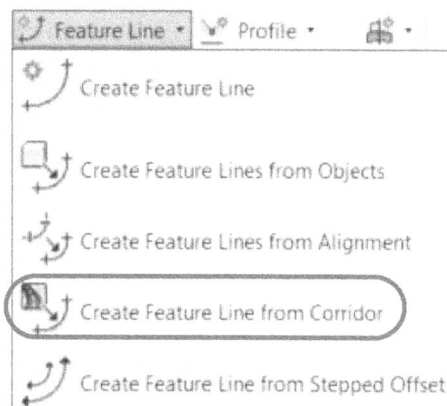

Figure 6–23

If it is difficult to select the corridor feature line, you can toggle on the selection cycling.

6. When prompted to select the corridor, click on Jeffries Ranch Rd.

7. When prompted to select the feature line, hover over the **north edge** line, which highlights in red. A tooltip appears with a **P2** designation, as shown in Figure 6–24. Select that line and press <Enter>.

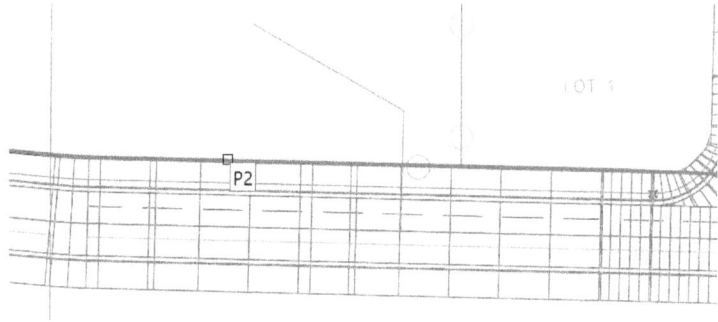

Figure 6–24

8. In the Extract Corridor Feature Line dialog box, complete the following, as shown in Figure 6–25:

   • In the *Site* column, select **Pond Site**.
   • Click **Settings**.
   • In the Extract Corridor Feature Line Settings dialog box, clear the **Dynamic link to the corridor** option, accept the remaining defaults, and click **OK** to close the dialog box.
   • Click **Extract**.

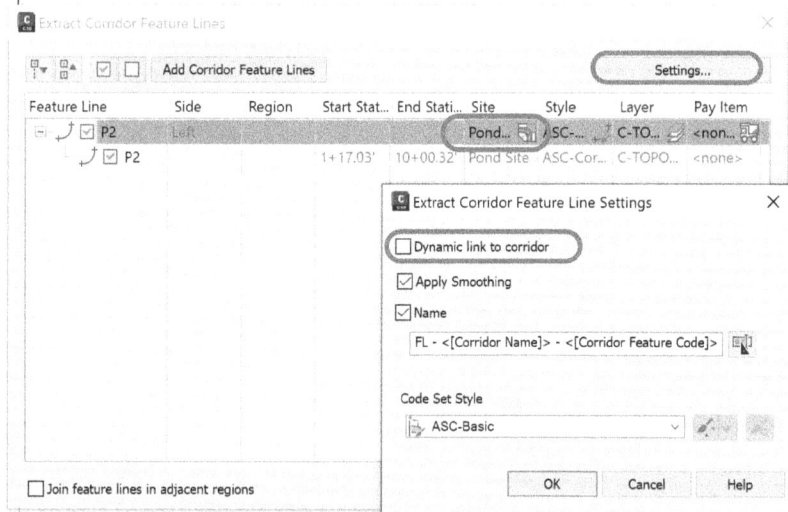

Figure 6–25

A message displays at the Command Line indicating that a feature line from <P2> has been created.

9. Save the drawing.

Task 3 - Edit feature line geometry.

1. Continue working with the drawing from the previous task.

2. In Model Space, zoom in to the southern edge of the pond, then select the newly created feature line, as shown in Figure 6–26. In the *Feature Line* contextual tab>Modify panel, click (Edit Geometry). In the Edit Geometry panel, click (Trim).

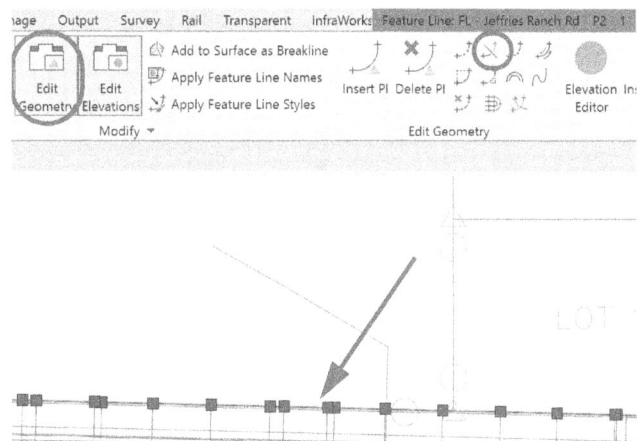

Figure 6–26

3. When prompted to select the cutting edge, select the east and west property lines of the pond and press <Enter> when done.

4. When prompted to select the object to trim, select the feature line at a point outside the pond property lines, west of the west cutting edge and east of the east cutting edge, as shown in Figure 6–27. Press <Enter> when done and press <Esc> to exit the feature object selection.

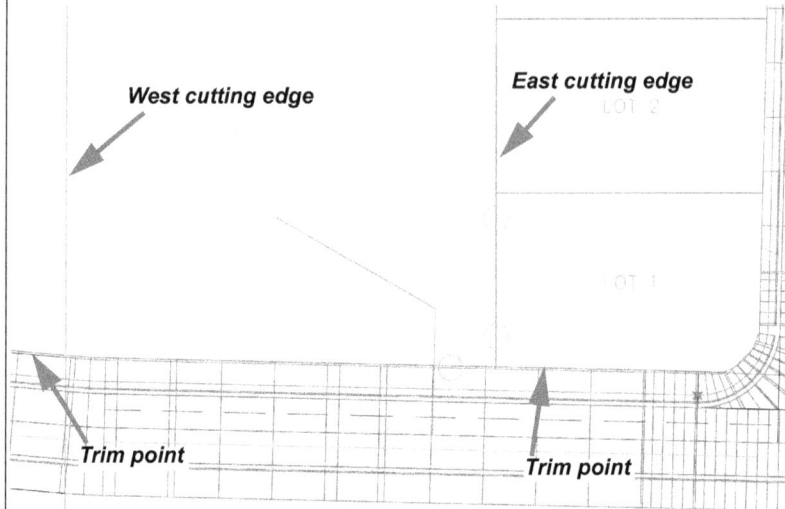

Figure 6–27

A feature line based on the corridor road design has now been created.

5. To ensure it has been properly trimmed, select the feature line once again and note the grips that indicate the extent of the feature line, as shown in Figure 6–28. If the grips extend beyond the green lines, repeat the trimming.

Figure 6–28

6. Press <Esc> to release the selection.

7. In the *View* tab>Views panel, select the preset view **Pond Corner SW** to zoom to the southwest corner of the pond.

8. Select the North-West Boundary feature line, and note by the grips that it extends beyond the Jeffries Ranch Rd corridor. The grips extend beyond the feature line you just trimmed, as shown in Figure 6–29.

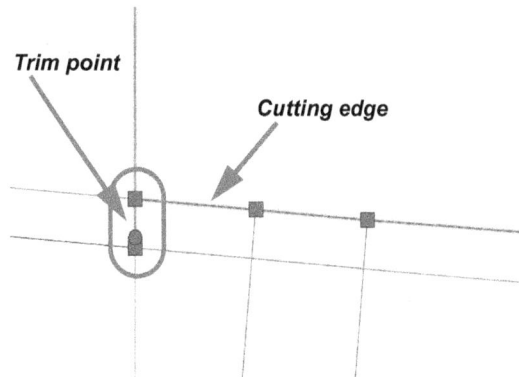

Figure 6–29

9. In the *Feature Line* contextual tab>Modify panel, click

   (Edit Geometry). In the Edit Geometry panel, click

   (Trim), then trim the North-West Boundary feature line as shown above in Figure 6–29.

10. In the *View* tab>Views panel, select the preset view **Pond Corner SE** to zoom to the southeast corner of the pond.

11. Select the East Boundary feature line, and note by the grips that it also extends beyond the Jeffries Ranch Rd corridor, as shown in Figure 6–30.

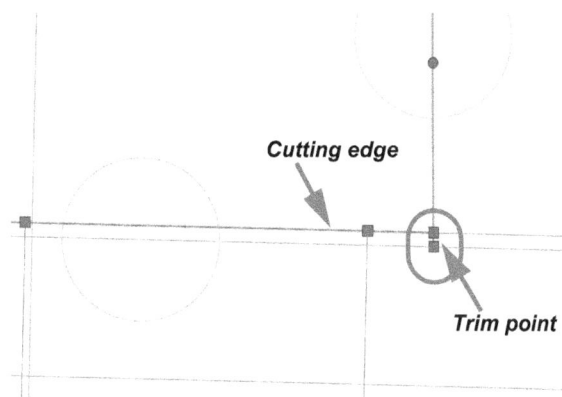

Figure 6–30

12. Repeat the trimming, picking the cutting edge and the trim point as shown above in Figure 6–30.

13. In the *View* tab>Views panel, select the preset view **Pond Edge South** to zoom to the southern edge of the pond.

14. To join the three feature lines, select the North-West Boundary feature line at the west side of the pond.

15. In the *Feature Line* contextual tab>Modify panel, click

    ⬜ (Edit Geometry) to display the Edit Geometry panel, and

    then click ↰ (Join), as shown in Figure 6–31.

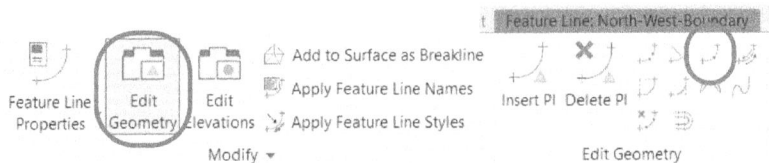

Figure 6–31

If the feature line fails to join any lines in this process, some grip editing might be required where lines do not intersect completely.

16. When prompted, select the feature line to the south and select the feature line to the east. Press <Enter> to end the command and press <Esc> to exit the feature line selection.

17. Save the drawing.

6.5 Creating Complex Grading Groups

An example of grading groups that use one baseline and project specific slopes until they find daylight (called *grading to a surface*) is shown in Figure 6–32.

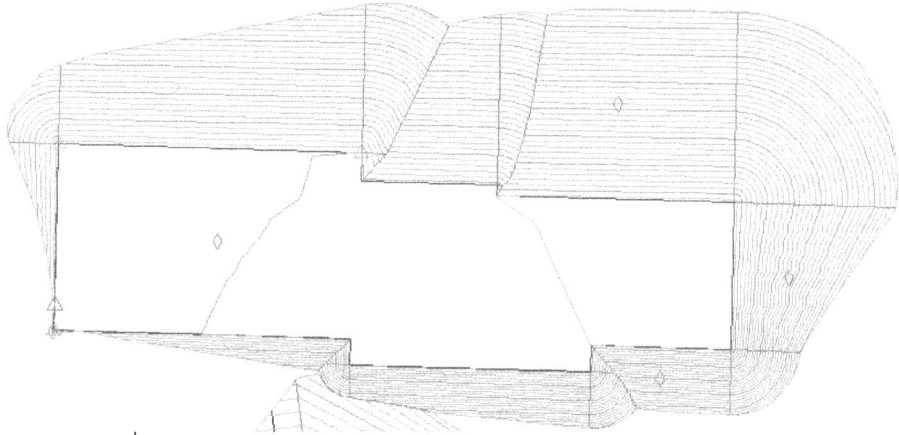

Figure 6–32

Unfortunately, real world grading projects are not always that simple. That is why the Autodesk® Civil 3D® provides a way to grade one grading object from another within the same site. When reviewing the pond grading parameters for the project, note that you need multiple grades for the interior of the pond, a maintenance road running along part of the pond, and then daylight from the maintenance road, as shown in Figure 6–33.

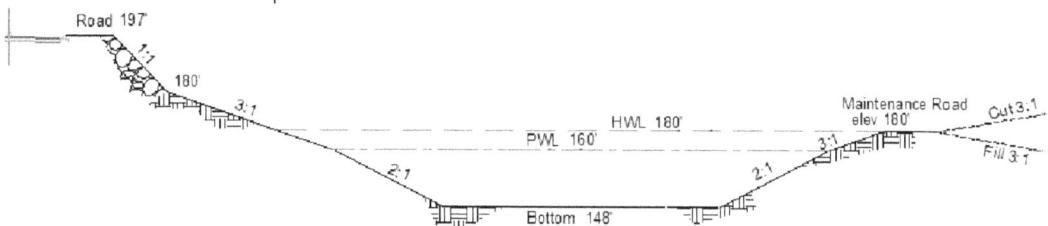

Figure 6–33

It is quite typical that pond grading projects use a minimum of three or four different grading criteria. Four types of grading criteria are available.

Grade to Elevation

When you need to keep a specific grade or slope to a specified elevation, the **Grade to Elevation** criteria is used. This enables you to set the target to be a specific elevation. It is often used in pond grading because the top of the pond needs to be level, as shown in Figure 6–34. Note in the front view that the pond bottom is sloped while the top is level.

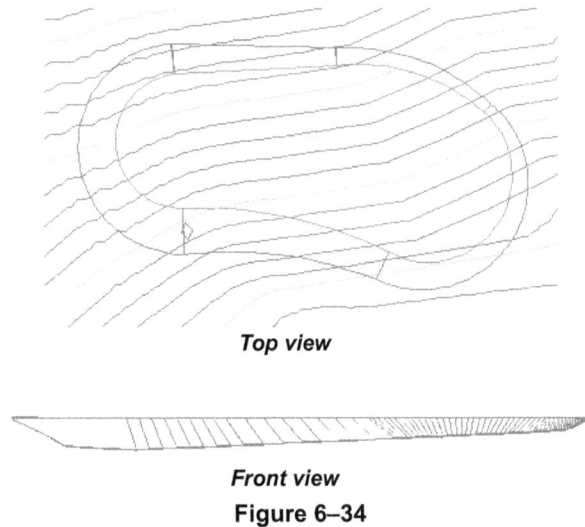

Top view

Front view

Figure 6–34

Grade to Relative Elevation

Sometimes you need to project a grade up or down a specific vertical distance. In this case, you would use the **Grade to Relative Elevation** criteria. Note that in the front view, both the top and bottom have the same slope (as shown in Figure 6–35), unlike the Grade to Elevation in which they had differing slopes.

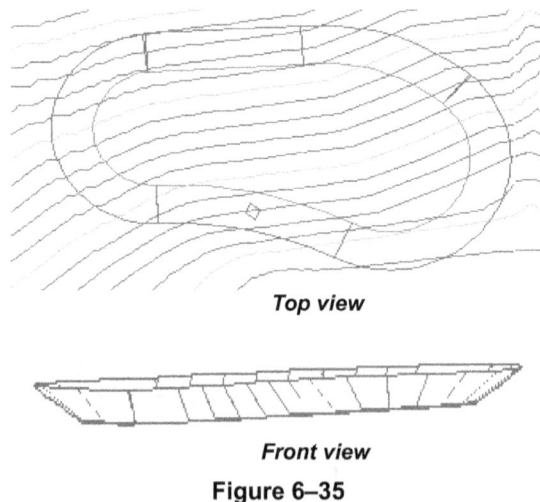

Top view

Front view

Figure 6–35

Grade to Distance

When you need to keep a specific grade or slope for a specified horizontal distance, you can use the **Grade to Distance** criteria. In pond grading, you might need to use this criteria to grade a maintenance road around the perimeter of the pond, as shown in Figure 6–36.

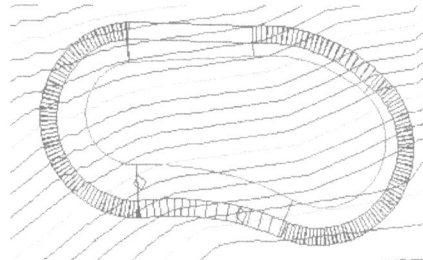

Top view

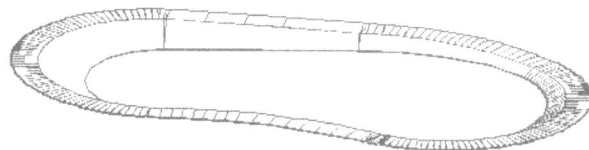

Isometric view

Figure 6–36

Grade to Surface

When you need to keep a specific slope until the projection finds daylight, you can use the **Grade to Surface** criteria. In pond grading, this is sometimes the first grading object that you create if you are starting from the outside and grading in. The pond in Figure 6–37 was graded from the inside out.

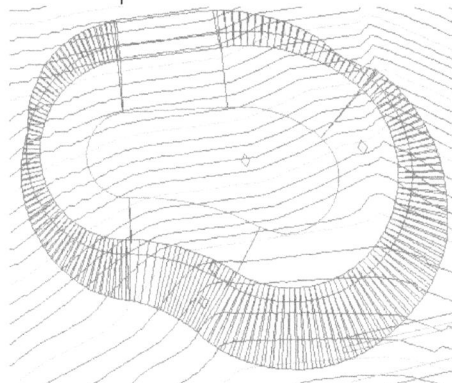

Top view

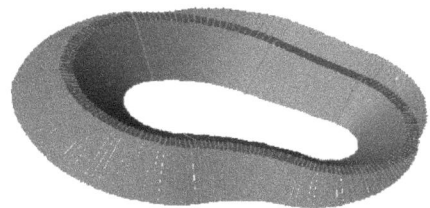

Isometric view

Figure 6–37

Practice 6c | (Optional) Pond Grading - Feature Line (Create Base Line)

Practice Objective

- Create and modify feature lines using grading objects and feature line editing tools.

In this practice, you will establish control feature lines at the north and south ends, as shown in Figure 6–38, and then create the pond outside rim feature line.

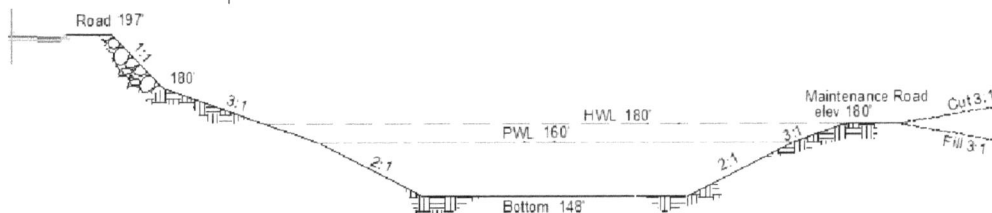

Figure 6–38

Task 1 - Establish control feature lines (south end).

1. Continue working with the drawing from the previous practice or open **POND-C.dwg** from the *C:\Civil 3D for Land Dev\ Working\Pond* folder.

2. In the *View* tab>Views panel, select the preset view **Storm Pond**.

3. In the *Home* tab>Create Design panel, expand the Grading drop-down list and click ![icon] (Grading Creation Tools).

4. In the Grading Creation Tools toolbar, click ![icon] (Set the Grading Group). Select **Pond Site** for the site, as shown in Figure 6–39, and click **OK**.

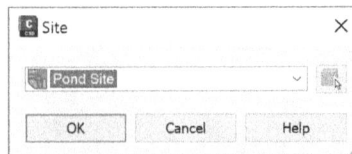

Figure 6–39

You will create a temporary grading object that creates pre-design information.

5. In the Create Grading Group dialog box, for the *Name*, enter **Temp**, as shown in Figure 6–40. Clear the **Automatic surface creation** option and click **OK**.

Figure 6–40

Establish a feature line with a **1:1** slope to an elevation of **180' using the following steps**.

6. In the Grading Creation Tools toolbar, set the *Criteria* as

Grade to Elevation and click [icon] (Create Grading), as shown in Figure 6–41.

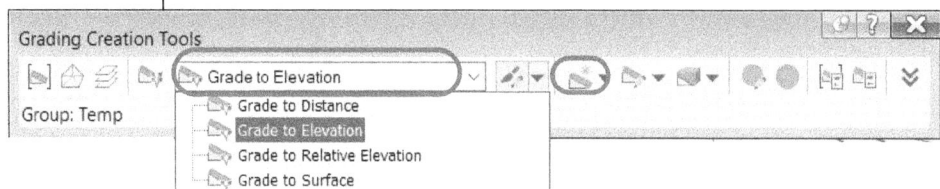

Figure 6–41

7. When prompted to select a feature, select the green pond boundary feature line that defines the perimeter pond site, as shown in Figure 6–42. If prompted to weed the feature line, select **Continue grading without feature line weeding**.

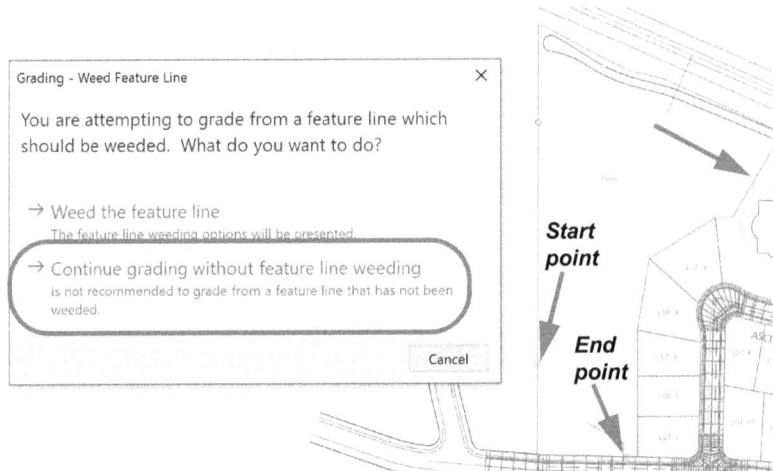

Figure 6–42

8. When prompted for the side to grade, select a point inside of the pond.

9. Select **No** when prompted to *Apply to the entire length*.

10. When prompted for the start point, select the center of the green circle located on the west feature line and press <Enter> to accept <20+09.87'> for the station.

11. When prompted for the end point or length, select the center of the green circle located on the south feature line and press <Enter> to accept <23+77.50'> for the station, as shown in Figure 6–43.

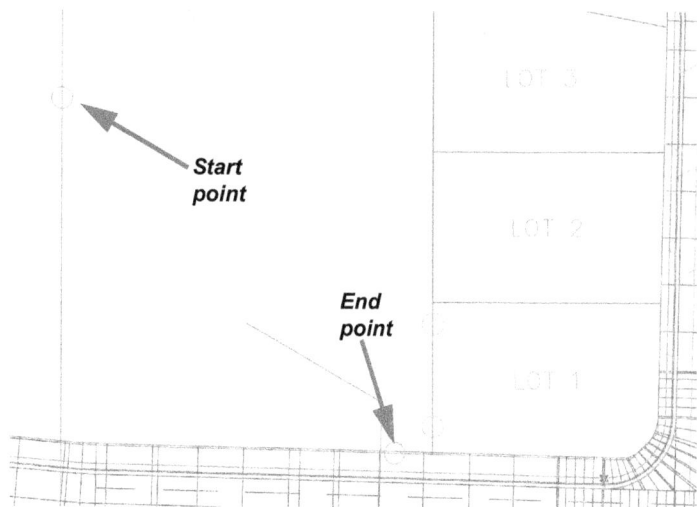

Figure 6–43

12. When prompted for the elevation, type **180** and press <Enter>.

13. When prompted for the cut format, select **Slope**. Type **1** and press <Enter> to indicate a cut slope of 1:1.

14. When prompted for the fill format, select **Slope**. Type **1** and press <Enter> to indicate a fill slope of 1:1.

15. This defines the 1:1 slope from the road, as shown in Figure 6–44.

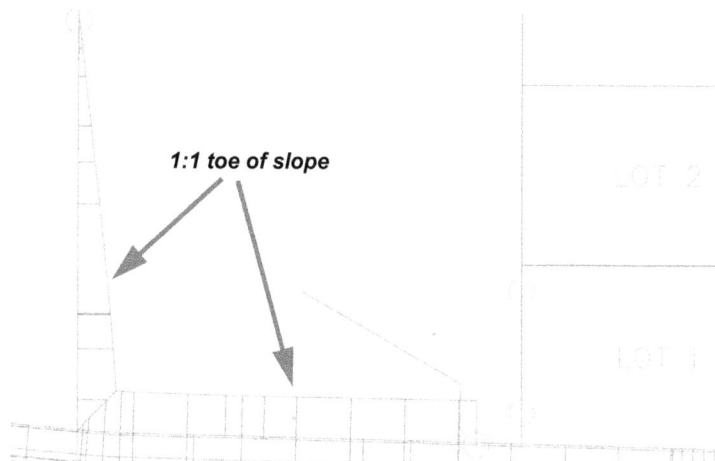

Figure 6–44

Next you will determine where the 3:1 slope from the parcels to the east intersects the 1:1 slope of the pond.

*At any time, if you accidentally close the **Grading** command, you just need to click*

(Create Grading).

16. When prompted to select a feature line, select the pond boundary feature line, which is the green line that defines the outer perimeter of the pond site.

17. When prompted for the grading side, select a point inside the pond.

18. When prompted for the start point, select the center of the southern-most cyan circle located on the east feature line and press <Enter> to accept <0+14.89'> for the station.

19. When prompted for the endpoint or length, select the center of the northern-most cyan circle located on the east feature line and press <Enter> to accept <0+69.25'> for the station, as shown in Figure 6–45.

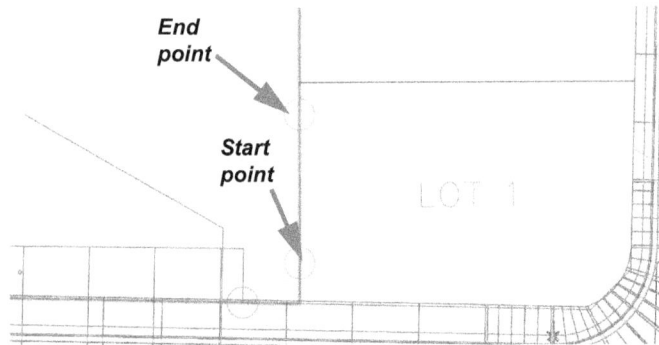

Figure 6–45

20. When prompted for the elevation, type **165** and press <Enter>.

21. When prompted for the cut format, select **Slope**. Type **3** and press <Enter> for a cut slope of 3:1.

22. When prompted for the fill format, select **Slope**. Type **3** and press <Enter> for a fill slope of 3:1.

This establishes the toe of slope where the 1:1 slope intersects the 3:1 slope.

23. Press <Esc> to end the feature line selection and select the **X** in the Grading Creation Tools toolbar to close the toolbar.

To use the toe of slope for further grading, the feature line that represents the toe of slope must be extracted from the grading object.

24. In Model Space, select the toe of slope feature line, right-click, and select **Move to Site...**, as shown in Figure 6–46.

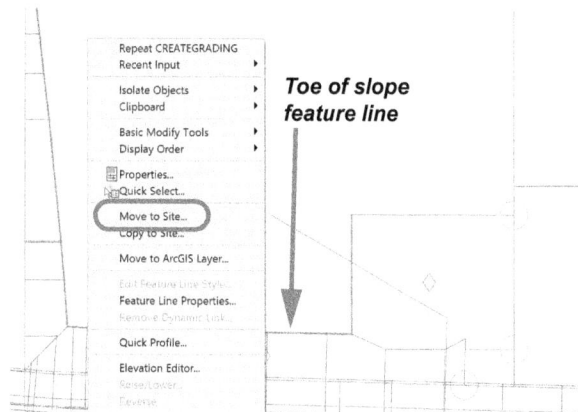

Figure 6–46

25. In the Move to Site dialog box, click **OK** to accept the default site, as shown in Figure 6–47.

It does not matter which site you place it in. By moving the feature line to a different site, the grading object is deleted, leaving just the toe of slope.

Figure 6–47

26. Select the feature line again and move it back to the **Pond Site**, as shown in Figure 6–48.

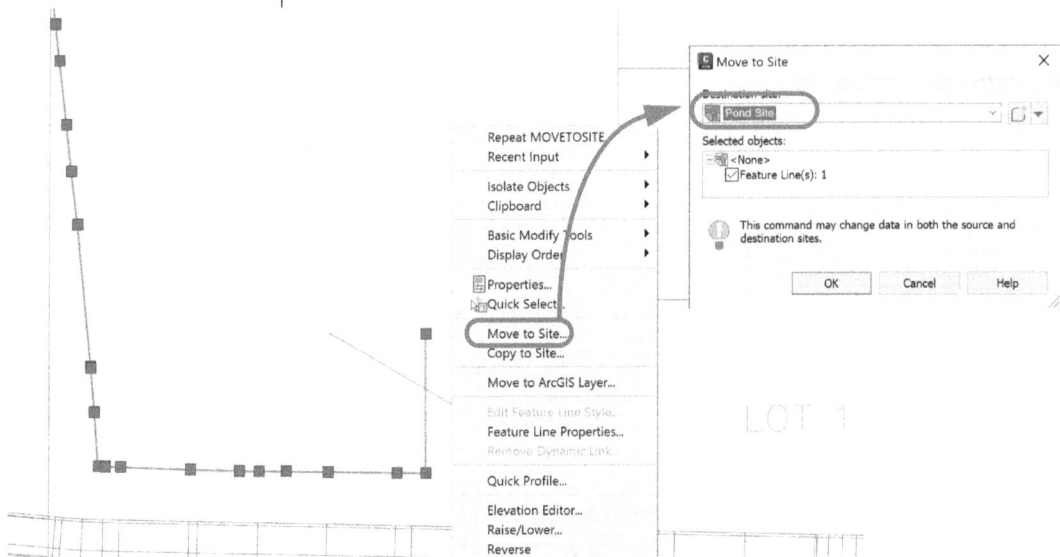

Figure 6–48

27. In Model Space, select the feature line. In the *Feature Line* contextual tab>Modify panel, click (Feature Line Properties).

28. In the Feature Line Properties dialog box, select the **Name** option and type **Toe of slope** in the *Name* field.

29. Stay in the Feature Line Properties dialog box and select the **Style** option. In the Style drop-down list, select the **ASC-Basic** style, as shown in Figure 6–49. Click **OK**.

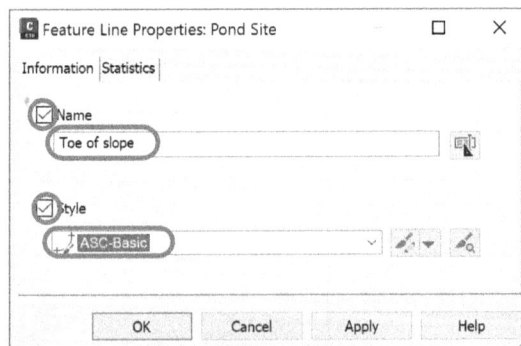

Figure 6–49

30. In Model Space, select the toe of slope feature line. In the *Feature Line* contextual tab>Modify panel, click 📷 (Edit Elevations). In the Edit Elevations panel, click ⚪ (Elevation Editor).

In the Grading Elevation Editor vista, the elevation shown for station 2+84.74' is 172.50', as shown in Figure 6–50. The correct elevation is 180'.

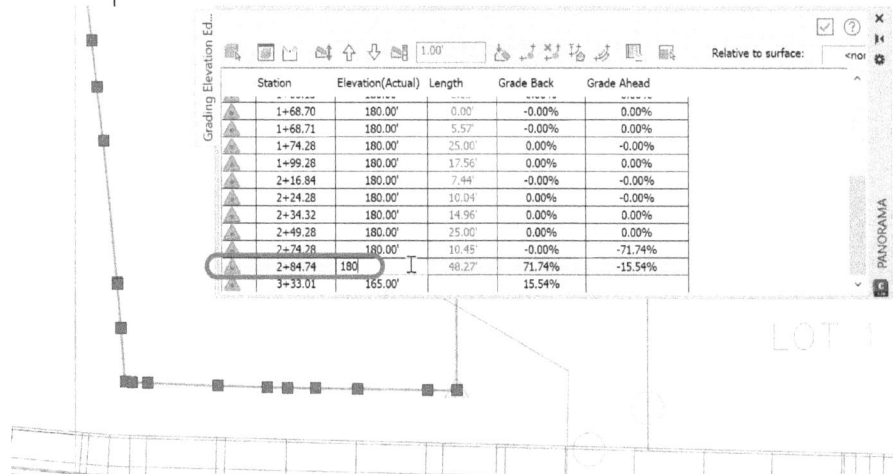

Station	Elevation(Actual)	Length	Grade Back	Grade Ahead
1+68.70	180.00'	0.00'	-0.00%	0.00%
1+68.71	180.00'	5.57'	-0.00%	0.00%
1+74.28	180.00'	25.00'	0.00%	-0.00%
1+99.28	180.00'	17.56'	0.00%	0.00%
2+16.84	180.00'	7.44'	-0.00%	-0.00%
2+24.28	180.00'	10.04'	0.00%	-0.00%
2+34.32	180.00'	14.96'	0.00%	0.00%
2+49.28	180.00'	25.00'	0.00%	0.00%
2+74.28	180.00'	10.45'	-0.00%	-71.74%
2+84.74	180	48.27'	71.74%	-15.54%
3+33.01	165.00'		15.54%	

Figure 6–50

31. Select the elevation field for station 2+84.74, type **180**, and press <Enter>.

32. Click ✔ to close the Elevation Editor vista.

33. To join the toe of slope feature line to the east pond boundary, select the toe of slope feature line and select the east feature line to display all of the grips.

34. Select the last grip on the toe of slope feature line and drag it to the intermediate point (as marked by the blue circular grip) on the east feature line, as shown in Figure 6–51.

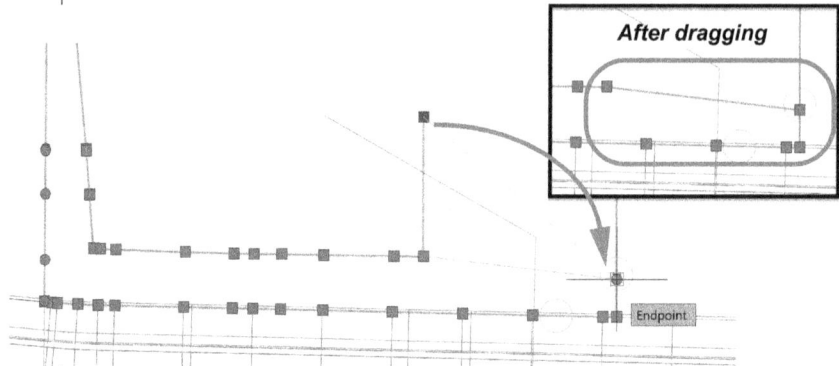

Figure 6–51

35. You have now defined the south pond feature line.

36. Save the drawing.

Task 2 - Establish control feature lines (north end).

In this task, you will define the north pond feature line by determining the location of the pond maintenance access road, based on a 3:1 grade from the existing boundary.

1. Continue working with the drawing from the previous task.

2. In the *View* tab>Views panel, select the preset view **Storm Pond**.

3. In the *Home* tab>Create Design panel, expand the Grading drop-down list and click (Grading Creation Tools).

4. In the Grading Creation Tools dialog box, set the *Grading Group* name to **Temp** (if not already set) and ensure that the grading criteria is set to **Grade to Elevation**.

5. Click ☀️ (Create Grading), as shown in Figure 6–52, and select the **Pond Boundary** feature line, which is the green line that represents the perimeter of the pond site.

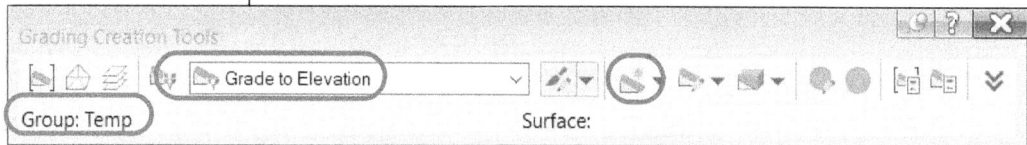

Grading Creation Tools

Grade to Elevation

Group: Temp   Surface:

Figure 6–52

6. When prompted to weed the feature line, select **Continue grading without feature line weeding**.

7. When prompted for the side to grade, select a point inside the pond. Select **No** when prompted to *Apply to the entire length*.

8. When prompted for the start point, select the center of the magenta circle located on the northeast corner of the feature line, as shown in Figure 6–53. Press <Enter> to accept <7+88.94'> for the station.

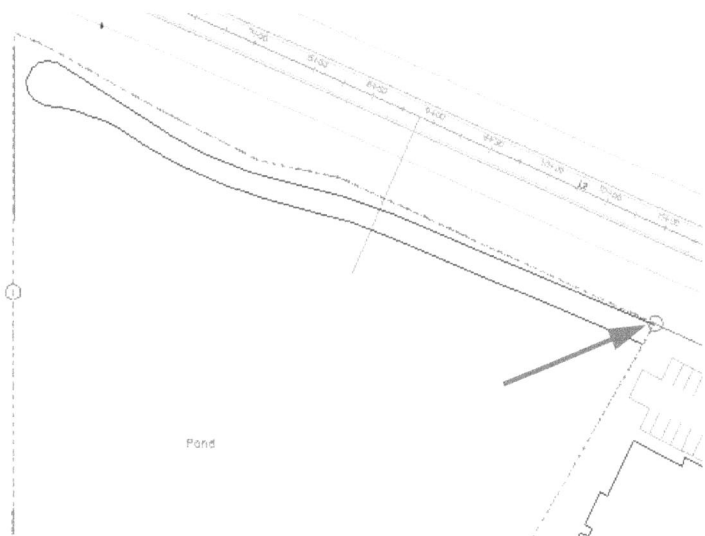

Pond

Figure 6–53

9. When prompted for the endpoint or length, select the center of the magenta circle located on the northern part of the west feature line, as shown in Figure 6–54. Press <Enter> to accept <15+31.82'> for the station.

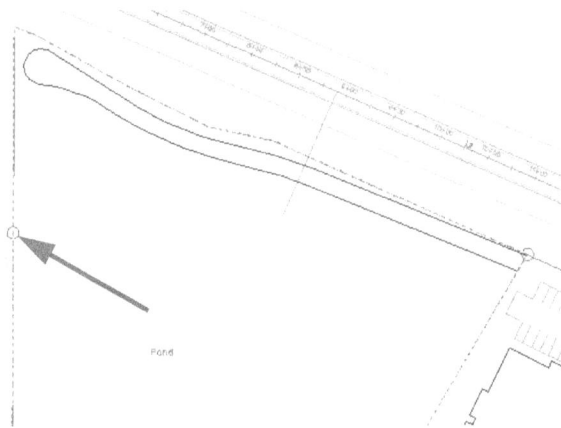

Figure 6–54

10. When prompted for the elevation, type **165.0** and press <Enter>.

11. When prompted for the cut format, select **Slope**. Type **3** and press <Enter> for a cut slope of 3:1.

12. When prompted for the fill format, select **Slope**. Type **3** and press <Enter> for a fill slope of 3:1.

13. Press <Esc> to exit the feature line selection. Select the **X** in the Grading Creation Tools toolbar to close the toolbar.

This grading object defines a 3:1 slope from the existing boundary and establishes the approximate location of the maintenance road. To save time, the access road has already been designed, as shown in Figure 6–55.

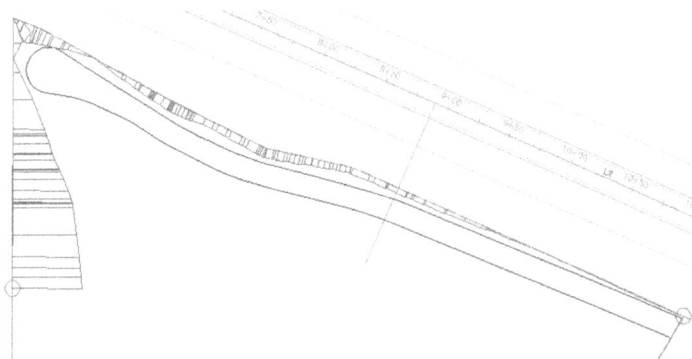

Figure 6–55

Based on the 3:1 cut and fill slope to an elevation of 164.4', you now have a feature line representing the access road. This access road has a maximum side slope of 3:1 to existing ground on the north side of the road. On the south side of the road, you continue to grade based on the design criteria for the pond.

14. You can erase the grading 3:1 maximum slope because it is no longer needed. In Model Space, select the grading object. In the *Grading* contextual tab>Modify panel, click

   (Delete Grading).

15. Save the drawing.

Task 3 - Create the pond's outside rim feature line.

---

1. Continue working with the drawing from the previous task.

2. In the *View* tab>Views panel, select the preset view **Storm Pond**.

3. In the *Prospector* tab, expand the *Sites>Pond Site* collection. Select **Feature lines** and note the grid view that is usually at the bottom of the pane.

This list displays the names of the feature lines, style, layer, and 2D length.

4. Select **Toe of slope** from the list, right-click, and select **Select**, as shown in Figure 6–56.

The Autodesk Civil 3D software highlights the appropriate feature line.

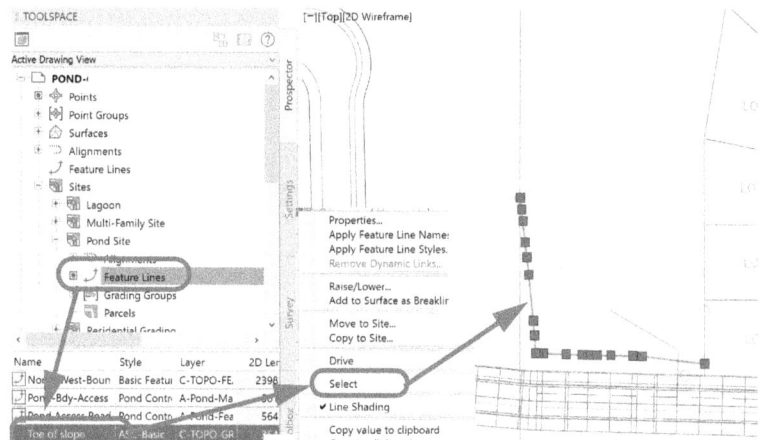

Figure 6–56

5. In the *Feature Line* contextual tab>Modify panel, click

   (Feature Line Properties).

6. In the Feature Line Properties dialog box, complete the following, as shown in Figure 6–57:

   • Change the *Name* to **Pond-Bdy-Control**.
   • Set the *Style* to **Pond Control Feature Line**.
   • Click **OK**.

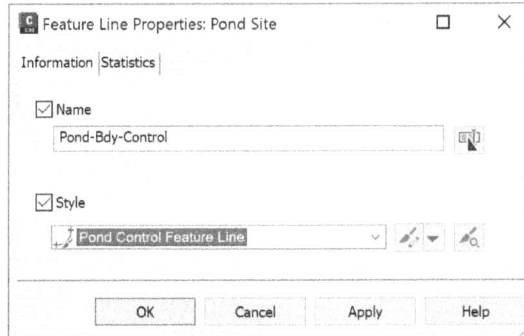

Figure 6–57

7. Press <Esc> to release the feature line.

8. Zoom in on the south end of the pond.

9. Select the feature line named **North-West-Boundary** that surrounds the pond.

10. In the *Feature Line* contextual tab>Modify panel, click
    (Edit Geometry) if it is not already displayed. In the Edit
    Geometry panel, click ⁺ᴶ (Break), as shown in Figure 6–58.

Figure 6–58

11. Select the **North-West-Boundary** feature line again. Type **F** at the Command Line so that you can select the first and second point of the break. Pick a point south of the cyan circle to the south of the control feature line for the first point, then pick the endpoint of the control line using Osnaps, as shown in Figure 6–59.

Station:0+13.00'
Endpoint

Pt. 2

Pt. 1

Figure 6–59

12. Select the **North-West-Boundary** feature line. In the *Feature Line* contextual tab>Modify panel, click 🗔 (Edit Geometry) if it is not already visible. In the Edit Geometry panel, click ↵ (Break).

13. Select the **North-West-Boundary** feature line again. Type **F** at the Command Line so that you can select the first and second point of the break.

14. Pick a point inside the green circle to the south of the control feature line for the first point. Then pick the endpoint of the control line using Osnaps, as shown in Figure 6–60.

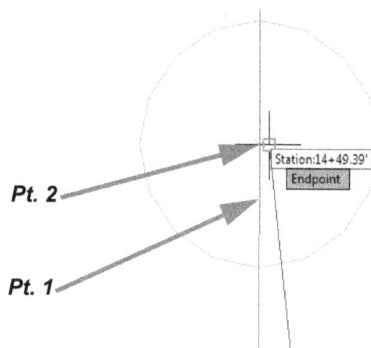

Station:14+49.39'
Endpoint

Pt. 2

Pt. 1

Figure 6–60

15. In the *View* tab>Views panel, select the **Storm Pond** view. Zoom in to the northeast corner of the pond.

16. Select the **North-West-Boundary** feature line. In the *Feature Line* contextual tab>Modify panel, click 🗔 (Edit Geometry) if it is not already displayed. In the Edit Geometry panel, click ↵ (Break).

17. Select the **North-West-Boundary** feature line again just north of the south line of the maintenance road (this is also the first point), as shown in Figure 6–61. Pick the endpoint of the south line of the maintenance road using Osnaps for the second point.

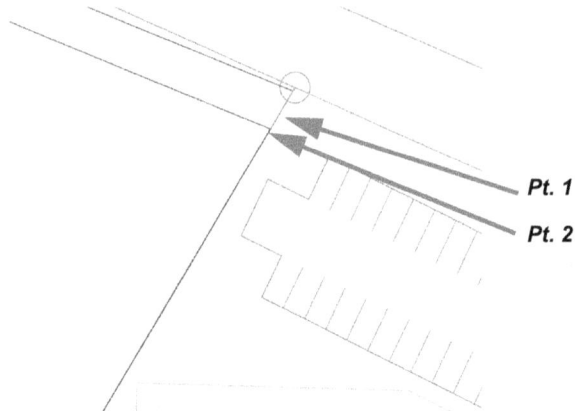

Figure 6–61

18. In the *View* tab>Views panel, select the **Storm Pond** view. Zoom in to the northwest corner of the pond.

19. Select the **North-West-Boundary** feature line. In the *Feature Line* contextual tab>Modify panel, click 🖼 (Edit Geometry) if it is not already displayed. In the Edit Geometry panel, click ↵ᵀ (Break).

20. Select the **North-West-Boundary** feature line again near the northwest corner of the pond (this is also the first point), as shown in Figure 6–62. Then, pick the endpoint near station 5+98.05' (using Osnap) for the second point.

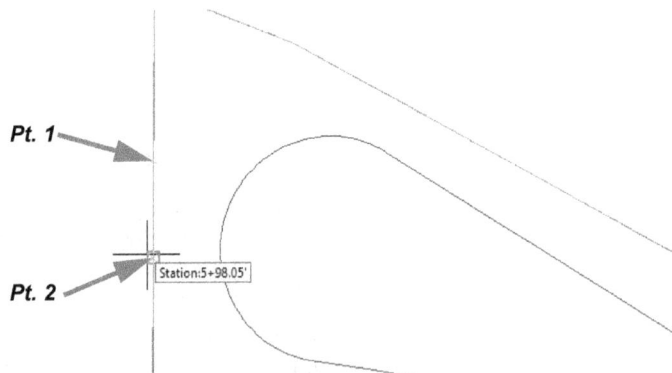

Figure 6–62

21. Select the west feature line. In the *Feature Line* contextual tab>Modify panel, click ⬜ (Edit Elevations). In the Edit Elevations panel, click ⬤ (Elevation Editor).

22. In the Elevation Editor vista, note that an elevation point is located at station **0+20.17** with an elevation of **170'**, as shown in Figure 6–63. You will turn this into a regular vertex.

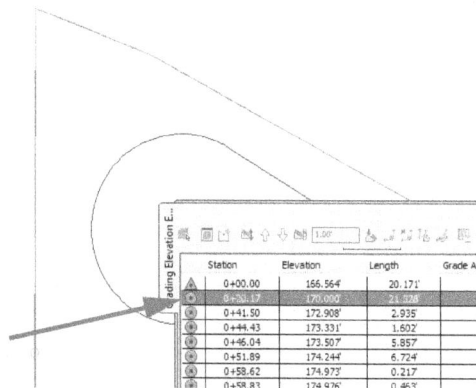

Figure 6–63

23. Select the feature line again. In the *Feature Line* contextual tab>Modify panel, click ⬜ (Edit Geometry). In the Edit Geometry panel, click ⬩ (Insert PI).

24. At the Command Line, for *Distance*, type **D** and press <Enter>. For the *Distance* value, type **20.17** and press <Enter>. For the *Elevation*, type **170** and press <Enter>. Press <Esc> to end the command.

25. Click ✓ to close the Elevation Editor vista.

26. Select the feature line. Using grips, move the first vertex to the endpoint of the southern boundary line of the maintenance road using Osnaps, as shown in Figure 6–64.

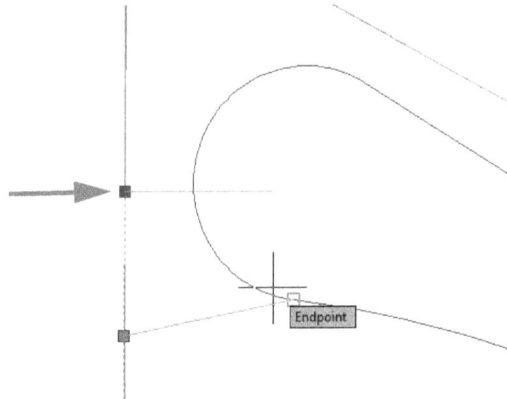

Figure 6–64

27. In the *View* tab>Views panel, select **Storm Pond** to restore the view.

28. To join all of the feature lines, select the feature line **Pond-Bdy-Control**. In the *Feature Line* contextual tab> Modify panel, click ⬛ (Edit Geometry). In the Edit Geometry panel, click ⬛ (Join), as shown in Figure 6–65.

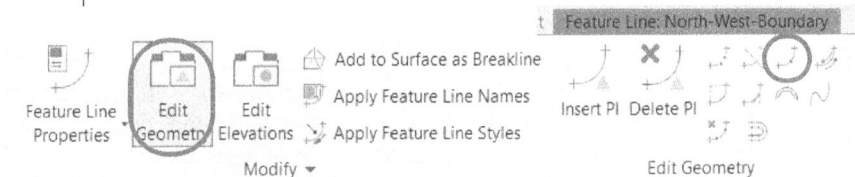

Figure 6–65

29. When prompted to select the connecting feature lines, select the feature line **Pond-Bdy-East** (2), **Pond-Bdy-North** (3), and **Pond-Bdy-West** (4), as shown in Figure 6–66. If you receive an error that they cannot be joined, you might need to grip edit the feature lines to snap them end to end.

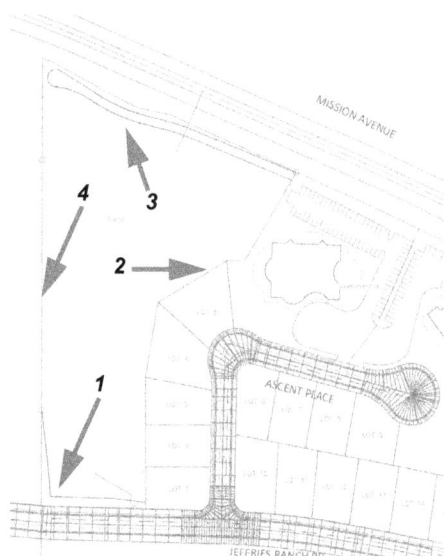

Figure 6–66

30. Press <Esc> to exit the feature line selection.

31. Select the feature line that runs along the Jeffries Ranch Road corridor to the south.

32. In the *Feature Line* contextual tab>Modify tab, click (Feature Line Properties).

33. In the Feature Line Properties, for the *Name*, type **Pond-Bdy-South**. Click **OK**.

34. Select the feature line that runs along the north of the pond.

35. In the *Feature Line* contextual tab>Modify panel, click (Feature Line Properties).

36. In the Feature Line Properties, for the *Name*, type **Pond-Bdy-North**. Click **OK**.

37. Save the drawing.

Practice 6d	# Pond Grading - Grading Object (Grading the Proposed Pond)

Practice Objective

- Create a complex grading group by grading one grading object from another.

In this practice, you will create a stormwater detention pond with feature lines and grading tools. With the control feature lines created, you can continue to grade the storm pond.

Task 1 - Create pond grading.

With the pond boundary established, the rest of the pond can now be graded as specified in the cross-section.

1. Continue working with the drawing from the previous practice or open **POND-D.dwg** from the *C:\Civil 3D for Land Dev\ Working\Pond* folder.

2. In the *Home* tab>Create Design panel, expand the Grading drop-down list and click ![icon] (Grading Creation Tools), as shown in Figure 6–67.

Figure 6–67

3. Ensure that the grading group is set to **Temp** (within the Pond Site site).

4. In the Grading Creation Tools toolbar, click ▣ (Set the Grading Group), as shown in Figure 6–68.

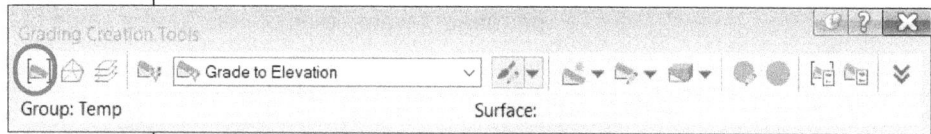

Figure 6–68

5. In the Select Grading Group dialog box, set the *Site name* to **Pond Site**, as shown on the left in Figure 6–69. To create a

   new group, click ▣ (Create a Grading Group). In the Create Grading Group dialog box, for the *Name* type **Pond** and clear the **Automatic surface creation** option, as shown on the right in Figure 6–69. Click **OK**.

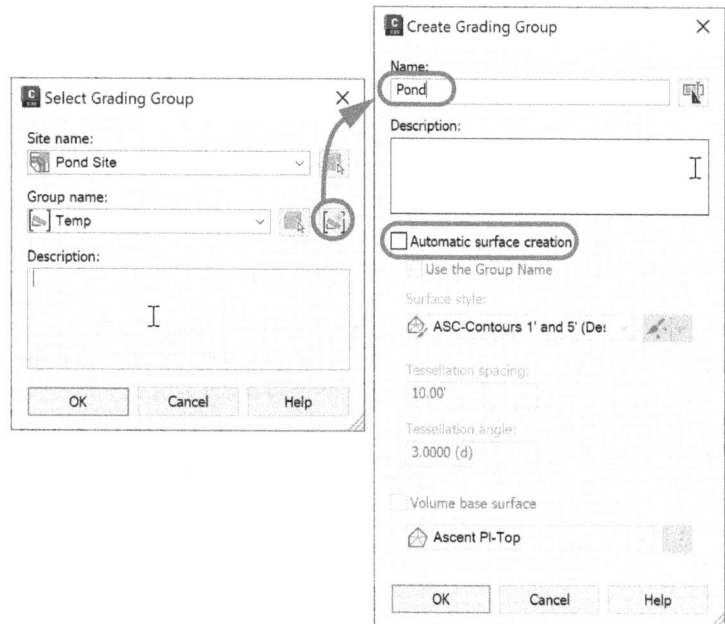

Figure 6–69

6. In the Select Grading Group dialog box, click **OK**.

7. In the Grading Creation Tools toolbar, set the grading criteria to **Grade to Elevation** and click (Create Grading), as shown in Figure 6–70. The first step is to grade to the permanent water level of 160.76 at a slope of 3:1.

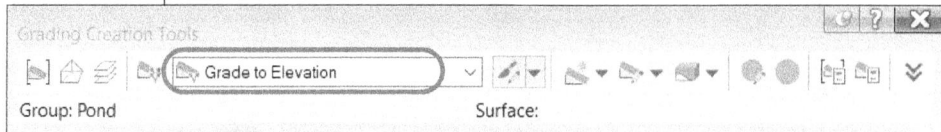

Figure 6–70

8. When prompted to select the feature line, select the **Pond-Bdy-Control** feature line. This feature line defines the inside rim of the pond.

9. When prompted to weed the feature line, select **Continue grading without weeding**.

10. When prompted to select the side to grade, select the inside of the pond. Type **Yes** when prompted to *Apply to entire length*.

11. Type **160.76** for the elevation.

12. When prompted for the Cut format, type **Slope** and press <Enter>. For the *Slope* value, type **3** and press <Enter> to signify a 3:1 slope.

13. When prompted for the Fill format, type **Slope** and press <Enter>. For the *Slope* value, type **3** and press <Enter> to signify a 3:1 slope.

14. You now need to grade to the bottom of the pond, which is 13' deep at a slope of 2:1. In the Grading Creation Tools toolbar, change the criteria to **Grade to Relative Elevation**, as shown in Figure 6–71.

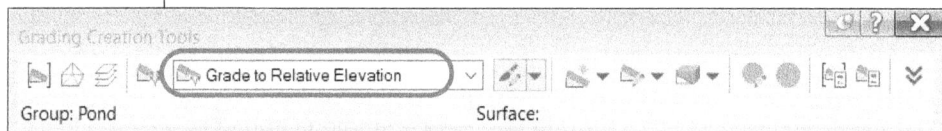

Figure 6–71

15. When prompted to select the feature line, select the inside of the pond feature line created by the last grading object, as shown in Figure 6–72. Type **Yes** when prompted to *Apply to entire length*.

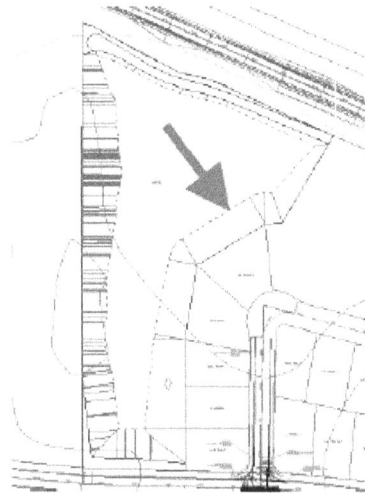

Figure 6–72

16. If prompted to select the side to grade, select the inside of the pond.

17. When prompted for the relative elevation, type **-13** and press <Enter>.

18. When prompted for the format, type **Slope** and press <Enter>. For the *Slope* value, type **2** and press <Enter> to signify a 2:1 slope.

19. In the Grading Creation Tools toolbar, expand the Create Grading drop-down list and click (Create Infill).

20. When prompted to select an area to infill, select the center of the pond, and press <Esc> to exit the command.

21. Select the diamond at the center of the infill that you just created.

22. In the *Grading* contextual tab>Modify panel, click (Grading Group Properties).

23. In the Grading Group Properties dialog box, select the **Automatic Surface Creation** option to automatically create the surface, as shown in Figure 6–73.

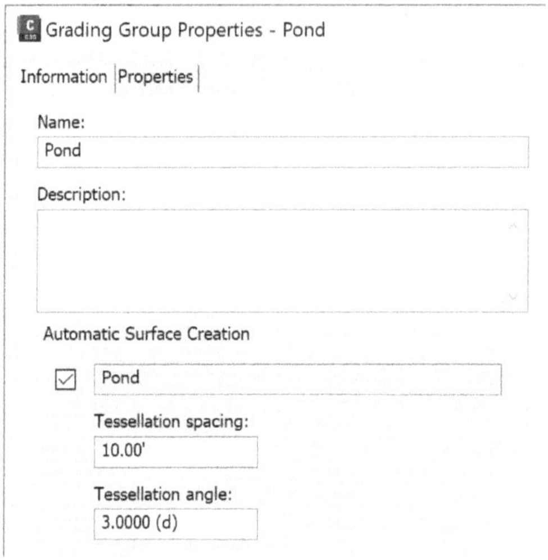

Figure 6–73

24. Click **OK** to close the dialog box. Click **OK** in the Create Surface dialog box. (If the Event Vista displays, close it.)

25. Save the drawing. (Before opening the Object Viewer in the next step, it is always prudent to save the drawing.)

26. Select the **Pond** surface (select one of its contour lines).

27. In the *Surface* contextual tab, click (Object Viewer). Set the view direction to **SW Isometric** and the style to **Conceptual**. Note the hole in the surface, as shown in Figure 6–74.

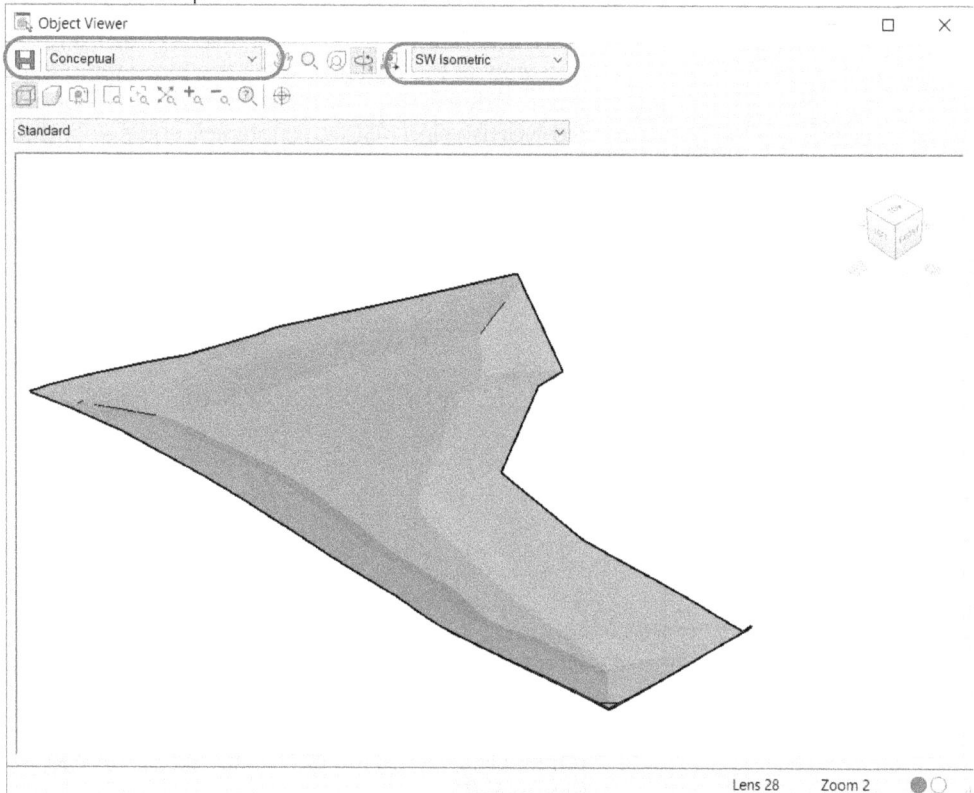

Figure 6–74

28. Press <Esc> twice to close the Object Viewer and release the selection.

Task 2 - Supplement the surface with feature lines.

Add feature lines to represent critical grade breaks and other important elevation breaklines on the surface. These lines accentuate the geometry and make the surface more accurate. In this task, you will add feature lines at the north and south ends of the site.

1. Continue working with the drawing from the previous task.

2. In the *View* tab>Views panel, select the preset view **Storm Pond**.

3. In the *Prospector* tab, expand the *Sites* collection, expand the site *Pond Site* collection, and select **Feature Lines**. In the grid view at the bottom, select the three feature lines **Pond-Bdy-North**, **Pond-Bdy-South**, and **Pond-Access Rd-North** using <Ctrl>. Right-click and select **Select**, as shown in Figure 6–75.

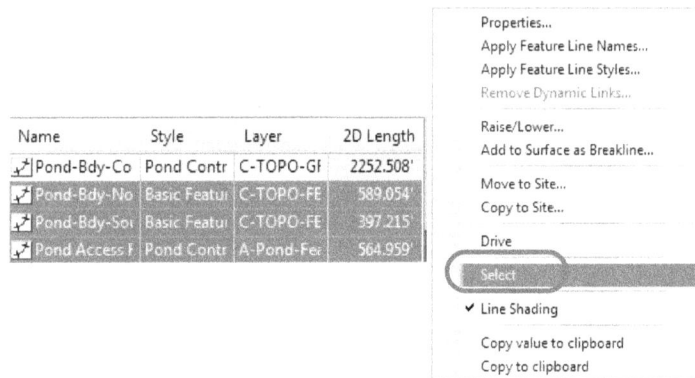

Figure 6–75

4. Once selected, the feature lines can be added to the surface as breaklines. In the *Feature Line* contextual tab>Modify panel, click [icon] (Add to Surface as Breakline), as shown in Figure 6–76.

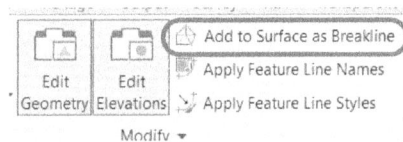

Figure 6–76

5. In the Select Surface dialog box, select the **Pond** surface, as shown in Figure 6–77. Click **OK**.

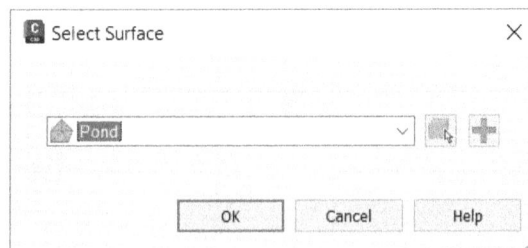

Figure 6–77

6. In the Add Breaklines dialog box, accept all of the defaults and click **OK**.

7. Press <Esc> to end the selection. You now have a pond surface that matches the proposed design of the parcels on the east side and Jeffries Ranch Road on the south side. The north and west sides of the pond have been graded to match the existing ground.

8. Save the drawing.

6.6 Pond Staging Volumes

An important part of designing ponds or basins is ensuring that the pond can hold the volume of water anticipated. This is often done using stage-storage calculations. Stage-storage defines the relationship between the depth of water and storage volume in the storage basin or pond.

Within the Autodesk Civil 3D software, you can calculate incremental and cumulative volumes using two different calculations, as shown in Figure 6–78 and described below. Whichever method is chosen, the Stage Storage command is used to complete the stage storage volume analysis.

- Average End Area: Calculates the volume between two cross sections.

- Conic Approximation: Calculates the volume between two sectional areas.

$$V = \left(\frac{A_1 + A_2}{2}\right)L \qquad V = \left(\frac{h}{3}\right)(A_1 + A_2 + \sqrt{A_1 A_2})$$

Average End Area   **Conic Approximation**
Method Equation   **Method Equation**

Figure 6–78

How To: Calculate the Stage Storage Volumes of a Pond or Basin.

1. Ensure that the contours are visible for the surface to analyze. This is done in the surface properties by selecting an appropriate surface style.
2. In the *Analyze* tab, expand the Design panel and click

    (Stage Storage).
3. In the Stage Storage dialog box, do the following, as shown in Figure 6–79:
    - Enter a *Report Title*.
    - Enter a *Project Name*.
    - Enter a *Basin Description*.
    - For the *Volume Calculation Method*, select either **Average End Area**, **Conic Approximation**, or **Both**.
    - For the *Basin Definition Options*, select either **Define Basin from Entity** or **Use Manual Contour Data Entry**, then click **Define Basin**.

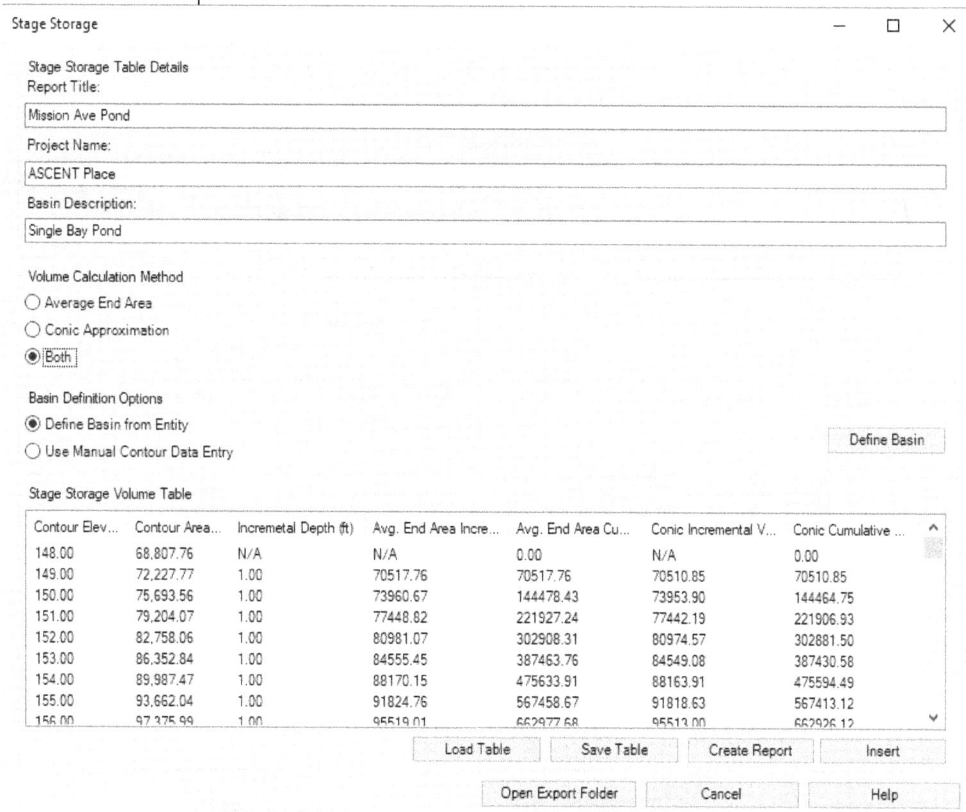

Figure 6–79

- If the **Use Manual Contour Data Entry** option is selected, a dialog box displays that enables you to manually enter the contour elevation and area, as shown in Figure 6–80.

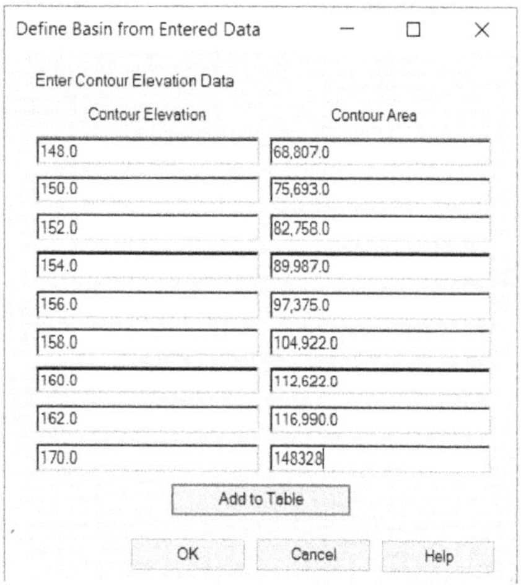

Figure 6–80

---

4. In the Define Basin from Entities dialog box, enter a *Basin Name*, and select one of the following options, as shown in Figure 6–81.

    *   **Define from Surface Contours:** Enables you to select a surface.
    *   **Define Basin from Polylines:** Enables you to select polylines representing surface contours.

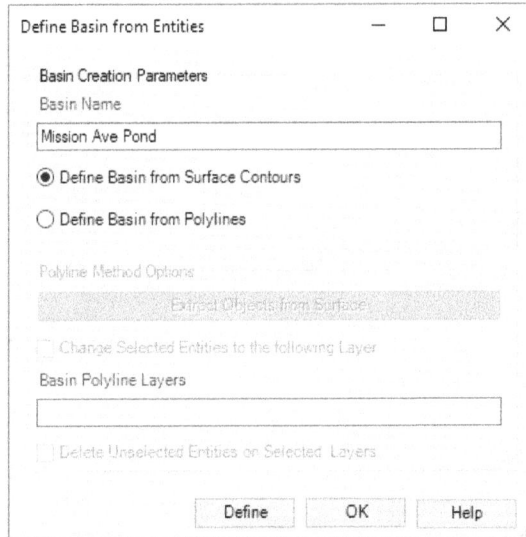

Figure 6–81

5. Click one of the following options to show the results:

    *   **Create Report:** Prompts you to save a *.txt file.
    *   **Insert:** Prompts you to select a point in the model to place the top-left corner of the volume table.

Practice 6e | Calculate Pond Staging Volume

Practice Objective

- Calculate the staging volume of the pond.

In this practice, you will calculate the volume of the pond at various depths, as shown in Figure 6–82, and then create a table showing those volumes.

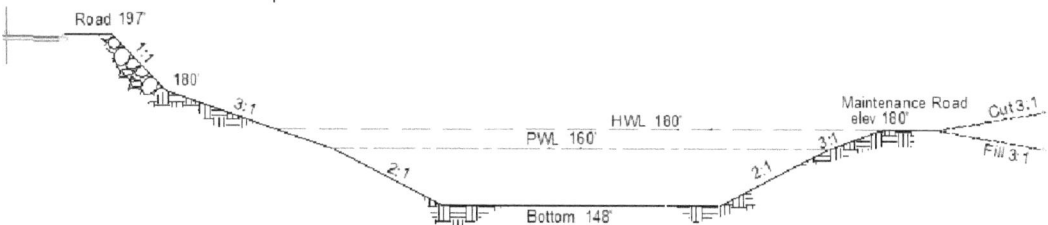

Figure 6–82

Task 1 - Calculate the staging volume for the pond.

1. Continue working with the drawing from the previous practice or open **POND-E.dwg** from the *C:\Civil 3D for Land Dev\ Working\Pond* folder.

2. Ensure that the contours are visible for the pond surface.

3. In the *Analyze* tab>expand the Design panel, and click

   (Stage Storage).

4. In the Stage Storage dialog box, do the following, as shown in Figure 6–83:

- For the *Report Title*, type **Mission Ave Pond**.
- For the *Project Name*, type **ASCENT Place**.
- For the *Basin Description*, type **Single Bay Pond**.
- For the *Volume Calculation Method*, select **Both**.
- For the *Basin Definition Options*, select **Define Basin from Entity**, then click **Define Basin**.

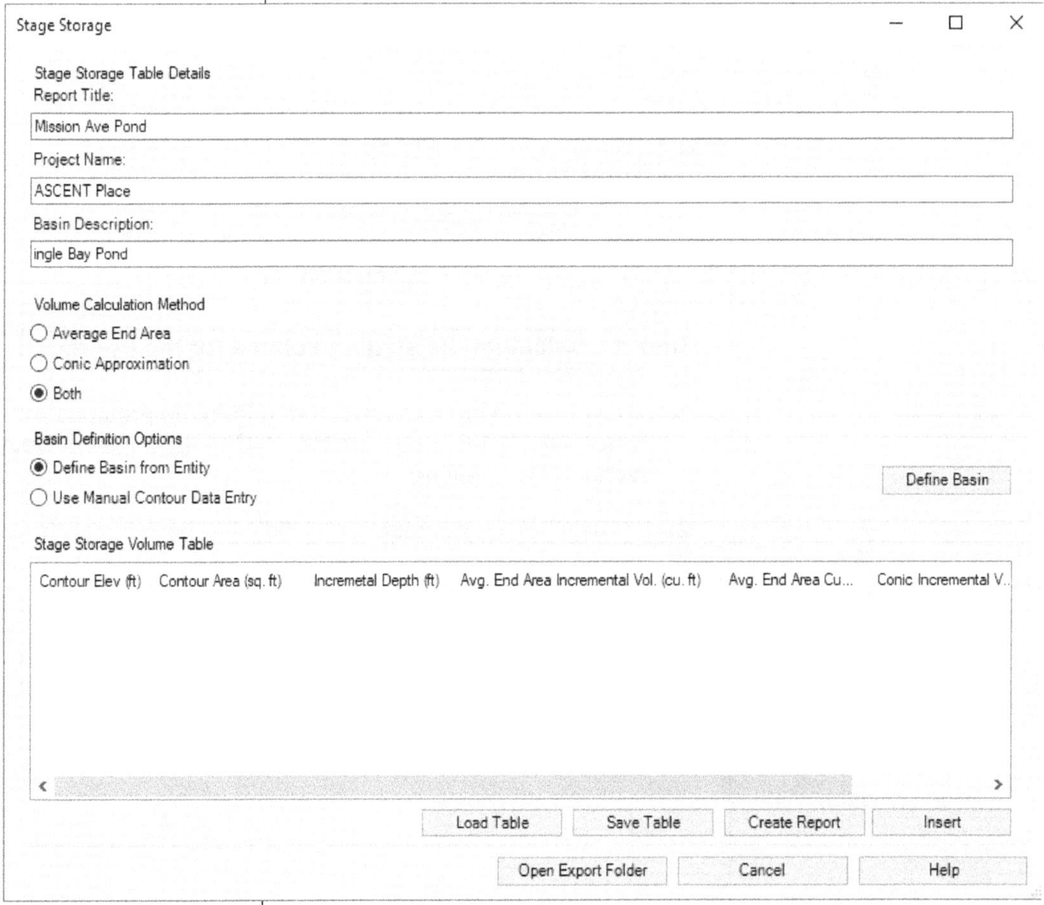

Figure 6–83

5. In the Define Basin from Entities dialog box, enter **Mission Ave Pond** for the *Basin Name*. Select **Define Basin from Surface Contours**, as shown in Figure 6–84, and click **Define**.

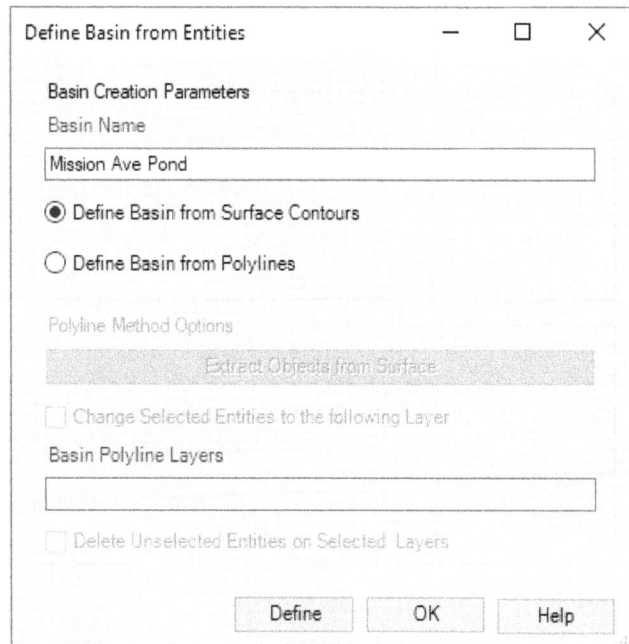

Figure 6–84

6. In the model, select the contours representing the pond surface.

7. In the Stage Storage dialog box, click **Insert**.

8. In the model, click to place the top-left corner of the table.

9. Close the Stage Storage dialog box.

10. Save the drawing.

Chapter Review Questions

1. Which icon in the *Feature Line* contextual tab>Modify panel enables you to edit feature line geometry?

   a.

   b.

   c.

   d.

2. Which icon in the *Feature Line* contextual tab>Modify panel enables you to edit feature line elevations?

   a.

   b.

   c.

   d.

3. Which icon in the *Feature Line* contextual tab>Edit Geometry panel enables you to trim a feature line at selected cutting edges?

   a.

   b.

   c.

   d.

4. Which icon in the *Feature Line* contextual tab>Edit Elevations panel enables you to insert a high/low elevation point?

   a.

   b.

   c.

   d.

5. Feature lines can be extracted from corridor models.
   a. True
   b. False

6. How do you calculate how much volume a pond can hold?
   a. This must be done manually since there is no way to do it in the software.

   b.

   c.

   d.

Command Summary

Button	Command	Location
	Add to Surface as Breakline	• **Ribbon**: *Feature Line* contextual tab> Modify panel • **Command Prompt:** FeatureAddAsBreakline
	Break	• **Ribbon**: *Feature Line* contextual tab> Edit Geometry panel • **Command Prompt:** BreakFeatures
	Create Feature Line from Corridor	• **Ribbon**: *Home* tab>Create Design panel, expanded Feature Line drop-down list • **Command Prompt:** FeatureLinesFromCorridor
	Delete Elevation Point	• **Ribbon**: *Feature Line* contextual tab> Modify panel, click Edit Elevations to display the Edit Elevations panel • **Toolbar**: *Elevation Editor* (*contextual*) • **Command Prompt:** DeleteElevPoint
	Feature Line Properties	• **Ribbon**: *Feature Line* contextual tab> Modify panel
	Insert Elevation Point	• **Ribbon**: *Feature Line* contextual tab> Modify panel, click Edit Elevations to display the Edit Elevations panel • **Toolbar**: *Elevation Editor* (*contextual*) • **Command Prompt:** InsertElevPoint
	Insert PI	• **Ribbon**: *Feature Line* contextual tab> Edit Geometry panel • **Command Prompt:** InsertFeaturePI
	Join	• **Ribbon**: *Feature Line* contextual tab> Edit Geometry panel • **Command Prompt:** JoinFeatures
	Stage Storage	• **Ribbon**: *Analyze* tab>Design panel • **Command Prompt:** _AeccStageStorage
	Trim	• **Ribbon**: *Feature Line* contextual tab> Edit Geometry panel • **Command Prompt:** TrimFeatures

Combining Surfaces

Grading objects can cause your drawing size to increase and slow down your computer. Therefore, when you are working on grading projects, you need to carefully plan the best way to organize your drawings before you start designing. This chapter reviews various ways of organizing your Autodesk® Civil 3D® projects. You will then use Data Shortcuts to create a final grading plan.

Learning Objectives in This Chapter

- List the three different ways in which Autodesk Civil 3D project drawings can be organized.
- Share design information with other members of a design team using Data Shortcuts.

7.1 Autodesk Civil 3D Projects

There are multiple ways of organizing Autodesk Civil 3D project drawings. Three of the most common approaches are as follows:

Single-Design Drawing Projects

Since Autodesk Civil 3D surfaces, alignments, and other AEC objects can be entirely drawing-based, a single drawing file can act as the repository for all of the design data. Realistically, this might only be feasible with the smallest projects and/or those worked on by only one person. The only external data would be survey databases, and possibly drawings containing plotting layouts that XREF the single design drawing.

Multiple Drawings Sharing Data Using Shortcuts

This approach permits multiple survey and design drawings to share data. For example, a surface could exist in one drawing and an alignment in another. A third could contain a surface profile based on the alignment and terrain model, and all could be kept in sync with each other using **Data Shortcuts**. This approach is usually preferable to the single-drawing approach, because it permits more than one user to work on the project at the same time (in the different design drawings). It does not create any external project data other than survey databases and XML data files that are used to share data between drawings.

Once an object has been referenced into the drawing and the drawing has been saved, the object is saved in the drawing. Therefore, it only needs access to the source drawing for validation and synchronization purposes if the source object changes. This makes it easy to share drawings with others because it ensures that the referenced objects display even if the source drawings are not available.

Shortcuts tend to be efficient for projects with a small number of drawings and project team members. Since the XML data files that connect drawings must be managed manually, keeping a large number of drawings and/or people in sync with shortcuts can be cumbersome. It is highly recommended that you establish procedures to ensure that data is not unintentionally deleted or changed. You need to document these procedures very carefully.

Multiple Drawings Sharing Data with Autodesk Vault

The Autodesk Vault software is a data and document management system (ADMS). It is used in conjunction with other Autodesk applications in different industries. When working with the Autodesk Vault software, all project drawings, survey databases, and references are managed and stored inside an SQL-managed database. Autodesk Vault consists of user-level access permissions, drawing check-in/out, project templates, automated backups, data versioning, etc. These benefits are offset by the additional time required to manage and administer the database, and in some cases purchasing additional hardware and software. If you work on large projects with multiple design drawings or have many team members (more than 10), you might find that the Autodesk Vault is the best way to keep those projects organized.

7.2 Sharing Data

In the Autodesk Civil 3D workflow, you can use two methods of project collaboration to share Autodesk Civil 3D design data: Data Shortcuts and Vault references.

Autodesk Vault and Data Shortcuts can be used to share design data between drawing files in the same project, such as alignment definitions, profiles, corridors, surfaces, pipe networks, pressure networks, sample line groups, and View Frame Groups. They do not permit the sharing of profile views, assemblies, or other Autodesk Civil 3D objects. Drawing sets using shortcuts typically use XREFs and reference other line work and annotations between drawings. Whether using Vault Shortcuts or Data Shortcuts, the process is similar.

The example in Figure 7–1 shows the sharing of data in a project collaboration environment. The data is divided into three distinctive levels. Using either Data Shortcuts or Autodesk Vault, these levels can be accessed and contributed to, on a local or remote server or across a WAN.

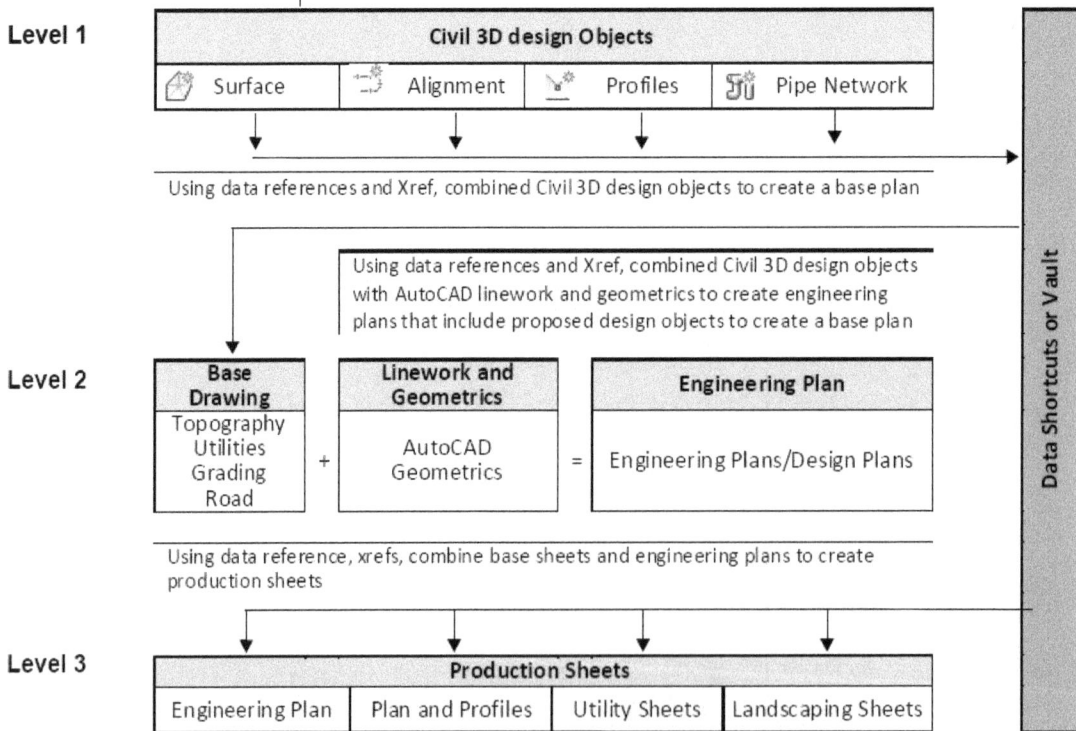

Level 1

Civil 3D design Objects			
Surface	Alignment	Profiles	Pipe Network

Using data references and Xref, combined Civil 3D design objects to create a base plan

Using data references and Xref, combined Civil 3D design objects with AutoCAD linework and geometrics to create engineering plans that include proposed design objects to create a base plan

Level 2

Base Drawing		Linework and Geometrics		Engineering Plan
Topography Utilities Grading Road	+	AutoCAD Geometrics	=	Engineering Plans/Design Plans

Using data reference, xrefs, combine base sheets and engineering plans to create production sheets

Level 3

Production Sheets			
Engineering Plan	Plan and Profiles	Utility Sheets	Landscaping Sheets

Data Shortcuts or Vault

Figure 7–1

7.3 Data Shortcuts

Data Shortcuts can be used to share design data between drawing files through the use of XML files. Using Data Shortcuts is similar to using the Autodesk Vault software, but it does not provide the protection of your data or the tracking of versions the way the Autodesk Vault software does.

Data Shortcuts are managed using the *Prospector* tab in the Toolspace in the *Data Shortcuts* collection, as shown in Figure 7–2. The shortcuts are stored in XML files within one or more working folders that you create. They can use the same folder structure as the Autodesk Vault software. This method simplifies the transition to using the Autodesk Vault software at a future time.

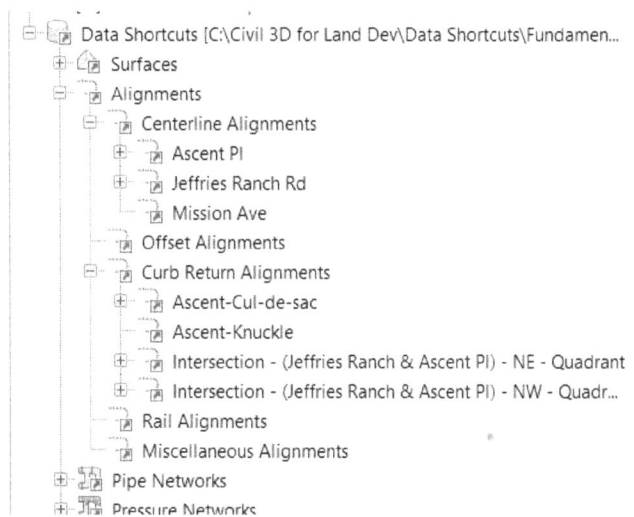

Figure 7–2

Whether using the Autodesk Vault software or Data Shortcuts, the intelligent Autodesk Civil 3D object design data can be consumed and used on different levels. However, this referenced data can only be edited in the drawing that contains the original object. As referenced data can be assigned a different style than those in the source drawing, you can separate the design phase (where drawing presentation is not critical) from the drafting phase (where drawing presentation is paramount). Therefore, after the styles have been applied at the drafting phase, any changes to the design have minimal visual impact on the completed drawings.

Changing the name of a drawing file that provides Data Shortcuts or the shortcut XML file itself invalidates the shortcut. Although the Data Shortcuts Editor outside the Autodesk Civil 3D software permits re-pathing if a source drawing moves, shortcuts might not resolve if the source drawing file name has changed.

Update Notification

If the shortcut objects are modified and the source drawing is saved, any drawings that reference those objects are updated when opened. If the drawings consuming the data referenced in the shortcuts were open at the time of the edit, a message displays to warn you of the changes, as shown in Figure 7–3.

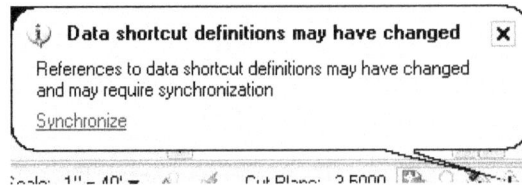

Figure 7–3

The following modifier icons help you to determine the state of many Autodesk Civil 3D objects.

▽	The object is referenced by another object. In the *Settings* tab this also indicates that a style is in use in the current drawing.
↗	The object is being referenced from another drawing file (such as through a shortcut or Autodesk Vault reference).
⬇	The object is out of date and needs to be rebuilt, or is violating specified design constraints.
◣	A project object (such as a point or surface) has been modified since it was included in the current drawing.
◢	You have modified a project object in your current drawing and those modifications have not yet been updated to the project.

Figure 7–4 shows how the modifier icons are used with an Autodesk Civil 3D object as it displays in the *Prospector* tab.

Figure 7–4

To update the shortcut data, select **Synchronize** in the balloon message or right-click on the object in the Prospector and select **Synchronize**.

Removing and Promoting Shortcuts

Shortcut data can be removed from the Shortcut tree in the Prospector by right-clicking on it and selecting **Remove**, but this does not remove the data from the drawing. To do so, right-click on the object in the Prospector and select **Delete**. This removes the shortcut data from the current list, so that the item is not included if a Data Shortcut XML file is exported from the current drawing.

You can also promote shortcuts, which converts the referenced shortcut into a local copy without any further connection to the original. You can promote objects by right-clicking on them in the Prospector and selecting **Promote**.

eTransmit Data References

Projects that use Data Shortcuts can be packaged and sent to reviewers, clients, and other consultants using the AutoCAD **eTransmit** command. With this command, all of the related dependent files (such as XML files, XREFs, and text fonts) are automatically included in the package. This reduces the possibility of errors and ensures that the recipient can use the files you send them. A report file can be included in the package explaining what must be done with drawing-dependent files (e.g., XML or XREFs) so that they are usable with the included files. The Create Transmittal dialog box is shown in Figure 7–5.

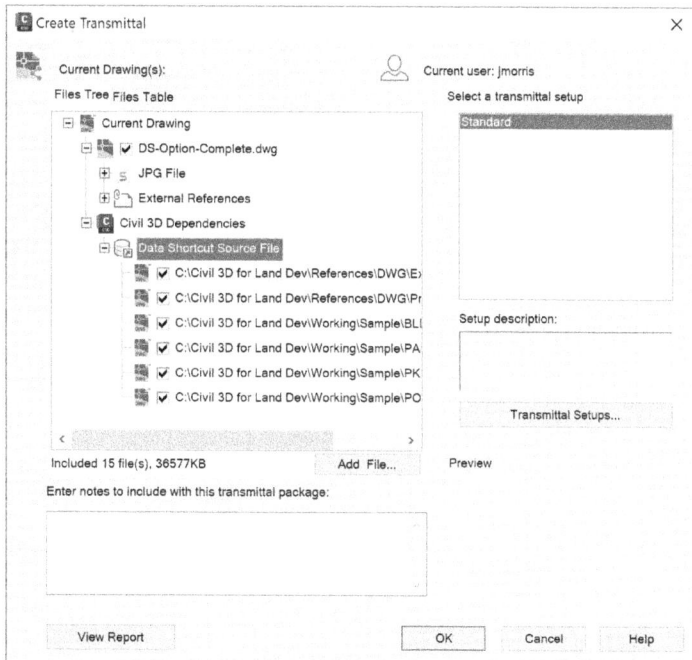

Figure 7–5

Data Shortcut Workflow

1. In the *Prospector* tab, right-click on Data Shortcuts to set the **Working Folder**. If it is not yet set up, you will need to create the folder.

2. ***Either*** select **Set the Shortcuts Folder...** if there is an existing project folder to be used ***or*** select **New Data Shortcuts Folder...** if you need to create a new project folder for all of your drawings.

3. Create or import the data that you want to share in the source drawing and save it in the current working folder under the correct project folder.

4. In the *Prospector* tab, right-click on Data Shortcuts and select **Associate Project to Current Drawing** (or **Associate Project to Multiple Drawings**).

5. In the *Prospector* tab, right-click on Data Shortcuts and select **Create Data Shortcuts**.

6. Select all of the items that you want to share, such as surfaces, alignments, or profiles, and click **OK**.

7. Save the source drawing (and close as needed).

8. Open, create, and save the drawing to receive the shortcut data. Expand the *Data Shortcuts* collection and the relevant object trees (*Surfaces*, *Alignments*, *Pipe Networks*, or *View Frame Groups*).Ensure that the proper the **Working Folder** and the **Shortcuts Folder** are still set.

9. Highlight an item to be referenced, right-click and select **Create Reference...** Repeat for all of the objects as needed. You are prompted for the styles and other settings that are required to display the object in the current drawing.

10. You might also want to add an XREF to the source drawing if there is additional AutoCAD® line work that you want to display in the downstream drawing.

11. The Autodesk Civil 3D tools for Data Shortcuts are located in the *Manage* tab (as shown in Figure 7–6), and in the *Prospector* tab.

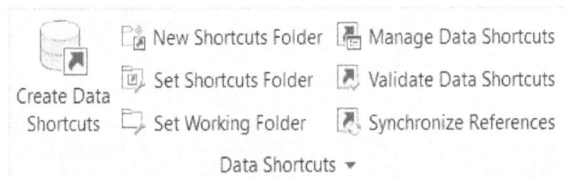

Figure 7–6

Advantages of Data Shortcuts

- Data Shortcuts provide a simple mechanism for sharing object data, without the added system administration needs of the Autodesk Vault software.

- Data Shortcuts offer access to an object's intelligent data while ensuring that this referenced data can only be changed in the source drawing.

- Referenced objects can have styles and labels that differ from the source drawing.

- When you open a drawing containing revised referenced data, the referenced objects are updated automatically.

- During a drawing session, if the referenced data has been revised, you are notified in the Communication Center and in the *Prospector* tab in Toolspace.

Limitations of Data Shortcuts

- Data Shortcuts cannot provide data versioning.

- Data Shortcuts do not provide security or data integrity controls.

- Unlike the Autodesk Vault software, Data Shortcuts do not provide a secure mechanism for sharing point data or survey data.

- Maintaining links between references and their source objects requires fairly stable names and locations on the shared file system. However, most broken references can easily be repaired using the tools in the Autodesk Civil 3D software.

Practice 7a | Data Shortcuts I

Practice Objective

- Create a new Data Shortcuts project with the correct working folder for the project being worked on.

In this practice, you will walk through the steps of creating project-based Data Shortcuts folders.

Task 1 - Start a new drawing.

In this task, you will set up a new working folder as the location in which to store Data Shortcuts projects. The default working folder for Data Shortcuts projects is *C:\Users\Public\Documents\ Autodesk\Civil 3D Projects*.

1. Start a new drawing from **ASC-GRD (CA83-VIF) NCS.dwt** from the *C:\Civil 3D for Land Dev\Working\Ascent-Config* folder.

2. If the Geolocation - Online Map Data dialog box appears, answer **No** to using Online Map Data, and also check the **Remember my choice** checkbox, as shown in Figure 7–7.

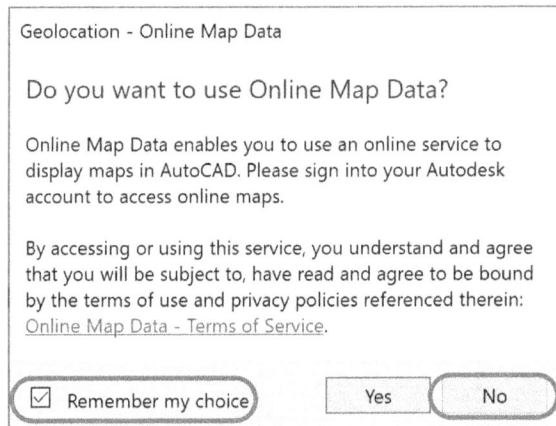

Geolocation - Online Map Data

Do you want to use Online Map Data?

Online Map Data enables you to use an online service to display maps in AutoCAD. Please sign into your Autodesk account to access online maps.

By accessing or using this service, you understand and agree that you will be subject to, have read and agree to be bound by the terms of use and privacy policies referenced therein: Online Map Data - Terms of Service.

☑ Remember my choice　　　Yes　　　No

Figure 7–7

3. Erase the message about the set coordinate system in the center of the screen.

4. Save the file in *C:\Civil 3D for Land Dev\Data Shortcuts\ Practice* folder and name it **DS-A-Shortcuts.dwg**.

5. In the *Manage* tab>Data Shortcuts panel, select **Set Working Folder**, as shown in Figure 7–8.

Figure 7–8

6. In the Browse For Folder dialog box, select the *C:\Civil 3D for Land Dev\Data Shortcuts\Grading* folder and click **Select Folder**.

Task 2 - Create new Shortcuts folders.

In this task, you will create a new folder for storing a set of related project drawings and Data Shortcuts. Create a folder name that reflects the project name and specify whether or not to use a project template to organize your data.

1. In the *Manage* tab>Data Shortcuts panel, select **New Shortcuts Folder**, as shown in Figure 7–9.

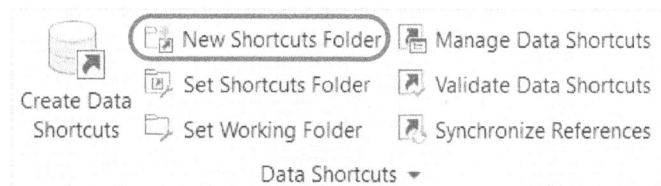

Figure 7–9

2. In the New Data Shortcut Folder dialog box, type **Ascent Phase 1** for the name and select the **Use project template** option.

Templates are found in the default folder C:\Civil 3D Templates; however, you will be using customized project templates.

3. Click the ellipses, as shown in Figure 7–10, and browse to *C:\Civil 3D for Land Dev\Ascent-Config\Ascent Project Templates.* Click **Select Folder**.

4. From the project templates available, select **Base Project**. Click **OK**.

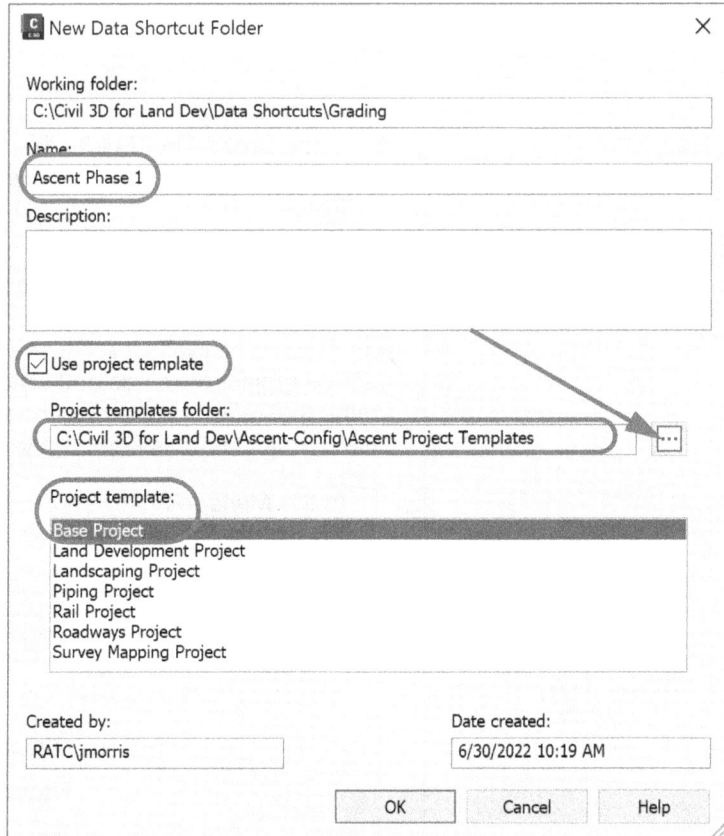

New Data Shortcut Folder   ✕

Working folder:

C:\Civil 3D for Land Dev\Data Shortcuts\Grading

Name:

Ascent Phase 1

Description:

☑ Use project template

Project templates folder:

C:\Civil 3D for Land Dev\Ascent-Config\Ascent Project Templates   ...

Project template:

Base Project
Land Development Project
Landscaping Project
Piping Project
Rail Project
Roadways Project
Survey Mapping Project

Created by: Date created:

RATC\jmorris   6/30/2022 10:19 AM

OK   Cancel   Help

Figure 7–10

5. The Autodesk Civil 3D software replicates the *Base Project* template folder structure and all included forms and documents in the Ascent Phase 1 project folder.

6. In the *Prospector* tab, a *Data Shortcuts* folder should be displayed in the *C:\Civil 3D for Land Dev\Data Shortcuts\ Grading\Ascent Phase 1* folder.

7. In Windows Explorer, verify that the *Civil 3D* folder structure has been created for this project, as shown in Figure 7–11.

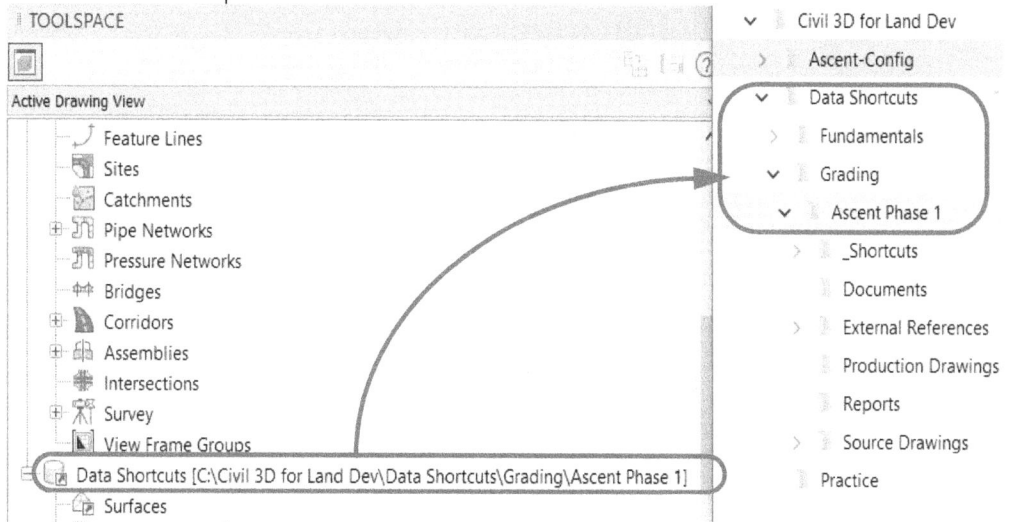

Figure 7–11

Task 3 - Associate the project to the drawings.

Associating drawings to the project is an important step to ensure that the data reference is inserted and an associate between project drawings is created.

1. In the *Prospector* tab, right-click on **Data Shortcuts** and select **Associate Project to Current Drawing**, as shown in Figure 7–12.

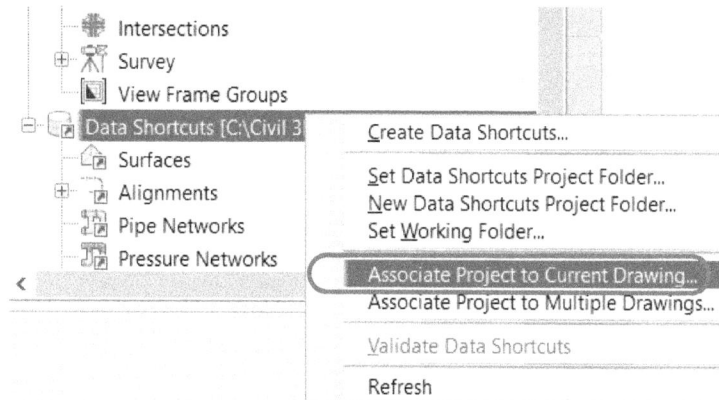

Figure 7–12

2. In the Associate Project to Current Drawing dialog box, click **OK** to accept the default working folder and project, as shown in Figure 7–13.

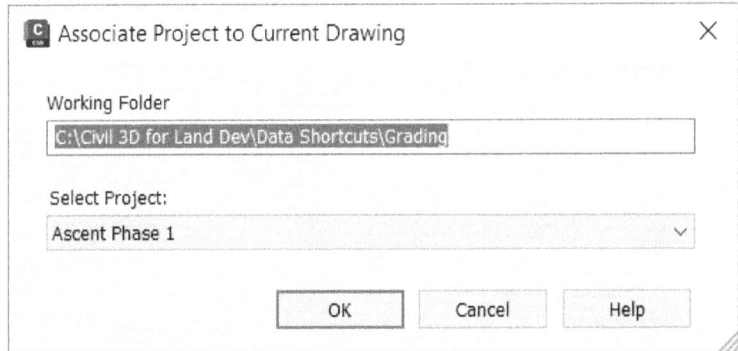

Figure 7–13

3. If you have any drawings from the *C:\Civil 3D for Land Dev\ Working\Sample* folder open, close them now. Otherwise you will get error messages in the next steps.

4. In the *Prospector* tab, right-click on **Data Shortcuts** and select **Associate Project to Multiple Drawings**, as shown in Figure 7–14.

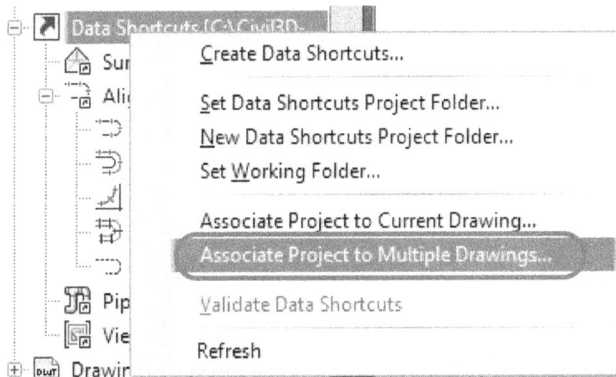

Figure 7–14

5. In the Associate Project to Multiple Drawings dialog box, click **OK** to accept the default working folder and project.

You will only associate the drawings in the Sample folder to the Ascent Phase 1 project so as not to disturb the other practice drawings which are associated with the Ascent Development project.

6. In the Browse for Folder dialog box, and in the Select a folder containing the drawings: dialog box, select *C:\Civil 3D for Land Dev\Working\Sample*, as shown in Figure 7–15. Click **OK**.

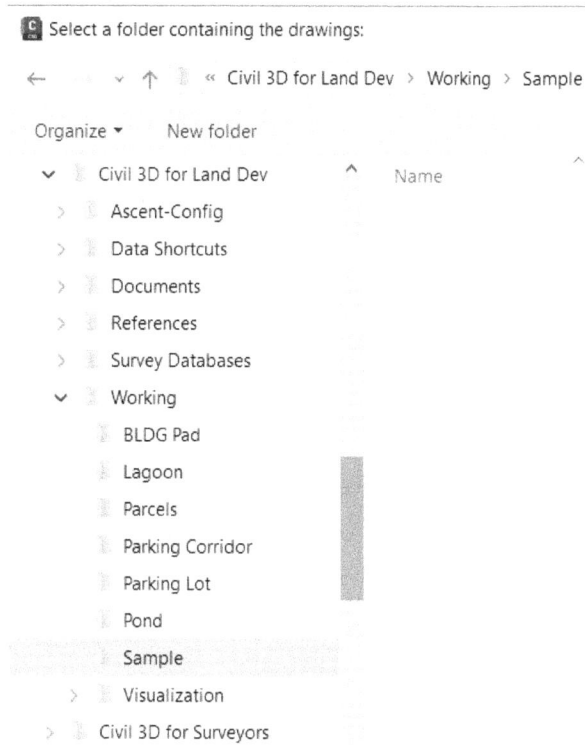

Figure 7–15

7. It will take a while for Civil 3D to process all the drawings, so be patient. If any of these drawings are currently open, you will get an error message on the Command Line.

8. Save and close the drawing.

Practice 7b | Data Shortcuts II

Practice Objective

- Create Data Shortcuts from objects in a drawing to share with other team members.

In this practice, you will create data shortcuts of the various surfaces within the *Sample* folder for the Ascent Phase 1 project you created previously. You will combine them into a finished ground surface,

Task 1 - Create Data Shortcuts.

1. Open **PARCELS-Complete.dwg** from the *C:\Civil 3D for Land Dev\Working\Sample* folder.

2. In the *Prospector* tab, verify that the Data Shortcuts points to the correct folder, as shown in Figure 7–16. If it is not, set the **Data Shortcuts Working Folder** to *C:\Civil 3D for Land Dev\ Data Shortcuts\Grading* folder and the **Data Shortcuts Project folder** to *Ascent Phase 1*, as you have done previously in this guide.

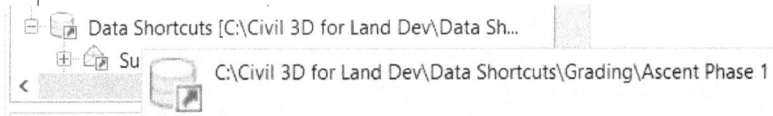

Data Shortcuts [C:\Civil 3D for Land Dev\Data Sh...
Su   C:\Civil 3D for Land Dev\Data Shortcuts\Grading\Ascent Phase 1

Figure 7–16

This drawing contains some surfaces for which you need to create Data Shortcuts.

3. Verify in the title bar at the top of the Civil 3D screen, the drawing name is displayed, as well as the **Ascent Phase 1** project the drawing is associated with (in square brackets), as shown in Figure 7–17. If it is not, then associate this drawing to the **Ascent Phase 1** project as you had done previously.

Autodesk Civil 3D 2023   PARCELS-Complete.dwg [Ascent Phase 1]

Home   Insert   Annotate   Modify   Analyze   View   Manage   Output   Survey   Rail   Transparent   InfraWorks   Collaborate   Help   Add-ins

Figure 7–17

4. In the *Manage* tab>Data Shortcuts panel, click [icon] (Create Data Shortcuts), as shown in Figure 7–18.

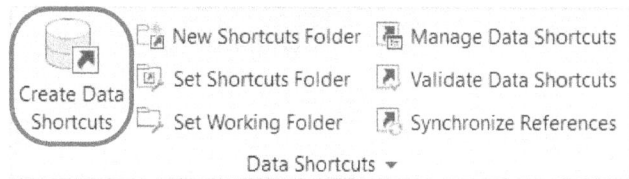

New Shortcuts Folder   Manage Data Shortcuts
Set Shortcuts Folder   Validate Data Shortcuts
Create Data
Shortcuts   Set Working Folder   Synchronize References

Data Shortcuts ▾

Figure 7–18

5. If you receive a message that the drawing has not yet been saved, click **OK**. Save the drawing and start the **Create Data Shortcuts** command again.

6. If you receive an error from the Event Viewer that the Jeffries Ranch Rd baseline hasn't been published, you can ignore it. That alignment is for another project. Click the green checkmark to dismiss the Event Viewer, as shown in Figure 7–19.

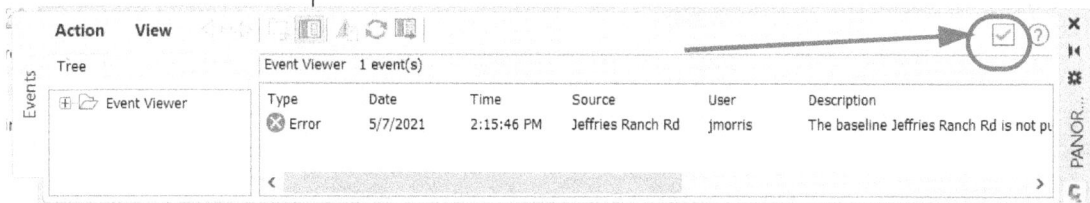

Figure 7–19

7. In the Create Data Shortcuts dialog box, a list of all of the objects available for use in shortcuts is displayed. Select **Residential Grading**, as shown in Figure 7–20, and click **OK**.

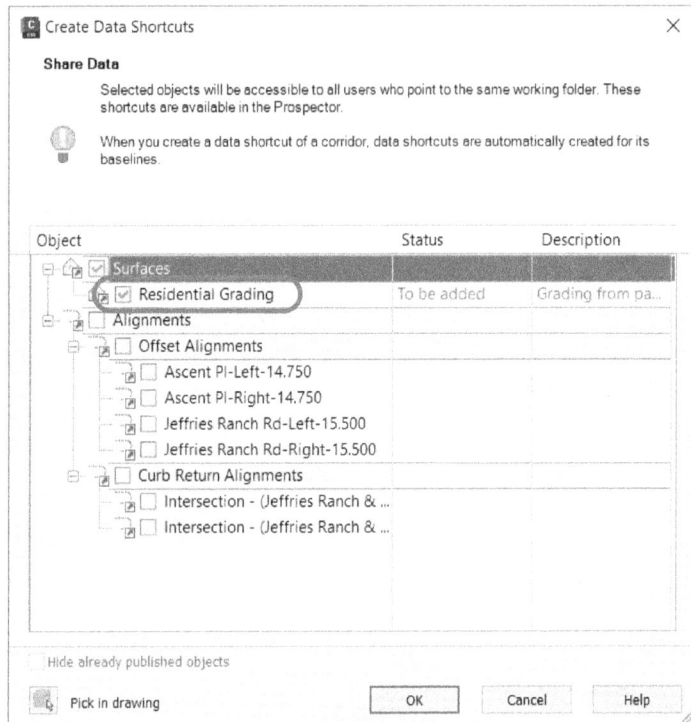

Figure 7–20

8. Save and close the drawing.

9. Open **PKLOT-Complete.dwg** from the *C:\Civil 3D for Land Dev\Working\Sample* folder.

10. In the *Prospector* tab, verify that the Data Shortcuts points to the correct folder, as shown in Figure 7–21. If it is not, set the **Data Shortcuts Working Folder** to *C:\Civil 3D for Land Dev\ Data Shortcuts\Grading* folder and the **Data Shortcuts Project folder** to *Ascent Phase 1*, as you have done in previous practices.

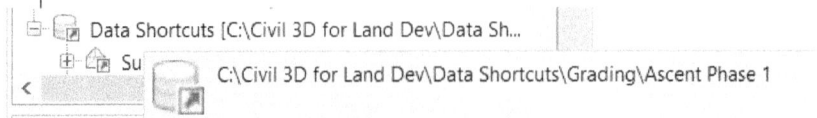

Figure 7–21

11. Verify in the title bar at the top of the Civil 3D screen, the drawing name is displayed, as well as the **Ascent Phase 1** project the drawing is associated with (in square brackets). If it is not, then associate this drawing to the **Ascent Phase 1** project as you had done previously.

12. In the *Manage* tab>Data Shortcuts panel, click ⬚ (Create Data Shortcuts).

13. If you receive a message that the drawing has not yet been saved, click **OK**. Save the drawing and start the **Create Data Shortcuts** command again.

14. In the Create Data Shortcuts dialog box, select the **Parking Lot** surface only **NOT** the Temp Parking Lot, as shown in Figure 7–22, and click **OK**.

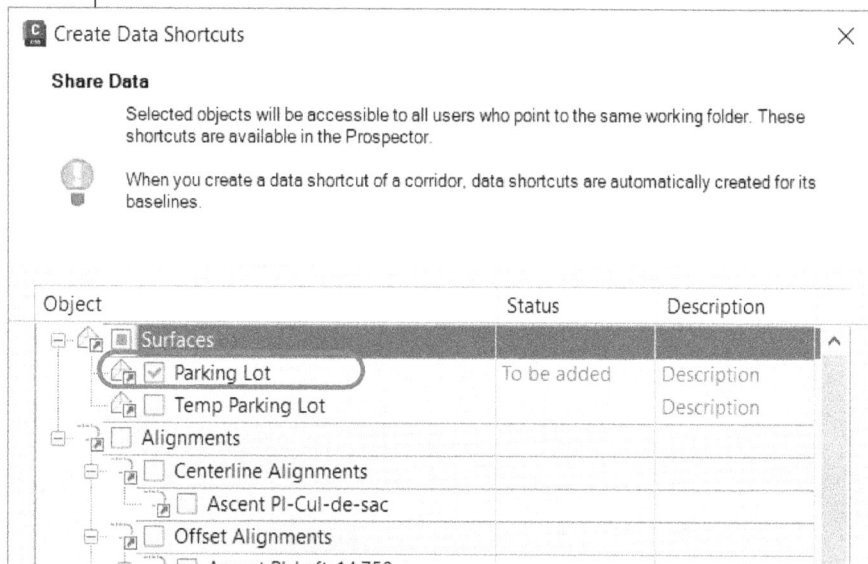

Figure 7–22

15. Save and close the drawing.

16. Open **BLDG-Pads-Complete.dwg** from the *C:\Civil 3D for Land Dev\Working\Sample* folder.

17. In the *Prospector* tab, verify that the Data Shortcuts points to the correct folder, as shown in Figure 7–23. If it is not, set the **Data Shortcuts Working Folder** to *C:\Civil 3D for Land Dev\ Data Shortcuts\Grading* folder and the **Data Shortcuts Project folder** to *Ascent Phase 1*, as you have done in previous practices.

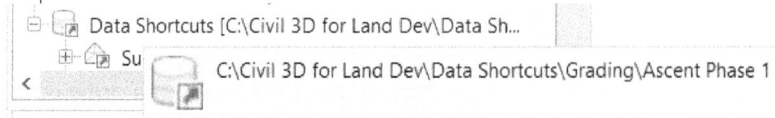

Figure 7–23

18. Verify in the title bar at the top of the Civil 3D screen, the drawing name is displayed, as well as the **Ascent Phase 1** project the drawing is associated with (in square brackets). If it is not, then associate this drawing to the **Ascent Phase 1** project as you had done previously.

19. In the *Manage* tab>Data Shortcuts panel, click (Create Data Shortcuts).

20. If you receive a message that the drawing has not yet been saved, click **OK**. Save the drawing and start the **Create Data Shortcuts** command again.

21. In the Create Data Shortcuts dialog box, select the **Building Pads** and the **Office Pad** surfaces only, as shown in Figure 7–24, and click **OK**.

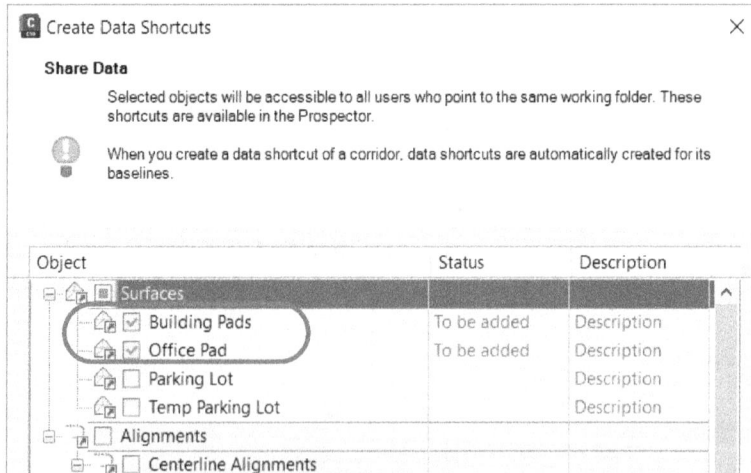

Figure 7–24

22. Save and close the drawing.

23. Open **POND-Complete.dwg** from the *C:\Civil 3D for Land Dev\Working\Sample* folder.

24. In the *Prospector* tab, verify that the Data Shortcuts points to the correct folder, as shown in Figure 7–25. If it is not, set the **Data Shortcuts Working Folder** to *C:\Civil 3D for Land Dev\ Data Shortcuts\Grading* folder and the **Data Shortcuts Project folder** to *Ascent Phase 1*, as you have done previously in this guide.

Data Shortcuts [C:\Civil 3D for Land Dev\Data Sh...

Su   C:\Civil 3D for Land Dev\Data Shortcuts\Grading\Ascent Phase 1

Figure 7–25

25. Verify in the title bar at the top of the Civil 3D screen, the drawing name is displayed, as well as the **Ascent Phase 1** project the drawing is associated with (in square brackets). If it is not, then associate this drawing to the **Ascent Phase 1** project as you had done previously.

26. In the *Manage* tab>Data Shortcuts panel, click (Create Data Shortcuts).

27. If you receive a message that the drawing has not yet been saved, click **OK**. Save the drawing and start the **Create Data Shortcuts** command again.

28. In the Create Data Shortcuts dialog box, select the **Pond** surface, as shown in Figure 7–26, and click **OK**.

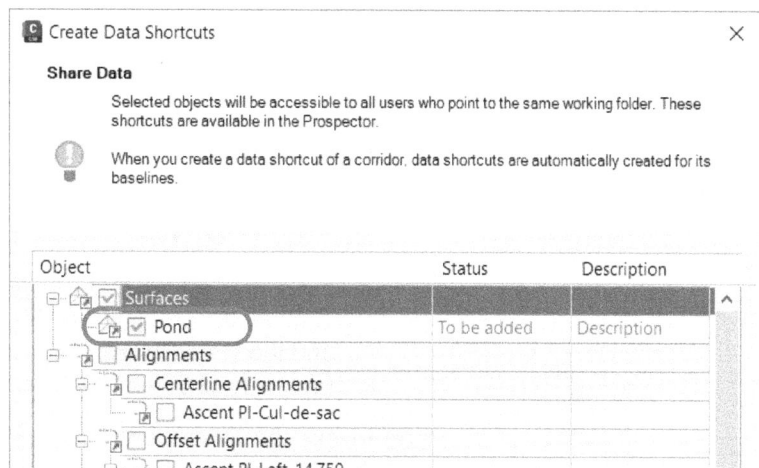

Figure 7–26

You have now created shortcuts for the surfaces. This means that if the shortcuts and drawings are in a shared network folder, anyone on the network has access to these Autodesk Civil 3D objects.

- Note that in the *Prospector* tab, under the *Data Shortcuts* and *Surfaces* collections, you can now access all of the surfaces. In the list view, the source file name and source path are displayed, as shown in Figure 7–27.

```
Data Shortcuts [C:\Civil 3D for Land Dev\Data Shortcuts\Gra
    Surfaces
        Building Pads
        Office Pad
        Parking Lot
        Pond
        Residential Grading
    Alignments
    Pipe Networks
```

Figure 7–27

29. Save and close the drawing.

Task 2 - Data-reference Data Shortcuts.

---

1. Start a new drawing from **ASC-GRD (CA83-VIF) NCS.dwt** from the *C:\Civil 3D for Land Dev\Working\Ascent-Config* folder.

2. Erase the message about the set coordinate system in the center of the screen.

3. Save it as **DS-Option.dwg** in the *C:\Civil 3D for Land Dev\ Data Shortcuts\Practice* folder.

4. In the *Prospector* tab, ensure that Data Shortcuts points to the *C:\Civil 3D for Land Dev\Data Shortcuts\Grading* folder.

   - If it is not, set the **Data Shortcuts Working Folder** to *C:\Civil 3D for Land Dev\Data Shortcuts\Grading* folder and the **Data Shortcuts Project folder** to *Ascent Phase 1*, as you have done in previous practices.

5. Invoke the External References panel by typing **XREF** at the command prompt.

6. In the upper-left corner of the External References panel,

   select ▦ (Attach DWG), as shown in Figure 7–28.

Figure 7–28

7. Select **Base-Proposed Engineering.dwg** from the *C:\Civil 3D for Land Dev\References\DWG* folder and click **Open**.

8. In the Attach External Reference dialog box, set the following:

   • *Scale*: Leave box unchecked and leave *X, Y* and *Z* values as **1.00**
   • *Path Type*: **Relative path**
   • *Insertion point:* Leave box unchecked and leave *X, Y* and *Z* values as **0.00**
   • *Rotation:* Leave box unchecked and leave *X* value as **0**
   • *Reference Type:* Set to **Overlay**

9. Click **OK**.

10. Close the External References panel.

11. In the *Prospector* tab, under the *Data Shortcuts* collection, expand the *Surfaces* collection (if not already expanded), as shown in Figure 7–29.

Figure 7–29

12. Under the *Surfaces* collection, right-click on the surface **Building Pads** and select **Create Reference...**, as shown in Figure 7–30.

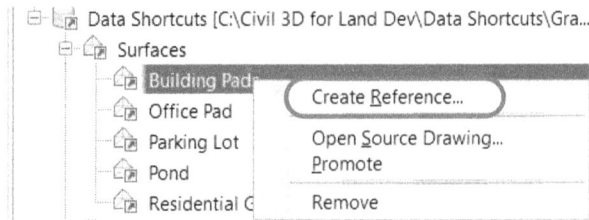

Figure 7–30

13. In the Create Surface Reference dialog box, complete the following, as shown in Figure 7–31:

- For the *Name*, leave as default.
- For the *Description*, type **Data referenced building pads.**
- For the *Style*, select **_No Display**.

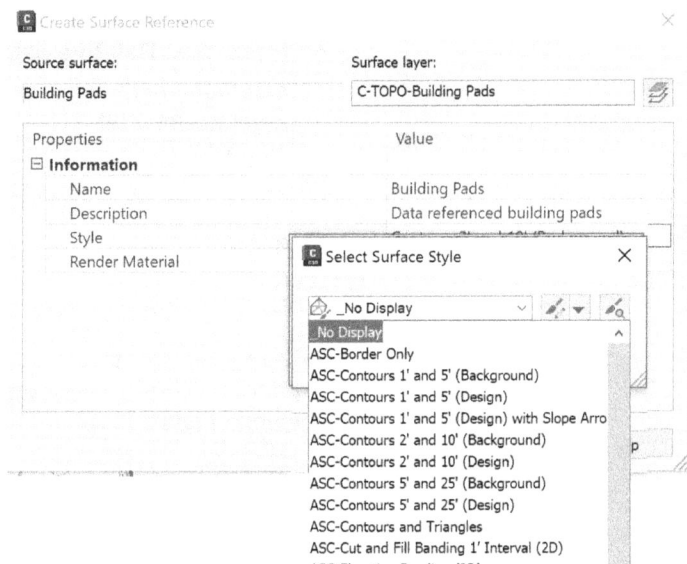

Figure 7–31

14. Click **OK** to close the dialog box.

15. Repeat Steps 6 to 8 to create references to the other four surfaces in the project, leave the names as the default, give appropriate descriptions and ensure that the surface style is set to the **_No Display** (which should be the default from the last surface reference creation).

16. Save the drawing.

Task 3 - Make the Ascent Development project current.

1. In the *Manage* tab>Data Shortcuts panel, click □ (Set Working Folder), as shown in Figure 7–32.

Figure 7–32

2. In the Browse For Folder dialog box, select the *Civil 3D for Land Dev\DataShortcuts\Fundamentals* folder. Click **Select Folder**.

3. In the *Manage* tab>Data Shortcuts panel, click 📝 (Set Shortcuts Folder), as shown in Figure 7–33.

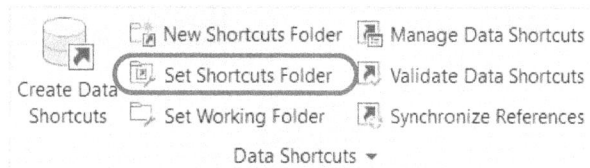

Figure 7–33

4. In the Set Data Shortcut Folder dialog box, select the **Ascent-Development** project, as shown in Figure 7–34.

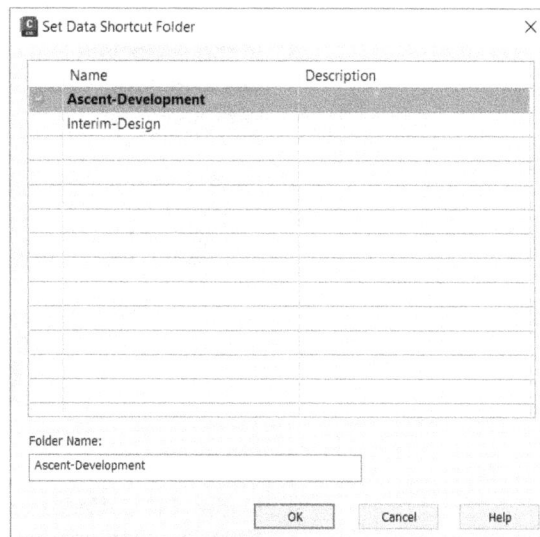

Figure 7–34

5. Click **OK**.

6. In the Toolspace, *Prospector* tab, verify that the Data Shortcuts points to the correct folder, as shown in Figure 7–35. By hovering over the Data Shortcuts heading, the full path gets revealed in the tooltip.

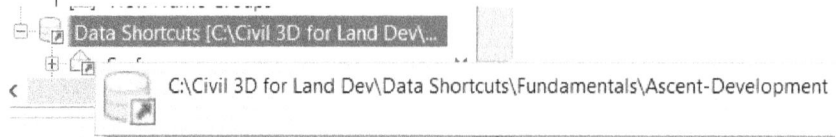

Data Shortcuts [C:\Civil 3D for Land Dev\...

C:\Civil 3D for Land Dev\Data Shortcuts\Fundamentals\Ascent-Development

Figure 7–35

7. In the *Prospector* tab, right-click on Data Shortcuts and select **Associate Project to Current Drawing**, as shown in Figure 7–36.

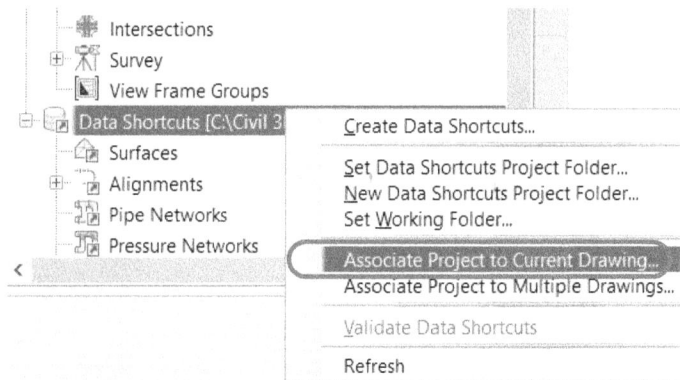

Figure 7–36

8. In the Associate Project to Current Drawing dialog box, click **OK** to accept the default working folder and project, as shown in Figure 7–37.

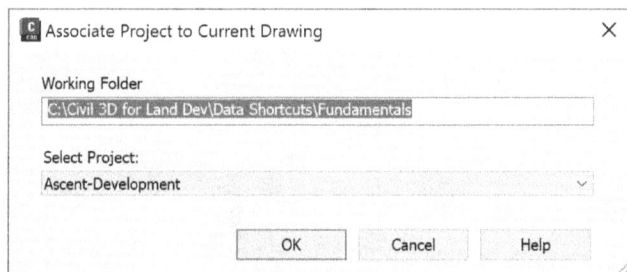

Figure 7–37

9. Under the *Surfaces* collection, right-click on the surface **Existing Site** and select **Create Reference**, as shown in Figure 7–38.

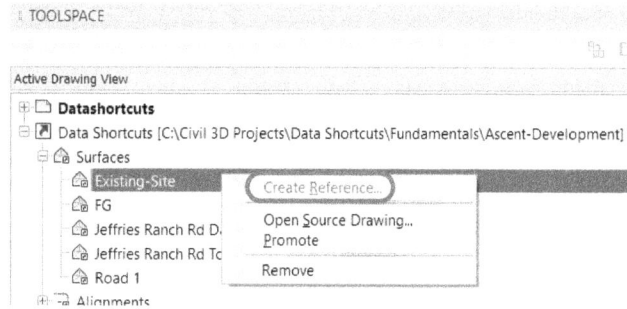

Figure 7–38

You can rename the reference surface and assign a different surface and render style.

10. In the Create Surface Reference dialog box, complete the following, as shown in Figure 7–39:

   • For the *Name*, leave as default.
   • For the *Description*, type **Data referenced existing surface**.
   • For the *Style,* set **ASC-Contours 5' and 25' (Background)**.

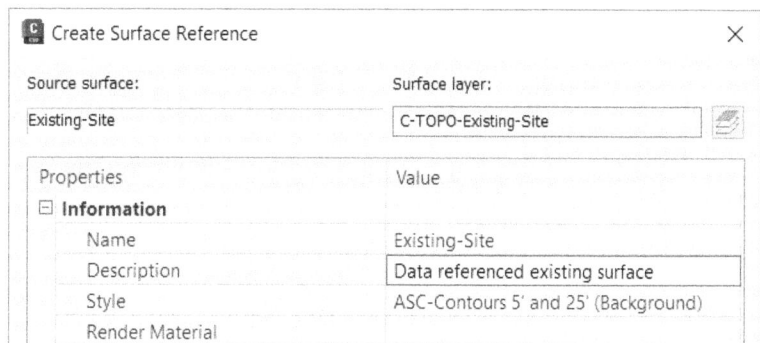

Figure 7–39

11. Click **OK** to close the dialog box.

12. Repeat Steps 9 to 11 to create references to the following:

   • **Ascent Pl Top**
   • **Jeffries Ranch Rd Top**
   • **Rand Boulevard Top**
   • **Roundabout (Jeffries Ranch - Rand Blvd) Top**

   Leave the names as default, provide appropriate descriptions, and set the surface style to **_No Display**.

13. Type **ZE** and press <Enter> to display the surface reference. The only surface to be displayed is the Existing Site, all others have been set to the *_No Display* style.

14. Save the drawing.

Task 4 - Combine surfaces into one.

1. Continue working in the drawing from the previous task.

2. In the *Home* tab>Create Ground Data panel, expand the Surfaces drop-down list and click ⌂ (Create Surface).

3. In the Create Surface dialog box, complete the following:

   - For the *Name*, type **Finished Ground - North Sector**.
   - For the *Description*, type **Combined finish grading surfaces from references**.
   - For the *Style,* select **ASC-Contours 2' and 10' (Design)**.
   - Set the *Rendering Material* to **Sitework.Planting.Grass.Thick**.
   - Click **OK** to close the dialog box.

4. In the *Prospector* tab, expand **Surfaces>Finished Ground - North Sector>Definition**. Right-click on Edits and select **Paste Surface**.

Hold down the <Ctrl> key to select multiple surfaces in the list.

5. In the Select Surface to Paste dialog box, select all the surfaces except for the Existing Site, as follows:

   - **Jeffries Ranch Rd Top**
   - **Ascent Pl-Top**
   - **Rand Boulevard Top**
   - **Roundabout (Jeffries Ranch - Rand Blvd) Top**
   - **Residential Grading**
   - **Pond**
   - **Parking Lot**
   - **Building Pads**
   - **Office Pad**

6. Click **OK** to close the dialog box.

7. Save the drawing. (Before opening the Object Viewer in the next step, it is always prudent to save the drawing.)

8. Select the **Finished Ground - North Sector** surface, right-click, and select **Object Viewer** to study it. Set the *Visual Style* to **Shaded with Edges** and navigate to the area of interest, as shown in Figure 7–40.

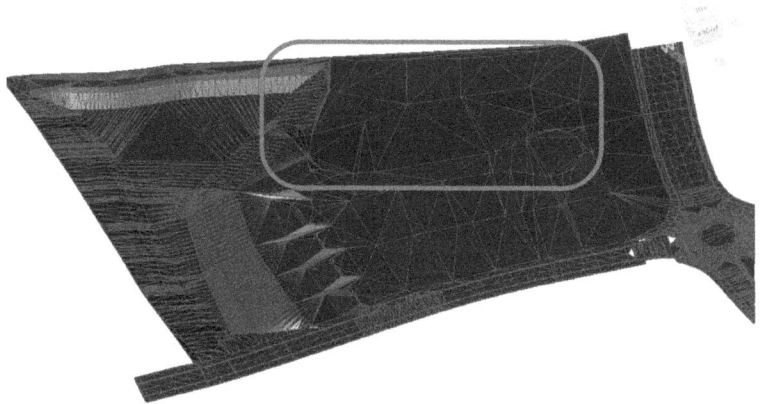

Figure 7–40

- The surface isn't correct; the parking lot and building pads are not present.

9. To ensure that the surfaces were pasted in the proper order, select the surface in the drawing. In the *Tin Surface* contextual tab>Modify panel, click ⬛ (Surface Properties).

10. In the Surface Properties>*Definition* tab, note the order the surfaces were pasted in, as shown in Figure 7–41.

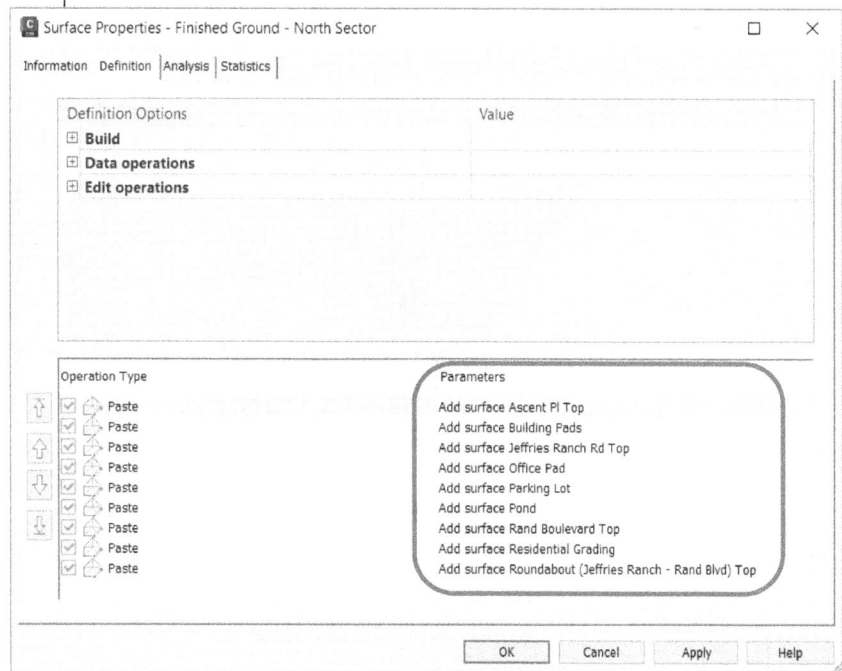

Figure 7–41

11. Arrange the Operation Type in the sequence that they would be created on the construction site, as outlined above in Step 5. You can order by selecting a **Paste** operation and moving it up or down with the arrows on the left, as shown in Figure 7–42. Each time you move an entry, a yellow alert icon appears.

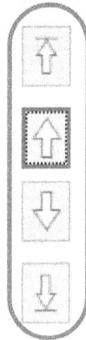

Add surface Jeffries Ranch Rd Top

Add surface Ascent Pl Top

Add surface Rand Boulevard Top

Add surface Roundabout (Jeffries Ranch - Rand Blvd) Top

Add surface Residential Grading

Add surface Pond

Add surface Parking Lot

Add surface Building Pads

Add surface Office Pad

Figure 7–42

12. Click **OK** to close the dialog box. Select **Rebuild the Surface** when prompted.

13. Note the difference in the surface. The building pads and parking lot are now apparent, as shown in Figure 7–43.

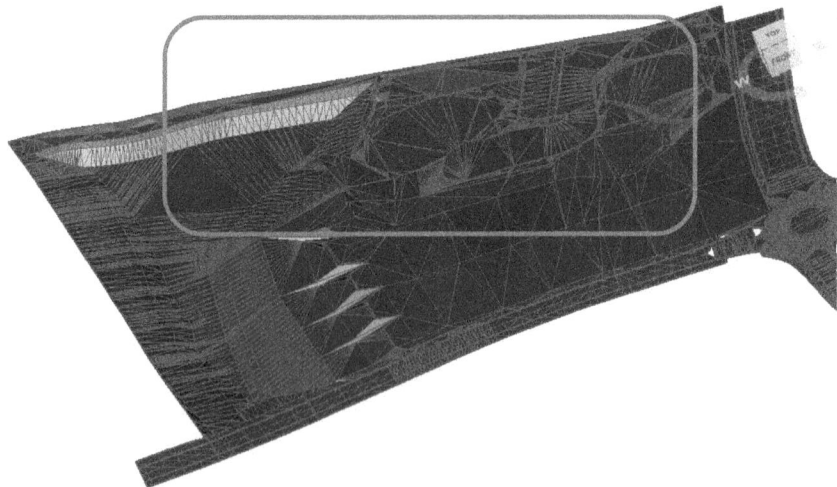

Figure 7–43

14. Save the drawing.

Practice 7c

Share Projects with Team Members Outside the Office Network

Practice Objective

- Create a transmittal package to send to other design professionals on the project team, which includes all of the referenced object drawings, XREFs, and other required files.

In this practice, you will create a transmittal to send the drawing and all its dependencies to other interested parties.

1. Continue working with the previously opened drawing.

2. Expand **C C3D** (Application Menu)>**Publish** and select **eTransmit**, as shown in Figure 7–44. If a warning dialog box opens stating that the current drawing is not saved, click **Yes** to save it.

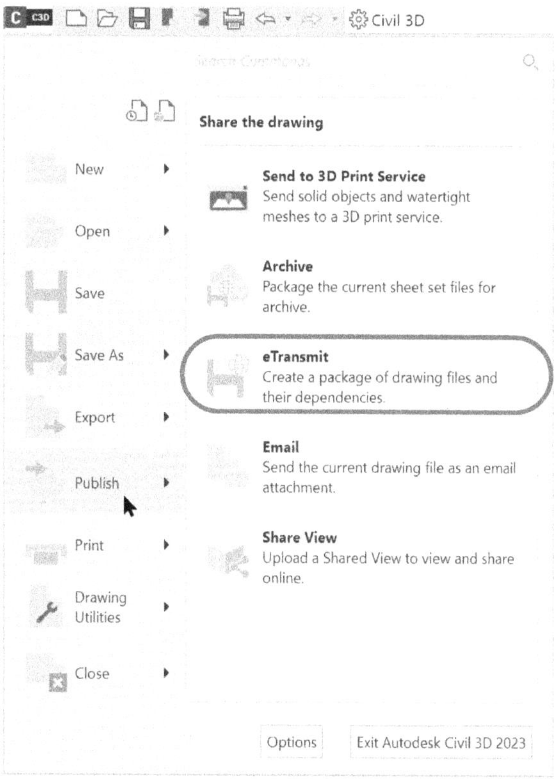

Figure 7–44

3. In the Create Transmittal dialog box, click **Transmittal Setups**, as shown in Figure 7–45.

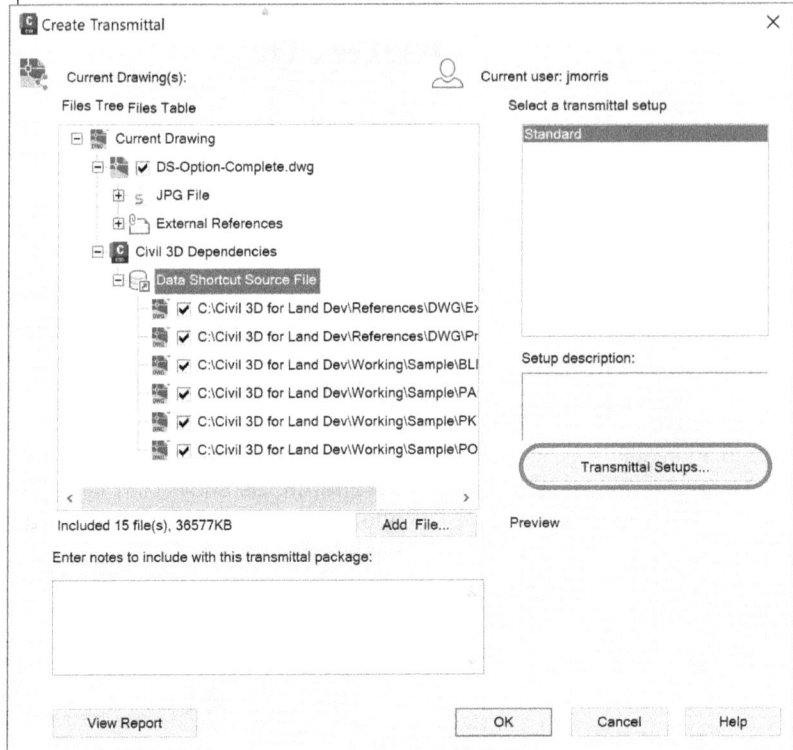

Figure 7–45

4. In the Transmittal Setups dialog box, select the **Standard** setup and click **Modify**, as shown in Figure 7–46.

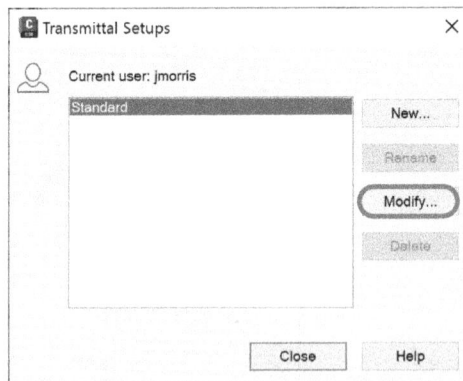

Figure 7–46

5. In the Modify Transmittal Setup dialog box (as shown in Figure 7–47):

- Accept the default for *Transmittal file folder*.
- Expand the *Transmittal file name* drop-down list and select **Prompt for a filename**.
- Select the **Keep files and folders as is** option.
- In the *Include options* area, select all of the options **except** the **Include unloaded file references** option.
- Type **Submittal for Municipality review** in the *Transmittal setup description*.
- Accept the remaining defaults and click **OK** to close the dialog box.

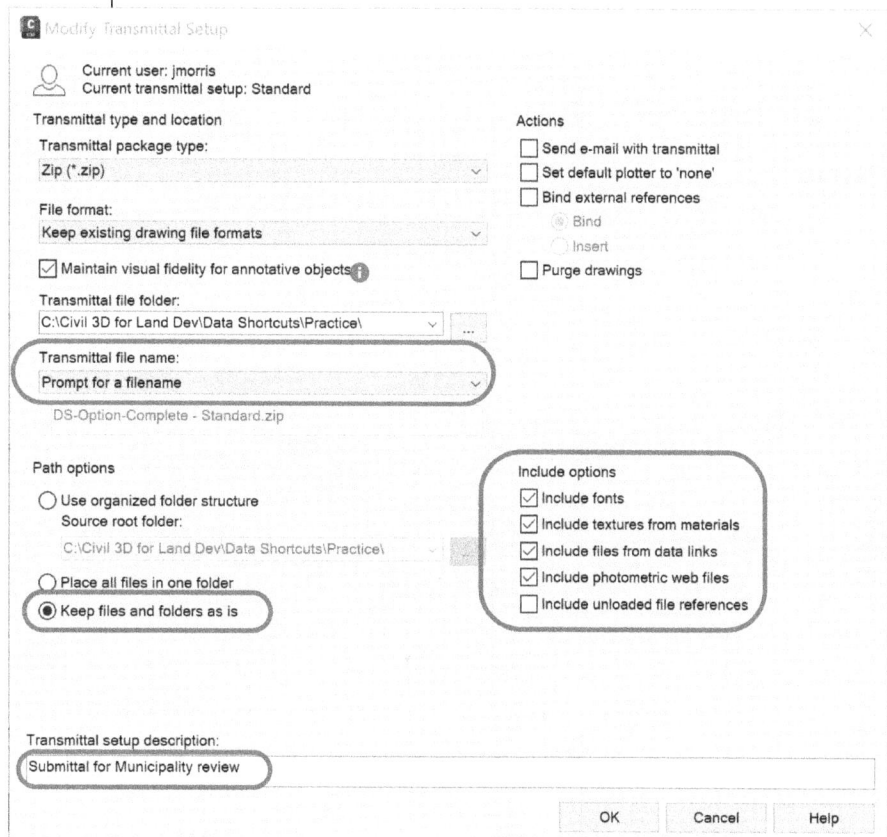

Figure 7–47

6. Close the Transmittal Setups dialog box.

7. Click **OK** to close the Create Transmittal dialog box and create the transmittal.

8. When prompted for the file name for the transmittal file, accept the default location and file name and save it. The Autodesk Civil 3D software will create a compressed file of all of the relevant data.

9. Save and close the drawing.

Chapter Review Questions

1. In the Autodesk Civil 3D workflow, what are the two main methods of project collaboration (or the sharing of intelligent Autodesk Civil 3D design data)?

   a. Windows Explorer and XREFs.

   b. Data Shortcuts and Vault references.

   c. XREFs and Data Shortcuts.

   d. Vault references and XREFs.

2. Why would you want to use Vault references over Data Shortcuts?

   a. Added security and version control.

   b. Permit more people to have access.

   c. It works more like the Autodesk® Land Desktop software.

   d. It works better with multiple offices.

3. How can you edit an object referenced through Data Shortcuts?

   a. Open the source drawing.

   b. With grips.

   c. Using the Panorama view.

   d. You cannot do it.

4. What is the file format that Data Shortcuts use to share design data between drawing files?

   a. SHP

   b. DWT

   c. DWG

   d. XML

Command Summary

Button	Command	Location
	Create Data Shortcuts	• **Ribbon:** *Manage* tab>Data Shortcuts panel • **Command Prompt:** CreateDataShortcuts
	New Shortcuts Folder	• **Ribbon:** *Manage* tab>Data Shortcuts panel • **Command Prompt:** NewShortcutsFolder
	Set Shortcuts Folder	• **Ribbon:** *Manage* tab>Data Shortcuts panel • **Command Prompt:** SetShortcutsFolder
	Set Working Folder	• **Ribbon:** *Manage* tab>Data Shortcuts panel • **Command Prompt:** SetWorkingFolder

Chapter 8

Using InfraWorks for Visualization

In this chapter, you will learn about Building Information Modeling (BIM) and how it is used in the Autodesk® InfraWorks® software. You will learn how to bring in a Civil 3D drawing and other source files, add details to the file, add visualization, and create a storyboard for output.

Learning Objectives in This Chapter

- Locate basic features and commands in the Autodesk InfraWorks software interface.
- Navigate a model.
- Connect to select data source types to display the model.
- Create water features in a model to represent a pond.
- Add predefined 3D buildings to a model.
- Create city furniture to add bike racks and other 3D models to a model.
- Add landscaping details to a model using trees and other vegetation.

Note: This guide is based on the 2022.1 release of the Autodesk InfraWorks software. There might be differences between the software used in this guide and newer versions of the software. ASCENT reviews newer software releases and the changes within; if differences are significant, ASCENT will issue Readme files within the training dataset.

Please check for such Readme documentation within the *C:\Civil 3D for Land Dev\Working\Visualization* folder. If present, those instructions supersede the steps outlined here.

8.1 Building Information Modeling

The Autodesk InfraWorks software is a powerful Building Information Modeling (BIM) program that streamlines site design and the design process for different types of infrastructure projects by using a 3D model. The BIM process supports the ability to coordinate, update, and share design data with team members throughout the design, construction, and management phases of a project's life cycle.

The Autodesk InfraWorks software creates data-rich models using information about the existing environment. Using these models supports more informed decision-making and an accelerated site design process. You can create multiple design alternatives in one model, enabling you to quickly estimate the budget, scope, and schedule with an appropriate level of detail from the beginning of a project. The high-impact visuals that are automatically created during the design process better communicate the design intent to stakeholders.

The Autodesk InfraWorks software coordinates with other software, such as the Autodesk® Civil 3D® software and the Autodesk® Revit® software, to reduce rework and seamlessly enable coordination between project team members.

Launching the Software

The Autodesk InfraWorks software can be launched by double-clicking on (Autodesk InfraWorks) on the desktop or selecting it from the Start menu.

When you open the software for the first time (and periodically thereafter), you must sign in to the Online Autodesk Account. The Autodesk Account Sign In screen displays automatically, as shown in Figure 8–1. Enter your username and click **NEXT**. Enter your password and click **SIGN IN**.

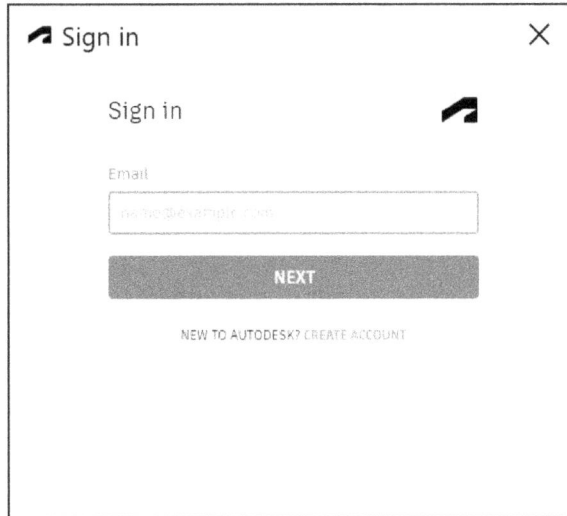

Figure 8–1

8.2 Overview of the Interface

The Autodesk InfraWorks user interface is designed for intuitive and efficient access to commands and views. It includes the Home Screen and the Model View.

Home Screen

When Autodesk InfraWorks is initially launched, the Home Screen displays, as shown in Figure 8–2. This screen enables you to:

- Preview recent models.

- Access Model Builder.

- Open existing or create new models.

- Toggle on and off available feature previews.

- Collaborate with others.

Preview thumbnails for recent models

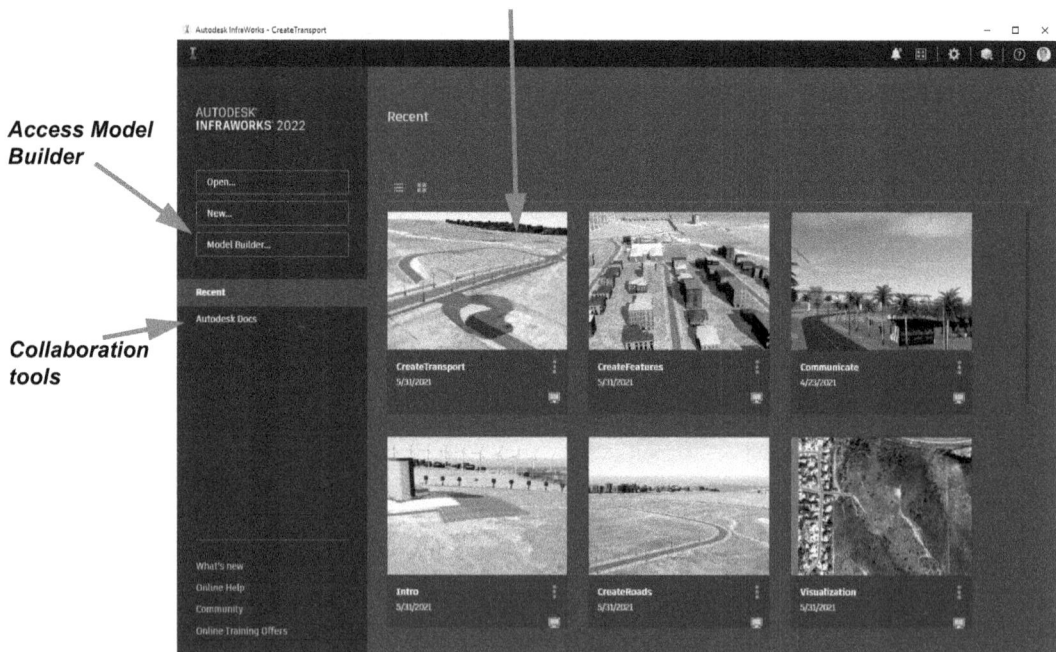

Access Model Builder

Collaboration tools

Figure 8–2

- Various icons display on each preview thumbnail, as shown in Figure 8–3.

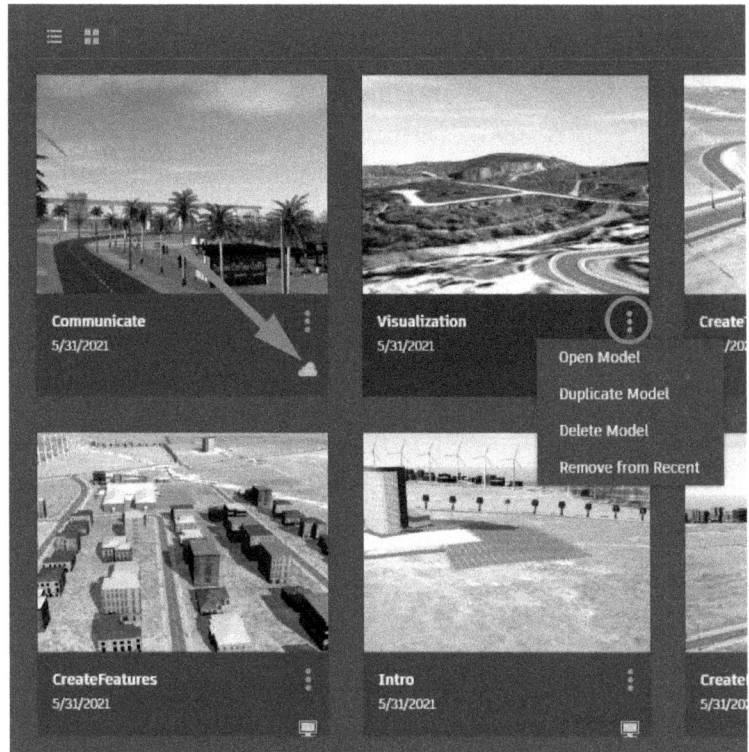

Figure 8–3

*A **Save** option is not available because the model is a database file (SQLite), which saves after every action. The **Duplicate** command, found under Settings and Utilities, enables you to save an existing model to a new file.*

When you hover over a thumbnail, ellipses (three dots) appear in the lower left corner of the thumbnail. Upon clicking on the ellipses, options become available to:

- Open the model
- Duplicate (copy) the model
- Delete the model
- Remove the model from the Recent list

How To: Open a Model

1. In the Home Screen, select tile or list view by clicking the required button at the top, as shown in Figure 8–4.

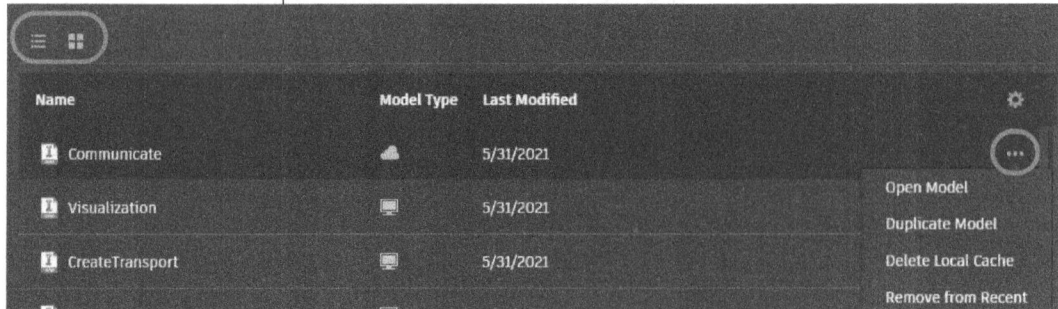

Figure 8–4

2. Click on the preview thumbnail for the model you wish to work in.

   - If the model you need to open is not visible on the Home Screen, click the **Open** button at the top. Then browse for the file location and click **Open**.

   - If the model you need to work with was saved in an older version of the software, you can either **Upgrade** the model or **Create a Copy**, as shown in Figure 8–5.

All team members should sync their changes before any cloud model is upgraded.

Figure 8–5

- If the model you need to work with was saved in a more recent version of the software, you cannot open the model as shown in Figure 8–6. A model cannot be saved to an earlier version, therefore you must upgrade your software to open the model.

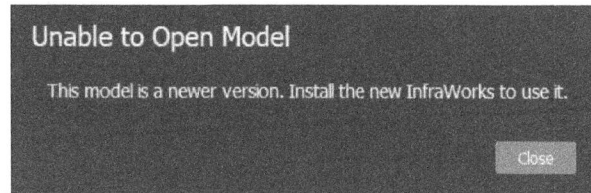

Unable to Open Model

This model is a newer version. Install the new InfraWorks to use it.

Close

Figure 8–6

Model View

The Model View displays when a model is created or opened from the Home Screen. Figure 8–7 shows the components in the model view user interface.

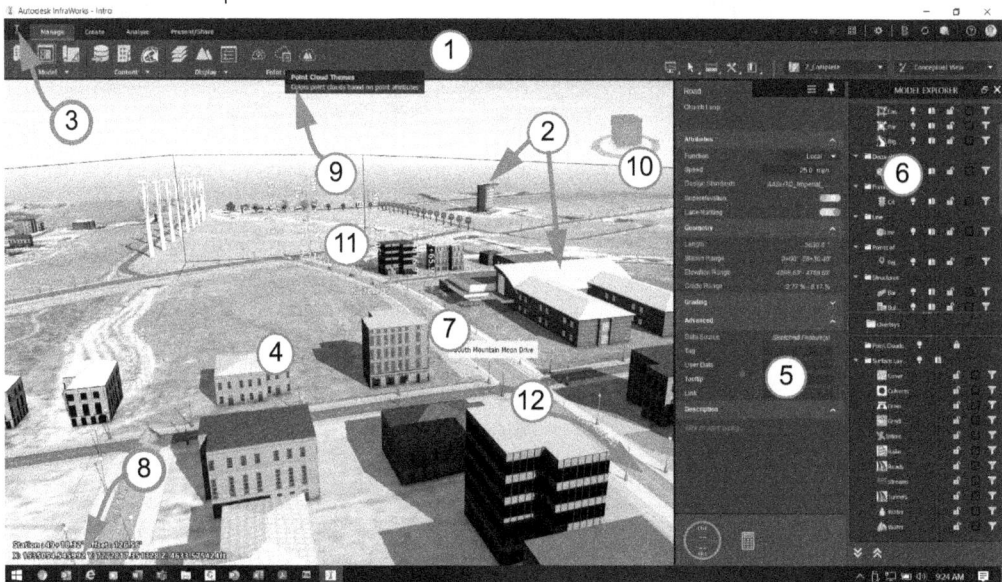

Figure 8–7

1. Toolbar	5. Asset Card	9. Tooltips
2. Buildings from Revit	6. Model Explorer	10. ViewCube
3. Switch to Home	7. Automatic Labels	11. Station labels
4. Buildings from Model Builder	8. Model Coordinates	12. Selected Feature

The following describe some of the elements in detail. For more in-depth coverage, consult the ASCENT InfraWorks guides.

1. Toolbar

The Toolbar provides a variety of frequently used tools. These tools are distributed over a series of tabs on the left side (shown in Figure 8–8). These tabs contain tools for a specific phase of work, coinciding with the workflow of a typical project – from left to right vis-a-vis from start to finish. These tabs are further separated into panels and drop-down menus, similar to those in the Civil 3D and a variety of other Autodesk programs.

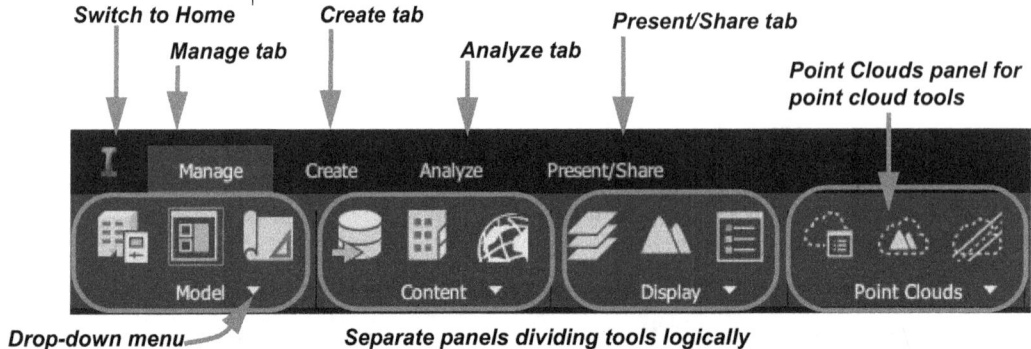

Figure 8–8

On the right-hand side of the toolbar are Common Tools, shown in Figure 8–9, enable you to switch views and proposals, undo/redo commands, and select or edit model components.

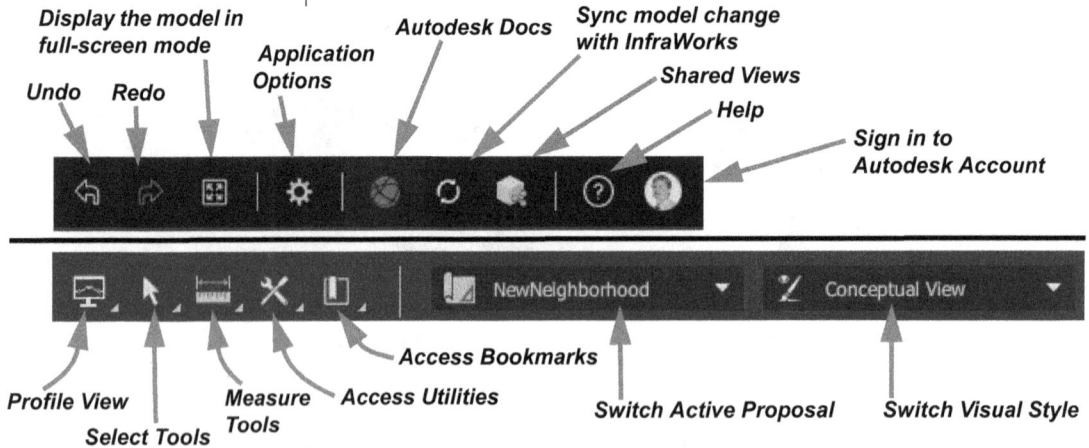

Figure 8–9

2.Toolbar Tabs

The tabs across the top contain a variety of tools for the creation, development, modification, analysis, presentation and sharing of the InfraWorks model, as shown in Figure 8–10.

Manage tab: Tools for adding content to the model, controlling the display, and point clouds.

Create tab: Tools for creating and editing roads, bridges, and misc model content.

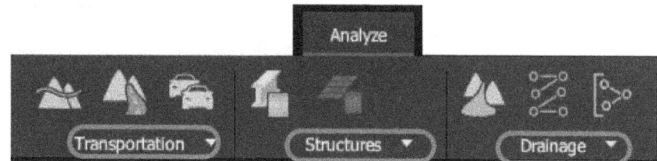

Analyze tab: Tools for analyzing roads, bridges, and drainage.

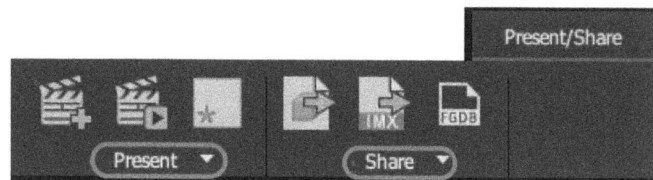

Present/Share tab: Tools for creating images/video, export and sharing options.

Figure 8–10

3.Toolbar Panels

Each tab is divided into panels, as shown above in Figure 8–10. These panels contain the most commonly used tools for the task the panel is named for. The panel is limited to three tools, but there are more tools available in the drop-down menu, which is accessible by clicking on the down arrow next to the panel name (Drainage ▼).

4. Drop-down Tool Menus

Within the drop down menus, as shown in Figure 8–11, are more tools available for the task at hand. Some drop-down menu may only contain three tools, while others can contain many more. Some tools may be grayed out because the tool is not valid for the present state of the model. For example, **Quantities** on the *Structures* drop-down menu would be grayed out if there are no bridges or other structural objects in the model to quantify.

Some drop-down menus with only three tools seem redundant, since the panel is already populated with those three tools. However, the drop-down menus reveal keyboard shortcuts available for these tools. These shortcuts are not visible in the panel itself.

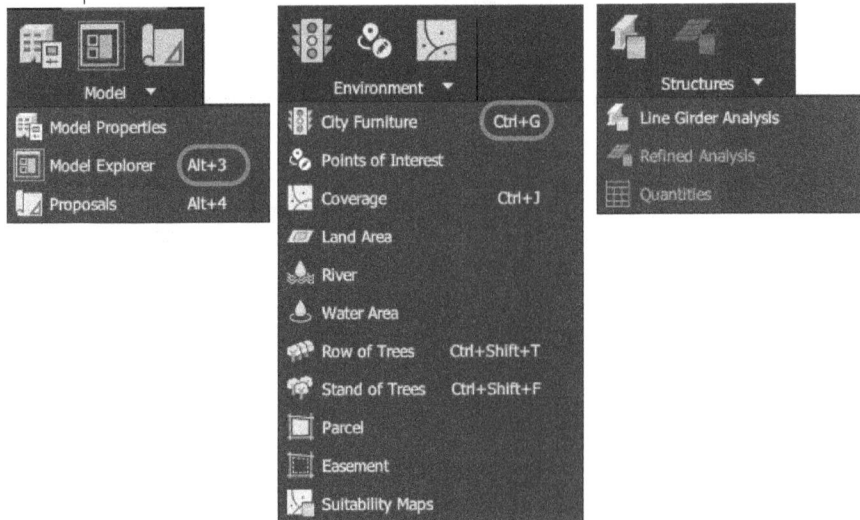

Figure 8–11

The contents within the panels can be rearranged. The panels are limited to three tools, however you can chose the tools,.

How To: Add Tools to a Panel

1. In the drop-down menu, hover over a tool, which causes vertical ellipses ( ) button to be revealed.
2. Click on the vertical ellipses and select **Pin to Toolbar** to put the tool in the panel, as shown in Figure 8–12.

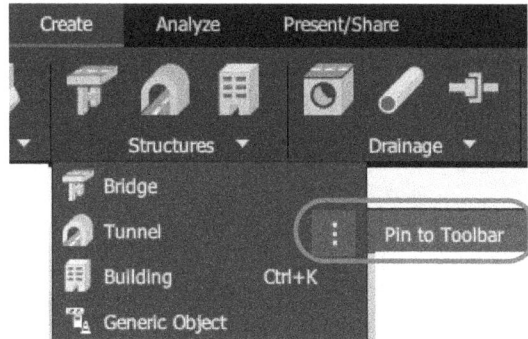

Figure 8–12

Hint: To change the order of the tools already in the panel, simply use the above procedure, picking the last tool you want in the panel first. The tool you chose to be pinned in the panel becomes the first tool listed.

5. Model Window

The Model Window (shown in Figure 8–13) is the working area in which you create model elements.

Figure 8–13

How elements display in the Model Window depends on the visual style selected in the Toolbar. Different view settings can be set up to support different work flows, as shown in Figure 8–14. When working on design roads, you might want to display the surface and buildings in wireframe in order to view their triangular irregular network (TIN). In contrast, when you are communicating the design to stakeholders, you might want a more realistic appearance to communicate what the design should look like when the construction is complete.

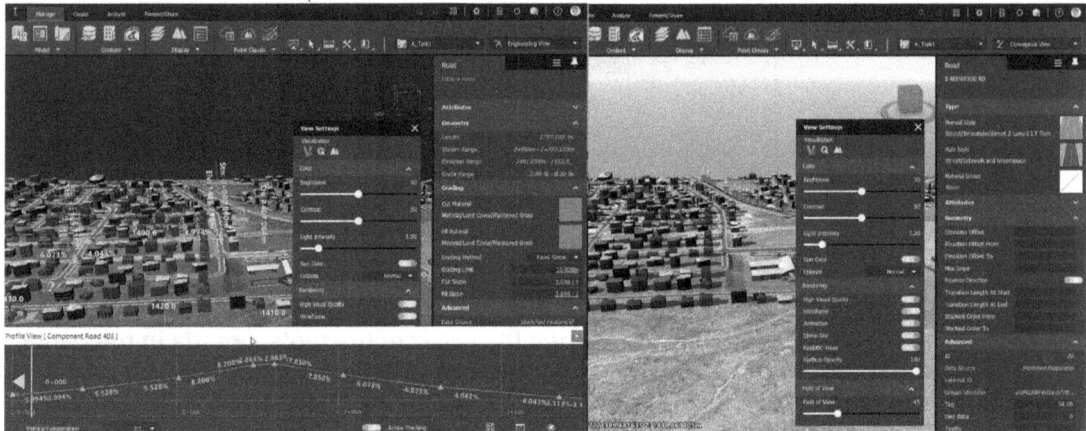

Engineering view style used for creating design elements   *Conceptual view style used for communicating the design*

Figure 8–14

6. Bookmarks

Bookmarks are saved views that quickly reorient the view from one location of the model to another. You can create, preview, and search bookmarks. In addition, you can share bookmarks via Shared Views. Just to the left of the Proposals drop-down list,

selecting ▢ (View bookmarks) produces a list of bookmarks with preview thumbnails displays, as shown in Figure 8–15.

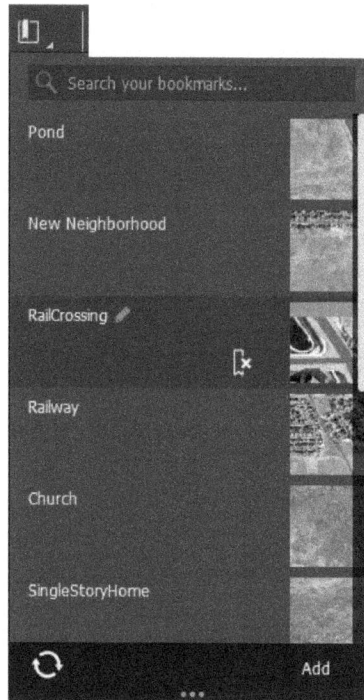

Figure 8–15

Hovering the cursor over a bookmark causes additional tools to display. The table below describes each tool available in the Bookmarks drop-down list.

Icon	Description
	Enables you to rename a specific Bookmark.
	Deletes the specific Bookmark.
	Refreshes the preview thumbnails for all Bookmarks according to what displays in the current proposal.
Add	Adds a new Bookmark for the current model view.

8.3 Creating an InfraWorks Model

All Autodesk InfraWorks models begin by importing existing data from various sources. These sources include building outlines, roads, utilities, terrain, images, etc.

Model Builder

To use this feature, access to the Internet is required.

The easiest way to find GIS data is to use the Model Builder. The Model Builder creates a new model and includes existing datasets from the following sources:

Data Type	Source
Elevation	Terrain data for the United States and its territories uses 10 and 30 meter DEMs from the National Elevation Dataset (NED). The rest of the globe uses SRTM 90m DEM data processed by CIAT-CSI.
Imagery	Satellite imagery from Microsoft® Bing® Maps is draped over the model terrain.
Roads and Highways	OpenStreetMap's (OSM) Highway and Railway datasets are readily available. They are used to create roads and railway features in the model. If feature names are available from OSM, they appear as tooltips and provide a hyperlink to the source feature that opens in the default web browser.
Buildings	The building data is also from the OpenStreetMap dataset.

How To: Create a New Model Using Model Builder

1. In the Home Screen, click **Model Builder**.
2. In the Model Builder dialog box, type the project address in the *Search by Location* field or zoom in on the project area using the map in the left pane, as shown in Figure 8–16.

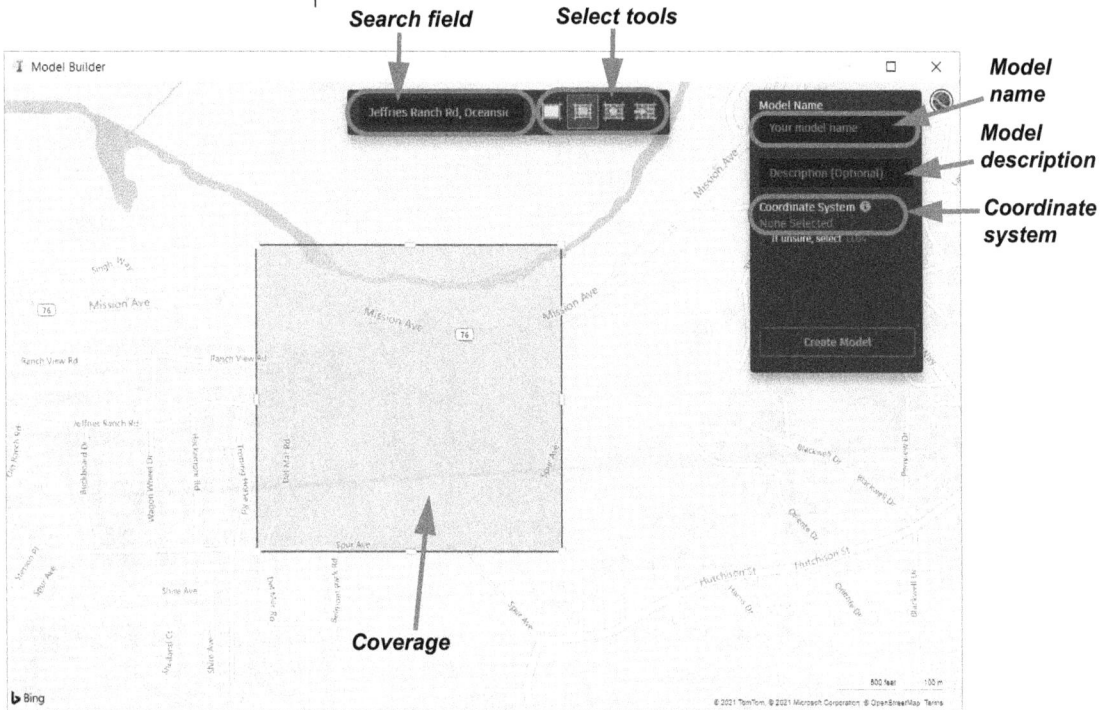

Figure 8–16

3. Use one of the Select tools to define the area of interest (AOI) to include in the model. (Note: There is a 200 sq. km maximum area limit.) You can choose between the following:
   - Select current map extents.
   - Draw a rectangle to select an AOI.
   - Draw a polygon to select an AOI.
   - Import a polygon to select an AOI.
4. Type a name for the model.
5. Type a description for the model.

6. Assign a **coordinate system** by opening the Select Coordinate System dialog box. You can type in the coordinate system's abbreviation, shown in Figure 8–17, or browse through the available systems in the list. Click **OK** when one is selected.

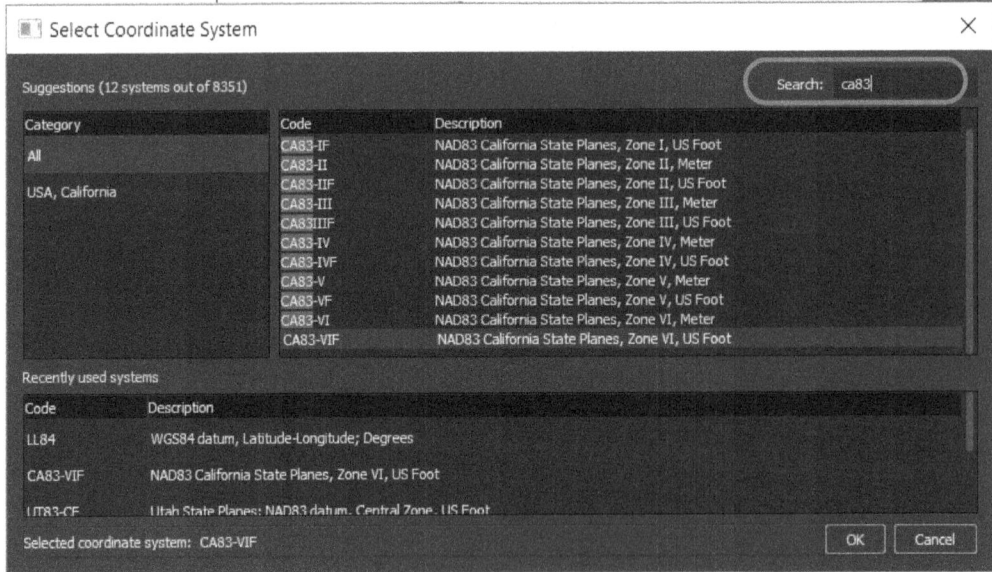

Figure 8–17

7. Click **Create Model**. The model is created in the background. Click **Close** in the Model Builder message box.
8. Close the Model Builder.
9. In the Home Screen, click on the newly created model to open it, as shown in Figure 8–18.

You are notified by email when the model is ready.

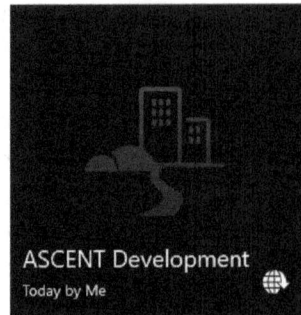

Figure 8–18

10. In the dialog box requesting where to store the model, click **Local** to save it to your computer's C Drive or **Autodesk Docs** to save it in a predefined Autodesk Docs project, as shown in Figure 8–19.

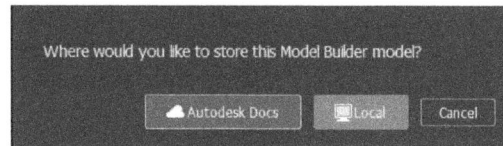

Figure 8–19

11. If you choose **Local**, the model will be stored in the default location with a cryptic folder name. The default location is *C:\Users\login-name\Documents\Autodesk InfraWorks Models\Autodesk 360*.

8.4 Connect to Data Sources

External GIS data is imported into the model as layers using the Model Builder or the Data Sources explorer, as shown in Figure 8–20. The Data Sources explorer opens when a new, empty model is created. If you close it before you have finished adding data, you can reopen it using the In Canvas tools.

In the Data Sources explorer, connected data is listed in the top area, while information about the data is listed in the bottom area. Two categories of data sources can be used in the model:

- File Data Source, which can be added by clicking

   (Add file date source).

- Database Data Source, which can be added by clicking

   (Add database data source).

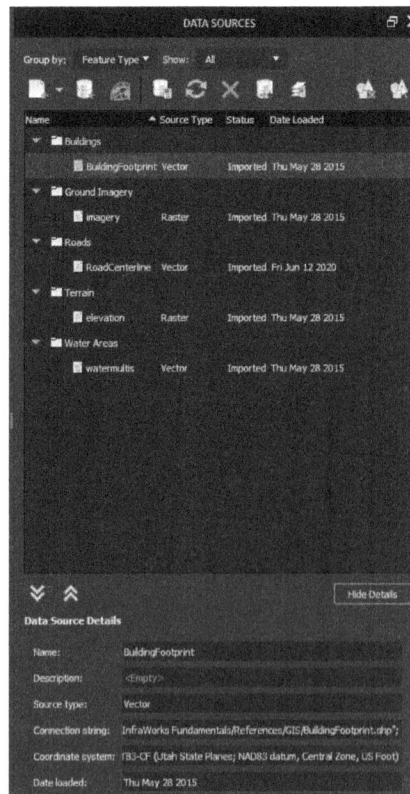

Figure 8–20

File Data Sources

A file data source can be a raster or a vector file. Several different file data sources can be imported into the Autodesk InfraWorks model, as shown in Figure 8–21. For each file data source type, multiple file formats can be used. To add a file data source, click (Add file data source) in the Data Sources explorer.

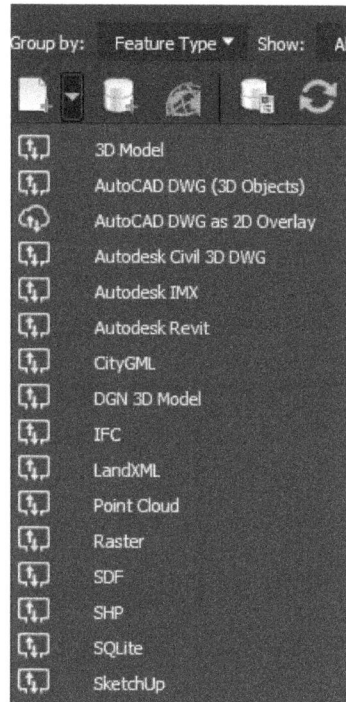

Figure 8–21

How To: Connect to File Data Sources

1. In the *Manage* tab>Content panel, click (Data Sources) to open the Data Sources explorer.

2. In the Data Sources panel, expand (Add file data source) and select the file format, as shown in Figure 8–21.

3. Browse to the directory in which the file is located. Select the required file(s) and click **Open**.

Hold <Shift> or <Ctrl> to select multiple files from the directory.

8.5 Configure and Display Data Sources

Although the source data has been connected, it does not display in the model because the data must be configured first. Configuring the data is important because it enables you to:

- Set the coordinate system in which the source data is located. If it is in a different coordinate system than the InfraWorks model, then the data will be transposed to fall into the correct position in the model.

- Map database fields located in the source data database file to the properties specified in the model template.

The more database fields you can map to your model, the more analysis can be done with the model. You can also add more accuracy to the model if database fields specify elevations, heights, and other numerical information about the raster or vector to which they pertain.

Data Source Configuration

Once a data source has been imported, it is configured in the Data Sources explorer by either double-clicking on the data source or selecting the data source and clicking [icon] (Configure Data), as shown in Figure 8–22.

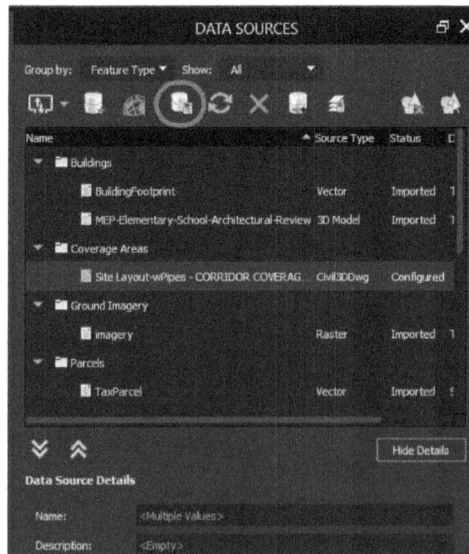

Figure 8–22

Hint: Terrain Data

It is essential that terrain data be added to the model first, since all other data sits on top of the terrain. Without a terrain surface, other data cannot be displayed. Additionally, only one terrain surface can display at any one time. If multiple terrain surfaces exist in a model, the visibility of the surfaces can be determined by setting the display order in the Surface Layers dialog box, as shown in Figure 8–23.

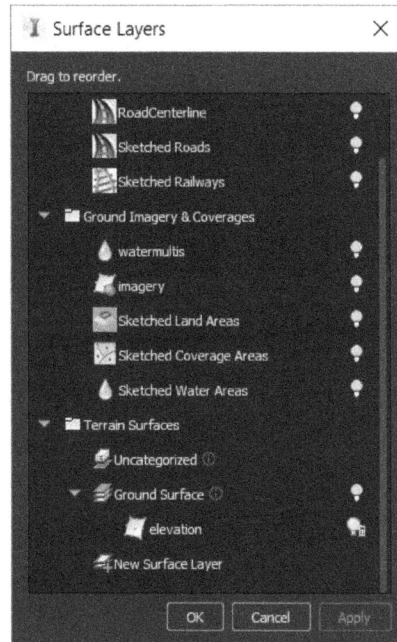

Figure 8–23

Surface Layers are available in multiple places:

- Click (Manage the order and visibility of surface data) in the Data Sources palette.

- In the Model Explorer palette, right-click on *Surface Layers* and select **Surface Layers**.

- In the *Manage* tab>Display panel, select (Surface Layers).

Data Source Details

When an item is selected in the Data Sources explorer, details about the source are listed in the Data Source Details panel, such as the name, description, source type, connection string (indicating where the source file is located), coordinate system, and date that the source was loaded into the model.

If a data source file is moved to a new location, the connection to the file is lost and errors might occur when working with features from that data source. Therefore, avoid moving files once you have connected them to an Autodesk InfraWorks model unless doing so is absolutely necessary.

If the data source files must be moved, you must reassociate them from the new location.

How To: Reassociate Moved Data Sources

1. Select the data source in the Data Sources explorer and click

   ![icon] (Manage paths of file data sources).
2. In the File Data Source Reconnection dialog box, click

   ![icon] (Browse) under the *New* column, as shown in Figure 8–24. Locate and select the file.

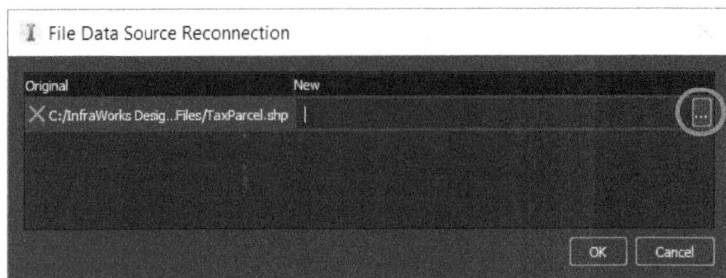

Figure 8–24

- This must be done for every proposal in which the data source is located.
- If more than one file is listed under the source data and both are located in the same directory, the paths for the additional files in the File Data Source Reconnection dialog box should automatically be populated.

General Information

In the *General* area at the top of the Data Source Configuration dialog box, every layer includes a *Name*, *Description*, *Source*, and *Type* field, as shown in Figure 8–25. The *Description* and the *Type* are usually the only two fields required to input information in the *General* area.

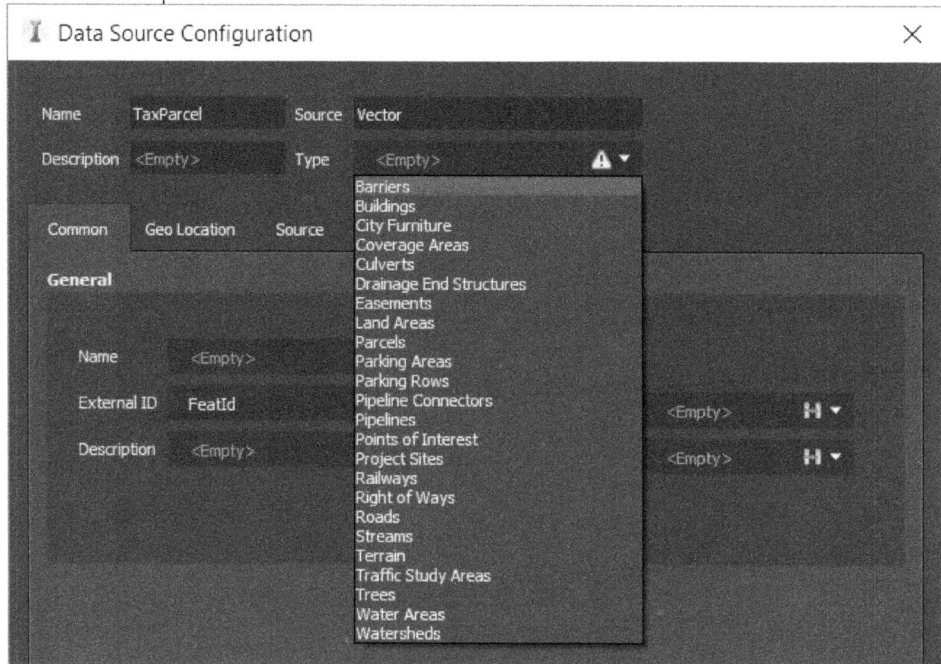

Figure 8–25

The *Type* field is the most important field in the *General* area. It determines the table and other settings that become available for the data source. Once the type has been configured in a model, it cannot be changed. The available configuration types are as follows:

• Barriers	• Pipelines
• Building	• Points of Interest
• City Furniture	• Project Sites
• Coverage Areas	• Railways
• Culverts	• Right of Ways
• Drainage End Structures	• Roads
• Easements	• Streams
• Land Areas (only available with A360)	• Terrain
• Parcels	• Traffic Study Areas
• Parking Areas	• Trees
• Parking Rows	• Water Areas
• Pipeline Connectors	• Watersheds

Common Tab

There are other ways to set styles in the Autodesk InfraWorks software as well (some will be covered later).

Note that each data type has different fields available on the various tabs.

The *Common* tab (shown in Figure 8–26) maps database fields to specific model properties and sets the styles to display the data source features.

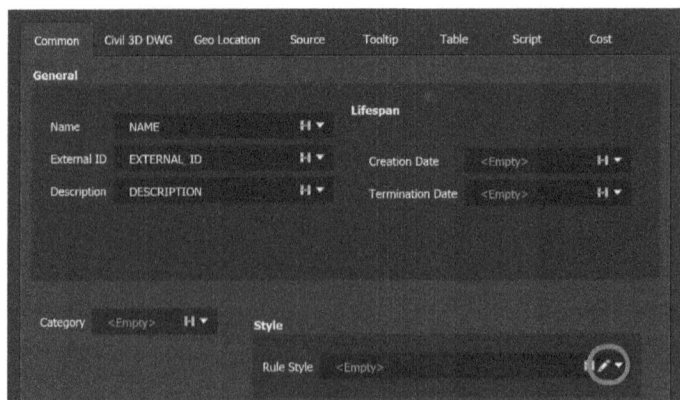

Figure 8–26

How To: Select a Style for Data Source Features

1. In the *Style* area, click ![pencil] (Style Chooser), as shown in Figure 8–26.
2. Select the required style in the Select Style / Color dialog box, as shown in Figure 8–27.

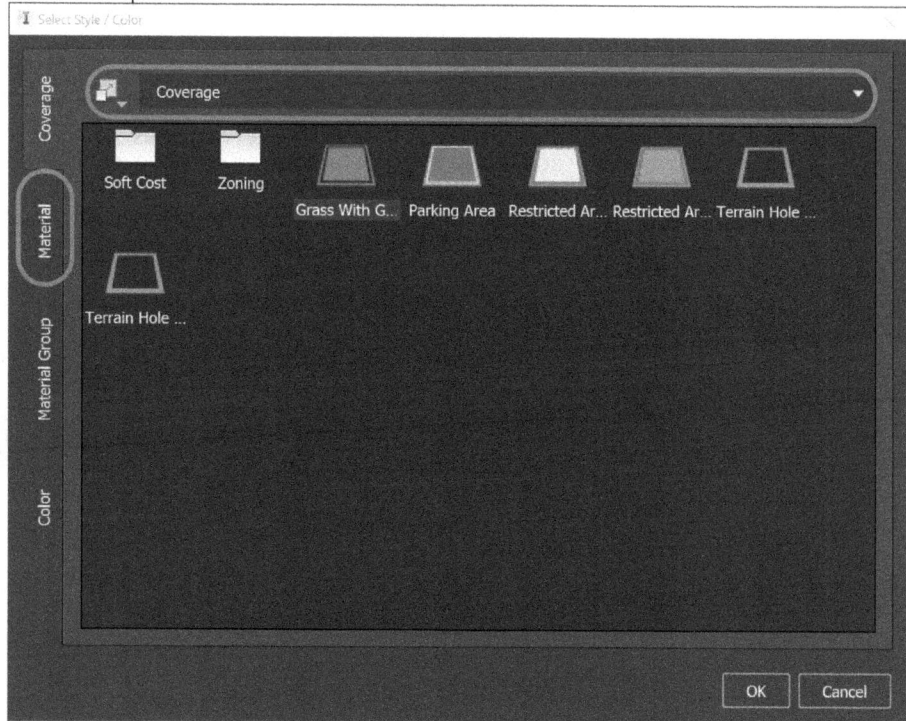

Figure 8–27

3. If necessary, select the proper vertical tab on the left-hand side.
4. Move to the appropriate folder if need be.
5. Select the appropriate style.
6. Click **OK**.

Geo Location Tab

The *Geo Location* tab (shown in Figure 8–28) sets the source data's original geographic coordinate system. It is important to ensure that the *Coordinate System* field is correct because it is used to project the source data to the model coordinate system. If the wrong coordinate system is selected, the features will display in the wrong location in the model.

If required, you can change the coordinate system using the Coordinate System drop-down list. Additional commands in the *Geo Location* tab enable you to manually set the insertion point, scale and rotation factors, or interactively place the data source.

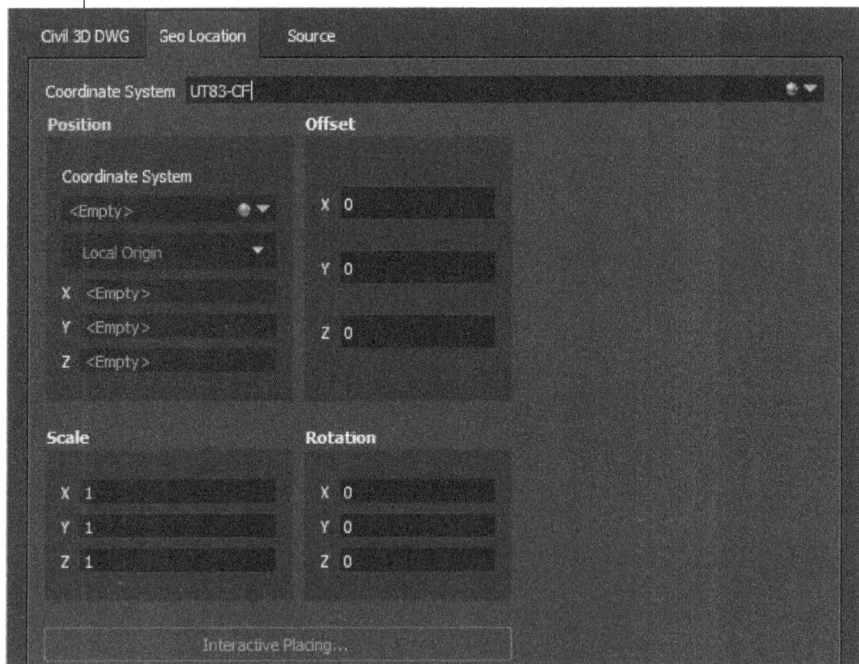

Figure 8–28

Source Tab

Clipping to the model extents helps keep the file size down.

The *Source* tab imports a subset of the original data by creating a source filter. The source filter can be a property filter or location filter. If the option to **Clip to model extent** is selected, the source data is automatically trimmed to the model extents.

The *Source* tab also enables you to control whether features are placed at a set elevation according to a property, or draped on the terrain surface. The following three options are available for the elevation:

Option	Description
Don't drape	Features are not assigned an elevation. Instead, they are imported at the elevation at which they were originally created.
Drape	Feature elevations are automatically taken from the terrain surface elevations.
Set Elevation	Enables you to select a field in the data table to be used to set the elevation.

If you are importing a source file that consists of polylines, you can select the option to **Convert closed polylines to polygons**, as shown in Figure 8–29.

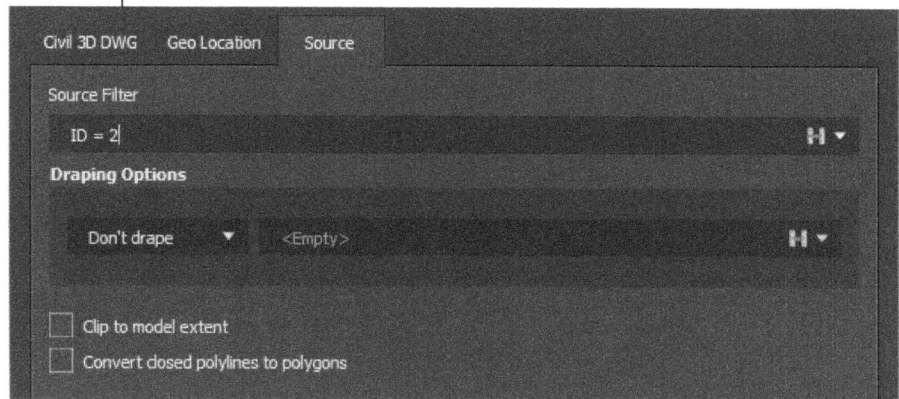

Figure 8–29

8.6 Share Design Elements with Autodesk Civil 3D

Autodesk InfraWorks models can be opened directly in the Autodesk Civil 3D software. Therefore, you do not have to recreate these design elements for the detailed design phase of the modeling process. Additionally, Autodesk Civil 3D drawing files can be imported into an Autodesk InfraWorks model to help communicate the final design to stakeholders by taking advantage of the high-definition graphics. In order to import an Autodesk Civil 3D DWG file directly, you must have the Autodesk Civil 3D 2022 or 2023 software installed on your computer.

How To: Import Autodesk Civil 3D AEC Objects from DWG Files

1. In the *Manage* tab, Content panel, select ![icon] (Data Sources).
2. In the Data Sources palette, expand ![icon] (Add file data source) and select **Autodesk Civil 3D DWG**.
3. In the Select Files dialog box, browse to the Autodesk Civil 3D DWG file, select it and click **Open**.
4. In the Choose Data Sources dialog box, select all of the AEC objects you want in the Autodesk InfraWorks model, as shown in Figure 8–30. Click **OK**.

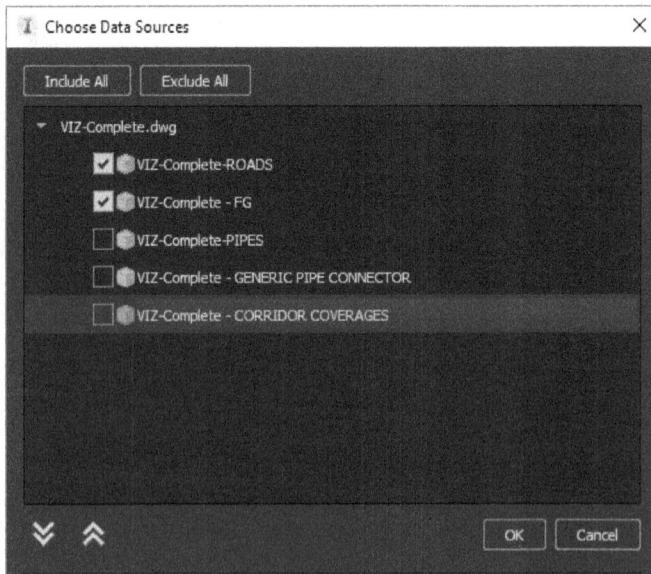

Figure 8–30

5. In the Data Sources palette, note that all of the imported AEC objects display under their appropriate source type and are selected, as shown in Figure 8–31. Click (Refresh data source).

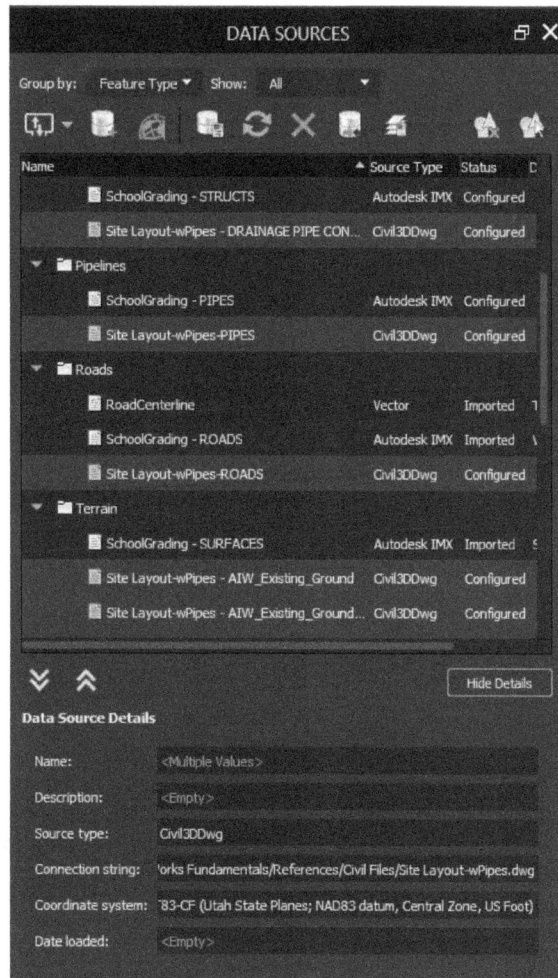

Figure 8–31

Civil 3D "Roads"

There are two types of roads that can be created in the Autodesk InfraWorks software: **planning roads** (existing roads) and **component roads** (proposed design roads). You can use the component roads to add engineering parameters to road designs and the rule-based tool sets to lay out a preliminary roadway design.

Visually, the unselected roads look similar, as seen in Figure 8–32.

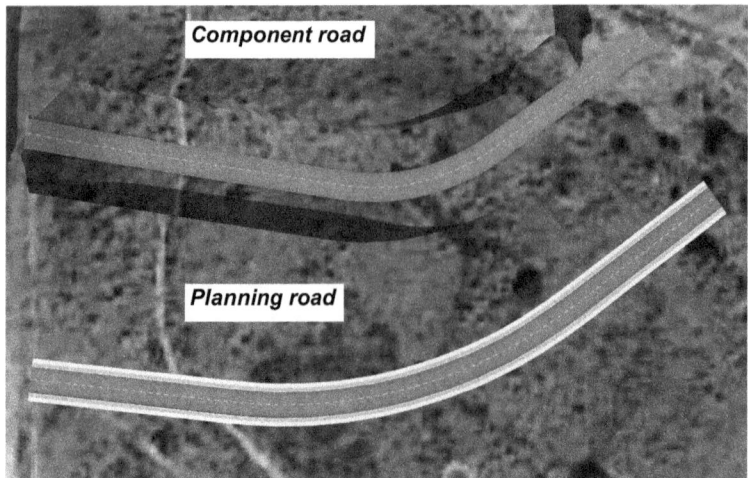

Figure 8–32

However, when selected, the grip clearly distinguish between the two types, as seen in Figure 8–33.

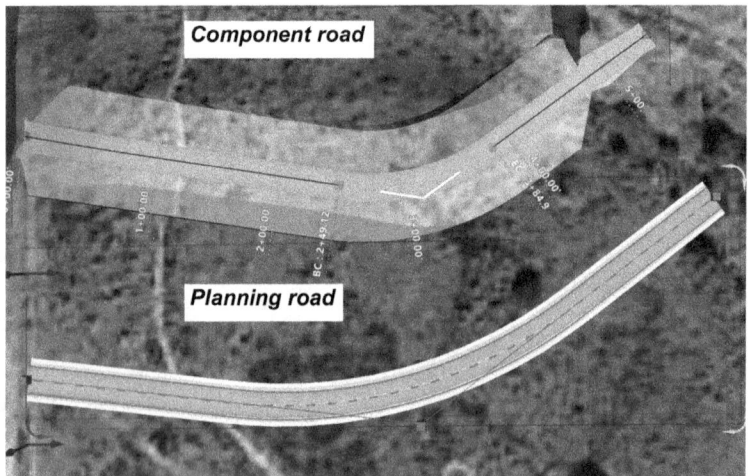

Figure 8–33

You can create either type of road in InfraWorks. However, when roads are created in the Model Builder, they are Planning Roads. You can convert Planning Roads to Component Roads. Planning Roads have road styles assigned to them, which can be swapped.Planning roads can be split into different parts, with the individual parts having different styles. There are several planning road styles set up in InfraWorks, as shown in Figure 8–34, and more can be created.

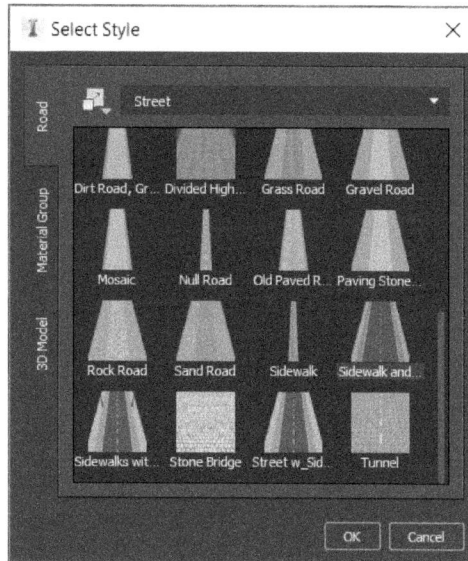

Figure 8–34

When roads are imported from Civil 3D (either alignments or corridors), they are Component Roads. Component Roads consist of *Road Assemblies* that can be replaced for sections of the road, and more components can be added, replaced, or deleted. There are Road Assemblies set up in InfraWorks, as shown in Figure 8–35, and more can be created.

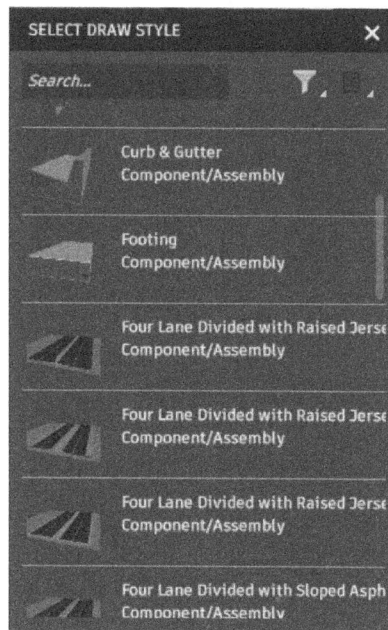

Figure 8–35

Drawing Overlays

When the Autodesk Civil 3D DWG data source type is selected, only the AEC objects are imported into the Autodesk InfraWorks model. In order to import other linework (such as parcel lines and utilities other than pipe networks), you can use an *AutoCAD DWG as 2D Overlay* data source type.

When working with terrain overlays, you can:

*   Move

*   Rotate

*   Scale

*   Control selectability

*   Control transparency, as shown in Figure 8–36.

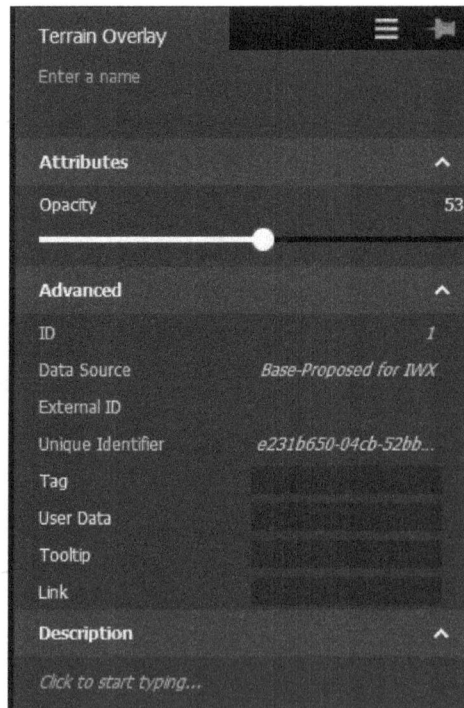

Figure 8–36

How To: Import Autodesk Civil 3D DWG File Linework

To use this feature, access to the Internet and an Autodesk 360 account are required.

1. In the *Manage* tab, Content panel, select ![icon] (Data Sources).
2. In the Data Sources palette, expand ![icon] (Add file data source) and select **AutoCAD DWG as 2D Overlay**.
3. In the Select Files dialog box, browse to the AutoCAD DWG file, select it, and click **Open**.
4. In the Data Import dialog box, when the following warning displays, click **Send**:

    • *This feature requires an Internet connection and an Autodesk 360 account. By clicking "Send", you will be transmitting data to InfraWorks 360 cloud-based services.*

5. In the Data Source palette, under *Terrain Overlays*, double-click on the imported DWG data source.
6. In the Data Source Configuration dialog box, adjust the **Scale** and **Rotation** as necessary. Click **Interactive Placing...** and double-click on a point in the model where the drawing should be located, as shown in Figure 8–37.

Set the Coordinate System, Location, Scale, and Rotation manually

or

Place interactively

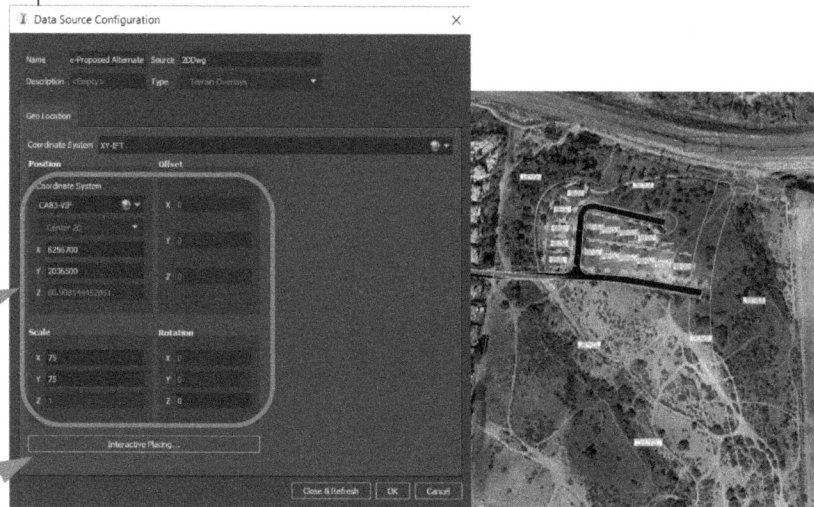

Figure 8–37

7. In the Data Source Configuration dialog box, click **Close & Refresh**.
8. In the model, select the overlay, then use the gizmos to move, scale, or rotate the overlay as required.

Practice 8a

To complete this practice, access to the Internet is required.

Create a New Model Using Model Builder

Practice Objectives

- Create a new model with existing GIS data.
- Import Civil 3D and AutoCAD data.

In this practice, you will create a new model using the Model Builder and add existing GIS data to it automatically during the creation process. Then, you will import Civil 3D data and AutoCAD 2D underlays.

Task 1 - Create a new model.

1. In the Home Screen, click **Model Builder**.

2. In the Model Builder dialog box, in the *Search by Location* field, type in the following address: **Jeffries Ranch Road, Oceanside, CA**. Pan over and click the Area of Interest and draw a rectangle as shown in Figure 8–38.

3. In the *Model Name* field, type **Visualization**. Provide an appropriate description of your choice.

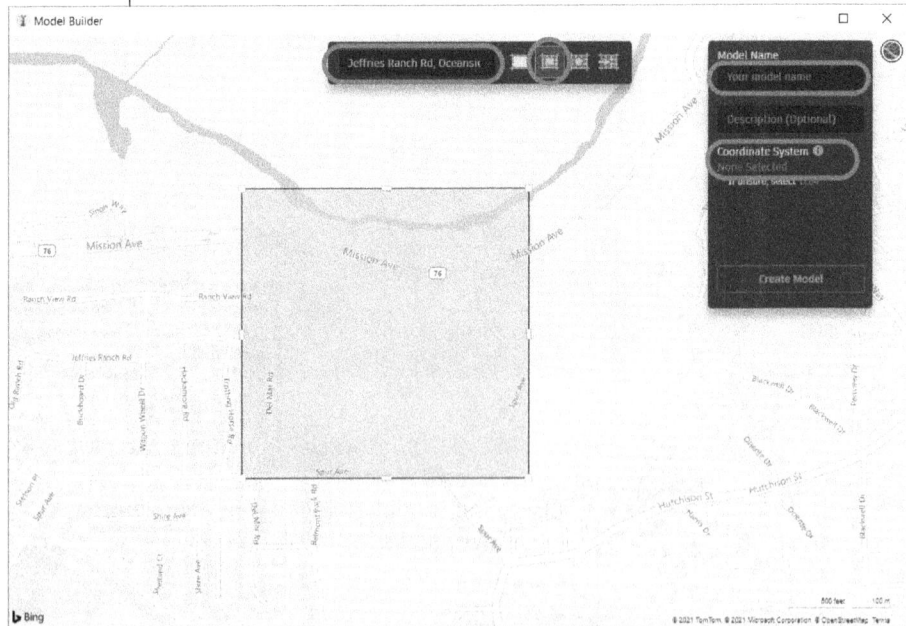

Figure 8–38

4. Under *Coordinate System*, click **None Selected**. In the Select Coordinate System dialog box, in the *Search* area, type **CA83** to narrow the selection choices, then select **CA83-VIF** at the bottom of the selection list, as shown in Figure 8–39.

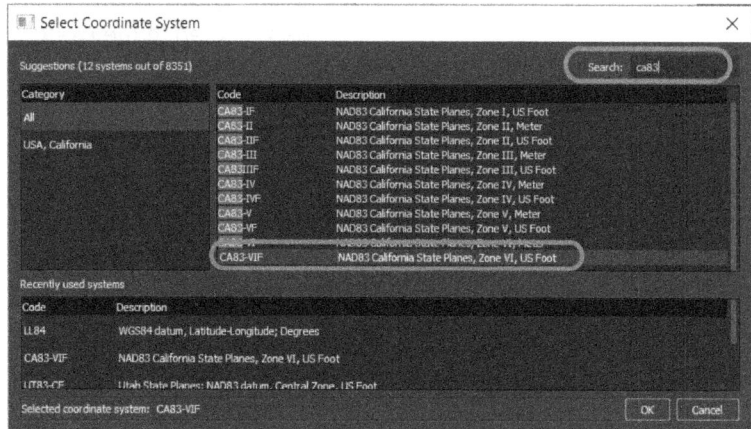

Figure 8–39

5. Click **OK** to close the Select Coordinate System dialog box.

6. In the Model Builder dialog box, click **Create Model**.

7. You are notified that the model is being prepared, as shown in Figure 8–40. When you expand the Show details section, you will see the tracking ID and other information. Click the **Continue** button to dismiss the notification.

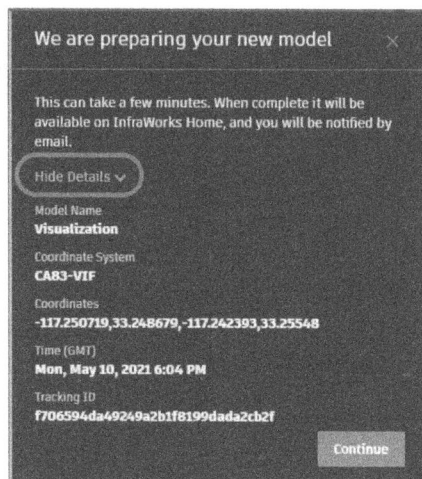

Figure 8–40

8. Close the Model Builder dialog box by clicking on the **X** in the upper right corner.

9. After a while, you will receive notification that your model is complete and it will appear on the Home Screen.

10. On the Home Screen, select the **Visualization.sqlite** model that was created in the cloud. If it is taking too long, you can open **Visualization-Local.sqlite** from *C:\Civil 3D for Land Dev\Working\Visualization* and, in the main Toolbar on the right side, expand *Switch Active Proposal* and select proposal **A_Task1**.

11. When initially opening a model created in Model Builder, select **Local** when prompted to select a location to store the model, as shown in Figure 8–41.

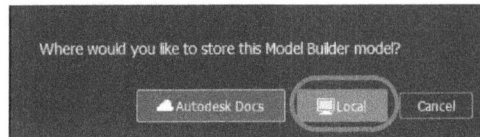

Figure 8–41

12. On the upper right corner of the Toolbar, click ⚙ (Application Options).

13. In the Application Options dialog box, select **Unit Configuration**. Expand the Default Units drop-down list and ensure that **Imperial** is selected, as shown in Figure 8–42.

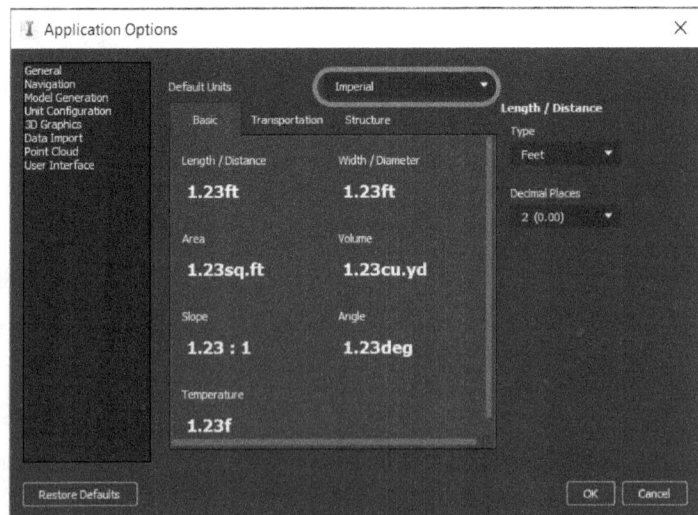

Figure 8–42

14. Click **OK**.

Task 2 - Open local file and import Autodesk Civil 3D data.

In this task, you will import the Autodesk Civil 3D surfaces, pipes, and roads from the detailed design phase of the project. Do not continue working on the previous file you created in Model Builder as there are proposals and adjustments made in the **Visualization-Local.sqlite** file contained in your practice files folder.

1. Open **Visualization-Local.sqlite** from *C:\Civil 3D for Land Dev\Working\Visualization*. It may take some time for the model to open.

2. In the main Toolbar on the right side, expand *Switch Active Proposal* and select proposal **A_Task1**.

3. In the Data Sources palette, expand ![icon] (Add file data source) and select **Autodesk Civil 3D DWG**.

   • If the Data Sources palette is not open, in the *Manage* tab,

   Content panel, select ![icon] (Data Sources) to open it, as shown in Figure 8–43.

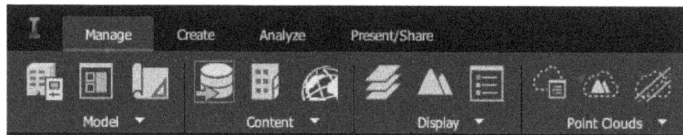

Figure 8–43

4. In the Select Files dialog box, browse to the *C:\Civil 3D for Land Dev\Working\Visualization* folder, select **VIZ-to-IWX.dwg**, and click **Open**. It may take some time for the drawing to be added.

The Top Corridor surfaces have already been pasted into the FG surface, so you need not import them.

5. In the Choose Data Sources dialog box, click the **Exclude All** button, then select the **VIZ-to-IWX-Roads**, **VIZ-to-IWX-FG**, and **VIZ-to-IWX-CORRIDOR-COVERAGES** objects, as shown in Figure 8–44. Click **OK**.

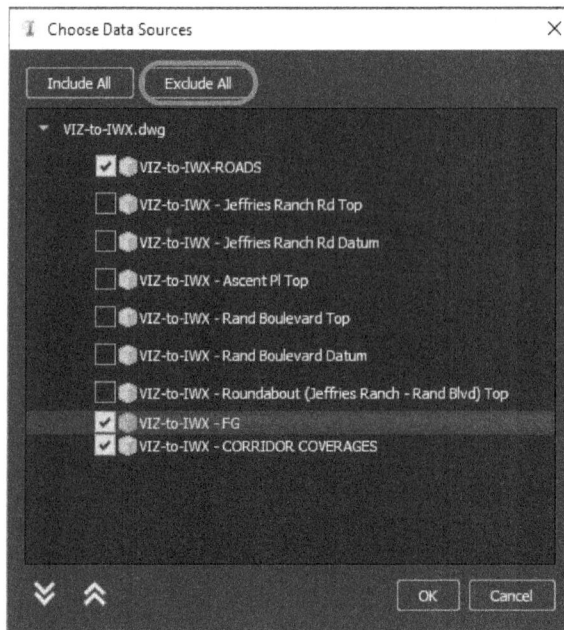

Figure 8–44

6. In the Data Sources palette, click (Refresh). This can take a while.

If this message does not appear, in the Manage tab>Display panel,

select (Surface Layers).

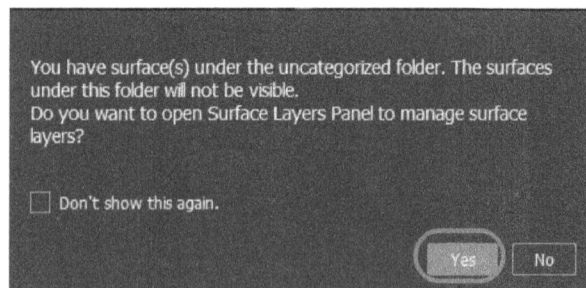

7. In the ensuing dialog box, select **Yes** to open the Surface Layers panel, as shown in Figure 8–45.

Figure 8–45

8. In the Surface Layers dialog box, drag the *FG* surface above *elevation1* and *elevation2,* as shown in Figure 8–46, and make it visible (by clicking the light bulb icon to turn it yellow).

Before   **After**

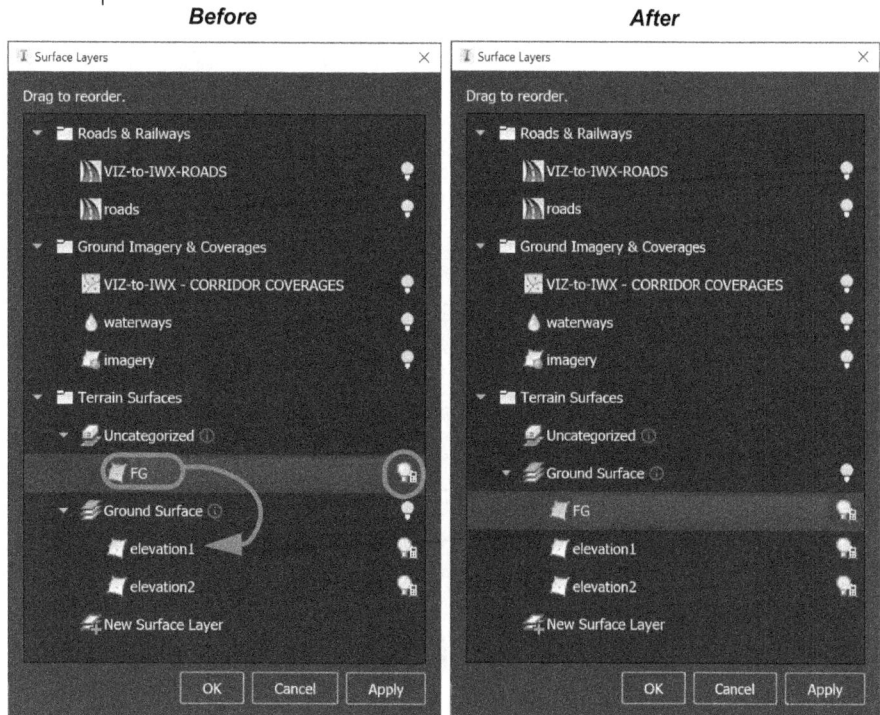

Figure 8–46

9. Click **OK** to close the Surface Layers dialog box.

10. The Civil 3D corridors and FG surface are imported, as shown in Figure 8–47. Note that the corridors are imported as Component Roads, as well as alignments without corridors (such as Mission Avenue to the north).

Figure 8–47

11. The Jeffries Ranch Road corridor overlaps the Jeffries Ranch Rd Planning Road (created from Model Builder), as shown above in Figure 8–47. This needs to be adjusted. Select the Jeffries Ranch Rd Planning Road by clicking on it.

12. Select the second last grip and in the right-click menu, select **Remove Vertex**, as shown in Figure 8–48.

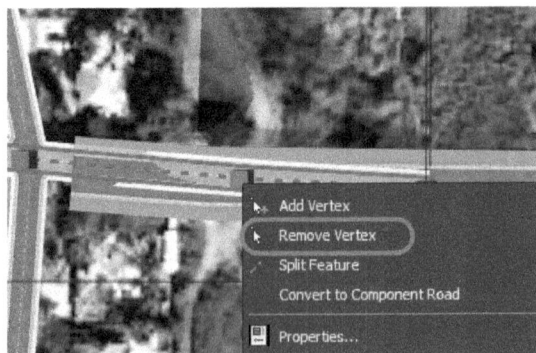

Figure 8–48

13. Now select the last grip and drag it to the beginning of the Jeffries Ranch Road corridor, as shown in Figure 8–49.

Figure 8–49

14. The Roundabout corridor was imported with a default Four-Lane Roadway assembly, which needs to be replaced for the Jeffries Ranch Road corridor sections. Pick on the Jeffries Ranch Road corridor and in the right-click menu, expand **Road Assembly** and select **Replace Assembly**, as shown in Figure 8–50.

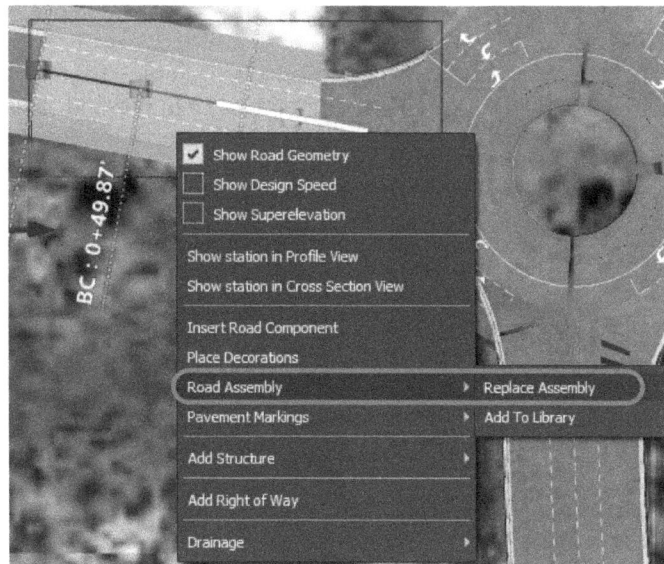

Figure 8–50

15. In the SELECT DRAW STYLE window, select the **Two Lanes** assembly (at the bottom of the list), as shown in Figure 8–51.

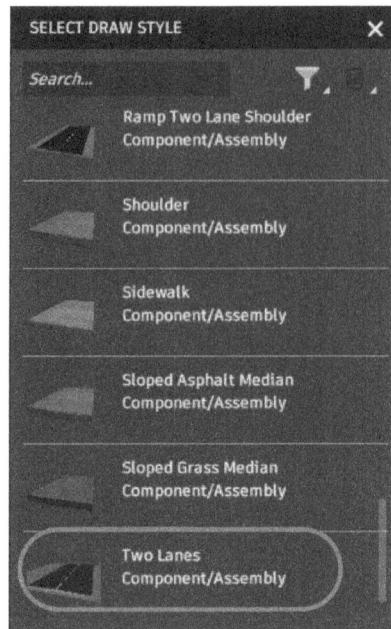

Figure 8–51

16. You are prompted for the range. Select the beginning and then drag it to the end, as shown in Figure 8–52. Press <Enter> to apply the assembly.

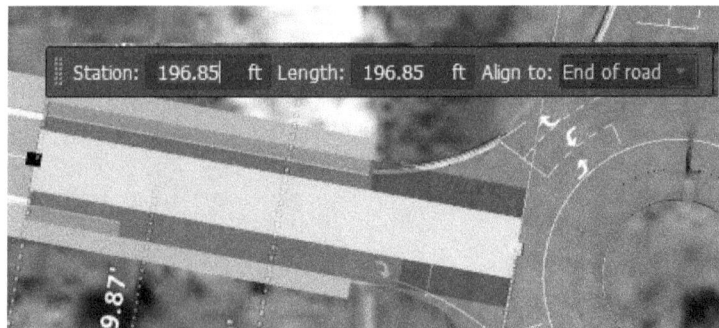

Figure 8–52

17. Time permitting, repeat the procedure for the other end of Jeffries Ranch Road corridor and the Roundabout.

Even though you haven't made any changes, InfraWorks still considers the terrain to be configured.

If you did not complete the last task, open Visualization-Local.sqlite from C:\Civil 3D for Land Dev\Working\Visualization.

Task 3 - Import a drawing overlay.

In this task, you will import a drawing overlay to display the linework created in a CAD drawing.

1. Continue working in the **Visualization-Local.sqlite** model from the last task.

2. In the main Toolbar on the right side, expand *Switch Active Proposal* and select proposal **A_Task2**. Here the Roundabout Lanes were also replaced with the **Two Lanes** assembly as you had done earlier.

3. In the *Manage* tab, Content panel, select ![icon] (Data Sources).

4. In the Data Sources palette, expand ![icon] (Add file data source) and select **AutoCAD DWG as 2D Overlay,** as shown in Figure 8–53.

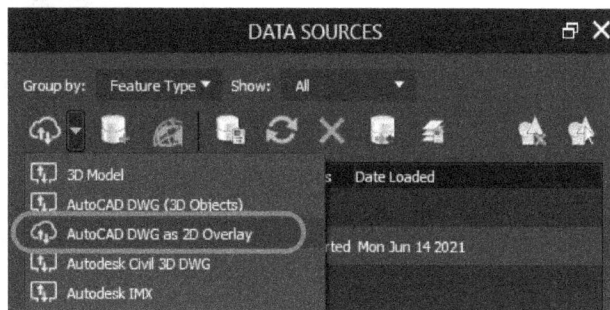

Figure 8–53

5. In the Select Files dialog box, browse to the *C:\Civil 3D for Land Dev\Working\Visualization* folder, select **Base-Proposed for IWX.dwg**, and click **Open**.

6. In the Data Import dialog box, click **Send**. This can take a while.

7. Once you note that the Status is no longer showing *Processing*, in the Data Source palette, under T*errain Overlays*, double-click on the **VIZ-to-IWX** data source, as shown in Figure 8–54.

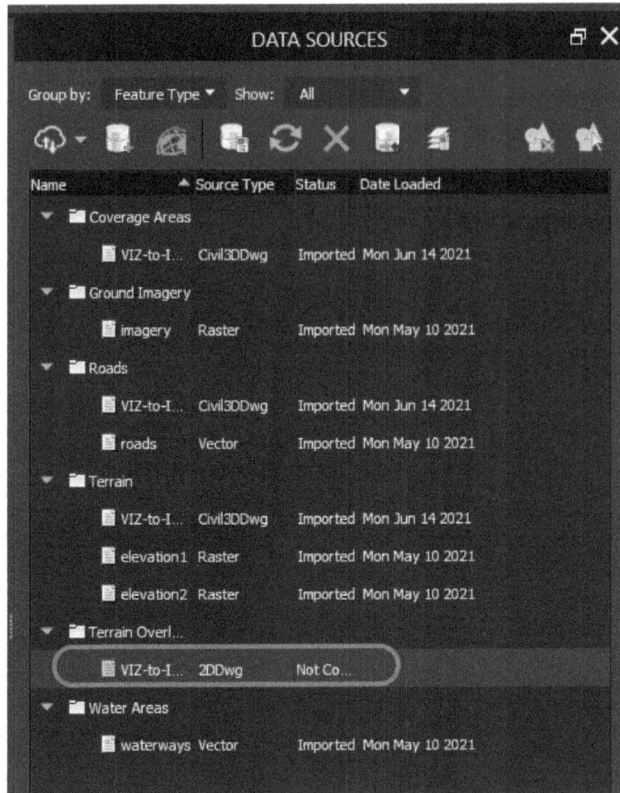

Figure 8–54

*If **CA83-VIF** is not in the drop-down list, click*

 (Choose Coordinate System) and search for it.

8. In the Data Source Configuration dialog box, do the following, as shown in Figure 8–55:

   - Leave the first *Coordinate System* as is (as **XY-M**).
   - In the *Position* area, under *Coordinate System*, expand the drop-down list and select **CA83-VIF**.
   - In the *X* field, type **6256700**.
   - In the *Y* field, type **2036500**.
   - In the *Scale* area, for both the *X* and *Y* fields, type **75**.

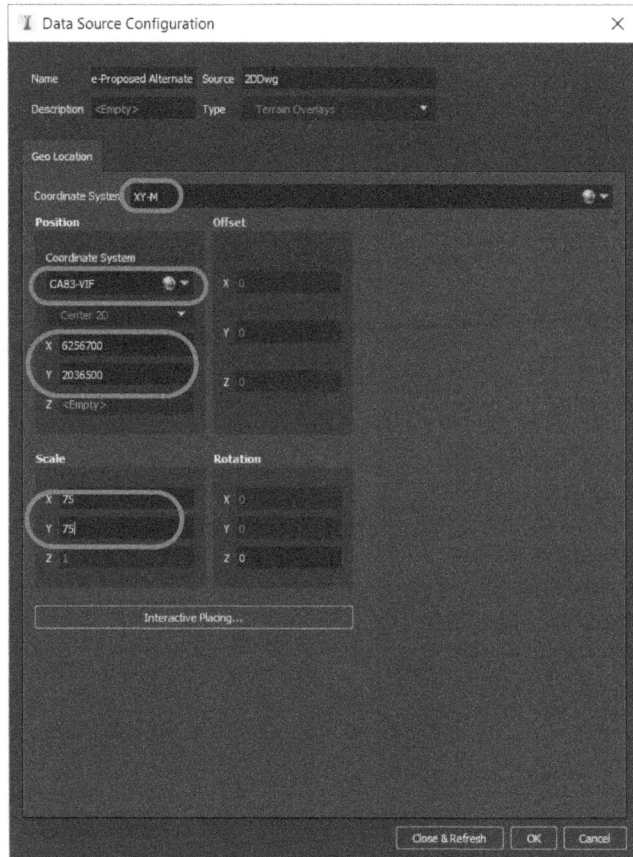

Figure 8–55

9. Click **Close & Refresh**.

10. You will notice the overlay is not lined up perfectly. Zoom into the intersection of Jeffries Ranch Rd and Ascent Place, as shown in Figure 8–56.

Figure 8–56

Experiment with pick points as suggested. Accuracy is not required here because the image will be properly positioned and scaled in the next practice.

11. Select the overlay and right-click to select **Place by Reference Point.** This command will allow you to select reference and destination points to move, rotate, and scale the overlay at once.

12. When asked to pick *point 1*, double-click on the point, and then double click where that point belongs in the model, as shown in Figure 8–57.

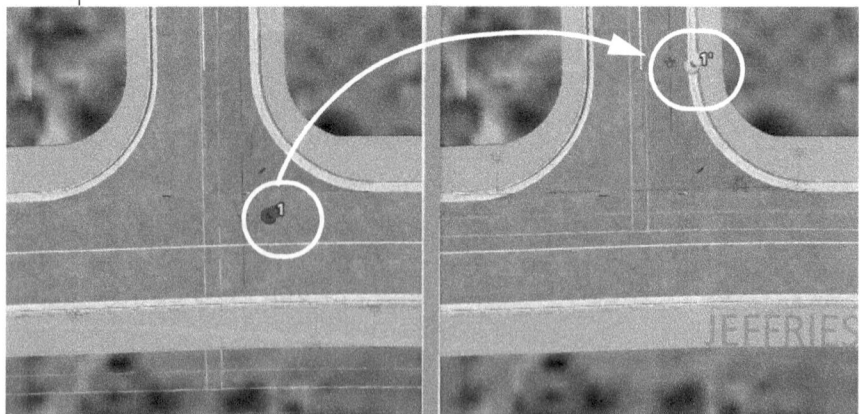

Figure 8–57

13. The command will stay active to select up to three references and destination points. Repeat this process two more times, selecting corners of the parking lot on the west and east sides, as shown in Figure 8–58 and Figure 8–59.

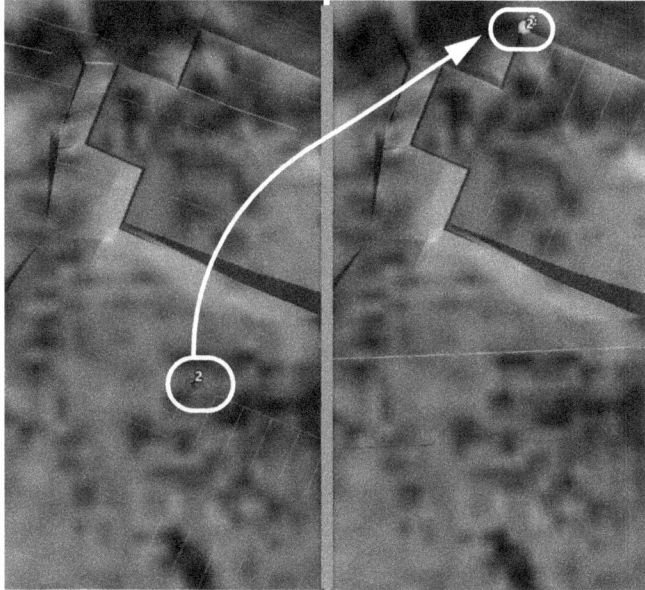

Figure 8–58

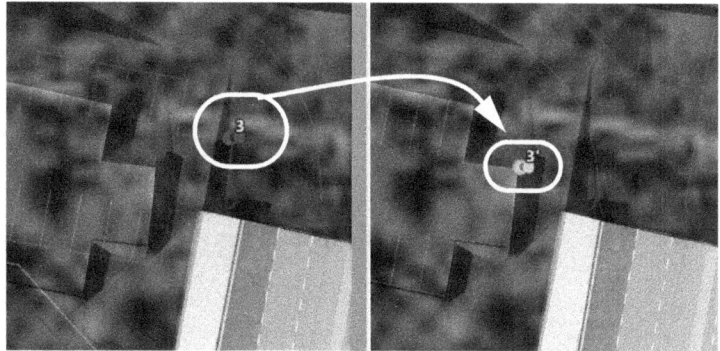

Figure 8–59

14. Review the overlay and notice it lays much better over the existing area.

15. Keep the InfraWorks model open for the next exercise. Remember, there is no "*Save*" command within InfraWorks.

8.7 Create Water Features in a Model

When designing a new community, water features are often required. Water features have a number of purposes. They can act as a water retention area that is used by local residents for drinking water, such as a reservoir. They can also be used to divert excess water away from homes and businesses to avoid flooding. This is often required when new hard surfaces prevent water from being absorbed into the ground, as it did before the land was developed. Finally, water areas can be used to provide recreation and make an area more visually appealing.

Water areas are a surface layer in the Model Explorer. You can create the following two types of water features:

- **Water Areas:** Enables you to create bodies of water, such as ponds, lakes, and wetlands. To create a body of water, you click to create points that will act as a boundary for the water area. Figure 8–60 shows a small pond water area.

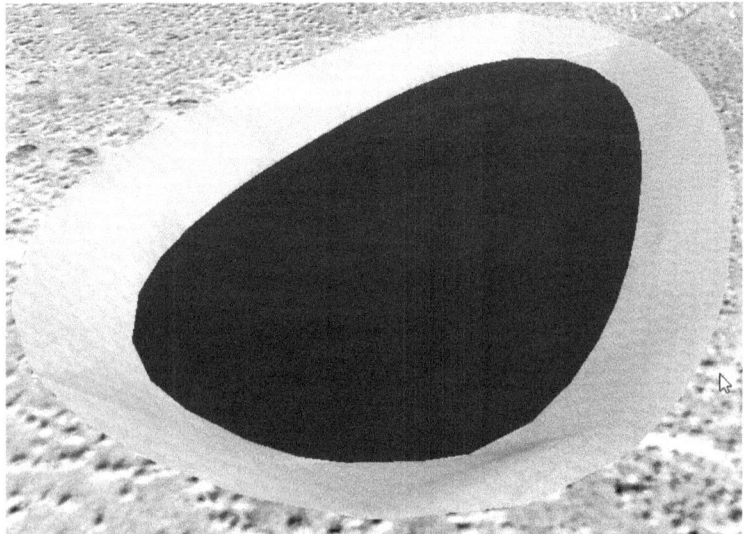

Figure 8–60

- **Rivers:** Enables you to create linear water features, such as canals, rivers, and streams. To create a river, you click to create points along a linear path. A buffer surrounds the water on either side. The buffer width is set in the Water asset card.

How To: Create Lakes or Ponds

1. In in the *Create* tab>Environment drop-down panel, select

    (Water Areas).

2. In the Select Draw Style asset card, select the required water style, as shown in Figure 8–61.

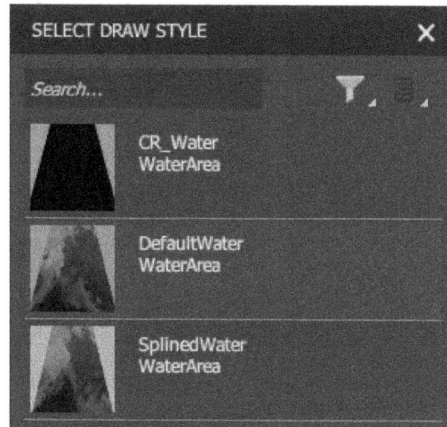

Figure 8–61

3. Click in the model to start the creation of the water boundary.
4. Move the cursor in the direction that you want the water boundary to follow. Type a distance for the length to the next point on the boundary and press <Enter> to set the distance. Click in the model to place the boundary point.
5. Continue clicking in the model until all of the boundary points have been created for the water area.
6. Double-click to place the last boundary point and end the command.

8.8 Create City Furniture in a Model

If you need to create multiple predefined 3D buildings or other 3D models in your model, it is recommended that you use

(City Furniture).

This command enables you to create multiple 3D models spaced along a path or a single feature at the location specified. Any type of 3D model style can be selected as city furniture, including trees and railway models. However, these models display in the *Furniture* category in the Model Explorer and are furniture features in the database.

The following 3D models can be added as city furniture to a model:

- **Buildings:** There are a number of predefined 3D building models. They fall into three categories from which you can select:
- **Furniture:** 3D models of roof-top items, such as solar panels and HVAC units.
- **Neighborhood:** A few common building types that are found in a typical city, such as gas stations, churches, and post offices.
- **Residential:** Multiple single-family home models.

These 3D model options are located in the *3D Model* tab of the Style Palette. The **Neighborhood** and **Residential** style options are shown in Figure 8–62.

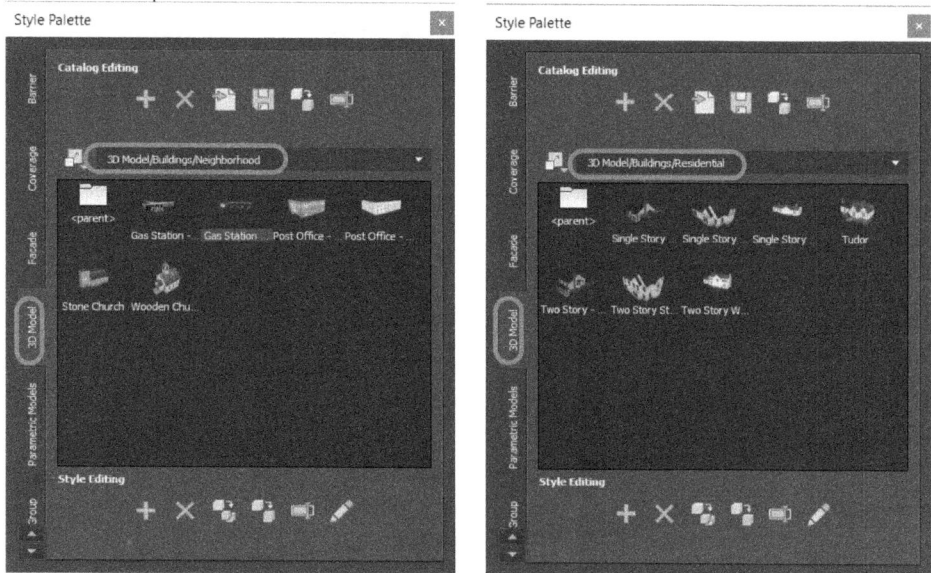

Figure 8–62

- **City Furniture:** Objects found in a city, including signs, fences, bike stands, parking meters, dumpsters, etc., as shown in Figure 8–63.

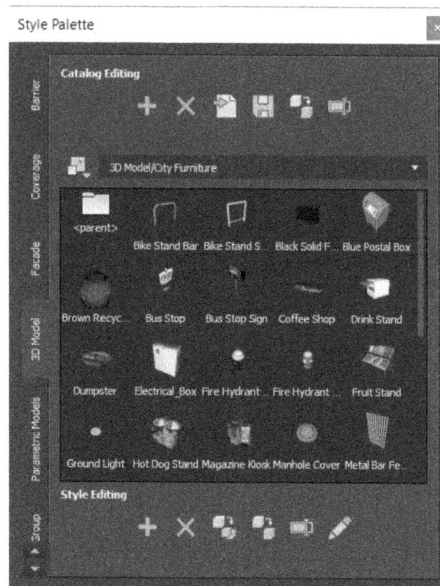

Figure 8–63

- **People:** One or more people walking or standing, as shown in Figure 8–64.

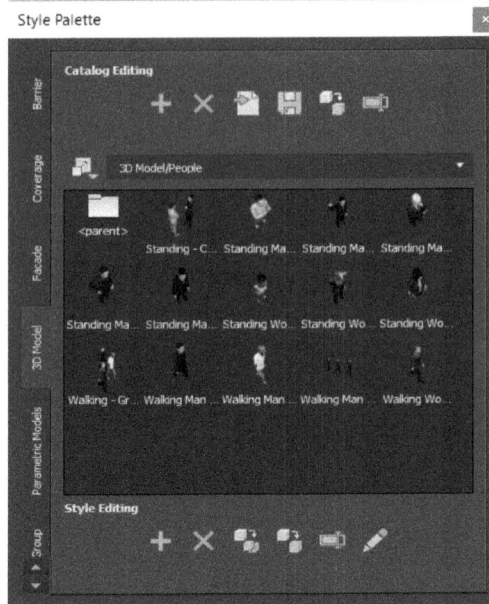

Figure 8–64

- **Vehicles:** Cars, trucks, vans, buses, and bicycles, as shown in Figure 8–65.

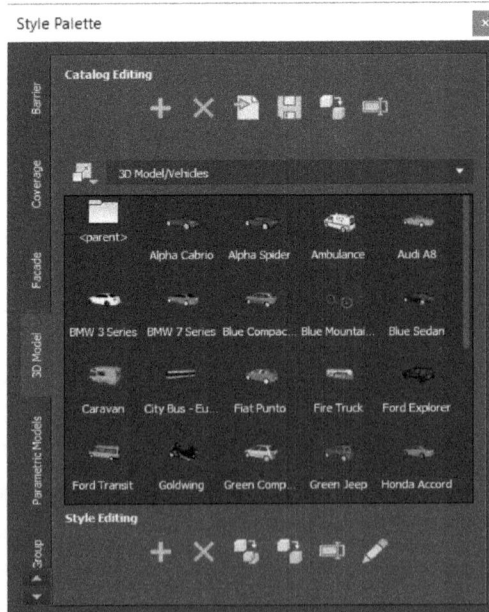

Figure 8–65

How To: Add One Predefined 3D Building or Single Piece of City Furniture

1. In in the *Create* tab>Environment panel, select (City Furniture).
2. The Select Draw Style asset card displays, as shown in Figure 8–66.

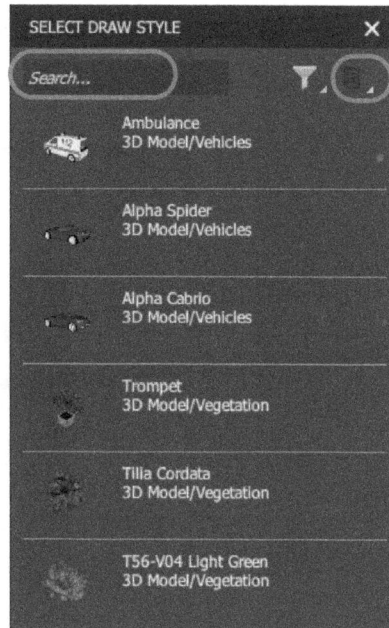

Figure 8–66

3. You can change the way the asset card displays its content by clicking on the icon in the upper right corner (it is difficult to see!), as shown in Figure 8–66. This reveals a collection of icons, as shown in Figure 8–67.

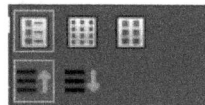

Figure 8–67

4. The upper row changes among:
   - Content items with thumbnails and text.
   - Content items with small thumbnails only.
   - Content items with large thumbnails only.
5. The lower row sorts either ascending or descending on the object's name.

6. Select a 3D model. (You can type in the search area to narrow down the selection options.)
7. In the model, double-click to place the 3D model and end the command. The size is not important because the 3D model size and shape are predetermined as part of the 3D model.
8. Press <Esc> to clear the selection of the newly created building.

How To: Add Multiple Predefined 3D Buildings or Other City Furniture

1. In in the *Create* tab>Environment panel, select ![traffic light icon] (City Furniture).
2. The Select Draw Style asset card displays, as shown in Figure 8–68. Select a 3D model. (You can type in the search area to narrow down the selection options.)

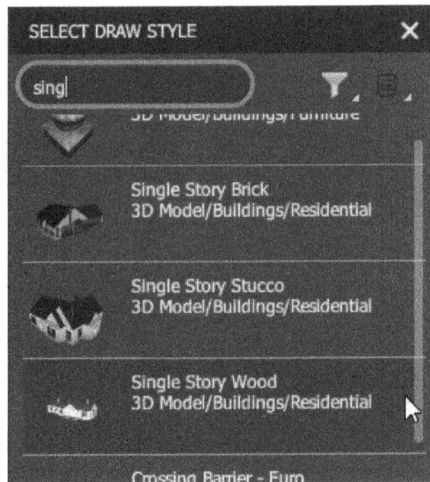

Figure 8–68

3. In the model, single-click to start the path to be followed by the 3D models.
4. In the model, move the cursor in the direction in which you want the 3D model path to follow. Type a distance for the length to the next point of intersection and press <Enter> to set the distance. Click in the model to place the point of intersection.
5. Continue clicking in the model until the full path has been created.
6. Double-click to place the last point and end the command.

7. To change the number of items that display along the path, slide the *Density* Slider (shown in Figure 8–69) until the model density is set as required.

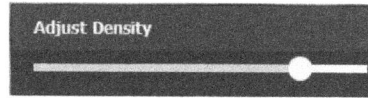

Figure 8–69

8. Press <Esc> to clear the selection of the newly created 3D models.
9. Move and rotate each 3D model by selecting it and using

 (Rotate Gizmo), (Height Gizmo), and (Move Gizmo) as required. If you need to change which 3D model displays at specific locations, you can drag and drop another 3D model in its place from the Style Palette, as shown in Figure 8–70.

Figure 8–70

8.9 Add Vegetation to a Model

Adding vegetation can add privacy, shade, noise barriers, and landscape appeal to a project. Trees and other vegetation can also help stakeholders to better understand how the project could look when completed. You can add vegetation in three different ways:

- **Single Plant:** A single plant is placed in the model when you double-click on an insertion point, no matter which vegetation tool is used. Figure 8–71 shows a single tree.

Figure 8–71

- **Row of Trees:** A group of plants are placed in the model along a line, as shown in Figure 8–72.

Figure 8–72

- **Stand of Trees:** A group of randomly spaced plants are placed in the model inside a polygon, as shown in Figure 8–73.

Figure 8–73

If you create vegetation along a line or in a polygon, you can set the number of plants that display using the Density Slider, as shown in Figure 8–74. The higher the density (slider moved to the right), the more plants that display.

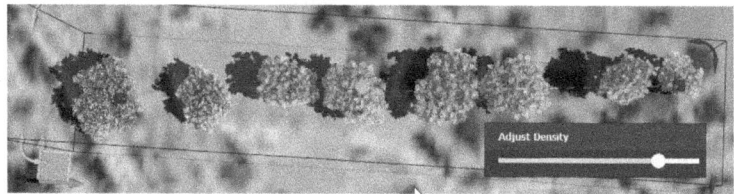

Figure 8–74

How To: Create Vegetation in a Group

1. In in the *Create* tab>Environment drop-down panel, select

    (Stand of Trees).

2. In the Select Draw Style asset card, select the type of plant required, as shown in Figure 8–75.

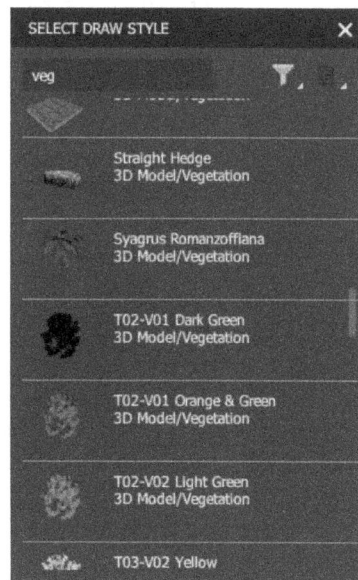

Figure 8–75

3. In the model, click to create the corners of a polygon for the vegetation group area. Remember to double-click on the final corner to finish the polygon.

4. Press <Esc> to make the Feature Density bar display. Slide the Density Slider (as shown in Figure 8–76) until the required number of plants displays in the model.

Figure 8–76

5. Press <Esc> to clear the selection of the newly created trees.

Edit Vegetation

When you select vegetation, gizmos display to enable you to modify the plants. 🔲 (Elevation Gizmo) enables you to adjust the height of the plants, while 🔲 (Height Gizmo) enables you to change the size and scale of the plants.

If you select a vegetation group (row or stand of trees), the Density Slider displays, enabling you to change the number of plants that display in the group. Move the slider left or right until the required number of plants displays in the model. If the Density Slider is not displayed, orbit the view to a plan view to make it display, as shown in Figure 8–77.

Figure 8–77

Practice 8b | Add Details to the Site

Practice Objectives

- Add a pond water area.
- Add predefined buildings.
- Add vegetation and other city furniture.

In this practice, you will enhance the site with a pond, buildings, trees and shrubs, and other details. An office building, hotel, and school have already been added to the site, as well as coverage areas to place homes along the pond area.

Task 1 - Add a water retention pond.

1. Continue working in the same model as the previous practice. If you did not finish the previous exercise, open **Visualization-Local.sqlite** from *C:\Civil 3D for Land Dev\ Working\Visualization*.

2. In the main Toolbar on the right side, expand *Switch Active Proposal* and select proposal **B_Task1**.

3. Just to the left of the Proposals drop-down list, click ▣ (View bookmarks) and select **Pond**.

4. In in the *Create* tab>Environment drop-down panel, select

    ▣ (Water Areas).

5. In the Select Draw Style asset card, select **Splined Water**, as shown in Figure 8–78.

Figure 8–78

6. Trace around the red polyline representing the pond, placing vertices as shown in Figure 8–79. If you can offset your picks inside the pond by about 3 feet, the pond will look better.

Figure 8–79

7. Double-click to finish the pond definition. Press <Esc> to exit the command (rather than creating another water area).

8. Right-click on the pond to edit vertices and adjust vertices, if needed, to make sure the pond is not overlapping any parcels or the office building (as shown in Figure 8–80).

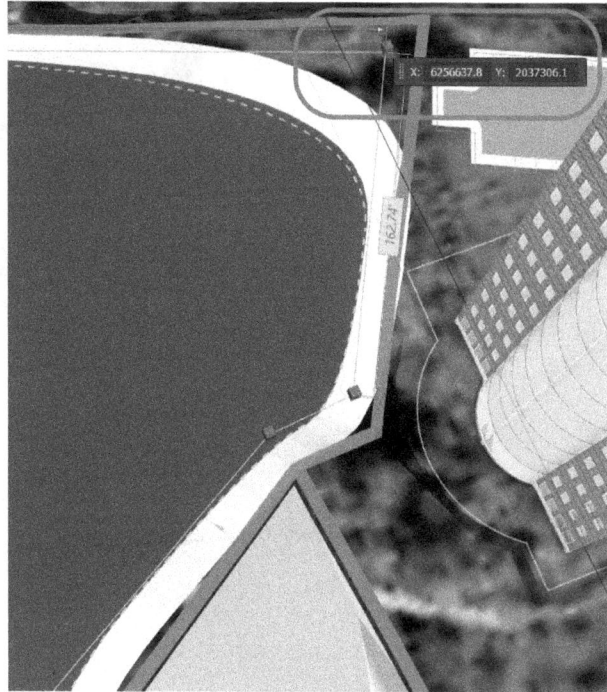

Figure 8–80

The AutoCAD Overlay may prevent you from selecting the pond. You may need to lock the overlay in the Model Explorer to prevent it from being selected. Also lock the Coverage Areas to avoid their selection.

9. In the *Manage* tab>Model panel, click (Model Explorer).

10. In the Model Explorer, in the *Overlays* section, click on the light bulb beside **Base-Proposed for IWX** to turn off the overlay, as shown in Figure 8–81.

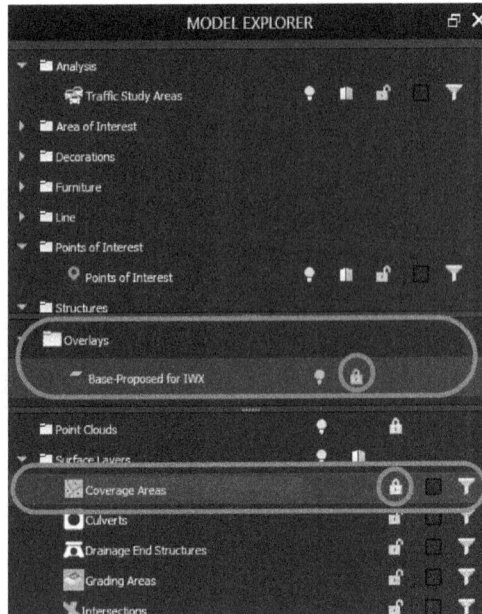

Figure 8–81

Task 2 - Add predefined buildings to the site.

1. Continue working in the same model as the last task.

2. In the main Toolbar on the right side, expand *Switch Active Proposal* and select proposal **B_Task2**.

3. Just to the left of the Proposals drop-down list, click (View bookmarks) and select **Subdivision**.

4. In the *Create* tab>Environment panel, select (City Furniture).

5. In the Select Draw Style asset card that displays, type **two stor** in the search field. Select the **Two Story Stucco** building, as shown in Figure 8–82.

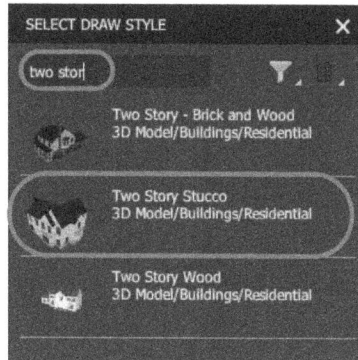

Figure 8–82

6. In the model, in the first lot, double-click in the center of the green coverage area to place the building, as shown in Figure 8–83. Press <Esc> to exit the command (rather than placing more buildings).

Figure 8–83

7. Use ⌒ (Rotate Gizmo), ⬆ (Height Gizmo), and

   ⬆ (Move Gizmo) as required to relocate it.

8. These lots were graded as walk-out basements and the city furniture buildings are slab-on-grade. Therefore, you won't be able to place the houses correctly on the surface as graded.

9. Continue this process for the other four lots, adjusting the building types as you add them. One example is shown in Figure 8–84.

Figure 8–84

Task 3 - Add vegetation to the site.

1. Continue working in the same model as the last task.

2. In the main Toolbar on the right side, expand *Switch Active Proposal* and select proposal **B_Task3**.

3. Just to the left of the Proposals drop-down list, click ▢ (View bookmarks) and select **Tree**.

4. In in the *Create* tab>Environment drop-down panel, select

   ▢ (Stand of Trees).

Note that the previous filter is still active; you need to change it.

5. In the Select Draw Style asset card, in the search field, type **veg** and scroll to select the **Syagrus Romanzoffiana** tree, as shown in Figure 8–85.

You can use the search window at the top of the asset card to find the proper tree if needed.

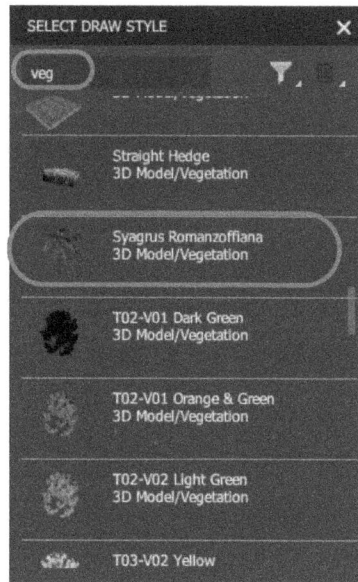

Figure 8–85

6. In the first lot, double-click at the corner of the lot to add a tree, as shown in Figure 8–86. Press <Esc> once.

Be sure to double-click on the spot rapidly, otherwise you will begin to draw a line for a row of trees. The similar feature for Stand of Trees will be covered later in the exercise.

Figure 8–86

7. Use (Height Gizmo) to adjust the height of the tree as needed. Press <Esc> when done.

8. In another lot of your choice, add some shrubs along the house. Select ![icon] (Stand of Trees) again. In the Select Draw Style asset card, type **hedge** in the search field. Select the **Straight Hedge**, as show in Figure 8–87.

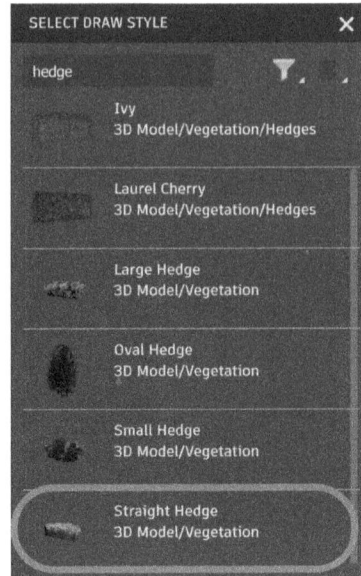

Figure 8–87

9. Double-click to add the first hedge at the front corner of one of the houses. Add five more hedges to the front of the house, as shown in Figure 8–88. You will need to use ![icon] (Rotate Gizmo) and ![icon] (Move Gizmo) to properly place the hedges along the front of the house.

Figure 8–88

10. Just to the left of the Proposals drop-down list, click ⬛ (View bookmarks) and select **Open Lot**.

11. In the *Create* tab>Environment drop-down panel, select

    ⬛ (Stand of Trees).

12. In the Select Draw Style asset card, in the search field, type **Ded** and scroll to select **Deciduous-V01 Tree**.

13. Create a polygon, as shown in Figure 8–89, to place an area of trees. Double-click to end the polygon. Press <Esc> when done.

Figure 8–89

14. To adjust the density of the trees, click once on a tree, then click again. This will bring up the Density Slider (as shown in Figure 8–90). Adjust the slider until you have the amount of trees you like.

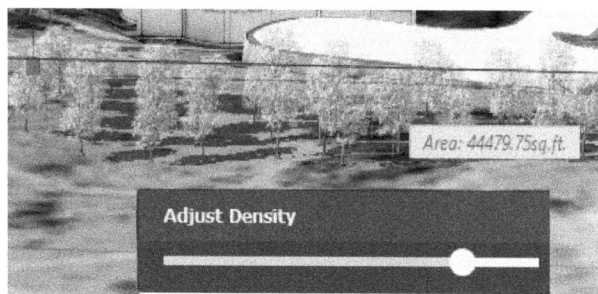

Figure 8–90

Task 4 - Enhance the site with city furniture.

1. In the main Toolbar on the right side, expand *Switch Active Proposal* and select proposal **B_Task4**.

2. Just to the left of the Proposals drop-down list, click (View bookmarks) and select **Church**.

3. In the *Create* tab>Environment panel, select (City Furniture).

4. In the Select Draw Style asset card that displays, type **church** in the search field. Select the **Wooden Church**, as shown in Figure 8–91.

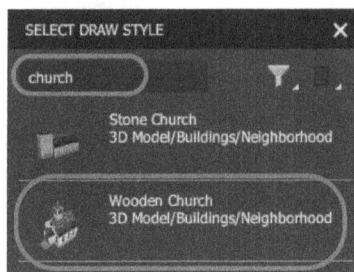

Figure 8–91

5. Double-click in the area shown in Figure 8–92 to add the church. You may need to use the Gizmos to adjust the rotation and position.

Figure 8–92

6. Click ▣ (View bookmarks) and select **Open Lot**.

7. In in the *Create* tab>Environment panel, select 🚦 (City Furniture).

8. In the Select Draw Style asset card, type **gas** in the search field. Select the **Gas Station with Convenience Store**, as show in Figure 8–93.

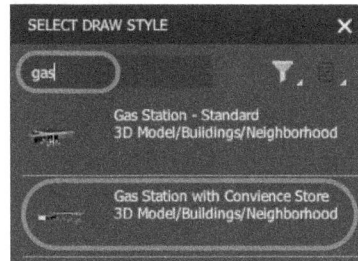

Figure 8–93

9. Double-click in the area shown in Figure 8–94 to add the gas station. You may need to use the Gizmos to adjust the rotation and position.

Figure 8–94

10. Time permitting, continue to add city furniture elements to the open lot, similar to those shown in Figure 8–95.

Figure 8–95

Task 5 - Hide CAD overlay.

1. In the main Toolbar on the right side, expand *Switch Active Proposal* and select proposal **B_Task5**.

2. In the *Manage* tab>Model panel, click (Model Explorer).

3. In the Model Explorer, in the *Overlays* section, click the light bulb beside **Base-Proposed for IWX** to turn off the overlay, as shown in Figure 8–96.

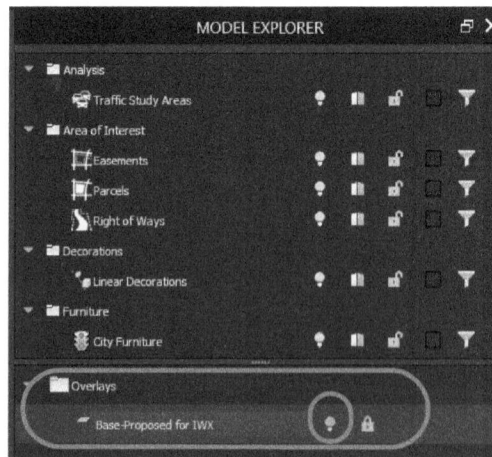

Figure 8–96

Chapter Review Questions

1. Which part of the user interface would you use to quickly change to an isometric view, for example a view from the upper north-east corner?
   a. In Canvas Tools
   b. ViewCube
   c. Model Explorer
   d. Model Window

2. How to do you change the density of a Row of Trees?
   a. By changing the style of the trees
   b. Through the Properties palette.
   c. Select the tree row, then select it again and use the slider to adjust the density.
   d. Once placed, you cannot change the density.

3. Which of the following should be used to display different design variations for the project?
   a. Bookmarks
   b. Proposals
   c. Coverages
   d. Model Explorer

4. Which of the following is not a category for a predefined 3D building model?
   a. Furniture
   b. Residential
   c. Neighborhood
   d. Commercial

5. Once placed, you can change the footprint of a building that has been created from a 3D model.
   a. True
   b. False

Command Summary

Button	Command	Location
⚙	Application Options	• **Home Screen** • **In Canvas Tools:** Settings and Utilities
▯	Bookmark	• **Toolbar**
N/A	Elevate Camera Down	• **Mouse:** Hold scroll wheel • **Shortcut Key:** <E> or <0> (zero)
N/A	Elevate Camera Up	• **Mouse:** Hold scroll wheel • **Shortcut Key:** <Q> or <1>
▮ / ⌂	Home	• **ViewCube** • **Keyboard:** <Home> or <F4>
N/A	Lock Above Terrain	• **View Settings>Interaction stack**
▣	Model Explorer	• **Toolbar** • **In Canvas Tools:** Build, manage, and analyze your infrastructure model> Create and manage your model
N/A	Open	• **Home Screen**
N/A	Pitch Down	• **Shortcut Key:** <W>
N/A	Pitch Up	• **Shortcut Key:** <S>
▱	Proposals	• **Toolbar** • **In Canvas Tools:** Build, manage, and analyze your infrastructure model> Create and manage your model
N/A	Tooltips	• **View Settings>Interaction stack**
N/A	ViewCube	• **View Settings>Interaction stack**
N/A	Zoom In	• **Mouse:** Scroll wheel • **Shortcut Key:** <+>
N/A	Zoom Out	• **Mouse:** Scroll wheel • **Shortcut Key:** <->
▣	Zoom Selected	• **Shortcut Key:** <F> • **In Canvas Tools:** Build, manage, and analyze your infrastructure model> Select model features • **In Model:** Double-click on point of interest

More Grading with Corridor Models

The Autodesk® Civil 3D® software provides tools that create multiple design scenarios in compressed time. Another benefit is the ease of making changes to a design. You can easily create a finished ground surface using parcel lines, feature lines, and grading objects. Unfortunately, they do not provide the level of flexibility that many projects require. As an alternative to the grading tools, this appendix explores using an Autodesk Civil 3D corridor as a grading design tool. The corridor and its tools provide easy design and editing capabilities. This is a non-standard approach to grading in the Autodesk Civil 3D software. Corridor subassemblies provide more daylighting options and the ability to add conditional grades to a finished ground surface. In this appendix, you will use the corridor and its tools to redesign a pond area to include a two-chamber lagoon.

Learning Objectives in This Appendix

- Create corridor baselines that can be used for a grading solution rather than a road design.
- Create profiles to be used in grading solutions.
- Determine the best subassembly to use for the type of grading being created.
- Create multiple baselines and regions in a corridor model to include multiple alignments, profiles, and assemblies in the grading solution.
- Modify a grading solution by changing the alignments, profiles, assemblies, target surface, or corridor parameters.
- Add feature lines to the corridor surface for additional grading control.

A.1 Corridor Baselines

Corridors can be used to create more than just roads; they can also create grading solutions. Corridors provide greater flexibility and make for easier designs and easier design changes over grading objects. Additionally, corridors provide material assignment options. For example, a graded parking lot using a corridor model enables the application of materials like asphalt to the parking surface, concrete for the curbs and gutters, and grass or some other material inside the islands. Not only does a corridor aid with design visualization, but a corridor model also creates material quantity takeoff values.

Baselines can be either alignments or feature lines. In a corridor, a baseline applies an assembly to create a corridor model. As the corridor applies an assembly along the baseline, the assembly stays perpendicular to the baseline. An example of this is in an intersection model: the edge of pavement baseline applies a curb return assembly perpendicular to the curb return alignment, as shown in Figure A–1.

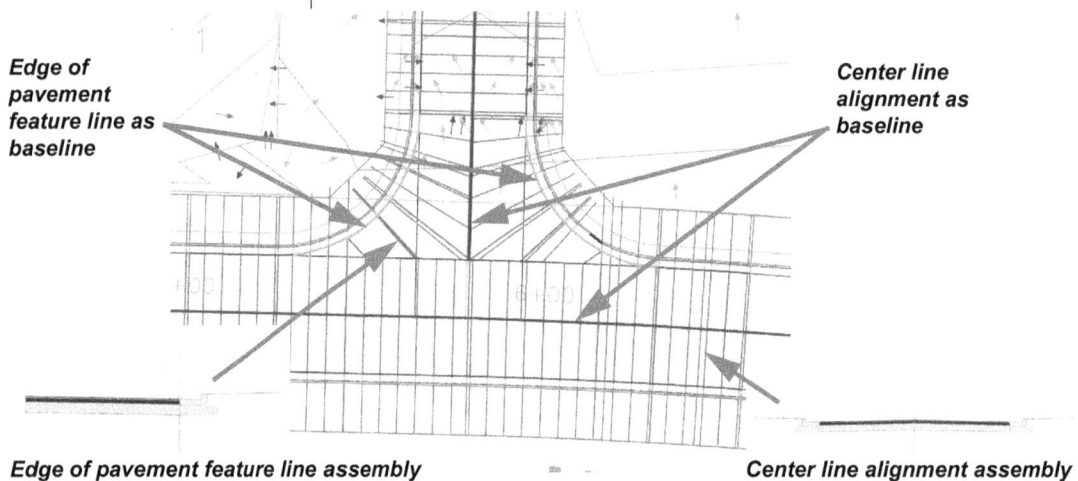

Edge of pavement feature line as baseline

Center line alignment as baseline

Edge of pavement feature line assembly

Center line alignment assembly

Figure A–1

Feature Line Baselines

Using a feature line for a corridor baseline enables you to quickly set both the horizontal and vertical location for a grading model. If the feature line needs to reference another entity for either the horizontal or vertical location, two options are available: **Create Feature Lines from Alignment** and **Create Feature Line from Corridor**. These options are found in the *Home* tab>Create Design panel> **Feature Line** command. When the command list for Feature Line is expanded, the drop-down list displays the two options, as shown in Figure A–2.

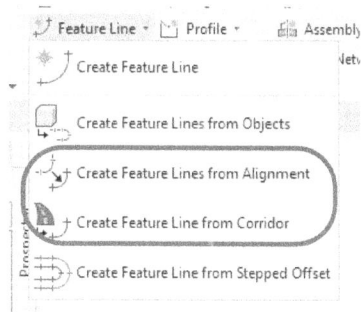

Figure A–2

Selecting the **Create Feature Lines from Alignment** option enables you to do the following, as shown in Figure A–3:

- Select the site in which to place the new feature line so that it interacts with other feature lines and grading objects.

- Name the feature line.

- Select a profile to use to assign elevations to vertices.

- Select a style.

- Determine if the feature line is dynamically linked to the alignment. The feature line updates to any change in the associated alignment.

Figure A–3

Selecting the **Create Feature Lines from Corridor** option enables you to do the following:

- Select which corridor feature lines are extracted, as shown on the left in Figure A–4. The options include:
  - All feature lines
  - Only those in a select region(s)
  - Only those within a select polygon

- Determine which settings to use, as shown on the right in Figure A–4:
  - Create a dynamic link to the corridor
  - Smooth the feature line
  - Name the feature line
  - Select a code set style

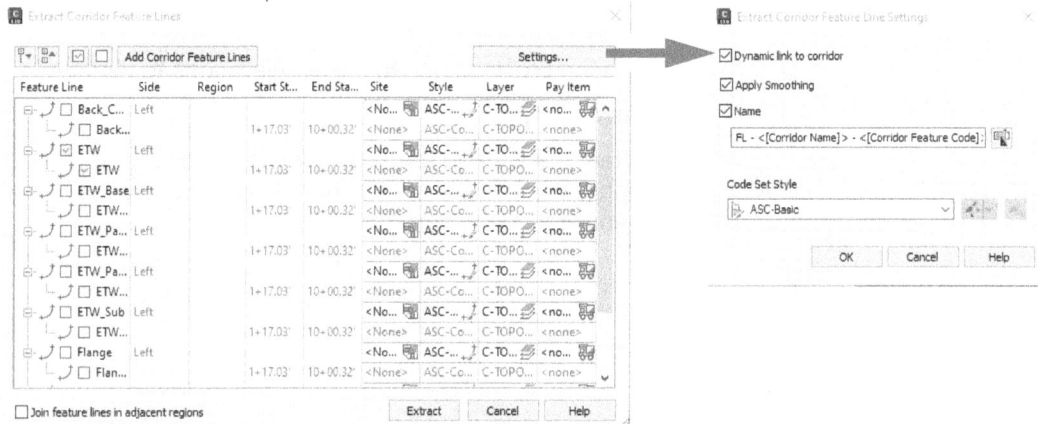

Figure A–4

Alignment Baselines

Even though a feature line can be a corridor baseline, horizontal and vertical alignments have more control during an editing session. For example, alignments keep arcs tangent to straight segments when using the free curve type as the corner treatment.

Grading solutions from alignments and corridor models do not have to be linear entities. The solutions include closed areas, such as parking lots, ponds, or lagoons. When grading a closed area, ensure that the alignment begins and ends along a straight (tangent) segment that does not contain any odd transitions, as shown in Figure A–5. This ensures that the corridor model built from the alignment correctly projects the grading slopes along the alignment's entire length.

Figure A–5

When using corridors as a grading solution, it is recommended that you include horizontal curves between tangents. Curves enable the corridor models to make smooth transitions between tangents rather than cut the corner off at an angle, as shown in Figure A–6.

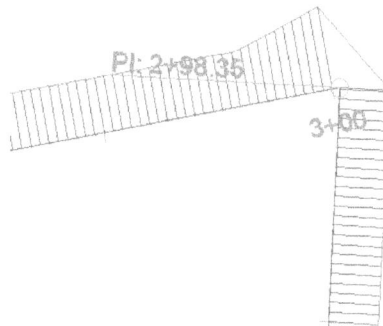

Figure A–6

How To: Create an Alignment for an Enclosed Grading Solution

1. In the *Home* tab>Create Design panel, expand the Alignment

   drop-down list and click ⟶ (Alignment Creation Tools).
2. Create the tangents and curves ensuring that the alignment begins and ends at the same location along a straight segment.

- To ensure that the beginning and ending of the alignment follow the same bearing, use the **Bearing and Distance** transparent command.
- Alternatively, you can create a line that spans one side of the area to grade. Begin the alignment at the midpoint of the line using Osnaps. Use the endpoint of the line to pick the second point. Loop the alignment around and use the other endpoint to begin the last segment. Use the **Midpoint** Osnap again to pick the last station of the alignment, as shown in Figure A–7.

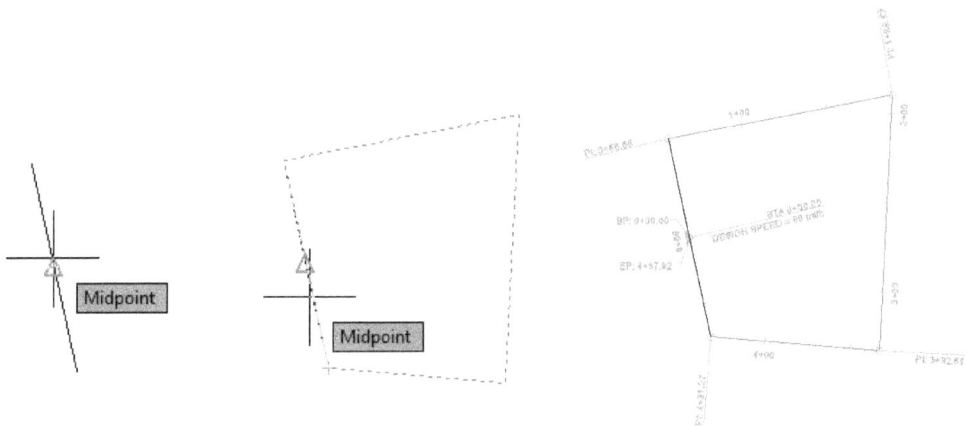

Figure A–7

Practice A1	**Create Grading Baselines**

Practice Objective

*   Create alignments representing the rim of the pond.

For the land development drawings in this guide, much of the preliminary work has already been done for the site development. The completed corridors for Jeffries Ranch Road and Ascent Place, the Ascent Place knuckle and cul-de-sac target alignments, the Mission Avenue alignment, and the Existing Ground surface have been referenced through Data Shortcuts.

In this practice, you will create alignments for the pond's rim, using polylines that are already in the drawing.

Task 1 - Create alignments from objects.

In this task, you will create two alignments that represent the pond's rim. One alignment closes on itself to create an enclosed area and acts as the pond's outer rim. The second alignment is in the pond's interior rim and represents the north bay. When selecting the polylines, it is important to pick them at the suggested location so that you end up with the same starting and ending points for each alignment.

The north bay is open because additional feature lines are used to grade a weir between the north and south pond bays.

1. Open **LAGOON-A.dwg** from the *C:\Civil3D for Land Dev\ Working\Lagoon* folder.

2. Hover over the Data Shortcuts and look at the tooltip that appears, as shown in Figure A–8. Ensure that your **Data Shortcuts Working Folder** is set to *C:\Civil 3D for Land Dev\ Data Shortcuts\Fundamentals* and the **Data Shortcuts Project Folder** to *Ascent-Development*.

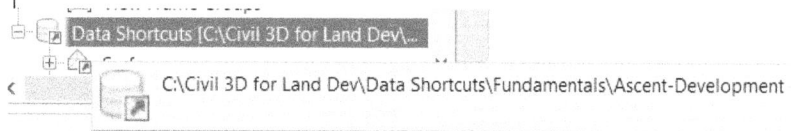

    *   If not, right-click on Data Shortcuts to set the **Working Folder** to *C:\Civil 3D for Land Dev\Data Shortcuts\ Fundamentals* and the **Data Shortcuts Project Folder** to *Ascent-Development*.

Data Shortcuts [C:\Civil 3D for Land Dev\...

C:\Civil 3D for Land Dev\Data Shortcuts\Fundamentals\Ascent-Development

Figure A–8

3. In the *Home* tab>Create Design panel, expand the Alignment

   drop-down list and click ⤵ (Create Alignment from Objects).

4. In the drawing, select the closed polyline representing the outer rim of the pond, as shown in Figure A–9. Press <Enter>.

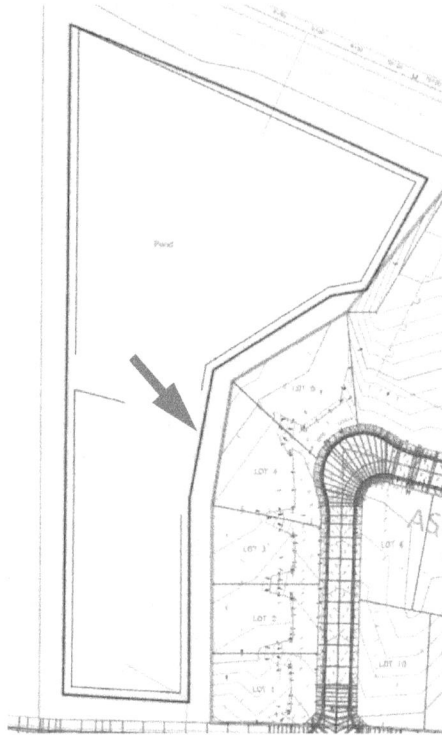

Figure A–9

5. Press <Enter> to accept the default direction.

6. In the Create Alignment from Objects dialog box, complete the following, as shown in Figure A–10:

- For the *Name*, type **Pond Outer Rim**.
- For the *Type*, select **Miscellaneous**.
- For the *Alignment style*, select **ASC-Proposed**.
- In the *Conversion options* area, set the *Default radius* to **60'** and toggle on **Erase existing entities**.
- Click **OK**.

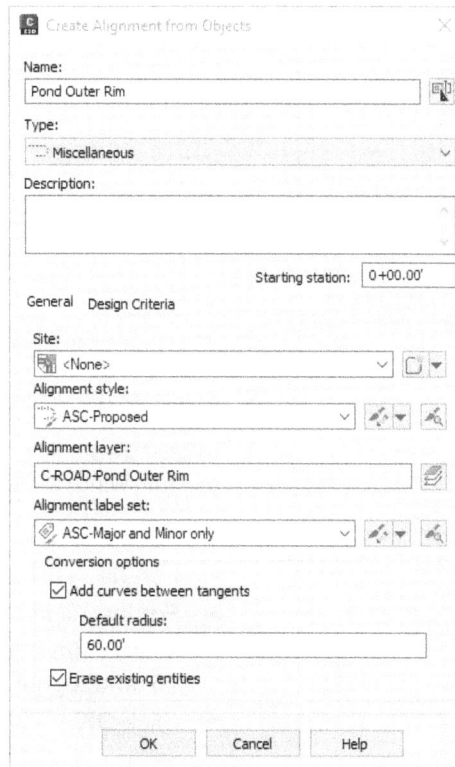

Figure A–10

7. In the *Home* tab>Create Design panel, expand the Alignment drop-down list and click ⟲ (Create Alignment from Objects).

8. In the drawing, select the polyline representing the northern interior rim of the pond's north bay, as shown in Figure A–11. Press <Enter>.

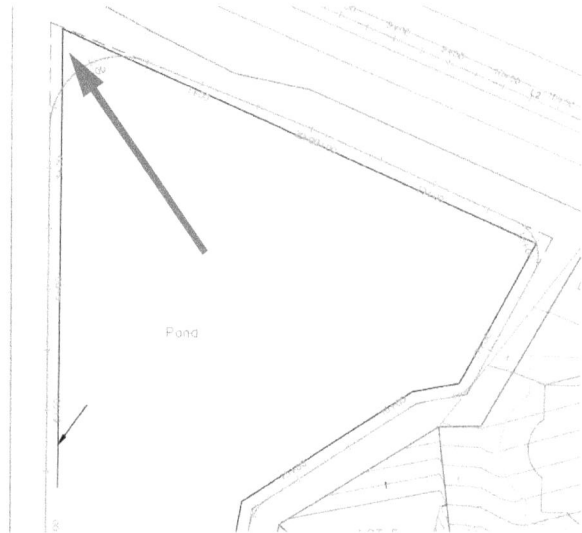

Figure A–11

9. Press <Enter> to accept the default direction.

10. In the Create Alignment from Objects dialog box, complete the following, as shown in Figure A–12:

- For the *Name*, type **Pond North Bay**.
- For the *Type*, select **Miscellaneous**.
- For the *Alignment style*, select **ASC-Proposed**.
- In the *Conversion options* area, set the *Default radius* to **75'** and toggle on **Erase existing entities**.
- Click **OK**.

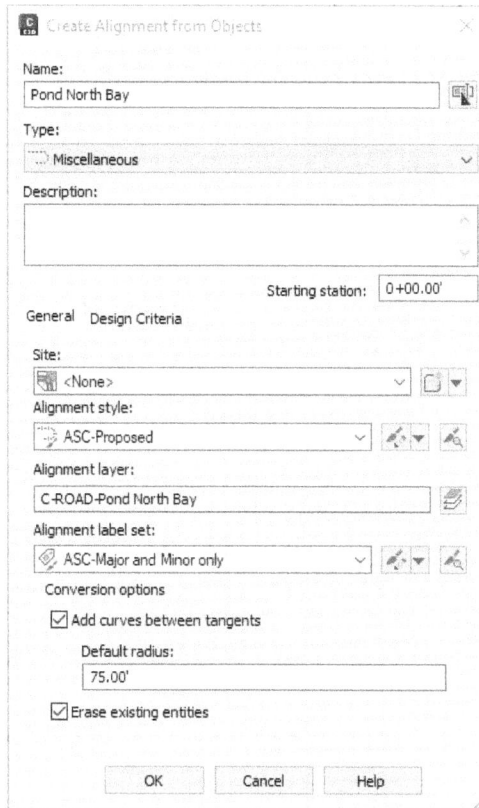

Figure A–12

Task 2 - Create a feature line to use as a baseline.

1. Continue working in the same drawing as the last task.

2. In the *Home* tab>Create Design panel, expand the Feature Line drop-down list and click (Create Feature Lines from Objects).

3. In the drawing, select the southern polyline representing the interior rim of the pond's south bay, as shown in Figure A–13. Press <Enter>.

Figure A–13

4. In the Create Feature Lines dialog box, complete the following, as shown in Figure A–14:

- For the *Site*, select **Pond Site**.
- For the *Name*, type **Pond South Bay**.
- For the *Style*, select **ASC-Pond**.
- In the *Conversion options* area, toggle on **Erase existing entities** and **Assign elevations**.
- Click **OK**.

Figure A–14

5. In the Assign Elevations dialog box, select **Elevation** and then set the value to **179**.

6. Click **OK**.

7. Save the drawing

Task 3 - Modify the curves and clean up the drawing.

In this task, you will modify the alignment curves to ensure the proper design radii. You will then remove the alignment labels and line extensions that are not required for the design documentation.

1. Continue working in the same drawing as the last task.

2. In Layer Properties Manager, freeze the following layers:

   • **C-ROAD-POND NORTH BAY**
   • **C-TOPO-FEAT-POND SITE**

---

3. In the drawing, select the **Pond Outer Rim** alignment, as shown in Figure A–15.

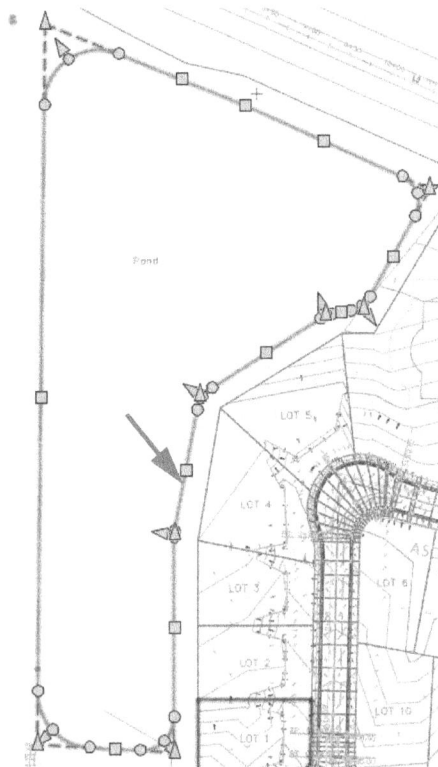

Figure A–15

4. In the *Alignment* contextual tab>Modify panel, click

   ⇗ (Geometry Editor).

5. In the Alignment Layout Tools toolbar, click ⦿ (Alignment Grid View).

6. Set the curve radius values according to those shown in Figure A–16.

No.	Type	Tangency Constraint	Parameter Constrai...	Parameter C...	Length	Radius
1	Line	Not Constrained (Fixed)	🔒	Two points	151.35'	
2	Curve	Constrained on Both Sides (Free)	🔒	Radius	116.24'	60.00'
3	Line	Not Constrained (Fixed)	🔒	Two points	646.64'	
4	Curve	Constrained on Both Sides (Free)	🔒	Radius	68.69'	45.00'
5	Line	Not Constrained (Fixed)	🔒	Two points	61.09'	
6	Curve	Constrained on Both Sides (Free)	🔒	Radius	73.14'	45.00'
7	Line	Not Constrained (Fixed)	🔒	Two points	167.19'	
8	Curve	Constrained on Both Sides (Free)	🔒	Radius	39.72'	215.00'
9	Line	Not Constrained (Fixed)	🔒	Two points	103.71'	
10	Curve	Constrained on Both Sides (Free)	🔒	Radius	53.95'	65.00'
11	Line	Not Constrained (Fixed)	🔒	Two points	122.95'	
12	Curve	Constrained on Both Sides (Free)	🔒	Radius	25.19'	65.00'
13	Line	Not Constrained (Fixed)	🔒	Two points	1.70'	
14	Curve	Constrained on Both Sides (Free)	🔒	Radius	53.31'	60.00'
15	Line	Not Constrained (Fixed)	🔒	Two points	53.27'	
16	Curve	Constrained on Both Sides (Free)	🔒	Radius	100.12'	60.00'
17	Line	Not Constrained (Fixed)	🔒	Two points	157.21'	

Figure A–16

7. Close the Alignment Grid View vista.

8. In Layer Properties Manager:

   - Freeze **C-ROAD-POND OUTER RIM**
   - Thaw **C-ROAD-POND NORTH BAY**

9. In the drawing, select the **Pond North Bay** alignment.

10. In the Alignment Layout Tools toolbar, click 🔘 (Alignment Grid View).

11. Set the curve radius values according to those shown in Figure A–17.

No.	Type	Tangency Constraint	Parameter Constrai...	Parameter C...	Length	Radius
1	Line	Not Constrained (Fixed)	🔒	Two points	264.17'	
2	Curve	Constrained on Both Sides (Free)	🔒	Radius	148.25'	75.00'
3	Line	Not Constrained (Fixed)	🔒	Two points	243.09'	
4	Curve	Constrained on Both Sides (Free)	🔒	Radius	125.15'	75.00'
5	Line	Not Constrained (Fixed)	🔒	Two points	25.69'	
6	Curve	Constrained on Both Sides (Free)	🔒	Radius	44.43'	50.00'
7	Line	Not Constrained (Fixed)	🔒	Two points	2.58'	
8	Curve	Constrained on Both Sides (Free)	🔒	Radius	27.32'	70.50'
9	Line	Not Constrained (Fixed)	🔒	Two points	134.85'	
10	Curve	Constrained on Both Sides (Free)	🔒	Radius	41.50'	50.00'
11	Line	Not Constrained (Fixed)	🔒	Two points	7.92'	

Figure A–17

12. Close the Alignment Grid View vista.

13. Close the Alignment Tools toolbar.

14. In Layer Properties Manager:

- Freeze **C-ROAD-POND NORTH BAY**
- Thaw **C-TOPO-FEAT-POND SITE**

15. In the drawing, select the **Pond South Bay** feature line.

16. In the *Feature Line* contextual tab>Edit Geometry panel, click
    (Edit Curve).

17. Select the curve shown in Figure A–18.

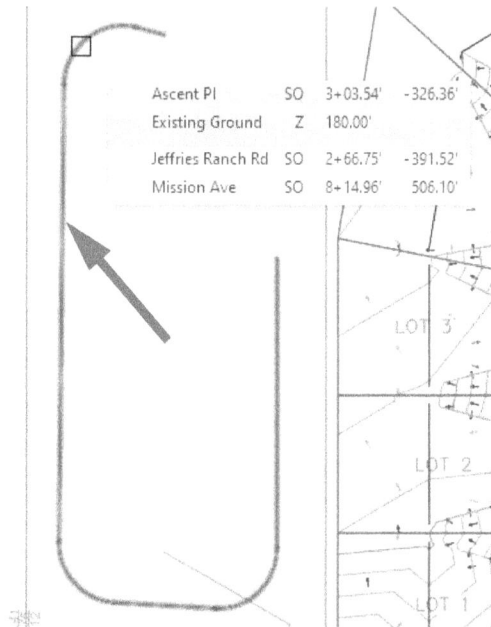

Ascent Pl	SO	3+03.54'	-326.36'
Existing Ground	Z	180.00'	
Jeffries Ranch Rd	SO	2+66.75'	-391.52'
Mission Ave	SO	8+14.96'	506.10'

Figure A–18

18. In the Edit Feature Line Curve dialog box, set *Radius* to **43** and click **OK** to change the curve's radius.

19. In Layer Properties Manager, thaw the following layers:

- **C-ROAD-POND NORTH BAY**
- **C-ROAD-POND OUTER RIM**

20. In the drawing, select one of the pond alignments and in the *Alignment* contextual tab>Modify panel, expand the Alignment Properties drop-down list and click ✏ (Edit Alignment Style), as shown in Figure A–19.

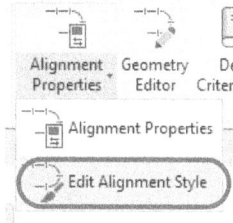

Figure A–19

21. In the Alignment Style dialog box, in the *Markers* tab, change the **Point of Intersection** marker style to **<None>**, as shown in Figure A–20. Click **OK** to close the Pick Marker Style dialog box, but remain in the Alignment Style dialog box.

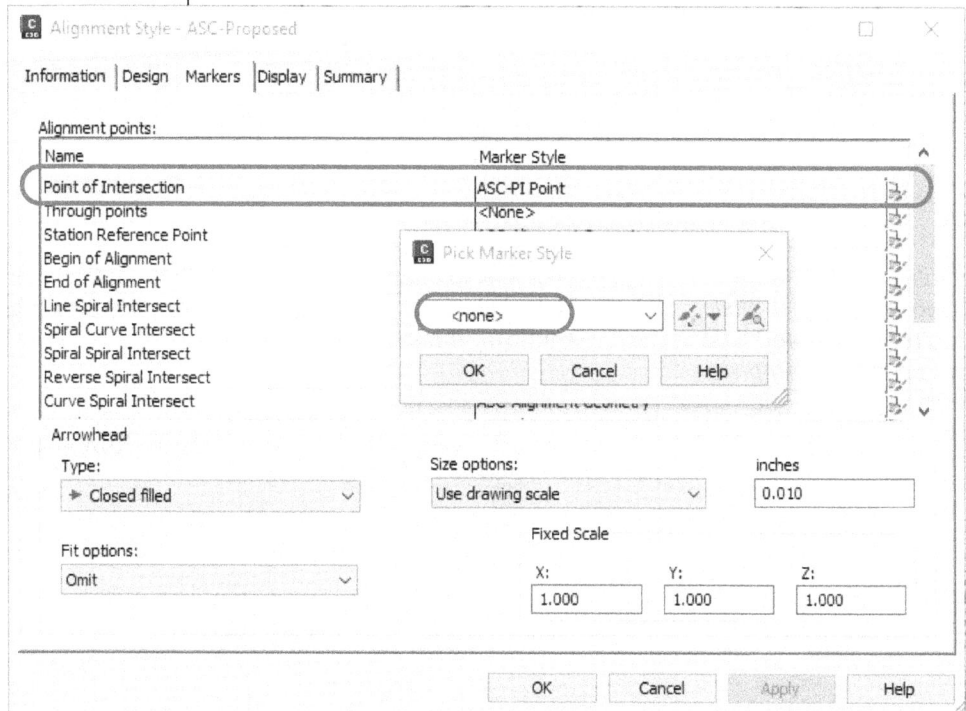

Figure A–20

22. In the *Display* tab, turn off the light bulbs next to **Line Extensions**, **Curve Extensions**, and **Tangent Extensions**, as shown in Figure A–21.

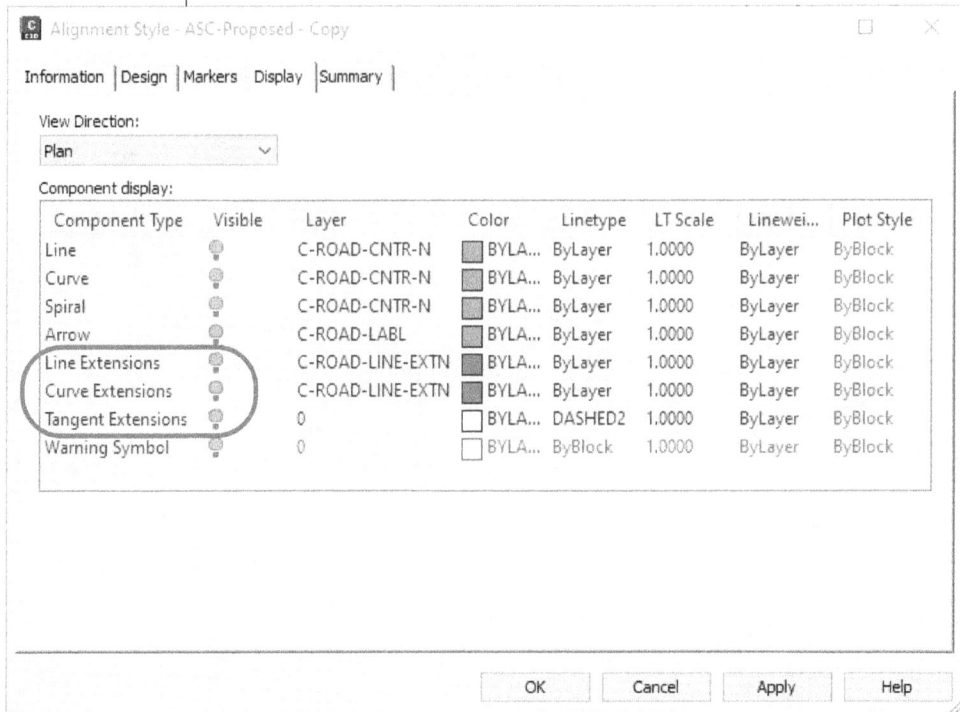

Figure A–21

If this is a style to be used on a regular basis, it is recommended it be set up in your template with its own unique name.

23. Click **OK** to close the dialog box. In the Edit a Reference Style dialog box, select **Make a local copy of the style with a unique name**.

24. Press <Esc> to deselect the alignment.

25. In the drawing, select the **Pond Outer Rim** alignment.

26. Right-click and select **Edit Alignment Labels**, as shown in Figure A–22.

Figure A–22

27. In the Alignment Labels dialog box, select **Import Label Set**. In the Select Label Set dialog box, select **_No Labels**, as shown in Figure A–23. Click **OK** twice to close both dialog boxes. The labels are now removed from the **Pond Outer Rim** alignment.

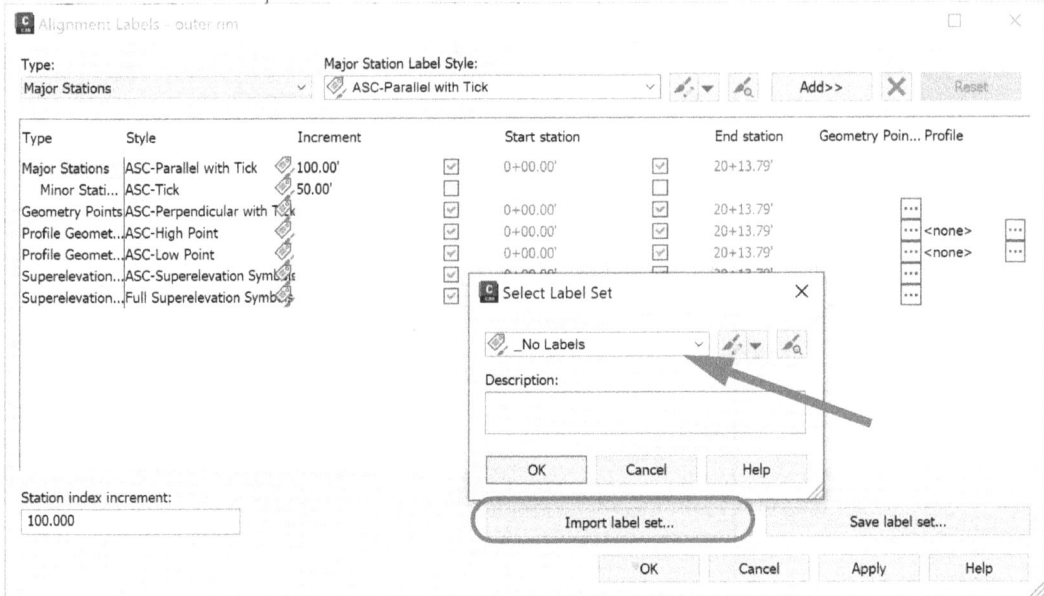

Figure A–23

28. Press <Esc> to clear the previously selected object.

29. In the drawing, select the **Pond North Bay** alignment.

30. Repeat Steps 26 to 28 for the Pond North Bay alignment.

31. Save the drawing.

A.2 Profiles

The process of creating a grading profile is similar to creating a profile for a road design. The same considerations and tools that are used in road design profiles are used in corridor-based grading design profiles. With a closed loop alignment (enclosed area), precautions are needed to handle a looped alignment's quirkiness.

First, if the alignment is modified, the alignment's stationing changes, and the surface profile updates to a new length. In a corridor, a region's stationing is not dynamically linked to any changes in the horizontal alignment. When the baseline's surface profile becomes longer than the region's length, a gap between the surface profile and the region's design stationing creates a station range with no vertical design elevations. When this gap occurs between the baseline's stationing and the region's stationing, the corridor assumes the region's design in the station gap is a zero elevation. To handle any change to a horizontal alignment, it is recommended that the design profile *ALWAYS* extends beyond the existing surface's profile by 10 or more feet, as shown in Figure A–24. This design profile extension ensures that the corridor model does not drop to elevation zero when the horizontal alignment (baseline) lengthens, and the region's stationing remains unchanged.

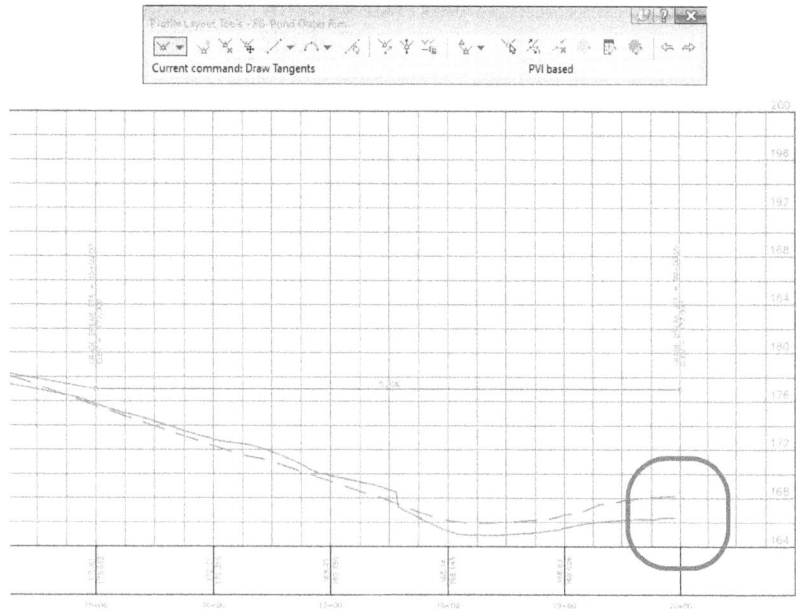

Figure A–24

Second, when working with loop corridors with grading enclosed areas, the design profile elevations must be the same elevation at the profile's beginning and end and, at the end, be 25 feet longer than the horizontal alignment.

In a road design, transitions between vertical grades are done with vertical curves. With grading corridor designs, vertical curves are optional. In a grading corridor, having smooth transitions between grades is not critical.

How To: Create a Surface Profile for Grading Solutions

1. Create a surface profile of the alignment and any required offsets. In the *Home* tab>Create Design panel, expand the Profile drop-down list and click ⎯ (Create Profile from Surface).
2. In the Create Profile from Surface dialog box, select the alignment. Select the surface(s) in the surface area and select **Add**. Select **Draw in profile view**.
3. In the Create Profile View dialog box, select **Create Profile View**. In the drawing, select a point for the profile view's insertion point, which will be the lower left corner of the profile view.

How To: Create a Design Profile for Grading Solutions

1. In the *Home* tab>Create Design panel, expand the Profile drop-down list and click ⎯ (Profile Creation Tools). In the drawing, select the profile view.

2. In the Create Profile dialog box, type a *Name* and select the *Profile style* and *Profile label set*, as shown in Figure A–25. Click **OK** to close the dialog box.

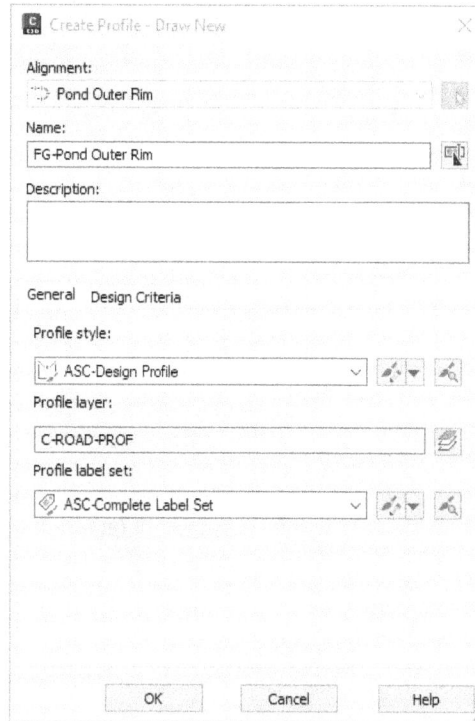

Figure A–25

3. In the Profile Layout Tools toolbar, click (Draw Tangents).

4. In the Transparent Tools toolbar, click (Profile Station Elevation).

5. In the drawing, select the appropriate profile view.

6. In the Command Line, enter the stations and elevations for the beginning and ending of the profile along with any intermediate PVIs.

7. Verify that the alignment closes on itself, and that the beginning and ending elevations match.

Practice A2

Create Grading Profiles

Practice Objective

- Create profiles representing the rim of the pond.

In this practice, you will create an existing ground surface and a design profile for the pond's alignments.

Task 1 - Create a profile for the outer rim of the pond.

In this task, you will create the pond's outer rim surface and design profiles. The outer rim alignment closes on itself and creates an enclosed area. Because the alignment is a closed loop, the design profile requires the beginning and ending elevations to be the same and that the design profile extend past the surface profile's ending station by 10 or more feet.

1. Continue working in the drawing from the previous task or open **LAGOON-B.dwg** from the *C:\Civil 3D for Land Dev\ Working\Lagoon* folder.

2. In the *Home* tab>Create Design panel, expand the Profile drop-down list and click ⎯ (Create Surface Profile).

3. In the Create Profile from Surface dialog box, do the following:

   - For the *Alignment,* select **Pond Outer Rim**.
   - For the *Select Surface*, select **Existing Ground**.
   - Click **Add>>** to add the surface profile.

4. With the Pond Outer Rim alignment still selected, add the following profile, as shown in Figure A–26:

   - Select **Sample offsets** and type **30** for the *Offset value*.
   - Select **Existing Ground** in the *Surface* area.
   - Click **Add>>**.
   - In the *Profile list* area, select **Existing Ground - 30.000** and change the *Style* to **ASC-Right Sample Profile**.

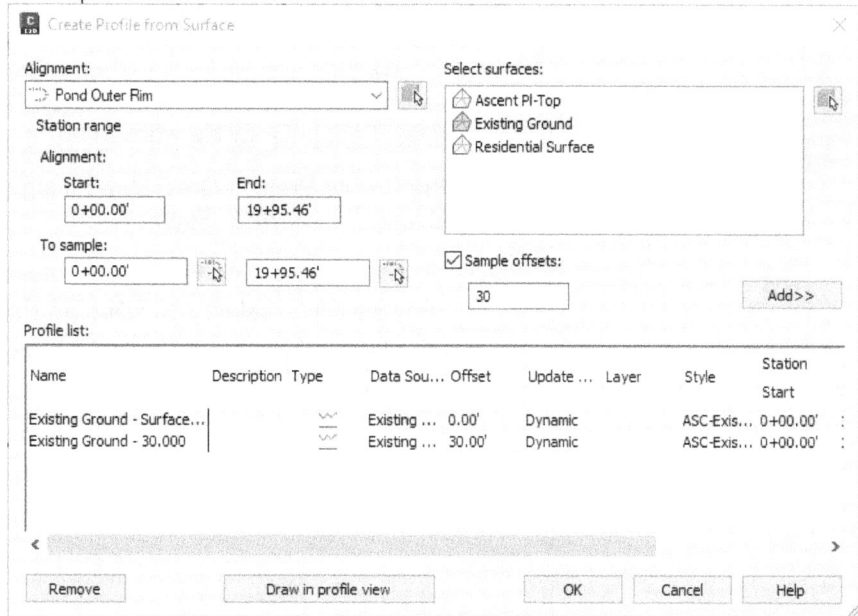

Figure A–26

5. In the Create Profile from Surface dialog box, select **Draw in profile view**.

6. In the *General* tab, set the profile view style to **ASC-Profile View**.

7. In the Create Profile View dialog box, click **Create Profile View**.

8. In the drawing, select a point above Mission Ave as the insertion point for the lower left corner of the profile view, as shown in Figure A–27.

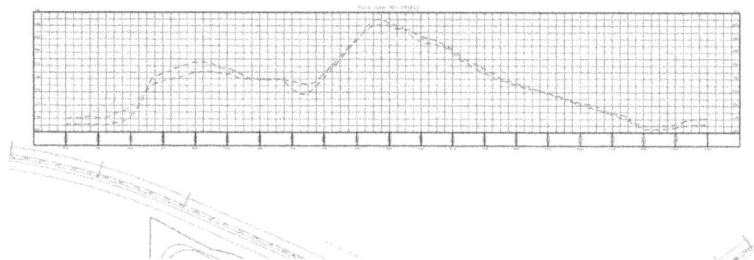

Figure A–27

9. Thaw the **C-ROAD-PROF-PROP** layer.

10. In the *Home* tab>Create Design panel, expand the Profile drop-down list and click ⎯ (Profile Creation Tools). In the drawing, select the Pond Outer Rim profile view to display the Create Profile - Draw New dialog box.

11. In the Create Profile - Draw New dialog box, complete the following, as shown in Figure A–28:

    • For the *Name*, type **FG-Pond Outer Rim**
    • For the *Style*, select **ASC-Design Profile**
    • For the *Profile label set*, select **ASC-Complete Label Set**.
    • Click **OK** to close the dialog box.

Figure A–28

12. In the Profile Layout Tools toolbar, click ⋎ (Draw Tangents).

13. In the Transparent Tools toolbar, click ⌐ (Profile Station Elevation).

14. In the drawing, select the **Pond Outer Rim** profile view.

15. In the Command Line, for the *Station* type **0** and press <Enter>. For the elevation type **177** and press <Enter>. Use the following table to set the remaining stations and elevations.

Note that you are going past the ending station. This ensures that if a curve changes (causing the alignment to lengthen or shorten), the corridor does not apply itself to elevation zero.

Station	Elevation
5+00.0'	177'
7+00.0'	180'
13+23.91'	180'
15+00.0'	177'
20+25.0'	177'

16. Press <Esc> to end the **Transparent** command. Press <Esc> again to end the command.

17. Close the Profile Layout Tools toolbar.

18. In the drawing, select the Pond Outer Rim profile view, right-click, and from the command list select **Profile View Properties**. You can also select the command from the contextual ribbon in the *Modify View* panel.

19. In Profile View Properties dialog box, select the *Bands* tab to make it current.

20. In the Bands panel, scroll right until the *Profile 1* and *Profile 2* columns are displayed.

21. Select the *Profile 2* value and from the drop-down list, select the **FG-Pond Outer Rim** profile, as shown in Figure A–29.

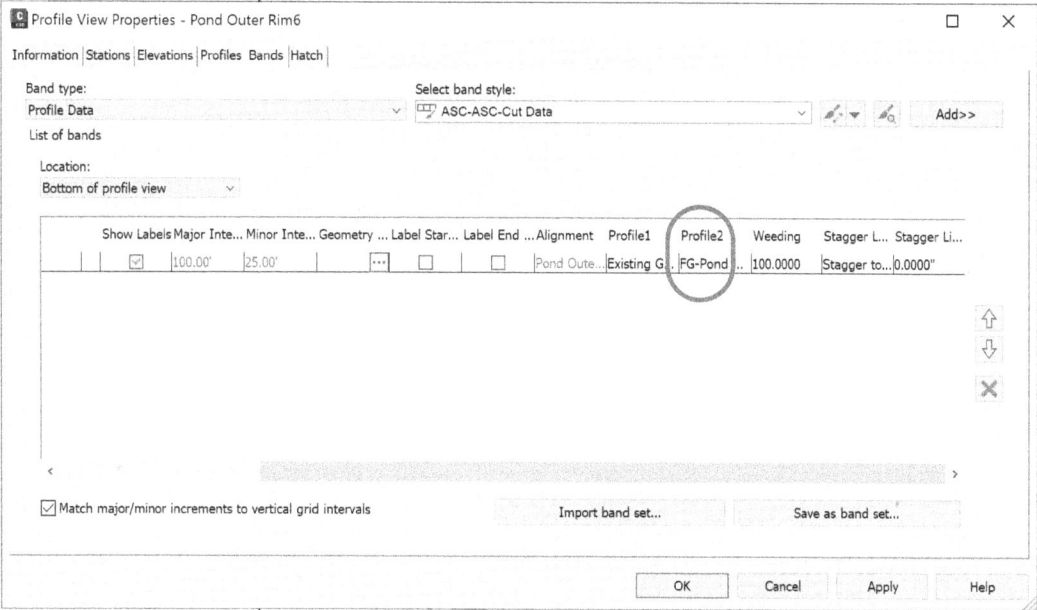

Figure A–29

22. Click **OK** to close the Profile View Properties dialog box.

23. Save the drawing.

Task 2 - Create the Pond North Bay alignment's surface and design profiles.

In this task, you will create a profile that represents the interior rim of the pond's north bay.

1. Continue working in the drawing from the previous task.

2. In the *Home* tab>Create Design panel, expand the Profile

   drop-down list and click ⎯ (Create Profile from Surface).

3. In the Create Profile from Surface dialog box, complete the following:

   - For the *Alignment*, select **Pond North Bay**.
   - In the *Surface* area, select **Existing Ground** and click **Add>>**.

4. Click **Draw in profile view**.

5. In the Create Profile View dialog box, click **Create Profile view**.

6. In the drawing, select a point above the Pond Outer Rim profile view as the insertion point for the lower left corner of the profile view.

7. In the *Home* tab>Create Design panel, expand the Profile

   drop-down list and click ⎯ (Profile Creation Tools). In the drawing, select the **Pond North Bay** profile view.

8. In the Create Profile dialog box, complete the following, as shown in Figure A–30:

   - For the *Name*, type **FG-Pond North Bay**.
   - For the *Style*, select **ASC-Design Profile**.
   - For the *Profile Label set* select **ASC-Complete Label set**.
   - Click **OK** to close the dialog box.

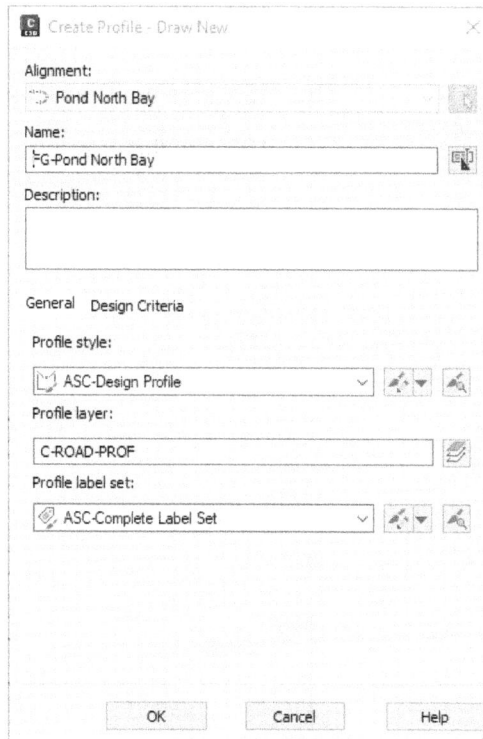

Figure A–30

9. In the Profile Layout Tools toolbar, click ⅄ (Draw Tangents).

10. In the Transparent Tools toolbar, click ⌐. (Profile Station Elevation).

11. In the drawing, select the **Pond North Bay** profile view.

12. In the Command Line, for the *Station* type **0** and press <Enter>. For the *Elevation* type **178** and press <Enter>.

13. Use the table below to set the remaining stations and elevations.

Station	Elevation
1+25.0'	177'
9+75.0'	177'
10+64.95'	178'

14. Press <Esc> to end the **Transparent** command. Press <Esc> again to end the command.

15. Close the Profile Layout Tools toolbar.

16. Save the drawing.

A.3 Create Grading Assemblies

The next elements to define are assemblies with associated subassemblies that create a grading solution from the previously defined baselines. There are three generic subassemblies that accomplish the same results as grading criteria would in a grading group. The three subassemblies and their grading criteria equivalent are as follows:

1. Link Width and Slope = Grade to Distance
2. Link Slope to Surface = Grade to Surface
3. Link Slopes to Elevations = Grade to Elevation or Grade to Relative Elevation

These subassemblies are accessed in the *Generic* tab in the Tool Palettes, as shown in Figure A–31.

Imperial Generic Subassemblies

LinkMulti
LinkOffsetAndElevation
LinkOffsetAndSlope
LinkOffsetOnSurface
LinkSlopeAndVerticalDeflection
LinkSlopesBetweenPoints
LinkSlopeToElevation
LinkSlopeToSurface
LinkToLaneMarker
LinkToMarkedPoint
LinkToMarkedPoint2
LinkVertical

Figure A–31

The Tool Palettes contains numerous subassemblies that act like grading scenarios. The subassembly used depends on the grading task, and the task determines when and how to use each subassembly. Most grading projects use link and/or daylight subassemblies. However, a grading solution may be more complex; for example, if a grading project is a parking lot, the design may include curb, sidewalk, and other specialized subassemblies.

Link Subassemblies

The Civil 3D Subassemblies Tool Palettes, *Generic* tab contains 14 subassemblies that create surface links between a grading alignment/profile and other drawing objects. Other Civil 3D objects may include offsets, elevations, alignments, profiles, surfaces, etc. These link subassemblies only have a top or datum link to create a surface and may not even have a point code. For more information on the link subassembly's parameters, right-click on the subassembly in the Tool Palette and select **Help**.

Link Width and Slope

The Link Width and Slope subassembly creates a link by specifying a link width and a link slope parameter. The link's inside point, closest to the assembly, is its attachment point. The link's fixed width and slope parameters can be overridden by targeting alignments, polylines, feature lines, or survey figures. The subassembly applies to an assembly's left or right side. An example is shown in Figure A–32.

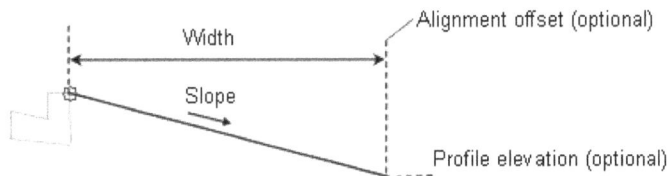

Figure A–32

Link Slope to Surface

The Link Slope to Surface subassembly creates a link by specifying a link slope parameter. The link's inside point, closest to the assembly, is its attachment point. The link's slope parameter is a given fixed value. The width of the link is determined by the link intersection with the closest target surface. The subassembly applies to an assembly's left or right side. An example is shown in Figure A–33.

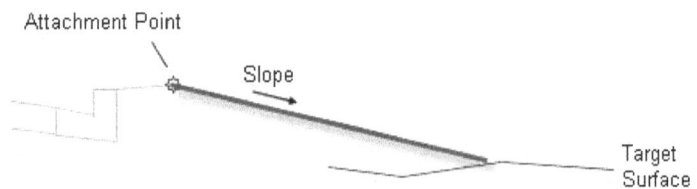

Figure A–33

Link Slope to Elevation

The Link Slope to Elevation subassembly creates a link to a user-specified target elevation by using a specified slope and elevation parameter. The link's length depends on the specified slope and target elevation. The link's inside point, closest to the assembly, is its attachment point. The link's elevation parameter can be overridden by targeting profiles, 3D polylines, feature lines, or survey figures. The subassembly applies to an assembly's left or right side. An example is shown in Figure A–34.

Figure A–34

Link Offset on Surface

The Link Offset on Surface subassembly creates a link by specifying an offset parameter and a target surface. The link's inside point, closest to the assembly, is its attachment point. The offset parameter is the distance from the assembly's baseline to a target surface. A positive value sets the offset to the baseline's right and a negative value sets the offset to the baseline's left. The link's offset parameters can be overridden by targeting alignments, polylines, feature lines, or survey figures. An example is shown in Figure A–35.

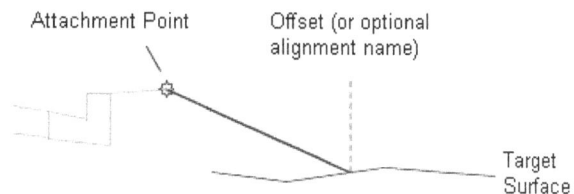

Figure A–35

Link to Marked Point

The Link to Marked Point subassembly creates a link from a subassembly point to a previously named marked point. The link's beginning point is a selected subassembly point. The link can go in any direction to connect to the named marked point. The link is to another subassembly within the assembly. An example is shown in Figure A–36.

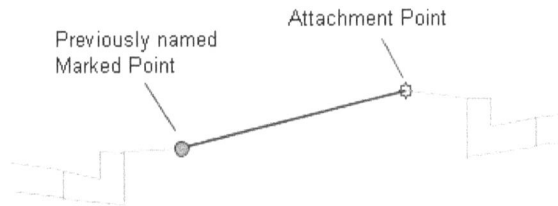

Figure A–36

Link to Marked Point 2

The Link to Marked Point 2 subassembly enables a link from the attached point to a previously named marked point. The link's beginning is the attachment point and the link can go in any direction. The named marked point's location determines the link's direction. The marked point can be on an adjacent corridor model. An example is shown in Figure A–37.

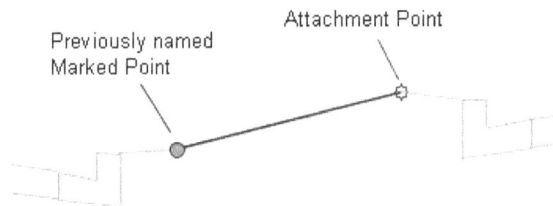

Figure A–37

Daylight Subassemblies

The *Daylight* tab in the Civil 3D Subassemblies Tool Palettes contains 17 subassemblies that create surface links between the grading alignment/profile and other objects in the drawing. In addition to creating links, materials can be assigned to the links to help with quantity calculations and visualization of the grading model. For more information on each daylight subassembly's parameters, right-click on the subassembly in the Tool Palette and select **Help**.

Daylight General

The Daylight General subassembly is a generalized solution to create cut and fill slopes from the edge of the grading design out to a target surface. This is the most commonly used daylight subassembly. However, it is seldom used to its full potential because many people do not realize the variety of cut and fill slope conditions it contains.

By default, the Daylight General subassembly attempts to create a cut first according to the parameter settings. The parameters can include up to eight different cut slopes, each with their own assigned material, before reaching the Cut Hinge Point, as shown in Figure A–38. You do not have to use all eight cut parameters. If only one slope is required, you can leave all of the other Cut Slope Width and Slope parameters set to zero. The slope after the Hinge Point can be set to define the final slope out to the target surface. It can vary according to the Max Cut Height settings. Therefore, the Flat Cut Slope (6:1 by default) is used if the height of the cut is less than the Flat Cut Height (5' by default). If the height of the cut from the Hinge Point to the surface is greater than the Flat Cut Height, but less than the Max Cut Height, the Medium Cut conditions are used automatically. The Medium Cut Slope enables the slope to be slightly more steep (4:1) than the Flat Cut Slope up to the Medium Cut Max Height (10'). If the cut is greater than the Medium Cut Max Height, the Steep Cut Slope (2:1) is used. The Steep Cut Slope does not have a maximum height parameter.

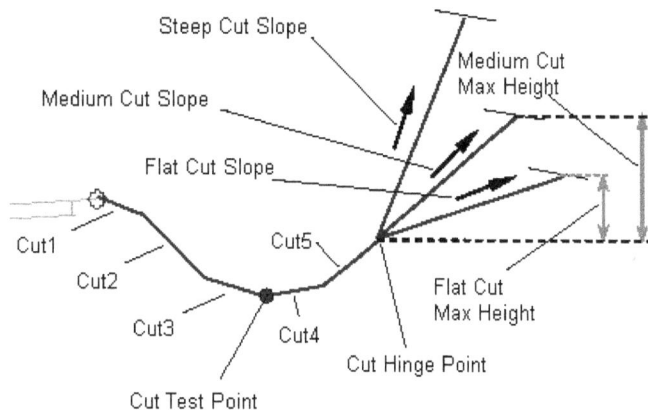

Figure A–38

If a cut condition is not found, a fill condition is used. Multiple fill conditions can be set similar to setting a cut condition, except that only three Fill Slopes can be set before the Fill Hinge Point. As with cut conditions, the fill conditions can include a Flat Fill Slope (6:1 by default) for a Maximum Height (5' by default), a Medium Fill Slope (4:1 by default) for a Maximum Height (10' by default), and a Steep Fill Slope (2:1) with no height restrictions, as shown in Figure A–39.

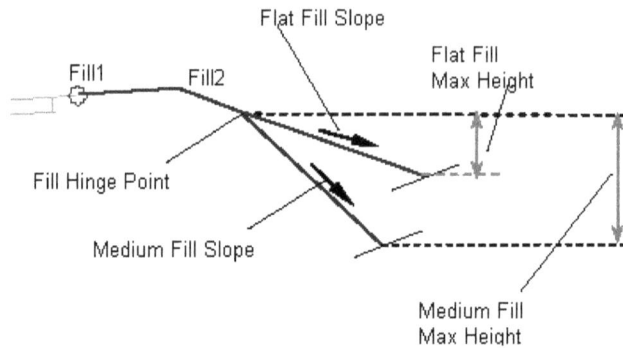

Figure A–39

If the Steep Slope is used in a cut situation, a guardrail can be incorporated into the design automatically by setting the guardrail parameter to **Include** and setting the slope, width and post position parameters, as shown in Figure A–40.

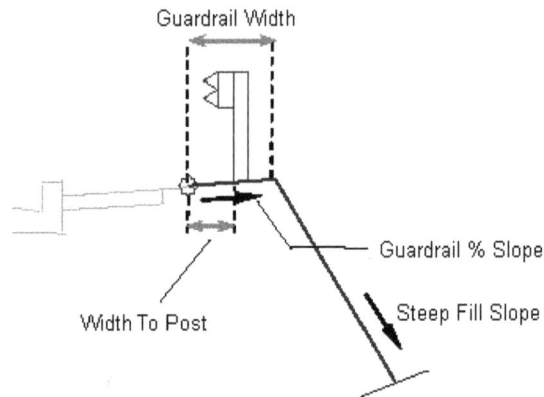

Figure A–40

Daylight Max Width

The Daylight Max Width subassembly creates a link that daylights to a target surface. The slope used is determined by the Maximum Width permitted. If the daylight link can touch the target surface within the Maximum Width parameter set, the slope is defined by the Slope parameter entered. If the daylight link cannot touch the target surface within the Maximum Width parameter set, the Slope parameter is ignored and the slope is defined by the Width parameter and the difference in elevation from the Hinge Point and the Target Surface at the Maximum Width permitted, as shown in Figure A–41.

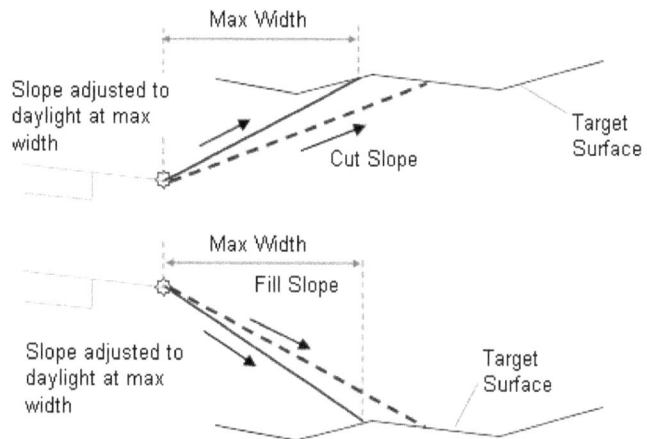

Figure A–41

Daylight to Offset

The Daylight to Offset subassembly creates a daylight link from the attachment point to a set offset from the baseline. This offset can be parallel to the baseline or target an alignment, polyline, feature line, or survey figure. Material types and depths can be assigned to the daylight link based on the slope's ranged values, as shown in Figure A–42.

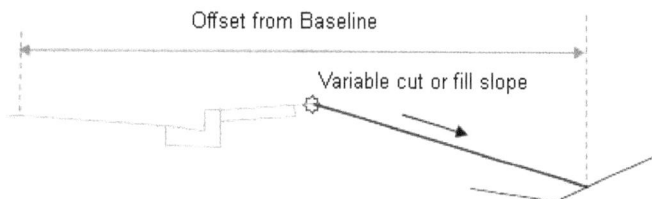

Figure A–42

Daylight Bench

The Daylight Bench subassembly creates repeating benches as needed at specified heights, widths, and slopes until it finds daylight on a target surface. The cut benches can have different parameters than fill benches if required, as shown in Figure A–43.

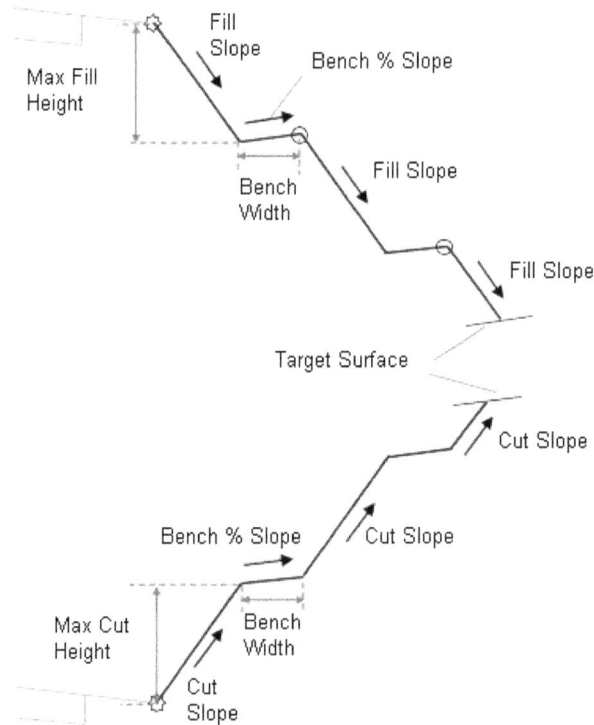

Figure A–43

How To: Create an Assembly for a Grading Solution

1. In the *Home* tab>Create Design panel, expand the Assembly drop-down list and click ![icon] (Create Assembly).
2. In the Create Assembly dialog box, type a name.
3. Set the *Assembly Type* to **Other**.
4. Click **OK** to accept all of the other defaults and close the dialog box.
5. In the drawing, select a point as the insertion point.

6. In the *Home* tab>Create Design panel, click ![icon] (Tool Palettes).

7. Select the required subassembly.
8. In the Properties palette, set the parameters in the *Advanced* area, as shown in Figure A–44.

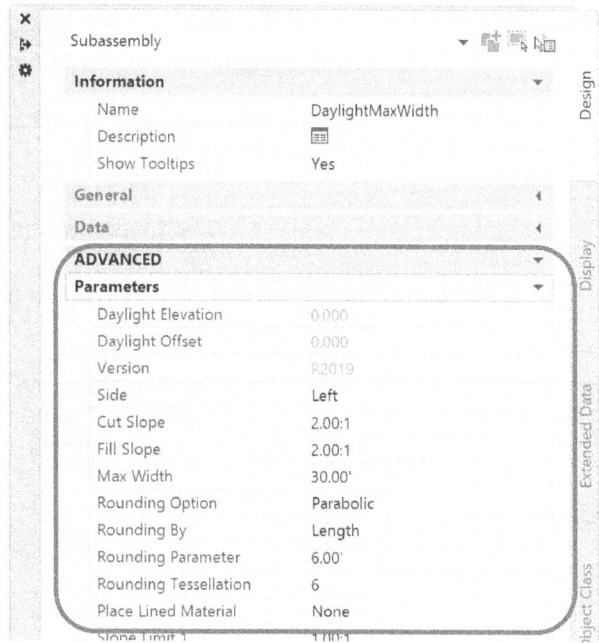

Figure A–44

9. In the drawing, select the assembly marker to which to connect the subassembly. Press <Enter> to end the command.
10. In the Tool Palettes, select another required subassembly.
11. In the Properties palette, set the parameters in the *Advanced* area.
12. In the drawing, select the required connection point, as shown in Figure A–45. Press <Enter> to end the command.

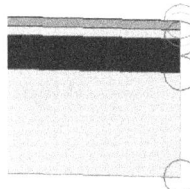

Figure A–45

13. Continue adding additional subassemblies as required.

Practice A3 | Create Grading Assemblies

Practice Objective

- Create typical grading corridor cross-sections by using assemblies and selecting appropriate subassemblies from the design specifications.

In this practice, you will create multiple assemblies for the pond grading.

Task 1 - Create assemblies for the outer rim of the pond.

In this task, you will create an assembly that represents the outer rim of the pond and daylights to the existing ground surface.

1. Continue working in the drawing from the last practice or open **LAGOON-C.dwg** from the *C:\Civil 3D for Land Dev\ Working\Lagoon* folder.

2. In the *Home* tab>Create Design panel, expand the Assembly drop-down list and click ⌗ (Create Assembly).

3. In the Create Assembly dialog box, complete the following:
    - For the *Name*, type **Pond Outer Rim**.
    - Set the *Assembly Type* to **Other**.
    - Set the *Code Set Style* to **ASC-View-Edit**.

4. Click **OK** to accept all of the other defaults and close the dialog box.

The Autodesk Civil 3D software automatically zooms in on the assembly marker.

5. In the drawing, select a point to the right of the Pond Outer Rim Profile view as the insertion point, so it visually relates to that profile.

6. In the *Home* tab>Create Design panel, click ⌗ (Tool Palettes) to display the Tool Palettes.

7. In the *Daylight* tab in the Tool Palettes, select **Daylight Max Width** to display the Properties palette.

8. In the Properties palette, set the parameters according to those shown in Figure A–46.

- *Side:* **Right**
- *Max Width:* **25'**
- *Rounding Parameter:* **3'**
- *Material 1 Thickness:* **1'**
- *Material 2 Thickness:* **0.5'**
- *Material 3 Thickness:* **0.33'**

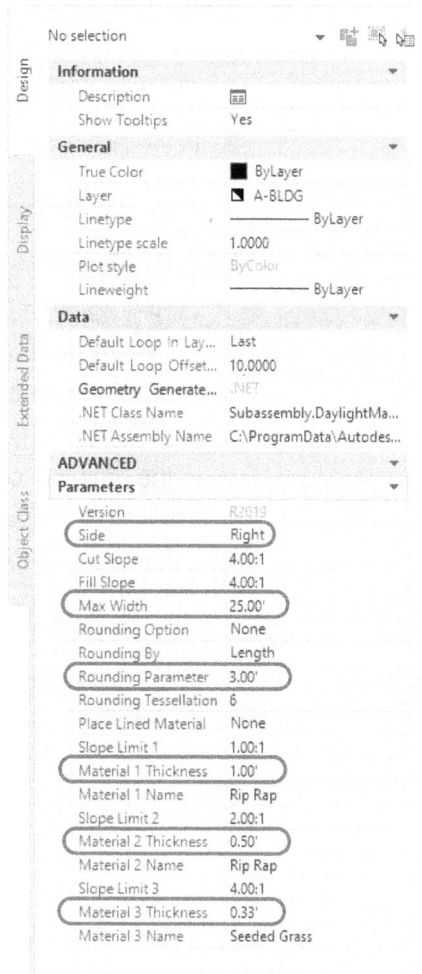

Figure A–46

9. In the drawing, select the **Pond Outer Rim** assembly marker to connect the subassembly.

10. Press <Enter> to end the command.

11. Save the drawing.

Task 2 - Create the north bay assemblies.

In this task, you will create three assemblies that represent the interior of the pond's north bay rim and daylights to the existing ground surface.

1. Continue working in the drawing from the previous task.

2. In the *Home* tab>Create Design panel, expand the Assembly drop-down list and click ⬛ (Create Assembly).

3. In the Create Assembly dialog box, complete the following:

   - For the *Name*, type **Pond North Bay 33 percent**.
   - Set the *Assembly Type* to **Other**.
   - Click **OK** to accept all of the other defaults and close the dialog box.

4. In the drawing, select a point to the right of the **Pond North Bay** profile view as the insertion point.

5. If the Tool Palettes is not already displayed, in the *Home* tab>Create Design panel, click ⬛ (Tool Palettes).

6. In the *Generic* tab in the Tool Palettes, select **Link Slope To Elevation**.

7. In the Properties palette, set the parameters according to those shown in Figure A–47.

- *Side:* **Right**
- *Slope:* **-33%**
- *Target Elevation:* **165'**

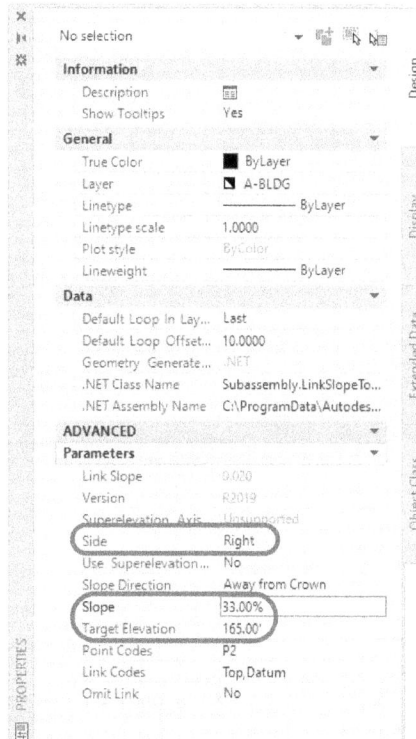

Figure A–47

8. In the drawing, select the **Pond North Bay 33** percent assembly marker to attach the subassembly, then press <Enter> to end the command.

Now you will create a copy of the Pond North Bay 33 assembly and change the slope for part of the north interior rim grading.

9. In the *Home* tab>Modify panel, click (Copy).

10. In the drawing, select the **Pond North Bay 33** assembly marker to connect the subassembly. Press <Enter> to end the selection.

11. In the drawing, pick two points of displacement to copy the assembly below the original, as shown in Figure A–48.

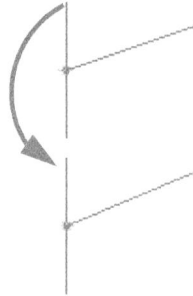

Figure A–48

12. Select the bottom assembly marker, in the *Assembly* contextual tab>Modify panel and click (Assembly Properties).

13. In the Assembly Properties dialog box, in the *Information* tab, for the *Name* type **North Bay 40 percent**.

14. In the *Construction* tab, complete the following:

    - Select **LinkSlopeToElevation**.
    - For *Input values*, for the *Slope Value,* type **40**.
    - Click **OK** to close the dialog box.

15. Press <Esc> to release the selection.

Now you will create an assembly with two links for part of the north interior rim grading.

16. In the *Home* tab>Create Design panel, expand the Assembly drop-down list and click (Create Assembly).

17. In the Create Assembly dialog box, complete the following:

    - For the *Name,* type **Pond North Bay - Double slope**.
    - Set the *Assembly Type* to **Other**.
    - Set the *Code Set Style* to **ASC-View-Edit**.
    - Click **OK** to accept all of the other defaults and close the dialog box.

18. In the drawing, select a point in the vicinity of the two existing pond north bay assemblies to locate the assembly in the drawing.

19. In the *Generic* tab in the Tool Palettes, select **Link Width And Slope**.

20. In the Properties palette, set the parameters as follows (as shown in Figure A–49):

- *Side:* **Right**
- *Width:* **30'**
- *Slope:* **-10%**

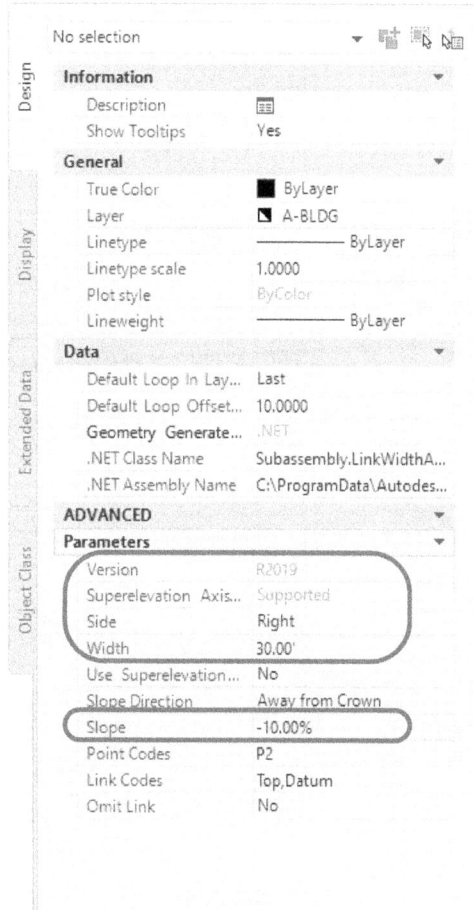

Figure A–49

21. In the drawing, select the **Pond North Bay Double slope** assembly marker to attach the subassembly. Press <Enter> to end the command.

22. In the *Generic* tab in the Tool Palettes, select **Link Slope to Elevation**.

23. In the Properties palette, set the following parameters (as shown in Figure A–50):

- *Side:* **Right**
- *Slope:* **50%**
- *Target Elevation:* **165'**

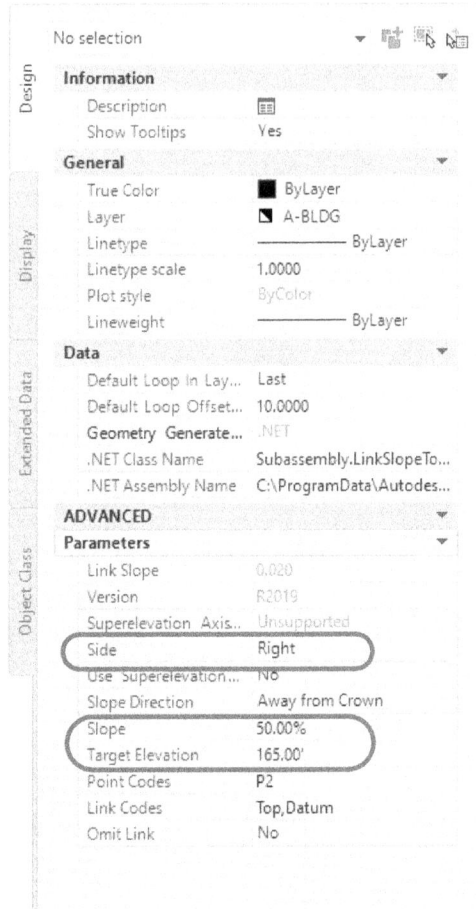

Figure A–50

24. In the drawing, select the **Pond North Bay Double slope** assembly's Link Width and Slope subassembly to connect the new subassembly.

25. Press <Enter> to end the command.

26. Save the drawing.

Task 3 - Create the pond's south bay assemblies.

In this task, you will create four assemblies for the pond's south bay assemblies.

1. Continue working in the drawing from the previous task.

2. In the *Home* tab>Create Design panel, expand the Assembly drop-down list and click ⊡ (Create Assembly).

3. In the Create Assembly dialog box, complete the following:

    • For the *Name,* type **Pond South Bay Bench**.
    • Set the *Assembly Type* to **Other**.
    • Set the *Code Set Style* to **ASC-View-Edit**.
    • Click **OK** to accept all of the other defaults and close the dialog box.

4. In the drawing, select a point below the **Pond North Bay** assemblies as the location for this assembly.

5. In the *Daylight* tab in the Tool Palettes, select **Daylight Bench**.

If the Tool Palettes is not already displayed, in the Home tab>Create Design panel, click

⊡ *(Tool Palettes).*

6. In the Properties palette, set the following parameters (as shown in Figure A–51):

- *Side:* **Left**
- *Cut Slope:* **3:1**
- *Max Cut Height:* **4'**
- *Max Fill Height:* **3'**
- *Bench Width:* **2'**
- *Bench Slope:* **-5%**
- *Rounding Parameter:* **1.5'**
- *Material 1 Thickness:* **1'**
- *Material 3 Thickness:* **0.33'**

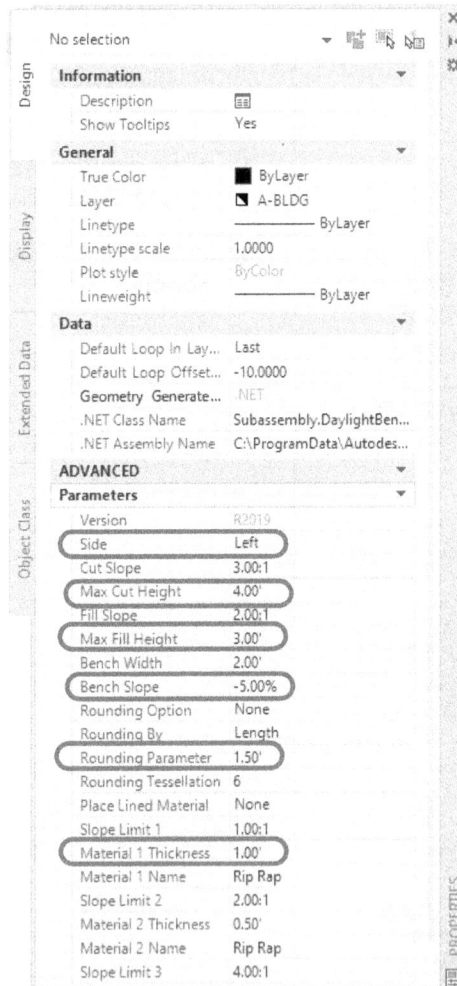

Figure A–51

7. In the drawing, select the **Pond South Bay Bench** assembly marker to attach the subassembly. Press <Enter> to end the command.

Now you will create the last three assemblies for the south bay. The first uses the Daylight Max Width subassembly and the other two are copies of the assembly with different slopes for part of the south interior rim grading.

8. In the *Home* tab>Create Design panel, expand the Assembly drop-down list and click ⬛ (Create Assembly).

9. In the Create Assembly dialog box, complete the following:

    *   For the *Name,* type **Pond South 2 to 1 slope**.
    *   Set the *Assembly Type* to **Other**.
    *   Set the *Code set style* to **ASC-View-Edit**.
    *   Click **OK** to accept all of the other defaults and close the dialog box.

10. In the drawing, select a point below the first Pond South Bay assembly as the insertion point.

11. In the *Daylight* tab in the Tool Palettes, select **Daylight Max Width**.

If the Tool Palettes is not already displayed, in the Home tab>Create Design panel, click

⬛ *(Tool Palettes).*

12. In the Properties palette, set the following parameters (as shown in Figure A–52):

- *Side:* **Left**
- *Cut Slope:* **2:1**
- *Fill Slope:* **2:1**
- *Max Width:* **30'**
- *Rounding Option:* **Parabolic**
- *Rounding Parameter:* **6'**
- *Material 1 Thickness:* **1'**
- *Material 2 Thickness:* **0.5'**
- *Material 3 Thickness:* **0.33'**

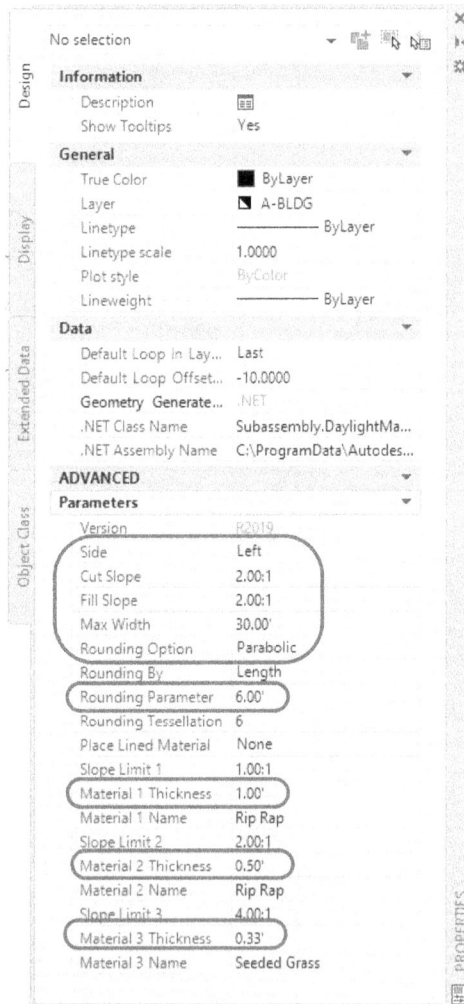

Figure A–52

13. In the drawing, select the **Pond South Bay 2 to 1 slope** assembly marker to attach the subassembly. Press <Enter> to end the command.

14. In the *Home* tab>Modify panel, click (Copy).

15. In the drawing, select the **South Bay 2 to 1 slope** assembly marker. Press <Enter> to end the selection process.

16. In the drawing, pick three points of displacement to make two copies of the assembly below the original, as shown in Figure A–53.

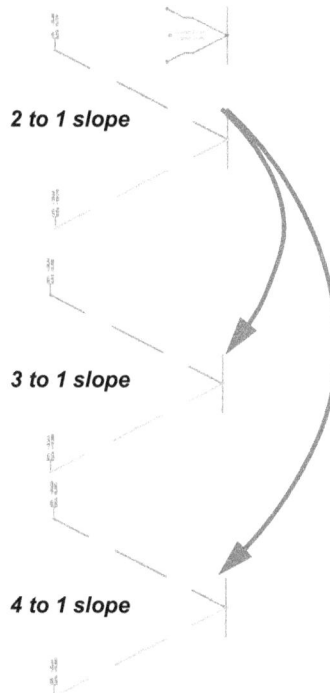

2 to 1 slope

3 to 1 slope

4 to 1 slope

Figure A–53

17. Select the middle assembly marker. In the *Assembly* contextual tab>Modify panel, click (Assembly Properties).

18. In the Assembly Properties dialog box, complete the following:

- In the *Information* tab, for the *Name*, type **Pond South Bay 3 to 1 slope**.
- In the *Construction* tab, select **DaylightMaxWidth**.
- In *Input values*, for the *Cut Slope* and *Fill Slope* values, type **3.0**.
- Click **OK** to close the dialog box.

19. Press <Esc> to release the selection.

20. Select the bottom assembly marker, in the *Assembly* contextual tab>Modify panel, click (Assembly Properties).

21. In the Assembly Properties dialog box, complete the following:

- In the *Information* tab, for the *Name*, type **Pond South Bay 4 to 1 slope**.
- In the *Construction* tab, select **DaylightMaxWidth**.
- In *Input values*, for the *Cut Slope* and *Fill Slope* values, type **4.0**.
- Click **OK** to close the dialog box.

22. Press <Esc> to release the selection.

23. Save the drawing.

A.4 Creating Complex Corridors

A complex corridor model is created by combining surfaces, baselines, assemblies, and subassembly targets. A simple corridor model uses one of each these Civil 3D objects. A complex corridor may contain several objects to create a corridor. For example, the Intersection Wizard creates an intersection that contains multiple baselines, regions, and assemblies. Each baseline and region may in turn use different assemblies and targets to create the intersection.

Corridor grading projects also create complex corridors that use multiple baselines, regions, and targets to create the grading solution. A grading solution can contain multiple grading slopes and non-parallel paths.

Baselines

Baselines represent a corridor model's path and are based on an alignment and profile or a feature line. The alignment controls the horizontal path, and the profile controls the vertical path. A corridor combines these two alignment types, horizontal and vertical, into a single string known as a baseline.

A single feature line defines both the horizontal and vertical paths because it is a three-dimensional object. By its nature, it is a baseline. A corridor may have multiple baselines and/or regions to permit multiple assemblies in the corridor's area or to change a corridor model's design elements.

How To: Add Baselines to a Corridor

1. In the *Home* tab>Create Design panel, click (Corridor).

2. In the Create Corridor dialog box, do the following, as shown in Figure A–54:

- Type a *Name*.
- Select the *Baseline type*.
- Select the *Alignment* or *Feature line*.
- Select the *Profile* (if an alignment baseline was selected).
- Select the *Assembly*.
- Select the *Target Surface*.
- Select **Set baseline and region parameters**.
- Click **OK** close the dialog box.

Figure A–54

3. In the Baseline and Region Parameters dialog box, click **Add Baseline**, select the alignment, and click **OK**.
4. In the Create Corridor Baseline dialog box, type a *Name* and select a *Horizontal alignment*, as shown in Figure A–55. Click **OK** close the dialog box.

Figure A–55

5. In the Baseline and Region Parameters dialog box, in the *Profile* value of the baseline, select **<Click here>**, as shown in Figure A–56.

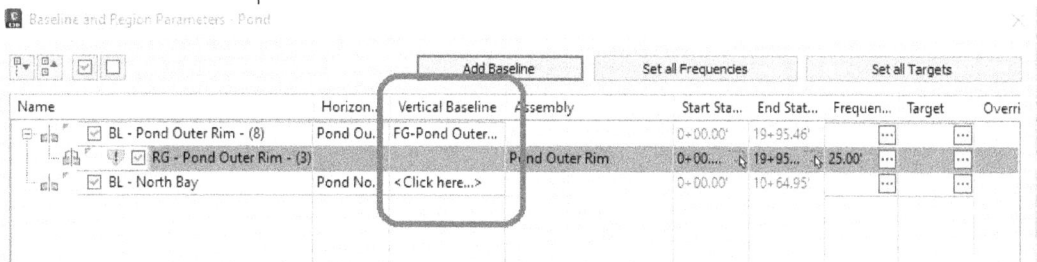

Figure A–56

6. In the Select a Profile dialog box, select a design profile, as shown in Figure A–57. Click **OK** close the dialog box.

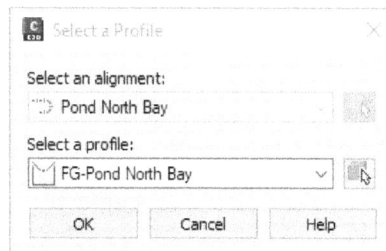

Figure A–57

Regions

Baselines consist of one or more regions. Each region is assigned its own assembly and provides a way to transition from one typical cross-section to another along the baseline. In addition, each region can target different subassembly points to modify an assembly's behavior.

How To: Add Regions to a Corridor

1. In the drawing, select the corridor. In the *Corridor* contextual tab>Modify Region panel, click ⬏ (Add Regions).
2. In the drawing, select the baseline alignment, as shown in Figure A–58.

BL - South Bay

Figure A–58

3. In the drawing, select a point or type a station number and press <Enter> for the beginning station, then select a point or type a station number and press <Enter> for the ending station.

4. In the Create Corridor Region dialog box, type a *Region name* and select an *Assembly*, as shown in Figure A–59.

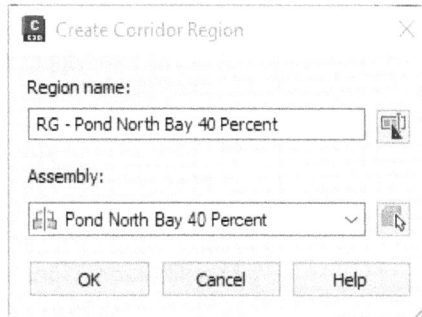

Figure A–59

5. In the Target Mapping dialog box, set the required targets, as shown in Figure A–60. Click **OK**.

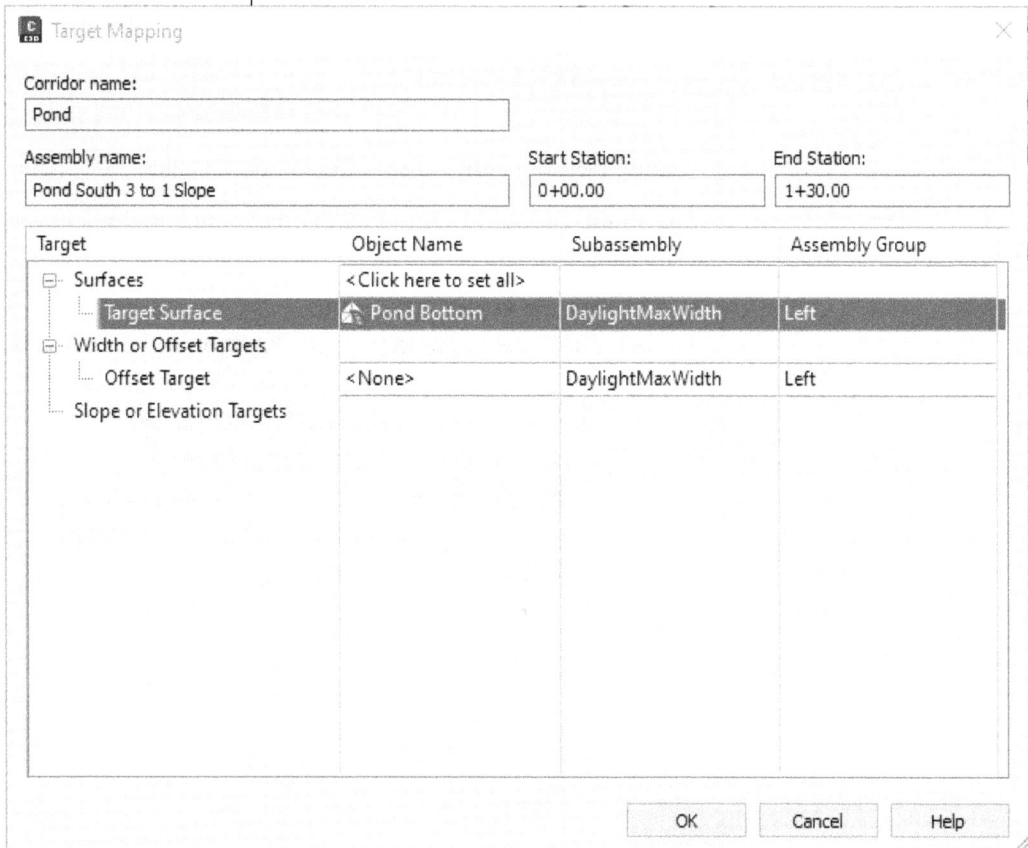

Figure A–60

Practice A4

Create Complex Corridors

Practice Objective

- Create a corridor model with multiple baselines and regions in the grading solution.

In this practice, you will create a corridor model with multiple baselines and regions to create a grading solution.The initial corridor is a single baseline and region. The corridor is made more complex by edits to the corridor that add additional baselines as alignments, profiles, or feature lines, regions, targets, and assemblies for each region. The corridor additions produce a corridor-based pond grading model.

Task 1 - Create a corridor with multiple baselines.

1. Continue working in the drawing from the last practice or open **LAGOON-D.dwg** from the *C:\Civil 3D for Land Dev\ Working\Lagoon* folder.

2. In the *Home* tab>Create Design panel, click   (Corridor).

3. In the Create Corridor dialog box, complete the following, as shown in Figure A–61:

   - For the *Name*, type **Pond**.
   - For the *Baseline type*, select **Alignment and profile**.
   - For the *Alignment*, select **Pond Outer Rim**.
   - For the *Profile*, select **FG-Pond Outer Rim**.
   - For the *Assembly*, select **Pond Outer Rim**.
   - For the *Target Surface*, select **Existing Ground.**
   - Toggle on **Set baseline and region parameters**.
   - Click **OK** close the dialog box.

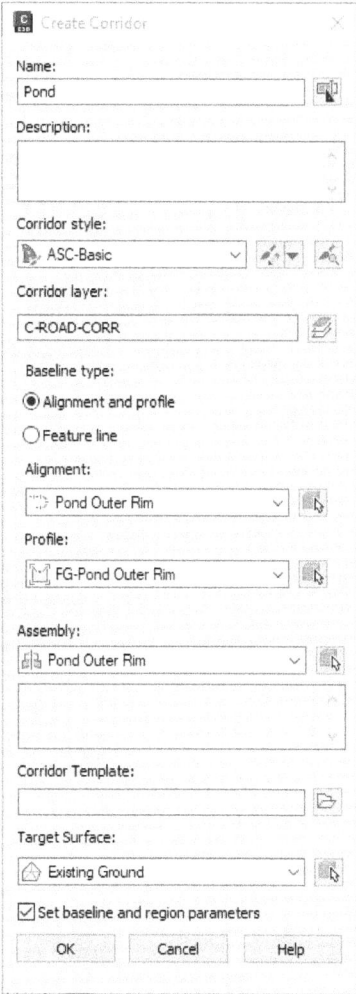

Figure A–61

4. In the Baseline and Region Parameters dialog box, click **Add Baseline**.

5. In the Create Corridor Baseline dialog box, complete the following, as shown in Figure A–62:

   - For the *Name*, type **North Bay**.
   - For the *Baseline type*, select **Alignment and profile**.
   - For the *Alignment*, select **Pond North Bay**.
   - Click **OK** close the dialog box.

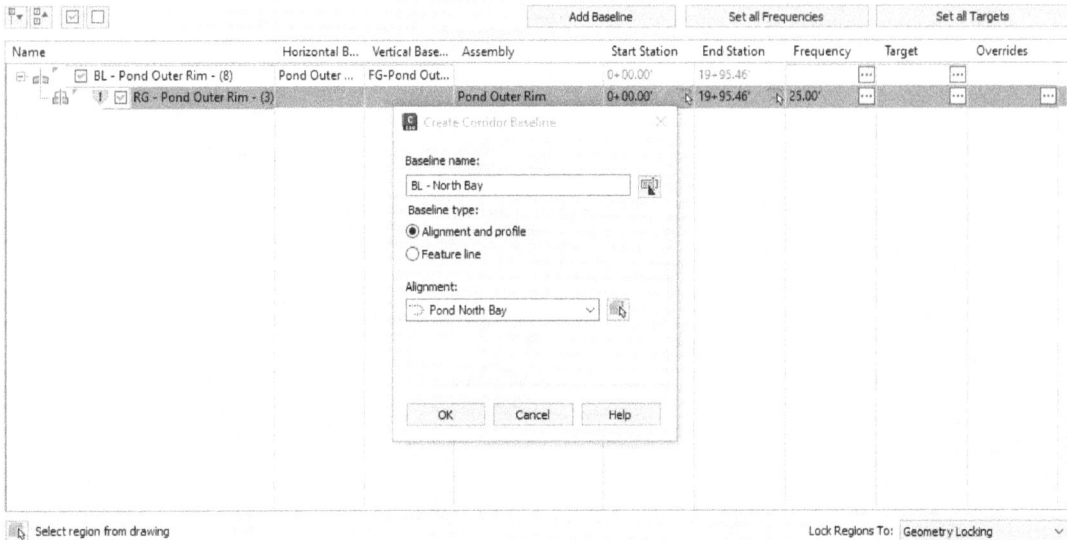

Figure A–62

6. In the Baseline and Region Parameters dialog box, in the Profile value of the North Bay baseline, select **<Click here>**, as shown in Figure A–63.

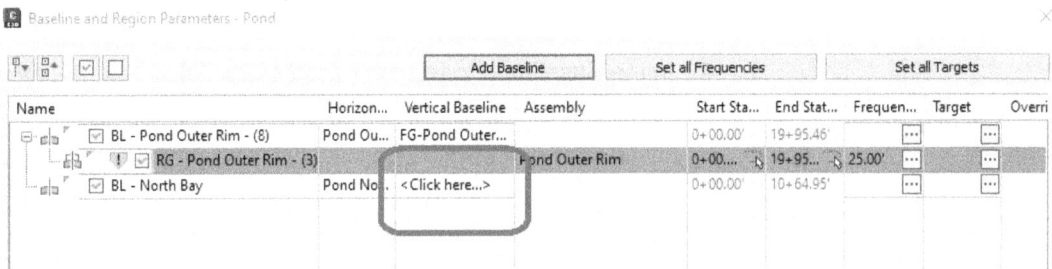

Figure A–63

7. In the Select a Profile dialog box, for the *profile* select **FG-Pond North Bay**, as shown in Figure A–64. Click **OK** close the dialog box.

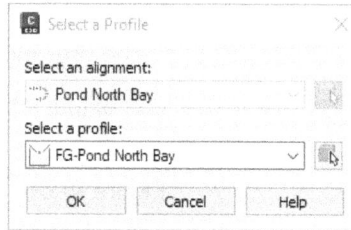

Figure A–64

8. In the Baseline and Region Parameters dialog box, click **Add Baseline**.

9. In the Create Corridor Baseline dialog box, complete the following, as shown in Figure A–65:

   - For the *Name*, type **South Bay**.
   - For the *Baseline, type* select **Feature line**.
   - For the *Site*, select **Pond Site**.
   - For the *Feature line*, select **Pond South Bay**.
   - Click **OK** to close the dialog box.

Figure A–65

10. Click **OK** close the dialog boxes and create the corridor model.

11. In the Corridor Properties - Rebuild dialog box, click **Rebuild the corridor**.

12. Save the drawing.

Task 2 - Add regions to the corridor to accommodate varying slopes around the north bay of the pond.

1. Continue working in the drawing from the previous task.

2. In the drawing, select the **Pond** corridor. In the *Corridor* contextual tab>Modify Region panel, click 🗐 (Add Regions).

3. In the drawing, select the **North Bay** baseline, as shown in Figure A–66.

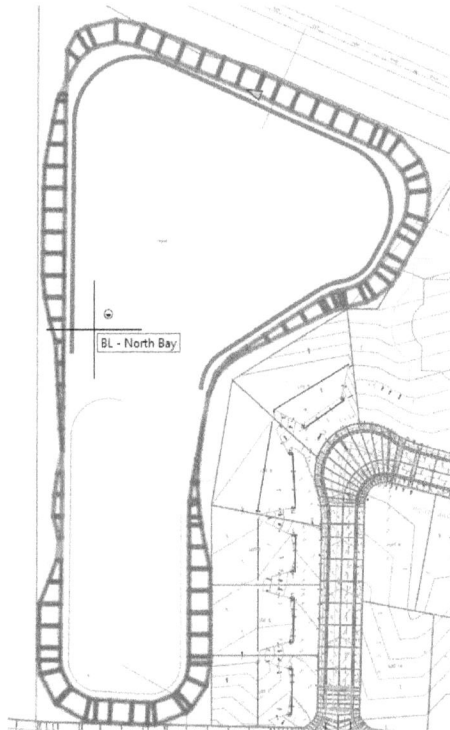

Figure A–66

4. In the Command Line, for the *Beginning Station*, type **0** and press <Enter>. Slide the cursor along the North Bay alignment to approximately station 4+20. For the *Ending Station*, type **420** and press <Enter>.

5. In the Create Corridor Region dialog box, for the *Region name*, type **40 Percent**. For the *Assembly*, select **Pond North Bay 40 Percent**, as shown in Figure A–67. Click **OK**.

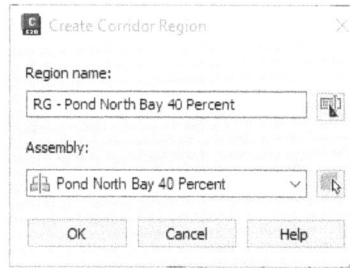

Figure A–67

6. Click **OK** to ignore the Target dialog box because the target elevation of 165' was already set when the assembly was created.

7. In the Command Line, for the *Beginning Station*, type **440** and press <Enter>. For the *Ending Station*, type **630** and press <Enter>.

8. In the Create Corridor Region dialog box, for the *Region name*, type **Double Slope**. For the *Assembly*, select **Pond North Bay Double Slope**. Click **OK**.

9. Click **OK** to ignore the Target dialog box because the target elevation of 165' was already set when the assembly was created.

10. Still in the **Add Region** command, in the Command Line, for the *Beginning Station*, type **650** and press <Enter>. Use the **Endpoint** Osnap to snap to the ending station in the drawing.

11. In the Create Corridor Region dialog box, for the *Region name*, type **33 Percent Slope**. For the *Assembly*, select **Pond North Bay 33 percent**. Click **OK**.

12. Click **OK** to ignore the Target dialog box because the target was already set when the assembly was created.

13. Press <Esc> to end the command.

14. Save the drawing.

Task 3 - Create a surface to set the pond bottom slope in the south bay.

In this task, you will create a pond bottom target surface for the pond's south bay area as a target for the correct slopes in this pond area. Feature lines in the pond's central area have already been drawn to aid in the design process.

1. Continue working in the drawing from the previous task.

2. In the *Home* tab>Layers panel, expand the layers and scroll down to the layer **C-TOPO-POND BOTTOM**. Select the light bulb to turn on the layer, as shown in Figure A–68.

You may have to enter **RE** *in the command line to regenerate the drawing in order for all of the feature lines to appear.*

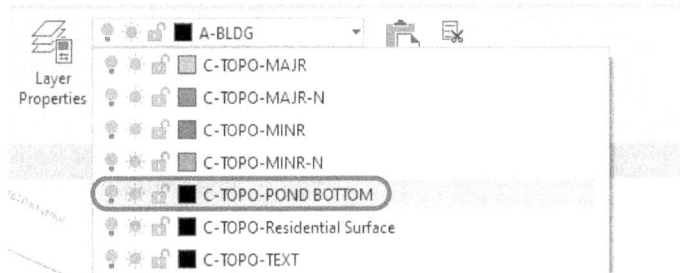

Figure A–68

3. In the *Home* tab>Create Ground Data panel, expand the Surfaces drop-down list and click (Create Surface).

4. In the Create Surface dialog box, for the *Name*, type **Pond Bottom**. For the *Style*, select **ASC-Border Only**. Click **OK** to close the dialog box.

5. In the drawing, zoom in on the south bay of the pond.

6. In the *Prospector* tab, expand **Sites>Lagoon**, and select **Feature Lines**. In the preview window below, select **Feature1** and **Feature2**, right-click and select **Select**.

7. In the *Feature Lines* contextual tab>Modify panel, click (Add to Surface as Breakline).

8. In the Select Surface dialog box, select the **Pond Bottom** surface and click **OK**.

9. In the Create Breaklines dialog box, set the following:

   * *Description*: **Pond Bottom FLs**
   * *Breakline type*: **Standard**
   * *Supplementing factors*: **25**

10. Click **OK** to close the dialog box. A surface is created.

11. Save the drawing.

Task 4 - Add baseline regions to define varying slopes around the south bay of the pond.

---

1. Continue working in the drawing from the previous task.

2. In the drawing, select the **Pond** corridor. In the *Corridor* contextual tab>Modify Region panel, click (Add Regions).

3. In the drawing, select the **South Bay** baseline, as shown in Figure A–69.

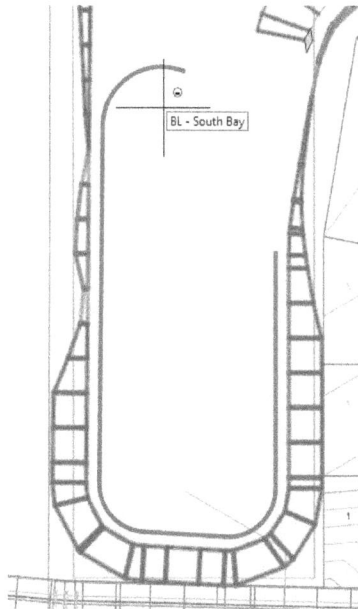

BL - South Bay

Figure A–69

4. In the Command Line, for the *Beginning Station*, type **0** and press <Enter>. For the *Ending Station*, type **130** and press <Enter>.

5. In the Create Corridor Region dialog box, for the *Region name*, type **RG - Pond South Bay 3 to 1**. For the *Assembly*, select **Pond South Bay 3 to 1 slope**, as shown in Figure A–70.

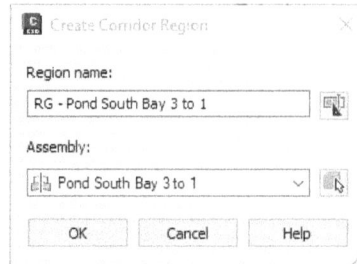

Figure A–70

6. In the Target Mapping dialog box, set the **Pond Bottom** as the *Target Surface*, as shown in Figure A–71. Click **OK**.

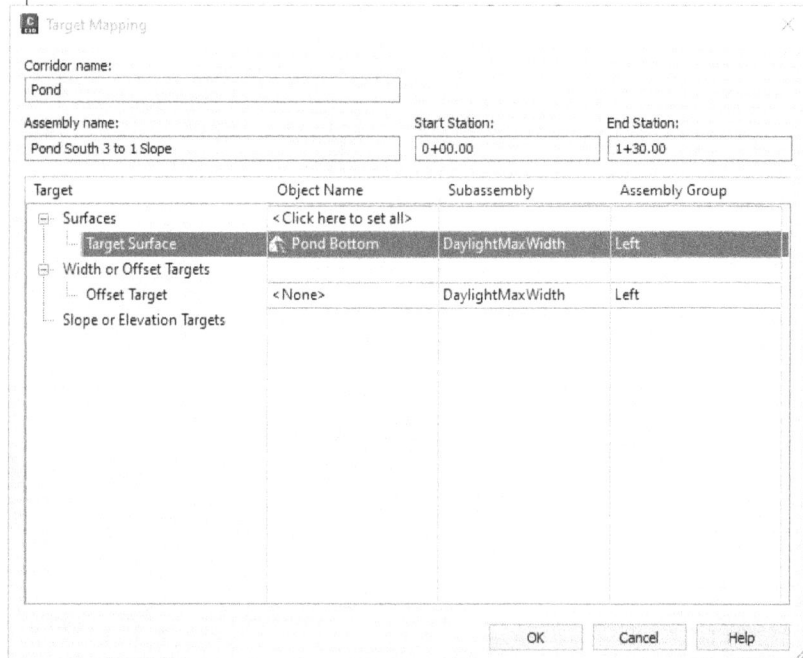

Figure A–71

7. Still in the **Add Regions** command, in the Command Line, for the *Beginning Station*, type **150** and press <Enter>. For the *Ending Station*, type **310** and press <Enter>.

8. In the Create Corridor Region dialog box, for the *Region name*, type **Pond South Bay Bench**. For the *Assembly*, select **Pond South Bay Bench**. Click **OK**.

9. In the Target Mapping dialog box, set the **Pond Bottom** as the *Target Surface*. Click **OK**.

10. In the Command Line, for the *Beginning Station*, type **320** and press <Enter>. For the *Ending Station*, type **550** and press <Enter>.

11. In the Create Corridor Region dialog box, for the *Region name*, type **Pond South Bay 2 to 1**. For the *Assembly*, select **Pond South Bay 2 to 1**. Click **OK**.

12. In the Target Mapping dialog box, set the **Pond Bottom** as the *Target Surface*. Click **OK**.

13. In the Command Line, for the *Beginning Station*, type **560** and press <Enter>. For the *Ending Station*, use the **Endpoint** Osnap and select the endpoint of the feature line.

14. In the Create Corridor Region dialog box, for the *Region name,* type **Pond South Bay 4 to 1 Slope**. For the *Assembly*, select **Pond South Bay 4 to 1**. Click **OK**.

15. In the Target Mapping dialog box, set **Pond Bottom** as the *Target Surface*. Click **OK**.

16. Press <Esc> to end the command.

17. Save the drawing.

18. Select the **Pond** corridor model, right-click, and select **Object Viewer**. Note that the pond is missing the weir between the two ponds, as shown in Figure A–72. The feature lines define the weir and are to be added as breaklines to the surface in the next task.

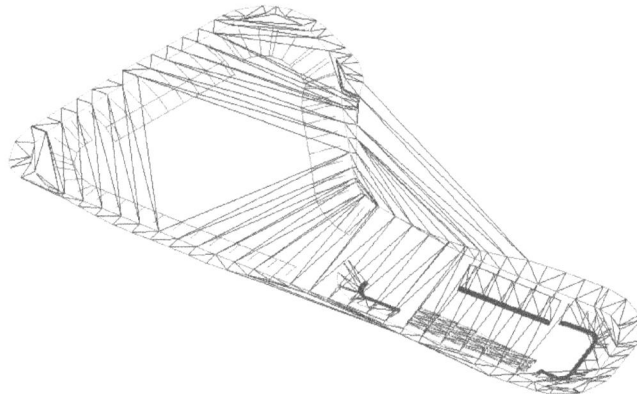

Figure A–72

19. Close the Object Viewer.

Task 5 - Create a surface from the corridor and add weir feature lines.

1. Continue working in the drawing from the previous task.

2. In the drawing, select the **Pond** corridor. In the *Corridor* contextual tab>Modify Corridor panel, click 🏠 (Corridor Surfaces).

3. In the Corridor Surfaces dialog box>*Surfaces* tab, click 🏠 (Create Corridor Surface).

4. In the Corridor Surfaces dialog box, select the **Pond** surface. Set the *Data type* to **Links** and the *Specify code* to **Top**. Click ➕ (Add surface item) to add the top codes to the surface, as shown in Figure A–73.

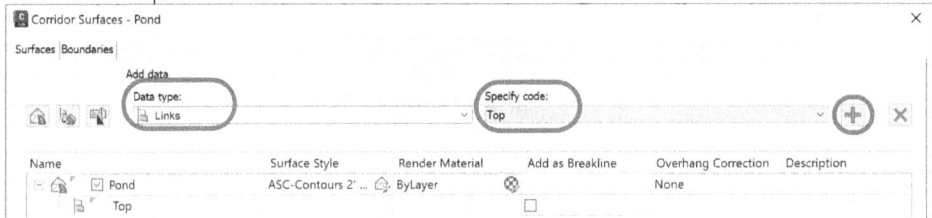

Figure A–73

5. In the Corridor Surfaces dialog box>*Boundaries* tab, right-click on the Pond surface, and select **Corridor extents as outer boundary**, as shown in Figure A–74.

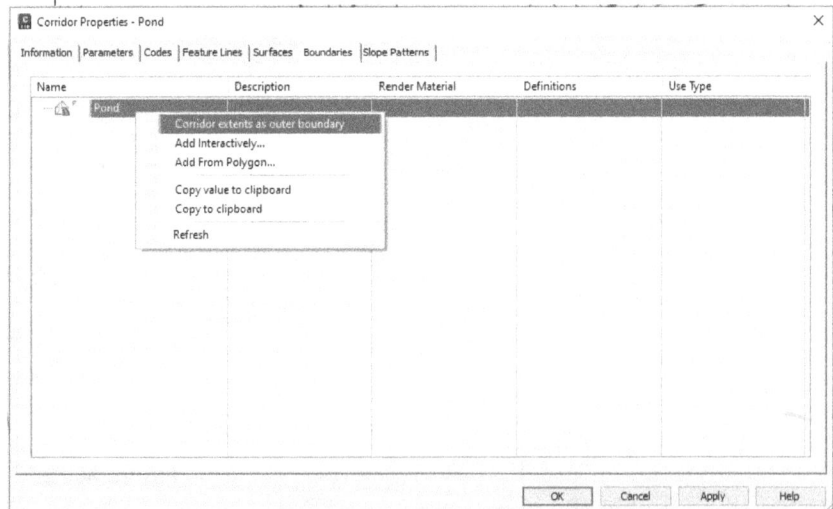

Figure A–74

6. Click **OK** to close the dialog box and create the surface.

7. Click **Rebuild Corridor Model**.

8. In the *Prospector* tab, expand **Sites>Lagoon**, and select **Feature Lines**. In the preview window, select **Feature3** and hold down <Shift> and select **South Bay bottom**, then right-click and select **Select**.

9. In the *Feature Lines* contextual tab>Modify panel, click

   (Add to Surface as Breakline).

10. In the Select Surface dialog box, select the **Pond** surface and click **OK**.

11. In the Create Breaklines dialog box, set the following:

    - *Description*: **Pond FLs**
    - *Type:* **Standard**
    - *Supplementing factors:* **25**
    - *Mid-ordinate distance:* **0.1**

12. Click **OK**. A surface is created that you control by modifying the two feature lines.

13. Press <Esc> twice to deselect everything.

14. Save the drawing.

15. Select the **Pond** surface, right-click and select **Object Viewer**. **Zoom** and **Orbit** around the pond, as shown in Figure A–75.

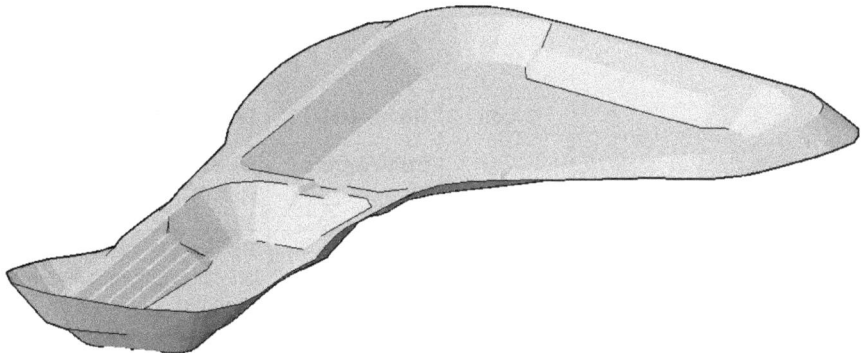

Figure A–75

16. Close the Object Viewer.

A.5 Modify Corridor Grading

Change occurs in any project. Using corridor models for grading projects speeds up the change process and makes it easier to edit slope values. A corridor provides additional tools to modify a grading solution.

Grip Editing

Grips can be used to edit a corridor model quickly. The

▷ (Triangle Grip) grips are located at the beginning and ending of regions and enable you to adjust the regions' stations. The

◁ (Diamond Grip) grip that is located between two regions enables the station adjustment of both regions' stationing at the same time. Triangular grips located at the diamond grip's location modify one region's stationing separately from the adjacent region's stationing.

Modify Regions

The Modify Region panel in the *Corridors* contextual tab provides all of the required tools for making changes to corridor regions, as shown in Figure A–76. The following table describes each command.

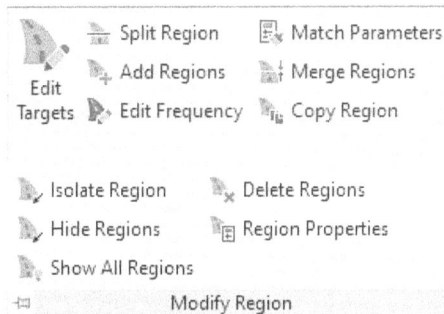

Figure A–76

Icon	Command	Description
	Edit Targets	Sets the targets for the assembly along the specific region only.
	Split Region	Splits a corridor region into multiple regions enabling different assemblies to be applied to a corridor.
	Add Regions	Enables an assembly to be applied to a gap on a corridor.
	Edit Frequency	Changes the frequency that an assembly is applied to a corridor within a region.

	Match Parameters	Match the assembly, target, and/or frequency of selected corridor regions.
	Merge Regions	Merges corridor regions along the same baseline.
	Copy Region	Copies regions along the same baseline.
	Isolate Region	Sets the visibility of all regions except the selected one to off.
	Hide Region	Sets the visibility of the selected region to off.
	Show All Regions	Sets the visibility of all regions to on.
	Delete Region	Removes a region from a corridor.
	Region Properties	Edits the assembly, beginning and ending stations, frequency, targets, and station overrides of a selected region.

Modify Corridor

The Modify Corridor panel in the *Corridors* contextual tab provides all of the tools required to make changes to the entire corridor at the same time, as shown in Figure A–77. The table below lists each command and describes what they do.

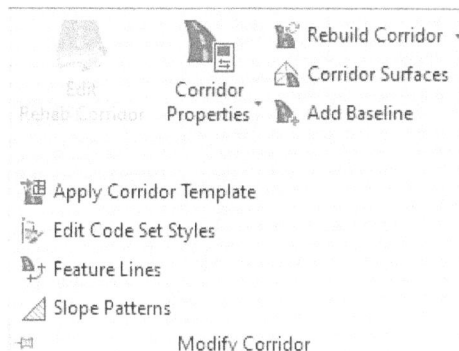

Figure A–77

Icon	Command	Description
	Corridor Properties	Edits corridor properties including *Name*, *Description*, *Object style*, Baselines, Regions, Targets, *Frequencies*, *Code sets*, *Feature lines*, *Surfaces*, *Boundaries*, and *Slope patterns*.

Icon	Command	Description
	Rebuild Corridor	Applies changes to a corridor that is out of date.
	Corridor Surface	Creates and manages surfaces built from links and codes assigned to assemblies used in the corridor.
	Add Baseline	Attaches alignments to a corridor to accommodate widening and non-parallel designs in road and grading projects.
	Edit Code Set Styles	Edits code set styles assigned to points, links, and shapes within subassemblies used in the corridor.
	Feature Lines	Edits feature line connections by indicating the point codes that are connected.
	Slope Patterns	Edits the patterns that are applied between any two feature lines.

Modify Corridor Sections

The Modify Corridor Sections panel in the *Corridors* contextual tab provides all of the tools required to make changes to the entire corridor at the same time, as shown in Figure A–78. The following table describes each command.

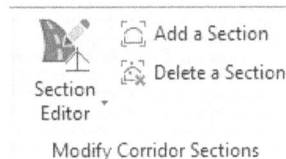

Modify Corridor Sections

Figure A–78

Icon	Command	Description
	Section Editor	Applies overrides to assembly parameters at specific stations.
	Add Section	Adds a section to the corridor at a defined location.
	Delete Section	Removes a selected section from a corridor.

Practice A5	# Modify Corridor Grading

Practice Objective

- Modify the corridor using grips and corridor parameters.

In this practice, you will create a new assembly for the outer rim of the pond, modify the corridor, and modify the frequency of the corridor and edit the corridor sections.

Task 1 - Create an assembly for the outer rim of the pond.

In this task, you will create an assembly that represents the outer rim of the pond and daylights to the Residential Grading surface.

1. Continue working in the drawing from the previous practice or open **LAGOON-E.dwg** from the *C:\Civil 3D for Land Dev\ Working\Lagoon* folder.

2. In the *Home* tab>Create Design panel, expand the Assembly drop-down list and click (Create Assembly).

3. In the Create Assembly dialog box, enter the following:

   - *Name*: **Pond Rim to Surface**
   - *Description:* **Pond Outer Rim-Tie to Residential Surface**
   - *Assembly Type*: **Other**
   - *Code set style*: **ASC-View-Edit**

4. Click **OK** to accept all of the other defaults and close the dialog box.

The Autodesk Civil 3D software automatically zooms in on the assembly marker.

5. In the drawing, select a point near the Pond Outer Rim Profile view as the insertion point to remember which profile it goes with.

6. In the *Home* tab>Create Design panel, click (Tool Palettes) to display the Tool Palettes.

7. In the *Daylight* tab in the Tool Palettes, select **Daylight to Offset** to display the Properties palette.

8. In the Properties palette, set *Rounding Option* to **Circular**. Leave all of the other parameters as their default value, as shown in Figure A–79.

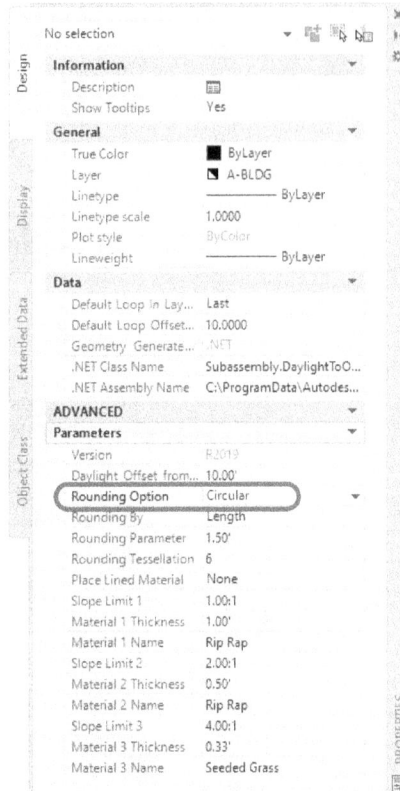

Figure A–79

9. In the drawing, select the **Pond Outer Rim-Tie to Residential Surface** assembly marker to attach the subassembly, as shown in Figure A–80.

Figure A–80

10. Press <Enter> to end the command.

11. Save the drawing

Task 2 - Modify the corridor.

In this task, you will adjust the corridor using grips. You will then create a polyline 6" inside the residential parcels to target and add the Pond Outer Rim-Tie to Residential Surface assembly to the corridor.

1. Continue working in the drawing from the previous practice.

2. In the drawing, zoom in on the weir that divides the pond into two bays. Select the pond corridor model.

3. On the east side of the north bay, the corridor encroaches on the feature lines that create the weir. Select the region grip at the endpoint of the North Bay baseline.

4. Using the **Midpoint** Osnap, move the grip to the midpoint of the curve, as shown in Figure A–81 and Figure A–82.

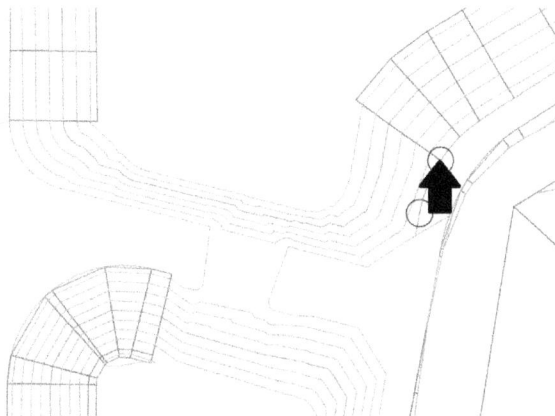

Figure A–81

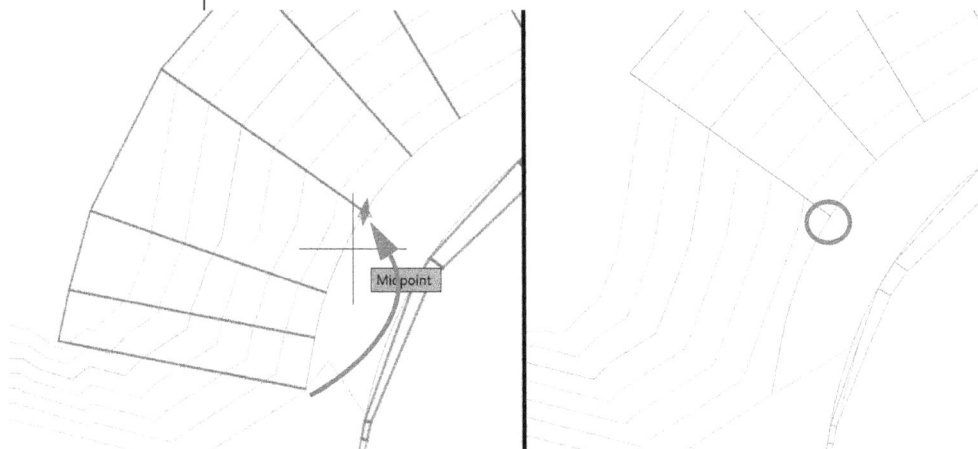

Figure A–82

Now you will create a target polyline that daylights the pond outer rim to the residential grading surface. To create the target, offset the pond parcel segment and trim the offset at Lot 1's northern boundary and Lot 5's northern boundary. This leaves a polyline target between Lots 1 to 5.

5. In the *Home* tab>Modify panel, click ⊆ (Offset). In the Command Line, for the *Offset value* type **.5 (6 inches)**.

6. In the drawing, select the **Pond** parcel segments, as shown in Figure A–83.

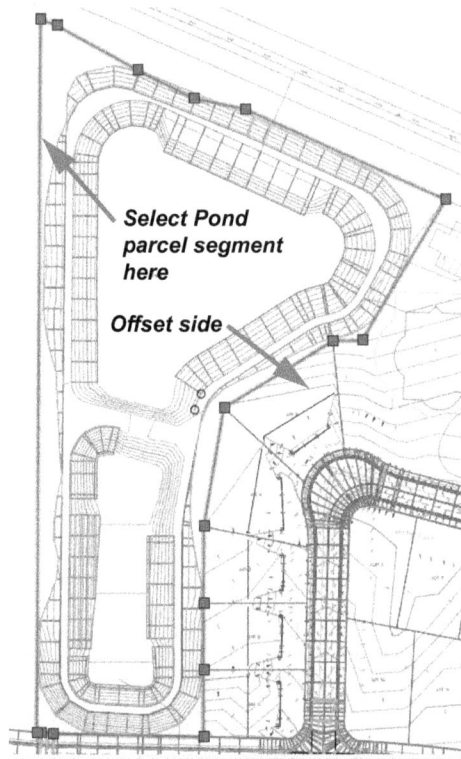

Figure A–83

7. In the drawing, pick an offset point outside the pond.

8. Press <Enter> to end the Offset command.

9. In the *Home* tab>Modify panel, click ✂ (Trim).

10. In the drawing, select the short segment to the east of Lot 5 and the southern segment bordering the road, as highlighted with red lines in Figure A–84. Press <Enter> to finish the Trim command.

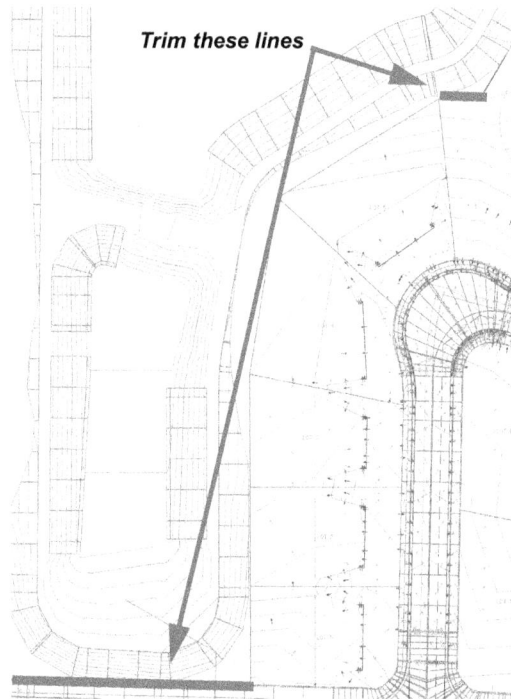

Figure A–84

11. In the drawing, erase the trimmed polyline that is in the northwest of the pond, so the only polyline that remains is the one to the rear of Lots 1 through 5, as highlighted with a red line in Figure A–85.

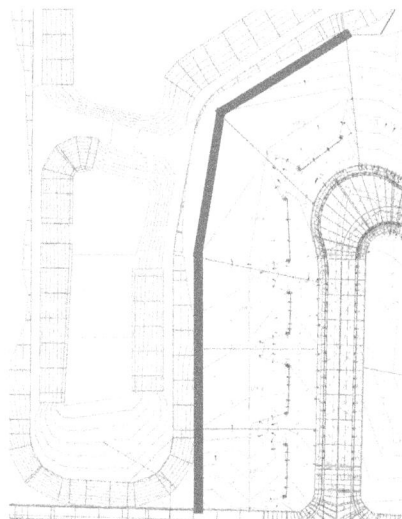

Figure A–85

12. Save the drawing.

Task 3 - Create a region for Pond Outer Rim.

1. Continue working in the drawing from the previous task or open **LAGOON-F.dwg** from the *C:\Civil 3D for Land Dev\ Working\Lagoon* folder.

2. In the drawing, select the **Pond** corridor. In the *Corridor* contextual tab>Modify Region panel, click ![icon] (Split Region).

3. In the drawing, select the **Outer Rim** region, as shown in Figure A–86.

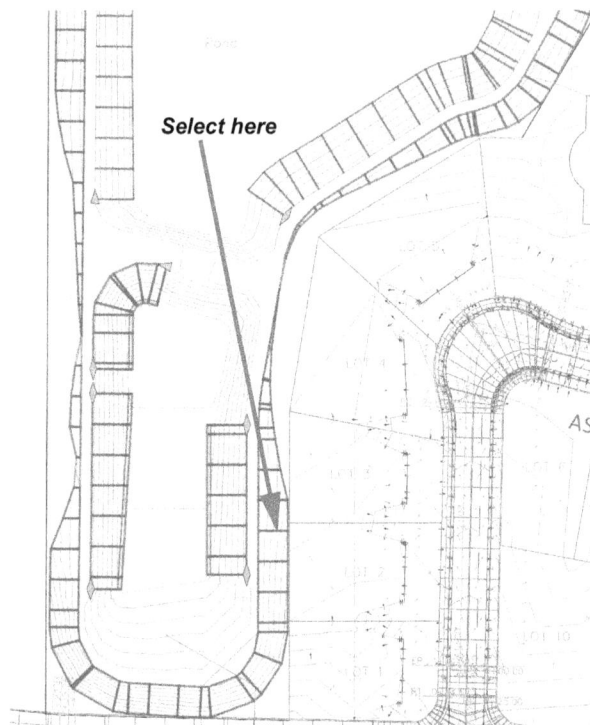

Select here

Figure A–86

4. For the first split point, in the drawing use the **Endpoint** Osnap to select the endpoint of the offset line at Lot 1's northern boundary as a region split point, as shown in Figure A–87.

5. You are prompted for another region to split. Select the same one as you did previously and also select at the northern boundary of Lot 5, as shown in Figure A–87.

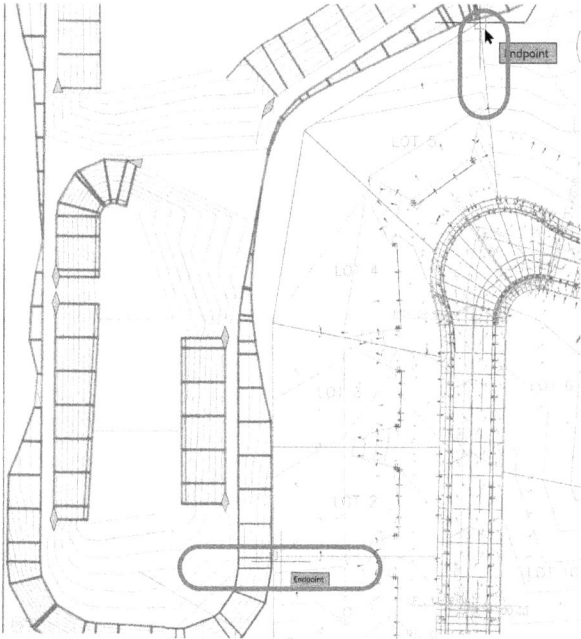

Figure A–87

6. Press <Enter> to end the Split command.

7. In the drawing, select the **Pond** corridor if no longer selected. In the *Corridor* contextual tab, expand the Modify Region

   panel and click (Region Properties), as shown in Figure A–88.

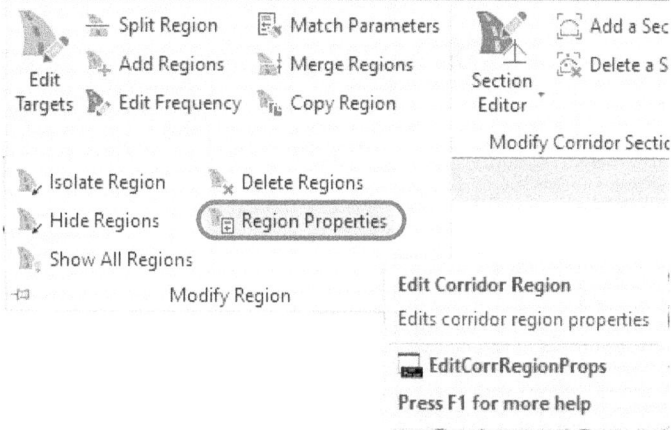

Figure A–88

8. In the model, click the Outer Rim Region on the east side of the pond, as shown in Figure A–89.

Figure A–89

9. In the Corridor Region Properties dialog box, in the *Assembly value* field, click ⊡ to open the Edit Corridor Region dialog box.

10. In the Edit Corridor Region dialog box, for the *Region name*, type **Residential Daylight**. For the *Assembly*, select **Pond Rim to Surface**, as shown in Figure A–90. Click **OK**.

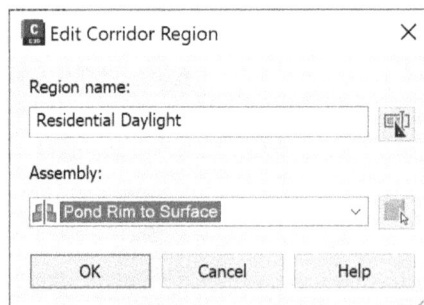

Figure A–90

11. In the Corridor Region Properties dialog box, rename the *Region Name* to **RG - Pond to Res surface**.

12. In the *Target value* field, click ⊡ to open the Target Mapping dialog box.

13. In the Target Mapping dialog box, set the *Target Surface* to the **Residential Surface**. Click **OK**.

14. Select the *Object Name* field next to *Target Alignment Daylight*, as shown in Figure A–91.

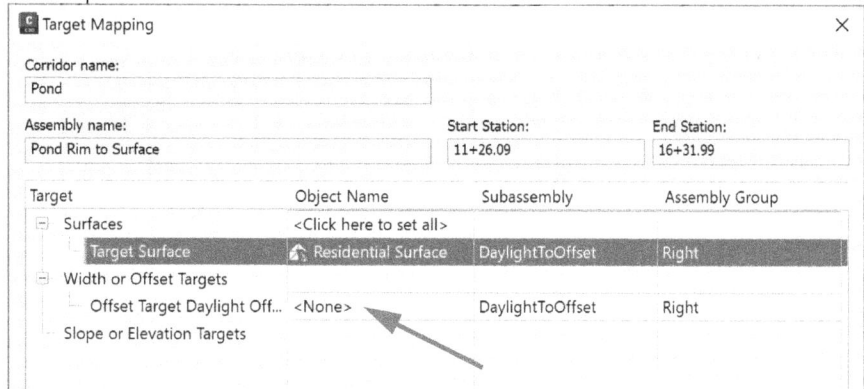

Figure A–91

15. In the Set Width or Offset Target dialog box, expand the Select object type to target drop-down list and select **Feature lines, survey figures and polylines**, as shown in Figure A–92. Click **Select from drawing**.

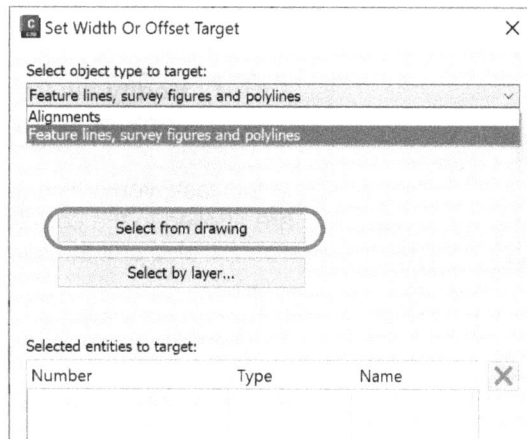

Figure A–92

16. In the drawing, select the polyline that was created from the Pond boundary offset, as shown in Figure A–93, and press <Enter> to finish the selection.

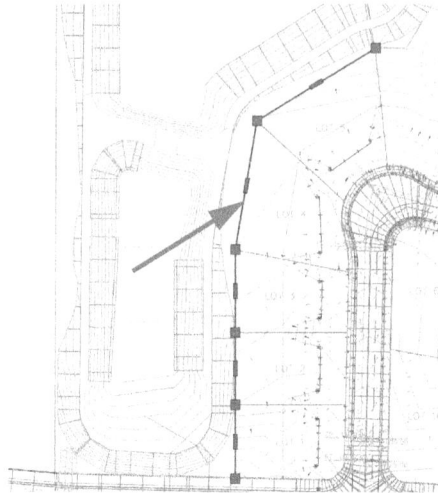

Figure A–93

17. In the Set Width or Offset Target dialog box, click **OK**.

18. In the Target Mapping dialog box, click **OK**.

19. In the Corridor Region Properties dialog box, click **OK**.

Task 4 - Modify the frequency of the corridor and edit the corridor sections.

In this task, you will change the frequency of the assemblies that are applied to the corridor to smooth transitions around curves. You will also edit the sections to accommodate another design change.

1. Continue working in the drawing from the previous task.

2. In the drawing, select the **Pond** corridor.

3. In the *Corridor* contextual tab>Modify Corridor panel, click

   (Corridor Properties).

4. In the *Parameters* tab or the Corridor Properties dialog box, click **Set all Frequencies**.

5. In the Frequencies to Apply Assemblies dialog box (as shown in Figure A–94):

- Set *Along tangents* to **10**.
- Set *Curve increment* to **3**.
- Click **OK** twice.
- When prompted, rebuild the corridor.

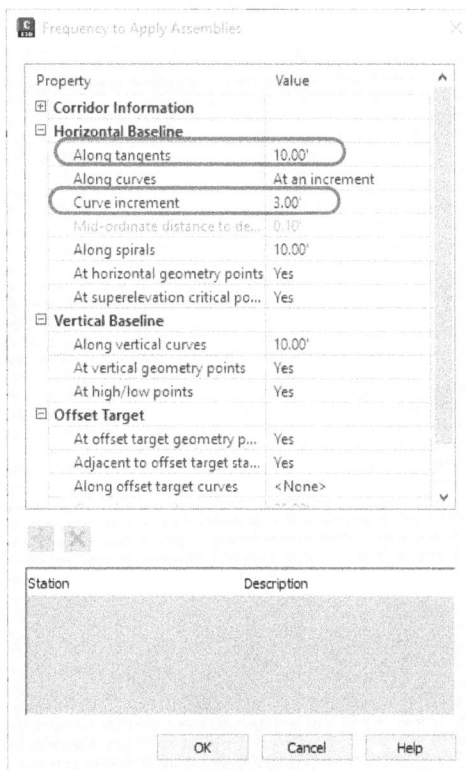

Figure A–94

Now you will edit a small section of the pond to extend the grade into the pond with less slope.

6. In the drawing, select the **Pond** corridor. In the *Corridor* contextual tab, click (Section Editor). This splits the drawing area into three viewports.

7. In the *Section Editor* contextual tab, in the Baselines & Offsets panel, complete the following, as shown in Figure A–95:

- For the *Baseline,* select **North Bay**.
- In the Station Selection panel, for the *Station,* select **5+00.00'**.
- In the Corridor Edit Tools panel, click ⬤ (Parameter Editor).

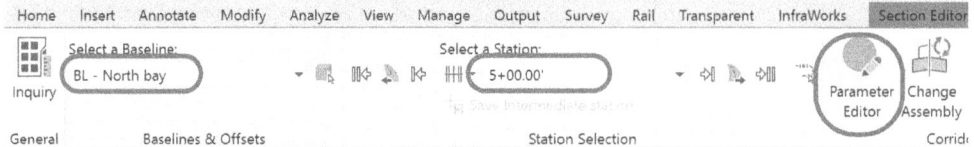

Figure A–95

8. In the Parameter Editor vista, expand the subassemblies. Under the *LinkWidthAndSlope* subassembly, change the *Value* of the *Slope* to **-3%** and the *Width* to **50.00'**, as shown in Figure A–96.

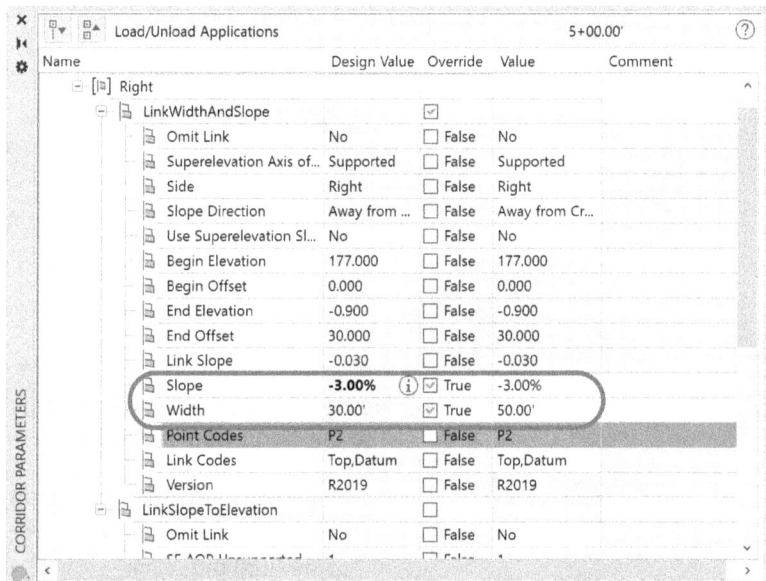

Figure A–96

9. In the *Section Editor* contextual tab>Corridor Edit Tools panel, click 🔳 (Apply to a Station Range).

10. In the Apply to a Range of Stations dialog box, for the *End station* value type **530**, as shown in Figure A–97. Click **OK**.

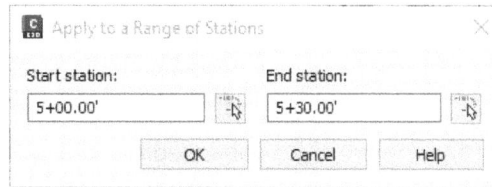

Figure A–97

11. In the *Section Editor* contextual tab, click the ✔ icon to close the Section editor.

12. Save the drawing.

13. In the drawing, select the **Pond** surface, right-click, and select **Object Viewer**. Zoom and orbit around the pond, as shown in Figure A–98.

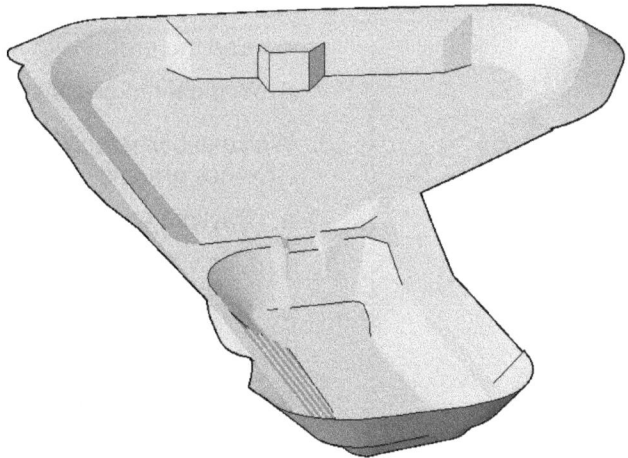

Figure A–98

14. Close the Object Viewer.

15. Close the drawing.

16. To view the final solution, open **LAGOON-ZZ-Complete.dwg** from the *C:\Civil 3D for Land Dev\Working\Lagoon* folder.

Chapter Review Questions

1. Which of the following is important to remember when grading an enclosed area with a corridor model?

   a. You cannot grade enclosed areas with corridor models.

   b. Begin and end the alignment for the corridor at a corner.

   c. Begin and end the alignment or feature line for the corridor along a straight segment.

   d. Begin and end the alignment for the corridor along a curve.

2. Which of the following is important when creating a profile for an enclosed area grading corridor model? (Select all that apply.)

   a. Begin and end the profile at the same elevation.

   b. Extend the design profile approximately 200 feet beyond the alignment to accommodate changes in length.

   c. End the profile with a tangent rather than a vertical curve.

   d. You cannot grade enclosed areas with corridor models.

3. Which subassembly does the same thing as the Grade to Distance grading criteria?

   a. Daylight General

   b. Link Width and Slope

   c. Daylight to Offset

   d. Link to Surface

4. If you need to have a corridor model follow multiple alignments or feature lines, which would you do?

   a. Add Baselines.

   b. Add Regions.

   c. Create a second corridor model.

   d. Split Regions.

5. What is assigned to a corridor region?

   a. Alignment

   b. Profile

   c. Subassembly

   d. Assembly

6. Which tool would you use to add a corridor region to a corridor to which an assembly has already been applied to its entire length?

a.

b.

c.

d.

Command Summary

Button	Command	Location
	Add Baseline	• **Ribbon:** *Corridor* contextual tab>Modify Corridor panel • **Command Prompt:** AddCorrBaseline
	Add Regions	• **Ribbon:** *Corridor* contextual tab>Modify Region panel • **Command Prompt:** AddCorrRegions
	Alignment Creation Tools	• **Ribbon:** *Home* tab>Create Design panel • **Command Prompt:** CreateAlignmentLayout
	Alignment Grid View	• **Toolbar:** Alignment Layout Tools (*contextual*)
	Assembly Properties	• **Ribbon:** *Assembly* contextual tab>Modify panel • **Command Prompt:** EditAssemblyProperties
	Corridor Properties	• **Ribbon:** *Corridor* contextual tab>Modify Corridor panel • **Command Prompt:** EditCorridorProperties
	Create Alignment from Objects	• **Ribbon:** *Home* tab>Create Design panel • **Command Prompt:** CreateAlignmentEntities
	Create Assembly	• **Ribbon:** *Home* tab>Create Design panel • **Command Prompt:** CreateAssembly
	Create Corridor	• **Ribbon:** *Home* tab>Create Design panel • **Command Prompt:** CreateCorridor
	Create Profile from Surface	• **Ribbon:** *Home* tab>Create Design panel • ***Command Prompt:*** CreateProfileFromSurface
	Draw Tangents	• **Toolbar:** Profile Layout Tools (*contextual*)
	Edit Alignment Style	• **Ribbon:** *Alignment* contextual tab>Modify panel>Alignment Properties drop-down list • **Command Prompt:** EditAlignmentStyle
	Geometry Editor	• **Ribbon:** *Alignment* contextual tab>Modify panel • **Command Prompt:** EditAlignment
	Profile Creation Tools	• **Ribbon:** *Home* tab>Create Design panel • **Command Prompt:** CreateProfileLayout
	Profile Station Elevation	• **Toolbar:** Transparent commands • **Command Prompt:** 'PSE

	Region Properties	• **Ribbon:** *Corridor* contextual tab>Modify Region panel • **Command Prompt:** EditCorrRegionProp
	Section Editor	• **Ribbon:** *Corridor* contextual tab>Modify Corridor Sections panel • **Command Prompt:** ViewEditCorridorSection
	Split Region	• **Ribbon:** *Corridor* contextual tab>Modify Region panel • **Command Prompt:** SplitCorrRegion
	Tool Palettes	• **Ribbon:** *Home* tab>Palettes panel • **Command Prompt:** ToolPalettes, <Ctrl>+<3>

Index

www.ingramcontent.com/pod-product-compliance
Lightning Source LLC
Chambersburg PA
CBHW060954210326
41598CB00031B/4821